David Hooper is a media and ......... p..., partner at Pinsent Curtis Biddle, a prominent London law firm involved in many of the actions described in this book. He is the author of two previous books, *Public Scandal, Odium and Contempt: An Investigation of Recent Libel Cases* and *The Official Secrets Act: The Use and Abuse of the Act.*

By the same author

PUBLIC SCANDAL, ODIUM AND CONTEMPT:
An Investigation of Recent Libel Cases

THE OFFICIAL SECRETS ACT:
The Use and Abuse of the Act

# REPUTATIONS UNDER FIRE

## Winners and Losers in the Libel Business

### DAVID HOOPER

WARNER BOOKS

A *Warner* Book

First published in Great Britain in 2000
by Little, Brown and Company

This edition published by Warner in 2001

Copyright © 2000 by David Hooper

The moral right of the author has been asserted

A CIP catalogue record for this book is
available from the British Library.

ISBN 0 7515 2993 1

Typeset in Rotis by M Rules
Printed and bound in Great Britain by
Clays Ltd, St Ives plc

Warner Books
A Division of
Little, Brown and Company (UK)
Brettenham House
Lancaster Place
London WC2E 7EN

www.littlebrown.co.uk

For my children James, Kate and Alice
and in loving memory of my son Edward

# ACKNOWLEDGEMENTS

I hope I have thanked personally the very many people who have assisted me in the preparation of material for this book. I would like to repeat those thanks here. A number of people will want their assistance to remain anonymous.

I would like particularly to thank Caroline North and Alan Samson at Little, Brown for their patience and support.

Finally, no one who writes a book of these dimensions in his spare time can fail to acknowledge with amazement and gratitude the tolerance of his family – in my case, particularly that of my wife Caroline.

# CONTENTS

# 1

# LIBEL:

## How it Works

The law of libel in England is rooted in the statutory offence created in the 1275 statute Scandalum Magnatum (scandal of magnates). This led to a system of royal proclamations and monopolies which controlled the press. In the sixteenth century seditious libel could result in the loss of a right hand and a slander in the removal of ears, presumably to prevent the slanderer from picking up any more gossip. Protection of reputation as overseen by the Court of Star Chamber was, in the seventeenth century, synonymous with the protection of the state. It was quick to punish 'unfitting worddes, unsemely words or evil opinions'. Libellers ran the risk of ingenious forms of mutilation and whipping round the streets of London. In the eighteenth century the laws of libel were felt to be so favourable to the state that Fox's Libel Act was passed in 1792 to enable juries to fix libel damages and to protect litigants from judges. Libel moved from being predominantly a criminal matter to a civil one, whereas in Europe it has remained predominantly a criminal matter. The tide turned in favour of private litigants, with English law developing a law of libel in the nineteenth and twentieth centuries which was to make London the libel capital of the world. Eventually newspapers, in a striking volte-face from Fox's Libel Act, turned to judges to protect them against the awards of juries.

Libel can be perpetrated in many forms. It can range from a defamatory waxwork of a person placed in the Chamber of Horrors at Madame Tussaud's to a kissogram. The Duchess of Windsor was dissuaded by the Duke's solicitors, Allen and Overy, from following the example of a Mr Monson, who had recovered one farthing's damages for libel against Madame Tussaud's. Their waxwork of her she considered 'appalling' and 'indecent'. A kissogram was sent to the church commissioners accusing, in verse, a finance company of being Shylocks. No less original was a damaging message about an oil company written in the sky with a plane's vapour trail by a disgruntled garage-owner, which entertained racegoers at the 1986 Cheltenham Gold Cup. Here the issue arose as to whether this constituted libel or slander, on the basis that, although the message was written, it was at the same time transitory.

The distinction between libel and slander is now archaic and virtually irrelevant: broadcasts and computer-generated transmissions are now defined as libel. The main distinctions between libel and slander are that the spoken word must be proved to have been uttered, while a libellous document can simply be produced. Additionally, in slander actual damage has to be proved. The salutary requirement is, however, undermined by the exceptions that cover most worthwhile slanders: imputing a crime or an infectious disease, accusing a woman (but apparently not a man) of adultery and disparaging a person regarding his or her business or occupation. Slander has its own special defence of vulgar abuse, a defence successfully used when a plaintiff complained of being called a tramp in the Cumberland Hotel in London. However, since this really goes to the question of whether there is a defamatory meaning, again there is no real difference between libel and slander.

The perception of libel cases is that they concern the rich and famous and the important events of the day. In fact people successfully bring libel actions for humdrum matters such as cheques being bounced, as happened in 1992 when Lloyds Bank had to pay substantial damages to a butcher's business. And in 1992 the solicitor Rex Makin recovered £750 from Merseyside Police on the basis that he had been libelled by the issue of a parking ticket, and the way in which the police chose to handle his complaint. His car had apparently been parked in the garage at the material time.

English libel law has looked increasingly remote and fundamentally different in principle from the law of other European states, except Ireland, where the injustice of the libel law is markedly more pronounced than in the UK, and different in its application from that of the United States. This has become more pronounced in an era of global publishing through the Internet. The Defamation Act 1996 has made some moves towards limiting the liability of those not primarily responsible for formulating the libel – such as Internet service-providers, printers, distributors and the operators of live phone-in programmes – even though they may have been involved in publishing it. (The Defamation Act 1996 is covered in detail in Chapter 21.)

In the past ten years, however, there has been a very striking shift in favour of freedom of speech, although it stops far short of the protection afforded by the First Amendment of the Constitution in the United States. In a case brought by Central TV in 1994 to prevent a mother trying to stop a programme about a paedophile being transmitted for fear that it might identify the child involved, Lord Justice Hoffmann noted that there was no question of balancing freedom of speech with other interests; rather, freedom of speech must always be the trump card.

In October 1977 Lord Denning gave a very powerful judgement when financier Jim Slater tried to rely on an earlier agreement with the journalist Charles Raw restricting the use of information Raw had obtained, while working for the *Observer*, from earlier interviews with Slater. *The Sunday Times*, which wanted to serialise Raw's book Slater Walker, successfully argued that it was not bound by any earlier agreement, particularly as

Slater was publishing his own book, the autobiography *Return to Go*. A court would not grant an injunction on the suggestion that there was a breach of contract except in the clearest possible case. It was of the highest importance that the press should be free to publish comments on matters of public interest. Lord Denning probably put the matter too strongly when he doubted whether any contract would be binding if it tended to hinder or place a fetter on a newspaper in the exercise of the freedom of the press to publish comments on matters of public interest, but it was a ringing endorsement of the freedom of the press by the English judges. The aspiration of the freedom of the press had, unfortunately, been undermined by the operation of the law of libel in practice. There has been a recognition since the government's attempt to stop publication of Peter Wright's book *Spycatcher* in the mid-1980s that English law is, or at any rate should be, in line with the protection of freedom of speech provided for in Article 10 of the European Convention of Human Rights. The convention has now by virtue of the Human Rights Act 1998 been incorporated into English law, which is likely to shift the balance of libel litigation more in favour of the media. The right of the press to publish responsibly matters of public interest in cases where it may be found impossible to prove the truth of the allegations has been recognised by the English courts in the ground-breaking case of Reynolds (see Chapter 16), a process started by the House of Lords in Derbyshire County Council v. Times Newspapers Ltd in 1993, where the court found that it offended principles of free speech to allow a county council to sue for libel for damage to its governing reputation. The lottery element of libel damages, which made the pursuit of speculative libel actions profitable and caused cautious newspaper proprietors to settle unmeritorious claims, has in large measure been ended by the decision in the Elton John case (see Chapter 15) and by the provisions of the 1996 Defamation Act.

The law of libel in England is still distinctly plaintiff-friendly, with its initial assumption in favour of the plaintiff that defamatory words are false and that he or she is of good reputation.

Equally helpful to a plaintiff is the fact that he or she does not have to prove actual damage as a result of the libel and that the burden of proving that what was said is true under the arcane laws of admissible evidence rests throughout on the defendant. England, therefore, remains the place where libel litigants prefer to sue.

The principal defence to a libel action is that what has been published is true. The fact that the burden of proof is on the defendant is the most onerous feature of English libel law. There is no obligation on the plaintiff to supply any evidence of falsity or to verify his or her claim on oath. The civil procedures introduced in the wake of Lord Woolf's suggested changes to civil litigation (see Chapter 21) go some way towards alleviating this. However, there is no discovery procedure comparable to that used in the United States, which permits a defendant to obtain documentary evidence before he has pleaded his defence of justification. He can raise that defence only if he has evidence to support it.

Publication need be to only a handful of people. The extent of publication will be relevant to damages, but even a small circulation of a libel can be very damaging if it is targeted at a person's business contacts.

At the heart of the law of libel is the mythical creature on the Clapham omnibus, the reasonable man or woman – in contemporary terms, the ordinary reader or viewer. This person – essentially fair-minded, not unduly suspicious or avid for scandal – is perceived by the courts to have been influenced by the first impression conveyed by an article or broadcast and not to analyse it in the sort of minute detail beloved by lawyers. The ordinary reader has to decide, looking at the context as a whole, whether the words used tend to lower the plaintiff in the estimation of right-thinking members of society generally (Lord Atkin in Sim v. Stretch, 1935), or whether they cause the plaintiff to be shunned and avoided (Youssoupoff v. MGM, 1934) – an authority which could be relied upon if the plaintiff was accused of having AIDS or of suffering from some misfortune which might not directly reflect discredit on him – or whether the words tend to expose the plaintiff to hatred, ridicule or contempt (Parmiter v. Coupland, 1840). This is a definition relied on by those who complain of satire.

Jokes tend to fall somewhat flat in the libel courts. A restaurant-owner recovered damages for what was meant to be a humorous piece headed 'CHARLIE'S PASTIES: LOOK BEFORE YOU BITE, IT COULD BE ROVER FROM NEXT DOOR'.

One working test is whether, if you were in the plaintiff's position, you could legitimately object if the offending words had been used about you.

In a surprisingly large number of libel actions the issue is what the words actually mean. As a result, there has often had to be a full trial, with allegations and counter-allegations, when all that has been needed is a ruling on the meaning of the words. One of the problems has been the courts deciding whether the words were *arguably* capable of bearing the meaning contended for by the plaintiff. As the libel claim will normally have been drafted by a specialist libel barrister, the contentious meaning is almost bound to be arguable, even if somewhat optimistic or far-fetched. In recent times, however, judges have taken an increasingly robust view of their powers when giving their rulings on meaning. In the case of Mapp v. News Group Newspapers Ltd in 1997, the constabulary at Stoke Newington in north London (Chapter 6) claimed that the *News of the World* headline 'DRUG QUIZ COP KILLS HIMSELF' – reporting that a Sergeant Carroll, the police station custody officer, had shot himself in one of the cells – suggested that he had done so to avoid confirming the guilt of his colleagues in drug-dealing and bribery. Applying the arguably capable test, the judge at first instance, Sir Michael Davies, felt unable to sling out this convoluted meaning. In the Court of Appeal Lord Justice Hirst reasoned that it was virtually unarguable to contend that the article suggested actual guilt. Reasonable readers could interpret Carroll's suicide in a number of ways. It was unreasonable to latch on to just the one meaning which was defamatory. The judge's role was to decide the range of meanings of which the words were *reasonably* capable. He had to consider what meanings a reasonable reader, guided only by general and no special knowledge, and not fettered by any strict legal rules of construction, would derive from the headline. Increasingly, judges have been required to consider what meaning the jury is likely to attribute to the words and to take a more hands-on approach. Under Section 7 of the Defamation Act 1996, courts are specifically required to decide such matters on the basis of what meaning the words are capable, as opposed to *arguably* capable, of bearing. The summary procedure introduced by the Defamation Act is likely to result in many more applications for rulings on meaning.

So at a libel trial the judge's role is to rule on what meaning the words are *capable* of bearing, while the jury decides what meaning they *in fact* bear. As meaning is decided simply by considering the words used as they would have been read or heard in a broadcast, in the 1998 Marks & Spencer v. Granada case the question was whether the jury had to hear all the evidence as to the truth or falsity of the allegations to determine the defamatory meaning of the broadcast, or whether it could decide the issue of meaning at the outset of the trial. Instead of letting the jury hear all the evidence before deciding what Granada Television's broadcast 'St Michael: Has the Halo Slipped?' meant, Mr Justice Popplewell asked them at the start to decide simply what meaning they felt the words bore, and a case which had been scheduled to last six weeks was over within three days. The key issues were whether – and if so the extent to which – the retail giant Marks & Spencer knew about any child exploitation at the Sicome factory in Menkes, Morocco, and whether goods manufactured in Morocco were being sold under a St Michael made-in-the-UK label. The jury never got to hear the rival arguments which described how girls as young as twelve were working ten-hour shifts for as little as 20p an hour.

As an exercise in shortening trials, and as a matter of legal logic, the Popplewell course had something to commend it. To decide what a broadcast meant, it should not be necessary to hear all the evidence. After all, the average viewer would make up his mind as the programme was transmitted into his home. The reality, however, is a little different. To understand the issues and to determine the right way of deciding the case, a jury really needs to hear the evidence. Rulings on meanings without hearing the evidence should be confined to the judge, who has experience of hearing such matters. There seems a distinct risk that a ruling on meaning before the evidence is heard may be determined by a few strong-willed jurors without all participating in the decision, and the whole process becomes something of a lottery.

It is difficult to predict when a judge will follow this course and what decision the jury will reach. A ruling on meaning may lead to a full trial, so the parties involved will have to incur the cost of preparing this in any event. It is much better for rulings to be given before a trial, so that everyone knows whether evidence will in fact need to be called. Juries are not trained to give rulings on meanings and are likely to function best when they have heard the evidence and have a feel for the issues at stake. The Marks & Spencer case showed how uncertain the outcome of such a ruling can be. On the central question of whether the programme suggested that Marks & Spencer knowingly and deliberately exploited child labour at the Moroccan factory, or whether, as Granada contended, it simply meant that Marks & Spencer did not make adequate checks to prevent exploitation of child labour, the jury rejected both Granada and Marks & Spencer's arguments. They produced what had all the hallmarks of an unholy compromise. They disregarded Marks & Spencer's words 'knowingly' and 'deliberately' and almost entirely accepted Granada's wording. However, as the jury ruled that the words implied Marks & Spencer had knowledge of the exploitation of child labour, and as Granada could not justify this, Marks & Spencer won. By agreement the retailer received £50,000 damages and £650,000 legal costs. The fact that the legal advisers to both parties almost felt it necessary to cross-question the jury as to what its somewhat Delphic ruling meant raised very real doubts as to whether justice had been properly done.

In March 1995, the House of Lords had to rule on a claim brought by two stars of the TV soap opera *Neighbours*, Ann Charleston and Ian Smith, against the *News of the World*. The paper had discovered that images of the actors, who played a married couple, Madge and Harold, had been used without their knowledge in a sordid computer game. To illustrate the point, in November 1992 the paper superimposed their heads on models in pornographic poses. It was classic tabloid mischief-making: 'STREWTH, WHAT'S HAROLD UP TO WITH OUR MADGE?' the headline bawled. In the photo Harold appeared to be astride Madge, with a map of Australia, bearing the helpful caption 'censored down under', covering their genital regions. 'Porn shocker for *Neighbours* stars', the strapline reported. Anyone perusing the article would have realised that the photographs were mock-ups. Studious readers would have digested the captions underneath (needless to say in much smaller print): 'Soap studs: Harold and Madge's faces are added to porn actors' bodies in a scene from the game.' The problem was the *News of the World* readers who did not bother with the small print and who might therefore believe that the actors had been involved in disreputable activities. The article had to be read as a whole, the House of Lords ruled. The bane of the headline was counteracted by the antidote of the article. At the same time their lordships deprecated gutter journalism and warned that those publishing defamatory headlines were playing with fire, as newspapers (as opposed to their readers) grew thicker and thicker and people read more and more selectively. In July 1992, however, the *Daily Sport* had to pay substantial damages to actress Sarah Lancashire of *Coronation Street* for publishing a mocked-up picture of her face on the body of a topless woman. Attempts by the paper to inform its readers that this was a spoof were inadequate and the actress won her case.

And in November 1999 a woman recovered substantial damages from the adult magazine *Fiesta* after her ex-husband sent the magazine private photographs for its 'Readers' Wives' photo section with the clear implication that she had consented to their publication, which she most assuredly had not.

Allegations of dishonesty, corruption, cowardice, plagiarism, incompetence in a person's work, sexual misbehaviour or plainly horrible and false allegations, such as accusing a celebrity with a deformed hand of offering it to people to shake as a practical joke, are self-evidently, according to the natural and ordinary meaning of the words, defamatory and have rightly resulted in the award of substantial damages. Other instances of libel are not so flagrant, but can be clearly established to be defamatory when the context of the comment is examined. For example, a musician recently recovered damages for being described in a book as 'that ghastly little man who played the mouth organ. I don't know who let him in.'

Libel may also arise through some innuendo known to a number of readers or viewers which renders libellous something which appears on the face of it to be harmless. In 1978 the *Daily Mail* had to pay the Labour Cabinet minister Michael Foot libel damages for a claim that he had been treated privately in a National Health Service hospital – a perfectly legitimate activity, but defamatory of a minister campaigning against the use of such 'pay beds'. Similarly, the photograph of a woman on a Kellogg's Cornflakes packet with the caption 'A pregnant mum doesn't have to be constipated' appeared harmless, if somewhat unappetising at the breakfast table. But add the fact that the photograph had been touched up, and that the subject was an unmarried and unpregnant nurse, and one had a claim for libel.

A jury is there to bring its knowledge of the world to bear on the meaning of words. It can decide that when *Private Eye* writes, 'There is no truth in the rumour that . . .', it means just the opposite. While a careful choice of words may avoid a claim for libel, a court will look at the reality of what has been written, as well as the words used and the reason why they have been selected. It applies its common sense. A court was not therefore fooled into thinking that the *Daily Star* had mere antiquities in mind when, in 1986, it wrote of 'the dashing poetry-scribbling minister Lord Gowrie' leaving the Cabinet suddenly to take up a more lucrative post at Sotheby's. 'What expensive habits can he have which he cannot support on an income of £33,000? I'm sure Gowrie himself would snort at suggestions that he was born with a silver spoon around his neck.' The unimpeachable Gowrie recovered substantial damages for the false libellous innuendo, which the paper evidently thought it could hint at without making a direct accusation.

Juries can award damages for the use of slang if, in the circumstances in which it has been used, it is defamatory. The pianist Liberace recovered £8,000 damages in 1959 for being described as 'fruit-flavoured' and as 'a deadly winking, sniggering, giggling, mincing, ice-covered heap of mother love and a mountain of jingling claptrap wrapped up in . . . a preposterous clown'. As he later faced a palimony action from a male live-in lover, the verdict that he had been unjustly accused of being homosexual was evidently wrong. And in 1943 a milliner called Thaarup doing his bit for the war effort sued for a caption of a picture of him: 'I only wanted a few pansies.' Lord Justice Scott commented, tongue in cheek, and with a veiled dig at his colleague's proclivities, 'I personally was not alive to the slang meaning of the word, nor, I think, was my brother McKinnon, but my brother Goddard' – later the lord chief justice who hastened Derek Bentley to the gallows – 'fortunately was quite alive to it, having had judicial experience as a result of which he had come to know about it.'

A plaintiff can recover damages even on a more esoteric use of slang if there are a number of people who understood the defamatory connotation. Gaynor Winyard, a beauty therapist, was awarded £75,000 for references in the *Tatler* in September 1989 in its feature about her health spa, entitled 'Sporran Partners'. There was no question that the allegations against her were false: the issue was what they meant. Was the description of Ms Winyard as an 'international boot' a meaningless insult? Was she was being called a haggard old woman, or did the expression bear the equally unjustifiable Scottish slang definition to be found in Beale's *Concise Dictionary of Slang*: 'an excessively compliant female'. A number of readers had spotted this esoteric meaning and she recovered £75,000 damages for the false attack on her reputation. The *Tatler* also had to pay her son, Stephen, £15,000 damages for its reference in this disagreeable article to his giving personalised massages – a generally harmless suggestion rendered defamatory in the context of the feature. By a majority the Court of Appeal upheld the award of £75,000 – one judge would have reduced it to £40,000.

References to a person's looks can in certain circumstances be defamatory if they might lead to that person being shunned, or if they amount to a reflection on that person's ability to pursue his or her chosen occupation. Often the recovery of damages will be made easier by the malicious tone of the piece containing such references. In 1985 Charlotte Cornwell, the actress, was awarded £10,000 against the *Sunday People* for a review which referred to her as an ugly, middle-aged rock star whose bum was too big. This highly offensive attack was made in a column by Nina Myskow entitled 'Wally of the Week'. The Court of Appeal was persuaded that the judge at first instance had been wrong to allow favourable evidence by the actor Ian McKellen of Ms Cornwell's qualities as an actress and singer and to permit reviews of her later plays to be shown to the jury. The defendants claimed this might have resulted in too high an award, but at the resulting retrial she recovered more money, £11,500. The paper had paid £5 into court. However, Cornwell ended up substantially out of pocket owing to the amount of her irrecoverable legal costs. With characteristic skill, the law of libel had conjured up a result which left everyone unhappy and defied all predictions.

Payment into court is a procedure designed to encourage plaintiffs to settle their cases. A defendant can pay into court, unknown to judge or jury until the end of the trial, what he estimates the jury will award if the plaintiff should win. The plaintiff is given twenty-one days to decide whether to accept the payment in or whether to fight on. If he accepts the sum, he will recover his legal costs to date. If he continues with his action and succeeds, but recovers less in damages than the figure tendered by the defendant, he has to pay all the costs incurred after the date of payment in. This system is a salutary reminder that such litigation is a form of gambling, and indeed it has led to the downfall of many an overambitious plaintiff.

The Court of Appeal, by a majority, held in 1997 that an allegation by the columnist Julie Burchill that the actor Steven Berkoff was hideous-looking was capable of being defamatory. Burchill's remark was certainly unpleasant. This slur had first been made in her review of the film *The Age of Innocence*; in her critique of *Frankenstein* she returned to the theme, describing the character of the Creature as 'a lot like Steven Berkoff, only marginally better-looking'. The Court of Appeal recognised the thin dividing line between ridicule in the area of professional activity and insults which would not diminish a person's standing. Again, a ruling was being sought as to what the words were *capable* of meaning. The trial to decide what they *actually* meant would have taken place later, but the parties settled after the ruling.

The differing approach of the members of the Court of Appeal underlines what a subjective matter meaning is. Lord Justice Neill focused on the suggestion that Berkoff was not merely physically unattractive but also repulsive. The perceived intention of the writer could colour the meaning. To say that someone in the public eye who made his living as an actor was repulsive was, Lord Justice Neill felt, capable of lowering his standing in the estimation of the public and making him an object of ridicule. Lord Justice Millett, on the other hand, felt that people must be entitled to poke fun at one another without the fear of litigation. To permit someone to sue for being called 'hideous-looking' was, in his view, an unwarranted restriction on free speech.

A similar issue came up in the Court of Appeal in November 1998, when the opera singer Jessye Norman sued the magazine *Classic CD*. The court felt it was a shame that she took such offence at what was a humorous article about her recording of

*Salome*. The reviewer's mind had evidently boggled at the image of 'the grand statuesque forty-nine year old' as 'a libidinous adolescent stripping off the seven veils'. This brought to mind, it was suggested, with reference to an old joke, the woman who was advised to turn sideways when she became trapped in some swing doors and replied, 'Honey, I ain't got no sideways.'

The court made a detailed analysis of the article and concurred with the decision of the judge at first instance, Mr Justice Buckley, rather than permitting the case to proceed to trial on the basis of somewhat fanciful interpretations. The article, it was noted, was extremely complimentary, drawing attention to Norman's education, her stable family background, her honorary doctorates and her clear grammatical and idiomatic English. That smartly kicked into touch the original pleaded meaning that she was uneducated. The case underlined the laboured and overelaborate meanings which are sometimes pleaded in libel actions. This complaint having been discarded, additional libellous meanings were added by way of amendment to the original claim some three to four years after the article was published. It was claimed that the singer was being accused of patronising hypocritical mockery, of using vulgar and undignified speech and of conforming to a degrading racial stereotype of a person of Afro-American heritage. One might, the court felt, have been able to accept some of those meanings if the words had been viewed in isolation, but the article as a whole portrayed Norman as a person of high standing and impeccable dignity. Her self-deprecating humour was quoted in the article in the comment that she simply didn't look the part for a heroine dying of consumption, even though she was referred to as the new slimmer Jessye.

The pop star Michael Jackson sued the *Daily Mirror* in 1992 for suggesting that his features had become hideously distorted and disfigured by plastic surgery in a quest for perfect looks and that he had banned close-up photographs of himself. The Court of Appeal ordered in 1994 that the action be stayed until Jackson submitted to a medical examination under proper lighting conditions and disclosed his medical records, whereafter it appeared to peter out – a decision reported by the press as Wacko Jacko putting his nose on the line. Four years after this decision the case was settled on confidential terms, reportedly without the payment of damages, but with a contribution to Jackson's legal costs. A London plastic surgeon was flown to Los Angeles, accompanied by miscellaneous London libel lawyers, to examine the unmade-up Jackson. The upshot was an acknowledgement that Jackson was not disfigured or scarred. The star was, however, successful in restricting the use the *Daily Mirror* could make of a close-up photograph they had of him on his European tour. They had breached their one-use-only agreement. The *Mirror* counter-sued for an allegedly defamatory press release issued on behalf of Jackson which accused the newspaper of publishing demonstrably cruel and false allegations about him.

The perils of suing for libel are numerous. So why do so many people do it? Unlike Evelyn Waugh, few are frank enough to admit the lure of tax-free cash. When he sued the *Daily Express* in 1957, having failed to persuade its editor to horsewhip the errant journalist, Nancy Spain, he wrote to his literary agent, A.D. Peters, 'I have waited a long time to catch the *Express* in libel', and to his brother Alec, 'I hope to earn a nice tax-free sum which will pay for Teresa's coming out. It is all very satisfactory. I think I can't lose. It is simply a question of how little or how much I get.' Clive Jenkins, the ASTMS union leader, was equally frank. He enjoyed suing for libel. 'My union fights the case and pockets the cost, while I keep the damages.'

Some have, however, spoken in lighthearted vein of the use to which they put their well-deserved libel damages. Lord Gowrie said he reroofed his house and Sir David Steel, the former Liberal leader, added the £100,000 he was believed to have recovered from the *Sun* and the *News of the World* in respect of articles in 1987 to grants from the Historic Buildings Council and his local council to renovate his Grade A-listed tower house in the Scottish borders.

The law of libel does provide remedies other than damages. A statement can be read in open court recording the exoneration of the plaintiff and any apology the defendant cares to make. The wording has to be approved by a judge beforehand. Once the statement has been read, it can be reported as a court hearing, which means that any fair and accurate publication of what has been said is privileged and libel-proof. Often the parties will, as part of a settlement, agree the wording of the statement. If the plaintiff decides to accept damages which have been paid into court, he can apply to a judge for leave to have a unilateral statement read in open court. This is the second-best option as it cannot, without the defendant's agreement, contain an apology, but it is nonetheless an opportunity for a plaintiff to remind the world of his unblemished reputation and his trouncing of the defendant. Just how fulsomely he can do so will depend on the level of damages he has obtained.

A plaintiff may also obtain an injunction preventing the repetition of the libel. This will normally follow a verdict in his favour, although this is not invariably the case, as the McDonald's litigation recounted in Chapter 7 shows. Breach of an injunction is a contempt of court, for which a defendant could be imprisoned.

Of greater interest to many plaintiffs is avoiding publication of the libel in the first place by obtaining an immediate injunction to prevent the offending article from seeing the light of day, or at least to limit its circulation. This can be done by a private (ex parte) application to a judge – by telephoning him at home if the matter is extremely urgent and publication is imminent. A successful use of this procedure occurred in October 1989, when the Countess of Avon, widow of Sir Anthony Eden, concluded that a defamatory reference to an unnamed woman in Richard Deacon's book about the Burgess and Maclean affair, *The Greatest Treason*, could be understood to refer to her. An injunction was obtained that evening by telephone. The publishers, Century Hutchinson, immediately accepted that there were no grounds whatsoever for casting suspicion on the conduct of Lady Avon. They recalled all copies of the book and pulped them. They did not try to set the injunction aside; moreover, they apologised in a statement in open court a few months later, deeply regretting that the book made any such allegations, which they entirely withdrew.

In granting an injunction, the judge will want to know why the plaintiff has not notified the other side and will give the injunction only for a limited period to enable the defendant to apply to have it lifted. The advantage to the plaintiff of a private hearing is that if it fails, the defendant may not find out that the application has been made in sufficient time to publicise the material in question as 'the story they tried to stop' – indeed, he may never get to hear of it at all. A plaintiff will not, under the rule in Bonnard v. Perryman, obtain an interlocutory injunction pending the trial if the defendant asserts that he intends to justify the allegations complained of. The 1997 case of Holley v. Smith showed that the courts would not in such circumstances grant an injunction against the repetition of contested allegations of fraud in relation to a trust unless the plaintiff could prove that they were plainly untrue.

Mohamed Fayed, the owner of the House of Fraser and its flagship store, Harrods, was unable to prevent the *Observer* from publishing in 1986 details about his financial past, his background and how he had financed the purchase of the House of Fraser, because the *Observer* proposed to justify what they intended to print. As Fayed was subsequently to be condemned by the DTI inspectors for his use of gagging writs, and as he later capitulated in his litigation against the *Observer* rather than give full disclosure of his finances, and paid the newspaper's legal costs in full, this was clearly a just result.

The tycoon Robert Maxwell made three attempts to injunct Tom Bower's book, *Maxwell the Outsider*, failing each time because Bower asserted he could justify what he had written. Having failed to suppress the book, Maxwell eventually dropped his libel action against Bower and his publishers Aurum Press, then part of the Really Useful Group, although not until after he had bought a substantial shareholding in the Really Useful Group in the forlorn hope of exerting pressure on its owner Andrew Lloyd Webber.

A court ruled that a Londoner could not be injuncted from inscribing over the flaking paint of his house abutting the South Circular Road, 'This house was painted with Carson's Paints'. The householder claimed that the brown paint used on his home had begun to turn green within six months, presenting, in the judge's view, 'a multi-coloured appearance not unlike military camouflage'. As he proposed to justify, the aggrieved paint company could not silence him until the trial. Crest Homes experienced the same problem with one of their customers, who was sufficiently upset by the defects in his cherry-red front door to unscrew it and fix it to the front of his Rolls–Royce, bearing the message, painted in yellow, 'This door, fitted by Crest Homes, is typical of the poor-quality materials used, and as with all other paintwork needed renovating within twelve months.'

The danger for a defendant of contesting an injunction on the grounds that he will justify the material he intends to publish is that if he fails to do so at a subsequent libel trial, and loses the case, higher damages may be awarded to the plaintiff.

Robert Maxwell recovered £50,000 exemplary damages from *Private Eye* when the magazine proved unable to justify its allegations that he had funded an African tour made by Labour leader Neil Kinnock in the hope of receiving a peerage, as it had asserted it would in order to defeat Maxwell's application for an interim injunction. When the defendants failed to do so they were penalised by a larger award in damages than would otherwise have been the case.

The Defamation Act 1996 gives the court new powers to try to put matters right other than simply relying on the undoubted attractions of an award of tax-free money (libel damages are tax-free unless they represent loss of income, which is taxable in the normal way). Under Section 9 of the act the court can declare material to be false and defamatory and can order the publication of a correction and apology. The court has not been given power to direct how any such correction or apology should be published – there would be obvious implications for the freedom of the press if a High Court judge was able to rearrange the front page of a newspaper. However, if the parties fail to agree on the form of the correction and apology, the court can give a ruling which must be suitably reported.

While the principal aim of libel damages is vindication of reputation, this can also have the useful side-effect of securing business objectives (Chapter 10). Less creditably, suing for libel has been viewed by writers of fiction as a means of somebody transferring wealth tax-free by arranging to defame a person to whom he wants to give some money without incurring capital transfer taxes. The nearest reality might have come to this scenario was in a criminal case in 1997, when Jack Robinson, previously chairman of Wigan Rugby League Football Club, was accused but acquitted of perverting the course of justice. The alleged plan, which bordered on farce, and which the jury clearly found incredible, was to mulct the *Wigan Observer* in damages. Robinson felt the newspaper had gone too far when it published a story claiming that the Wigan squad had been on an all-night drinking binge while on a team holiday in Tenerife. The article was illustrated by a picture of their international player Neil Cowie, who had been skiing in Scotland at the time. In retaliation, Robinson was alleged to have hit on the wheeze of persuading another club-owner to claim that he had withdrawn a fictitious bid to buy Cowie as a result of the newspaper coverage. He and Robinson would split the libel damages fifty-fifty. Not surprisingly the other man said he dropped the telephone when he heard this and immediately retorted that they would both end up in jail if they did it. Robinson was said to have subsequently adjusted this to sixty-forty, at which point the other chairman told him to bugger off. After Robinson explained that a misunderstanding had arisen – he had made the approach as a favour to a third party and knew it would be rejected out of hand – he was acquitted.

A plaintiff has to prove three things in a libel action: that the words used were defamatory; that they referred to him; and that they were published to a third party. He does not have to prove his good reputation, or that he suffered actual damage as a result

of the libel. It is not necessary to show that the plaintiff was
named in order to establish reference. In a defamatory article in
1978, for which he recovered £50,000 in damages from the
*Sunday Telegraph*, Jack Hayward was referred to simply as 'a
wealthy benefactor of the Liberal Party' in a discussion about the
events which led to the charging (and acquittal) of Jeremy
Thorpe, the former Liberal leader, for conspiracy to murder.
Wealthy benefactors of the Liberals were few and far between,
and as a further report the following week made it clear that the
paper had intended to refer to Hayward, the jury had little difficulty in deciding reference, even though the first article,
somewhat artificially in the circumstances, had to be interpreted
as readers would have interpreted it that first Sunday.

The fact that a libel was unintended is not in itself a defence,
although it is likely to be relevant to the level of damages. In
1994 the London *Evening Standard* had to pay damages to the
distinguished chancellor of Glasgow University, Sir Alec
Cairncross, whose photograph wrongly adorned its report about
a suspected member of the Cambridge spy ring, John Cairncross,
his brother, who had worked at the Government Code and
Cypher School at Bletchley. And an English QC recently recovered damages when his name was wrongly attached to a
photograph of a similarly named Scottish QC accused of sexual
misconduct. The *Guardian* had to fork out damages believed to
be £15,000 to Labour MP George Howarth for recounting an
entertaining but incorrect story of boorish and drunken behaviour when Howarth was said to have bumped into the writer Fritz
Spiegl in Soho and mouthed expletives at him. The newspaper
had the wrong man – Howarth had never met Spiegl.
Regrettably, the newspaper failed to accept its mistake from the
outset and did not apologise to Howarth until after he had
incurred the expense of taking the case to court.

Even typographical errors can result in libel awards, for
readers might not appreciate that an error has been made. One
newspaper had to pay damages to the head of a car-distribution
business for its report of the damages he himself had to find for

road-testing the wife of a wronged husband. The piece had been headlined: 'CAR THIEF TO PAY £1,000 TO HUSBAND'.

In 1999 Patti Boulaye, the Nigerian-born singer and actress, accepted damages of £15,000 from the *Guardian*. In explaining her decision to seek a seat as a Conservative in the Greater London Assembly, she had said it was time 'to support a party'. In quoting her as saying it was time to support apartheid, the newspaper gave a very different and offensive impression of her views.

A respectable resident of Hans Place in Knightsbridge was likewise awarded damages because a photograph accompanying a story headlined 'VICE DEN IN SNOB SQUARE' featured an arrow unhelpfully pointing to her flat. And David Morgan, a council caretaker who had already won £2,100 in damages from Haringey Council in London, whom he had accused of wrongfully sacking him because of his sexual proclivities, recovered damages believed to be £6,000 for a letter written by the council's human resources manager to the opposition group leader. The letter stated that Morgan had been sacked because he could not get on with black caretakers and for falsifying council notebooks. Not only had Morgan not falsified the documents, but the manager had meant to write *block* caretakers.

It is perhaps scant consolation that a defendant has to prove only that what he or she published was true. He does not have to justify why he published it. He can repeat any old piece of gossip, however unpleasant, provided it is true. Only if he maliciously refers to a conviction which is deemed 'spent' under the Rehabilitation of Offenders Act 1974 can he be sued for telling the provable truth. If the defendant can prove the bulk of what has been alleged, he may have a complete defence under Section 5 of the Defamation Act 1952 or a partial defence which will reduce the damages.

If a defendant can prove that what he published was comment, and not an allegation of fact; that the comment was on a matter of public interest; that the comment was based on facts which were substantially true; that it was a view which a fair-minded person might honestly hold; then he has a defence of fair comment – however bigoted his opinion.

In certain circumstances the courts will uphold a defence of privilege where there is sufficient common interest in enabling people to communicate freely with each other, even if what is said cannot be proved to be true. Certain publications are absolutely privileged, such as words spoken in court or in Parliament. Under Section 14 of the Defamation Act 1996, fair and accurate contemporaneous reports of court proceedings enjoy absolute privilege. However, the courts are reluctant to expand this defence. In 1997 an unfortunate bank clerk, Lynne Griffiths of Portardawe, found it did not extend to a libel claim brought against her by a convicted rapist. She had complained to the police about his prospective release on parole on the grounds he had been bombarding her with letters and phone calls. He asserted that her denial of any romantic attachment was libellous and would prevent him from getting parole. The court refused to strike out the case on the ground that the facts were in dispute and the action was not bound to fail leaving Mrs Griffiths with the prospect of £30,000 in legal fees. It was a case which could have been efficiently and economically determined under the summary procedure laid out in the Defamation Act 1996, which had not yet been brought into force.

Certain publications will enjoy qualified privilege if there is a duty to communicate the information and a corresponding interest in receiving it. This means that the defendant will have a defence, even if what he or she wrote was defamatory and false. An example would be in the giving of a reference. That would be covered by qualified privilege, so no action could be brought even if the reference contained false and defamatory comment unless malice could be proved. In the absence of malice, the only basis on which someone can sue for a bad reference is if it has been negligently provided. This was established by the House of Lords in the case brought in 1991 by Graham Spring, who successfully claimed that Guardian Assurance had owed him a duty of care when they gave Scottish Amicable a reference which was the kiss of death for his career in insurance. This defence has been expanded by the decision in the Reynolds case, dealt with in Chapter 16. Reports of various public bodies or meetings are protected by qualified privilege, although in some instances a paper can be asked to publish a statement in reasonable explanation or contradiction of (but not an apology for) what has been said at, for example, a company meeting. To defeat a defence of qualified privilege, the plaintiff has the burden of proving malice on the part of the defendant. This can include not only ill will but improper conduct or motive.

It is no defence to assert that the defendant has simply repeated what someone else has said. In Stern v. Piper (1997), the *Mail on Sunday* had written about a well-known property developer, William Stern, who was being sued for £3 million. It quoted from an affidavit seeking to give evidence that Stern had failed to meet his commitments. The paper could show that such an affidavit had been sworn, but not that the allegation itself was true, and in March 1998 paid substantial damages to Stern. Only when the contents of the affidavit were read into proceedings held in public would they become privileged, unless qualified privilege under the Reynolds case could be established. Normally the repetition of a rumour will involve a defendant in having to prove the truth of what was being said rather than proving that there was such a rumour. The decision in Aspro Travel v. Owners Abroad Group (1996), that a defendant could rely on the existence of a rumour of insolvency as opposed to actual insolvency, was doubted in two cases in 1998: Bennett v. Mirror Group and Shah v. Standard Chartered Bank. In the latter example, defamatory allegations were repeated relying on an affidavit by a Bank of England official (although the point complained of did not feature in a subsequent Bank of England report). The Court of Appeal followed the Stern case rather than the Aspro decision. In other words: if you repeat someone else's defamatory words, you may have to prove that what was said was true, not simply that it was said.

Meanwhile, Stern's own triumph was limited. In April 2000 he was banned from being a company director for twelve years owing to his 'objectionable' conduct in relation to the collapse of one of his firms with debts of £11 million – a relatively modest sum compared to the £118 million involved in a more spectacular failure of some of his companies back in 1979.

If it is a reasonably foreseeable consequence of an original libel that it will be republished, a defendant may face a claim for such republications. Accordingly, in 1990 the Court of Appeal held that former Detective Chief Superintendent Jack Slipper could sue the BBC not only for its wholly inappropriate depiction of him in its film *The Great Paper Chase* (based on the book *Slip-up*) as a ridiculous buffoon in his attempts to bring Ronald Biggs, the convicted Great Train robber, back to the UK, but also for the reviews which repeated the allegation. Slipper of the Yard subsequently trousered £50,000 in damages.

A person who has agreed not to repeat a libel but then does so faces an additional peril. In November 1995, Baron Stephen Bentinck recovered £50,000 damages against the *Daily Mail* gossip columnist Nigel Dempster for suggestions that he was a creep and had been mean to his sick wife when he divorced her. Dempster gave an undertaking not to repeat the libel. In October 1997 he unwisely wrote of Bentinck's former wife receiving 'a tax-free £5,000-a-month settlement but no lump sum'. Those last four words were ruled by Judge Richard Walker to be a breach of the undertaking. Had the breach been deliberate, he would have committed Dempster to jail for a significant period of time, but it was found to be due rather to ineptitude and negligence. Dempster was fined £10,000 and his newspaper £25,000 with £20,000 costs.

Even apologies can give rise to libel claims. In 1954 journalist Honor Tracy recovered £3,000 from *The Sunday Times* when the newspaper apologised, without consulting her, to the Doneraile parish priest after she had written a piece criticising the money spent on building him a house. And in 1991 a freelance journalist obtained £20,000 damages against the *Derby Herald and Post* for another uncleared apology, before the decision in Derbyshire County Council v. *The Sunday Times*, to Derbyshire County Council.

Even before the procedures introduced by the Defamation Act 1996, moves were being made, albeit in an unstructured fashion, to simplify the law of libel. Surprisingly few libel actions in fact turn on the killer document, so judges are reluctant, bearing in mind the costs involved, to allow discovery which is too extensive or to prolong cases by permitting side-issues. A fine balance must be struck between cost on the one hand and allowing a plaintiff artificially to narrow the issues and confine the battleground to the only area where he feels safe. On occasion the courts seem to go too far in narrowing the issues when there is no real danger of the defendants oppressively expanding the scope of the action. In doing so, it could be argued that they are following the lead of Parliament which, surprisingly, removed Clause 13 of the 1996 Defamation Bill, which would have repealed the rule in Scott v. Sampson (1882). This allows evidence of the general bad reputation of the defendant to be given in mitigation of damages, but specific instances of misconduct cannot be led in evidence.

The absurdity of this rule was illustrated by the 1961 case of Plato Films Ltd v. Speidel. Speidel, by then a leading NATO general, was less than happy with a film *Operation Teutonic Sword*, depicting him during the war as having betrayed Rommel and murdered King Alexander of Yugoslavia and the French minister, Jean-Louis Barthou. Plato Films wanted to prove in mitigation of damages that Speidel had a bad reputation earned by his other war crimes in Russia and France. The House of Lords ruled that details of unrelated war crimes were inadmissible and the defendants could only assert his bad reputation in general and unspecific terms. It was a ruling that later proved helpful to scoundrels such as Robert Maxwell.

In United States Tobacco International v. BBC (1988), the BBC's consumer programme *That's Life* accused the tobacco company of marketing its Skoal Bandits chewing tobacco, which was alleged to be carcinogenic, to young people in breach of

DHSS guidelines. The company chose to sue only for the breach of the guidelines libel and not for the cancer allegation. The BBC was not allowed to justify its allegations about cancer, as to do so would have enormously prolonged the trial, but the court noted that the company's failure to sue on this far more serious allegation could be the subject of strong comment at the trial.

The fast-track procedure introduced by the Defamation Act of 1996 was to some extent foreshadowed by the use of an arbitrator, Lord Williams of Mostyn QC, then chairman of the Bar Council, to assess the claim for damages brought by Mr Justice Popplewell, the libel judge, against the now defunct *Today* newspaper in 1992. The paper had by then admitted libelling him by falsely suggesting that he might have fallen asleep during a case. Williams awarded the surprisingly low figure of £7,500 damages to the judge for what was unquestionably a very serious libel. He was left having to pay part of the costs, having rejected the tendered sum of £10,000. The experiment itself was otherwise a success. The case was over within an hour, and took less than seven weeks from start to finish. It was estimated that the procedure might have saved as much as £20,000 in costs by avoiding a full trial. It was, however, a painful and spectacular reminder of the uncertainties of libel litigation. This type of arbitration procedure was recently successfully used by the Rowntree charity to resolve a libel claim against *The Sunday Times*. Once a QC had decided that the charity had been libelled, an apology was quickly published and Rowntree's legal costs paid.

A potentially complex claim brought against the same newspaper by the magazine publishers Haymarket Publications over a motor racing matter was likewise swiftly resolved once an arbitrator ruled on the meaning of the contentious words. Mediation was also used by a firm of solicitors in Manchester to resolve eleven claims arising out of comments made by a disc jockey on a radio station. The settlement involved the novel but sensible remedy of a face-to-face apology.

Straightforward cases have tended to come up for trial within six to nine months of the writ being issued, and that has resulted in the saving of costs. Even contested cases can be heard in a short time. The record appears to be the case brought by the boxing entrepreneur Frank Warren against the *Mirror* in 1990 for its distasteful comment, five days after he was shot, allegedly by the boxer Terry Marsh: 'Frank Warren started in the gutter and almost ended up there.' The sole issue in Warren's action against the *Mirror* was whether the words had any defamatory meaning or were simply a passing insult. The jury awarded Warren £10,000 and the case was over within a creditable three hours. Ironically, the motive alleged against Marsh at his criminal trial was that he was trying to 'abate' a separate libel action brought by Warren against him by killing the plaintiff. If this had been true, it would have constituted a novel application of the principle that libel actions cannot be brought by or continued on behalf of or against dead people. Clearly it was not: Marsh was eventually acquitted of the attempted murder of Warren. Moreover, Marsh successfully defended the libel action brought against him by his rival. The jury found that Warren had consented to the words spoken about him by Marsh in the course of the television interview in question. Of thirty libel actions brought by Warren, this is the only one he has lost.

In the past decade a wide spectrum of people has processed through the libel courts. The oddest of all, perhaps, was a five-year-old branded by the *Sun* in 1991 as the worst brat in Britain. Contrary to the implication of the newspaper's description of him, he had neither killed the family cat nor cut off his own ear; sadly, he had suffered from meningitis and had a behavioural disorder. To the paper's credit, it settled the case within six days, even though, as the falsely accused 'terror tot' was a minor, the settlement of £35,000 damages had to be approved by a judge, as in the case of Lester Piggott (see Chapter 19).

Until recent times members of the royal family have not sued for libel. In 1789, the editor of *The Times* was jailed for sixteen months for commenting on the insincerity of the joyous response of the Prince of Wales and the Duke of York to the recovery of George III from his illness. Edward Mylius, editor of the *Liberator*, ended up in prison for two years when he accused George V of bigamy. And in Victorian times the Prince of Wales, later Edward VII, did not enjoy having to give evidence in the Gordon–Cumming baccarat libel action.

In March 1990, however, the Queen's nephew, Viscount Linley, recovered £35,000 damages for libel, of which £30,000 were exemplary damages against *Today* for unregal allegations that the Viscount had behaved like an upper-class lager lout in the Ferret and Firkin pub in Chelsea. The newspaper did not contend that the allegations were true. When *Today* appealed against the form of the award, the damages were by agreement – and to the annoyance of the trial judge, Mr Justice Michael Davies – adjusted to £30,000, with any suggestion of them being exemplary damages removed. In March 1997, Princess Diana received damages against the *Sunday Express* of £75,000 (which she donated to the Aids Crisis Trust and the Royal Marsden Hospital) for suggestions that she would be pocketing half the proceeds from the sale of eighty of her evening dresses, which were being auctioned in New York. The paper, it transpired, had been the victim of an elaborate forgery.

As luck would have it, in April 1999 the same newspaper group found itself forking out substantial libel damages in almost identical circumstances, this time to Princess Diana's brother, Earl Spencer. Apparently as a result of a sub-editing error, he was wrongly accused of using the proceeds of a concert at Althorp House, the Spencer family seat, to meets its running expenses, when in truth they were going to the Princess of Wales Memorial Fund,

Those on the fringes of the royal family, or who have been connected with the royal family, have also sued. In Penny Junor's first book on the Prince of Wales, *Charles*, published in 1987, a picture of Lady Camilla Fane, with the caption, 'Charles missed his chance but some say he had never been so much in love', was inadvertently included. It was wrongly stated in the text that Lady Camilla had married Andrew Parker Bowles and that Charles had continued to visit her home after his marriage.

It was, of course, Camilla Shand who had that honour. The author had completely muddled her Camillas. In fact Camilla Fane had been a friend of Prince Charles before either of them had married, and Penny Junor had assumed that she was the Camilla who became Camilla Parker Bowles. The mistake was no doubt annoying for Camilla Fane, who, by that time, had become Lady Camilla Hipwood. In the event worthwhile damages were paid not only to Camilla Hipwood but also to Andrew Parker Bowles. It is not immediately apparent how his friends and acquaintances would have thought the worse of the Roman Catholic brigadier as a result of the error in Junor's book. One divorce, one remarriage and a much-discussed private life later, it is possible that Parker Bowles would not now have sued Junor.

Less successful was the suit brought by James Hewitt in 1992 against the *Sun* over allegations about his relationship with Princess Diana. He nobly dropped his action in 1993, partly on the grounds of expense, but partly, he explained, because the court ordeal would have been too horrendous for her. It was perhaps just as well. Given that Anna Pasternak's book *Princess in Love*, published in 1994, described Diana's letters to Hewitt, away in the Gulf War – how every night she lay awake thanking God for bringing him into her life and aching with desire to be in his arms – denial of the affair would indeed have proved an ordeal. Pasternak was herself to sue the *Daily Mail* with some success for unkind comments made about her after the publication of the book. *Princess in Love* was followed by Hewitt's own magnum opus *Love and War* – his epic account of his time between the sheets and in the Gulf – which probably did more damage to his reputation than anything the *Sun* was capable of.

As we have seen with Mr Justice Popplewell, judges, too, have sued for libel. In 1996 Judge Griffiths recovered damages for an inaccurate court report put out by a news agency concerning a sentence he had passed on a sex offender. The judge's reference to the fact that the victim would have forgiven her attacker if he had apologised was wholly misrepresented and exaggerated by a headline-grabbing and false summary. Likewise Judge Brooks, in

1994, was awarded damages against *Hello!* magazine, which was unwise enough to publish the comments of the convicted socialite Darius Guppy on the judge's handling of his fraud trial. *Hello!*, with its sugary profiles, seems an unlikely libel defendant, but this is not the only such case in which it has been involved: in 1991 it was sued by a solicitor for a suggestion he had defrauded his client.

In 1994 another member of the legal profession, Judge James Harkess, whose wife and daughters had featured in the salacious diaries of politician Alan Clark, deservedly recovered substantial damages from *The Sunday Times* for its provocative article 'Revenge of a Cuckold', which suggested that he had been motivated by money in the public comments he had made about Clark's diaries, and that he was so right wing that he had been denied citizenship in South Africa. Clark was reported to have himself consulted lawyers about untrue allegations made in the *Sun* that he had fathered a love child and exposed his penis to gay friends. Sadly, this intriguing case never reached court, as Clark became a columnist for the *Sun*'s sister paper, the *News of the World*. However, many people do feel under greater pressure to sue to clear their names in England than they do in, say, the USA, where such an action by a public figure would almost certainly fail irrespective of its falsity.

More rarely, judges have also proved to be the perpetrators of libel. When Michael Argyle QC, a retired Old Bailey judge, wrote an article in the *Spectator* attacking the defendants in the *Oz Schoolkids* issue obscenity trial of 1971, he overlooked the fact that he did not enjoy the absolute privilege against libel which had covered his utterances on the bench. These had earned him the nickname 'Maximum Mike'. Argyle was stirred into action by Felix Dennis's review of the book *Hippy Hippy Shake*, written by his co-defendant Richard Neville published in 1995. *Oz Schoolkids* had been put together under the editorship of Dennis and Neville, following *Homosexual Oz* and *Acid Oz*. It featured a well-endowed Rupert Bear and the Furry Freak Brothers.

During the six-week obscenity trial the judge had epitomised the clash of cultures. He had memorably interrupted George Melly's evidence about cunnilingus to ask, 'For those of us who did not have a classical education, what do you mean by cunnilinctus?' Melly had also testified to similar effect, and without Latin, in describing 'yodelling in the canyon'. Felix Dennis in his closing remarks, had said: 'I emerge from the trial confirmed in my views about the lack of communication and understanding between myself as a young person and you as a judge.'

Argyle had been subjected to a lot of abuse at the trial. Marty Feldman, the comedian, had gone unpunished when he commented, 'Sorry, Judge, am I waking you up?' after calling him a boring old fart. Argyle had been burned in effigy outside the Old Bailey. In his summing-up, the judge had poured scorn on the defence case ('Homosexuality' [one of the defendants said], 'is not a perversion, well . . . there we are') and denigrated its expert evidence ('so-called defence experts who you may think either had to admit they were wrong or tell a lie'). The three defendants – Dennis, Neville and Jim Anderson – were convicted of publishing an obscene article, but acquitted of a conspiracy to corrupt public morals. Argyle remanded the defendants in custody, and on their return to the court with a decent haircut he sentenced the twenty-four-year-old Dennis to nine months, as opposed to the fifteen months he had dished out to Richard Neville. Dennis received the lesser sentence because he was said by the judge to be 'very much less intelligent than his two co-defendants'. The convictions for obscenity were quashed by the lord chief justice, Lord Widgery, on the grounds of misdirection. The conviction for sending indecent material through the post was upheld, although the prison sentences were suspended.

By 1995, the 'less intelligent' Dennis had established a £100 million computer publishing company; Argyle had retired and felt able to share his bizarre reminiscences with readers of the *Spectator*. Among these was the recollection that he had ordered a glass from which John Peel, the disc jockey, had drunk some water in court to be destroyed after Peel admitted in the witness box to having had VD. More pertinently, he described how he had had four special branch officers and two Alsatian dogs guarding him twenty-four hours a day because of threats made against him. In fact these threats had come from someone wholly unconnected with the *Oz* defendants. Argyle madly suggested that behind *Oz* lay a conspiracy of criminals who were trying to sell drugs at school gates and youth clubs. He commented that when the accused were sent to prison, the trafficking seemed to slacken, and when the convictions were quashed, it appeared to pick up. Dennis successfully sued him for libel for the false suggestions that he had been supplying drugs to children and had put the judge's life at risk. The *Spectator* paid damages believed to be £10,000, which were donated by Dennis to the National Library for the Blind and a Down's Syndrome charity.

Despite these perhaps less than promising precedents, in February 2000 the lord chancellor proposed that judges should, where so advised, receive assistance from public funds for libel actions. It was, however, explained that the public purse would have the first call on any damages recovered to reimburse any irrecoverable costs and that judges would be required to give the surplus to charity. A similar proposal was put forward to protect members of Parliament involved in libel actions as a result of work carried out in their capacity as MPs. This was raised after Peter Luff MP successfully defended a claim by a convicted murderer, Denzil Walker, who was serving a sentence for strangling an Australian backpacker. Walker had taken Luff to court when the MP criticised him for suing a postmistress who refused to deliver the *Financial Times* to him in jail.

The Argyle case was the second time the *Spectator* had been sued for libel in relation to the *Oz* trial. In a background sketch of the trial published at the time, it had referred to the journalists covering the proceedings as a bunch of drunken hacks. As they were not named, the question arose as to whether this slur was actionable. Surprisingly, the journalists had little difficulty in establishing that they had been identified from this description and they recovered damages.

Even more unwisely, *Private Eye*, in 1991, libelled the

renowned libel lawyers Peter Carter-Ruck and Partners and had to pay substantial damages for allegations concerning the way the firm handled an action. In 1990 the newspaper *Today* had to stump up similarly substantial damages for leading libel solicitor Oscar Beuselinck, for a jocular reference that he breached clients' confidences. Beuselinck was not a man to be crossed, as the *Mail on Sunday* found to their cost when they published in their *You* magazine what they believed to be a friendly profile of him and his actor son. Both collected damages for false allegations of disloyalty and hypocrisy in 1992.

The *Independent on Sunday* set some sort of record in 1990 by attracting litigation before the newspaper was even launched. A dummy issue sent to advertisers earned a writ from James Gatward, chief executive of TVS, concerning problems relating to the acquisition of the television company MTM in the USA. And PR consultant Mathew Freud managed to be successfully sued by a property company for his 1988 Christmas card, which invited people to guess whether it was a) that company and one of its directors, b) Emma Freud or c) Frank Bough who had not paid their bill that year. In fact there had been a dispute about the bill and part of it had been paid. Like many jokes, it fell disastrously flat in the libel courts. The director of the property company was awarded £10,000 damages. Freud's company was nearly ruined by sums which at that time it could scarcely afford to lose. The following year's card invited clients to guess whether the previous one had cost the company £1,000, £5,000 or £50,000.

Other members of the Freud family have been more successful in libel litigation. Mathew's father, Clement Freud, the bon viveur who later became a Liberal MP, won damages against Kemsley Newspapers in 1956, although they amounted to less than the sum paid into court, for portraying him as a chubby nightclub owner retiring to his club to drink brandy after his nightly run. Mathew's nephew Tom Freud recovered damages for misleading reports in the *Daily Mail* about a murder case in which he was a witness, and the artist Lucien Freud, Mathew's uncle, recovered damages for an unfortunately worded profile in the *Daily Telegraph* in which the careless use of a wrong name confused family relationships and resulted in a wholly unintended meaning.

The Freuds are an example of a libel-prone family; multiple individual plaintiffs abound, as will become clear later in this book. Self-confessed multiple defendants are rarer. One such, the gossip columnist Taki Theodoracopoulos, has been sued four times and lost on each occasion. In 1986 he had to pay socialite Rosemary Marcie Riviere £15,000 for a vitriolic and wholly unfounded attack on her in the *Spectator* after he had been refused admission to a lunch party she was giving in Spetsai. 'Multiple face-lifts and multi-millions do not a lady make,' he wrote, as he laid into what he saw as her breeding, recently acquired money, sexuality and lack of taste, as well as working over her entourage and family. The case is estimated to have cost £150,000. Taki's counterclaim for her comments about him in *Women's Wear Daily* was rejected. In 1991 he had to pay actor Sylvester Stallone substantial damages for falsely suggesting that he had gone to work in Switzerland in preference to fighting in Vietnam.

There is, after the McDonald's case (covered in Chapter 7), a little more latitude as to the nature of the evidence required for a defence of justification. But the burden of proof on a libel defendant remains a heavy one. The opportunity for a plaintiff to exploit this situation was illustrated by the injunction that Charles St George, a Lloyd's underwriter, was able to obtain in 1986 against Godfrey Hodgson's book *Lloyd's of London: a Reputation at Risk.* Hodgson claimed that St George, one-time head of the discredited Oakeley Vaughan Group, had been suspended from Lloyd's. St George had resigned from Oakeley Vaughan, and had not in fact been suspended. A writ was immediately issued.

Not only did Hodgson have the burden of proving that what he had said was true, or at any rate substantially true, but he had to do so very swiftly if he was to prevent his book from being injuncted. Hodgson had heard from a source at Lloyd's that disciplinary proceedings had been taken against St George in 1981, but he had been unable to obtain firm proof of this. In fact, three directors of Oakeley Vaughan had been adjudged to have fallen short of the standards expected of Lloyd's and had been suspended for two years. St George had been expected by his colleagues to resign as chairman of Oakeley Vaughan and to cease to exercise management or control over the company after an inquiry by a leading underwriter, Henry Chester, followed by a special audit by the accountants Ernst & Young to investigate massive overwriting and the acceptance of risks from dubious sources in the United States.

This, however, was not St George's plan. Instead, Oakeley Vaughan 'names' were reassured that Chester's inquiry was not unusual, and purely of a technical nature. St George, by then a pillar of the British establishment and a leading racehorse-owner, was ordered to be reprimanded and a notice of the penalty was to be posted at Lloyd's. After discreet discussions between leading figures at Lloyd's, this was downgraded to a private reprimand. The Chester Report was not published – not even a summary of its findings was announced – and 'names' were not informed about what was happening. The group collapsed with debts of over £5 million six years later. 'Names' who looked to the group's errors and omissions policy to help them meet some of their losses found that the funds available under the policy had already been claimed by those ahead of them in the game. The group's computer records were subsequently destroyed in a fire which broke out not very long after a court order had been made for their production.

It might have been thought that there was a significant degree of public interest in an investigation of the byzantine affairs of Charles St George and the Oakeley Vaughan Group. However, such a defence was not then permissible under English libel law. The question was whether Hodgson could justify what he had written. Clearly he could not justify that St George had been suspended, because he had not been, but he would have stood a reasonable chance of substantiating the sting of what he had claimed if he had had access to the findings of the inquiry, or if a plaintiff such as St George had been required to verify the facts underlying his own claim. But St George was under no obligation to produce documentary evidence to establish the facts in respect of which he was seeking an injunction. He certainly did have a copy of the Chester Report which condemned his activities. Hodgson asked Lloyd's if he could see a copy of the Chester Report for the purpose of filing his defence. Ironically, Lloyd's felt unable to comply for fear of itself being sued for libel.

Faced with an injunction, Hodgson had no alternative but to withdraw the book and make changes which satisfied St George. St George's tactics had, however, ensured that an unjust decision had been obtained. In practice, when the publication of a book has to be postponed in such circumstances it is difficult to relaunch it with the same prospect of success, and its authority is weakened by the acknowledgement of significant 'errors'.

A classic example of the use of the law of libel to prevent light being cast on one's own activities was Kunwar Chander Jeet Singh, who ran two licensed dealers in securities, London Venture Capital Market (LVCM) and Ravendale Securities. He also had a group of share shops, City Investment Centres, until it was wound up by the Department of Trade and Industry (DTI) in November 1986, owing its investors over £1 million. In the early to mid-1980s the *Observer* ran a series of investigative articles probing Singh's activities and his links with what the FBI termed 'LCN' (La Cosa Nostra) business associates. Of particular interest to the financial journalist Lorana Sullivan were the seemingly false rumours which had hyped the share price of one of Singh's companies, Bio-Isolates, from 33p, its issue price, to 350p. Successively it was said to be on the point of collaborating with SmithKline, obtaining a US share quotation, attracting a takeover bid from Rank Hovis MacDougall and even linking up with McDonald's. None of these attractive rumoured plans materialised. Bio-Isolates Holdings had been floated on the unlisted securities market by LVCM.

Before the implementation of the Financial Services Act of

1986, private investors were very much at the mercy of licensed dealers and greatly at risk if the dealer defaulted. The *Observer*'s exposure of unscrupulous dealers provided a very real service to the investing public, particularly when the DTI had insufficient resources or will to intervene promptly.

In January 1984 the *Observer* published an article entitled 'Chander Singh's Major Error of Judgement'. This stated that one quarter of Ravendale Group plc's issued capital had been allotted to New York sportsman and restaurateur Abraham Margolies, whose name, the paper alleged, featured in FBI reports on organised crime. The *Observer* received what appeared to be gagging writs from Singh, Ravendale and Margolies. Margolies subsequently withdrew his action and paid a substantial contribution to the *Observer*'s costs. This action by Singh was dismissed in 1987, when he failed to provide £125,000 security for costs. He had by this time moved to India after the failure of his City Investment Centres share shops.

In 1985 Singh had issued another writ against the *Observer* for Sullivan's article in December 1984, 'Chander's SEC Problems', which described what Mr Justice Macpherson called the 'unedifying' history of Singh's dealings with the American *Penny Stock News* tipsheet. The report detailed the Securities and Exchange Commission's proceedings in respect of a $20,000 payment by Singh for a favourable article about Bio-Isolates Holdings.

The *Observer* defended its reports as true. Singh showed reluctance to attend court. On the first trial date, 8 February 1988, he was found to be languishing in the Taj Mahal Hotel in New Delhi with 'suspected amoebic hepatitis, fever and a tender liver'. Successive orders for security for costs in a total sum of £55,000 were made against Singh. These were satisfied by his solicitor's personal undertaking to meet these sums if called upon to do so. As luck would have it, on the next trial date, 4 May 1988, the *Observer* legal team turned up at court to discover that Singh was claiming to have been prevented by overzealous Indian emigration officials from boarding his plane – they had apparently received a tip that a Mr K.C.J. Singh would be travelling on a forged passport. By the next scheduled hearing, 26 May 1988, Singh had at last reached London. He was not in court but was said to be willing to come. Singh proved evasive about who had put his solicitor in funds to give the £55,000 undertaking. First it was family and friends, then a Mr and Mrs Chopra, whose names were subsequently withdrawn. Eventually, in March 1989, Mr Justice Macpherson dismissed the action, ordering Singh to pay the costs and to identify the maintainer of the action and the guarantor for the £55,000.

Singh's exploitation of the advantages given to a plaintiff by English libel law left the *Observer* with legal expenses of £250,000. The irrecoverable cost of justifying the truth of what had been written and the absence of a viable qualified privilege defence meant that few newspapers were now prepared to fund this type of investigative journalism. The tendency of English libel law has been to give an increasing say to the accountants in the matter of what will be published in newspapers and to avoid stories which might attract a writ, however ill founded.

The libel defendant has to formulate the meaning he or she seeks to prove, and it must relate to the charge made in the words complained of. He cannot raise matters which would simply serve to mitigate damages. If the evidence is allowable for other reasons, it can, however, be taken into account to reduce the damages. So a legal executive, Barry Pamplin, who sued the *Sunday Express* in 1983 for calling him 'a slippery, unscrupulous spiv' when he registered his car in the name of his five-year-old son to avoid having to pay parking fines, received only ½p damages. The uncertainty of libel law is well illustrated by his case. At the first trial he had been awarded £12,000 before the Court of Appeal ordered a retrial. He had rejected an offer of £5 and had to pick up all costs.

Libel actions cannot be brought or even continued if the plaintiff or defendant dies. Robert Maxwell's libel action against the publishers Faber and Faber and author Seymour Hersh came to an abrupt end in 1991 when he fell off his boat to his death. This applies however late in proceedings such a death occurs: it was the consequence in 1958 when a Mr Frederick Webb collapsed and died in the court corridor while awaiting the jury's verdict in his otherwise unnoteworthy libel action against George Holder about caravans in Luton. Each side has to pay its own legal costs.

However, dead plaintiffs have a nasty habit of occasionally turning out to be alive after all. In his controversial 1968 play *Soldiers*, Rolf Hochhuth blamed the pilot, among others, for the wartime air crash in which the Polish general Wladyslaw Sikorski was killed. It transpired that the pilot, Captain Edward Maximilian Prchal, notwithstanding two broken legs and a broken arm, had been rescued from the sea and was very much alive in California and in touch with libel lawyers. He recovered £50,000 in damages.

It is a defence to a libel action if a plaintiff has consented to what has been published. The consent must be an informed consent, in the sense that the plaintiff must know what it is he is consenting to. Giving an interview to a journalist may well be held to be consent. So, for example, a man who told a tabloid reporter about his sexual exploits could not complain about a headline such as 'I BEAT UP TRAGIC DEB'.

Since the Defamation Act 1996, the limitation period for bringing a libel action has been reduced to one year. Book publishers may not benefit from this time limit: each sale of a book containing the libel is a new act of publication and creates a fresh cause of action. In 1849 the Duke of Brunswick was able to bring an action by the simple expedient of sending out his servant to buy a copy of a book published seventeen years previously (although arguably he was thereby consenting to publication to himself of the libel). And in 1989 a firm of loss-adjusters who republished a book written in 1933 called *The Fire Raisers*, which described the fraudulent activities of Leopold Harris, found themselves having to apologise to the blameless Harris Assessors plc, who were worried about being associated sixty years later with such behaviour.

The advantages which exist in English law for plaintiffs have made England a popular forum for wealthy foreigners wanting to bring a libel action, as we shall see in Chapter 20. Conversely, the cost and uncertain outcomes of libel actions have discouraged many less well-off plaintiffs. They may be able to take advantage of the simplified procedures of the Defamation Act 1996. In the meantime there has been an increase in the number of malicious falsehood actions brought. In such cases a plaintiff has to prove that the defendant maliciously published false words to a third party which caused him damage. Unlike in cases of alleged defamation, the plaintiff has to prove falsity, malice and actual damage. Damages, being fixed by a judge, tend to be lower and more difficult to win. The advantages, however, are that legal aid can be obtained, and that the action can be continued after the plaintiff's death.

In one such action, in 1993, a former lady's maid to the Princess Royal, Linda Joyce, received damages thought to total £25,000 for a false allegation in *Today* that she had stolen intimate letters from Princess Anne to her future husband, Commander Tim Laurence, and had as a result been dismissed. She had in fact resigned for personal reasons, and indeed had not taken the letters. The newspaper had not sought to assert that these highly defamatory allegations were true, but equally it had not apologised, perhaps on the assumption that Linda Joyce could not afford to sue for libel.

In November 1999, the Court of Appeal upheld an award of £20,000 for malicious falsehood to an Iranian woman who sued after a mock-up photograph falsely suggested that she was involved in telephone sex services.

Kirk Brandon, a post-punk singer with Theatre of Hate and Spear of Destiny, was less successful when he sued pop star Boy George and his publishers in 1997 for references to a short-lived but intense homosexual affair between the two singers. In his autobiography *Take it Like a Man*, George had written movingly of 100 nights of love. 'Kirk talked socialism while I sucked beer through a straw to protect my lipstick. Sleeping with Kirk wasn't sex. It was absolute love.' Unfortunately for Brandon, Mr

Justice Douglas Brown concluded that, while the plaintiff was a decent man who had conducted his case in person with unfailing courtesy, he did not believe him. 'I am satisfied he has not been truthful about his physical relationship with Mr O'Dowd [Boy George],' who had come across as 'a truthful, impressive witness'.

One of Boy George's brothers fared rather better. He recovered libel damages from IPC Magazines for the inappropriate use of his photograph in place of that of another relative in a feature entitled 'Embarrassing Siblings'.

Many feel that suing for malicious falsehood, which places the burden of proof on the plaintiff, strikes a more appropriate balance between protecting reputation and maintaining the freedom of the press. Libel actions are in any case becoming more uncertain and less profitable for those who bring them, though procedural changes under the Lord Woolf reforms and the Defamation act of 1996 will make it easier for plaintiffs to bring small claims. Even so, the likelihood is that reputation will continue to be safeguarded by the more plaintiff-friendly law of libel.

# 2

# MAXWELL:
## Libel Terrorism

Charles Dickens and Anthony Trollope vividly captured the villainy of rich and powerful industrialists involved in financial scandals in the nineteenth century in their respective characters Merdle, the swindling financier in *Little Dorrit*, and Augustus Melmotte in *The Way We Live Now*. When it came to the real thing in the twentieth century, the British media proved markedly less successful in charting the crooked ways of Robert Maxwell – at least until after his death in November 1991, when the libel laws which Maxwell had so ruthlessly exploited could no longer protect him.

Over a period of thirty years Maxwell developed a policy of using the law of libel to terrorise his opponents. His libel actions covered every aspect of his career: publishing, politics, newspapers and football. As his business empire collapsed, so he fired out his last bevy of writs to muzzle the press.

Yet there were people who did take on Maxwell in his lifetime, and their record is more successful than is generally realised. In 1969 *The Sunday Times* published several articles about the reason why two DTI inspectors, Owen Stable QC and

Ronald Leach, had concluded that Maxwell was unfit to be trusted with the stewardship of a public company. The newspaper was repeatedly sued, but after three years Maxwell dropped his five writs against them. In the early 1980s, the trade magazine the *Bookseller* was sued for its description of an industrial dispute at Pergamon Press. The magazine stood firm; Maxwell dropped the case, capitulated and paid every penny of its legal costs. Aurum Press, then part of Andrew Lloyd Webber's Really Useful Group, published Tom Bower's biography *Maxwell: The Outsider* in 1988. After years of litigation, including three attempts to obtain injunctions, Maxwell dropped that case as well. His last titanic libel action before his descent into the Atlantic in 1991 was against Faber and Faber, the publishers of *The Samson Option*, and Seymour Hersh, the book's author. Maxwell's claim perished with him, but his company, Mirror Group Newspapers, sought unsuccessfully to continue the action before wiser counsel prevailed. Their claim was struck out and they agreed to pay substantial libel damages to Faber and Faber and Hersh for Maxwell's mendacious attacks on them, plus their legal costs in full. As the lawyer who had acted for the *Bookseller*, Tom Bower, Aurum Press, Faber and Faber, Seymour Hersh and George Galloway MP, I was viewed by Maxwell as part of some ill-defined conspiracy against him. Yet, as a libel lawyer, I had a rare reason to regret the passing of the old villain and the source of so much business.

Robert Maxwell learned early in his career that English libel law was an extremely useful device for concealing the truth about his reputation and his business methods. Defendants had to prove the truth of what he had striven successfully to cover up, and that was both costly and difficult. Maxwell's litigiousness was evident as far back as 1959, when he first stood for Parliament as a Labour candidate in Buckingham. His Conservative opponents produced a bulletin about his background, his dealings with the fraudsters Peter Baker (a former Conservative MP who had been sentenced to seven years in prison) and Kurt Wallersteiner (himself an exponent of the gagging writ – Wallersteiner v. Moir, 1974) and his controversial asset-stripping activities at the publishing wholesalers Simpkin Marshall. They soon received a libel writ.

Maxwell's campaign was perhaps most memorable for his suing the first Conservative supporter to question him about his background, his business dealings as described in the *Sunday Express* and his use of non-union labour at his publishing company Pergamon Press. He also sued the Conservative agent Frank Smith, Tory candidate Sir Frank Markham – and, for good measure, Markham's wife – as well as the *Buckingham Advertiser* and the *Northampton Chronicle and Echo*, both of which had unwisely published a letter from Lady Markham. At the election count, Maxwell bombastically announced that he had served libel writs on three of the Conservatives present. The result of the election was an increased majority, from 1,140 to 1,746, for Sir Frank Markham.

Maxwell had acquired the taste for bullying his way to a reputation he did not deserve. The local newspapers in Oxford (home of Pergamon Press) regularly had to apologise to him and pay damages to some high-profile cause. In 1969 the actor Robert Morley had to pay *The Times* to publish an apology for his perfectly reasonable observation on BBC's *Any Questions* that it was disgraceful for Maxwell's private family businesses to hive off the profits of a public company – an activity later shown to be the key to Maxwell's frauds. 'On reflection I recognised that such a criticism of Mr Maxwell's accounts would be wholly unjustified,' Morley was obliged to write. 'I have no personal knowledge of anything which reflects on Mr Maxwell's record of integrity and public service to his adopted country in the army, in politics and in business or in his accounts. To mark any regret for the slur on Mr Maxwell's reputation, I have paid a substantial sum to a charity of Mr Maxwell's choice.' Morley also had to apologise in open court. It was despicable bullying of an actor who was in no position to take on Maxwell, whose companies picked up the legal bills for protecting the reputation of their crooked chief executive.

Thereafter Maxwell the litigator never looked back. He sued

around the world, issuing one of his earlier libel writs against a Murdoch-owned newspaper, the *Sydney Daily Mirror*, in 1969 for a series of perceptive articles, entitled 'Racket in Sale of Books', about Maxwell's fraudulent accounting techniques in his encyclopaedia-selling operation through the grandly named company International Learning Systems Corporation Ltd (ILSC).

Maxwell's first concerted attempt to silence the press came with his three-year battle against the Insight team at *The Sunday Times*. Although he ultimately dropped his five actions without any payment of costs or damages, he extracted some benefits in that he persuaded the editor, Harold Evans, to give him the opportunity to comment on the proposed articles before publication, and was permitted to put his version of the facts when the litigation was settled in 1972. It was scant reward, but it did enable him to give a clear warning that in future the publication of unfavourable articles, however true, could carry a large legal bill. At the same time, it put him on notice that the media were prepared to stand up to him.

The *Sunday Times* articles examined Maxwell's murky business career and played a part in undermining the proposed takeover of Pergamon Press by Saul Steinberg's Leasco. The newspaper examined, as did the DTI inspectors, the massaging of ILSC's profits in 1968 within the Pergamon accounts. Maxwell's position had been achieved by what the inspectors called a 'remarkable sale' of 5,000 complete sets of the *New Caxton Encyclopaedia* to Pergamon's subsidiary, PPI, in New York. The sale was 'remarkable' in that there was no written order for it, the books did not exist in a deliverable set, and the transaction had been back-dated to just before the end of ILSC's accounting date, and was promptly reversed thereafter. Not surprisingly, PPI never got its encyclopaedias.

The *Sunday Times* also revealed Maxwell's manipulation of the House of Commons Catering Sub-committee's accounts during his tenure as its chairman. A huge deficit was turned into a profit less by Maxwell's claimed entrepreneurial skills than by flogging the contents of the wine cellar – an action *The*

*Sunday Times* described as the 'ballet of Robert Maxwell, caterer extraordinary to the House of Commons'. Maxwell complained about this, to no avail, to the Committee of Privileges. He also wrote to Lord Thomson, the paper's owner, claiming that Godfrey Hodgson, Insight's editor, had been fired by the *Observer* for theft – a complete fabrication.

Maxwell's tactics ranged from the paranoid to the threatening to the corrupt. Indeed, it was his bluster and reaction to the impending articles that persuaded Hodgson of the truth of the allegations against Maxwell. Hodgson's dealings with Maxwell produced an offer of a job at £100,000 a year, dark references to the secret work Maxwell had done for Her Majesty's government, the brandishing of a knife and a threat to hang Hodgson from as high as the dome of St Paul's Cathedral.

Maxwell was up to every trick in the book. When he was – at his request – sent a copy of an article by Hodgson he promptly issued a writ for libel. *The Sunday Times* were confident that they could call a solicitor to give evidence that Maxwell had sworn a perjured affidavit, only to discover that Maxwell had dealt with this potential problem by retaining the unsuspecting lawyer in question to act on his behalf.

The final skirmish followed publication in September 1975 of an article in *The Sunday Times* which investigated Maxwell's running of the *Scottish Daily News* and the acquisition by a workers' co-operative commandeered by Maxwell of the *Scottish Daily Express*. Its message was apparent from the headline: 'HOW MAXWELL SABOTAGED THE WORKERS' DREAM'. Wisely, *The Sunday Times* hired the services of John Wilmers QC, a much-feared cross-examiner of whom even Maxwell was genuinely afraid. Nevertheless, he mistakenly believed that he could steamroller *The Sunday Times*. His solicitors wrote to editor Harold Evans to the effect that Maxwell could not believe he was personally responsible for what had happened, and could only assume that he had 'lost control' of Bruce Page, the executive editor responsible for the Insight article. Maxwell received the dusty answer from Evans: 'I do not want you to be under the misapprehension that I am not in full control of this newspaper.' A writ was issued, but it was countered by a claim for slander by Evans. Again Maxwell achieved nothing other than the delivery of a very public warning to anyone who might be thinking of writing something hostile about him. The case was settled four years later, each side bearing its own costs and the paper making it clear that it had not been conducting a vendetta against Maxwell. He never issued another writ against *The Sunday Times*.

Maxwell then turned his attention to the satirical magazine *Private Eye*, which was prepared to publish the stories many national newspapers would not touch. The *Eye* had started to track his transference of the ownership of Pergamon to Liechtenstein to prevent the public from discovering the true state of his finances. Maxwell sued *Private Eye* in 1975 and obtained damages for the suggestion that he had borrowed £10,000 from journalists' redundancy money to help finance the *Scottish Daily News* and that he had lied about the circulation figures of the paper. In the light of the failure of that venture, these seemed fairly mild criticisms. Nevertheless *Private Eye* was reluctant to run the financial risk of taking on Maxwell in the courts. It paid a sum to the *Scottish Daily News* welfare fund.

If the law of libel had required proof of actual damage, rather than a mere tendency of words to damage reputation, Maxwell would have had difficulty in bringing such cases for libel. He used his power in the press to give as good as he got, just as he bullied his own staff. Workers at the *Scottish Daily News* had to endure tannoy announcements ordering, 'Attention, this is your chairman speaking.' Maxwell would then denounce employees who had displeased him in terms which he must have learned from the neo-Stalinist leaders such as Ceausescu, Zhivkov, Honecker and Husak, whose sycophantic biographies he published in his 'World Leaders' series. The workers would have to listen to Maxwell's co-chairman, Allister Mackie, and executive council member James Russell being insulted by him as 'fools, knaves, the enemies in our midst, who are seeking deliberately to put the company into liquidation'.

*Private Eye* committed the cardinal sin of exposing the ego-maniac to its trademark ridicule, and in 1983 Maxwell hit upon the tactic of taking action over the jokes the magazine made about him. He successfully sued it for its transposition of his photograph with that of the gangster Ronald Kray in its 'looka-like' feature, with the outlandish implication that Maxwell was a crook. This was a stratagem he was soon to use again. By 1985 Maxwell had acquired the Mirror Group, and in two issues that July, the *Eye* lightheartedly probed the relationship between the owner of the only Labour-supporting tabloid newspaper and the Labour Party. Their first article raised the question of whether 'Kinnochio, the Welsh windbag', then the Labour leader, would disclose whether Maxwell was acting as paymaster for his official trip to Dar-es-Salaam and Nairobi, and speculated on how many more Kinnock freebies Maxwell would have to provide before he was recommended for a peerage. Neil Kinnock's office denied that Maxwell had paid for the tour, and as for Maxwell wanting a peer-age – perish the thought. The second piece reported problems with the guest list for the *Mirror*'s 'glittering champagne-all-the-way party marking Captain Bob's first glorious year at the helm'. Kinnock, it suggested, had decided not to attend. Maxwell was alleged to have told Julia Langdon, the political editor of the *Mirror*, that if the Labour leader did not come, the paper would not be reporting his Africa tour. 'Mindful of his master's voice,' wrote *Private Eye*, 'Kinnock duly turned up.' It seemed the story arose out of a misunderstanding as to whether Kinnock had been intending to go instead to a party at *The Times*.

At an early stage Kinnock let it be known through his press secretary, Patricia Hewitt, that he did not plan to get involved in Maxwell's confrontation with *Private Eye*. Maxwell retorted that Kinnock could not be ambivalent, claiming that he was bringing his action on behalf of the Labour Party. He happily sued, using his paper to attack *Private Eye*, or Public Lie, as it was hilariously dubbed in a piece in the *Mirror* diary entitled 'Another Whopper'. *Private Eye* counterclaimed on this article, but in the end thought better of it and let the matter drop.

Here, Maxwell thought, was an opportunity to destroy *Private Eye* and to nail the prevalent perception that he did not have the courage to go into the witness box. He exploited a problem the *Eye* had: that their distinguished informant in the Labour Party would not break rank and give evidence on their behalf. Maxwell told his lawyers he wanted £250,000 damages. His advisers saw his psychopathic qualities at first hand as he set about his mission. All previous libels admitted by *Private Eye* must be detailed, and all dirt on its editor, Richard Ingrams, exhumed, Maxwell ordered as he took control of the libel action. Every back copy of the magazine was purchased. Every cutting in the *Mirror* cuttings library under 'I' for Ingrams and 'P' for *Private Eye* was excavated, as was every article Ingrams had written for the *Sunday Telegraph*. It was pointed out to the obsessed Maxwell that Ingrams' column in the *Sunday Telegraph* of 3 August 1986 could not be used as it discussed the issue of the DTI inspectors' report – the very issue Maxwell had been specifically advised not to raise.

Initially Maxwell sought an injunction to prevent *Private Eye* from repeating their allegations. Relying on the case of Bonnard v. Perryman in 1891, *Private Eye* was able to defeat that manoeuvre by asserting that they would prove that what they had written was true. In such cases the courts do not grant injunctions on the basis that freedom of speech is to be upheld. If, as was to happen in this case, the defendants do not at trial prove the truth of the allegations, they are likely to be punished by a large award of damages.

Maxwell was convinced he understood the arcane laws of libel better than his advisers. He was unable to sit back and exploit *Private Eye*'s difficulties in proving the truth of what they had said. Instead he insisted, despite the dangers pointed out to him by his barristers, on calling evidence of his own *good* character. This meant that *Private Eye* was entitled to call evidence of Maxwell's bad character. So, while Maxwell sought to portray himself as a successful entrepreneur, philanthropist, socialist and upholder of trades-union rights, *Private Eye* was able to show that he was in fact an unprincipled bully. Richard Hartley QC felt Maxwell's proposal to call evidence of his good character was so foolish that he gave Maxwell written advice to this effect.

Those advising Maxwell became familiar with his ever-changing moods and his desire to humiliate. The lawyers' meetings with Maxwell were constantly interrupted by a series of visitors and telephone calls. Many of the routine administrative tasks had to be performed by former diplomat Peter Jay, Maxwell's subservient chief of staff, who would be summoned to copy documents by a shout for 'Mr Ambassador'. Maxwell's solicitor had started the case with an early-morning forty-minute walk round town with his client, who reassuringly told him that he would establish him as the best libel lawyer in town. As the case progressed and the foolishness of Maxwell's strategy became apparent, his abuse of his legal team increased. The solicitor was told, amid a foul-mouthed denunciation of the size of the barristers' fees, to relay to them how pissed off he was. He was summoned on the first Sunday after the trial had begun to Maxwell's home, Headington Hill Hall in Oxfordshire, to join a team of people inexplicably combing through Maxwell's antecedents to establish how much he had suffered in the Holocaust, and how much dirt could be dug up about Ingrams. Maxwell decreed that Ingrams was to be put on the rack for several days of cross-examination, and eventually two boxes of documents for the cross-examination of Ingrams were prepared. Maxwell kept telephoning his legal team to tell them how they should do this work, but to his fury they had retreated to the golf course. After hours of ranting, Maxwell had the documents delivered by Rolls-Royce to his lawyers in London at midnight for them to study for discussion in conference with him at 9am the next day before the court resumed.

Hartley's view was that the documents were worthless and that the whole exercise was a waste of time. Moreover, he was not going to be told how to cross-examine. If Maxwell insisted on these matters being put to Ingrams, he and his junior, Tom

Shields, would resign from the case and leave Maxwell to represent himself. They told their client this when he finally turned up at the conference, twenty-two minutes late, complaining unjustifiably about the lack of preparation of the case. In the end, he reluctantly allowed his lawyers to conduct the case as they felt appropriate.

During the case Maxwell was enraged by an article written by John Smith, formed self-styled 'Man of the People', in one of his own newspapers, the *People*, on 29 December 1985, during the litigation. Headed 'BUY YOUR OWN GONG', it continued, 'Every tycoon knows that the short cut to a title is to cough up cash to the party in power.' This was uncomfortably close to what *Private Eye* was suggesting. Maxwell's paranoia convinced him that the story had been planted in the *People* by *Private Eye*'s solicitor, Oscar Beuselinck. Maxwell set about seeing if he could, despite the lack of any proof, report Beuselinck to the Law Society. Ironically, he was later to hire the solicitor as his in-house legal adviser.

To establish his good name, Maxwell called a former lord chancellor, Lord Elwyn-Jones; Alex Kitson, a former deputy secretary of the Transport and General Workers' Union and chairman of the Labour Party; Michael Foot, the former leader of the party; and Michael Cocks, a former Labour chief whip. When Lord Elwyn-Jones gave evidence in court, the judge, Mr Justice Simon Brown, rose to his feet and bowed politely in greeting to the former lord chancellor. Maxwell had not extended such courtesy to the eminent witness called to speak on his behalf: asked to give a statement of evidence, Lord Elwyn-Jones had been obliged to join a queue of people waiting outside Maxwell's office. The tycoon was not even in the building at the time.

After a case which ran into three weeks, the jury awarded Maxwell a mere £5,000 for the damage to his general reputation, rather than the £25,000, at least, which he would have received but for his own crass interference, plus £50,000 punitive damages for *Private Eye*'s conduct in swearing an affidavit contending that they would prove the first article was true but failing to do so, and publishing a second defamatory article. This was due to Maxwell's insistence on unsuccessfully trying to show his good character. But he gave an upbeat press conference in the well of the court, denouncing *Private Eye* and expressing delight at the result. Privately he was incensed by the modesty of the award – he felt he should have received £250,000. Yet it was unquestionably a significant success for Maxwell and very expensive for *Private Eye*.

Maxwell announced that the damages would go to AIDS research, so that money from one infected organ could go to another. He summoned his solicitor and the barristers to berate them, finally dismissing the lawyer with the words, 'Mr Solicitor, call Mr Carter-Ruck and tell him to come for a glass of champagne. He will do my libel work instead of you.' In the heat of the moment no one could find Peter Carter-Ruck's number, and the poisoned chalice was instead passed to Lord Mishcon. Nevertheless the QC, Richard Hartley, praised the way the long-suffering solicitor had handled the case. Despite their victory, the lawyers were united in their view that Maxwell was the rudest and most arrogant person they had ever acted for and vowed never to represent him again.

Maxwell's contempt for the serious business of reputation was in a sense demonstrated by his response after the case. He instructed his *Mirror* journalists to produce a booklet, entitled *Not Private Eye*, which depicted Richard Ingrams as Hermann Goering looking over a map of Europe with Adolf Hitler, saying, 'If anyone objects, we will say we were only doing it for a laugh.' This Nazi joke seemed a little rich. In court Maxwell had managed to weep when shown a spoof 'lookalike' letter from *Private Eye* from a Mrs Ena Maxwell of Headington Hill Hall, illustrated by transposed photographs and captions of the Duke of Edinburgh and Adolf Eichmann. 'My family was destroyed by Eichmann,' Maxwell said, and in the moving terms of his mouthpiece, Mirror Group political editor Joe Haines, 'it was several minutes and a number of questions from his counsel later before Mr Maxwell felt it safe to push his handkerchief back in his pocket.' This was not the only sycophantic reportage given by Haines. At one point in court Lord Elwyn-Jones had described the moment when Field-Marshal Montgomery had pinned the MC to Maxwell's chest. 'For the second time during the case,' wrote Haines sickeningly of his employer's reaction, 'his eyes filled with tears and he dabbed them with a handkerchief.'

One of the issues at the trial was Maxwell's megalomania. He firmly denied an allegation made by the investigative journalist John Pilger that the *Mirror* had been turned into a family album. 'The gentleman was an employee of ours, very highly paid, who did no work for us. We were very happy to be shot of him – he was a disgruntled employee' Maxwell lied. In truth Pilger was absolutely on target. The judge, Mr Justice Simon Brown, expressed some surprise that Maxwell should have thought it relevant to the *Mirror*'s business for him to personally interview a head of state. Maxwell explained to the court that it was his job, as publisher of the *Mirror*, to interview someone as important as Mr Zhivkov of Bulgaria to obtain his opinions and views about relations with our country and on world peace.

After the trial Joe Haines – who was later to write the hagiography *Maxwell* to counter Tom Bower's book *Maxwell: The Outsider* – was encouraged, with other *Mirror* journalists, to write Maxwell's account of the trial, *Malice in Wonderland*, which was published and printed by Maxwell-owned companies. The book was, Haines tells us rather unnecessarily, Maxwell's idea. In Appendix 2 the reader was treated to Maxwell's diary of the trial, ending with his 'business achievements of the year'. We were breathlessly told how, at the trial, notes were passed through a chain of hands to Mr Maxwell, either ending up in his jacket pocket or prompting him to rise, give a long bow to the judge and take control of whatever situation had arisen by means of a portable telephone held for him in the corridor. The book featured many photographs of Maxwell, including one of Captain Bob with the Prince of Wales and Prince William, plus facsimiles of a letter from the Queen thanking him for the splendid royal wedding souvenir book and of a doctorate of science degree bestowed on him by the Polytechnic Institute of New York.

*Malice in Wonderland* also listed all the previous successful libel actions against *Private Eye*, which Haines described as having become the Joe McCarthy of British journalism. This interesting piece of research showed that Sara Keays, a House of Commons secretary, had recovered damages in March 1984 and Cecil Parkinson MP likewise in July 1985 – not for the true suggestion they had slept with each other, but for false allegations that they had respectively had affairs with another MP and another House of Commons secretary.

In terms of closing down *Private Eye*, or even deterring it from writing hostile stories, Maxwell's battles with the magazine were counterproductive. Readers responded generously to an appeal to help fund the libel action and ultimately, in 1991, the *Eye* was able to help expose Maxwell's pension frauds. In the meantime, Maxwell had further financial successes against the magazine. In October 1983 *Private Eye* had to pay more damages to the National AIDS Trust when it prematurely accused Maxwell of 'classic asset-stripping'. In December 1988, it had to fork out yet more damages after suggesting that the *Mirror* Ethiopia Fund was being improperly administered. In 1989 Maxwell secured an undertaking from the magazine not to repeat allegations about safety shortcomings in his company British International Helicopters. In June 1990 an issue of 258,000 copies had to be withdrawn when the allegations were repeated. The offending article was hastily replaced by a cartoon announcing, 'Nobody's read the last *Eye*', with a bubble comment: 'Just like the *European*.' *Private Eye* remained unbowed by Maxwell's activities. Its stance was epitomised by an illustration featured in the magazine in 1989: an enlargement of an almost subliminal squiggle in a *Mirror* cartoon by Griffin which, on magnification, could be seen to consist of the words 'Fuck Maxwell'.

Another unsuccessful attempt by Maxwell to suppress criticism and sanitise his public image had come in 1981, this time in a second action against the long-established organ of the book trade, the *Bookseller*. Maxwell was reduced to a state of apoplexy by a seemingly unexceptionable report, printed under the headline 'PERGAMON SACKINGS ATTACKED', which dealt with a dispute he was having with members of the NUJ at Pergamon Press in Oxford. The article recounted how questions had been raised by Jonathan Hammond, the NUJ vice-president, as to whether Maxwell's behaviour was 'consistent with the standards required by his membership of organisations such as the Oxford City Labour Party and the Oxford branch of [the trade union] ASTMS'. This was too much for Maxwell to stomach. He had harboured a grievance against the *Bookseller* since the magazine's exposure of his behaviour towards Simpkin Marshall in the 1950s; he also, curiously, prided himself on his reputation as a trades-unionist. Maxwell had been reluctant to talk to the *Bookseller*, telling it, improbably, in 1980, 'As you will have seen in recent years, I have been shunning publicity, having learned from experience that overexposure leads to negative results.'

Maxwell's initial attempt to browbeat David Whitaker, the publisher of the *Bookseller*, failed. He called Whitaker and told him he was tired of the *Bookseller* libelling him when it felt like it.

'Balls,' Whitaker replied.

'What did you say?' asked Maxwell.

'Rubbish,' said Whitaker, in an attempt to be conciliatory.

'Are you saying I'm lying?'

'No, just very, very mistaken.'

Matters remained unresolved and Maxwell issued a statement to *The Times*. 'What was written was untrue and the *Bookseller* knows it to be untrue. Whitaker will now have the privilege of proving how reliable, true and accurate their stories are. Whitaker has brought it on himself. I have no option but to go to court unless they want to make a grovelling apology.' A writ followed alleging that the article had portrayed Maxwell as a bad and oppressive employer and a hypocrite, and his behaviour as inconsistent with the standards he was required to observe by his membership of ASTMS and the Labour Party. The full-frontal-assault approach to libel litigation may have appealed to

Maxwell, but it proved to be very foolish. By needlessly expanding the scope of his complaint, he gave the *Bookseller* the
opportunity to justify its article by producing evidence of a wide
range of misconduct on his part.

Indeed, the activities of the Labour-supporting trades-unionist
chairman of Pergamon did not stand up to scrutiny. For a man so
anxious to resort to libel writs, he showed a remarkable capacity
to libel those who displeased him. His press releases about the
dismissed 'Pergamon Nine' referred to them deliberately sacking
themselves in an attempt to misuse industrial relations for militant party political purposes. He denounced their childish claims
of trades-union and Labour movement support. They were, he
said, politically motivated musketeers supported by their drunken
rent-a-mob friends. They were all loonies, Trotskyists and hooli-
gans guilty of despicable behaviour, wanton acts of sabotage and
of trying to damage the British economy in the belief that this
would usher in an era of true Marxism. More objective observers
found these descriptions difficult to reconcile with the picture
they had of the people involved, who included a doctor of philosophy, four bachelors of science and a bachelor of art.

I was called upon to represent the *Bookseller* in the action.
Provided with the opportunity of showing that Maxwell was
indeed a hypocrite and a lousy employer, I then discovered that
he had been lying to industrial tribunals. Maxwell's tactics were
to maximise the normally irrecoverable legal costs dismissed
employees incurred when bringing claims against his companies
in order to wear them down. If he could obtain repeated adjourn-
ments of a case, the claimants' costs could outstrip what they
stood to recover at the tribunal. Andrew Nopper had been dismissed in September 1981 as financial director of Caxton
Publishing (Scandinavia) Ltd after ten years' service. When his
case eventually reached the industrial tribunal hearing on 22
March 1982, Maxwell was said to be on a business trip to South
Africa and Japan. Previously he had said he would not be attending the hearing; now he wanted it adjourned so he could be
there. Nopper discovered that Maxwell's Rolls-Royce was parked

outside Maxwell House, the offices occupied by his British Printing Corporation (BPC), in Worship Street in the City of London. His chauffeur helpfully revealed that Maxwell was working in his office.

By then the tribunal had been adjourned, but Nopper did tip off a former colleague, Adrian Warbey, who was the following week bringing his own case for unfair dismissal after eleven years' service from his post as group financial director of Caxton Publishing Holdings Ltd. Warbey was among many who suffered when BPC was taken over by Maxwell. He had not endeared himself to Maxwell for having perspicaciousy recommended that the tycoon's conduct in relation to the Leasco takeover should be referred to the Fraud Squad – a step which might have spared Maxwell's pensioners much pain ten years later. Thus forewarned, Warbey took the precaution before attending his industrial tribunal hearing of establishing that on that day Maxwell had a full diary of appointments in Oxford and was due to attend a dinner in London in the evening.

Once more the tribunal was told that Maxwell was away in South Africa and Japan, but on this occasion the hearing was adjourned while Warbey's claim that Maxwell was in fact in Oxford was checked. Maxwell was unable to explain away his lies.

Maxwell fired his lawyers, Lewis Silkin and Partners, a month before the libel trial. They were replaced by Denton Hall and Burgin. Maxwell then claimed that the trial estimate of eight to ten days was wrong: now he said it would take at least six weeks, and he would be calling fifty or sixty witnesses. He tried unsuccessfully to adjourn the case. In an attempt to find favourable advice and a way out of the litigation, Maxwell turned from Peter Bowsher QC to Anthony Hoolahan QC to John Matthew QC to Derry Irving QC. Sam Silkin QC, a former attorney-general and later deputy chairman of the renamed Maxwell company BPCC, telephoned to indicate that Maxwell would be prepared to settle for as little as £1,000. The *Bookseller* had on the recommendation of The *Sunday Times* lawyers retained the intimidating John Wilmers QC, secure in the knowledge that Maxwell would never agree to be cross-examined by him. The *Bookseller* stood firm and Maxwell capitulated. He withdrew the case, paid every penny of the magazine's £30,000 legal costs and received no apology at all, much less a 'grovelling' one.

Emboldened, however, by his successes against *Private Eye* and by the death of John Wilmers, Maxwell felt more inclined in 1988 to challenge the biography *Maxwell: The Outsider*, written by Tom Bower and published by Aurum Press, then part of Andrew Lloyd Webber's Really Useful Group. He commissioned the Mirror Group political editor Joe Haines to write a 449-page 'authorised version' of his life to try to steal Bower's thunder. Bower's book was hit by an avalanche of writs when it was published, as was a second hostile biography, *Maxwell: A Practice of Power*, by journalists Peter Thompson and Anthony Delano. Maxwell explained that he had acted against these 'purported biographies' because they told lies and were full of libels. 'Regrettably, the British media suffers from the desire to attack people of standing on the principle they all have feet of clay. Occasionally it is good for them to receive a kick up the backside to disprove their fanciful theory.' Maxwell tried to persuade *The Sunday Times* not to serialise Bower's book. He sued any book chain which continued to stock it after receiving a warning from his solicitors. Actions were started against W.H. Smith, John Menzies, Waterstone's, Hatchard's and Blackwell's. He made repeated but unsuccessful attempts to obtain an injunction banning the book. On each occasion Bower could show that he was able to justify what he had written.

Maxwell's action against Bower was unsuccessful. He managed to intimidate bookshops into not stocking the book, but he never brought the case to trial. His tactics were to try to wear down the defence by numerous applications to court for an injunction. He even bought a stake in the Really Useful Group in a vain attempt to put pressure on its publishing company. This was libel terrorism of the first order, coupled with the use of his media power to promote the authorised Haines version of his life.

Maxwell was more successful against the Thompson and Delano biography. This, Maxwell complained, contained 'thirty serious libels, a devastating catalogue of libels which is wholly destructive of [his] character and reputation'. The authors were not as fortunate as Bower, for Maxwell was able to catch them out on their suggestion that he had, in revenge for the paper's coverage of his 1959 election campaign, bought and closed down the Conservative-supporting *Bletchley Gazette*. Maxwell could show that the paper was never in fact closed. The book was republished in paperback with the offending passages deleted, but Maxwell managed to get even that edition pulped when he did not care for the blurb on the back cover.

The case against Bower was memorable for the improper tactics used by Maxwell. Alarmed that Bower, having been able to speak to Anne Dove – a former Maxwell secretary living in South Africa with whom Maxwell had been in love – the tycoon had her followed and watched when she came to the UK and as she lunched with Bower. To discourage her from any further contact with Bower, he sued her in South Africa for alleged breach of confidence. The threat worked. Maxwell never pursued the case – presumably he had never intended to actually bring it to court.

Maxwell's people were deputed to keep Bower, too, under observation. Tony Frost, an assistant editor at the *Mirror*, sent a memo to former ambassador to the United States, Peter Jay, then reduced to working as chief of staff at Maxwell Communications Corporation. It contained details of discussions about Bower with his local newsagents, the registration number of his BMW and the helpful observation that his house looked to be very tastefully and expensively decorated inside. The memo was circulated among senior Mirror Group staff. Maxwell's next wheeze was to see whether Bower could be prosecuted for failing to register his computer-held research as a data-user under the Data Protection Act 1984. His barrister, Stephen Nathan, was pessimistic that the director of public prosecutions could be made to interest himself in such non-subversive activities. Maxwell got Lord Mishcon and Anthony Julius of Mishcon de Reya to investigate whether Bower's computer records could be seized under an Anton Piller order* without Bower receiving advance notice.

The lawyers at Mishcon de Reya agonised over whether they should ask me – Bower was my client – about his computer records, but understandably concluded that I might smell a rat, legal or otherwise. Lord Mishcon had to explain to Maxwell that Anton Piller orders existed to seize documents for the investigation of fraud or systematic dishonesty. Without apparent irony, Jay noted that, legally speaking, this was not (quite) the situation with Bower. Still, it was decided to see if evidence could be obtained to found an application to seize Bower's computer source material. Jay called in specialist investigators Control Risks to investigate the possibility of discovering what was in Bower's computer records to find out who was providing information to him. Control Risks were evidently doubtful about such a project. They pointed to the levels of background radiation and the need for extremely sophisticated equipment, which would cost an estimated £50,000. Even then they had reservations about the possibility of obtaining the evidence Jay required and the likelihood that such an operation could be kept covert.

It was an astonishing way to proceed in a case brought to protect Maxwell's good name. Eventually Jay accepted that it was not really practical to proceed. In retrospect, he acknowledged that he had acted in craven fashion in trying to suppress Bower's book – and, predictably, thereby ensuring its huge success – and in the way he had administered Maxwell's unwise legal actions.

Notwithstanding Maxwell's experiences with the *Bookseller*, those who wrote about his industrial-relations problems were likely to receive a writ. In August 1988 he sued the NUJ for an article in its paper *The Journalist* about the sacking of a hundred *Mirror* journalists in Manchester. In May 1990 SOGAT, the print

*A search order.

union, was sued for what it had written in its union journal about Maxwell's treatment of its members. In June of that year Maxwell discontinued actions against BBC Scotland and the *Glasgow Herald*, without payment of damages or costs, for comments made on radio in 1986 by the paper's editor concerning an industrial dispute at the *Daily Record* and *Sunday Mail*. Originally he had sought £500,000 damages, dropping this to £10,000, but still he got nothing more than a statement in the *Glasgow Herald* recording that the editor's comments had been made on a matter of public interest and that there had been no intention of casting aspersions on the personal integrity of Mr Maxwell.

And a number of Maxwell libel writs centred on another of his interests – football. BBC Radio Derby's coverage in May 1991 of Maxwell's rejection of a local businessman's offer for Derby County – of fans shouting, 'Take the money, Maxwell,' and chanting, 'He's fat, he's round, he's never at the ground' – resulted in a writ, a complaint to the Broadcasting Complaints Commission and a barring of the station's journalist Graham Richards from the club.

The case brought in June 1989 by Ken Bates, chairman of Chelsea Football Club, against Maxwell illustrated the tycoon's abuse of power and his contempt for the law of libel. In December 1987 the Football League Management Committee had prevented Maxwell from buying Watford FC from the pop star Elton John, on the grounds that Maxwell already had interests in Reading, Oxford and Derby football clubs. Maxwell thought he could attack Bates, as a member of the Management Committee, in the pages of the *Mirror*, as Bates had interests not only in Chelsea but also in Wigan. The fact that Bates had severed his links with Wigan when he acquired Chelsea posed something of a problem here. The deputy sports editor, on legal advice, spiked the story. Maxwell was reported to be 'not at all pleased' when he saw that the story was absent from the first edition of the paper. As Harry Harris, chief football writer of the *Mirror*, recounted at the trial, Maxwell felt that remarks reported to have been made

by Wigan chairman Bill Kenyon 'had a valuable point to make
and ought to go into the paper. See there is fair play and let the
readers decide' – an uncharacteristically even-handed attitude.
Whether or not this was a sanitised version of Maxwell's order,
the second edition carried the headline: 'BATES SLAMMED: HE'S THE REAL
KING OF CLUBS'. Bates recovered £75,000 damages, of which £3,500
were paid by Bill Kenyon, the chairman of Wigan.

Later that year Maxwell had to pay substantial libel damages
to Stewart Steven and Joe Melling, respectively editor and football editor of the *Mail on Sunday*, in respect of a wholly false
allegation by Maxwell that they had fabricated a story about
him.

Sometimes it seems that Maxwell sued purely as a recreation.
In May 1989 he brought proceedings against the publishers of
*Chronicle of the Twentieth Century* regarding a reference to a different Robert Maxwell who had been freed from Libya in 1987
after facing trumped-up charges of being a British spy. Precisely
how this Robert Maxwell was likely to be confused with the
publisher was far from clear. In the year of his death Maxwell's
real aim in firing out libel writs – to curtail discussion of the
state of his financial empire – emerged. In July 1991, Maxwell
Communications Corporation sought an injunction against the
*Independent* to prevent publication of eight defamatory allegations, including the damaging but true assertion that Peter
Walker, the former Cabinet minister, had changed his mind about
becoming chairman of MCC after reading an internal report
which indicated that MCC's claimed profit of £145 million in the
previous year was in reality a loss of £8 million. In September
the stream of writs became a cascade when *Panorama* broadcast
their programme 'The Max Factor', which examined the state of
the Maxwell empire and dealings in MCC shares by Goldman
Sachs. Maxwell's dishonesty was exemplified by *Panorama's*
exposure of the running of the *Mirror* 'Spot the Ball' competition. The ball's position was decided after all the entries had
been submitted and the chairman of the judges was none other
than Maxwell himself. The *Sun* gleefully ran headlines such as

'MAXWELL TRICKED *MIRROR* READERS OUT OF £1 MILLION SAYS *PANORAMA*' and 'SPOT THE CHEAT'. It was promptly sued.

Shares in Mirror Group Newspapers and MCC fell sharply. Maxwell sued the BBC for libel and malicious falsehood and issued a general threat to any newspaper, periodical, news service or other electronic medium which reprinted or disseminated any of the libels or falsehood from the *Panorama* programme. He brazenly dictated an editorial for the *Sunday Mirror* attacking the BBC 'who caused needless anxiety to pensioners in our group who are better treated than they would have been by their former employers.'

Worse was to follow for Maxwell. In October Faber and Faber published *The Samson Option* by Pulitzer-winning journalist Seymour Hersh. This was a book about the development of Israel's nuclear bomb. Alarmingly for Maxwell, it accused him of involvement in arms-dealing, along with the *Mirror*'s foreign editor, Nicholas Davies. It was alleged, among other things, that they supplied TOW missiles to the Iranians and were responsible for the arrest of Mordecai Vanunu, who had revealed some of the secrets of the Dimona nuclear plant in Israel to *The Sunday Times*. Maxwell and Davies issued vigorous denials – 'a ludicrous and total invention'. Writs followed. One of Hersh's documents linking Davies to an Ohio arms-dealer was claimed to be a forgery and, what was more, Davies's expense account seemed to provide an alibi for his presence in England in the form of bills from a number of plush London restaurants. Eyebrows were raised at the idea that journalists' expense accounts proved anything other than that an expenses claim was being made, and the *Daily Mail* duly published a photograph of Davies with the American arms-dealer at his home in Ohio. The case never came to court, so Davies was unable to give his account and make good his denials. Maxwell's version of events was never heard, either. On 5 November 1991, he mysteriously disappeared from his yacht in the Atlantic, from which his body was fished out twelve hours later.

Before his death, Maxwell had rashly libelled two MPs, Rupert

Allason and George Galloway, who had raised the Hersh allegations in Parliament. They respectively recovered £230,000 and
£150,000 in damages and costs. Maxwell's actions abated with
his death, but Mirror Group Newspapers – which had been party
not only to Maxwell's actions but also to the counterclaim for
libel brought by Hersh and Faber and Faber for articles in the
*Mirror* accusing them of reckless libel – remained caught up in
the machinery of the law. These actions had a suitably inglorious
end. The Mirror Group Newspapers action was struck out, as the
court held that in law the words published by Faber and Faber
and Hersh could not be said to be defamatory of the company. In
August 1994 MGN paid very substantial damages and costs to
Hersh and Faber and Faber. Thus Maxwell's ill-fated foray into
libel litigation had ended posthumously.

After Maxwell's death his son Kevin struggled to protect what
little of his father's reputation remained after Captain Bob's
abuse of the *Mirror* pension fund had been exposed. Kevin persuaded the attorney-general in February 1994 to ban Evan
Steadman's *Maxwell: The Musical*, with music by Sir Arthur
Sullivan and Gilbertesque lyrics adapted by a *Spitting Image*
writer – 'I am the very model of a modern megalomaniac.' This
was felt to be likely to prejudice the impending trial of two of
Maxwell's sons, who stood accused of involvement in their
father's fraudulent practices. The enforced closure of the production appears to have cost Steadman £500,000, but ironically,
it seems to have been financed out of the money he had received
from Maxwell on the acquisition of his exhibition-organising
business. The BBC *Have I Got News For You* also fell foul of the
court case: the programme was fined £10,000 for its injudicious
remarks about the Maxwells *fils* during their criminal trial. No
objection was raised, however, to the very much more helpful
autobiography of Maxwell's widow, Betty, *A Mind of My Own*,
which was published without incident before the trial.

The ultimate unreality of Maxwell's attempt to massage his
reputation with the aid of his *Mirror* newspapers was reflected in
their coverage of his death. He was mourned with the headline

'THE LAST TYCOON'. 'Nobody has come from less and achieved more,' grieved the *Mirror* on 6 November. By December this had become 'MILLIONS MISSING FROM *MIRROR*' and 'THE LIE'. There followed headlines about more Maxwell lies, his love life and his bugging of employees. Dickens' Merdle had come full circle. Grief at his death had been dampened by the realisation that he was the greatest forger and thief ever to have cheated the gallows.

The final verdict on Maxwell must be that the evidence of his dishonesty had been uncovered by the DTI inspectors as early as 1969. People like Maxwell do not tend to change their business practices, and a more energetic press could have exposed him much earlier. However, his career shows how the law of libel can be used to muzzle critics, and how easy it is simply to issue writs and to rely on the inability or reluctance of defendants to bear the cost of having to prove the truth of what they have written. The absence of any usable public interest, public figure or qualified privilege defence meant that the only defence to a libel writ from Maxwell could be one of justification. This could be an intolerable burden, and one which Maxwell was quick to exploit.

# 3

# ARABIAN TALES –
# As Told in Knightsbridge

### Mohamed Fayed's Tale

For someone determined to conceal a carefully constructed web of deceit about his origins and his wealth, the law of libel is a handy weapon. It assumes he is a man of good reputation and it throws upon his critics the not inconsiderable burden of proving the truth. The issue of a writ casts doubt on what his opponents are saying and discourages the press from pursuing the matter.

The names of Mohamed Fayed and his brothers Ali and Salah became well known in Britain when their bid to buy the House of Fraser, which included the famous flagship department store, Harrods, finally succeeded in 1985. In the process Mohamed Fayed earned the undying enmity of Tiny Rowland, proprietor of the *Observer*. Rowland had placed his shares in the company with Fayed for safekeeping, only to discover that they had been used to support Fayed's takeover bid, which was backed by funds from the Sultan of Brunei. Four years later, the Fayeds were found to have lied about their assets in order to purchase the House of Fraser.

For the next decade Rowland sought to destroy Mohamed

Fayed's reputation, producing evidence for the DTI inspectors of Fayed's lies about his background and wealth. The aristocratic 'Al' he added to his name was mere embroidery; his background of nannies and private education an invention.

The problem for Mohamed Fayed is that he has failed to realise that libel is about the protection of reputation. It involves being prepared, as Robert Maxwell was, to enter the witness box to assert one's claim to a good name. This Fayed was never prepared to do until the Hamilton case (see Chapter 18) came on for trial. Although he was prepared, when surrounded by lawyers, to give evidence to parliamentary committees and to face some mild questioning, he lacked the courage of his convictions when it came to giving evidence in contested litigation – certainly when he was a plaintiff. Instead he viewed libel litigation initially, but unsuccessfully, as a means of silencing or intimidating the opposition, and latterly as a means, again unsuccessfully, of massaging an expensively manipulated reputation.

Fayed, like Maxwell, has never been slow to resort to the law. One of his earliest forays into libel litigation was in 1983 when, as Muhammed Fayed, he issued a writ against the ambassador of the United Arab Emirates, Mahdi Al Tajir. Like his later litigation, it came to grief, but on this occasion owing to an interesting point of law in the Court of Appeal.

On 7 September 1982 the ambassador had written an internal memorandum, which ultimately fell into Fayed's hands, expressing dismay that Mr Mohamed Fayed had been given two passes to enter Heathrow Airport in his car in the name of the embassy. It contained a number of highly defamatory allegations about Fayed's behaviour at London Airport and his status as a representative of the government of Abu Dhabi. The memo was in the nature of a severe reprimand to a member of the embassy staff, who was told that he was being transferred to the head office of the Ministry of Foreign Affairs in Abu Dhabi and that the matter was being referred to the ministry so that it could take whatever action it deemed necessary.

Evidently Fayed disputed these allegations, as he issued a writ on 3 May 1983 vigorously denying the allegations of misconduct. But it was open to question whether Fayed could sue in respect of such a document. The ambassador had briefly resigned, but as he ultimately took responsibility for the defamatory memorandum, no issue turned on that. However, both Lord Justice Stocker, at first instance, and the Court of Appeal held that the English courts could not entertain an action based on an embassy document. They took the view that such a memorandum would be covered by absolute privilege and should be the subject of litigation, if anywhere, in the emirate of Dubai. This ruling deprived Fayed of the opportunity to clear his name.

In November 1984 Fayed issued a writ against Dr Ashraf Marwan, son-in-law of former President Nasser of Egypt and sometime chief of staff in President Sadat's private office. Marwan was also a business associate of Tiny Rowland, with whom Fayed had by then fallen out. In January 1985 he served another writ on Marwan for allegations he had made linking Fayed with the Sultan of Brunei over the purchase of the Dorchester Hotel.

And in March of that year Fayed sued Melvyn Marckus, the city editor of Rowland's newspaper the *Observer*, for his article 'The Bloody Harrods Battle', in which he accused Fayed of dishonesty about his background.

Fayed's use of the libel law attracted strong criticism in 1990 from the DTI inspectors Henry Brooke QC (later Lord Justice Brooke) and Hugh Aldous. They concluded that the Fayed brothers had dishonestly misrepresented their origins, their wealth, their business interests and their resources to the secretary of state, the Office of Fair Trading, the press, the shareholders and board of the House of Fraser and their own advisers. The inspectors took particular interest in the libel writs Fayed issued against the *Observer*. The first of what was to become an avalanche of such writs arrived at the newspaper's offices on the Wednesday following the publication of Melvyn Marckus's article. The inspectors found that, far from gagging the *Observer*, it drew their financial journalists, Melvyn Marckus, Lorana Sullivan,

Michael Gillard and Peter Wickman, closer to Rowland in terms of whatever documentation they had than might otherwise have been the case. The inspectors concluded:

> We are, however, concerned at one rather sinister aspect of the evidence before us: a constant and unprincipled process of 'gagging' the press which was set in operation by Mohamed Fayed . . . On the one hand Mohamed Fayed was telling lies about himself and his family . . . on the other hand he gave instructions to his very able lawyers to take legal action against any who sought to challenge his claim that he and his brothers beneficially owned the money with which they bought the House of Fraser. To a great extent he succeeded in his aims. Most newspapers and magazines considered that discretion was the better part of valour and preferred to write about other things than get involved in an expensive libel action with a rich man. As a result of what happened, the lies of Mohamed Fayed and his success in 'gagging' the press created, as Mr Fisher [a director of Warburgs and a former *Financial Times* journalist] put it, a new fact: that lies were the truth and that the truth was a lie.

There was a time when people thought that the issue of a writ for libel rendered the particular subject *sub judice* and journalistically out of bounds. That misconception was nailed by Lord Denning in the case of Wallersteiner v. Moir in 1974. Wallersteiner, a wealthy business colleague of Robert Maxwell, was accused by a stockbroker, M.S. Moir, of various acts of fraud. Moir wanted to warn shareholders that Wallersteiner's Rothschild Trust had nothing to do with the famous bank and was an obscure concern of little worth registered in Liechtenstein. Moir argued that Wallersteiner was guilty of fraud and Mr Justice Geoffrey Lane, later the lord chief justice, agreed with him. He awarded Moir £500,000 damages for fraud, misfeasance and breach of trust and dismissed Wallersteiner's claim for libel. On appeal Lord Denning emphasised that matters of public interest should be, and are, open to discussion notwithstanding the issue of a writ. Fair comment does not prejudice a fair trial.

Only if an article creates a substantial risk of serious prejudice to a trial is it likely, under Section 1 of the Contempt of Court Act 1981, to constitute a contempt of court. Libel actions being, for the most part, jury actions, do carry a risk of contempt of court, once the action has been set down for trial. There is, however, a heavy burden in establishing a contempt. Certainly the mere issue of a writ does not stifle comment.

As the role of accountants in newspapers has increased, the resources which proprietors are prepared to devote to investigative journalism have shrunk. In practice, if not in strict legal theory, a person who is known to embark on costly libel litigation, even if it is likely ultimately to be unsuccessful, and who is skilled in cajoling and flattering journalists is unlikely to suffer many difficulties with the press. Fayed learned this lesson early.

In the first year after he acquired control of the House of Fraser, its accounts revealed that the company which previously had concentrated on the running of its staid stores had spent £80,000 on libel actions against the press. The *Observer* bore the brunt of these. On 11 June 1986, Fayed issued a writ for nine articles published in the period between 27 October 1985 and 18 May 1986. He sought an injunction to prevent the paper from repeating allegations about his financial dealings with the Sultan of Brunei and that he had insufficient funds to purchase the House of Fraser on his own account. He claimed that such allegations were an abuse of freedom of speech, part of a persistent and irresponsible journalistic campaign against him and part of Tiny Rowland's vendetta against him. The *Observer* told the court it proposed to justify the allegations and, predictably, an injunction was refused: courts do not grant injunctions pending trial where a defendant asserts he or she will justify what was written. In the end, when in 1990 Fayed faced the prospect of having to disclose documents about his wealth, he hauled up the white flag, as was his wont when faced with an imminent appearance in court. He paid the *Observer*'s legal costs of £500,000.

He had continued all the while to fight the *Observer*. On 15 June 1986 the newspaper had published an article by Peter Wickman about the Fayeds' background. The DTI inspectors were satisfied that Wickman was a meticulously thorough journalist who had carried out his own completely independent research. The attack on his journalistic integrity was deplorable and ought never to have been made; that the Fayeds continued to attack him in this way was, in the opinion of the inspectors, disgraceful.

Fayed did not care. He attacked the inspectors' findings; he peddled disgraceful lies about one of the inspectors, of whom he spoke on tape in characteristically abusive and revolting terms, claiming to have compromising photographs of him. In an attempt to have the findings of the DTI inspectors set aside, he applied to the European Court of Human Rights, claiming that he had been deprived of his right to a fair and public hearing by an independent and impartial tribunal. When that failed, he called the European judges thirteen old farts.

The inspectors also noted and deplored the use made by Fayed of the law of libel against the *Far Eastern Economic Review*, the *Financial Times* and the *Institutional Investor*. Fayed extracted an apology from the *Far Eastern Economic Review* for any embarrassment caused by its suggestion of a financial link between himself and the Sultan of Brunei. He also secured an apology from the *Financial Times* in respect of its article 'The Mystery of the Al Fayeds', which correctly cast doubt on the veracity of their claims about their wealth. Threats of a libel action had also resulted in a considerably toned-down article in the *Institutional Investor* of 13 January 1986 entitled 'The Brunei Mystery – How the World's Richest Man Manages his Money'.

The inspectors' conclusion was: 'In consequence of watching them [Mohamed and Ali Fayed] give evidence we became reluctant to believe anything they told us, unless it was reliably corroborated by independent evidence of a dependable nature. As month after month of our investigation went by, we uncovered more and more cases where the Fayeds were plainly telling us lies.'

In March 1989, Mohamed Fayed sued the publisher Century Hutchinson over the publicity material they released to advertise the launch of *By Hook or by Crook*, a book written by a Washington lawyer, Steven Martindale. It was a rare libel victory for Fayed, as it resulted in the book being pulped. It had reproduced the controversial Swami Tapes – recordings of conversations between the distinctly worldly guru Chandra Swamiki and Fayed in June 1985, in which they were apparently discussing the financing of the purchasing of the House of Fraser. Fayed disputed the authenticity of the tapes, although the voice analysis conducted for the DTI appeared to support it.

Yet over the years, through a mixture of libel writs, spirited entertaining of leading media and public figures and aggressive public-relations tactics, Fayed seemed to turn the tide of public opinion in his favour. The findings of the DTI inspectors, that Fayed had been deceitful and dishonest in his acquisition of the House of Fraser, had with the passage of time and repeated denials faded from public memory. Many had reservations about the fairness and reliability of the Star Chamber procedures of the DTI procedure. Some had a sneaking sympathy for the larger-than-life character who had snatched Harrods from under the nose of Tiny Rowland. A number of journalists gratefully succumbed to the blandishments of Fayed, accepting his hospitality and hampers and idly regurgitating the beautifully wrapped public-relations stories they were fed. Insidiously the public were persuaded to doubt whether it really mattered who ran the upmarket department store and whether there was much to choose between Fayed and Rowland anyway. But unfortunately for Fayed, Rowland continued to fight and £20 million was spent on a battle which included the circulation of the evidence against the Fayeds and the production of a midweek issue of the *Observer* to publish the DTI findings.

Fayed's Achilles' heel was the refusal of the British government to grant him the citizenship to which he apparently felt his honour and business and charitable activities entitled him. It rankled with him that he had to get visas to return to the UK and was treated as a foreigner on his arrival – particularly when he had to deal with immigration officers who he felt were less British than he was. Things were very different in France, where he had been awarded the Légion d'Honneur for his restoration of the Villa Windsor, home of the exiled Duke and Duchess of Windsor, and the Ritz Hotel. Fayed's contribution to the debate was immortalised on tape: 'They have to give us the British passport and kiss my arse, right – ten times for all the things I have done.'

The refusal of the British establishment to give Fayed British citizenship sufficiently interested Graydon Carter, the editor of the American magazine *Vanity Fair*, to prompt him to commission a major profile of Fayed. This attitude seemed to epitomise all that was worst about Britain. He chose the experienced journalist Maureen Orth to write the article. They both envisaged a sympathetic portrait of a man who had suffered from the prejudices and unjustified hostility of the British authorities. But Orth soon got hold of the DTI report, and then, as she researched the subject, she interviewed a large number of witnesses who talked of the extraordinary regime that operated at Harrods. Beneath the tranquil surface of the department store lay a security network which bugged telephones and energetically but unsuccessfully attempted to prosecute people like the former deputy chairman Christoph Bettermann (of whom more later).

Notwithstanding Orth's discoveries, her published profile, 'Holy War at Harrods', was not wholly unsympathetic to Fayed. She acknowledged his achievements and remarkable career, recounted his difficulties with the British government, and interviewed Fayed's supporters and sympathisers. Many felt he was at worst a lovable rogue and made the point that perhaps it did not really matter who owned a shop like Harrods. It was at the point when the article examined Harrods' slogan – 'Enter a different world' – with its sinister connotations that Fayed's fury seems to have been aroused. Here Orth cited a number of cases where

Fayed had been accused of racial discrimination and harassing his female staff with unwanted sexual approaches and, perhaps most disgusting of all, requiring AIDS tests and intimate gynaecological examinations of selected female employees. Fayed was, it seems, also riled by the description of his personal security staff of thirty-eight. He treated them with contempt, like 'donkeys', bugging and sacking them, and they appeared to have had a similarly low opinion of him. Precisely why Fayed feels he needed such massive personal protection and why it is that visitors to Harrods are cocooned in such a sinister web of security are questions which remain to be answered.

The profile also described Fayed's treatment of Christoph Bettermann and of his wife, Francesca, who had been the Harrods solicitor. Mrs Bettermann had to undergo two internal examinations, whereas her successor and predecessor, both women, but less striking-looking, who were both doing precisely the same job, were not required to do so at all. One of the puzzling features of the subsequent libel case was what medical purpose the doctors involved thought they were fulfilling when they carried out these tests and gynaecological procedures. A number of female employees were to complain that reports found their way to Fayed.

The article also referred to Fayed's obsession with sex. He would brandish a two-foot plastic penis at male visitors, asking, 'How's your cock?' This unappealing object was later to surface, together with a package which had evidently delighted Fayed – a grow-your-own-pecker – which he had presented to surprised visitors. Harrods director of security Bob Loftus had also been required to laugh sycophantically as his employer handed him an aphrodisiac with a note stating that it should be inserted in every orifice. However, the majority of the *Vanity Fair* piece was devoted to the strange financial manoeuvrings of Fayed as he sought to purchase Harrods, and to the lies which were told about his background, his wealth and his 'caper' in Haiti, where he posed as Sheikh Mohamed Fayed from Kuwait.

Fayed was persuaded by his advisers, including the devoted

ex-BBC royal reporter Michael Cole, that he had to sue for libel. Otherwise the press could no longer be cajoled into refraining from publishing hostile material about him. A writ was issued which complained of a handful of allegations in the twelve-page article. The complaint focused on what had been written about Fayed's behaviour to his female and non-white employees, his phobia about germs and his charitable activities. Conspicuously, it did not complain about the findings of the DTI inspectors. Fayed had unsuccessfully litigated such matters in his cases against the *Observer*, but although he continued to dispute the DTI findings, he did not sue *Vanity Fair* for its account of his financial operations.

The decision to sue proved to be a very unwise one. The pro-file was defensible even under English libel law. As it was, the vast bulk of the circulation of *Vanity Fair* was in the United States, where, as a public figure, Fayed would have no prospect of success in a libel action as he could not, of course, prove that the allegations had been published with knowledge of their fal-sity. One of his objectives may have been to try to secure in England an apology which could have been published in the United States, even though he would not have been entitled to it under American law.

Although there were many who were worried about giving evidence against Fayed, his treatment of his staff made it inevitable that some ex-employees would come forward. Indeed, there were a number who had successfully taken him or Harrods to an industrial tribunal, where their claims tended almost invariably to be settled for substantial amounts at the last moment. More often than not they had simply fallen out of favour, but this did not prevent allegations of wrongdoing against them. The description of Fayed's behaviour towards his staff was well known at Harrods and evidence of it proliferated. This rendered the pursuit of the action a reckless gamble. He was, after all, a man renowned for his reluctance to enter the witness box – an essential requirement for a libel plaintiff.

The industrial tribunal's decision in the case of Mrs Gillian Elmi

roundly condemned an act of blatant racial discrimination by a
senior personnel officer at Harrods. Harrods had seemingly felt it
appropriate to dispense with her services by describing her as
'unclean' and 'unkempt', and as having 'untamed hair' and 'unpol-
ished speech'. The contrasting fortunes of black and white
applicants for jobs at Harrods were contrasted by the Carlton TV
programme *White Christmas*, which reported how, for a time,
prospective employees were required to submit photographs of
themselves. Mrs Elmi's case, together with those of Maria Remick
and Annaparna Seeley, revealed how the store could use its dress
code and other arbitrary means of withholding approval to disqualify ethnic minorities from employment.

The litigation was made even more hazardous for Fayed by
the contents of secret tape-recordings, which he would have
known existed and were likely to be produced in evidence.
Recording had become such a big operation at Harrods that tapes
were run at half-speed so that each tape could hold twice the
usual amount of material. Old tapes were recycled and occasionally previous recordings remained unerased. Fayed could be
heard, on obtaining planning permission in Cannes, France, to
say: 'I do not want to complicate them because the fucking guy,
if you go and pay him half a million francs, he will give me the
planning permission.' He could also be heard discussing increasing an employee's wages from £5,500 to £8,000, and his cash
payment from £2,000 to £4,000 plus housing and food – something which did not lie easily with either his claim that
conversations were not taped or his denial of paying part of his
employees' wages in cash, with consequent tax savings. And in
a case where issues of racism and obsession with sex arose, it
was scarcely helpful for him to be revealed on tape saying to
Rowland, 'Get me one of those nigger cocks, because I want a
bigger one. I want a transplant now they can transplant. Yes, and
I talk about transplants – heart, liver – what about the fucking
penis?'

The Bettermanns gave detailed accounts of their ordeals at the
hands of Fayed, as did female employees from every part of the

globe. One even contacted the defence from the Far East. Some of the accounts given were very harrowing; some bordered on the bizarre, although even here a common theme, the exploitation of naïveté, recurred. A Portuguese cleaner, Hermina da Silva, was arrested on suspicion of theft after she complained of unwelcome advances from her employer at his Surrey home. No charges were preferred against her and she received a £12,000 pay-off to settle her industrial tribunal claim. A nanny who was summoned late at night to Fayed's apartments at his Surrey house found herself being propositioned for sex and her breasts being squeezed. Fayed was always asking his female employees if they had had a good fuck at the weekend, and if so with how many men. All of them viewed his behaviour as very unpleasant; many found it very distressing.

Most damaging of all to Fayed's case was the willingness of the Harrods head of security, Bob Loftus, to give evidence. Fayed denied the existence of a system of bugging his employees, but Loftus knew how and where it was done and who was doing it. He had hundreds of tapes and transcripts. When Loftus turned down Harrods' proposed severance package, his ex-employers destroyed his prospects of taking up his appointment of director of security at Harvey Nichols by giving him a reference likely to render him unemployable in the security field, despite the glowing reports of his work given before his dismissal.

Loftus was subsequently quoted on many occasions in articles hostile to Fayed. For all Fayed's denials, Loftus had been required to return a Geemarc slow-speed recording device and a black recording briefcase when he left Harrods. Bizarrely, he also had to give back some black balaclavas and a Bruni Automatic 8mm-calibre KN starting pistol which had been used by security staff to carry out an unsuccessful mock kidnap of Fayed in Harrods to check the reflexes of his bodyguards.

It was a far cry from listening to the familiar calls of the Harrods lift-operators to be examining tapes and transcripts of those spied upon in the concessionary jewellers, toy, audio and TV, man's shop, menswear, restaurant, ladies' fashion, Way In,

visual merchandising and artistic design and the Turnbull and
Asser departments. Also recorded were managing and financial
directors, engineers, bodyguards, chauffeurs and secretaries. Even
the communications between Harrods USDAW union representatives (before the union's derecognition) and their lawyers were
captured. Many employees had spoken indiscreetly about their
private lives, in spite of expressing anxieties as to whether it was
safe to talk about personal matters on the phone. Loftus
recounted how it was part of his duties to pass on to Fayed any
salacious details, such as discussions of sexual threesomes.

There were moments when it was easy to forget that one was
dealing with the operations of a department store rather than a
bunch of inept security police. Talented business people whom
Fayed had been happy to employ were treated as criminals when
they fell out of favour. The financial director of the House of
Fraser, Graham Jones, was arrested for alleged fraud as he sat on
the tarmac waiting to fly home to Australia. He was released
after questioning by police, but not until after his arrest had
been dramatically recounted in the newspapers.

Peter Bolliger, who resigned as managing director of Harrods
in April 1994 after three years in the post, found himself vitri-
olically denounced in the press by Fayed's faithful mouthpiece,
Michael Cole. Bob Loftus was directed to complain to the police
that Bolliger had dishonestly made personal phone calls from his
company house which he had not paid for. The complaint
referred to calls costing £1,810.69 in the period 1991 to 1993,
mainly to South Africa and Switzerland. The fact that Bolliger
had immediately agreed to pay his 1993–4 bill of £2,176.25
when asked counted, it seemed, for nothing, despite being obvious evidence of his honesty. The criminal investigation into
Bolliger was widely reported in the press, and next he was falsely
accused of a £2 million fraud. His assets to the value of £400,000
were frozen under the terms of a Mareva injunction.* There was
covert surveillance of his home, and members of his family were

---

*A court order restraining the use of assets.

photographed as they came and went. Not surprisingly, Loftus was soon instructed to ask the police to discontinue their inquiries, and shortly afterwards the proceedings against Bolliger were halted. Bolliger was completely vindicated when Harrods paid him in excess of £50,000 and his daughter over £2,000 and, as a final expunging of the insult which had been added to injury, his furniture was released to him from Osterley, where it had been impounded.

Similar unsubstantiated allegations had been made in 1995 against Gerhardt Eggert after he resigned as director of Harrods Information Systems. A complaint was made to the police alleging the theft of commercially sensitive information. The complaint was not pursued by the police. Later that year, Sandra Lewis-Glass, another dissident employee – who had helped Fayed make millions from his lettings, which were paid to a Liechtenstein management company – was arrested for the purported theft of two computer disks worth 80p after she had made allegations about irregularities concerning tenancies at 55–60 Park Lane. She was not, of course, charged with any wrongdoing, despite the best efforts of the Fayed security forces who trailed her to eavesdrop on her leaving dinner in a Bayswater restaurant.

One of the things which becomes evident in contesting a libel action brought by Fayed is that somewhere along the line he loses sight of the purpose of such an action: to restore a good reputation. In the *Vanity Fair* case, when it became apparent to him that Loftus might be prepared to assist the defence, he launched one of his 'sting' operations. His head of personal security, Paul Handley-Greaves, stepped forward. Handley-Greaves was deputed to come to our offices – we were representing *Vanity Fair* – with a harrowing tale. He had, he said, been dismissed for breach of the non-fraternisation with staff rule – a variation on the store's prohibition of fingering the goods – after impregnating his partner. However, he had a compromising video, he was instructed to tell me, of Fayed breaking precisely the same rule with another employee. He offered to strip at our offices to show (falsely) that he was not carrying any recording

device, having correctly calculated that I would have some distaste for inquiring that closely. This charade increased my
suspicion that Handley-Greaves might very well be a plant. He
had, as part of his cover, had his employment amicably termi-
nated – or so Fayed told his solicitor. No matter that this was not
true. What, after all, was one more lie about the employment
status of his head of personal security? Handley-Greaves was
later to emerge as part of the security team protecting the
Princess of Wales.

Handley-Greaves' story raised the question of whether there
was a tape, which would have been the killer punch, or whether
Fayed was in effect defaming himself by claiming sexual
encounters with employees – precisely the charge on which he
was suing *Vanity Fair*. Handley-Greaves' objective was apparently to try to establish that I was prepared to purchase stolen
property. I reviewed the matter and took the appropriate sound-
ings, and it was clear that it might be permissible to purchase a
document on tape if it were not otherwise obtainable, and if the
document effectively spoke for itself. However, the situation can
be contrasted with paying a witness of fact for his testimony,
which is seldom likely to be proper. We would, of course, have
needed to examine the tape and the circumstances in which it
came into existence before any decision could be made about
any possible use of it, and the fact that such a tape had been purchased and the price would have to be disclosed to the other side.
In any case, no action would have been taken until the facts had
been established and reviewed.

Handley-Greaves' imbecilic plan seemed to revolve around
whether the tape was the original, in which case it could be said
that the plastic enclosing the tape was stolen property, or
whether it was a copy, in which case it could not be, although
taking it could have constituted a breach of copyright. The
slant of the questions raised by the former captain in the Royal
Military Police suggested that this was a carefully rehearsed
'sting' operation. It was in any event a complete waste of effort.
It was made clear in writing to Handley-Greaves that nothing

would be done until I had examined anything he had to show me and had reviewed the material with leading counsel. This was unfortunate and no doubt disappointing for him since he was taping and videoing our conversations to record any nuance that could be seized on by those who, as the Bettermann incident and secretly recorded lunches between Fayed and Rowland had demonstrated, were skilled editors of tapes.

No video was ever produced of Fayed *in flagrante*, as in truth there was none. There was no stolen property, and therefore no potentially dishonest handling of it, but this did not stop Fayed complaining to the director of public prosecutions about my activities, those of Henry Porter, *Vanity Fair*'s London editor, and, for good measure, Bob Loftus. The complaint was swiftly consigned to the dustbin, and neither Porter, Loftus nor I were ever questioned about our alleged wrongdoing. Fayed appears to have had no scruples about lying to the DPP in stating that he had ended the employment of Handley-Greaves on amicable terms. It was somehow appropriate that Fayed, while making unfounded allegations of dishonesty against others, should at the very moment be acting dishonestly himself. The truth was that Handley-Greaves, for all his lies to me, had been since 1995 and was still Fayed's head of personal protection – a job requiring him to stay in close proximity to Fayed.

The libel action was resolved in the autumn of 1997 before it came to trial. In this highly publicised and often bizarre piece of litigation, it was inevitable that even the discussions between the parties received publicity. Somewhat unusually, the opening overtures, but fortunately not the closing ones, were conducted in the nude and were the subject of an unflattering cartoon on the front page of the *Independent*, conjuring up the image of Nicholas Coleridge, managing director of *Vanity Fair*'s owners Condé Nast, and Michael Cole, Fayed's media man, talking peace in the steam room of their London club – with not a hidden wire in sight.

The allegations against Fayed were published in detail in the press and on television, yet no writs followed from the man who

had been so fond of litigation. There is no question that Fayed
was far worse off bringing these libel proceedings than he would
have been had he let the *Vanity Fair* article pass. He had enjoyed
a fair degree of support for his position over the whole DTI and
citizenship saga, and his acquisition of British citizenship should
only have been a matter of time under a Labour administration.
But now his unpleasant activities had been investigated and
uncovered, and initial sympathy for a father who had in August
1997 tragically lost his son in the notorious Paris car accident in
which Princess Diana was also killed soon evaporated in the
wider knowledge the press now had of his lies, and in their belief
that he would not now be so quick to reach for a libel writ.

The speed with which this sympathy turned to hostility and
the eagerness to question Fayed's allegations regarding the fatal
Paris crash was due in part to the light the libel litigation had
cast on his extraordinary lifestyle. The early denial of the driver
Henri Paul's drunkenness, the claims that Fayed had been
'vouchsafed' Princess Diana's last words – which were retold in
a variety of improbable and conflicting forms made all the less
likely by the sad fact that she never recovered consciousness
after the accident – and that he had reached the hospital before
the official party consisting of the French minister of the interior
and the British ambassador, and before Diana was pronounced
dead, and his account of a conversation with an untraceable
nurse who had treated her were all met with incredulity. So, too,
were the claims of an engagement between his son Dodi and
Diana, of a mysterious Fiat Uno – promoted to 'the grassy knoll
of the investigation' by the mellifluous Michael Cole – having
caused the accident, of a blinding light in the tunnel and of
Fayed's 99.9 per cent certainty that this was no accident. In reality the Fiat was at most no more than a near victim of the
homicidal drunken driving of the unqualified Henri Paul. In any
event, it was an improbable choice of vehicle for assassins trying
to kill the occupants of a speeding bullet-proof Mercedes on an
unpreplanned route. Moreover, there was something profoundly
unpleasant about Fayed's allegations of a conspiracy, about his

vow: 'I will not rest until I have established exactly what happened,' and about his attacks on members of Princess Diana's family.

The most damaging consequence of the libel action was that it destroyed the image Fayed's advisers had created for him. The *Vanity Fair* article could have been ignored, and any damaging effect offset by the sycophantic pieces that appeared in much of the British press. As it was, settlement of the libel action opened the door to hostile media coverage in a steady drip of bad publicity which the press now felt able to publish. The harassment and bugging of staff were widely publicised. The *Observer* on 30 November 1997 described the hundreds of secret tape-recordings made of the conversations of Harrods employees. On 18 December 1997 Carlton's *Big Story*'s 'Sex, Lies and Audiotapes' broadcast allegations of Fayed's groping and trying to kiss female members of staff and making obscene remarks, and the tapes were played back to outraged victims. The story of the nanny who had been propositioned by Fayed secured two days' exposure in a national newspaper. The London *Evening Standard* called for an investigation into why so many dissident employees had been the subject of inconclusive police investigations. On 16 November 1997 *Scotland on Sunday* published, under the headline 'DODI'S UNCLE, COCAINE AND THE EX-POLICE CHIEF . . . HOW DRUGS TRAIL LED TO FAYED'S COCAINE FIND BUT PROCURATOR FISCAL CHOSE NOT TO PROSECUTE', an odd tale of a bag containing some crack cocaine and thousands of pounds having been traced to Salah Fayed and his female assistant after it was left in an Aberdeen cab driven by a special constable, who had handed the items in to the police.

Then came Tom Bower's unauthorised biography of Fayed. Bower, too, found himself the object of an unsuccessful entrapment operation by an intermediary who claimed to have incriminating information but who had been equipped by Fayed's henchmen with recording devices.

Quite independently of the libel action, Harrods director of security Bob Loftus supplied Tiny Rowland with details of how his Harrods safety deposit box came to be broken into at the instigation of Fayed, John Macnamara (head of security at Harrods Holdings), Mark Griffiths (personal secretary to Fayed) and Paul Handley-Greaves in December 1995. This was to lead to a claim by Rowland for the value of items rifled by Fayed and his confederates. A locksmith called Roy Hamilton had been called in to pick the lock. When Hamilton was first asked by police about the incident, he denied that it had taken place. Commenting on the payment he was supposed to have received for his services, he told the press: 'If I had been handed an envelope with £50 notes in it, I would certainly remember it, and I can't remember anything like that ever happening. But the original break-in had indeed taken place, and the box had been rifled on two further occasions. By the time Rowland's claim for damages for the disturbance of his private effects and the removal of gems worth over £200,000 had come to trial, Hamilton's memory had improved. He *had* received about £200 in £50 notes on each break-in.

Harrods' much-vaunted 'citadel of security' was, it seems, secure against all depredations except those of the management. Rowland had been filmed as he visited Harrods to examine the contents of his box on 6 December 1995. When Loftus reported this to Fayed, his boss's orders were unequivocal: 'You don't know he has a fucking box here – you fucking go and find out.' Loftus's observation to Macnamara – 'There's loyalty, blind loyalty and downright fucking stupidity' – fell on deaf ears. Harrods initially denied Loftus's account of the break-in, which had been disclosed by Neil Hamilton MP to a House of Commons committee. 'Loftus is a disgruntled former employee of Harrods [who has] made a number of false allegations against the management of Harrods, one of which was referred to by Mr Neil Hamilton,' a Harrods press release claimed. Michael Rogers, Harrods' legal director, was quoted in *The Sunday Times* later, on 19 October 1997, as having described the allegation of theft as 'malicious, vindictive and wholly without foundation'.

But Rowland reported the break-in to the police, and Fayed and his confederates were arrested and interviewed by Scotland

Yard's organised crime group. Presumably Fayed was also fingerprinted – an unpleasant experience for a man used to his bodyguards handing him Roger & Gallet wipes to rid himself of germs after he had shaken hands with someone. They were not charged with a criminal offence, but they were sued. After the action had run for nine days, Fayed and his colleagues, by this time having recalled that there had indeed been a break-in, during which documents had been removed for copying, capitulated. Fayed agreed to reimburse Rowland for the items now missing from his so-called safety deposit box now valued at £1.65 million, and to pay legal costs of £1 million as well as his own legal bills, which probably themselves totalled at least £1 million.

Fayed had some success in persuading the Police Complaints Authority that his arrest had been unjustified. He was also cleared of any criminal involvement in the purloining of documents belonging to Neil Hamilton's lawyers (see Chapter 18). Nonetheless it was a case of humiliating surrender rather than settlement. Evidently having been warned of the very dire perils they faced if they continued to defend the case, and if they were cross-examined on oath about their story that the break-in had been all Loftus's idea, they consented to judgement against them on the grounds that they had induced a breach of contract. They agreed to pay all the costs on the higher-indemnity basis and their ill-judged third-party proceedings against Loftus were dismissed, again with an order for indemnity costs. Fayed's boast that 'if Loftus starts throwing pebbles at me, then I will throw some dynamite back' had rebounded on him. The case illustrated the usefulness of compelling the production of mobile telephone records. In this instance these cast interesting light on who talked to the locksmith and when.

In September 1999 Fayed was obliged to pay Loftus 'generous' libel damages when the previously withdrawn allegations against his former head of security were repeated in an *Observer* article published in Fayed's name, though not actually written by him.

Following further litigation brought by Loftus against Fayed, no fewer than six police officers turned up on Loftus's doorstep at 7am to investigate at Fayed's behest the alleged theft of a secret tape-recording of Rowland. In this lavish use of police resources no one seems to have noticed the inconsistency between the apparently unjustified arrest of Fayed in connection with the actual disappearance of property worth £1.65 million and the apparently justified arrest of Loftus for the alleged theft of a tape probably not worth much more than a pound. Needless to say no further action was taken,

The *Vanity Fair* libel action had ended up doing far more damage to Fayed's reputation than the original article. It had focused unwelcome attention on his activities and undermined his hitherto reasonably successful strategy in dealing with the press.

As we will see, Fayed successfully defended the action brought against him by Neil Hamilton, but even that was not without its drawbacks. As details of Fayed's weekly cash withdrawals of £120,000 to maintain his lifestyle emerged in the evidence, they seem to have caused raised eyebrows at the Inland Revenue. Clearly unimpressed by Fayed's response to Desmond Browne, QC for Hamilton – 'It's none of your bloody business' – it sought to renege on the agreement to limit his annual tax liability to £240,000.

The Hamilton case showed how Fayed was able to turn his bad reputation to advantage, as did the rejection by the Court of Appeal of the *Sun*'s claim that it was entitled to publish film footage of Princess Diana's visit to the Villa Windsor just before her death. The copyright belonged to one of Fayed's companies, but the *Sun* sought to justify its use of the material on the basis that it exposed the falsity of Fayed's claim that Diana was there to measure up the drapes for her future home. The Court of Appeal refused to accept the newspaper's ingenious argument that publication was in the public interest. It could have made its point without using the pictures, the court ruled, and in any event Fayed's claims were patently ridiculous, as were his fabricated assertions about his son Dodi buying a ring to mark his engagement to Diana, having seen their bodies and having been informed of the Princess's last words.

## Christoph Bettermann's Tale

In addition to using the law of libel (not always successfully) to protect his own reputation, Mohamed Fayed demonstrated the ease with which powerful people can defend libel actions, irrespective of the strength of their defence. In Christoph Bettermann, however, he met his match, despite the oppressive tactics he used.

At the age of forty-three, German-born Bettermann, by training a lawyer, was deputy chairman of Harrods and chairman of Harrods Estates. In addition he was in charge of many of Mohamed Fayed's business interests in Dubai, being president of the Gulf-based International Marine Services Inc. (IMS), which provided offshore maritime services, chief executive of Dubai Trade Centre Management Co. Ltd and managing director of Dubai Trade and Trust Company. He had also married the Harrods company solicitor.

Bettermann had met Fayed in 1981 when he was managing director of IMS. He evidently made a good impression on the entrepreneur, as in 1984 Fayed bought IMS, stipulating that Bettermann should be its president. Bettermann turned the company round, transforming a loss of $20 million into a profit of $15 million, the bulk of which went into Fayed's pocket. When he took up his Harrods appointments, he started to commute between Dubai and Knightsbridge and rapidly became Fayed's right-hand man.

Working at these close quarters with Fayed, Bettermann became increasingly concerned at the very idiosyncratic way he ran Harrods. He found Fayed's attitude to his attractive female staff unacceptable, and this worry was compounded by the growing strain of commuting between his jobs in Dubai and London. He happened to mention his travelling pressures to a business associate, Hamid Jafar, who was chairman of Crescent

Petroleum in Dubai. Jafar asked the New York-based industrial
psychologist Dr Mortimer Feinberg to suggest to Bettermann
that he consider going to work in the Gulf for Crescent.
Bettermann and Feinberg met in April 1991. The idea of working
in one country had its attractions, and Bettermann discussed
Feinberg's offer with Fayed. Fayed proposed that Bettermann
work for him in Dubai and then return to London and become a
director of his holding company, Al Fayed Investments Ltd, at a
salary of $500,000. Bettermann decided to turn down the
Crescent offer and take up Fayed's suggestion. So in May 1991
he resigned from Harrods Ltd and Harrods Estates in order to do
more for Fayed in Dubai.

At first Fayed seemed relaxed about this development. He
circulated a memorandum praising Bettermann's contribution to
Harrods. However, things were seldom as they seemed at
Harrods. On 28 May 1991 Bettermann received a letter from
Fayed claiming he had overcalculated his bonus from IMS.
Bettermann replied that the basis of the calculation had been
agreed in 1984. Fayed asked him to come to London to discuss
the matter. Before the meeting, scheduled for 24 June,
Bettermann decided to resign from his remaining Harrods posts
and drafted his letter of resignation on 21 June.

The meeting started auspiciously enough. Fayed accepted that
Bettermann had not cheated on his bonus. In fact, he said, he had
been underpaid. But Fayed could not resist the sense of power he
experienced from secretly bugging people. He produced a transcript of Bettermann's conversation with Feinberg in April 1991
and accused Bettermann of betraying his trust by speaking about
such matters to Feinberg and Jafar. Bettermann, who had earlier
been told by Fayed's security chiefs that telephones were rou-
tinely bugged, realised this procedure had been extended to the
telephones at the Fayed-owned flat he had occupied at 60 Park
Lane. He told Fayed that the bugging had destroyed his trust and
that he would resign. Fayed accused him of being arrogant. 'You
don't go back to Dubai,' he added ominously. 'It will be very
embarrassing for you, Feinberg and Hamid Jafar.'

Bettermann did return to Dubai, but he was told not to set foot in the IMS office. Significantly, in the light of the allegations he was later to make, Fayed, through his London solicitors Allen and Overy, paid Bettermann £160,000 compensation for his dismissal from IMS.

While working at Harrods Bettermann had fallen in love with the company solicitor, Francesca Armitage. At the time he felt he should inform Fayed that he was seeing Francesca so that Fayed could, if he wished, ask for the resignation of one or both of them. Fayed did not do so. Instead he suggested others among his employees with whom Bettermann could also enjoy himself and made a number of gratuitously offensive and slanderous remarks about Francesca and her family. He even offered to show Bettermann the two gynaecological reports which he had wholly inappropriately had prepared on Francesca by his tame doctor, ostensibly as part of the requirements of employing someone as a company solicitor at Harrods. And as we have already seen, AIDS tests were apparently necessary in case the legal work took a turn for the horizontal.

After Francesca resigned in May 1991 to travel to Dubai, she was told to clear her desk immediately, and Harrods staff were forbidden to attend the Bettermann wedding on 31 August. One of Francesca's colleagues was told by Harrods Holdings head of security, John Macnamara, on the preceding Thursday that it would be better if she did not go. She had already bought an outfit for the occasion and a wedding present. One of the photographers outside the church was posted there expressly to check that no Harrods employee had disobeyed orders.

Shortly before this Bettermann had been contacted in Germany by Macnamara, a former detective chief superintendent in the Fraud Squad. He wanted to talk to Bettermann about the payments made to IMS arising from the salvage of an oil tanker, the *York Marine*, which had been hit by fire from Iranian gunboats in the Mubarak Oilfield in the Gulf. The deal had had a distinctly Middle Eastern flavour to it. Crescent Petroleum owned the cargo and were due to pay IMS $900,000 after the ship had been salvaged. There were no insurers involved and a series of complicated interlocking transactions were agreed for local political reasons so that all parties could be paid in full. Bettermann had gained no personal benefit, but IMS had received payment in full for its services, resulting in its owner, Fayed, being better off to the tune of $150,000.

Fayed decided now, in August 1991, two and a half years after payment had to his apparent satisfaction been made to IMS, that IMS had been defrauded. Bettermann agreed to meet Macnamara in Malaga to explain the transaction to him. His experience of working for Fayed prompted him to ask Macnamara at the outset whether he was recording their conversation. No, the former policeman asserted unblinkingly on tape. With a nose for dodgy dealings honed by his twenty-six years in the police force, Macnamara accused Bettermann of defrauding the insurers – a difficult manoeuvre to perform considering that there had been no insurers to defraud. Macnamara had reached his startling conclusion on the assumption that Holman, Fenwick and Willan were the insurers' loss-adjusters. A quick look in the London telephone directory would have told him that Holman, Fenwick and Willan were in fact a long-established firm of maritime solicitors in the City of London who were in this instance acting for the Dutch salvage firm, Smit Tak.

A further meeting, also secretly recorded, took place at the Intercontinental Hotel in London on 29 August 1991, at which Macnamara repeated his allegations. A complaint was made to the Dubai police, and on 28 September 1991 Bettermann was interviewed about the transaction. On 2 October Fayed wrote in Arabic to the Sheikh Bin Al Qasimi, ruler of Sharjah, where Bettermann was then working, copying in the deputy ruler, claiming that Bettermann had been fired from IMS for dishonesty (when he had in fact been paid £160,000 compensation) and that he had embezzled $900,000 of IMS's money in the matter of the *York Marine*.

Bettermann turned to Peter Carter-Ruck and Partners and sued for libel. They succeeded in establishing jurisdiction in London for a letter written in Arabic to the Gulf about someone resident in the Gulf. Fayed's allegations in any case cut little ice with the Petroleum and Mineral Department of the government of Sharjah. In November 1991, Bettermann was informed by the ruler that he had been exonerated. He was not so fortunate in Dubai. On 17 December he was ordered to return to the police station in Dubai, his passport was impounded and he was granted bail only on the lodging of financial guarantees. His criminal trial, which was accompanied by a civil claim from IMS, started on 22 February 1992. It did not end until 25 December 1993, when he was acquitted after twenty-five court appearances which involved standing with other prisoners in a caged dock while yet another application for an adjournment was made. Bettermann found that the allegations against him were published in the Arabic-speaking press and also in *Private Eye*. The civil claim by IMS was dismissed too, although the company appealed twice to the Court of Cassation, the appeal court in Dubai. His acquittal was unsuccessfully appealed, and eventually, on 22 October 1994, all proceedings ceased and IMS was ordered to pay $160,000 costs to Bettermann.

Fayed's tactics in the libel action were revealing. He unleashed the forces of his solicitors, D.J. Freeman, where he had entrusted the case to Lawrence Harris, a young partner, an aspiring Conservative MP destined for disappointment at the forthcoming election and a speaker on law-and-order matters such as closed-circuit television. Fayed, it seemed, employed Harris despite his politics rather than because of them. Harris demanded that Bettermann should lodge £322,393.93 as security for costs as he was resident abroad. This application hit the rocks when it was discovered that Bettermann was by then based in Germany, a member of the European Union, and security for costs could not be ordered. Having to ante up some £320,000 as well as finding his own legal expenses would have made the cost of proceeding crippling for Bettermann, particularly after the two-year, Fayed-inspired interruption of his life.

Fayed's affidavit evidence exhibited a seven-page summary of

Macnamara's conversation, which the ex-copper had prepared in place of a full transcript. By a curious oversight Macnamara had felt it unimportant to include the first few sentences of the conversation in which he had lied about not recording the conversation.

Bettermann's case was due to come to court in February 1996. Fayed gave every sign of contesting the case, including delivering a brief to, among others, the redoubtable but costly George Carman QC. Fayed's defence claimed, rather bizarrely, that he had been under a moral or social duty to report an apparent fraud to the authorities. At the last moment, however, Fayed cravenly capitulated – having been warned, no doubt, that his behaviour put him beyond the scope of Carman's forensic skills. He paid Bettermann £125,000, which was right at the top of the scale of damages suggested in the Elton John case (see Chapter 15), plus every penny of Bettermann's legal costs of £287,500, which meant, with the inevitable element of irrecoverable legal costs, had Fayed insisted on them being 'taxed' (assessed by a court official), that the real level of damages was in the bracket of £150,000 to £175,000 – a very high figure for two private letters in Arabic, even if they did wreak enormous damage.

In the statement in open court, Fayed said he regretted having written the letters and acknowledged the falsity of the allegations. He conceded that Bettermann had left Harrods and IMS on agreed terms which neither involved nor reflected any criticism on his past service. He undertook not to repeat the allegations he had made to the ruler of Sharjah.

Clausewitz has written of war being an extension of politics. Sometimes it seems that Fayed has a similar view of the law of libel. In the summer of 1997, he was once more inviting Bettermann to his office at Harrods and putting various business proposals to him, while his minions were telling Sir Gordon Downey, the parliamentary commissioner, that he had settled the libel action only because he could not get witnesses to come forward.

Mohamed Fayed finally got his comeuppance in May 1999, when the home secretary, Jack Straw, concluded that he did not have the good character required under the British Nationality Act 1981 to qualify for British citizenship. Fayed's attempt to get the courts to annul this decision in October also met with failure. His involvement in the Rowland safety deposit box break-in and corrupt payments to MPs, and his wild allegations about the role of the royal family and the British establishment in the deaths of the Princess of Wales and his son Dodi and in subsequently covering them up, appear to have counted against him. Precisely why Fayed wanted citizenship in the first place is unclear. 'I piss on the British. I bought Harrods so I can sit up here and piss on them as they pass down there. I want them to come here every day so I can piss on them. And when I am dead. I'll be buried in a mausoleum on the roof and I'll still piss on them. I hate them.'

# 4

# THE DESTRUCTION OF JONATHAN AITKEN

There have been many cases in which the wrong verdict has been obtained by dubious evidence. The libel action brought by former Conservative Cabinet minister Jonathan Aitken was of a different character, involving as it did evidence that was not only dubious, but elaborate and perjured.

Aitken had entered Parliament as MP for Thanet South in 1974 at the age of thirty-one (he would have got in four years earlier at Thirsk but for a brush with the Official Secrets Act in the company of the editor of the *Sunday Telegraph*, Brian Roberts). In 1985 he successfully defended a libel action brought by an irate constituent, Mrs Hazel Pinder-White, who had taken exception to a jocular reference to her as a 'Sue Ellen of *Dallas*' type character: Aitken had reviewed the shortcomings of the law of libel in an article in the *UK Press Gazette* – entitled 'Lessons of the Sue Ellen Case: Why the Lottery of Libel Law needs Reform'. His career during the Conservatives' eighteen years in office would have progressed faster but for the fact that he had dated Mrs Thatcher's daughter Carol. The prime minister believed that he had upset her and took the view that she was damned if she was going to give him a job. Nor was an MP likely to prosper by saying to a Cairo newspaper of Mrs Thatcher: 'I wouldn't say she is open-minded on the Middle East so much as empty-headed. She probably thinks Sinai is the plural of sinus.' But things improved when John Major became prime minister. In 1992 Aitken became minister of state for defence procurement, and in 1994 he joined the Cabinet as chief secretary to the Treasury.

Aitken's spectacular downfall came as a result of libel actions he brought against the *Guardian* and Granada Television. In the wake of the collapse of the cases in June 1997, the *Guardian* exulted with the headline: 'HE LIED AND LIED AND LIED'. Alan Rusbridger, the editor, revelled in the paper's triumphant exposure of Aitken: 'For three years he has lied to newspapers, lied to the Cabinet secretary, lied to the prime minister and lied to his colleagues. Now he has made his fatal mistake by lying on oath to the High Court.' Aitken separated from his Swiss wife, Lolicia, to whom he had been married for eighteen years. 'Recent events have shattered me and broken my family,' he observed sadly. He resigned from the Privy Council, having already lost his seat in the 1997 election by converting an 11,500 majority into a deficit of 2,878 votes, a swing of 15 per cent. He faced a claim for legal costs of £2 million, his own costs were £800,000, and he was charged with and subsequently pleaded guilty to perjury and perverting the course of justice. It was a fall to earth experienced by few since Icarus.

Following the trial someone in the Land Registry tipped off the *Guardian* that Aitken's share in his London home in Lord North Street was about to be transferred to his wife. His assets were frozen under the terms of a Mareva injunction, under which his living expenses had to be approved by the court, and he was compelled under threat of imprisonment to give proper disclosure of his assets. By that stage the *Guardian* and Granada had an order for him to pay 80 per cent of their legal costs, which amounted to something in the region of £2 million, and were concerned that his assets should not be spirited abroad. Aitken declared himself bankrupt. The transfer of the £1.75 million house was blocked by the court on the grounds that it was a manoeuvre to defraud his creditors, and the trustee in bankruptcy laid claim to it, along with his Rolex watch and cufflinks. Eventually he had to admit defeat and put the house on the market, inviting offers of over £2 million, in order to pay the *Guardian*'s and Granada's legal costs.

He also suffered the anguish of seeing his own seventeen-year-old daughter Victoria being arrested for conspiracy to pervert the course of justice, although she was not in the end charged with any offence: three months after Victoria's arrest the Crown Prosecution Service decided to take no action against her, having secured Jonathan Aitken's confession, which was probably their objective in the first place.

A biography of Margaret Thatcher which Aitken was scheduled to write in a deal said to be worth £1 million was passed instead to Charles Moore, editor of the *Daily Telegraph*. A consultancy Aitken had with GEC Marconi to advise on sales to Saudi Arabia was not renewed. The White House, his £500,000 home in Sandwich Bay, was sold as the case proceeded.

Hopes that it would provide a source of funds to reimburse the *Guardian*'s and Granada's legal costs were dashed when it emerged, to the evident surprise of the defendants, that the Panamanian company which owned the house in fact belonged to Lolicia's Serbian grandmother. After the trial Aitken sought to make a voluntary arrangement with his creditors, claiming debts of £8 million. The *Guardian* and Granada calculated his debts to be a fraction of this sum. They claimed Aitken had been lying over his assets, as he had at the trial.

Contested libel cases tend to engender all-out warfare, and that certainly seemed to be the case with the *Guardian*. They continued to savage Aitken, seeing him as libel-proof, and for good measure Granada broadcast a new version of their offending *World in Action* programme. The newspaper's attitude to Aitken was conditioned by their view that he had been dishonestly seeking to extract massive damages in a libel action which he knew rested on perjury. But their pursuit of the politician and the tactics they themselves adopted raise interesting questions as to how far the press should exercise its powers against its perceived enemies holding elected office in an administration which a particular newspaper happens to dislike.

On one view the lies Aitken told concerned a relatively insignificant matter: who paid a bill at the Ritz Hotel in Paris of no more than £1,000, a sum well within Aitken's means. As is so often the case, it was the cover-up rather than the original offence that made the matter so serious. The *Guardian*'s and Granada's view was that the fact that this hotel bill had been picked up by Aitken's Saudi associates was a graphic illustration of their contention that he was in the pocket of the Saudis, notwithstanding his position in government, and that he was engaged in arms-dealing on his own account. His decision to lie so elaborately about the matter was, they suggested, typical of the man. What was extraordinary was that Aitken did not either come clean about the hotel bill at the outset or refrain from specifically complaining in the libel action about who paid the hotel bill. Aitken had not, after all, sued the *Guardian* in respect of their article of 10 May 1994, 'The Minister, the Mandarin, the Premier and the Editor'. By citing the question of the hotel bill in his claim, he opened up the disclosure of documents process that was ultimately to seal his fate. Libel plaintiffs can to some extent delineate the battlefield by picking and choosing the parts of broadcast or newspaper article on which to sue. Aitken would, of course, have been severely criticised for his failure not to sue in respect of the hotel bill allegation, but that need not have presented an insurmountable problem to someone as plausible as him. Instead, Aitken showed himself to be the ultimate poker player.

It all began on 10 April 1995, when Aitken was hit by a twin-pronged attack. Granada Television broadcast a budget programme entitled 'Jonathan of Arabia', which suggested that Aitken was in the pay of the Saudi Arabians. A camel hired from Chester Zoo was filmed in the distinctly uneastern setting

of a Merseyside beach, with reporter David Leigh, as if on loan
from central casting, dressed as a Bedouin Arab, shown outside
Aitken's Westminster house in an attempt to reconstruct a
meeting between Aitken and businessman Fouad Makhzoumi.
Makhzoumi, Lebanese by origin, was an English citizen who did
not wear such Arab clothes. Of this programme Aitken was to
complain: 'Clearly this was a hatchet job. It was character assassination television, not current affairs television. There was no
attempt at balance or objectivity. It was destroy Aitken time.'

The programme had been trailed in that morning's edition of
the *Guardian* under the front-page headline 'AITKEN TRIED TO ARRANGE
GIRLS FOR SAUDI FRIENDS'. The report accused Aitken of asking staff to
procure women for Arabs at the Inglewood Health Hydro in
Berkshire, in which the minister had had an interest and which
the *Guardian* dubbed 'Inglenookie'. On its inside pages the paper
alleged that Aitken was involved in arms deals with Iran and Iraq
and with the Makhzoumi brothers, Fouad and Zaid, and that he
had received gifts from the Saudis. The first edition was faxed to
Aitken in Switzerland where he was skiing. He read it in the
small hours.

Shocked by its contents, Aitken perhaps got a little carried
away at the trial when he described his reaction.

It was almost the equivalent of having a heart attack in the
terms of shock and pain I felt reading it. I was so astonished
to read on the front page of a serious newspaper an allegation of this seriousness that I knew in my heart to be untrue
and I felt such pain because it was a sordid story. I remember burying my head in my hands and saying to nobody in
particular, 'The *Guardian* has said I am a pimp.' My twelve-
year-old son asked, 'What's a pimp, Daddy?' I felt that the
*Guardian* had moved from the vendetta they had been running for some time against me to all-out war, because the
allegations were so serious and devastating.

Spurred on by a mixture of hubris, anger and sleeplessness,

Aitken penned his fateful 'Sword of Truth' speech. He flew back to London to read it off autocue at Conservative Central Office at 5pm, a few hours before the Granada programme was due to be broadcast. 'If it falls to me to start a fight to cut out the cancer of bent and twisted journalism in our country with the simple sword of truth and the trusty shield of British fair play, so be it, I am ready for the fight,' he declared. 'The *Guardian*'s report is one of deliberate misrepresentations, falsehoods and lies and is clearly part of the paper's long campaign of sustained attempts to discredit me.' This was fine fighting stuff – until Aitken lost the case. Alan Rusbridger, by then the *Guardian*'s editor, was able to throw it back in his face. 'Jonathan Aitken seems to have impaled himself on the simple sword of truth: he made the fatal mistake of lying on oath to the High Court.' Thereafter many a report on Aitken's downfall was accompanied by his overconfident 'Sword of Truth' address.

To support its accusations that Aitken was in the pocket of the Saudis, the *Guardian* suggested that his house in Lord North Street had been bought in 1982 with money from Prince Mohammed Bin Fahd, son of the Saudi King. Tipped off by Mohamed Fayed, who owned the hotel, the paper also claimed that Aitken had had a business meeting with two Arab arms-dealers at the Ritz in Paris. By maintaining his business relationship with the Saudis when in government, it was alleged, Aitken had broken the rules governing such matters in the Questions of Procedure for Ministers, and had used his position as minister for defence procurement to push contracts the way of his former business associates.

A number of the allegations were very old: the Inglewood accusation dated back to 1982; and the suggestion that the Saudis had supposedly purchased a Jaguar for him and paid for his House of Commons notepaper went back as far as 1975–6. The 'pimping' question was never resolved. Granada and the *Guardian* claimed that the allegation was not one of pimping, but one of pandering to the needs of his Arab associates by providing liberal-minded young ladies from Newbury. The issue was to some extent complicated by further suggestions that Aitken might have been responsible for the supply of like-minded air stewardesses, but these allegations were not pursued, apparently owing to the discovery that one of the air stewardesses turned out to be the respectably married wife of a City solicitor. In any case, there were a number of former Inglewood staff prepared to support the claims and the defence believed that their stories hung together, notwithstanding Aitken's response that these were disgruntled ex-employees. Aitken, meanwhile, was confident he could show that all the allegations were false.

The evidence, though, was never heard because in the end Aitken abandoned his case. What impact the evidence of events fifteen years earlier would have had on the trial judge, Mr Justice Popplewell, and whether it would have been sufficient either by itself or in conjunction with other evidence to convince him that Aitken was lying, is something that is unlikely ever to be known. In a sense it mattered little whether the lie about the hotel bill was, as Aitken perceived it to be, a small part of the case and a corner which could, in the light of the other libels, be cut. The issue had been extensively canvassed in correspondence and had entailed lying to the Cabinet secretary. Aitken has also assured the prime minister that he had been in Paris on family business. The elaborate web of deceit it involved rendered what may or may not have been a valid libel claim fraudulent.

The *Guardian*'s pursuit of Aitken brought them a strange bed-fellow in Mohamed Fayed. Fayed had over the years been savagely attacked for his unethical business practices by the *Guardian*. When Fayed's lies were exposed by the DTI inspectors in 1990, the *Guardian* was at the forefront of those condemning him. 'LIES, LIES AND MORE LIES: THE MOUNTAIN THAT CAME FROM MOHAMED. THE 15-YEAR STORY OF THE BID THAT TURNED INTO A SCANDAL'. Their editorial was even more scathing: 'If there is one thing more damning than yesterday's report on the way the brothers Fayed lied their way to control of the House of Fraser group, it is the thought that the government is doing nothing about it. The Fayeds are found to have lied about their origins again and again, they produced birth certificates they knew to be false.' In spite of these salvos, the agendas of the *Guardian* and Fayed did overlap in their mutual desire to bring down the Conservative government. In January 1995, Fayed could be heard, in one of his secretly taped meetings with Tiny Rowland, bragging that Aitken would go (from the government) in two or three weeks. To this end, in the summer of 1993 the *Guardian* had approached Fayed to see if he could assist in securing the settlement of a libel action which had been brought against them by Prince Bandar Bin Sultan, the Saudi ambassador to Washington, for the wholly false allegation that he had given £7 million in cash to the deputy prime minister, Michael Heseltine.

Prince Bandar was the negotiator for the reinstatement of the £4 billion Al Yamamah arms sale contract with Britain. On 22 June 1993 the *Guardian* ran a story initially headlined: 'TORIES FACE SAUDI CASH CLAIM'. In the first edition, for legal reasons, reference was made merely to an unnamed Cabinet minister. By the time of the second edition Labour MP Clive Soley had, in a fortuitously timed debate on party-political funding, read out a letter falsely stating that Heseltine had met Prince Bandar to solicit funds. The allegation now became privileged as a parliamentary report. The *Guardian*'s headline changed, amid allegations of dirty tricks, to 'LABOUR MP ALLEGES HESELTINE MET SAUDI ROYAL TO SOLICIT GENERAL ELECTION FUNDS'. Soley subsequently apologised for having named Heseltine; meanwhile, the *Guardian* wrongly believed it had fallen upon a scandal which would bring down the Conservatives.

As it turned out, Fayed could not help, but the then editor of the newspaper, Peter Preston, did note Fayed's diatribe against the Conservatives and his claim to have two junior ministers, Neil Hamilton and Tim Smith, on his payroll. And Fayed then telephoned arms-dealer Wafic Said at his home in Marbella, claiming to be 'a close friend' of Preston's, and tried to broker a settlement by offering favourable coverage of Prince Bandar in the *Guardian*. The Prince, it seems, felt his life could go on in Washington without the undoubted attraction of favourable coverage in that newspaper.

Fayed made a similar and equally unsuccessful approach to Prince Mohammed Bin Fahd when he stayed at the Paris Ritz on 3 September 1993, again claiming to speak on behalf of the *Guardian*. In the event the paper realised it had got the story wrong and paid £10,000 to a charity of Prince Bandar's choice, apologised unreservedly, and accepted that no such meeting between Heseltine and Bandar had taken place, nor had any such donation been made.

But the link between the *Guardian* and Fayed had been forged, and after Jonathan Aitken stayed in Paris at the Ritz, on 17 September 1993, Peter Preston met Fayed and was shown, in the third week of October 1993, a copy of Aitken's bill, or *libelle*, as it was appropriately captioned. It was for 8,010.90 francs and marked 'Debiteur a/c M. Ayas # 626/7'. Fayed explained that, walking around the hotel, he had happened to see a 'government minister' sitting with two men he described as major arms-dealers, Said Ayas, private secretary and adviser to Prince Mohammed, who had been involved in the Al Yamamah arms deal, and Wafic Said. He likened the scene to seeing the attorney-general sitting with Al Capone. Understandably, Fayed was worried about a possible breach of confidentiality in disclosing details of a client's hotel bill. David Pallister of the *Guardian* wrote to Aitken on 19 October 1993 inquiring about his meeting at the Ritz with prominent Saudis. He replied that the purpose of his visit was to meet up with his wife and daughter – who was going to her new school – and that he had not met Said Ayas or Wafic Said that weekend.

To allay Fayed's concerns, Preston then set about an astonishing act of forgery which he later sought to excuse on the grounds that it was not intended to deceive, claiming that he was merely trying to protect a source. Preston described it euphemistically as a 'cod fax' and as part of a legitimate journalistic ruse, but it was nonetheless a forgery. Although this was probably not strictly an offence as defined in Section 1 of the Forgery and Counterfeiting Act 1981, Preston was clearly using a false instrument upon which he had forged the signature of Aitken's private secretary in order to gain an advantage over his target. But the Ritz knew that Preston's confection was a fake. So what was involved could therefore be presented in law as more of a covering of tracks than a forgery.

The document was a letter typed on what appeared to be Aitken's House of Commons notepaper, although it now featured a *Guardian* telephone and fax number. It was sent on 21 November 1993 to a number given to Preston by Fayed. This was not the main Ritz number, but it purported nevertheless to be a request directed to the Accounts Department of the hotel. 'I wonder if you could kindly assist me with a matter,' Preston wrote. 'Regrettably I seem to have mislaid my copy [of the bill], which I require for personal accounting reasons. Could you please confirm that billing arrangement and send me a copy of my account at the above fax number? Thank you for your co-operation. Yours faithfully, Jonathan Aitken.' The forged signature was that of Jeremy Wright, Aitken's private secretary, who was falsely represented as having signed the letter on Aitken's behalf.

On receipt of the forged letter Fayed was happy to oblige and a copy of the bill was sent to Preston, who later admitted to the House of Commons Privileges Committee that he had been wrong to send this fax. 'It was a stupid and, as I rapidly learned, discourteous thing to have done and I would not do it again.' He accepted that the reputation of the Ritz would not be enhanced if it was regularly sending clients' bills to newspapers. It was certainly wrong to have sent this fax, he conceded, and he totally regretted using the House of Commons notepaper for this purpose. He added that it had not occurred to him at all that his action might have been used to promote a vendetta of Fayed's against the minister. He was asked whether he viewed Fayed as a truthful man. 'I know Mr Al-Fayed is a controversial man,' he replied guardedly.

He was asked if he was out to get Jonathan Aitken. He had known Aitken for a large number of years, he replied; he had shared platforms with him and been to parties at his home, and had a generally good relationship with him. 'We were on a very friendly basis and spoke for the freedom of information campaign during the 1980s, so I consider Mr Aitken, if you like, more of a friend than anything else in political life'. Indeed, the early exchanges between Preston and Aitken proceeded on amicable first-name terms. Aitken, however, at the trial, spoke of Preston telling him at a dinner in late 1993, 'We will get you in the end.' In a sense he did, as Preston's letter of 11 January 1994 elicited on 13 January the fateful lie which Aitken never recanted: that Lolicia, his wife, had paid the Ritz bill 'with money given to her for that purpose'. Coupled with his answer to Pallister's letter, this was the trap sprung by Aitken.

After the exposure of his forged letter to Aitken by the *Daily Telegraph* in October 1994, and the embarrassment of the revelation in the *Spectator* in December 1994 that Richard Gott, a senior *Guardian* executive, had received payments for travel expenses from the Soviet Union, Preston resigned from the Press Complaints Commission and stood down as editor of the *Guardian*, to be replaced by Alan Rusbridger, and was booted upstairs as editor-in-chief of the *Guardian* and *Observer*. The House of Commons Privileges Committee concluded that in their eagerness to follow up the story, Preston and the *Guardian* were guilty of unwise and improper conduct. It was a contempt of the House to purport an act in the name of Right Honourable or Honourable members of that House without that member's authority.

It was, the committee ruled, unacceptable for anyone other than a member of Parliament, or a person directly acting on that member's authority, to use official notepaper; it was even more unacceptable when the notepaper and signature were used deliberately to give the impression that that authority had been given. Fayed told the committee that in retrospect he regretted that he had not simply handed over the bill. However, he resented the insinuations of certain members of the committee. 'The gentleman is trying to incriminate me as if I am a criminal, not the minister who is the criminal,' he protested. Fayed also opaquely but unambiguously complained to the committee about the prime minister's lack of decency in not apologising to him. 'What is the harm about a letter being sent to uncover the malpractice of very, very high office occupied by a person who is a liar, who is an arms-dealer himself . . . somebody like me who had contributed over thirty-nine years of his life giving billions of business, employing tens of thousands of people, this is the attitude, you have been insulting me.' No doubt Preston equally regretted that in his anxiety to secure the necessary evidence he had cut corners.

Once Preston was in possession of the Ritz bill, a correspondence started between the *Guardian* and Aitken as to who had paid the bill for his stay at the hotel. Aitken, unaware of how much the *Guardian* had discovered about the method of payment, mistakenly believed that the Saudis' relationship with the Ritz was sufficient to prevent the truth from coming out. In fact the correspondence Aitken had had with the Ritz was being copied to the *Guardian*.

The truth of the matter was that the entire bill for the Saudi party of eight, including Aitken, which totalled 117,008 francs (£14,000), had been paid by cheque by Madame Manon Vidal, who worked for Prince Mohammed Bin Fahd. Subsequently, she had paid, in cash, 4,256.80 francs for the outstanding extras. Aitken's portion of the bill, as we have seen, had been 8,010 francs (£1,000). After several months of correspondence and repeated denials that he had breached Section 126 of the Questions of Procedure for Ministers, Aitken was required in March 1994 to explain the position to Sir Robin Butler, the Cabinet secretary. Still in the dark as to the extent of the *Guardian*'s knowledge of the payment of the bill and the cooperation that was taking place between the Ritz and the *Guardian*, Aitken took advantage of what he had been told by Frank Klein, the manager of the Ritz: that 'a brunette lady of European aspect speaking French paid the cash sum of 4,257 francs in favour of the account of Mr Ayas.' The lady was Manon

Vidal, but Aitken, latching on to a means of escape, wrote to
Butler saying that this was a reasonably accurate description of
his wife, who was a French-speaking Swiss national of European
parentage and appearance and a brunette. He omitted, however,
to tell Butler that the sum paid was only half the bill of 8,010
francs.

When this letter had been disclosed as a relevant document to
the *Guardian*, they felt they had the evidence they required to
prove that Aitken was lying. He himself had to admit that it was
a regrettable subterfuge. He did not intend to deceive the Cabinet
secretary, but he was trying to throw dust into the *Guardian*'s
eyes. This was to be a difficult area of cross-examination for him
at the trial, but Aitken got over it and his lies were not exposed
until documentary evidence was produced that proved his wife
could not have been in Paris at the time.

Aitken's story was that he was in Paris to meet up with Lolicia
and daughter Victoria in Paris before installing Victoria at
Aiglon College in Switzerland. When he checked in at the Ritz at
10.30pm on Friday 17 September, he discovered they had already
left for Switzerland. His wife, he said, was too tired to return the
following day for their planned romantic evening and had spent
the Saturday night at the Hotel Bristol in Villars. Aitken said she
had returned to Paris on the Sunday morning, paid the bill at
3pm, and that he had left for Geneva at lunchtime, leaving
Lolicia in the bath at the Ritz. At the trial he produced a doctor's
appointment for her in Paris. In fact she had been in Switzerland
throughout.

Lolicia, he explained, had paid his bill out of $3,000 taken
from the safe at home. It was said that, owing to her dyslexia,
she preferred paying cash to using a credit card. This excuse
faded out of the earlier witness statements when documents were
disclosed on discovery which showed that she had in fact paid
her own bill at Hotel Bristol in Switzerland by credit card. The
explanation then became more convoluted. She had by mistake
paid only half the bill. When the error was spotted, Jonathan
Aitken had sent a cheque for the balance of £426.88 to Abdul

Rahman, Ayas's nephew, to whom the balance of his account, he said, had been wrongly assigned. The problem was that it was Prince Mohammed's treasurer and not Rahman who had paid the bill. Aitken explained that there was a muddle, rather than a conspiracy, as a result of wrong information.

The first flaw in the story appeared when it was pointed out in cross-examination that a call had been made from Jonathan Aitken's room at the Ritz to the Hotel Bristol at 10.15am on Sunday 19 September, by which time Lolicia would, according to his account, have been en route for Paris. Details of this call had appeared on the hotel bill – one of the first parts of the paper trail that was to destroy him. Aitken had an answer for that: he had been dutifully talking to his mother-in-law, who, he said, had been sharing Lolicia's room in Switzerland. The problem there was that Lolicia had secured a reduction of 70 Swiss francs by claiming single occupancy of her room. In fact documents obtained on subpoena and discovery showed that Lolicia had not been to Paris at all.

As each piece of paper emerged, Aitken's account became more convoluted. George Carman QC accused him at the trial of creating a web of thirteen lies concerning his stay at the Ritz. His story was 'a catalogue of improbability heaped upon improbability'.

Had Aitken been candid about the matter from the outset rather than embarking on an elaborate set of lies, his weekend at the Ritz would probably not have ended his career, despite the questions that had been raised about his improper acceptance of hospitality at the hotel. The rules were in the nature of signposts rather than commandments. Ministers must not accept hospitality which put them under a sense of obligation, but judgement of this was largely left to the good sense of ministers. However, there was at the time a feeding frenzy at any suggestion of misconduct, sexual or financial, on the part of any Conservative MP, let alone a Cabinet minister. To be shown to have accepted payment of a hotel bill by Saudis who were involved in the arms contracts for which Aitken, as defence procurement minister,

might have had responsibility could possibly have led to his resignation. But the bill was a fairly small one, and well within his
means, and the people he had met were friends – Ayas was godfather to one of his children.

Aitken had demonstrated an aptitude for giving explanations
of his activities. Furthermore, the government had shown a willingness, if not an eagerness, to accept his assurances. He had,
after all, been promoted to the Cabinet notwithstanding the
May 1994 article in the *Guardian*. By April 1995, either confident that his story could not be unravelled or unaware as to how
much information the *Guardian* and Granada had gathered, he
felt that attack was the best form of defence when he was publicly criticised. While the *Guardian* and Granada were convinced
that what they published was securely founded in fact, Aitken,
for his part, believed that he had been accused of a number of
things which he had not done, that he would be able without
too much difficulty to secure a verdict in his favour and that the
truth about the Ritz bill would never be uncovered. Indeed, he
rejected attempts by the advertising mogul Lord Saatchi to
broker a settlement shortly before the trial. This would have
been a 'walkaway' settlement, with each side bearing its own
costs, and would probably have salvaged Aitken's political
career.

Aitken sought the advice of Peter Bottomley MP, who had
himself successfully withstood cross-examination by George
Carman to win £40,000 damages in a libel action. Bottomley
pointed out that reaching decisions in libel cases was an assy-
metrical business. He counselled: 'If in your life you have done
something significantly wrong, no matter how many things you
have done right, don't sue. If in the article there is a significant
thing which they have got right, again, don't sue.' Unfortunately,
Aitken chose not to heed this warning.

Aitken would have been encouraged to act so by Said Ayas's
success against the *Independent on Sunday*, which had, in
November 1994, published a report headed: 'AITKEN FRIEND IN FBI
PROBE'. This had alleged that one of Said Ayas's companies had

been the subject of a probe during the Iran-Contra scandal. Ayas and Aitken had both been directors of Prince Mohammed's British investment company Al Bilad (UK) Ltd. The day after the *Guardian* article appeared, Ayas had been paid substantial damages by the *Independent on Sunday*. And Aitken had himself recovered damages in December 1996, against *The Times*, which had included him among the ministers involved in the 'cash for questions' affair.

Moreover, in April 1995 the *Independent* had published a story accusing Aitken of being involved, as a director of Bmarc, an arms company, in the illegal supply of cannon for installation on Iranian gunboats. The fact that they paid £30,000 into court led Aitken to believe it likely that the *Guardian*'s action would also eventually collapse. The *Independent* tried to have that sum paid back out of court and sought its legal costs from Aitken after the collapse of the case against the *Guardian*. The matter was held in abeyance pending the criminal prosecution. Aitken also sued *Private Eye* for allegations that he had told a lie in a television interview when he said that he had had no defence experience prior to joining Bmarc. That case was never resolved.

Thus it was that, unfazed by the risk of his lie being exposed, Aitken embarked on his attritional libel actions. In July 1995 he announced that he would be resigning in the next government reshuffle as he could not continue to carry out the onerous responsibilities of being chief secretary to the Treasury during the public expenditure survey when he would at the same time be heavily engaged in the preparation for legal battles with his adversaries. A few days later the *Sunday Mirror* published details of an affair in 1980 with a prostitute who specialised in bondage and chastisement. Aitken had unwisely spoken to her on the telephone, telling her to 'tough it out, and above all don't open your mouth'. Unfortunately for him the conversation was being recorded by a *Mirror* journalist. This interlude caused Aitken some embarrassment, as he had previously claimed that it was the *Guardian* article that had severely damaged his political career. The *Guardian* gleefully relied on the *Sunday Mirror* article as the real cause of his resignation, and Aitken had to ask the court to allow him to withdraw that part of his claim.

There were other moments of embarrassment for Aitken during the trial. He had to apologise for falling short of good candid business practice in failing to disclose the Saudi interest in the British television station TVam, which arose out of the investment by Al Bilad UK Ltd in Aitken Telecommunications Holdings Ltd. He was also reminded of a letter of 12 July 1988 to Sheikh Abdul Aziz Ibrahim thanking him for his 'most generous gift of that magnificent watch', which he had not declared in the Register of Members' Interests as it did not amount to personal enrichment. Indeed, he had by that time given it away. He had to admit that he had dissembled about his role as managing director of Inglewood, allowing the *Newbury Weekly Times* to describe him as 'master of all he surveys' and not disclosing the fact that the health club was owned by the Saudi Arabian Al Athel family. These were, however, minor setbacks and seemed to cut little ice with Mr Justice Popplewell.

Although in his Sword of Truth speech Aitken had indicated that he would defend his reputation 'not only before the jury of the courts but before the wider jury of all fair-minded people', his tactic before the trial was, by pointing out the complexity of the issues and the weight of documentation, to argue for trial by judge alone. The *Guardian*, meanwhile, believed that their best chance lay with a jury.

In May 1997 Aitken succeeded in obtaining the ruling he wanted from the Court of Appeal under Section 69(1) of the Supreme Court Act 1981, which was felt to be a further restriction on the use of juries in libel actions. The lord chief justice, Lord Bingham, felt that on balance, given the proliferation of issues and subissues and the volume of documents, it would be appropriate for a judge to hear the case alone and deliver a reasoned judgement which would settle the issue once and for all, rather than for the case to be heard by a jury. A general verdict by a jury could leave room for doubt as no reasons would be given, and the interests of justice would be best served by a painstaking, dispassionate, impartial and orderly approach to deciding where the truth lay.

When the ruling went against the newspaper, they were advised to make a payment of damages into court and to try to settle the case. Thus far each attempt to settle matters with each side bearing their own legal costs had been rejected by Aitken. Negotiations had floundered principally on the unwillingness of the *Guardian* or Granada to apologise. The defendants refused to pay into court, hoping that they would be able to expose Aitken as a liar.

After he had given his evidence, however, whatever embarrassments had arisen in the course of the trial, it seemed that Aitken would win and receive enormous damages ('The *Guardian* is buggered,' one reporter was quoted as declaring graphically). Although the defence remained to be heard, Aitken had scored a notable victory over the arms-dealing allegations. In 1996, while a non-executive director of Bmarc, he had been cleared by a parliamentary committee of complicity in sales of weapons to Iran. Mr Justice Popplewell ruled that the meaning of the *Guardian* article and *World in Action* programme was that Aitken *had* known about the illegal Bmarc arms sales to Iran and not, as they argued, that he *should have* known. The defendants had no evidence that Aitken had known, and they therefore had to withdraw their defence of justification. George Carman gloomily told his clients that he had not broken Aitken in cross-examination.

The *Guardian* and Granada seemed at that stage to be making no headway with the judge on the other allegations, either. The charges against Aitken were always difficult to establish as they had in part been levelled by ex-employees who had left his companies in acrimonious circumstances. Aitken, meanwhile, had acquitted himself well in the witness box and had not been significantly damaged in cross-examination by Carman. He felt that specific allegations about financial gifts from the Saudis in the form of houses, Jaguars and notepaper could be shown to be false and that he could provide evidence that he had not been involved in or benefited from a telephone contract in Saudi

Arabia or a Phillips–GEC streetlighting or electrification contract in Riyadh.

The defence, on the other hand, were adamant that they could
establish that Prince Mohammed had received huge commissions from the Phillips telephone contract in Saudi Arabia, that
Aitken was aware of this and that he and Ayas had worked for
the Prince soliciting commissions from British companies such as
GEC in return for contracts. They remained convinced that they
could prove that Aitken's business career and fortune depended
on his links with the Saudis. In the event the judge never got to
hear their witnesses, but whether their evidence would, in the
absence of incontrovertible proof that Aitken was lying, have
been sufficient to persuade a judge who was perceived to have
been impressed by him that Aitken had not been libelled, and to
reach a decision that would effectively have destroyed his reputation and career, was at that point doubtful. It was very much
on the cards that Mr Justice Popplewell could have formed the
view that the main thrust of the defence allegations related to
activities that were not unlawful, which had taken place, if at all,
some time ago and which were part and parcel of the way that
business was conducted in the Middle East. Insofar as the judge
might have found that some of the allegations against Aitken
were proved, he might have felt that these matters related to the
time before Aitken joined the government and that the implication of what had been published – that he remained in the pocket
of the Saudis – was not borne out. Aitken's character witnesses
were still to come – and they included two former speakers of the
House of Commons.

Some indication of the despondency of the defendants arose
out of the fact that George Carman QC was indicating that on the
TVam issue he might, surprisingly, want to call the judge's wife,
Lady Popplewell, who was a member of the Independent
Broadcasting Authority. Cynics felt this was a ploy to try to
obtain a retrial, as the judge would be discomforted by having to
decide a case in which his wife was a witness.

Granada's insurers had instructed their own lawyers and were becoming nervous about their financial exposure. The *Guardian*, who were not insured, were determined to see the case through, and it is likely that Granada would have continued to fund the case themselves even if their insurers had withdrawn.

But the cavalry, as it turned out, were just over the horizon and, in the best traditions, arriving at the last moment. A three-day search of the basement of the Hotel Bristol in Villars – which had since closed down – unearthed print-outs of guest lists and bill payments, among them Lolicia's payment by American Express of her hotel bill of 575 Swiss francs. The hotel records showed Lolicia arriving late on 17 September and staying there alone on the night of Saturday 18 September. A subpoena sent to British Airways established that Lolicia had flown from Heathrow to Geneva accompanied by Victoria on Friday 17 September 1993 at 8.30am on BA 724. Had she flown Swissair, the lawyers would not have been able to access this information. Her American Express records confirmed that she had hired a car at Geneva airport at 12.02pm on 17 September. It was returned in the centre of Geneva at 6.25pm on Sunday 19 September. The document trail further showed that she had returned to London on Monday 20 September on the 7.05pm British Airways flight. As a foreign national, her passport had been stamped on re-entry into England. It was later established that the Aitkens had stayed the night of Sunday 19 September at the Hilton Hotel in Geneva as the guests of Prince Mohammed. Here was proof that the story of the trip to Paris, set out in painstaking detail – which involved her taking the ferry on Thursday 16 September to Calais and spending the night at Said Ayas's daughter's flat in Paris, as recounted in statements by Lolicia and Victoria and declared in their witness statements to be true to the best of their knowledge and belief – was a fabrication.

Aitken subsequently admitted that it was a 'shameful mistake' to get Victoria to corroborate his false story. It was all part of his 'web of deceit'. He had written out the statement and asked her to sign it. He had scarcely done Lolicia any favours, either – an international arrest warrant was issued against her in respect of her false witness statement. She left for Switzerland, where she would not be extradited.

On 18 June George Carman QC pointed out the significance of this documentation to the judge. The judge asked Charles Gray QC, Aitken's counsel, whether he wanted to consider this turn of events overnight. Applications were made the following day for a BA employee, Wendy Harris, to prove these matters formally and for Aitken to be recalled as a witness. In his book *Pride and Perjury*, published after his release from prison, Aitken described his 'confidence exploding as flying shrapnel' when he saw Harris's statement. He knew at once that he had lost the libel case and that with it he 'had lost his whole world'. He realised he had been caught red-handed and admitted that he had been arrogant and dishonest. In the event no more was to be heard from Aitken, for in a very short hearing on 20 June it was announced that he was abandoning the cases and was going to pay 80 per cent of the *Guardian*'s and Granada's legal costs.

The humiliation of Jonathan Aitken was complete.

The most astonishing features of the case are why Aitken sued at all, why he lied, and why he did not structure his claim to avoid making the Ritz bill a central issue upon which the *Guardian* and Granada could obtain full discovery of documents. True, he did have the embarrassment of the Saudis having paid his bill in breach of the Question of Procedure for Ministers, but he could probably have overcome that. The trip was recorded in his official diaries, and he had registered in an up-front fashion as a British minister. The point is made against Aitken that not only did he lie to the government about payment of the bill, but there are no governmental records of his discussions. Much would have depended on the judge's view of what Aitken was doing in Paris. The defence had at that stage made only limited progress: it would have been arguable that it might have been in the national interest to maintain friendly relations with those who had some influence over the implementation of the Al Yamamah arms contract. Yet instead Aitken chose to lie his way out of it. Why?

When the *Guardian* had started asking who had paid his Ritz bill, Aitken had called Said Ayas on a yacht in the Caribbean. Aitken says he was told that the Saudis wanted the meetings he had with Prince Mohammed and his representatives, including the payment of the Ritz bill, kept secret. Ayas pointed out that Aitken's bill had been paid in cash by Manon Vidal. Why not say that Lolicia had paid it? The fatal flaw in this concocted story was that what Vidal had been paying was not Aitken's bill (8,010 francs) but the shortfall and extras on the Saudi party's bill (4,257 francs). Aitken was thus locked into a story which was eventually unravelled.

Aitken's explanation of the need for secrecy was that there had been from January 1993 a series of high-level meetings to prevent the possible loss of the extension of the Al Yamamah arms contract, Al Yamamah 2 to the United States. This was worth over £4 billion in exports and 100,000 jobs could have been depending on it. A meeting had been arranged for Aitken and his officials with Prince Mohammed in Dhahran, in the eastern province of Saudi Arabia. The outcome had been relayed to King Fahd, on holiday in the desert, who had flown to Riyadh to see Aitken and the British ambassador. The King had given instructions for negotiations on Al Yamamah 2 to be reopened and Aitken had been able to pass on information about the threat posed to Saudi Arabia by the activities of Iran's new kilo-class submarines. The upshot was that another meeting was arranged, between King Fahd and the British prime minister, John Major, on his way back from India, which was also attended by Aitken. The Al Yamamah 2 contract was reinstated and extended, the British agreed to pass on intelligence about Iran to the Saudis and in the following six months there were several more secret rendezvous. These events had taken place; the question was whether they had any relevance to the events of September 1993 at the Ritz. In any event this explanation was not canvassed in court.

In September 1993, Aitken claimed, Prince Mohammed gave instructions for another meeting to be fixed up with Aitken.

According to Ayas, he wanted to discuss the threat of Iranian
submarines laying mines off the Saudi coast. The appointment
had originally been scheduled for Cannes, but had to be
rearranged in Paris at the Ritz. Ironically, Prince Mohammed
himself decided not to meet Aitken at the Ritz for fear that the
hotel was bugged, and it was agreed they would meet in Geneva
instead. Prince Mohammed ordered that the bill be paid in accordance with Arab hospitality and without any knowledge of the
governmental rules to which Aitken was subject. This secret
channel of communications continued to be used on several
occasions in the autumn of 1993, culminating in an occasion
when Aitken was able to pass on an MI6 report of an Iranian plot
to destabilise Saudi Arabia with a terrorist bombing campaign. It
was in these circumstances, Aitken asserted, that he had covered
up what had happened at the Ritz. He saw no reason why he
should not lie about this to maintain the confidentiality of the
meetings. He believed that the Saudis had attended to the details
and that the *Guardian* would never be able to disprove the story
of the cash payment. He did not see why he should compromise
his relationship with the Saudis by revealing the truth to the
*Guardian*, and he was loth to allow what he considered a detail
to stand in the way of obtaining recompense from the *Guardian*
for libels. In the end he learned the harsh lesson that truth is not
an à la carte menu, and that one cannot lie on matters which
strike one as unimportant, or where one feels there is some overriding public interest in concealing the truth.

When details of Aitken's account were published in the *Daily
Telegraph*, the *Guardian* vigorously disputed his account, pointing out that he had confessed to having written Ayas's statement,
which contained a number of matters which were not true. In
essence the paper highlighted the lack of formal documentation
which they would have expected to come into being in relation
to such meetings, even if talks were conducted on an unofficial
basis. They accused Aitken of playing the M16 card to create a
security smokescreen to give credence to his account and to get
Ayas off the hook. Indeed, it may very well have been a most

unwelcome prospect for a trial of Ayas to take place in which the conduct of these arms negotiations would have been open to public view.

Armed with an affidavit, which Ayas had prepared in defence of a $231 million claim brought against him by Prince Mohammed for misappropriation of funds, and which they had obtained in circumstances which were never made clear, the *Guardian* suggested that Aitken's motive for lying about the Ritz had been to cover up a meeting to discuss arms deals from which Aitken and Ayas stood to make very large commissions. The *Guardian* disclosed the existence of an account set up in Switzerland, to which Ayas was a signatory, to receive commissions under the name of Marks 1. Aitken was accused of seeking to skim off commissions from arms contracts which he might, as a government minister, be able to direct the way of companies willing to pay commissions.

'If there was a more serious act of corruption in post-war British politics, we would be interested to know of it', the paper commented. This act of corruption relied, however, on an act of faith, because Ayas and Aitken had been business partners, remained friends and shared an office in Westminster, and because there must have been a reason for Aitken to have constructed such an edifice of lies. The paper published details of Aitken's promotion of contracts from which Ayas stood to benefit. The deals, however, do not appear to have gone through, nor did the *Guardian* have any direct evidence that Aitken would have personally benefited.

The newspaper had no doubt that this was not merely a question of a small lie concocted to dispose of an embarrassing truth, but of an elaborate cover-up designed to prevent exposure of Aitken's promotion of arms contracts from which he stood to secretly make millions in commission while defence procurement minister.

The *Guardian* adopted a distinctly triumphalist tone when, on 22 May 1998, Jonathan Aitken was, with Said Ayas, charged with conspiracy to pervert the course of justice. Aitken was

additionally charged with perjury. Alan Rusbridger denied that
his paper had been involved in the prosecution and 'hounding' of
Aitken. 'I wrote to Sir Paul Condon, Metropolitan Commissioner
of Police, asking him to look at whether an offence had been
committed . . . since writing the initial letter I have made no contact with the police or the Crown Prosecution Service – some
hounding!' Rusbridger wrote in *The Times*.

David Leigh's book *The Liar*, in a sense the *Guardian*'s official
version of the trial, paints a rather fuller picture. A letter was sent
not only to Condon, but also to the DPP, speaking of incontrovertible evidence that Aitken had perjured himself on oath.
Witness statements had been tendered which were directly dishonest, Rusbridger informed the DPP. 'There is therefore,' he said,
'the clearest evidence of a well-laid and carefully co-ordinated
conspiracy to pervert the course of justice – not only [on the part
of] Jonathan Aitken but also his wife and seventeen-year-old
daughter. The *Guardian*'s solicitors have all the documents to
support this charge and would be happy to assist you in any
inquiries.' These documents were subsequently handed to
Scotland Yard's Special Operations Unit by the *Guardian*'s
lawyers. The newspaper's determination to secure a prosecution
was also displayed in its editorial of 25 March. 'There is a small
swell of sympathy for Mr Jonathan Aitken as the net closes
round him. That is understandable and predictable. He rose high
in his political career, he has made many friends. But for all that
it is right that Mr Aitken should be prosecuted.'

When Aitken was charged, in May 1998, the *Guardian*'s editorial was straplined: 'Aitken's friends – waiting for the truth in
court'. The newspaper lamented its inability to attack those who
had spoken up for Aitken in the *Daily Telegraph*. Rusbridger's
appearance on television to tell the world that these were very
grave charges contrasted with the attitude of Granada which,
pending the trial, maintained a dignified silence. The television
company had played its part, by uncovering the car-hire documentation, in establishing the truth but appeared content now to
let events take their course. Although different considerations, in

relation to their output, apply to a daily newspaper and a television company, it must be almost unprecedented for a newspaper to seek to undermine a potential defence before a guilty plea and subsequently to try to shoot down what it anticipates a plea in mitigation will be when the defendant comes to be sentenced. The *Guardian* seemed to be gunning for a hefty jail sentence.

Ayas's plea of not guilty to charges of perverting the course of justice were accepted in May 1999 in the face of Aitken's confession. Nevertheless he took out a full-page newspaper advertisement apologising to Prince Mohammed bin Fahd for his behaviour. In June Jonathan Aitken was sentenced by Mr Justice Scott Baker to eighteen months' imprisonment. Mr Justice Scott Baker condemned his calculated perjury, pursued over a long period of time, which he viewed as a gross and inexcusable breach of trust. It was also, said the judge, a very grave feature that he had involved his young daughter. The irony of Aitken, still haunted by his 'Sword of Truth' speech, looking up as he was sentenced at the sword mounted on the wall of Court number 1 behind the judge, was not lost on the media.

On his release from jail Aitken went to study theology at Oxford University. He announced that he had forgiven the reporters at the *Guardian* and Granada, although it was unclear whether he had withdrawn his accusation against David Leigh of dabbling in witchcraft and anonymously sending statuettes with pins stuck in them to his house in Lord North Street.

It was the first time since 1977 that a libel action had resulted in a prosecution for perjury. In June of that year, Tommy Docherty, formerly manager of Manchester United, had been charged with perjury arising out of evidence he had given in a libel action he had brought, also against Granada Television, after he had been described as 'about the worst manager there has ever been', and accused of having had an affair with the wife of one of the team's medical staff. One of his former players, Willie Morgan, was recorded as saying, 'When he goes, I think the rejoicing in Manchester will be like winning the Cup again, and when that happens, it will be a good club again.' Docherty's

case collapsed when he was asked by John Wilmers QC, 'You told
a pack of lies to the jury about this, didn't you?'

'Yes, it turned out that way.'

At this, Docherty abandoned his case and scurried out of
court, accompanied by the woman in question.

He was acquitted of perjury at the Central Criminal Court
three years later. There had been no intention of lying or misleading the jury: it transpired that he had simply misunderstood
what the word 'probity' meant. For a man who had once on the
radio advocated capital punishment for football thugs and then,
on being asked whether he in fact meant corporal punishment,
had replied, 'It might even come to that,' this seemed plausible.

Jonathan Aitken was less fortunate. He had the unhappy distinction of becoming the first party to a libel action to actually
be convicted of perjury having pleaded guilty to the charge. The
moral of the case is self-evident. A plaintiff must realise that
media organisations are now very much more prepared to fight
such libel actions rather than settling them. The likelihood is that
in the course of such litigation lies may be uncovered by the discovery of incriminating pieces of paper. If Aitken's case proves
anything, it is that the risk of lying, even if on a small part of a
case, is out of all proportion to any imagined benefit.

The best coda came from one of his contemporaries at school,
who said he had always thought Aitken would end up either in
the Cabinet or in prison. He had never imagined he would end up
in both.

# 5

# ARCHER –
# Fragrant Justice?

With Jonathan Aitken we saw how devastating the consequences of the loss of a libel action can be. But success – even huge success – is no guarantee that a plaintiff's reputation will be preserved. In July 1987 Jeffrey Archer, later Baron Archer of Weston-super-Mare, received what was then the largest-ever award of damages from an English jury: £500,000 from the *Star*, with an additional £50,000 and £30,000 costs from the *News of the World*. Yet in 1999, when I asked Archer – at that time seeking election as London's first mayor – for his comments on the libel action he had brought in 1986, he immediately sent me a message declaring that he had nothing to say on the matter. The revelation that November that he had concocted a false alibi before the trial explains why.

Even before his disgrace and public humiliation, which compelled him to stand down as the Conservative candidate for mayor, the damages award of twelve years earlier, massive though it was, had not proved the resounding vindication of his reputation which it had appeared to be at the time. The blurring of fact and fiction in the life of the ex-MP, former deputy chairman of the Conservative Party and bestselling author ultimately seemed to put him beyond the protection of the libel law.

Yet at an early stage of his career, Jeffrey Archer saw what the law of libel could do for him in terms of suppressing adverse publicity. In 1967 he was hired as a fund-raiser by the chairman of the United Nations Association, Humphrey Berkeley. An acrimonious dispute about the expenses Archer was claiming ensued in 1968. This resulted in Archer refunding the association £150 – not in those days such an insignificant figure. In 1969 he was selected to stand as a Conservative candidate at Louth in a by-election necessitated by the death of Sir Cyril Osborne MP. Berkeley distributed a dossier to Tory officials in London and Louth and to selected journalists alleging that Archer was an unsuitable candidate and sharing with the Louth electorate the saga of the expenses. 'Parliament? He should be in a remand home,' Berkeley spluttered.

Happily for Archer, Berkeley's credentials were somewhat dented by the fact that, having himself been a Conservative MP, he had switched to the Labour Party. Nevertheless, with Berkeley retailing lurid accounts of sixty-nine claims relating to meals and car journeys, Archer was told by Conservative leaders that he must either sue or stand down. So Archer sued Berkeley for libel and slander. The issue of the writ removed the topic from the political agenda and he was triumphantly elected, increasing the Conservative majority from just over 4,000 to 10,000.

In February 1973 Archer's libel action was discreetly settled. Berkeley did not apologise, and Archer paid the defendant's costs of £17,000 and his own of some £23,000. The matter did not, however, entirely disappear, and in March 1998 – when Archer was the 3–1 favourite with William Hill for mayor of London – the investigative journalist Paul Foot brought it up again in an article in the *Evening Standard* unflatteringly entitled 'Why this man is unfit to be mayor'. The terms in which Foot recounted Berkeley's allegations were highly defamatory, and Archer was compelled to issue a firm denial: the charge that he had systematically fiddled the UN Association was complete fiction. 'If I had wanted to be on the fiddle, I would have made considerably more than £150,' he declared, which was perhaps not the most convincing argument.

He had, he said, settled the libel action out of court because of Berkeley's precarious financial position. Berkeley, on the other hand, was convinced that Archer had caved in. He received nothing except confidentiality about the terms of settlement. It was odd, however, that Archer had paid Berkeley's costs. A man in Archer's fortunate financial position could have withstood the irrecoverable cost of the proceedings if Berkeley could not afford to pay him. Furthermore, libel actions are difficult to sustain for those in a financially precarious position and they are often themselves anxious to settle. Berkeley, by then dead, could not give his account. Certainly the *Standard*, which had republished Berkeley's defamatory allegations against Archer, was not sued. Archer had clearly had a change of heart about bringing libel actions.

It was all very different when, on 26 October 1986, the *News of the World* published a lurid story under the headline 'TORY BOSS ARCHER PAYS VICE GIRL'. Archer was then deputy chairman of the Conservative Party. The report told of a prostitute called Monica Coghlan, who worked under the name of Debbie, being offered by Archer's friend Michael Stacpoole an envelope three-quarters of an inch thick crammed with £50 notes. It was guessed that the cash amounted to at least £2,000 – a sum which acquired the slang term of an 'Archer' – but it may well have been much more. The *News of the World* also published the transcript of a conversation in which Archer told Coghlan to 'go abroad as quickly as you can'. Very wisely, the *News of the World* did not go so far as to suggest that Archer had slept with Coghlan. It did, however, publish the claims of one of Coghlan's clients, a lawyer called Aziz Kurtha, who claimed to have seen Archer going with Coghlan to a hotel near Victoria Station. This dubious piece of evidence was clearly disbelieved by the jury at the subsequent trial of another tabloid, the *Star*.

The *News of the World* had taped six telephone calls between Archer and Coghlan. She told him that reporters were on to her. Archer consistently denied that they had met, but said that he had nevertheless offered to help her financially to leave the country. Archer consulted his solicitor, Lord Mishcon, who asked him, 'Did you sleep with the prostitute?'

'No.'

'Have you gone with any other prostitute?'

'No.'

'Do you still want to pursue a political career?'

'Yes.'

A statement was put out in which it was conceded that Archer had shown a lack of judgement in allowing himself to fall into a trap which the newspaper had played a reprehensible part in laying. This was a shrewd move, as it began to shift the focus away from him and towards the sleazy behaviour of the press. Mishcon's direct approach was reminiscent of the pithy advice Lord Goodman once gave one of his clients: 'There are two people to whom you must tell the truth, your solicitor and your clap doctor.'

The story was then picked up by the *Star* and its ill-fated editor Lloyd Turner. The report was headlined 'POOR JEFFREY: VICE-GIRL MONICA TALKS ABOUT ARCHER – THE MAN SHE KNEW'. 'Inter-city hooker yesterday told for the first time about her part in the downfall of Tory party boss Jeffrey Archer,' the story misleadingly began. In fact the paper had not talked to Monica. They had spoken only to her dodgy nephew, Tony Smith, who had wisely put the modest value of £400 on what he had to sell the paper. The tale the *Star* ended up telling was at the heart of the libel action, for it cast doubt on Archer's denial. It published further improbable details of Aziz Kurtha's account, which had him apparently recognising Archer as the driver of a Daimler flashing its lights at about 12.45am to pick up Coghlan, who had first enjoyed the pleasures of the flesh with Kurtha at the Albion Hotel, Victoria.

This was a doubtful story resting on shaky foundations. Understandably, *Private Eye* had turned it down. Coghlan had convictions for prostitution, Smith was distinctly flaky and there was an inherent improbability to the idea of Archer scouring the streets after midnight for the consumer-tested charms of Monica Coghlan. But Archer did not help his cause by initially denying offering money to Coghlan, unaware that his conversations had been recorded. ('What if a friend of mine helped you financially to go abroad again? Would that interest you?') He explained that he had denied paying her as it might have implied he had slept with a prostitute; instead, he had given her money as he felt sorry for her as the victim of a smear campaign. With Archer, context was everything.

Mishcon now issued writs against both papers. Wisely, he chose to proceed first against the *Star*, as it had in effect accused Archer of sleeping with Coghlan – something that he asserted was not true. In July 1987, after an application for a speedy trial, Archer's action against the *Star* came up for hearing before Mr Justice Caulfield and a jury. The paper had rashly turned down an offer to settle the case on payment of £16,000 damages plus all Archer's legal costs and a front-page apology. The defendant apparently felt there was something which did not ring true in Archer's account. After all, canny politicians do not normally pay £2,000 or more to ladies of the night whom they do not know. The *Star* also had two witnesses – in the form of Adam Raphael, the political editor of the *Observer*, and Rupert Morris, a journalist with *Sunday Today* – who claimed that they had had a conversation with Archer in which he had admitted that he had in fact once met Coghlan casually six months earlier, which contradicted Archer's assertion that he had never met her.

But Archer's confidence had increased as the date of the trial approached. He had retained the leading advocate of the day, Robert Alexander QC, later Lord Alexander of Weedon. Alexander warned Archer of the perils of the case and the doubts the jury was likely to have about the reasons for the payment of at least £2,000 to a prostitute. Archer telephoned Lord Stevens, chairman of Express Newspapers, owners of the *Star*, to

demand £100,001 damages. Even with the various inconsistencies in his case and the lack of a convincing explanation as to
why Archer had felt it necessary to give Coghlan £2,000, there
would have been something to be said for the finality of a settlement out of court. The newspaper clearly had got its story
wrong. In its obsession with Archer's sex life and its vain
attempt to destroy his alibi for the night in question, the *Star*
overlooked two other possible motives for payment: that Archer,
according to one story, seemingly with substance, that was
doing the rounds, was trying to keep his political career afloat,
or that he was producing cash to bail out one of his colleagues.
In any event, Archer did not settle and the enormous award of
damages was to engender a degree of hostility and suspicion
towards him in the press.

When the case commenced on 26 July 1987, Robert Alexander
QC reminded the jury of the words of Richard II: 'The purest
treasure mortal times afford is spotless reputation.' Alexander
was, of course, far too skilled an advocate to highlight the view-
point of Iago in *Othello*: 'As I am an honest man, I thought you
had received some bodily wound. There is more sense in that
than in reputation. Reputation is an idle and most false imposi-
tion; oft got without merit and lost without deserving.' Archer
explained how on 8 September 1986 he had been dining at Le
Caprice with his publishing editor, Richard Cohen, and his wife,
and that he had talked to a number of people at other tables. He
had later been joined by Terence Baker, his film agent. Prior to
the trial Archer had announced to his legal team that he had an
alibi. Their hopes that this involved addressing the Mothers'
Union in his former Lincolnshire constituency had soon been
dashed: Le Caprice was only a few minutes' walk from Shepherds
Market in Mayfair, where Coghlan had been plying her trade.

The *Star* had decided that it needed a ferocious cross-
examiner to take Archer's story to pieces. It chose Michael Hill
QC, a barrister who had practised in the criminal courts rather
than in the specialist area of libel. It is a tactic that seldom works
(George Carman QC is the exception to the rule). Michael Hill

QC's other high-profile libel action took place in November 1987, when he defended the *Mail on Sunday* over utterly false a-llegations that a former Royal Navy lieutenant, Narendra Sethia, who was not named in the article, had stolen a log from the sub-marine HMS *Conqueror* after the Falklands War. Sethia was awarded £260,000 by the jury, although the action was said to have been later settled for a smaller sum.

Hill boldly set about his task of suggesting that Archer had fabricated his alibi. He accused Archer of lying to the *News of the World* journalist when he denied paying Coghlan. No, Archer replied, that was grossly unfair. His admittedly untrue answer had to be seen in terms of context and what was on the record, he said, somewhat opaquely. Archer emerged relatively unscathed from eleven hours' cross-examination. There were some inconsistencies, such as the fact that one witness of Archer's had spoken of him being at a 'function' with forty people. There was no inconsistency, said Archer. There had been fifty people in the restaurant.

No real inroads were made into Archer's case. His position was immeasurably strengthened firstly by his wife Mary's evidence – they had a happy marriage and, as it was delicately put, a full life – and then by the defence case. Depending as it did on the word of a member of the oldest profession and on that of mem-bers of two of the more disliked professions – journalism and the law – the defence was always likely to have problems against the charismatic Jeffrey and Mary Archer. Monica Coghlan, who cut a tawdry figure, said that the hotel had been well lit and that Archer had commented how lovely she was. He was quite taken aback by her nipples, she said. However, the lighting cannot have been that good as she described his back as spotty. Either her eyesight had failed her or she was thinking of some other bastion of the Conservative Party.

Archer did not make the same mistake as former Liberal Party leader Jeremy Thorpe had made in failing to rebut the claims of his *soi-disant* homosexual lover Norman Scott that Thorpe had 'nodules' on his back. Instead Mary Archer was recalled to confirm her husband's lack of dorsal blemishes. Coghlan went through the loveless details of her encounter, for which she had been paid a modest £70. More significantly, she did much to undermine the credibility of her hapless nephew, Tony Smith. Asked about his claim that 90 per cent of her clients wanted kinky sex, she said, 'He is a compulsive liar,' and, in a strange phrase, 'He romances a lot.' As Smith was the *Star*'s principal source, this was scarcely helpful.

The paper's case was fatally damaged by the impression created by Aziz Kurtha. Being colour blind, he was not even able to describe accurately the colour of the Daimler. This affliction produced the best jokes from the judge in his summing-up. He wondered whether Kurtha would be much good as a television commentator on *Pot Black*, or at a rugby match. Would he have to wait to hear 'Bread of Heaven' being sung to know whether it was the Reds of Wales who had won at Cardiff Arms Park or the Greens of Ireland? Kurtha gave the impression of being unreliable and untrustworthy, out to damage Archer politically.

Nine witnesses were called for the *Star*. The potentially damaging evidence of Raphael and Morris, about the conflicting account given by Archer of his knowledge of Coghlan, was buried in the overall seediness of the paper's case. Morris seemed less certain as to what Archer had actually told him, and Archer dismissed Raphael's account as bunkum. Raphael had written an article in the *Observer*, headlined 'ARCHER TO QUIT OVER CALL-GIRL', accurately predicting Archer's resignation. It was a measure of how potentially damaging this story was. The jury may not have liked the conventional journalistic practice adopted by Raphael in not revealing the identity of his source and attributing Archer's remark to him to a friend of Archer's. But Raphael forcefully made the point that he had then asked Archer where he had met her and Archer had not replied. He said that if Archer had denied meeting Coghlan, he would have asked the obvious question: 'Why on earth, if you have never met this woman, did you pay her off?' For his pains Raphael was savaged in an editorial written by Stewart Steven, a friend of Archer's on the *Mail on Sunday*, for having

betrayed a source – an unwise move that was to cost the paper
£25,000 in libel damages and £20,000 in legal costs.

Alexander made much of the failure of the defence to call any
witnesses from the *Star* itself. Editor Lloyd Turner had been in
court but was not called. 'Does he have the power of speech?'
Alexander asked rhetorically. Rather more to the point was the
absence of the 'bag man', Michael Stacpoole. The *Star* would
dearly have liked to call him as a witness, but he had left the UK.
He now says that his move to Paris was lubricated by £40,000,
paid to him by Lord Archer in instalments, in return for staying
out of the country until the trial was over.

The case is perhaps best remembered for the dotty remarks of
the elderly judge, Sir Bernard Caulfield, who had been entrusted
with libel actions in the run-up to his retirement. The jury can
have been in no doubt what verdict he was gunning for: a
decision against Archer, he told the jury at the outset of his
summing-up, would mean that Archer was destined to 'endure
the rest of his life as a social leper in a social workhouse for
hypocrites'. There would be 'a graveyard for lost reputations'
with a monument acknowledging the co-operation of 'Monica
Coghlan, a well-known trader in Shepherds Market, and of Aziz
Kurtha, one of the many thousands of satisfied customers of
Monica'. He got a little carried away in his summary of Mary
Archer's evidence. Matters of evidence are essentially for the
jury to decide, and the judge's role is to explain the law and
summarise the conflicting relevant parts of evidence. Caulfield,
however, had clearly been much taken by Mrs Archer. 'Your
vision of her will probably never disappear. Has she elegance?
Has she fragrance? Would she have, without the strain of this
trial, radiance? What is she like in physical features, in presen-
tation, in appearance, how would she appeal? Has she had a
happy married life? Has she been able to enjoy rather than
endure her husband Jeffrey? Is she right when she says to you –
you may think with delicacy – Jeffrey and I lead a full life?'

Of Jeffrey Archer the judge, applying his experience of the
world, asked: 'Is he in need of cold, unloving, rubber-insulated

sex in a seedy hotel around about quarter to one on a Tuesday morning after an evening at Le Caprice?' He compared Coghlan with Little Red Riding Hood, whose goodies in this instance came in a suspender belt rather than a basket. He said that one of the issues of the case was whether Jeffrey Archer had enjoyed the body of Monica Coghlan – if enjoyment was the word for it. Archer's history was 'worthy and healthy and sporting', and he had had 'the great honour of being appointed president of the university athletics club'. Was it likely, the judge wondered, that Archer would have breached the rules of grammar by saying, as Monica alleged, 'I hope you don't mind *me* following you?' But that is what the girl had said. If jury members found the article defamatory, the judge told them, they had to ask themselves how 'filthy' it was.

After a retirement of four and a quarter hours the jury awarded Archer damages of £500,000. Archer announced that he would be giving a substantial part of the damages to various charities. There was no appeal against the amount awarded, although there was unsubstantiated talk of an accommodation being reached privately between Archer and Lord Stevens. He collected a further £50,000 damages plus £30,000 costs from the *News of the World*, which had the good sense to see which way the wind was blowing. At the *Star*, Lloyd Turner resigned and his career never recovered.

The size of the award and the bizarre and troubling nature of the case kept the eyes of a number of journalists, notably Michael Crick and Paul Foot, on Archer's career. They took a particular interest in the profit of £77,219 made on a strikingly canny purchase of 50,000 Anglia TV shares on 13 and 14 January 1994 at a price of £4.85 each, and their sale, on 18 January, at £6.54 after approval of a takeover bid by MAI. The transaction was conducted in the name of Archer's Kurdish friend Broosk Saib, and Archer is adamant that he himself made no profit whatever out of the deal. But the press latched on to the coincidence that Archer's wife, who had no involvement in the transaction, was a director of Anglia TV. The shares had been bought and sold in the fortnightly accounting period, which meant that no cash needed to be produced. Charles Stanley, the stockbroker, referred the transaction to the Stock Exchange Insider Trading Group, who investigated the matter. Initially, when asked about the matter by *The Times*, Archer retorted, 'It is completely untrue – I did not buy any shares. I am not going to make a statement. That sort of accusation is libellous.'

Why had he so assiduously given the orders for the purchase and sale of the shares, acted as guarantor of the purchase price and provided the mailing address for the profits? As in so many instances in his life, Archer's conduct was unexplained and indeed inexplicable.

Archer instinctively reached for the libel law, but wiser counsels perhaps prevailed, as he did not sue. The DTI decided in July 1994 not to take any further action, and they did not publish the findings of their inspectors, Roger Kaye QC and Hugh Aldous. They did, however, reopen their inquiry to look into a story published in the *Mirror* about possible links between Archer and a woman called Karen Morgan-Thomas who had bought Anglia shares. Again, though, no further action was taken. In August Archer admitted that he had made a grave error and apologised for the embarrassment needlessly caused to his wife. He reiterated that he had not personally made a profit, nor had he received inside information from his wife. The subject had come up at dinner with Sir Nicholas Lloyd, editor of the *Daily Express*, he explained later, which led him to start buying over a period of two days on 13 and 14 January. Lloyd was contacted but his diary showed that such a conversation took place significantly later, on 18 January – the day of the profitable sale, and, of course, after the purchase. The whole incident was part of the overlap between fact and fiction which seems to crop up in Archer's life – curiously, the subject of insider dealing had featured in his 1987 play *Beyond Reasonable Doubt*, in his books *Not a Penny More, Not a Penny Less* and *Kane and Abel*, and, for good measure, in one of his short stories, *Twelve Red Herrings*.

In July 1995 Archer failed to be appointed chairman of the

beleaguered Conservative Party, a job for which he had been widely tipped in the forthcoming government reshuffle.

When Michael Crick wrote his appropriately named biography on Jeffrey Archer, *Stranger than Fiction*, he was threatened with an action for libel. Archer did not sue. Nor has he sued Paul Foot or Crick for the doubts they cast on his explanation of his decision to buy the Anglia shares at the critical moment, or for their unflattering dissection of the many conflicting accounts of controversial incidents in his life. Archer's father was not a colonel in the Somerset Light Infantry, nor had he won the DCM, but he was a convicted fraudster. His grandfather had not been lord mayor of Bristol. His fellowship from the International Federation of Physical Culture hailed not from an American campus but from an office block in Chancery Lane. One mystery is how Oxford University archives could record Archer as having A Levels in English, history and geography, when he admits he has no A Levels – although he does have three O Levels – and denies telling Oxford he had them. Although he ran for the university, he did not get a degree. Another mystery is whether in 1967 he filled in GLC councillors' expenses and claimed 10 per cent for doing so. He angrily denied this in 1994 to Crick's publishers. 'At no time did I fill in members' expenses and claim 10 per cent. If the question is asked again, I shall place matters in the hands of my solicitors,' he wrote. He now says he 'did help them a bit – there was nothing wrong or illegal in doing so. The sums involved were minuscule.'

There was a misunderstanding, Archer explained, when he was stopped on suspicion of shoplifting in Toronto. He had been confused by the layout of the Simpsons store and exited it innocently by mistake with a couple of suits on a hanger while looking for the shirt department. Fortunately, this was all amicably resolved. Archer had, however, undone the benefit he had obtained for his reputation in the *Star* libel action by denying in 1987 – at the very time of his libel action – to Paul Foot that he had ever been involved in any such incident. Instead he had replied to Foot's 1998 article with his own piece, 'Why I am Fit to be Mayor' in June. He said he had not wanted to give any assistance to a left-wing journalist who was campaigning against him. Perhaps he was wrong not to have clarified what had happened as this would, as he pointed out, have 'described the entire trivial incident in all its glory', thereby clearing him of any wrongdoing.

In October 1999, Archer recovered undisclosed damages, which he controversially claimed amounted to £100,000, for false allegations in *The Times* that he had had access to inside information which he had used help him defeat Steven Norris, his Tory rival as mayoral candidate. The paper had at once realised its mistake and apologised within a week. Archer told journalists that after the election he would be bringing libel actions against those who had lied about him.

He may well have felt that this success neutralised *The Times*' hostility to his mayoral aspirations, but his triumph must have been tempered to some extent by continuing demands for yet another DTI inquiry and claims made by the *Economist* about the Anglia share transactions. The latter produced threats of an action for aggravated and exemplary damages from his new solicitors, Eversheds, who now suggested a variant on the explanation that their client had bought the shares after dining with Sir Nicholas Lloyd. His recommendation to Mr Saib to buy the shares, they said, was based upon reports in the previous week's *Daily Mail*. Eversheds' letter to the *Economist* disclosed for the first time that Archer had, as the husband of a director who was privy to price-sensitive information, given a written undertaking in August 1992 not to buy Anglia shares between the end of December every year and the middle of the following March – a commitment which makes the Saib transaction even more puzzling. For a letter threatening libel proceedings, this communication had an unusual and unintended consequence: it led the trade and industry secretary, Stephen Byers, to consider whether the fresh disclosure merited a new inquiry. He decided they did not.

Finally in November 1999, the libel law exacted its revenge on Archer and he was obliged to resign in disgrace as Conservative mayoral candidate. A former friend, Ted Francis, produced for the *News of the World* documentary evidence that in January 1987 he had been asked by Archer to write to Lord Mishcon to support a fabricated alibi in the *Star* case for 9 September 1986 – the day on which the *Star* originally suggested Archer's tryst with Coghlan had taken place. Once more Archer had been taped being indiscreet on the telephone, admitting to 'porkies' and to this discreditable plot. In fact the *Star* had mixed up their dates and the key evening was actually that of 8 September, for which Archer had the more promising Le Caprice alibi. However, as purpose of the 9 September alibi was to conceal the fact that Archer had been dining with his personal assistant, Andrina Colquhoun – an engagement which ought not to have required such secrecy – it is likely that, had the jury got wind of the attempt to deceive them, they would have taken a very different view of Archer's fragrant personal life and found against him out of an instinctive mistrust of liars rather than any conviction about Coghlan's tale.

As it was, the 9 September alibi was not needed and so no question of perjury at the trial arose.

The law of libel initially served Jeffrey Archer reasonably well; the electors of Louth rather less well. He proved, until recently, surprisingly successful in controlling what was said and written about him with the mere threat of a libel action because of a perception in the media that he was someone who invariably won such cases, even though there was a considerable body of evidence to the contrary.

Archer's libel litigation showed what a chancer the man was and revealed much of the arrogance and willingness to cut corners with the truth that bedevilled Jonathan Aitken. The real scandal was the picture of marital fidelity he painted to the jury that trustingly awarded him £500,000 in his action against the *Star* when, as it later emerged, he was a well-practised adulterer.

Thereafter disaster followed disaster. Archer was expelled from the Conservative Party for dishonest and disreputable conduct after lying to the party in June 1999 during the vetting procedure for the mayoral election. He had declared that no new substantial, potentially damaging allegations could be levelled against him. He was arrested in April 2000 on charges of perjury and perverting the course of justice. The perjury charges related to false statements about his appointments diary – he was accused of falsifying it to support his version of the events of 9 September 1986 – that he made on oath in the *Star* case.

Astonishingly, Archer spent part of his time awaiting trial acting the role of the defendant in his play *The Accused*, in which he relished the opportunity to indulge his love of mixing fact with fiction. In a dig at Monica Coghlan's evidence in court, he would strip to the waist, revealing a scar on his back to disprove the testimony in the play of a nurse who had described it as unmarked. As for his acting, one critic commented that to call him wooden would be an insult to furniture, and few were surprised when *The Accused* ended its run six weeks early.

In July 2001 Archer was sentenced to four years for perjury – described by Mr Justice Potts as the most serious instance of it he had known – and for perverting the course of justice. Ted Francis was acquitted. The trial was a disaster. Archer's barrister, Nicholas Purnell QC, fell out dramatically with the judge over his tactics. Archer's decision not to give evidence, while attacking in cowardly fashion his former PA's honesty, backfired. The jury was directed that they could conclude that Archer had no answer to the prosecution's case. Mary Archer's reputation after the delivery of her unconvincing evidence changed from fragrant to whiffy.

This shameful episode could cost Archer well over £4 million: the *Star* and *News of the World* claimed £2.5 million for the damages, costs and interest of the libel actions, and Archer had to pay £175,000 in prosecution costs. His bill from his somewhat uninquisitive solicitors, Mishcon de Reya, for the libel and criminal trial may exceed £1.5 million. His disgrace was epitomised by the announcement of problematic legislation to prevent convicted criminals from resuming their seats in the House of Lords.

# 6

# LIBELLING THE POLICE:
## Garage Actions

There is no legal aid for libel actions. Such litigation tends therefore to be the preserve of the rich. The main exception to this rule of thumb is the backing given by the Police Federation to actions brought by police officers. The federation's policy is that, in view of the 'very high profile, very high risk and very high costs' of defamation proceedings, 'we only take cases where an officer's career or reputation could be destroyed'. However, a general perception has grown up that the police are too thin-skinned and a little too enthusiastic when it comes to libel actions. Until February 1997, when they lost an action involving the Stoke Newington station in north London, the police had enjoyed an almost unbroken line of victories.

There was the occasional reverse, as in February 1991, when two West Country policeman lost their case against the *People*, which had accused them of doing nothing to help colleagues who were being beaten up by lager louts, landing the federation with a £200,000 bill.

But for the most part the statistics speak for themselves. In 1993 thirty-nine cases were won against national and regional newspapers, netting police officers £370,000 in damages. From 1994 to 1997 they had brought and won ninety-five defamation actions, netting £1,567,000 damages. Against that, £500,000 was reported to have been paid out in the period 1992 to 1996 for the claims of malicious prosecution and false imprisonment against officers from Stoke Newington Police Station. Indeed, so successful was their record that libel actions were jokingly known in police circles as 'garage actions' for the enhancement they brought to the officers' suburban homes.

This record is relied upon by the federation as evidence that only valid claims are brought, and that there is no policy of suppressing criticisms of the police. Over the last five years only 150 of the 1,200 complaints to the Police Federation have resulted in proceedings. But even that is a high proportion, and this willingness to sue does seem to produce a chilling effect, particularly on provincial papers wishing to publish criticism of the police. Even weaker cases in which officers are not named tend to be settled because of the expense of fighting them and the difficulty of contesting the identification evidence. The police argument is said to be only against irresponsible reporting. They argue that they need to protect themselves against those they view as self-interested liars. Newspapers should confine themselves to publishing what is true or covered by privilege. However, things are not that clear cut, and it is arguable whether use of the libel law is appropriate in all circumstances. A distinction needs to be drawn between cases where serious allegations are made against genuinely identifiable police officers, and those which relate to criticism of policing methods. It is no doubt unpleasant for the police to read of their methods being vilified, but these are matters of public interest, which the police ought to be able to tolerate along with the many other difficult and unpleasant facets of their job.

Many cases are brought by police officers who are not named, but who are, inevitably, identifiable to some of their colleagues, who would know which officers attended the particular incident described. The public, however, are very unlikely to be aware of the identity of the officers, nor are their views of the police likely to be much influenced by an event of which they know little. Such cases therefore proceed rather shakily on the word of officers who have apparently shunned a colleague in the police canteen, which conjures up an image of police looking warily at their oppos over the top of their *Guardians* after reading of some contentious policing incident. If all that is happening is that some police officers are being given a wide berth by their colleagues, it does seem very questionable whether the full panoply of a libel action, as opposed to an internal police inquiry, is necessary to discover where the truth lies.

On the other hand, there clearly is a legitimate interest in discussion of how the community, and in particular certain sections of it, is policed. It may well be that the decision in the Reynolds case (Chapter 16) will make it easier for the media to raise a qualified privilege defence based on a duty to report such matters of public interest.

A balance needs to be drawn between freedom of speech and the protection of reputation. It is difficult to see how many of the libel actions brought by the police actually impact on reputation, when the reference to a particular officer will only have been picked up by a colleague who knows the allegation is false and is sufficiently cynical not to believe everything he or she reads in the press. False or inaccurate reports may well be matters of considerable annoyance or distress to the police officers concerned, but it is questionable whether they actually damage reputation. They will often be matters which a disciplined organisation accustomed to the difficulties of dealing with the public should be able to take in its stride. The armed forces do not find it necessary to make such frequent recourse to the law courts for damage to their reputation; the National Association of Head Teachers, which was in the 1980s quick to protect its members by issuing writs, has now changed its policy and the sky has not fallen in. A system of apologies, corrections or statements in rebuttal seems preferable to libel actions of this kind.

Even more disturbing is the pattern of delay in bringing such actions. The courts have repeatedly said that libel actions should be brought very promptly (as in the Oyston case covered in Chapter 13). The limitation period for initiating libel cases was three years until the Defamation Act of 1996, when it was reduced to one. Yet in the Stoke Newington case, seventeen writs were issued against the *Guardian* and the Murdoch press on 25 January 1995, almost three years after the publication of the articles in question. Granada TV was sued in June 1987 by two police officers two years and seven months after the programme complained of, and in April 1995 an action was brought against *Time Out* for reports published in October 1992. Some of these delays are caused by waiting for disciplinary inquiries to take place. Nevertheless, it would be fairer, and certainly possible, for the Police Federation to issue a writ and seek to leave it in abeyance pending the outcome of an inquiry. The defendant would then be on notice of the claim and could collate the evidence needed to defend the action. As it was up to 1996, receiving a writ almost three years after the event made the task of defending such cases almost impossible. Sometimes a letter of complaint is sent, but those who receive them say they are not specific. Often they do not identify the officers who are complaining or the nature of the complaint, but simply require all documents relating to a report or programme to be preserved. Furthermore, the fact that a disciplinary inquiry is taking place ought to be a matter which the defendants can raise by way of public interest.

Assuming that a police officer bringing a libel action is readily identifiable, it is easy to sympathise with him or her when specific serious allegations have been made without justification. In the last ten years, cases have been successfully brought by officers accused of such misdemeanours as leaking a sex offender's previous convictions; passing on information to car-ringing criminals; being involved in a plot to allow IRA prisoners to escape; cheating in an exam to gain promotion; bungling a drugs raid in which an officer was shot; inventing a defendant's confession and being involved in a suspect's death; taking bribes from a prostitute; concealing evidence in a child sex abuse inquiry and engaging in a dirty tricks campaign against social workers; being involved in a plot to smear a leading police-woman; suggesting that a senior anti-terrorist officer was dismissed for incompetence and being racist and undermining a murder case. The last example related to the case of the murdered black teenager Stephen Lawrence. The officer was unnamed, and in view of the later findings of Sir William Macpherson (albeit not against that officer), the case brought into sharp relief the issue of public interest in such matters.

A clear example of a case in which a former police officer needed to clear his reputation, and succeeded in doing so, was that of Superintendent Gordon Anglesea in December 1994. Anglesea had retired after thirty-four and a half years' police service – four and a half more than normal. He described himself as an old-fashioned policeman who joined the force after seeing Jack Warner in *The Blue Lamp*. He was a school governor, a Methodist, a rotarian and a Freemason. Superintendent Anglesea was accused by the *Independent on Sunday*, the *Observer*, HTV's *Wales This Week* and *Private Eye* of assaulting boys at the troubled Bryn Estyn Children's Home in Wrexham. The libels were described by his counsel, Lord Williams of Mostyn QC, as the filthiest lies which had blown his reputation out of the water and shattered his life. Understandably, the ex-officer told the jury he felt like a leper. This poison had polluted his life and that of his family. In truth he had simply visited the home on various occasions as a uniformed inspector to caution the boys and he had had nothing whatsoever to do with any of the persons convicted of offences in relation to the running of the home.

After a three-and-a-half-week trial Anglesea was vindicated by the jury's finding that he had been libelled. Unusually, the jury had been invited first to consider the issue of liability, then to decide on the amount of damages. After they had been considering damages for three hours, the parties reached agreement among themselves and Anglesea recovered a total of £375,000, split into £107,500 each against HTV and the *Independent on*

*Sunday* and £80,000 each against the *Observer* and *Private Eye*. He also subsequently recovered very substantial damages from *Take a Break* magazine, which, in a thinly veiled account of the case, falsely suggested that there might have been substance to the allegations.

And armed with information supplied to him by Julian Lewis MP (see Chapter 18), Anglesea recovered substantial damages from the printer, distributor and retailers of *Scallywag*, a scurrilous magazine with no money but a well-developed love of publicity, which not only republished the libels but claimed it was all a masonic conspiracy.

It is more difficult to sympathise with many of the group actions brought on behalf of police officers. All members of a group can sue if the group is sufficiently small and its members identifiable. The Police Federation has also successfully supported actions in which individual police officers were not named, and were identifiable only to their colleagues, and in which it might be thought that, whatever the truth of the allegation, legitimate matters of public interest relating to police conduct or methods of policing were involved. On some occasions newspapers have not themselves made allegations against the police, but have merely reported allegations others have made. However, it is no defence to say that you are simply repeating what others have said. Yet allegations made by responsible members of the community against the police may well be a matter of legitimate interest – even if, on investigation, they turn out to be groundless. As the law stands, the police are entitled to bring such claims, but it is questionable whether they ought to be able to do so with such ease.

Doubtless it was annoying for the members of Banbury CID in 1979 to find the *News of the World* republishing in tabloid style the crazy rantings of the inaptly named David Brain, who falsely suggested that his wife had been raped by the CID. But it seems highly unlikely that anyone could have seriously considered that the newspaper was suggesting there was any substance to his claims. Brain, who was holding his wife hostage at gunpoint, had bizarrely required a *News of the World* reporter to be present before he gave up his siege. The paper had published a somewhat selective report under the headline: 'EXCLUSIVE: SIEGE MAN TELLS US WHY HE DID IT'. Nevertheless, each of the ten male members of the CID recovered £300 damages, plus £25,000 exemplary damages, while there was not even a consolation prize for the sole female CID member who, by the nature of Brain's allegations, was excluded from the windfall. One other officer did not bother to sue. The exemplary damages award was considered excessive by the Court of Appeal and was sent for retrial.

In 1995 eight London police officers recovered £30,000 libel damages and costs from the *Camden New Journal*, which had reported allegations of racism and violence made by a lady arrested at a local electricity board showroom. Undoubtedly her allegations against the police were serious, and her case was enthusiastically taken up by the Camden Race Equality Council. The officers were not named but were identifiable to their colleagues as having attended the incident. They were said to be appalled to read of her accusations of brutality and racism. But unpleasant as they were, these might have been seen as the sort of false claims regularly made against the police. The newspaper had not suggested that they were true, and had published them in good faith as a matter of public interest, and the police were exonerated by a security video.

And in 1983 a plain-clothes officer had either the good or bad fortune, depending on how you look at it, to walk out of West End Central Police Station during filming for a *World in Action* programme on Operation Countryman, aimed at rooting out corruption in the Metropolitan Police. In the finished film the clip was shown as the voice-over informed the viewers: 'Since 1969 repeated investigations show that some CID officers take bribes.' The officer was not otherwise identified in the programme, nor was it suggested that he was guilty of such conduct – he was merely present in a background shot providing a context for the commentary. Not surprisingly, his guest appearance was the subject of some comment among his colleagues, but any injury to his reputation was undoubtedly made good by the award of £20,000 libel damages against Granada.

There was a bizarre twist to another group action brought in 1997: the damages were recovered against the *Police Review*, the professional weekly journal of the British police. Twelve dog-handlers were awarded substantial libel damages for an article entitled 'Nazi Humour Forces Jewish PC to Quit'. It is easy to understand why the officer's colleagues would want to nail the lie that they had given Nazi salutes at a Christmas party, sung the Nazi Party anthem and threatened to plant drugs on him. However, accusations of this type of unpleasant and untrue behaviour in other workplaces would not normally result in a libel action.

Indeed, a number of the cases brought by the police fall short of being career-threatening, although they might have damaged an officer's prospects or constituted a disciplinary offence. In 1995 a former senior member of the Obscene Publications Squad recovered £15,000 from a women's magazine which alleged that he was a transvestite and a hypocrite, and in 1990 a detective superintendent was awarded £2,000 against a newspaper television review in *Today* which branded him ploddish and stupid.

So, given the support for such actions from the Police Federation, newspapers publish defamatory material about police officers at their peril, whereas in different occupations such insults might pass unchallenged. In 1990 a police sergeant recovered £10,000 and £5,000 libel damages paid into court by the *Sun* and the *Mail on Sunday* respectively after Stewart Steven, editor of the *Mail on Sunday*, wrote at inordinate length about the officer's conduct in arresting him for improper use of the car horn (for which magistrates had convicted Steven). The editor ungraciously commented: 'I have withdrawn nothing and I have not apologised.' He was lucky not to have been sued again.

The *News of the World* were not so fortunate that year when they were sued for breaching a settlement agreement under which they had paid a police officer £60,000 damages and costs for an article headlined 'NEIGHBOURHOOD WATCH NICK SEXY PC ON THE JOB'.

For reasons of its own, the *News of the World* had added the unremarkable words 'under a previous editor' to the text of the apology so that the new editor could avoid personal blame for libel. Damages were also paid for a story headlined ROOKIE NOOKIE.

And in 1995 two police officers recovered a second lot of damages when they found that a libellous account of their conduct in arresting the cricketer Ian Botham for possession of cannabis, first published in the hardback edition of his autobiography, had inadvertently not been removed from the text in the paperback. Damages were said to be substantial. One of the officers commented: 'We are sorry this all happened, but are satisfied with the outcome. This has cleared up a serious slur on our name.'

In December 1995, in one of the first cases after guidelines for damages had been laid down in the Elton John action (see Chapter 15), a jury gave an indication that it did not consider substantial damages should be awarded in cases in which officers were not named. PCs Christopher Wright and Peter Callaghan recovered the relatively modest sums of £12,500 and £4,000 after the *Panorama* programme 'Race Hate UK', in dealing with the arrest of an Asian shopkeeper, suggested that they were racists. The programme had been seen by 2.8 million viewers, and the BBC had argued that they were not identifiable. The BBC, meanwhile, was landed with a bill for legal costs of £200,000.

The controversial backing of such actions by the Police Federation came into sharp focus in July 1988 when, after a twenty-two-day trial, eleven Metropolitan Police officers recovered sums ranging from £10,000 to £30,000, totalling £160,000, for two articles published in the *Evening Standard* in February 1986. Legal costs were at least double that figure. The newspaper had demanded an inquiry into an unprovoked attack on five schoolboys in Holloway in north London and that the officers responsible be brought to justice. The assault, during which the boys had been kicked, punched and beaten with truncheons by police from an unidentified van, and after which two had needed hospital treatment, had taken place in August 1983. The news-paper had published its article after a two-and-a-half-year police investigation had failed to find the culprits. It suggested that there had been a conspiracy of silence. The first article was head-lined 'CALL SIGN NOVEMBER THREE ZERO – WE TRACE THE SUSPECT VAN'. Although Three Zero had originally come under suspicion, its occupants had in fact had nothing to do with the attack. A few days after the article appeared, the crew of another van, call sign November Three Three, were arrested and in July 1987 five officers were convicted at the Old Bailey and sent to prison.

Clearly, the occupants of Three Zero were wronged. During the trial they explained that they were appalled by the article and described how they had been shunned and abused by their col-leagues because of a widespread belief that they were responsible for the assault and the subsequent cover-up. They had every sympathy for the victims, and felt that a libel action was the only way they could establish their innocence. Outside court they declared that money had never been their motivation. The news-paper accepted that they were innocent, and had made an error of judgement in not publishing an apology, even after the offi-cers in November Three Three had been convicted.

Bearing in mind the fate of the officers in November Three Three, the allegations against those in November Three Zero were potentially very serious. However, the case did raise ques-tions (in the days before the Reynolds decision) as to whether there should be a defence of qualified privilege on a matter of undoubted public interest. The *Standard* complained with some justification that the outcome of the case would seriously inhibit the freedom of the press to investigate matters of public impor-tance. There had been an intolerable delay in bringing the guilty men to justice, after all, a limited number of police vans had attended the incident. As the law stood, their defence was almost bound to fail, however good their intentions, for there was no mechanism in law to raise the shortcomings of the police investigation and the misconduct of the Three Three officers in the claim by the Three Zero officers.

In December 1988 the eleven were reluctantly back in court, along with more officers from another van, one of whom now lived in Australia, to trouser another £175,000. On this occasion they were collecting damages from Gerald Kaufman MP, the BBC and Thames TV for ill-advised remarks Kaufman had made as shadow home secretary on the BBC's *London Plus* and *Thames News* suggesting that the officers from all three vans, guilty and innocent alike, should be dismissed.

But if the tide was turning against such actions, the Police Federation did not seem to notice it. In January 1992 the *Guardian* published two articles headlined: 'POLICE SUSPECTED OF DRUG DEALING' and 'DISQUIET DOGS COMMUNITY POLICE STATION'. It reported how eight unidentified officers had been transferred from Stoke Newington Police Station following allegations of drug-dealing and corruption in the wake of Operation Jackpot. This operation, which involved the investigation of complaints against forty-four officers, many of which originated from drug-dealers, had taken four years and resulted in only one conviction. The *Guardian* article stated that the eight officers had not been suspended and made it clear that one of the persons making the allegations against the police was serving a sentence for drug offences. The view had been taken by the deputy assistant commissioner, Michael Taylor, that the best course was to transfer the officers, bearing in mind the paramount importance of maintaining public confidence in the police in an area like Stoke Newington.

The five officers who sued the *Guardian* in 1995 complained of the sensational terms of the report. It had spread through the police district, leading to a lot of speculation, and they had been approached by dozens of people in connection with it. One of the officers, Reynold Bennett, was asked why it had taken him three years and two months to serve a writ if he was genuinely shocked. He said that his action was backed by the Police Federation and that he had been advised to await the outcome of Operation Jackpot. Another, Detective Constable Paul Goscomb, recalled how 'awful' and 'sick' he had felt on reading the offending articles. PC Gerald Mapp was even more graphic: he had felt 'dismayed' and 'abandoned', his 'guts fell through the floor and the room fell away'. Detective Sergeant Robert Walton was stunned when he saw the pieces while in Jamaica investigating the financial affairs of a drug-dealer. Detective Sergeant Bernard Gillan had been 'sickened' and felt that he had failed to gain promotion as a result of the reports. No disciplinary action had been taken against them as a result of Operation Jackpot. Their case, as put by Tom Shields QC, was that the impression had been given that they were guilty of serious misconduct. Not so, argued George Carman QC; their claim was strained and contrived. One of the purposes of a newspaper was to provide the public with more information than the authorities were prepared to give out. No fair-minded reasonable reader of the *Guardian* would conclude that the officers were guilty of any misconduct.

The summing-up by Mr Justice French was notable for his comment that the defence of qualified privilege was not available and that the defence of justification had been abandoned. 'Mr Carman says, and rightly so, that he has abandoned the defence of justification except in the very limited sense which I reminded you of yesterday,' he told the jury opaquely. Carman then pointed out that the defence had *not* abandoned the plea of justification. The plea had been the same from start to finish. The judge replied that if he (Mr Justice French) had said that, then he had been wrong to do so. The judge retired a few months later.

By a majority the jury found in favour of the newspaper after a retirement of five and a half hours. The costs of the two-week action were believed to be £600,000. The verdict was upheld by the lord chief justice, Lord Bingham, in the Court of Appeal: no wrong or miscarriage of justice had been occasioned by any misdirection or non-direction. There was some solace for the five losing plaintiffs when settlement was announced shortly afterwards of a claim against *Time Out* they had brought along with three other officers, Bruce Galbraith, David Osborn and Paul Sweeney. The police complained that the magazine had been at the forefront of the campaign against them. In this action the plaintiffs recovered a total of £120,000 damages, plus costs, for a repetition of the Operation Jackpot allegations coupled with a strong suggestion that the allegations of corruption and planting drugs were true. Osborn and Sweeney had not in fact been transferred from Stoke Newington – they had been mistakenly identified. The *Time Out* articles went much further than the *Guardian*'s, but the settlement had been agreed in principle before the outcome of the *Guardian* case was known.

A writ had also been issued by the Stoke Newington five against the *News of the World* in respect of its story, published on 2 February 1992, headlined 'DRUGS QUIZ COP KILLS HIMSELF'. This was an account of Sergeant Carroll shooting himself in a cell at Stoke Newington Police Station. Three other officers – Galbraith, Palumbo and Lyons – issued writs on 25 January 1995, just before the expiry of the limitation. As Galbraith had been suspended from duty from June 1992 to September 1994 for allegedly causing damage to a safe at a drug suspect's house and leaving a blank space in his notes relating to the arrest of another suspect, and Lyons and Palumbo had been charged with conspiracy to pervert the course of justice, they did not serve their writs (although no action was taken against Galbraith and Lyons and Palumbo were acquitted). They claimed that the *News of the World* piece implied that they were guilty of involvement in drug-dealing and bribery, and that Carroll had killed himself because he would otherwise have had to confirm their involvement. Mr Justice Drake declined to rule that the words were incapable of bearing that meaning.

A fortnight after the *Guardian* case had been lost, the Court of Appeal ruled that the words complained of could not reasonably be read as imputing guilt to the plaintiffs as contrasted with reasonable suspicion of guilt. The prominent reference to the sergeant's suicide did not transform them so as to bear that meaning, since a reasonable reader could interpret the reference in a number of different ways. The words were incapable of bearing the meaning attributed to them by the plaintiffs (Mapp v. News Group Newspapers Ltd).

It was not the end of the action: there was a further appeal, as a result of which it was ruled that the defendants had insufficient evidence to argue that the police officers could reasonably be suspected of involvement in unlawful activities. And indeed the case continued, despite pointed comments about time-consuming procedural applications to court, for over seven years before it was eventually settled on confidential terms.

While the Police Federation were winning their cases, the legal costs could be recovered and were not a significant drain on their funds. The Stoke Newington litigation is likely to have cost the federation £500,000 or £600,000, depending on whether they were able to offset the *Time Out* damages. In the aftermath of that action, media defendants are likely to feel increasingly emboldened to fight cases against the Police Federation. A ruling by the Court of Appeal in 1992 (R. v. Bromell ex parte Coventry Evening Newspapers Limited) may make it easier for them to do so. In this case the *Coventry Evening Telegraph* had been sued for its story in April 1991 headlined, 'WHY THE CHIEF CRACKED DOWN ON HIS CRIME STAFF'. Each of the two officers suing for libel had previously recovered £40,000 libel damages from the *Independent*, the *Guardian* and the BBC. The newspaper was able to gain access to documents in the possession of the Police Complaints Authority which had resulted in the quashing of Michael Bromell's conviction, based on a disputed confession obtained by the West Midlands Serious Crime Squad. These documents would normally have been protected from disclosure under the terms of a public interest immunity certificate. While the court did not prejudge the defence of justification, the lord chief justice felt it would be repugnant to justice if these officers could continue to mulct the press in damages while the courts disabled their adversaries from access to the documents which might enable them to raise a defence to the libel claims brought against them. Henceforward the playing field may be more even.

In September 1998 police officers Sergeant Peter Bleakley and PC Emyln Welsh, together with former PC Paul Giles, recovered £100,000 each for allegations that they had fabricated evidence and committed perjury at the trial of Malcolm Kennedy for murdering Patrick Quinn in his cell at Hammersmith Police Station on Christmas Eve 1990. The *World in Action* programme 'A Time to Kill' was a dramatisation of Kennedy's account: lying in the cell in a drunken sleep, he claimed he was woken by a struggle between Quinn and a uniformed officer. After the programme was shown his conviction for murder was quashed, but at the retrial he was convicted of manslaughter, a conviction upheld by the Court of Appeal. At the retrial a computer-aided police dispatch report was produced establishing that the police officers were indeed telling the truth about the timings they had given in their evidence. It also proved that the officers were not even in Hammersmith Police Station at the time of the killing.

This conclusive evidence was not obtained until eighteen months after the broadcast and underlined the perils of such programmes. The allegations were very grave ones, and despite all the care that went into researching the programme, the only defence could have been justification. A Reynolds-type defence of qualified privilege (see Chapter 16) would certainly have failed, probably on the duty test and inevitably on the test of the reasonableness of the defendants' conduct. Granada accepted that the allegations made in their programme that the officers had given false evidence or fabricated documents were wrong, and apologised both in court and on television. Additionally they paid the Police Federation costs of £1.2 million, as well as their own of £500,000. The case had cost £2 million. Granada's mistaken conviction that it had uncovered a miscarriage of injustice and serious wrongdoing on the part of the police resulted in this very high libel settlement in a case which did not reach the stage of a trial.

There was a less happy outcome for the police in the case brought by Detective Inspector Trevor Gladding of the Gloucestershire Constabulary against Channel 4 and Headline Books, which illustrated the uncertainties of libel law and the risk of costly legal errors. Gladding sued in respect of a *Trial and Error* programme broadcast in 1994 and a book *Trial and Error* by reporter David Jessel which claimed that Gary Mills and Tony Poole had been wrongly convicted of the 1989 murder of drug-dealer Hensley Wiltshire in a fight in a Gloucester flat. Mills claimed he acted in self-defence. Poole denied he was involved at all. It was suggested that Gladding had tried to persuade a witness, Neville Juke, not to attend the committal proceedings. At the murder trial he had denied any such conversation with Juke, but a tape-recording had then been produced.

As was recognised at the libel action before Mr Justice Morland in October 1998, these were very serious allegations against Inspector Gladding. In effect he was being accused of perverting the course of justice by warning Juke off giving evidence in favour of the accused at the committal proceedings and of perjuring himself at their trial at Bristol Crown Court in January 1990 in his evidence about his conversation with Juke. The Police Federation foolishly seems to have allowed itself to be influenced by the gravity of the allegations rather than by the prospects of success in the libel action. It seems also to have underestimated Channel 4's determination to uphold the integrity of its programme and reporter, and to have overestimated the anxiety inevitably caused by the costly litigation. The upshot of this disastrous miscalculation was a potential seven-figure depletion of the Police Federation's funds, for which a more sensible use could surely have been found.

Providentially, Juke had, on his mother's advice, recorded Gladding's ill-judged remarks when he telephoned Juke a few days before the committal proceedings for the murder trial. 'Paid any fines lately?' Gladding had inquired, pointedly commenting that there was a warrant out for Juke's arrest. In fact this related not to non-payment of fines but to non-attendance at court. Gladding said he didn't want to see Juke at court that Monday or Tuesday, as his attendance would 'cause other problems'. He did not want to see him until the Wednesday. There was a protracted discussion about whether Juke had received formal written notice to attend court – he was one of the principal eye-witnesses to the murder and had twice been interviewed by Gladding. 'Right. You have not received official notification that you are required at court. Do not go to court on Monday. Ring me up on Wednesday, will you do that for me? I am telling you, deny all knowledge. You have not received that letter to go to court Monday,' Gladding told Juke.

At the murder trial Gladding had testified that a witness summons had been served on Juke and that he had expected him to turn up. Asked whether he ever told Juke not to come to the Magistrates' Court, Gladding replied, 'No, I did not.'

Unlike the preceding examples, this was not a case where unexpected new evidence emerged at a very late stage to cast a new light on the matter. The Court of Appeal, while upholding the murder convictions in a case where criticisms had at varying stages and by various people been made of some barristers, solicitors, police and doctors, had roundly condemned Gladding's behaviour. It was unfortunate that the incident had resulted in Wiltshire's death, and Mills and Poole were a little unlucky to have been convicted. But Gladding had, the court ruled, behaved in 'an exceedingly unwise manner . . . he should never have gone so far as to threaten Juke that he would be arrested if he were to attend court. It is most unfortunate that he answered proper questions in cross-examination so readily in an improper and misleading manner. We apprehend that his conduct will have been dealt with by disciplinary procedures.' This was not the case: evidently the Police Complaints Authority was satisfied that Gladding had made a genuine mistake in not recollecting his conversation with Juke.

He put his failure to remember his telephone call seven months earlier down to forgetfulness. Bearing in mind the Court of Appeal's comments and the existence of the tape which cast doubt on Gladding's truthfulness, it was astonishing that the Police Federation felt it prudent to commit such massive resources to Gladding's case. The judge indicated that the jury might feel the detective inspector was brushing aside the Court of Appeal's criticisms of his conduct as being of little or no consequence. It was, as Mr Justice Morland pointed out at the libel trial, an 'extraordinary telephone conversation' and 'an extraordinary lapse of memory, if forgetfulness is the true and honest explanation for the wrong answers'. It was perhaps hardly surprising that at the libel trial the jury returned a unanimous verdict for the defendants within two hours.

Most unusually, the jury had been discharged twice, resulting in three trials being necessary to achieve the final result. At the first trial David Jessel, the programme's reporter and author of the book, had been scheduled to give evidence, but Gladding's counsel had taken objection to the whole of Jessel's evidence on the grounds of its inadmissibility. Unwisely, Gladding's counsel had proceeded in his closing speech to the jury to attack Jessel for not having the courage to go into the witness box. Channel 4's counsel, George Carman QC, protested that the reality of the situation had been misrepresented to the jury. As a result of the objection to Jessel's evidence, there was no testimony he could validly have given. Mr Justice Eady agreed with Carman, despite Gladding's counsel's assertion that there was other evidence Jessel could have given, such as evidence on the question of aggravation or mitigation of damages. The judge adjourned the case overnight for Gladding's counsel to reflect on the wisdom of his attack on Jessel. When, the next day, he rashly declined to withdraw it, the jury was discharged from giving a verdict in a case which had by then lasted two weeks. This process was held up while the Court of Appeal itself reviewed the judge's decision regarding the relevance or otherwise of any evidence Jessel could give. Noting that it would only very rarely overrule a decision to discharge the jury, a retrial was ordered.

When this took place, in October 1998 in front of a new judge, Mr Justice Morland, that jury was also discharged after the inappropriate fashion in which the case had been opened to the jury by Gladding's counsel. The judge felt compelled to act because of the way in which counsel had asked the jury to view the television programme. His comments had wrongly suggested that the jury could determine what the programme meant, not simply by what it in fact said and portrayed, but also by what it did not say, or should have said, which was not the way ordinary television viewers would watch a programme. This time the trial lasted only one day.

After this chapter of disasters came the curious spectacle of Gladding's counsel disclosing in advance at the third trial what he proposed to say to the jury, almost by way of a dry run, to avoid further mishaps. Another two-week trial, again before Mr Justice Morland, ended with a verdict in favour of Channel 4 and a bill of £1.5 million costs for the Police Federation. The lack of wisdom of the Police Federation's conduct was underlined by the fact that they had rejected the £202 paid into court by both Channel 4 and Headline Books in an attempt to resolve Gladding's unmeritorious claim.

In this accident-prone case the verdict was the decision of only eleven jurors, as the Metropolitan Police had managed to nick one of them the previous weekend for obstructing the police. He was discharged from the jury after he very properly brought the matter to the attention of the judge, voicing his intention to sue the police for wrongful arrest.

Another officer, Inspector Patrick Geenty, did succeed in obtaining substantial damages from Channel 4 in relation to their account of his involvement in the Wiltshire case after the Court of Appeal ruled that the programme was capable of meaning that he had contributed to the drug-dealer's death. As the television company had not intended to make any such suggestion, they settled his claim.

With the extension of qualified privilege defence in the Reynolds case and the incorporation of the freedom of speech provisions of Article 10 of the European Convention on Human Rights, which provides for a greater latitude for criticism of the police on grounds of public interest (Thorgeirson v. Iceland, see Chapter 21), there is likely to be a welcome decline in actions brought by them.

# 7

# McDONALD'S:
# The McFolly of McLibel

English libel law permits companies to sue for damages to their trading reputation, and it is all too easy for them to do so: they do not have to prove actual financial damage, and like other libel plaintiffs they can cast the burden of proving the truth of what was said on the defendants. Not only are they likely to have greater resources than the vast majority of individuals, but they can offset their legal costs against the taxes they have to pay, and reclaim the VAT on their bills, whereas an individual will normally have to pay all his or her legal bills out of taxed income. This can make already costly litigation twice as expensive for an individual as for a company. An impecunious libel litigant cannot get legal aid even as a defendant. The benefits of libel law are freely available to companies, and they are in the same position as any individual litigant – there are no special rules relating to companies suing and no additional protections for freedom of speech.

The rules covering government bodies, however, are different. In 1993, in the case of Derbyshire County Council v. Times Newspapers Ltd, the House of Lords held that a county council could not sue in libel and overruled a contrary decision in the case Bognor Regis Urban District Council v. Dutton for what was termed 'injury to its governing reputation'. Freedom of speech required, the House of Lords ruled, that people should be able to criticise government bodies. An action could only be brought by a council upon proof of malice. Merely asserting that what was said was false and defamatory would no longer be sufficient in such cases.

With no such restrictions applying to companies, the mighty McDonald's Corporation of Chicago has never been slow to try to keep the gloss on its reputation by frequent recourse to libel writs. Some time in 1986 the fast-food giant learned that it was under fire from a minuscule and virtually unknown outfit called London Greenpeace. London Greenpeace, on a good day, could muster thirty members. Formed in 1971, it was the original Greenpeace group in the UK but never became part of the international environmental organisation. McDonald's had been in business for over thirty years. Its annual sales in 1990 were $18.75 billion and increasing and its operations were supported in the UK by its subsidiaries, Goldenwest Foods and McKey Food Services. Having opened its first restaurant in the UK, in Woolwich, south London, in 1974, it was expanding at a prodigious rate: its advertising and public-relations budgets were measured in billions of dollars and were well able to deal with pinpricks of criticism. Corporate policy, however, seemed to dictate that there was no nut too small for the McDonald's sledgehammer.

The case which McDonald's brought against two penniless protesters underlined the need for some restrictions on the at present unfettered right of powerful corporations to sue for libel. It also showed that even a verdict awarding damages can prove to be a public-relations disaster.

What had upset McDonald's was the publication of a leaflet consisting of six sides of A5 paper entitled 'What's Wrong with McDonald's? – Everything They Don't Want You to Know', and illustrated with graphics. 'McTorture, McGarbage, McCancer,

McMurder, McWasteful, McGreedy, McDollar and McProfits'. The low-budget pamphlet contained a number of strongly worded claims against the business practices of McDonald's and the food industry and modern capitalism in general, focusing on the environment, people's health, employees' rights, animal welfare and unethical marketing. It was the converted preaching for the most part to the converted. The leaflet ran counter to McDonald's carefully projected image of itself, as personified by the clown Ronald McDonald and his stomach-churning confederates, Mayor McCheese, the Fry Kids and the Happy Meal Guys, and the less politically correct Hamburglar, and as reflected in Ronald McDonald children's charities, Ronald McDonald House and commercial tie-ins with children's entertainment characters such as the Flintstones and the Lion King.

What was worse was that the company actually believed in all this mush. According to Paul Preston, chairman and chief executive of McDonald's UK and seemingly one of the moving spirits behind the subsequent litigation, acknowledged company folklore included the memorable remarks 'McDonald's isn't a job, it's a life. Our employees have ketchup running in their veins.' Although companies are allowed to use the libel law to defend their trading reputation, they cannot sue for hurt feelings. But it was difficult to escape the conclusion that in this case McDonald's motivation, in addition to their cynical policy of stamping on any criticism, featured an element of umbrage.

McDonald's were in a position to exploit any imprudent use of language in the leaflet. They could set the agenda of what London Greenpeace had to prove and sit back in the knowledge that this tiny pressure group was most unlikely to be able to fly in witnesses and testify, for example, about the state of the rainforest areas in Central America or labour disputes around the world. Yet astonishingly, McDonald's felt sufficiently threatened by the activities of London Greenpeace to call in Sid Nicholson, their head of security and a UK vice-president, a former South African police officer and superintendent in the Metropolitan Police. Through contacts with Special Branch, he learned the names of some of those involved with London Greenpeace but was told that the police were not interested in the group as it was not concerned with any illegal activities.

Sight was soon lost of the fact that the actions of London Greenpeace were essentially those of activists demonstrating against a network of family restaurants. The heavy-handed actions of McDonald's were more in line with attempts to protect the defence of the realm at the height of the cold war. Two separate firms of private detectives were hired to infiltrate the group over a period of eighteen months. Neither agency was told about the other's existence. Nicholson said that he told Paul Preston he wanted at least two teams to work independently of one another with a view to achieving McDonalds' objective, which was to stop the distribution of the leaflet. London Greenpeace meetings at that time drew at most ten people and the agents were noticeably more diligent in their attendance than those they were spying on. Member Dave Morris, later to be on the receiving end of a McDonald's writ, was attending on average eight meetings a year, whereas one keen infiltrator notched up twenty-six in seven months. One gathering in 1990 had a turn-out of only four people, two of whom were McDonald's paid spies. Consequently the agents had little to do other than to report on the suspicious activities of their unknown allies.

Seven private detectives in all were hired to keep tabs on London Greenpeace and to exhibit varying degrees of enthusiasm for the activities of the group in order to conceal their true affiliations. This took a wide range of forms. In one instance, according to the *Observer*, it involved the seduction of a red-blooded member of London Greenpeace, a case perhaps of McPenetration and McPillowtalk. The fact that the relationship lasted six months testified, it seems, to no more than the devotion to duty of the agent in question. In others it led, embarrassingly, to McDonald's security filming sleuths handing out leaflets outside their HQ. In fact as a number of the leaflets were handed out by McDonald's agents, an issue was unsuccessfully raised at the trial that McDonald's had by such conduct consented to their distribution. Moreover, only two years earlier, it was claimed, solicitors acting for McDonald's had given their clients' formal consent to a virtually identical version of the pamphlet, produced in tens of thousands in Nottingham.

Genuine members of London Greenpeace who did attend its meetings were followed home and letters sent to the group were analysed, and in some cases purloined. The organisation's offices were broken into by means of a phonecard used to swipe the lock. At the trial private eye Allan Clare explained how this was done, prompting an intervention by the judge, Mr Justice Bell, to the effect that if the witness was asked any question the answer to which he thought might put him in peril of any criminal proceedings, he was entitled not to answer it.

Another agent ended up as a defence witness at the trial, telling the court: 'I felt uncomfortable doing that type of job. I did not like the deception, prying on people and interfering with their lives. I did not think there was anything wrong with what the group was doing.'

The product of this espionage was a libel writ, McDonald's Corporation and McDonald's Restaurants Ltd, issued in September 1990 against five members of London Greenpeace. Three of the five – Paul Gravett, Andrew Clarke and Jonathan O'Farrell – regretfully decided that discretion was the better part of valour and reluctantly agreed, in January 1991, to make a statement in open court apologising for their criticisms of McDonald's. But hopes that Dave Morris, a thirty-six-year-old single father and former postman, and Helen Steel, a twenty-five-year-old ex-gardener, would likewise kow-tow proved illusory. Soon it became apparent that, despite the gross inequality of resources, they were prepared, with some pro bono* support, to take on McDonald's, and not to capitulate or even settle.

What united Steel and Morris, who had worked together in Haringey community action groups supporting the miners' strike

*An unusual instance: lawyers acting for nothing.

and opposing the poll tax, was their strong conviction about the malpractices of McDonald's and a determination not to be bullied into making an apology for statements which they believed were true. They claimed that all the criticisms in the pamphlet were directed at the food industry in general, and were all widely held views on matters of public importance.

Evidently it never occurred to McDonald's that two people living on £42 to £45 per week income support would take on the multinational corporation. The company would have realised that they would reap no financial benefit from the litigation: the most they could hope for was a demonstration that such libellous dissent would not be tolerated. Yet the futility and counter-productive nature of suing a couple of the distributors of this pamphlet seems to have altogether escaped McDonald's. The Big Macs were determined to squash the small fries, come what may. By the time the writ was issued, 5,000 copies of the pamphlet had been circulated and it was out of print. There were no plans to reprint. McDonald's were perfectly well aware of this from the intelligence provided by their sleuths. In contrast, by the time the case had ended, in June 1997, well over 2 million leaflets had been printed and distributed, with a further 450,000 going out in a week on the back of the publicity generated by the verdict. Five hundred of the 750 McDonald's outlets in the United Kingdom were leafleted, and all told 3 million copies were circulated.

The publicity thus given to the views of the defendants must have exceeded McDonald's worst nightmares. Certainly it must have dented any promotion the company's annual advertising budget of $2 billion could have bought. In 1990 the McLibel Support Campaign, which later linked up activist groups in thirty countries, was established. In 1996 the McInformation Network set up a website, McSpotlight. By the end of the trial McSpotlight, with its 21,000 files, had been visited 7 million times, and by 1999 that figure reached 65 million, 3.2 million visits being made in the month following the verdict. There is now even a McSpotlight CD Rom, which enables the browser to access any article, programme, or even a theatre script, which

McDonald's have, at great expense, attempted to have banned, along with the complete transcripts of all the evidence and legal arguments in the McLibel trial. The whole débâcle spawned a book by the journalist John Vidal, *McLibel: Burger Culture on Trial*, an unflattering three-and-a-quarter-hour reconstruction of the trial on Channel 4 and a video, *McLibel – Two Worlds Collide*.

Had there been an obligation for McDonald's to prove actual damage – not an unreasonable requirement for a corporate plaintiff – they would never have got to first base. It was hard to see how their American company could be adversely affected by the actions of two activists in England. The company has grown inexorably, doubling in size since 1984. During the course of the trial 2,500 new restaurants opened worldwide and in the UK the number of outlets swelled from 380 in 1990 to 650 in 1995, a rate of about one per week after the case began. At the start of the trial it was calculated that 489 million McDonald's meals were being consumed annually in the UK alone. There are now over 25,000 restaurants in 117 countries and annual growth of 13.9 per cent, 40 million people eat at McDonald's each day and a horrendous 100 billion burgers have been consumed since the business started in 1954 – it has been calculated that if all these burgers were placed end to end, they would stretch to the moon and back five times. By 1995 the annual worldwide turnover of the McDonald's Corporation had risen to $30 billion from $18.75 billion at the start of the litigation. In 1997 its turnover was $35 billion and McDonald's had 760 outlets in the UK visited by 10 million customers a week, producing annual profits of £45 million.

McDonald's instinctive reaction to sue the pants off anyone who said, wrote, filmed or acted anything which corporately they did not care for was unwise and, as is usually the case with inveterate litigants, it eventually came disastrously unstuck. Before this happened, McDonald's sued on a global scale: national, local and student newspapers, television shows, magazines, trades unions and green groups. In 1995 Big Mac even turned its guns on a restaurant of the same name which had been open for twenty-six years in Kingston, Jamaica. Although the US claim won in the end, like Steel and Morris, the owner refused to be bullied and held out against the corporation. The restaurant was even granted an order preventing the corporation from operating in Jamaica under the name McDonald's until the litigation was complete.

Reports that the company took action against a topless bar in Australia called McTits seem to be apocryphal. However, when, in March 1991, McDonald's spotted a piece in the *Glasgow Evening News* about *McBurger's – Real Neat Scotch Fayre*, a comic play set in an unnamed fast-food restaurant written by Steve Brown and Jenny Frazer for a youth theatre group and supported by East Kilbride District Council, their lawyers swung into action. McDonald's did not care for the play's portrayal of the exploitation of young employees. Their lawyers graciously allowed the first performance to go ahead with some changes to the script to avoid 'great disappointment to the young persons involved in the production' (and presumably also potential McDonald's customers). On that occasion their clients would not exercise their 'undoubted legal remedies', but thereafter they might 'enforce vigorously their rights against the author or authors in respect of any future unauthorised performances'. The world premiere of *McBurger's* was attended by a grey-suited London lawyer on £200 an hour plus expenses, who sat in the front row with his lawyer's yellow notepad discreetly placed on his knee. Despite all these efforts the script of *McBurger's* can be found on the McSpotlight CD Rom.

In October 1989 McDonald's solicitors complained about remarks attributed to a Liberal councillor, Richard Stokes, in the *Slough, Eton and Windsor Observer* about the destruction of rainforests by McDonald's. The councillor was reminded that McDonalds' support for the conservation of wildlife and natural resources throughout the world was a major part of their philosophy. Unless he agreed within seven days to apologise in open court, pay the full legal costs of the maligned corporation and procure the publication of an apology in his local paper, would be hit by a claim for damages. And in February 1990 the *Bournemouth Advertiser* found itself having to apologise and acknowledge the high ethical concerns of the McDonald's Corporation and the great care it took to ensure its slaughtering methods were humane after running a story headlined 'DEMO BEEFS OVER CATTLE' on animal rights protesters' allegations about cruel slaughter policies. At the McLibel trial Mr Justice Bell was rather more critical about the company's animal welfare policies.

The *Guardian* also had to apologise to McDonald's, for an article entitled 'The Squalor Behind the Bright Fast Food Lights', published on 21 August 1987, by Steven Percy and Harriet Lamb. They accused the corporation of exploiting young people by making them work in degrading conditions for excessively low wages and commented on its aversion to trades unions. The *Guardian* decided not to take on McDonald's. Instead a statement in open court was read out making it clear that no employee had been sacked or victimised for union activities, although the corporation certainly required its employees to work hard and to be committed.

Interestingly, in 1996 at the McLibel trial, although Mr Justice Bell eventually acquitted McDonald's of exploiting disadvantaged groups, he did find that the company paid low wages in Britain, which depressed the going rate for other workers in the catering industry. However, he also found that the London Greenpeace pamphlet had libelled McDonald's because they had failed to prove that the company had a policy of preventing unionisation by getting rid of pro-union workers.

Channel 4, too, had had to say sorry for its documentary *Jungleburger*, broadcast on 12 March 1989. Their public apology included a statement that McDonald's were not engaged in destroying rainforests in Costa Rica and that their restaurants there used only suppliers who could prove that their beef came from long-established cattle ranches and not from rainforest land. BBC's *Nature* programme had likewise apologised in 1984 for the suggestion that McDonald's meat came from cattle ranches built l as a result of deforestation in Central America. ewspaper, *The Sunday Times*, *Time Out*, the ld the satirical television programme *Spitting Image* had ~~...~~ felt the wrath of the McDonald's organisation over allegations they had published or broadcast. But the libels are now repeated, seemingly with impunity, on the McSpotlight website.

For the most part these libellers have been raising matters of public interest. The burden of proving what may or may not have happened in a strip of Central American rainforest at a given time is intolerable for the average defendant, who would need to find witnesses and persuade them to come to this country. So, in the short term, the prospect of such actions does send a chill down the spine of media organisations. However, the general McSchadenfreude when the libel defences were breached resulted in more hostile publicity than would have been the case had these matters been calmly countered by the company through its large advertising and public-relations machine.

In December 1992 Steel and Morris made an unsuccessful application to the European Commission of Human Rights, claiming that the absence of legal aid in such a complex libel case negated freedom of expression. In the run-up to the beginning of the trial in April 1994, statements were obtained from a total on both sides of 180 witnesses from twenty countries, and senior personnel at McDonald's had to devote inordinate amounts of time to the case. One senior vice-president, Stan Stein, who flew over to Britain from Chicago, was described by a journalist in court as looking as happy to be there as a cat in a swimming pool, and fuming like a tourist with a heavy suitcase on a hot day waiting at a taxiless cab rank. He was in the witness box for nine days.

There were seven defence applications to the Court of Appeal. One produced a very important ruling as to the quality of evidence on which a defendant could rely when seeking to prove that a libel was in fact true. The Court of Appeal held that previous rulings that a plea of justification (truth) would be struck out if it lacked sufficient particularity and supporting evidence placed an unfair and unrealistic burden on a defendant. The criteria for a plea of justification should be that the defendant believed the words complained of were true, that he or she intended to support the plea or justification at the trial, and that he or she had some evidence to support the plea, or reasonable grounds for supposing that sufficient evidence to prove the allegation would be available at trial. Although the Court of Appeal felt that some parts of Steel and Morris's defence (in particular areas of the international evidence) were very weak, they might have been improved or transformed by the date of the trial. The test was whether the plea was incurably bad. This meant that a defendant could rely on what evidence he or she might reasonably expect to obtain on subpoena, cross-examination and the discovery process. This extension of the law was the sort of wing and prayer that Steel and Morris, as litigants in person, required.

McDonald's had succeeded in December 1993 in obtaining an order for trial by judge alone. Under English law, either party in a libel action is entitled as of right to trial by jury, unless, under Section 69 of the Supreme Court Act 1981, it can be demonstrated that the complexity of the case will be such that it will involve a detailed examination of documents. The judge held that this was just such a case. The judge who drew the short straw of hearing the proceedings was the recently appointed Mr Justice Bell. Richard Rampton QC, for McDonald's, estimated that the case would last six or seven weeks with a jury but a mere three or four if tried by judge alone. By the time the full hearing started the trial estimate had increased to three months. However, the issues slowly proliferated and in the event the case was to last 314 days, spanning a period from June 1994 to June 1997, and in the process to spawn 19,000 pages of court transcripts at a daily cost of £700 and 40,000 pages of documents.

McDonald's made two fundamental errors which were greatly to prolong the trial. The first was to sue on everything in the 'What's Wrong with McDonald's?' pamphlet. This meant that Steel and Morris could try to justify every allegation it contained. Although McDonald's were, particularly in view of the

extravagance of some of the leaflet's language, on strong
ground regarding the allegations of their contribution to starvation in the Third World, and to the destruction of vast areas
of Central American rainforest, their use of recycled paper and
the minimum risk of food poisoning – the interpretation of the
words accepted by the judge but disputed by the defendants –
the fast-food giant faced problems over accusations that they
promoted unhealthy food, exploited children through their marketing and advertising, were cruel to the animals destined to
end up as Big Macs and McNuggets and treated their employees
badly. However, when they saw which way the wind was blowing, they managed to amend their case by means of some fancy
legal footwork so that the burden of proof became even greater
for Steel and Morris. Originally McDonald's complained that the
pamphlet alleged that some of the contents of typical
McDonald's meals were *linked to* cancers of the breast and
bowel and heart disease. When it appeared that there might
indeed be such a link, McDonald's shifted their ground to claim
that the leaflet accused them of *causing* such cancers and heart
disease in their customers. McDonald's no doubt feared that if
they did not sue for every allegation, they would be perceived
to be admitting that parts of the pamphlet were true, but they
were wrong to follow this path. They had well-paid lawyers and
PR men to explain why they had chosen the worst allegations
without conceding that any of the others were true. It seemed
they simply wanted to crush their opponents.

Having sued on everything in the pamphlet, McDonald's
found themselves having to justify their trade practices in an
increasingly environmentally conscious and diet-aware country
where methods of beef production were being questioned in the
light of the emerging links between BSE and Creutzfeldt-Jakob
disease.

Their second major strategic error was to themselves libel
Steel and Morris. Either they should not have sued and fought
fire with fire, relying on the very much greater heat of their
own furnace, or they should have shut up and brought the case

to court as swiftly as possible. Ineptly, McDonald's tried to do both. On the eve of the trial they produced for distribution in their restaurants 300,000 copies of a leaflet entitled 'Why McDonald's is Going to Court', which was backed up by a flurry of press releases.

This counter-attack accused Steel and Morris of persistently spreading lies and making numerous false statements about McDonald's, thereby deceiving the public and consequently harming their staff, customers, employees and franchisees. The case was, they high-handedly claimed, not about freedom of speech, but about their right to stop people telling lies. In so doing they had shot themselves in the corporate foot. The defendants were able to counterclaim for libel. Their action greatly widened the issues of the trial and effectively reversed the burden of proof. Now McDonald's had not only to prove that they did not pay low wages and target children with marketing, but also that Steel and Morris *knew* that what they had written was untrue. The upshot was an open season on virtually every aspect of the McDonald's business, to the extent that the company was accused of everything from being anti-trade union to watering down milkshakes.

At the conclusion of the case the judge held that the London Greenpeace pamphlet was defamatory, but he ruled that McDonald's own leaflets were defamatory as well, and, not justified. They were entitled as a matter of law to claim 'qualified privilege', and to respond in suitably vigorous terms to the original attack on them, but this was scant consolation for the unnecessary widening of the issues. The judge felt unable, with litigants in person, to impose a rigid timetable for presenting the case, as happened in the no less complex Upjohn litigation dealt with in Chapter 9.

Hearing the evidence took over two years; the judge took six months to write his 762-page judgement and even the forty-five-page summary of his findings took two hours to read out. More records fell than on a bad day for England at a Test match. It became the longest libel action by March 1995, the longest

English civil case by December 1995 and the longest English trial of any kind by November 1996. Only the 391-day Piper Alpha disaster case in Scotland was longer in Britain's history. Taking into account all McDonald's American legal costs and the expense of the preparation, the acquisition of expert evidence and the getting the witnesses to court in the UK, the case would have cost McDonald's in excess of £10 million.

The bullying tactics of McDonald's which had hitherto served them well had now ensnared them. The litigation gathered its own momentum. McDonald's had failed to appreciate that Steel and Morris were determined campaigners who considered their concerns to be far more important than money. Despite the immense burden of proof on them and their lack of resources, they did at least have time to devote to the case and they were receiving increasing financial and practical support from the public. After three months, McDonald's flew over two board members from Chicago, Dick Starmann and their senior legal adviser, Shelby Yastrow, to try to broker a settlement and exploit the potential window of opportunity afforded by the summer adjournment. They had again miscalculated. They could not impose on Steel and Morris conditions of confidentiality requiring them not to disclose this approach. If they did not quite raise the white flag over the golden arches, they were close to doing so. McDonald's no longer wanted an apology, and were even prepared to pay money to a third party nominated by Steel and Morris. The negotiations floundered mainly on Steel and Morris's insistence that McDonald's should guarantee not to sue their critics in future. In May 1995, after the case had been running for over a year, at the McDonald's AGM in Chicago, their chairman and chief executive Michael Quinlan was asked whether it was in the interests of the shareholders to continue the action. He replied optimistically that it was 'coming to a wrap soon'. In fact Mr Justice Bell was not to give his judgement until June 1997.

Ordinarily the embarrassing matters which inevitably emerge in a case of this length would have been buried in the tedium and weight of evidence. However, in this case the apparatus for distributing any damaging evidence existed on a scale never before seen. The McLibel Support Campaign was pumping out press releases and hand-outs to thousands of activists and the McSpotlight website carried blow-by-blow accounts of the trial. Attempts to justify the unhappy existence of the 27 million chickens which annually passed through the hands of McDonald's bordered on the idiotic. It was established in the course of the evidence of one McDonald's expert witnesses that the company's egg suppliers kept five chickens in each battery cage, providing less floor space for each bird than the size of an A4 sheet of paper and allowing no freedom of movement or access to fresh air or sunshine. These were the conditions which Ed Oakley, chief purchasing officer for McDonald's in the UK, described as 'pretty comfortable'. He claimed McDonald's had a very real feeling that animals should be kept and slaughtered in the most humane way possible. Dr Sidney Arnott, a cancer expert called by McDonald's, did little good for the corporation's case on the potential health risks of its food when, in reply to a question about whether it was a reasonable statement to say that 'a diet high in fat, sugar, animal products and salt and low in fibre, vitamins and minerals is linked with cancer and heart disease', he commented: 'If it is being directed at the public, then I would say that it is a very reasonable thing to say'. He was then informed that this was the key quote from the London Greenpeace pamphlet on this issue.

The case also involved McDonald's having to lift the veil on its attitude towards trades unions and staffing generally. It was pointed out that there was a very high turnover of staff, about three or four times the average in the catering industry, and that there was no trade-union representation in the UK. The company employed 1.5 million people in total, and 30,000 in the UK, 64 per cent of whom were under the age of twenty-one. Paul Preston did not consider the starting wage of £3.10 per hour to be low pay.

Mr Justice Bell felt compelled to ask: 'Are any members or

employees of McDonald's in this country members of any union at all?'

Paul Preston replied unconvincingly, 'They may well be. I do not know. It is their right to form one if they so choose.'

The judge then said, 'I asked you whether any employee of the English company was a member of the union.'

Preston responded, somewhat testily, 'I said they may very well be.'

'They may very well be?'

'It is their right to join one if they so choose.'

It emerged, however, that McDonald's had serious disputes with unions in fifteen countries. The corporation's attitude appeared to be that as they had 'company rap sessions' for workers to express their views to managers or supervisors, there was no real need for unions. The reality seemed somewhat different. This was something successfully exploited by Steel and Morris and the McSpotlight website set up an international 'debating room' for disgruntled McDonald's employees. Other awkward evidence included a claim by a former McDonald's employee, Siamak Alimi, that he had been instructed to continue cooking food in a kitchen flooded with sewage.

McDonald's denials of allegations that their marketing exploited children led to further embarrassment. An examination of their 666-page confidential operations manual, which incorporated the McDonald's philosophy, 'The System', revealed such inanities as 'Ronald loves McDonald's and McDonald's food. And so do children, because they love Ronald. Remember, children exert a phenomenal influence when it comes to restaurant selection. This means that you should do everything you can to appeal to children's love for Ronald and McDonald's.' In evidence their UK marketing service manager stated: 'It is our objective to dominate the communications area . . . because we are competing for a share of the customer's mind.'

David Green, US senior vice-president of marketing, found himself in court for four days. He agreed that McDonald's spent $1 billion on advertising each year in the US alone. From one point of view that made the cost of this litigation small fries. From another it led one to wonder why, with that sort of spend, McDonald's needed to take on Steel and Morris. Green agreed that children between the ages of two and eight were impressionable and likely to be susceptible to the image projected of Ronald McDonald. But, he explained, rather unattractively, Ronald was their friend. This may have been a cynically correct assessment of the market, but it looked bad expressed in the written word. It simply underlined the foolishness of suing for everything in the Steel and Morris pamphlet and the inadvisability of McDonald's bulldozer tactics.

More entertaining was the raking over of a controversy concerning the Duke of Edinburgh which had been recounted in a letter by one of the witnesses to the incident. In his capacity as president of the World Wildlife Fund Prince Philip had attended a cocktail party in Canada in 1983, where he was introduced to George Cohon, president of McDonald's restaurants in Canada. The Prince greeted him with the corporately incorrect statement: 'So you are the people tearing down the Brazilian rainforest and breeding cattle?' Cohon's face changed swiftly from the colour of McDonald's highly sugared strawberry milkshake to a ketchup shade as he replied, 'I think you are mistaken, sir.' The Duke is said to have retorted 'Rubbish,' or words to that effect, and turned on his heel. Anguished top-level letters from McDonald's eventually elicited the response that Prince Philip did not recall having said what he was reported to have said.

This incident appeared to provide some support for Steel and Morris's contentions, as did a range of expert witnesses called by the defence. McDonald's defended the accusation of deforestation on fairly narrow grounds. They made the point that as the corporation owned no land, apart from that which its restaurants and offices occupied, no cattle and no beef-supply companies, it was in no position to destroy a single rainforest tree. However, the argument went wider: global beef consumption did result in deforestation, and the company was forced to concede that it had imported some Brazilian beef for its UK restaurants in the mid-1980s and used former rainforest land in Costa Rica for its outlets there. The question was, what did Steel and Morris mean by 'recently deforested'? Within the previous twenty-five years, or what other period?

Even more bizarre was the evidence uncovered by Steel and Morris in an officially sanctioned book *Behind the Arches*. This featured a claim made by Den Fujita, the president of McDonald's' Japanese subsidiary, that 'Japanese people are so short and have yellow skins because they have eaten nothing but fish and rice for two thousand years . . . If we eat McDonald's hamburgers and potatoes for a thousand years we will became taller, our skin will become white and our hair blond.' As only twenty-five years have elapsed since this statement was made, the jury seems still to be out on that one.

More significant than that type of distasteful mishap were the claims made by McDonald's in their advertising that their meals were 'nutritious'. What they meant, they said, was that their food contained nutrients, rather than intending in the more widely accepted sense of the word as meaning wholesome, healthy for the body and providing energy. One of the large number of experts called by McDonald's, Professor Verner Wheelock, agreed that a typical McDonald's meal was high in saturated fat and sodium (salt). He argued that this had to be kept in perspective. People could attain government dietary recommendations if they ate McDonald's food sparingly. He seemed to be saying that McDonald's provided you with a satisfying meal provided you did not go there too often. The statistics showed that in the UK 80 per cent of McDonald's customers did eat there only once a week or less, and just 2.4 per cent were unwise enough to eat there every day. An over-user would, it seems, have been someone who ate McDonald's three or more times weekly. US company statistics, on the other hand, showed that a staggering 77 per cent of customer visits were made by 'heavy users', who ate an average of three times a week at McDonald's. Much, in health terms, would depend on what other fast food that person ate.

On 19 June 1997, six months after the evidence concluded, Mr

Justice Bell gave judgement. Technically, there was no question that McDonald's were the victors, but Steel and Morris had won most of the main points concerning the corporation's core business practices.

The health issue was a very mixed bag as far as McDonald's were concerned. It could not be right, the judge found, to say that eating McDonald's meals would bring a very real risk that you would suffer cancer of the breast or bowel or heart disease. However, he observed that the small number of customers who ate at McDonald's several times a week *would* run a very real risk of heart disease if they continued to do so throughout their lives, encouraged by McDonald's advertising. It was likewise true only of this small proportion of people that eating McDonald's would make for a diet high in fat, animal products and salt and lacking in vitamins and minerals. The risk of bowel cancer would probably be increased to some extent, but this was only possibly true for breast cancer.

The judge found that McDonald's did exploit children as being more susceptible to advertising than adults in order to encourage them to pressurise their parents into going to McDonald's. He also found that McDonald's falsely advertised their food as nutritious. Claims of positive nutritious benefit did not match reality. Mr Justice Bell did not find McDonald's food unhealthy as such, but his praise was coloured with distinct criticisms. The meals were high in saturated fat and sodium and low in fibre. And indulgence in Big Macs did increase the risk of breast and bowel cancer and heart disease to some extent. This was a disastrous finding for a company which prides itself on its wholesomeness. Seldom can a group of restaurants have received such a lukewarm endorsement.

The judge also held McDonald's guilty of paying low wages, thereby depressing wages in Britain's catering trade. He acquitted them of discriminating against disadvantaged groups, particularly women and black people – everyone, a cynic listening to the judge might have felt, was treated equally badly. The judge did not care for the practice of sending crew members home early and not paying them for the remainder of the shift when business was slack. This was most unfair as it deprived the crew of pay for a time which they had set aside to earn money. Since the basic rate of pay was so low (by then £3.25), the savings to McDonald's were not vast, whereas the losses were significant to their employees. He was also unimpressed that a number of staff effectively earned less than the basic rate due to the absence of overtime pay.

McDonald's were culpably responsible for cruelty to the animals reared for their products. Broiler chickens and pigs were badly treated by being given too little room to move. Even Dr Neville Gregory, McDonald's own expert, had conceded that dairy cows were subjected to stress, pain, exhaustion and disease by being forced to be constantly pregnant and milked. He agreed that some stunning and killing methods, and stocking densities, did not comply with the government's code of practice. McDonald's were also culpably responsible for the cruel practice by which a small proportion of the millions of chickens slaughtered annually were fully conscious when their throats were slit, and for cruelty shown by a very limited number of egg suppliers.

So McDonald's had won on points, but their victory was a public-relations disaster. They might have won a technical knock-out on the counterclaim, but that was always a tactical sideshow.

The company line was expressed by a dour Paul Preston, who set some sort of dubious record by being cross-examined intermittently over a period of twenty-three months. He stated at their post-trial press conference that the company was broadly satisfied with the judgement. 'For the sake of our employees and customers, we wanted to show these serious allegations to be false and I am pleased to have done so.' There had been a thorough audit of their business and he believed their customers and employees would be reassured by the overwhelming evidence given in support of their case. The defendants' press conference, meanwhile, was more like a victory rally, with hundreds of members of the public cheering the upbeat and defiant stance.

The companies, McDonald's Corporation in the US and McDonald's Restaurants Ltd in the UK, were each awarded £30,000 damages, £27,500 being awarded against Steel and Morris jointly, and an additional £5,000 against Morris, as a reflection of his greater responsibility for the publication of the allegations in the pamphlet. The judge ruled that the pair had not proved that McDonald's were responsible for starvation in the Third World, or that they caused the destruction of rainforests, either by clearing them for ranching or to fulfil paper requirements, or that they were guilty of lying about the percentage of recycled paper they used, or that they produced food which caused cancer of the breast or bowel or heart disease if eaten occasionally, or that they sold food which contained undue residues of antibiotics, growth-promoting hormone drugs or pesticides. These were scarcely startling acquittals after seven years of litigation.

The futility of the libel action was underscored by the fact that McDonald's were unable to recover any damages from the impecunious defendants. They were allowed to apply on four weeks' written notice for costs, but they never bothered to do so and even foreswore their damages. More significantly, and even though this was their stated aim, McDonald's shied away from applying for an injunction forbidding further publication of the leaflet, something which would normally flow from a finding of libel and the awarding of damages. The defendants had made it clear that they and thousands of supporters might well disobey any such order. Even McDonald's could envisage what a public-relations disaster it would be if Steel and Morris were to be jailed for contempt. In this regard they acted sensibly, but the consequent lack of an injunction served to make their victory seem even more of a Pyrrhic one. Certainly McDonald's harvested a distinctly paltry return on the £10 million they had spent on the case.

Then there was the galling spectacle, for a company which

appeared to use the law of libel as a part of their public relations, of the public perception of the case as a victory for David (Dave and Helen) against Goliath (Ronald). Inevitably the focus of the media was on the findings made against McDonald's and on comments made by the judge which were critical of McDonald's, even when McDonald's may have won that particular issue, because of the meaning attributed to the words. The press were less interested in the findings that McDonald's had not acquired vast tracts of land in Costa Rica, Guatemala or Brazil by evicting families and tribal people from their land, or that they had not used poisons to destroy areas of Central American rainforest to create pastures. Nor that the company was not liable for litter outside its restaurants, although litter patrols did on occasion break down, or indeed that McDonald's were not guilty of wrecking the planet by creating ecological havoc.

And still the agony is not over for McDonald's. Steel and Morris's appeal challenged the judge's findings and rulings on sixty-three closely argued points. Four weeks in the Court of Appeal in March 1999 resulted in a 309-page judgement, another £200,000 of legal costs, two further victories for Steel and Morris and more misery for McDonald's. The court ruled that it was fair comment for Steel and Morris to have said that McDonald's workers worldwide do badly in terms of pay and conditions, and that they were justified in claiming that if one eats enough McDonald's food, one's diet may well become high in fat, animal products and sodium, leading to the very real risk of heart disease. Damages were reduced from £60,000 to £40,000. McDonald's won on the remaining points, but it was another Pyrrhic victory for the corporation.

In March 2000 the House of Lords refused Steel and Morris leave to appeal. In July 2000, however, they recovered £10,000 in an out-of-court settlement from the police in respect of their claim that confidential data relating to them had been passed to McDonald's.

There are likely to be substantive challenges in Europe to the English law of libel, including the right of corporations to sue for libel and the imbalance of the law against defendants fighting libel claims. Steel and Morris also intend to oppose the lack of a right to a jury trial, and to argue that the absence of legal aid, coupled with the heavy burden of proof imposed on an individual when he or she is sued for libel by a powerful corporation, is an abuse of process. It is an argument destined to end in the European Court of Human Rights, and McDonald's unwise litigation could very well result in a European ruling which will prevent repetition of such a case.

Had the Reynolds action dealt with in Chapter 16 been decided before the McLibel case, there might have been some rulings in favour of Steel and Morris that some of what had been published was covered by a public information qualified privilege. This would have saved them from having to prove the truth of such allegations. Under the changes in civil procedure introduced by Lord Woolf, which took effect in April 1999 (see Chapter 21), the court is now required to conduct a trial in a manner which is proportionate to the issues involved and to take account of the relative strengths and weaknesses of the parties in deciding how it is to be run. But both these changes came too late for Steel and Morris.

Maybe the last word on this tangled litigation should be given to Mr Justice Bell. 'For better or worse, the law of defamation has grown up in its own special way over the last 150 years, and whereas in ordinary negligence claims, if you don't know what the law is you can say what you think is sensible and there is a 90 per cent chance of you being right, I'm not sure the percentage isn't the reverse of that in the law of defamation. But there we are.'

# 8

# NOMURA:
# A Case of Foolish
# Corporate Bullying

A particularly outrageous example of a powerful company trying to use the law of libel to muzzle its critics was the case brought by the Japanese company Nomura against an English publisher and an American author. Nomura ruthlessly exploited the situation whereby the burden of proof in a libel case rests upon the defendants. Subsequent financial scandals in Japan underlined the absolute folly of bringing libel proceedings and vindicated many of the book's allegations.

In 1990 Albert Alletzhauser, an American author and a former senior executive at James Capel & Co. in Tokyo, published *The House of Nomura: The Rise to Supremacy of the World's Most Powerful Company*, subtitled 'The Inside Story of the Legendary Japanese Dynasty'. The book was by no means unfavourable to Nomura. It described how Nomura Securities' dominance of the Japanese stockmarket had countered the collapse of Western markets: for three days Nomura had bought stock and prevented a collapse of the Japanese market in the October 1987 crash. It had successfully exploited the power of a company with 5 million individual and 200,000 corporate accounts, 132 domestic branches, a massive turnover and the power generated by its salesforce's informal discretionary *eigyo tokkin* investment funds to buy shares when everyone else was selling.

Alletzhauser's studiously researched book had been published in the UK by Bloomsbury Publishing, a respected literary house founded in 1986, and was due to be released in Japan by Shinchosha, one of Japan's most distinguished publishers. It had been read before publication by two leading members of the Nomura family no longer involved in the management of the company, who were sufficiently impressed by its contents to make a number of helpful suggestions for the text. They were Tomohide Nomura, a grandson of Tokushichi Nomura, the founder of the company, and Kozo Nomura, Tokushichi's nephew and himself chairman and founder of Nomura Microscience Company, president of the Nomura Japan Corporation and a member of the main board of Nomura Securities from 1952 to 1982. When I met Kozo Nomura in Tokyo while preparing the defence of the case for libel which Nomura had by then brought in England, he told me he had bought thirty-six copies of Alletzhauser's book.

No one had ever written in so much detail about the history and, to Western eyes, distinctly Eastern practices of Nomura. Alletzhauser described the curious tradition of paying off corporate blackmailers known as *sokaiya* (*sokai* being the Japanese for annual general meeting) to prevent them from publicly airing the peccadillos of the directors or their assorted corporate misdeeds. The *sokaiya* would buy stock in companies and threaten to disrupt company meetings. They were instantly recognisable from their chalk-striped suits, black shirts, white ties and the gold chains round their necks – not to mention the missing top joints of their little fingers, amputated as a token of loyalty to their underworld leaders.

Payments to *sokaiya* had been banned in 1982, and by 1984 their numbers had shrunk from 6,800 to 1,700. However, they still operated openly and could be found in the Tokyo phone book, even if payments to them now had to be disguised as research costs or fees for worthless publications. Alletzhauser recounted how Nomura would pay the *sokaiya* group Rondan Doyukai for valueless economic research to prevent disruption to its public meetings. He also described how Nomura manipulated the stockmarket and passed inside information to favoured clients to enable them to make a risk-free killing, and how Nomura would on occasion 'churn and burn' their clients' accounts (the practice of unnecessarily buying and selling shares to generate brokerage) to maximise their commission. Many of these practices would have been illegal in England, but they were at the time common currency among all the Japanese brokerage houses, of which Nomura had proved to be the most successful.

Alletzhauser explained how the structure of the Japanese stockmarket, and particularly of Nomura in that era, guaranteed profits. Profits from trading in stocks and bond issues were to be made available to favoured clients. Each Thursday at its *mokuyokai* meeting, Nomura would highlight the stocks it intended to push. With its 5 million clients, aggressive domestic branches and discretionary investment funds, price increases in these stocks were a self-fulfilling prophecy. The only variable was how early particular customers were granted access to the relevant information. There was also a selective release of price-sensitive information. Alletzhauser detailed, for example, the sales campaign run by Nomura in Asahi Chemical shares from April to June 1984. The share price had been 600 yen in April; by June, and after the announcement of a new cancer drug called TNF, it had soared to 1,000 yen. Alletzhauser also claimed that convertible bond issues enabled Nomura's special clients to purchase bonds at 100 yen in companies such as Mitsubishi Heavy Industries, which, by the time they were traded, would have painlessly reached a price of 225 yen by vigorous promotion of the bond.

When *The House of Nomura* was published in 1990, the de facto head of Nomura was its chairman, Setsuya Tabuchi, known as Big Tabuchi. Its president and ex-officio head, an unrelated Tabuchi, Yoshihisa Tabuchi, was known as Little Tabuchi. They decided to take action against the book, overriding the caution of London-based Nomura executives and of their London solicitors, Linklaters and Paines. Yoshihisa Tabuchi argued that if Nomura failed to react it would have been tantamount to admitting to the improper acts described in the book, such as releasing confidential information selectively, training its sales force to use aggressive tactics and paying money to gangsters, extremists and blackmailers to cover up illegal acts. Nomura therefore demanded the immediate withdrawal of the book, claiming that it had damaged the company's reputation. Nomura obviously imagined that, faced with the threat of being put out of business by the cost of the litigation, a small publishing house such as Bloomsbury would capitulate to such a potentially large claim.

Alletzhauser flew out to Tokyo to try to resolve the matter. He met Nomura's legal counsel, a man named Sori. Alletzhauser sensed trouble when Sori refused to bow or shake his hand – something unheard of in Japan. Instead Sori barked out his demands: 'You apologise. You withdraw book. You pay us damages.' This attempt to protect what was perceived to be Nomura's honour was a miscalculation. Alletzhauser was having none of it and he walked out of the room with the melodramatic words: 'Mr Sori, I have tried to be accommodating, but this is an attempt to destroy my family and me. I cannot tolerate this and from now on you are no longer the hunter, you are the hunted.'

Nomura seems to have been driven by a desire to control what could be written about it and to deter publication of the book in Japan, rather than by any real concern about damage to its reputation. A company of the power, size and advertising and PR clout of Nomura was well able to resist the slings and arrows of Alletzhauser and Bloomsbury. Accordingly, Nomura's London arm, Nomura Securities Co. Ltd, was ordered to sue the author and his publishers. The issue of proceedings merely served to attract far wider publicity for the book and to maintain its position in the UK bestsellers' list.

In another miscalculation the company used the blunderbuss approach to litigation. This involves confronting a less powerful opponent with a wide range of complaints which then have to be justified. It was a tactic subsequently followed, as we have seen, by the fast-food giant McDonald's, with disastrous consequences. It had the distinct disadvantage that it likewise enabled Alletzhauser and Bloomsbury to raise a very wide range of allegations of corporate misconduct. Nomura complained in their statement of claim that the book meant they had succumbed to the demands of gangsters, extortionists, blackmailers; that they had conspired with blackmailers to misuse shareholders' funds to make payments to blackmailers; that they habitually engaged in the practice of insider trading and the misuse of confidential information; that they were habitually rude, arrogant and irrational in the treatment of recruits; that they 'churned and burned' clients' funds; that they revealed inside information to favoured clients; that they manipulated the Japanese stockmarket for their own benefit and that their sales staff habitually gave advice to clients, regardless of whether it was in the clients' best interest, in order to maximise their own brokerage commission.

Nomura had completely underestimated the tenacity of its opponents. Bloomsbury and Alletzhauser counterclaimed for allegations that they had recklessly promoted the book as a serious story when it was nothing of the kind, and for false rumours allegedly circulated by Nomura about Alletzhauser. The defence and counterclaim ran to forty-five pages seeking to justify allegations of methods and illegal conduct ranging from payments to *sokaiya*, ramping shares and promoting what were known as campaign stocks, which enabled politicians to fund their election campaigns from the profits they had been allowed to make.

Alletzhauser and I travelled to Tokyo, Hong Kong and the United States to prepare the defence, which detailed penalties imposed on Nomura by the New York Stock Exchange and the Securities Exchange Commission and judgements obtained in Japan by shareholders against Nomura for churning their stock.

In response to Nomura's scattergun approach the defence raised issues about the bank's conduct in the United States and Brazil, and about its transactions regarding the Matsushita Electrical Industrial Company, Honda, Asahi Chemical and the Shokusan Mutual Housing Company.

A grim picture of working at Nomura was painted by the defendants. It was known as 7–11 – get in at 7am and leave at 11pm – or *heto heto* (work until you drop). Many of the stockbrokers lived in dormitories, where they were woken at 5.45am. Another nickname was 'Noruma Securities', *noruma* being the word for the quota its stock salesmen, the *kabuya*, had to achieve. At a meeting each morning the *sagami-kai*, members of the trading and sales team, would meet with other Nomura affiliates to decide the day's strategy. Once a stock had been chosen, the sales force would start trading it to drive up the price. Female employees were taught to bow by ex-Japan Airlines stewardesses: the formal 45-degree bow was replaced by a more businesslike 40 degrees, reduced to 30 for quick greetings and a mere 15 when passing superiors in the corridor. One salesman was accused in the defence of throwing things at people who did not perform adequately and of hitting them over the head when they did not reach their targets. (It was alleged that foreign trainees who arrived late at head office could find themselves lined up against a wall being hit on the head with a newspaper.) The defence suggested that the term *pero wo kiru*, 'writing tickets', meant churning stock to generate commission.

Nomura had then to submit themselves to the indignity of having to respond in writing in their thirty-six-page reply and defence to counterclaim, stating which of the allegations they admitted and which they denied. They admitted that in 1984 they had been ordered by the Tokyo District Court to pay a Mr Dhana Baines 17,042,239 yen (£84,397), effectively for churning his stock. They admitted that they had agreed to pay penalties imposed by the New York Stock Exchange and the Securities Exchange Commission, but said they had done so because of an honest difference of opinion between the NYSE and Nomura Securities Inc., and without conceding the facts alleged against them.

Indeed, Nomura denied any wrongdoing. It was, however, surprising that they should bring proceedings which would have enabled an English court to examine the large number of transactions that the defendants sought to question. Having failed to force Bloomsbury and Alletzhauser into submission, sound commercial sense prevailed, and in July 1992 Nomura dropped their claim for damages and had to pay their own legal costs. The expense of the action to Nomura was estimated at £2 million. They received no apology.

The case demonstrated the dangers of abrasive senior executives trying to muzzle their opponents and to litigate in foreign countries. It had, however, been costly to defend, and unfortunately that factor in itself serves as something of a deterrent to those intending to write about potentially litigious companies. Nomura may well have been taken aback by the ferocity of its prey's counter-attack. Alletzhauser moved the battle to Japan and acquired the distinction of becoming the first Westerner, in conjunction with a Japanese shareholder activist, to lay a criminal charge against a large Japanese company when he filed a complaint with the Ministry of Justice that Nomura had unlawfully pushed up the share price of Tokyu Corporation. Nomura was subsequently censured by the Ministry of Finance and subjected to severe financial penalties.

The Nomura case also brought into focus the question of whether it is proper to allow public companies an unfettered right to use their power and money to sue their critics for libel. As we have seen, county councils can no longer sue in the absence of proof of malice (Derbyshire County Council v. *The Sunday Times*). The Australian courts have expanded the law of qualified privilege to enable a great discussion of matters of public interest (ABC v. Lange) and this has to some extent been followed by the House of Lords in Reynolds v. Times Newspapers Limited (see Chapter 16). Even if English courts are unwilling to introduce such defences for claims against companies, it would be desirable to require a higher standard of proof of actual or likely damage to the firm. The damage likely to be done to a multibillion-dollar corporation like Nomura by Alletzhauser's book scarcely justified libel proceedings. As it was, the libel proceedings themselves resulted in damage to Nomura's reputation.

Major financial scandals in Japan spanning the events of many years were to expose Nomura's activities and provide powerful evidence that Alletzhauser had been on target. The company was able to exploit the assumption in English law that the plaintiff is of good reputation, and the fact that the burden of proving the truth of allegations rests on the defendant. The absence of any requirement to assert the falsity of what was written, or to verify on affidavit the truth of the facts underlying the complaints, makes it all too easy for a plaintiff like Nomura to bring a libel action which it must have realised was ill-conceived. At the forefront of Nomura's complaint was the suggestion that it protected favoured clients against losses and that it paid off the *sokaiya*.

In 1991 the Japan Securities Dealers' Association listed the 231 companies, public bodies and individuals who had received over $1 billion to cover stockmarket losses in the 1987 and 1989 crashes from four of the largest and best-known Japanese brokerage companies, one of which was Nomura. The true extent of Nomura's wrongdoing emerged when Susumu Ishii, head of the second largest *sokaiya* group, Inagawakai, who had retired on the grounds of ill health, was dying that year. He had become a client of Nomura Securities in 1986. In April 1989 he had borrowed 2 billion yen (£10.25 million) to help build up a 2 per cent stake of 27 million shares in a railway company, Tokyu Corporation – the company about which Alletzhauser had filed his criminal complaint. This coincided with the promotion of the stock by Nomura, and in a few weeks the price moved from 2,000 yen to 3,060. When Ishii was asked about the loan, he claimed it had been used to purchase membership certificates in a golf club. The club in question, however, was open to the public, and did not recognise private membership. Problems had arisen when the market fell and even gangsters had difficulties in maintaining the interest payments. Inagawakai members began to threaten Tokyu officials, demanding that the company buy back their shares at four times the price they had fallen to.

A criminal investigation was instituted by Nohuhiko Itsumo, director-general of the Japanese Ministry of Finance Securities Bureau, in September 1991. Article 54 of the securities and exchange law prohibited excessive recommendation of a particular stock. Nomura admitted it had excessively recommended Tokyu shares between October 1989 and January 1990. Its principal client for Tokyu shares had been the gangster Ishii.

However, Setsuya (Big) Tabuchi insisted that Nomura had not broken the law concerning stock manipulation. The investigation reached the same conclusion, and Nomura was exonerated from a charge of stock manipulation under Article 125. Big Tabuchi suffered the indignity of losing his position as vice-chairman of the Keidanren, Japan's powerful big-business lobby. Little Tabuchi likewise endured the humiliation of a rebuke from the minister of finance.

Big and Little Tabuchi both resigned to 'purify the company', but in May 1995 they both returned to the board. It was announced that in principle their diplomatic skills would be used exclusively abroad. In the meantime they had remained advisers to the company with no official executive control. Hideo Sakamaki, who had become president of Nomura, admitted: 'There was excessive business activity in the Tokyu shares, which almost doubled in price after a crime syndicate leader bought a stake in the company in 1989.' Nomura took out full-page advertisements in nine Japanese daily newspapers declaring: 'Following the recent brokerage scandal we have resolved to wipe clean all of our past errors,' and sent out letters to its 5 million customers apologising for its misdeeds. And along with fifteen other brokerage houses they acknowledged paybacks totalling $1.26 billion to nearly 600 favoured customers.

Such compensation was not then illegal in Japan, unless it

had been guaranteed in advance – brokers were forbidden by law to guarantee yields on investments. However, the Ministry of Finance had issued guidelines in 1989 to prevent such practices. Seventy-nine of Nomura's eighty-seven officers were suspended by the Ministry of Finance for one month, the remaining eight being suspended for six weeks. Nomura were estimated to have lost 3 billion yen (£15.37 million) in consequence. They were also banned by the Ministry of Finance from handling the offering of debt issues during November. Two senior board members resigned, and various senior executives took a 20 per cent pay cut for three months. The atmosphere of financial scandal was such that the finance minister, Ryutaro Hashimoto, felt compelled to resign.

No doubt these sorts of problems hit the best-ordered financial houses from time to time. It should also be remembered that most of these activities, though repellent to British eyes, were not illegal under Japanese law. These were not just isolated acts by overenthusiastic employees, and Nomura was not the only company behaving in this way: in the period 1987–9, twenty-one Japanese brokers had reimbursed a total of 173 billion yen (£887 million) to favoured corporate and individual clients for stock and bond investment losses, of which Nomura was responsible for in excess of 20 billion yen (£102 million). What was disgraceful was that Nomura had seen fit to launch a libel action complaining of those activities it was later to so cravenly admit to the Japanese Ministry of Finance.

As a consequence a number of changes were made to the law. Brokers were banned in 1991 from making discretionary transactions on behalf of clients, and in July 1992 the Securities and Exchange Surveillance Commission was established.

That was not, however, quite the end of the story. In its effort to distance itself from the scandals of the past, Nomura launched internal probes. In March 1997 it was discovered that two directors had made discretionary deals and funnelled the stock-trading profits to a corporate client run by a relative of a corporate racketeer. Nomura had in 1993 opened a brokerage

account for a *sokaiya* called Ryuichi Koike. The account was in
the name of a building company. It was a discretionary account,
an *eigyo tokkin*, which permitted orders to be placed without the
clients' specific approval – something which had been made illegal the previous year. The plan had been for hot share tips to be
passed to the account, the deals being recorded on handwritten
order forms rather than the normal computer printouts. But the
account was a disaster, and Nomura had to funnel profits of 370
million yen ($1.9 million) it had made on its own account to pay
off Koike's losses. Interestingly, the Japanese have a word for the
practice of reimbursing favoured clients' losses – *tobashi* (not, of
course, to be confused with Tabuchi). Nomura were found to
have 10,000 other so-called VIP accounts which received prefer-
ential treatment in share dealing.

Normura's headquarters and the homes of a number of senior
executives were searched. Three of their number were arrested
and fifteen left the firm. Leading companies excluded Nomura
from their underwriting arrangements. Three very senior officials
admitted in December 1997 at their trial in the Tokyo District
Court that they had violated the commercial code and securities
and exchange law. In July the Ministry of Finance had ordered
Nomura to halt stock-trading on its own account, including
stock options and index trading, from 6 August to 31 December.
In August, when the penalties took effect, Nomura's stock-trading volume dropped 30 per cent from the previous month.
However, it recovered by 37 per cent the following month, owing
to similar bans being applied to four other large brokerages.

In December 1997 Ryuichi Koike appeared at his trial in the
Tokyo District Court in handcuffs and with a rope around his
waist. He admitted that he had extorted tens of millions of dollars from Nomura as well as other leading brokerage houses
Daiwa, Nikko, Yamaichi and Dai-Ichi Kangyo Bank (DKB). He
had bought shares in these financial institutions so that he could
hold their company meetings to ransom. Three former executives
of Nomura Securities told the court they had paid Koike $3 mil-
lion in 1995.

The head of DKB, Miyazaki, hanged himself, while the president of Yamaichi, Shohei Nozawa, wept at a press conference and, bowing deeply, snivelled, 'We don't know how to ask the forgiveness of our customers, shareholders and other associates.' Yamaichi went bust a few months later in one of Japan's largest post-war bankruptcies.

Nomura's president, Hideo Sakamaki, having admitted making payments to the extortionists, resigned somewhat less emotionally. However, he remained an adviser to the company. The new president, Junichi Ujiie, admitted at a hearing at the Ministry of Finance that there had been illegal stock transactions for the *sokaiya* corporate racketeers and pledged: 'We will accept administrative penalties sincerely.' It was probably no coincidence that the prime minister at the time was Ryutaro Hashimoto, who must have experienced a particular schadenfreude at Nomura's discomfort, having been forced to resign as finance minister on account of the company's misdeeds.

The embarrassment to the company far exceeded anything Alletzhauser's book could have caused. It also had many salutary effects at Nomura. VIP accounts were abolished; a compliance officer was appointed to cultivate a 'culture of compliance', with some 222 general compliance officers to double-check. A whistle-blowing system to enable any irregularities to be reported was put in place. The scandals of Nomura are now a thing of the past, and under new management the company has resumed its position as a reputable and profitable securities company.

# 9

# THE HALCION
# NIGHTMARE

On 19 June 1988 Mrs Ilo Grundberg, a fifty-seven-year-old citizen of Hurricane, Utah, pumped nine bullets into the head of her mother, eighty-three-year-old Mildred Coats, while she was asleep in her trailer home. Unusually, Mrs Grundberg left a cheerful birthday card in her mother's hand. When the sheriff arrived, she handed him a written confession explaining: 'I didn't kill her because I didn't love her, I love her very much.' This was not a case of euthanasia, yet charges of second-degree murder were dropped when the prosecution was persuaded that Mrs Grundberg had been involuntarily intoxicated by the sleeping pill Halcion.

Mrs Grundberg sued Upjohn, the manufacturers of Halcion, for $6 million for compensatory and punitive damages, and her mother's estate claimed $15 million for the octogenarian's loss of life expectancy. Their complaint was that Halcion had made Mrs Grundberg psychotic and that Upjohn had wrongfully and wilfully misrepresented information to the American Food and Drugs Administration (FDA) about the known hazards and risks associated with the use of the drug. Upjohn got up to every trick in the book of litigation, even seeking (to no avail) to bar access on copyright grounds to information about their drug trials – a move which prompted District Judge Thomas Greene to comment: 'Upjohn intended to use copyright laws to thwart accessibility to the public of information . . . which may be offered into evidence in court proceedings.' But in July 1991 Upjohn settled with Mrs Grundberg for 'a substantial sum' on otherwise confidential terms. However, Upjohn's belief that it could put a lid on the facts about Halcion was to prove illusory.

At the time Halcion was sold in ninety countries and had annual sales of $240 million, of which $100 million were in the USA. In the 1980s it had become the most prescribed sleeping pill in the world, and it was Upjohn's second most profitable product. What had made the drug so popular was its short half-life – the time it takes for the concentration of the drug in the blood to fall to half. In other words, it reduced the hangover of drowsiness associated with many sleeping pills. However, it had a very chequered history. The first new drug application for it had been turned down in 1977, when the FDA ruled that the safety of Halcion had not been demonstrated. It was finally approved for sale in the USA in November 1982. In 1979 the *Lancet* published a letter from a Dr C. Van der Kroef setting out the alarming side-effects he had noted in connection with the drug since it had been licensed in Holland in 1977 in dosages of 0.25, 0.5 and 1 mg. His observations, based on 1,100 reports, recorded symptoms ranging from paranoid reactions, severe suicidal tendencies and hallucinations to restlessness and amnesia. These side-effects might have been tolerated in a cure for a life-threatening ailment, but in a sleeping pill they were extreme.

The Dutch Ministry of Health suspended Halcion for six months, announcing that it could be reregistered in August 1980 in dosages of 0.25 and 0.125 mg. In something approaching corporate sulking, Upjohn declined the offer. Yet in 1987 it discontinued production of the 1 mg tablet and by 1988 the 0.5 mg tablet had been withdrawn at the request of the French, German, Icelandic and Italian authorities. Halcion was finally reapproved in the Netherlands in dosages of 0.25 and 0.125 mg in 1990.

Mrs Grundberg's case had not been a quirkish claim brought by some wildly optimistic US plaintiff attorney. An analysis produced in the court proceedings was based on two years' examination of the data relating to Upjohn's drug trials by Professor Ian Oswald, a psychiatrist and emeritus professor of psychiatry at Edinburgh, who had thirty years' experience of studying sleep. Professor Oswald had been a thorn in Upjohn's corporate side for some years. In 1982 he had, with Dr Kevin Morgan, shown in the *British Medical Journal* that Halcion caused daytime anxiety. In 1986 Oswald and Dr Kirstie Adam had produced a report at the European Sleep Congress which indicated that Halcion in 0.5 mg doses caused anxiety and paranoid reactions. Upjohn had prevented this unwelcome report from being published in academic journals for three years.

Oswald's conclusion for the Grundberg case was not that Halcion had serious adverse psychiatric side-effects in all cases, but that it was capable of causing them, depending on the dose and the period over which the drug was taken. His earlier work played an important role in ensuring that Halcion was not sold in a dosage of over 0.5 mg, was not recommended for use for any longer than fourteen days (Mrs Grundberg had been taking it for thirteen months) and that proper warnings were given in the package inserts of the potential dangers of the pill.

The problems with Halcion had manifested themselves in tests conducted in 1972 on prisoners in Jackson Prison, south Michigan, who were attracted to take part by the chance to get out of their cells and by the pittance they were paid for being experimented upon. It was designed as a double-blind study, with twenty-eight prisoners taking 1 mg tablets of Halcion and nineteen taking a placebo for forty-two days. Neither the prisoners nor those in charge were meant to know who was taking Halcion and who the placebo. Professor Oswald discovered that the results were incorrectly reported, giving the erroneous impression that Halcion was no more likely than a placebo to

cause paranoia, and that a misleading summary of the results
had been prepared by Upjohn.

Oswald established that seven out of the twenty-eight prisoners taking Halcion had shown signs of paranoia. Upjohn reported
only two. Upjohn claimed that two of the nineteen taking the
placebo showed signs of paranoia. Oswald found that only one
did. His analysis reflected that of Dr Van der Kroef in Holland.
The numbers were not that great, but the significance was enormous.

So the evidence had been there in 1972 to show that the drug
could cause nervousness, memory lapses, depression and paranoid reactions. Upjohn claimed that errors which resulted in
some of the side-effects being wrongly attributed to placebo
patients, and the failure to record some of the symptoms, were
purely accidental, having been caused by tabulation errors when
one of their employees was interrupted in the course of his work.

A 1991–2 FDA investigation, conducted at a time when the
FDA had ranked Halcion number 1 in the list of 329 prescription
drugs reported in association with hostile behaviour, had been
discontinued after four months. However the FDA decided to
reinvestigate Halcion in 1994. Reviewing the matter, the FDA
described Upjohn's excuse of 'transcription errors' in the 1972
tests as false and misleading. Upjohn had been well aware of the
threat from the FDA. Indeed one of their employees had noted in
1983 in a memorandum: 'If my sources are anywhere near correct, the FDA will never approve Halcion without tremendous
pressure. We have the people willing to exert the pressure, but we
must orchestrate it.'

It was unfortunate for Oswald that the findings of the FDA's
first investigation were not released until the end of his subsequent trial for libel in April 1994 – and were not accepted into
evidence. The agency concluded then that there was at minimum
a gross and seminal failure to properly tabulate the data.
Although it was not able to determine to a high degree of certainty that the omissions in the final report for the Jackson
Prison Study (Protocol 321) were intentional, the FDA's review of

the documents and interviews with the people involved indicated that there was an awareness of the Study 321 adverse effects. One of the prisoners who had participated in Protocol 321 had set fire to his bed in the course of the tests. In a *Panorama* documentary in 1991 he said: 'Half the guys started to have after-effects and then they didn't know . . . their friend, they didn't know the person that they are most close to.'

On 24 August 1991, in the wake of the Grundberg settlement, Oswald wrote to the *Lancet* explaining his findings in the case. On 2 October the licence for Halcion in the UK was suspended by the Committee on Safety of Medicines on the basis that it had been given incomplete information on the adverse effects and withdrawals from the clinical trials in the original product licence application. On 9 June 1993 health minister Dr Brian Mawhinney finally revoked the licences. Thirteen countries were to suspend sales of Halcion following the British regulatory action. The damage caused to Upjohn by the ban was severe. From the launch of the product in 1978 to 1991, in the UK 674 million Halcion tablets had been sold, and in 1990 alone 1.7 million prescriptions for it had been written. By 1992 the drug was in crisis. In the first nine months of the year, sales of Halcion had declined by $83 million (45 per cent) over the previous year.

The *New York Times* reported the outcome of the Grundberg case on 20 January 1992 under the headline 'MAKER OF SLEEPING PILL HID DATA ON SIDE EFFECTS, RESEARCHERS SAY'. Professor Oswald was quoted as saying: 'I have concluded that the whole thing has been one long fraud. Upjohn have known about the extent of Halcion's adverse effects for over twenty years and have concealed those truths from the world.'

By this time Oswald had become an expert witness in the trial in Missouri of Nila Wacaser, who had killed her children and who claimed that the balance of her mind had been affected by Halcion. Mrs Wacaser was convicted of murder at her retrial and committed suicide before she was sentenced. Oswald was also the expert in the Alfano case in Ohio, where the suicidal tendencies of a man who had stabbed himself to death were

alleged to have been brought about by Halcion. With his articles
about the dangers of Halcion, and his status as an expert witness
about the drug, Oswald had consolidated his role as Upjohn's
*bête noire.*

The decision to sue Oswald seems curiously to have been
taken by the appropriately named Upjohn Business Strategy
Group a month *before* the *New York Times* interview was published. However, this article seems to have been the *casus belli.*
Oswald was later to deny using the words attributed to him,
claiming they were a synthesis of the allegations and counter-
allegations being made by both sides. However, as he admitted
the remainder of the interview, and as the words imputed to him
were not far from his views of Upjohn's conduct, the judge at the
subsequent libel trial held that on the balance of probabilities he
had spoken those words. Thereafter what should have been an
issue about the extent of Upjohn's knowledge of the ill effects of
Halcion unfortunately became an issue of whether or not Upjohn
was guilty of fraud.

What was remarkable in this case was the use made by Upjohn
of the law of libel, and in this regard the jurisdictional basis for
Upjohn bringing such a claim was questionable. Oswald, by now
a retired professor living in Scotland, was sued in England for
remarks reported in the *New York Times* about a Kalamazoo-
based company in relation to an American piece of litigation.
The case was allowed to proceed on the flimsy grounds that
Upjohn had a small English subsidiary in Crawley; that 100
copies of the 1,200,000 print run of the *New York Times* were
sold in England – presumably mostly to Americans working or
on holiday in the UK – that the comments had been picked up by
the *International Herald Tribune*, which had a large sale in
England; and that they were similar to remarks made by Oswald
on the *Panorama* programme 'The Halcion Nightmare', broadcast
on 14 October 1991.

It was wholly oppressive that Upjohn was permitted to bring
such an action in English as opposed to American courts. In the
principled stand which characterised its actions, Upjohn did not

sue the *New York Times* or the *International Herald Tribune*, which had published Oswald's opinions to their readers, preferring the softer target of a retired Scottish professor. It placed on Oswald the burden of proving words he disputed having spoken in the first place. Upjohn did not have to prove actual damage as a result of the sale of these 100 copies of the *New York Times*. The only viable defence for Oswald was one of justification. The fact that there were issues of the utmost public interest – was this drug safe and fit for sale, and the work done by Oswald to make it safer – was not itself a defence.

Upjohn's action was a deplorable case of forum-shopping – a classic example of how a rich and powerful company can exploit the English law of libel. Upjohn sued *Panorama* after weighing up the business implications; it did not, however, have sufficient courage of its convictions to sue the American television company CBS, which repeated the allegations on its *60 Minutes* programme in the USA, nor the ABC programme *20/20*. Instead it contented itself with attacking *60 Minutes* as 'poor entertainment and even poorer journalism'.

Upjohn's internal memoranda on the decision to sue were interesting. One example read:

We are not in the position to assess the legal ramifications of such action, but we can assess the *business* ramifications. The strong message we had received from our physician thought leaders and consultants is that the Upjohn company appears unwilling to defend Halcion in the medical or public arena. This image was exacerbated by settlement of the Grundberg case. Initiation of legal action would publicise our intent to defend Halcion against unjust action. The message would encourage both thought leaders and primary care physicians to continue writing Halcion prescriptions.

Presumably Upjohn reached this view on the basis of Oswald's comments on *Panorama*. A Halcion strategy memorandum of 4

December 1991, the month before the *New York Times* article was published, showed that the company was for this reason contemplating an action against Dr Oswald, Professor Anthony Kales, another interviewed expert critical of the drug, *Panorama* reporter Tom Mangold and the BBC. However, in the event it was Royston Drucker, vice-president of Upjohn's Division of Medical Affairs, and not the company itself, who sued Oswald for what he had said on *Panorama*. And Upjohn did not stop at suing for libel. It set about libelling Oswald at the same time. It accused him of practising junk science and of being influenced by the fees he had been paid in the Grundberg case – allegations firmly rejected by the trial judge, Mr Justice May.

The trial, which took place in 1994, proved to be one of massive proportions. The particulars of justification ranged over the events of twenty-two years; the oral hearings lasted sixty-two days and would, but for a very strict timetable laid down by the judge, have lasted for the best part of a year. The exhibits ran to over 36,000 pages. There were so many witnesses that the judge observed he had not counted them. Upjohn had an additional advantage: since most of their witnesses were living abroad they had the option of deciding whether or not to produce those witnesses in court to give oral testimony and be cross-examined, or whether to simply produce their written evidence, which could not be questioned. It was a privilege they would not have enjoyed if those witnesses had lived in England.

Upjohn's legal tactics were honed by a United States law firm renowned for its successful defence of tobacco suits. It is a moot point whether the tobacco companies have learned from the drug companies how to fight product liability cases or vice versa. Whatever the case, there were obvious advantages for Upjohn in discrediting Oswald. It was, in fact, what the company had been doing for over a decade. One of Upjohn's hired hands had dismissed the Oswald and Morgan 1982 paper as 'crap' and one of their employees had called it 'sensational, unsubstantial and unscientific speculation'. Mr Justice May found that Upjohn had, over a period of three years, been striving behind the scenes to discourage the *New England Journal of Medicine*, the *Archives of General Psychiatry* and the *Journal of Psychiatric Research* from publishing Oswald and Adam's 1986 paper on Halcion. 'So far we have been successful in having it stop,' wrote Dr Robert Straw of Upjohn, his grammar flying out of the window in his excitement.

Somewhere along the line the distinction between the obligation of a pharmaceutical company to look after the health of its customers and the pursuit of its commercial interests had become blurred and Upjohn had ended up believing its own propaganda. Central nervous system (CNS) products represented the major source of Upjohn's profits. As these products came under attack, Upjohn established its CNS Product Support Committee in 1983. A Halcion Defense Group was set up. As the FDA noted, employees who criticised Halcion left under a 'special contract', Upjohn-speak for early retirement. Dr William Barry, director of worldwide drug experience, was not destined to remain at the company for long when he wrote a memo in September 1989 – the time of a FDA Psychopharmacological Drugs Advisory Committee (PDAC) meeting to review the effects of Halcion – headed 'Borderline Personality Disorder Patients'. Under the subheading 'Action', he recommended 'clear and adequate warning in the package that paranoia and disinhibition can occur and that dyscontrol in patients with underlying borderline disorders may result in aggressive and anti-social behaviour'. Precisely Oswald's point. Barry was present at the PDAC meeting but not invited to speak. He left Upjohn shortly afterwards. Mr Justice May, however, held that the evidence did not suggest that Barry should have spoken, or that he was prevented from speaking when he was bursting to do so. Given that Barry had given a chilling account of the machinations of Upjohn to the FDA, not surprisingly, Upjohn did not call him as a witness at the libel trial, so the court was never able to discover why he had left the company. The view of the FDA, which perhaps had its ear a little closer to the ground, seems more sceptical.

Upjohn also sued the BBC and reporter Tom Mangold for libel

in the *Panorama* programme. Interestingly, Professor Anthony Kales had made many of the same points as Oswald had about Upjohn on *Panorama*. Yet he was not sued – an indication, perhaps, that Oswald was the target. Kales had highlighted some major disadvantages of Halcion, such as amnesia and brain impairments including paranoia and hallucinations. Upjohn, a company committed to the Association of the British Pharmaceutical Industry practice that the clinical and scientific opinions of members of the health profession should not be disparaged, nevertheless saw fit to condemn Professor Kales as having made a career out of attacking Halcion. On 16 December 1991, the company had issued a press release accusing Kales of 'passing himself off as an expert on Halcion'.

In his *Panorama* interview Oswald had been highly critical of Royston Drucker, the vice-president of Upjohn's Division of Medical Affairs, who had told the 1989 PDAC meeting: 'I would also reassure you that there is no information available to the Upjohn company, outside of this meeting, that would tend to substantiate [the early warning] signal[s] about Halcion. It is my personal belief as a physician, and the belief of Upjohn company, that Halcion is a safe and effective hypnotic.' Oswald accused him of lying. He claimed that as Drucker was speaking on behalf of the Upjohn company, he must have been aware of research such as the papers of Morgan and Oswald, Adam and Oswald and Professors Bayer and Pathy. Drucker explained that he had had no dealings with Halcion before January 1988. Surprisingly, as of September 1989 he had not heard of the flawed test at Jackson Prison. He had been referring to the epidemiological data, not all the scientific papers which had been published. He evidently did not consider the published material hostile to Halcion relevant to that point, and nor were the memoranda that he had very recently received about Oswald's findings. He believed what he was saying was true, and had not made the statement dishonestly knowing it to be false. Mr Justice May accepted that Drucker's evidence was honest.

It was regrettable that the veracity of Drucker was attacked. He was, however, there as a representative of Upjohn, and this criticism was made in the context of a serious scientific debate. Drucker said he had personally taken the decision to sue Oswald, but his legal bills were picked up by Upjohn. Interestingly, he did not sue the BBC as well. Mr Justice May noted that many of Drucker's answers were circumlocutory, long and in part evasive, and that he was on occasions agitated and concerned when giving evidence. He had also, in the judge's view, been well rehearsed to answer the precise question only and to give nothing unnecessary away. Yet he had given many frank answers in circumstances where frankness could readily have been avoided. The judge decided that Drucker had been libelled and awarded him the somewhat high figure – for a man who lived in the USA – of £75,000.

The judge had accepted that it was no part of the trial to decide whether Halcion was a safe and effective hypnotic, taking the view that it was for the regulatory agencies to decide between the conflicting expert opinions on the safety of the drug. In 1994, after its first investigation, the FDA concluded that Upjohn had attempted to minimise post-marketing surveillance reports of adverse effects made in a 1989 meeting with them, and that the company had supplied incomplete information to the members of the conference to influence the conclusions reached. Even so, they were initially doubtful that the facts withheld would have been material to the technicalities of the new drug approval process (though the Halcion task force in May 1996 subsequently concluded that the errors in Protocol 321 should have been considered material).

Unfortunately, Mr Justice May felt unable to pay much, if any, heed to the conclusions of the FDA on matters which he felt he had to decide. It might be thought that the agency was better equipped to do so. So the position was somewhat curious. It underlined the unsuitability of the English law of libel to decide the serious issues arising out of this case. Everything turned on the minutiae of the words believed to have been spoken, and on the question of whether allegations about state of mind had been proved to the high standard required by English law. Upjohn, not having to prove damage to its reputation, or to face a qualified privilege defence based on Oswald's duty to raise matters of legitimate public interest, was able to use the law of libel as a blunt instrument with which to batter him. As it was, Oswald's defence would fail unless he could in effect prove fraud.

The judge's rulings on meaning resulted in Oswald having to prove that Upjohn had for twenty years deliberately and fraudulently concealed from the FDA data adverse to Halcion, and that Upjohn had deliberately concealed the drug's side-effects from Protocol 321 in 1972. Mr Justice May similarly ruled that the BBC had to prove that Upjohn had known since Protocol 321 that Halcion gave rise to the most unusual and disturbing reactions; that the company had continued, despite this knowledge, to deny there was anything wrong with Halcion; that Upjohn's public statements following Van der Kroef's revelations were dishonest; that Upjohn, through Drucker, had lied at the 1989 PDAC meeting, and that the symptoms reported by individual prisoners in Protocol 321 were intentionally left out of the report. This imposed a very heavy burden on Oswald and the BBC, and the lack of a public interest defence gave Upjohn an enormous advantage.

Mr Justice May found that the summary of Protocol 321 was misleading and that the British Medicines Control Agency had reached the same conclusion in 1991. But he decided there was no dishonesty. He felt that it was rather a grey area – a situation where someone is genuinely trying to present in its best light a case in which he believes, but in doing so produces material which the judgement of hindsight considers to be less than frank. Upjohn, in the judge's view, had not been guilty of the deliberate concealment of serious side-effects to Halcion known to them from the trials going back to 1972.

The FDA in 1994 was more censorious. It reported that 30 per cent of the serious adverse reactions which had been known to senior management had not been reported to the FDA in the Protocol 321 submission. Handwritten corrections to the original tabulations were omitted in the final report. Responsible management *was* aware of serious side-effects, which included confusion, amnesia, agitation, hallucinations and bizarre behaviour. The clinical investigator conducting the study had felt that the 1 mg dose was too high. Yet Upjohn had sought approval of the 1 mg dose, even though there was an awareness that at this level the drug caused serious side-effects in a significant number of cases. Approval for long-term use was sought even though the evidence at hand suggested that taking the drug for longer than fourteen days was potentially dangerous. The FDA had unearthed an internal Upjohn memorandum suggesting that data from some studies (Protocols 6045, 6047 and 6065) should be omitted in the interests of gaining approval for Halcion for treatments of more than fourteen days, noting, 'A fourteen-day limit could reduce projected sales by 50 per cent over a ten-year period.' Upjohn's claims that the use of Protocol 6045, which had been conducted by a disqualified investigator, had had no effect on conclusions as to safety and efficacy were condemned by the FDA as false and misleading.

The FDA observed that this was perhaps the most incriminating evidence, because it showed that the company chose to disregard the potential harm of inappropriate use in order to maximise sales. It concluded: 'It appears that Upjohn misrepresented the data in order to persuade the FDA reviewers to waive the proposed fourteen-day duration of use limit.' The only caution statement regarding usage in the original package insert was the advice: 'It is recommended that Halcion is not prescribed in quantities exceeding a month's supply.'

The FDA also reported that Upjohn had taken no corrective action after reports of numerous reactions at the 1 mg level in the Low Countries, and had supplied incomplete and inaccurate information in response to inquiries from the French and Japanese government drug agencies. While Upjohn reported 'thorough and exhaustive' reanalysis of data to both the Dutch Ministry of Health and the FDA after receiving reports of adverse effects, they were actually engaged in attempts to discredit the reports and did not conduct a reanalysis. The FDA criticised

attempts to discredit reports by Oswald, to prevent publication of
a hostile article by him in the *New England Journal of Medicine*,
and to provide flawed, misleading data to a Boston study group.
It appeared that it was not until the examination by Oswald in
1991 of the original case report forms in the Jackson Prison
research that Upjohn's lawyers discovered the errors which had
been made.

Mr Justice May considered that Oswald's case was overloaded
with hindsight and his judgement of people and their intentions
and motives was seriously awry. He rejected Oswald's argument
that dishonesty was a corporate culture within the manufacturing company. He accepted that Upjohn was convinced that
Halcion was a safe and effective hypnotic. He considered that the
view of the earlier trials of the 1970s, when drug-testing trials
had been in their infancy, had been distorted by the application
of the standards of the 1990s. The judge seems to have been
impressed by the evidence of Ley Smith, Upjohn's president, who
said that in normal circumstances Upjohn would not contemplate
suing a physician and that the company had absolutely no objection to the free exchange of proper scientific research and views.

At the trial Smith was asked about the documents which had
emerged as a result of the libel action, including a memorandum
dated 23 August 1991 which read: 'There are some real concerns
because of some manipulation of data by one of our people
and . . . the involvement of this individual in other product submissions.' He replied: 'I think manipulation of data is a bad
choice of words.' Smith complained that Oswald's conduct since
1989 had amounted to an unrelenting and increasingly virulent
campaign against Upjohn. Clearly the judge was unimpressed by
the making and subsequent withdrawal by Oswald of allegations of fraud in relation to another test, Protocol 6048, when
Upjohn's explanation of what had appeared to be altered sample
numbering, resulting in distorted results, was finally produced.

The nearest the judge came to looking at whether the action
against Oswald was, in US parlance, a 'slapp suit' – that is to say
an action designed to knock out your opponent – was in his

consideration of how Upjohn behaved in relation to Van der Kroef. One of Upjohn's employees had written in the appropriately named Halcion Crisis File, 'We must stop further publication by Van der Kroef in major journals. We must expose the Dutch regulatory action and bring their motives under intense scrutiny and criticism. We must learn everything possible about Van der Kroef and be prepared to use the evidence. It should be clear that someone is going to get hurt and this is going to be a long tough battle.' The judge tamely observed that this was strong stuff and could be seen in a poor light as an expression of commercial ethic. However, acting within the constraints of the trial imposed on him by his ruling on the meaning of the article, he did not consider it was material which justified what he decided Oswald had said.

Mr Justice May awarded Upjohn £60,000 against the BBC and £25,000 against Oswald.

By having embroiled the retired Professor Oswald in years of litigation, Upjohn had effectively silenced one of its most knowledgeable critics. Nevertheless the evidence of other experts was there for all to see. In addition to the testimony of Professor Anthony Kales, Graham Dukes, professor of drug study policies at the University of Groningen, stated that it was his regretful conclusion that it was not credible that Upjohn's errors could have been accidental. At the trial the judge found his evidence impressive and, subject to the fact that he held committed opinions about Halcion, balanced. Professor Frank Ayd, clinical professor of psychiatry at West Virginia University, and the man invited by Upjohn to set up a Boston symposium to send out the message that the Dutch findings about Halcion were misguided, said that it was now his opinion that Halcion should be withdrawn from the market. Reducing the dose had not totally eliminated side-effects, and even some patients on 0.125 mg doses could experience some reactions. He felt he had been misled by Upjohn regarding the information available about Halcion in September 1979. It had not been until 1991 that he had learned about Protocol 321. The judge observed: 'I do consider there was no more impressive witness in this case than Dr Ayd. His evidence was notable for its true impartiality.'

Oswald's case had also been supported by Professors McGuffin and Pathy and Dr Davidson. Upjohn had had its own very distinguished experts, including Sir Martin Roth, Dr Nutt and Dr Greenblatt. But their case would have had greater intellectual respectability if Upjohn had not embarked on a campaign of denigrating their opponents and had left the discussion of Halcion as a subject of scientific debate.

It was the libelling of Oswald, which gave rise to his counter-claim, that revealed what sort of a company Upjohn was. The judge ruled that they had to prove that Oswald had brought false and reckless charges against them about Halcion for questionable motives, that he had deprived millions of people of a safe, effective and well-tolerated sleeping medicine, that he practised 'junk science' and that, as a result of the fees he was paid for the Grundberg case, he was biased and partisan. The judge held that it was absurd to suggest that Oswald's findings were influenced by his fees. He found that Upjohn had, in 1987, been striving behind the scenes to discourage publication of Adam and Oswald's paper. This, he felt, was unacceptable, and the public would not expect a pharmaceutical company to suppress adverse reports about their product. The evidence established that Adam and Oswald were entitled to hold a place in the literature about the drug and deserved proper consideration.

Objectively, he ruled, no fair-minded person could have described Oswald's work in the Grundberg case, let alone his other work, as 'junk science'. In publishing this allegation Upjohn had, he held, published untrue, defamatory material recklessly, without considering or caring whether it was true or not. Although in June 1991 Upjohn had been fined $600,000 in relation to false records of drugs given to doctors for marketing purposes, he was not persuaded that they had a general bad reputation in the country. The judge refuted the allegations of dishonesty against Upjohn in relation to the serious errors

and omissions in the reporting of Protocol 321. He awarded
Oswald £50,000 in respect of the libels of him by Upjohn.

Mr Justice May found that Upjohn were at the very least reckless in relation to the use of disqualified investigators in a
number of the pivotal studies to establish the safety of Halcion
(Protocols 6041 and 6045 and 6415). Upjohn had used three doctors subsequently disqualified, Franklin, Sanguily and Fuerst.
The company was, the judge held, aware by 1989 of the fact that
they had employed a disqualified doctor, Fuerst, in Protocol
6415. Yet they had submitted this protocol to the Medicines
Control Agency in September 1991, when it was investigating
the safety of Halcion as a result of the Grundberg case. The use
of a disqualified investigator was disclosed to the MCA only
after Dr Straw of Upjohn, who had personally considered the
effects of Fuerst's disqualification in 1984, had, deliberately, in
the judge's view, relied on Protocol 6415 in his *Panorama* interview, only to be reminded by reporter Tom Mangold that
Protocol 6415 was invalidated for this reason. Upjohn's handling of these investigators was considered by the judge to be
thoroughly discreditable. It was scarcely credible that Upjohn,
and especially Dr Straw, had overlooked, even in the heat of the
moment in 1991, the fact that Dr Fuerst had been disqualified.
Upjohn's damages, which were seemingly high for a corporate
plaintiff, should, the judge ruled, be significantly reduced as a
result of their conduct in this matter. Unethical product support
and discrediting science did not do much, in the judge's view, to
take the sting out of allegations that Upjohn deliberately concealed known adverse data, but he did take them into account.
These findings underlined that this was always high-risk litigation for Upjohn, and a case in which the likelihood of such
findings made the advantages of suing Oswald questionable.

It was litigation which Upjohn were unwise to have brought
for another reason, too. They had to disclose thousands of pages
of documents which now came into the public domain, having
previously been successfully bound up in confidentiality orders
in the United States. It meant that plaintiffs in product liability

suits against Upjohn could order transcripts of the evidence in the Oswald case and could pinpoint documents which could help establish the claims they were making against Halcion. Indeed, Upjohn settled a number of cases against such plaintiffs in the USA in the wake of the Oswald case.

Had the FDA report of April 1994 been available at the beginning of the trial, Oswald's minority voice in the wilderness might have rung somewhat louder and the case might have turned on questions of public interest rather than on arguments about fraud.

As the FDA report of 1994 stated, the FDA's own earlier investigator had been instructed to discontinue his investigations into Upjohn's testing of Halcion and their dealings with the agency. The Oswald litigation appears to have revived the FDA's interest in this aspect of the drug. A Halcion Task Force was established by the FDA, and in 1996 it recommended a Department of Justice investigation of Upjohn to find out whether any crimes had been committed when the company submitted faulty data in its application for approval of the sleeping pill. The FDA did not itself make any recommendation of criminal prosecution, but it noted that if the case had been referred to the Justice Department during the FDA's probe from December 1991 to March 1992, additional information might have been obtained. The FDA had made a mistake in failing to make the referral to the Department of Justice earlier, although the task force did conclude that there was no indication of criminal conduct by any FDA employee in this regard.

The FDA felt that it had bungled its own inquiry into Halcion and had allowed bureaucratic in-fighting over scientific evidence to continue for five years without any resolution. The matter was referred to the US assistant district attorney in Michigan. No charges were preferred, but it was an inglorious end to what Upjohn must have hoped would be a worthwhile libel action in England. Nor did they succeed in bringing back Halcion to the market in the UK. In 1995, with no major drugs in development and slow sales growth, Upjohn merged its business with the Swedish company Pharmacia, a merger described as more of a collision than a combination of Swedish and American management styles and cultures – a marriage of US top-down and Swedish team-orientated management.

Although the findings of the FDA in April 1994 had no significant impact on the trial, the fact that we, as Oswald's lawyers, had been able to obtain the FDA report under the US Freedom of Information Act had clearly caused some concern to Upjohn. They complained to the FDA Office of Internal Affairs that the conduct of Dr Robert Young, a lawyer and doctor with the FDA and a signatory of the 1994 report as a representative of their Division of Scientific Investigations, demonstrated 'gross impropriety' and 'called into question his fairness and integrity'. It was suggested that he had assisted Oswald's lawyers but not those of Upjohn – allegations contested by Young. For his part, Young claims that his career suffered as a result of the investigations he carried out into Halcion. It all looked very familiar: attacking your enemy is the best form of product defence.

Young himself felt compelled to sue Upjohn for libel for allegations made in a letter written by an attorney acting for the company, a copy of which had been sent to the FDA's office of internal affairs by 'an unknown source'. Young was exonerated of any misconduct. His libel action was, however, rejected by the Maryland District Court on the basis that such a letter would be covered by absolute privilege. The reason given for this was that the letter was intended to put an end to the criminal investigation of Upjohn by providing information about errors or improprieties perpetrated by the FDA.

In December 1997 the FDA upheld an Institute of Medicine report which found Halcion safe when taken as recommended – 0.25 mg for seven to ten days – a far cry from the higher doses and longer periods Oswald had criticised. The FDA remained to be convinced about Halcion. More studies were needed of a lower starting dose and of long-term use. In spite of the recommendations, the average use of Halcion was still eighteen months, and short-term studies were probably not enough to judge safety and tolerance, it was suggested. Halcion had, however, been banned in five countries, including the UK, and there was an active Public Citizen's Health Research Group lobbying the FDA to take it off the market in the USA as well. In January 1999 the European Court of Justice disallowed Upjohn's challenge to the procedure the health authorities had followed in banning Halcion.

It was little short of a scandal that Upjohn was able to sue Oswald for libel in the UK and recover costs of over £1 million. If the claim belonged anywhere, it was in the USA, where virtually all the witnesses lived and where the FDA was based. Fortunately, Oswald was insured, although payment of the damages dented his pension fund. In many countries Professor Oswald might have received commendation for alerting the world health community to the dangers of the drug, particularly if taken in high dosage and over a long period of time. As a result of his ground-breaking research, the misleading research of Upjohn was exposed, sales of Halcion in dosages of 0.5 mg ceased and the recommended period was reduced by stages to seven to ten days. Yet the English court awarded Upjohn damages against Oswald and the BBC – a decision which must raise real questions about the ability of the law of libel to deal with such matters.

# 10

# VIRGIN LIBEL

Unlike the wealthy businessmen who have used their power to try to suppress hostile criticism and to prop up a reputation they scarcely deserve, entrepreneur Richard Branson, head of the Virgin empire, has used the law of libel selectively, with calculation and to great commercial effect. In his litigation against British Airways and the lottery giant GTech he put his opponents to the sword and derived a considerable advantage from doing so. Although these two actions arose in different circumstances, there were striking similarities in Branson's approach to each case – and in the consequences for the losers.

## British Airways

In June 1984, Branson's airline, Virgin Atlantic, started a service between the UK and America. Initially, Lord King, the chairman of Britain's national carrier, British Airways, underestimated Branson. 'If Richard Branson had worn a pair of steel-rimmed glasses and a double-breasted suit and shaved off his beard I would have taken him seriously,' he remarked. 'As it was, I couldn't.' But BA soon noticed the success and profitability of the Virgin operation and the popularity of its Upper Class service. Already making inroads into BA's business, Virgin were seeking a foothold in Britain's principal airport, Heathrow, and planning to launch a competing service on BA's profitable Tokyo route. BA wanted to know how Branson was succeeding so well and how he could be stopped. No longer could he be dismissed by the BA chairman as 'the grinning pullover': now the suits at BA decided that the threat he posed had to be taken seriously.

The methods BA chose to counter this threat were to lead to accusations of paranoia, hostile campaigns in the press and dirty tricks. The paranoia was allegedly manifested in the launch of Operation Covent Garden, which involved hiring private detectives – who were, on occasions, billing BA £15,000 a week – to discover what was behind Branson's publicity blitz against BA. BA were convinced that there was a mole within their company who was leaking confidential information to Branson, and that he was himself using private detective agencies to get hold of their commercial secrets. These fears were exacerbated in March 1992, when Branson returned to Sir Colin Marshall, chief executive and deputy chairman of BA, a tape which had been sent to him anonymously. This was a recording of a discussion between Marshall and another director, Robert Ayling, about their problem with Virgin. It prompted BA to try to place a story with Frank Kane of the *Sunday Telegraph* alleging that Virgin was bugging BA's phones.

In Operation Barbara, so called because all this talk of virgins had apparently conjured up Barbara Cartland in the minds of their senior executives, BA hired the services of a leading financial PR consultant, Brian Basham of Warwick Corporate, to produce, at a cost of £46,000, a report on the threat posed by Virgin. There was public-relations-inspired badmouthing of Virgin in the financial press as a series of unfavourable articles were fed to receptive journalists. On 31 March 1991, The *Sunday Telegraph* published a piece headed: 'VIRGIN HEADING FOR STORMY SKIES', speculating about Branson's ability to finance his expansion. On 2 October, the *Guardian* asked: 'Will Richard Branson's balloon burst? Behind the man with the Midas touch there is a picture of a highly indebted and not very profitable conglomerate.' Rumours also started to circulate about Virgin being unable to pay for their fuel at Heathrow.

These reports on the state of Virgin's finances bore such noticeable similarities to one another that Branson suspected a concerted campaign. His suspicions were well founded. On 24 October, one of Brian Basham's calls was to Chris Hutchins, a columnist for *Today*. This was followed by a meeting at Basham's house, which was secretly taped. Speaking, unbeknownst to him, into Hutchins' microphone, but asking as a precaution, 'I take it that this is all just between the two of us?', Basham warned that he and BA must not be associated with any story run in *Today* as a result of their conversation. He mentioned that Branson was now getting Japanese investors, asserting that this was a dangerous way to operate, though all right so long as one's reputation was intact. He then turned unambiguously to Branson's ownership of the gay nightclub Heaven. This was a dangerous activity for a serious businessman. There was, Basham alleged, a huge heap of rubbish outside the British Aerospace office in the Strand which backed on to Heaven. The council refused to touch it for fear of AIDS-infected hypodermic syringes. There was a danger, he suggested, of the club being raided and of charges being brought. Virgin was a dicky business, Basham claimed, changing tack; it was appallingly run and risked going bust. One day one of its planes was going to fall out of the sky. *Today* decided not to publish the story. Indeed, the call turned out to be a bad move by Basham, because Hutchins' tape ended up with sound-enhancers at Virgin's Town House Studios.

As part of BA's so-called dirty tricks, another Barbara was brought into play. This was BABS, the acronym for BA's booking system, which included its computer reservations system, CRS. This held details not only of BA's bookings but also those of other airlines. BA had agreed that the bookings of other airlines would remain confidential, but now Branson accused BA of hacking into Virgin's computerised departure control system (DCS) to find out how much they were making on each flight and which of their ticket deals and marketing strategies were working. Some of this information would be released six months later by the Civil Aviation Authority, but BA, Branson claimed, wanted immediate access to it so that they could establish the load factor and target potential Virgin customers in the meantime.

Using this information, BA was said to have assembled a selling team of seventeen staff to offer upgrades and limousine services to existing and prospective Virgin customers. Apparently, such was BA's enthusiasm for their task that when one of their own lawyers booked with Virgin to fly to New York, he was offered an upgrade to change to BA. 'Do you know who I am? I'm BA's bloody lawyer, and you are not supposed to be doing this sort of thing,' he berated the caller. Branson discovered later that Virgin passengers were also being told by BA agents that Virgin services were cancelled, and being offered BA flights instead. Another complaint was that BA refused to handle long-haul Virgin passengers seeking connections via BA flights to other European destinations.

Branson launched a counter-attack in the press. On 3 November 1991, *The Sunday Times* published a report headed: 'BRANSON ATTACKS BA TRICKS'. But the bad publicity against Virgin had been highly damaging. As Basham pointed out, many of Branson's predecessors, such as Laker, British Caledonian and Air Europe, had failed. Even if false, the stories about him having to pay for his fuel in cash could become self-fulfilling prophecies. If this happened, with fuel representing 20 per cent of Virgin's running costs, cashflow could be badly affected. Lloyds Bank were showing signs of nervousness about Virgin's £55 million overdraft and Salomons were finding it difficult to raise £20 million on a sale of equity. Branson was now considering legal action, possible in the area of anti-competition law, an uncertain and lengthy procedure.

On 11 December he wrote an eleven-page open letter with an eight-page appendix to BA's non-executive directors, alleging that BA was orchestrating a dirty-tricks campaign against his airline, a campaign which included leaking damaging stories to newspapers, sharp sales and marketing practices and the use of private investigators against his business. The letter expressed dismay that British Airways could be associated with such disreputable activities. Sir Michael Angus replied that it was inappropriate for him and his fellow non-executive directors to respond. Sir Colin Marshall, the chief executive, told Branson that the allegations were without foundation. 'Would it not be better if you were to devote your undoubted energies to more constructive purposes?' It was wholly without foundation and unjustified, he said, to suggest that BA was involved in a deliberate campaign to damage Virgin's business, or that it sought to compete other than through normal promotional efforts. Branson's motive, he suggested, was to secure publicity.

A Thames Television programme, 'Violating Virgin', produced by Martyn Gregory and broadcast on *This Week* on 27 February 1992, aired Branson's allegations of dirty tricks. BA declined to appear on the programme, responding instead in *BA News*, their staff newspaper, which had a circulation of 50,000 worldwide, with an article headed: 'BRANSON'S DIRTY TRICKS CLAIM UNFOUNDED'. This accused Branson of stirring up controversy with BA to create publicity for himself and his company and to inflict serious damage on the reputation of BA, and of inventing the allegations. Lord King replied in similar vein to television viewers who wrote to *BA News* complaining about the company's conduct.

The libel was spotted by Virgin's director of corporate affairs, Will Whitehorn, when he picked up a copy of *BA News* at Gatwick. It was difficult to see what further damage could be said to have been done to Branson and Virgin by the repetition of these well-aired allegations in a piece commenting on the television programme in a staff newspaper. However, the libellous words gave Branson a weapon with which to retaliate. Attempts to obtain an apology proved, not surprisingly, unproductive. BA and Lord King reacted by counter-suing Branson and Virgin for libel in the letters sent in December 1991 to the non-executive directors. It seems that the last straw for Branson was hearing in March 1992 that the *Sunday Telegraph* was planning to publish a story alleging that he had hired private detectives to spy on BA. He was able to persuade the newspaper that the story was false. Thus began what was described with some hyperbole as 'the mother of all libel battles' as writs were served on BA and Lord King. Any weakness in their reason for suing BA was, it was felt, removed by the discovery of BA's alleged malpractices, many of which had been unknown to Virgin when the litigation started.

Amid the publicity as the case was prepared for trial, witnesses came forward with first-hand accounts of BA's campaign against Virgin. One, Sadig Khalifa, gave evidence that Virgin's confidential computer data had been accessed by BA. He described how a special services unit had been set up under the reassuring cover of the Helpline section. When not pushing the halt and lame in wheelchairs to their planes, they were accessing BABS to obtain, in breach of the undertaking of confidentiality, the records of passenger names, which gave such personal details as their telephone numbers and booking records, and information about the splits as between upper class and economy.

Virgin received evidence from customers who said they had been targeted by BA. Marcia Borne now realised how it was that BA had come to ring when she had booked to fly Virgin to ask her why she was using that airline instead of BA. Yvonne Parsons now knew why she had received a number of calls telling her falsely that her Virgin flights were overbooked, or that some other booking error had occurred, which meant she could not take her flight as planned. Another customer had been telephoned the night before she was due to fly Virgin to Tokyo and offered an upgrade to first class, plus two free tickets to Paris, if she switched to BA.

Evidence was also obtained from Ronnie Thomas, director of limousine services at New York's John F. Kennedy Airport, who reported that passengers were being approached at the kerbside and offered better-class BA tickets and free flights in exchange for their Virgin tickets.

A former BA undercover man told Branson, who had been fixed up with a concealed microphone to record the conversation, about Operation Covent Garden. Another witness described how the records of Operation Covent Garden had been shredded. Had the trial actually taken place, George Carman QC had planned to open Virgin's case with the line: 'The "world's favourite airline" has a favourite pastime. It's called shredding documents which are liable to be misconstrued.'

Meanwhile, there was a degree of dissent in the BA camp. BA appeared to be blaming their public-relations consultant, Brian Basham, for the hostile and discreditable stories which had appeared in the press about Virgin. This was certainly not the way Basham remembered things. He was adamant that he had acted in accordance with his instructions throughout. He made the point that he had counselled caution in the opening sentence of his Operation Barbara Report, which began: 'There are certain misconceptions about Virgin.' Basham had been asked by BA to sign a thirty-four-page statement. Basham was not happy with this. He felt it gave the impression that he had orchestrated the campaign, and that others at BA who, in his view, had been involved were being exonerated. He eventually agreed to sign an alternative six-page statement.

The action was settled before the trial, on 11 January 1993. Among the weight of evidence against BA, it was that of Sadig Khalifa, relating to the BABS breach of confidentiality, that seems to have persuaded BA that they had to settle the case. On 7 December 1992, a month before the trial was due to start, on the advice of their solicitors, Linklaters and Paines, BA paid into court the enormous sum of £485,000 damages. The purpose of this was to protect BA's position on the costs of the action if Branson and Virgin recovered a lesser sum. After negotiation it was agreed that £500,000 should be paid to Branson personally and £110,000 to Virgin. Each member of Virgin Atlantic received £166 from Branson as a bonus as a result of the litigation. All the legal costs, which were said on each side to exceed £1 million, were to be paid by BA. A statement in open court was read, asserting: 'Both British Airways and Lord King apologise unreservedly for the injury caused to the reputation and feelings of Richard Branson and Virgin Atlantic for the article in *BA News* and letters written by Lord King which they published. In particular they wish to apologise for having attacked the good faith and integrity of Richard Branson'.

It was stressed that the directors of British Airways were not party to any concerted campaign against Richard Branson and Virgin Atlantic. The board accepted that Mr Branson did have reasonable grounds for concern, and it was therefore wrong to suggest otherwise. The regrettable conduct revealed by the investigation was confined to a relatively small number of unconnected incidents involving a very small number of employees. In the hyperbole of the case, this was described as 'the mother of all climbdowns' or, as the *Sun* headlined it, 'VIRGIN SCREWS BA', although doubtless their headline-writers would have preferred the opposite result. As BA had likewise attacked Thames TV's 'Violating Virgin' programme as 'a figment of the imagination', they also had to pay Martyn Gregory, as the programme's producer, £30,000 in damages in a separate action later in the year.

After the action was settled, Brian Basham retained his own QC, Patrick Milmo, to add a rider to the BA statement in open court that he 'did not accept that the references to him were an accurate summary of his actions on behalf of British Airways'. He made the point that he had tried to discourage BA from disparaging and circulating unsubstantiated rumours about Richard Branson and Virgin. He vigorously disputed the attempt by the board of BA to wash their hands of responsibility and to place the blame on him. In April 1993 he was to feature in *World in Action*'s documentary 'BA's Virgin Soldiers', produced by Martyn Gregory. When, in the wake of the affair, Gregory's book *Dirty Tricks – BA's Secret War Against Virgin Atlantic*, was published, Basham – who had initially welcomed the book, saying that the author had found out a tremendous amount that had been kept secret – recovered £20,000 damages for passages which might have been taken to suggest that he had lied to the City about Virgin's activities, a meaning which had not been intended. The award was upheld on appeal. Any omissions in the summing-up of what was a straightforward case did not flaw it so as to require a retrial.

In February 1993, after the case ended, Lord King resigned as chairman and became president of BA five months earlier than planned. Other senior executives also left, albeit with sizeable pay-offs. Sir Colin Marshall announced that BA was taking fair but effective action to ensure there was no repetition of the regrettable conduct. Their solicitors, Linklaters and Paines, were instructed to prepare a report into the débâcle.

This was not the end of the affair. The litigation between Virgin Atlantic and BA continued with claims for compensation for the misuse of computer information and the poaching of passengers. Eventually Virgin accepted £265,000 paid into court although, as there had been a delay in reaching this settlement, they had to pay £400,000 costs. In 1997 the company lodged a complaint about BA's anti-competition practices with the European Commission, which resulted in 1999 in a £4 million fine for BA. However, a similar claim in the USA was rejected in the courts there.

It was difficult to escape the impression that BA's apology had been made through gritted teeth and that there was a reluctance to learn the necessary lesson from this costly and embarrassing litigation. In May 1998 chairman Sir Colin Marshall had to apologise to Branson again after BA accused him in *BA News* of hypocrisy in attacking their reward schemes, designed to attract business from travel agents. Virgin, it was said, operated a similar system. After a complaint that the words were defamatory, Marshall wrote: 'I too think it is a pity that the press release used the word hypocrisy. It should not have been used. I regret it and apologise for it. We have taken steps to ensure this does not happen again and have withdrawn this week's edition of *BA*

*News* which included the same statement and every effort will be made to destroy all of our copies. By all means publish our exchange.' Branson needed no second bidding.

## GTech

It was a lunch of baked salmon followed by meringue in the conservatory of his Holland Park office on 24 September 1993 which led to Branson's most successful libel action. He was one of the bidders for the seven-year franchise to run the UK's first national lottery. He wanted the lottery to be run on a non-profit-making basis, along the lines of the Irish equivalent. His lunch guest was Guy Snowden of GTech, a company which ran 70 lotteries, 27 of the 37 in the USA and 43 on behalf of foreign governments. GTech had attracted more than its fair share of controversy. In the USA it had apparently seen six FBI investigations into possible illegal payments, federal grand jury investigations and questions raised in seven states over the award of contracts, although no charges had been brought. The company, founded in 1984 by Guy Snowden and Victor Marcowicz, produced 70 per cent of the global market lottery equipment. Since 1994 it has received £74 million as suppliers to Camelot – the eventual winners of the UK franchise, for whom it provides the technical expertise – plus £12 million in dividends from its 22.5 per cent shareholding in Camelot. Snowden's salary in 1997, including bonuses, amounted to £2.5 million.

Back in 1993, Snowden and GTech were determined to become involved in the running of the British National Lottery. 'Everything I have done in my life has been a dress rehearsal for this,' he was quoted as saying in April.

Branson's non-profit-making bid was clearly causing concern to Camelot and GTech. There was a lot at stake: in the first five years, tickets worth £25 billion were sold. Under the National Lottery Act of 1993, 5p in every pound would go to the operator, and in 1997, for example, this worked out at £70.8 million pre-tax profits for Camelot. But for these profits to benefit a commercial operator, Branson's bid would have to be neutralised. It is apparent from a memorandum dated 2 March 1994 from a GTech employee, Charles Cousins, that Branson's bid was perceived as a threat. In it Cousins described a meeting he had had with Colin Moynihan, a former Conservative minister and retained as a consultant at £60,000 a year by GTech. Moynihan had told him that 'he believes HMG will not support the Branson bid', although he agreed that 'we must find an elegant way to get the director-general off the political hook'. A good case would have to be made as to why a profit-making organisation such as Camelot should be preferred to a consortium which would donate all profits to charity.

It was in this context that Snowden lunched with Branson at his Holland Park office. Also present was John Jackson, the co-ordinator of Branson's lottery bid, a former chief executive of the Body Shop who had launched Mates condoms with Branson. Snowden and GTech were to be asked to supply equipment for Branson's bid. The discussion started reasonably enough. Branson explained why he believed that all lottery profits should go to charity. Snowden's argument was that such an important role should be left to companies with the greatest expertise – his, not surprisingly. Branson's talk of charities benefiting to the tune of £1 billion did not cut much ice with Snowden. 'Everybody needs something. I don't know how to phrase this, Richard. There is always a bottom line. I'll get to the point. In what way can we help you? I mean, what can we do for you personally?'

Although there was some dispute about it at the subsequent trial, Snowden, an overweight man of fifty-two, was said to have been agitated, sweating profusely and mopping his brow as he spoke these words. In Snowden's world of fixers and revolving doors, this may have been no more than an offer of partnership. From one point of view it was simply a case of Snowden appealing to the self-interest of a businessman and seeing if they could pool their efforts. Unhappily for Snowden, that was not how Branson and Jackson saw it. 'What do you mean?' asked Branson.

'Everybody needs something,' replied Snowdon.

Branson said: 'The only thing you can do for me is to join our bid where all the profits go to good causes. Thank you very much, but I am quite successful. I only need one breakfast, one lunch and one dinner a day. The only way you could have helped us is by joining our consortium.'

Snowden's recollection of the conversation was rather different. He said that Branson had told him he wanted to give the money away to charity, but that he, Snowden, was probing him as to what his commercial motives might be. 'I said, "What's the real agenda here, what are you trying to accomplish?" I think I upset him. He said, "Look I am a very charitable person."'

Branson and Jackson, however, had no doubt that this was an attempt at bribery. Branson left the room and had the presence of mind to scribble down a written record of the conversation, which became known as the 'loo note' at the trial. On his way back to the conservatory, he met two of his secretaries, to whom he confided, 'You won't believe what's happened – somebody's tried to bribe me.' Jackson said he nearly fell off his chair when he heard Snowden's words. It was clear to him, a man of thirty-four years' experience of business, what was being said. He was amazed that Snowden could have been so crass. As George Carman QC, for Branson, observed at the subsequent trial, Snowden had picked the wrong man and said the wrong thing in the wrong place at the wrong time. In court Jackson confirmed that he believed Snowden had been offering Richard Branson a bribe to stay out of the lottery competition. 'He was not explicit in what he was offering, but because the implications were so huge, I took it that there was going to be a considerable bribe offered.' After the meeting Jackson and Branson had discussed what had been said.

'I wasn't mistaken was I, that was a bribe?'

'That was most definitely a bribe attempt, Richard.'

Branson's view may have been reinforced when he received a call four days later from Sir Tim Bell, Camelot's PR consultant, described by George Carman QC at the trial as the ultimate spin doctor, who said that he hoped there had been no misunder-standing about what had been said at the lunch.

Many people might have drawn a veil over Snowden's crude approach, especially since it never progressed beyond first base. Branson, however, determined to use it to his advantage. Curiously, in view of his apparent shock at what Snowden had said, he did not officially raise the matter with the authorities until May 1994 – on the day after Camelot were awarded the franchise. Then he told Peter Davis, the director-general of Oflot, the lottery regulator, about it. The reason he gave for not mentioning it before was that he had not wanted to muddy the waters and detract from the merits of his own bid by publicising the issue. At the trial Davis denied that Branson had raised it with him. He did, however, recollect a conversation that day with Sir Ron Dearing, chairman of Camelot, in which Sir Ron had told him about GTech's record in the USA in connection with obtaining state lottery contracts.

Branson decided to go public with the incident on *Panorama* in December 1995. He duly accused Snowden of trying to bribe him. This carefully calculated throwing down of the gauntlet was bound to cause regulatory difficulties for Snowden and GTech. They would either have to take Branson's words on the chin or sue for libel. If they took the latter option they would face the difficulty of making their less attractive features and past stand up against the qualities of Britain's most popular businessman. Snowden recognised this problem. 'Richard Branson has put a wire brush up a wild cat's ass,' he expostulated. Branson rejected his protests and challenged him: 'If I am wrong, sue me. If you are calling me a liar, I will sue you.' Snowden was asked for an explanation by Peter Davis of Oflot. He accused Branson of not telling the truth about their conversation. So Branson got his retaliation in first, suing Snowden, GTech and their public-relations director, David Rendine, for libel on 4 January 1996. Snowden and GTech issued their writ against Branson for his accusation of bribery on *Panorama* and his repetition of the charge to Peter Davis on 13 January.

An inquiry ordered by Davis in February 1996 was chaired by Anne Rafferty QC, chairman of the Criminal Bar Association. It found in July 1996 that there was insufficient evidence to support the allegations that Snowden had tried to bribe Branson. It noted, however, that 'there came a time when he [Snowden] may have used words which conveyed or were meant to convey his willingness in a way unconnected with the lottery to co-operate with Richard Branson as an experienced businessman might, but he denied strongly any untoward motive.' Branson described the report, which was based on written submissions from Snowden, as worthless and toothless. He himself had declined to take part in the inquiry, preferring to rely on the libel action to establish the truth. He was suspicious of an inquiry set up by Davis in which Davis himself might have been a witness.

Faced with Branson's determination to undermine his business standing in this country, Snowden felt he had no alternative but to sue himself, even though he was under no illusions about the difficulties of squaring up to such a man. 'I always knew it was going to be an uphill battle taking on a figure of the importance and success of Mr Branson. A lot of people along the way tried to get me to settle or otherwise opt out, but I decided to see this through, even knowing what the bookmaker's odds were likely to be.' The upshot was a three-week trial in January 1998.

Snowden had the additional disadvantage of not being on his home turf. The millions he had made from the lottery would have been a cause for congratulation in the USA; in the UK they astonished the jury.

Branson's case, as put by George Carman QC, was that there should be no shilly-shallying about the matter. There was no room for doubt, misunderstanding or misinterpretation about what Snowden had said, he claimed. Branson was about to join seven other consortia bidding for a franchise. His non-profit-making venture, with all proceeds going to good causes, presented a problem. The conversation at lunch had been a desperate gamble by Snowden to disarm a rival who might have been about to deprive him of his dream, the jewel in the crown.

Branson had to endure some ferocious but ultimately ineffective cross-examination by Richard Ferguson QC, for Snowden and GTech. It was suggested that he had added the word 'personally' to Snowden's question: 'What can I do for you?' to embellish and strengthen his case. 'There's nothing that needs strengthening, and I don't embellish things,' Branson retorted. 'I have been accused of being a liar in the strongest possible terms. Millions of people put their trust in me every year. We have people who invest their money with us, and people have got to trust you.'

Branson was accused of being a crass amateur when it came to plans to run the lottery and of pursuing the case for its 'razzmatazz' value. On a number of occasions the normally confident Branson became hesitant in giving his answers and several times lost his cool as he was taken through the untransmitted *Panorama* material. He admitted he had jotted down only the key words of the conversation, but he had no difficulty in remembering it. He admitted that Snowden had not specifically asked him to drop his bid, but maintained that the implication had been clear. Eventually he came out fighting. He agreed that the allegation was likely to destroy Snowden, but asserted that if people thought bribery was wrong, then his reputation ought to be destroyed. He said he knew that *Panorama* had described six different FBI investigations into GTech America relating to allegations of illegal payments to secure contracts. When Ferguson accused him of raking up dirt on Snowden, Branson replied that as far as he was concerned, there was not much of a reputation to be destroyed. He described Snowden as the most odious man he had ever met. Branson's account of the crucial conversation was supported at the trial by John Jackson, and by the fact that this was not the first occasion on which such allegations had been made against GTech.

In his evidence Snowden said there was no possible way that

his conversation with Branson could have been construed as offering a bribe.

> I was invited to his house. I was happy to go there for the purpose of demonstrating my expertise and to see if there was any possible thing with which we could co-operate. We had a lot of competitors but Richard Branson would not have ranked very high at that point in time based on the degree of preparation he had undertaken. I had the world at my feet. I had a great company. I was very successful. I had founded it and built it and brought it to this point of success of perfection of being recognised as world experts at what we do. I had British companies on my side. Richard Branson had become annoyed during the lunch when I asked him what commercial gain he wanted to get out of running the lottery. What was the real purpose for wanting to be associated with the lottery? Branson seemed to bristle at this so I attempted to move on.

GTech public-relations director David Rendine testified that the allegations were outrageous and completely untrue. Richard Branson posed no threat to GTech, and Guy Snowden had absolutely no reason to offer him money. The judge had earlier ruled that Rendine could not be responsible to Branson for any defamatory material broadcast or published on behalf of GTech, and that the case against him was dismissed. Peter Davis, who had, with some insight, described himself as solid, middle-aged and dull, gave evidence on behalf of Snowden as to the inquiries which had been made into GTech, and why there had been no objection to Camelot being granted the franchise when they relied so heavily on the American company's expertise.

However, his evidence was not as helpful to Snowden as he might have thought. The inquiries into GTech had not been extensive and had taken place only in the three months between the final submission of bids and the announcement of the winner. Davis also had to admit to having accepted free flights from GTech in the United States on a trip to look at the operation of lotteries there, and to having visited a New York financier, Carl Menges, a friend who had a major stake in GTech, just before the launch of the UK lottery. This was subsequently condemned by the House of Commons Public Accounts Committee as a serious error of judgement. Davis said he had accepted the free flights to save the taxpayer money. After the trial he announced: 'I am going to continue to do the job given to me by the Lottery Act.' Chris Smith, the secretary for culture, media and sport, had other ideas. While stressing that there was no question-mark whatsoever against Davis' integrity, he did require his resignation. Davis was unceremoniously dumped with a £42,000 pay-off within twenty-four hours of the verdict, since the political judgement was that there had to be public confidence in the lottery. Having come to Oflot after an unremarkable career at Harris Queensway and Sturge Holdings at Lloyds, Davis lacked the political antennae necessary for the job.

After a retirement of three hours the jury decided that Branson had not lied and that Snowden had indeed attempted to bribe him. Branson was awarded £100,000 damages, which he announced he was giving to charity. Costs were estimated to total over £2 million.

The consequences for Snowden and GTech were catastrophic. Snowden immediately resigned as a director of Camelot and GTech UK. With masterly understatement, he commented: 'In hindsight, I wish I had not accepted Mr Branson's invitation to lunch.' Branson had obtained, in winning this libel action, much of what he had failed to obtain from Oflot. The prospect of Camelot continuing to operate the lottery after the expiry of their licence in 2001 now seemed bleak. Davis lost his job, and John Stoker, the acting director-general of Oflot, required GTech to satisfy Oflot under the National Lottery Act 1993 that it was fit and proper as a supplier to the lottery operator, and to satisfy him as to its fitness to remain one of five Camelot shareholders. 'You cannot just be a bit fit and proper,' Stoker was reported to have observed somewhat pointedly. Although GTech had never been found guilty of any wrongdoing, Stoker required to be satisfied as to its business practices – an inquiry which the House of Commons Public Accounts and Culture, Media and Sport Select Committees and the National Audit Office felt should have been made some years previously. GTech sold its 22.5 per cent stake in Camelot, which was worth £51 million, a sum which was distributed among its other shareholders.

Snowden subsequently resigned from GTech Holdings Corporation. The parting was softened by a $13 million pay-off, which GTech said arose out of a complete reordering of the company by a refocusing of the way they conducted business. Of this sum, $9 million represented Snowden's golden goodbye, and $4 million his salary payments to the end of 1998. Snowden also retained 1 per cent of GTech's shares, then valued at £48 million. A hundred staff, representing 20 per cent of the company's workforce in the UK, were to be dismissed, along with another 800 employees around the world. The job cuts were said to have affected 14.5 per cent of GTech's global workforce of 5,500. Snowden denied that the redundancies were connected to the libel action, but it was obvious that the consequences of losing the case had been momentous. An appeal heard in June 1999 failed to overturn the verdict: the court held that the irregularity of the production of inadmissible documents by the plaintiff was not enough to cast doubt on the integrity of the jury's decision.

It looked as if Branson's victory against GTech had paid dividends when, in August 2000, the Lottery Commission, under Dame Helena Shovelton, eliminated Camelot from the bid for the new franchise to run the lottery, leaving Branson's People's Lottery as the only competitor in the race. The commission was influenced by Camelot's failure to disclose minor faults in the GTech software. This decision was overruled by Mr Justice Richards as being conspicuously unfair and amounting to an abuse of power. Shovelton resigned to be replaced by Lord Burns, the former permanent secretary at the Treasury, and in

December 2000 the commission finally awarded the franchise to Camelot.

While the record of businesses litigious in the libel field has not been universally good, Virgin and Branson, considerably assisted by the latter's personal charisma, have hitherto enjoyed complete success as well as commercial advantage. However, experience would suggest that what Richard Ferguson QC described scathingly in the GTech case as their 'new product' of 'Virgin libel' would benefit from selective exposure.

# 11

# THE PITFALLS OF LIBEL

The pitfalls of bringing a libel action, some of which we have already seen, are legion. One frequent danger is that what might originally have seemed a strong case may, in the course of the litigation, prove to be both weak and ruinous. Challenging the findings of two investigative television documentaries resulted in the destruction of the careers of Dr Frank Skuse and Dr Peter Nixon. Even winning a case may on occasion ultimately prove to be disastrous. Both Dr Malcolm Smith and Patricia Eaton faced years of litigation in unsuccessful attempts to enforce their judgements. Dolly Kiffin had part of her libel damages taken away from her by a judge at the Old Bailey. And Professor Frederick Hartt won his case, but the criticisms made of his conduct by the judge at the libel trial when awarding him damages outweighed the harm of the original libel. Other plaintiffs have won their cases but ended up substantially out of pocket because they did not recover more than the sum paid into court.

Dr Frank Skuse was the forensic scientist whose tests for explosives helped convict the so-called Birmingham Six for the 1974 pub bombing at the height of the IRA's campaign in

mainland Britain. Seventeen years later, in 1991, they were found
to have been unjustly convicted. Skuse's career in forensic science spanned twenty years and included the development of the
breathalyser and the investigation of the Welsh arson campaign
in the 1970s. He was notably successful in the detection of those
suspected of handling explosives. However, he had been criticised
in 1992 when Judith Ward successfully appealed against her
conviction for the 1973 IRA bombing of a coach on the M62.

In 1985 a *World in Action* programme, 'In the Interests of
Justice', portrayed Dr Skuse as lacking the proper skill, knowledge and care required of a forensic scientist in testing for
nitroglycerine. Skuse was outraged and wanted to sue for libel.
He was advised by Peter Carter-Ruck and Partners to await the
outcome of the Birmingham Six appeal. To protect his legal position, he issued a writ on 26 March 1988 alleging that the
programme suggested he had, at the trial, negligently misrepresented the effect of his scientific tests. At that time leading
counsel advised that his prospects of success in a libel action
were 65 per cent. On this understanding, the businessman Sir
James Goldsmith had agreed to fund the case, as Skuse appeared
to be the victim of politically motivated left-wing journalism.
Goldsmith supported the case from January 1987 to October
1989, when he pulled out because it seemed to be 'far more of a
political than a civil matter'. Such considerations had not previously deterred Sir James, but the activities of his foundation in
supporting libel actions were coming under scrutiny from
Granada's solicitors, Goodman, Derrick & Co. They sought disclosure of the funding and an order that the foundation would
agree to pay Granada's legal costs if Skuse lost.

From then on things started to go badly wrong. Estimates of
the legal costs steadily mounted to £280,000. Skuse's solicitors
required legal charges over his three homes in Sardinia,
Blackpool and Wigan. His life savings evaporated as he traipsed
from QC to QC. George Carman QC advised that his chances of
success were no better than 20 to 30 per cent. He fared no better
with Desmond Browne QC. Another £20,000 had gone in fees.

Hemmed in by the costs of his litigation but convinced of his innocence, Skuse insisted on bringing the case to court in October 1995. He can scarcely have derived much comfort from the advice of his new QC, Geoffrey Shaw, that Skuse had 'not a cat's chance in hell of winning' or his remark that he had never seen 'such a stone-cold loser of a libel action'. After a ten-day adjournment, Skuse dropped the case without receiving any apology, damages or contribution to his legal costs.

He had already paid out £156,582 in legal fees. His solicitors had reduced their bill by £100,000 from £388,478, but they wanted to be paid the outstanding balance of £131,896. Eventually they sued him and he embarked on the perilous course of countersuing them for negligence and breach of contract. That action also failed. Skuse's real problem was that he had a weak case which was always likely to be contested and that he had begun litigation he could ill afford. The libel action spanned seven years and, with some bitterness, he complained it had ruined him.

Similar misfortunes can befall those who win their cases against those who either cannot or will not pay. In October 1991 Dr Malcolm Smith, a thirty-five-year-old Northampton doctor, was awarded £150,000, the highest-ever damages for slander, against his forty-seven-year-old partner in his surgery, Dr Alanah Houston. She had accused him of sexual harassment, falsely alleging that he had groped her, feeling her breasts and pinching her bottom. She had tried to get him removed from the surgery. Dr Smith claimed that the slander was part of her campaign to evict him. After five and a half hours' deliberation, the jury unanimously rejected Dr Houston's charges against Dr Smith. In December 1993 the Court of Appeal reduced the damages to £50,000 because of the limited circulation of the slander, nevertheless taking into account the lurid publicity such a case inevitably engendered.

Although Dr Smith was exonerated by the verdict, it was also to wreck his life. There followed years of litigation to enforce the judgement. He was paid only £2,000 of the damages and legal costs owed to him by Dr Houston. He lost his house, his surgery and his practice, and was reduced to surviving on the charity of his family as he pursued the case as a litigant in person. The action left him with debts of £300,000.

Dr Houston had declared herself bankrupt in the face of the order for costs and damages against her of £300,000. She was, however, subsequently discharged from her bankruptcy and able to earn a living as a family-planning practitioner and forensic medical examiner in rape and child abuse cases. In July 1998, Dr Smith was able to establish that Dr Houston had lied about her assets to the court and had disposed of £50,000 in breach of an injunction in order to avoid paying Dr Smith. Dr Houston was jailed for three months, but the court could not on that occasion order the debt to be paid. The simplified procedures of the Defamation Act 1996 (see Chapter 21) would have assisted Smith in obtaining swifter and cheaper justice, although it would not have helped directly in his recovering his damages and costs from Houston.

Patricia Eaton, a physical education teacher at Avery Hill College in south London, was awarded in 1983 £12,000 damages against an art teacher at the college with whom she had had an affair. He had unquestionably libelled her in 1980 by sending a letter, which he copied to six other members of staff, falsely accusing her of blackmail and sexual harassment. The defence, though rejected by the jury, had been luridly reported in the tabloid press as 'The Sex Slave Case'. The teacher had been 'asked for sex by gym mistress' and the college had been labelled a 'sin bin'. Ms Eaton was owed £20,000 legal costs, of which the defendant paid her £2,000 before declaring himself bankrupt. He was discharged from his bankruptcy in 1989, by which time Eaton had received only £6,000 towards her legal costs.

The art teacher had been briefly suspended by the Inner London Education Authority but had then been transferred to another school and promoted. Avery Hill College became part of Thames Polytechnic and after a six-week suspension Eaton found herself redundant, despite her long service. The college

then became part of the grander-sounding University of
Greenwich. In 1990 ILEA had set up an inquiry into Eaton's
case, chaired by a QC, but it got lost in the system as ILEA was
absorbed into first the London Residuary Body and then the
London Pensions Fund Authority. Eaton's career and health suffered as she struggled to seek compensation from ILEA and to
contest the art teacher's discharge from bankruptcy. Over a
period of fifteen years, she attended fifty court hearings. As the
years went by, her legal costs mounted to £200,000.

In 1996, ironically as a litigant in person, Eaton did at last
enjoy some success in the courts but no thanks were due to the
law of libel. She obtained £400,000 damages from the London
Pensions Fund Authority and an apology on behalf of ILEA for
their breach of contract and their refusal to believe her innocence. The case had been listed for six weeks but the authority
backed down at the court door. It was scant consolation as she
was by then sixty-two and unlikely to work again.

Even when you win and receive libel damages, your problems
may not be over. Dolly Kiffin, a community leader on the
Broadwater Farm estate in Tottenham, north London, recovered
£84,000 from various newspapers which had unjustifiably
alleged that she had misappropriated the Broadwater Farm Youth
Association's funds. In July 1989 she was convicted of two
offences of perverting the course of justice. The prosecution had
not alleged that there was any fraud involved – and Kiffin
strongly denied that there was – rather that the handling of
grants totalling £508,263 required proper accountability. Kiffin
had taken the records to Jamaica, where she had unfortunately
decided to bury them in her mother's grave three days before a
court deadline to hand them over to the police. To add to her
misfortune, the grave had been lost in the floods of 1986 and the
records could no longer be exhumed. When Judge Brian Capstick
QC heard of her £84,000 award, as well as handing out a three-
month suspended prison sentence he ordered her to pay £25,000
towards the prosecution's costs.

People are not usually obliged to sue for libel, and both the

expense involved and the fact that many libels are soon forgotten are extremely good reasons for not doing so. Yet many do
sue even when the wiser course would have been to do nothing.
Dr Peter Nixon, a seventy-one-year-old retired cardiology consultant, featured in February 1994 in a Channel 4 documentary
called 'Preying on Hope', produced by Duncan Campbell as part
of the *Undercover Britain* series. The programme followed Ian
Hughes, an AIDS sufferer, as he traipsed round assorted practitioners to be offered expensive remedies ranging from extracts of
shark to bleach. Not surprisingly, they did Hughes little good;
indeed he was dead before the libel action started. Dr Nixon, who
practised near Harley Street, recommended more medically
respectable remedies than those offered by some of the charla-
tans who appeared in the programme. He charged Hughes £275
for a consultation, in which he told him that his AIDS-induced
fatigue was the product of hyperventilation, the cause, he said, of
a wide range of illnesses, ranging from Gulf War syndrome to
pre-menstrual tension, as well as AIDS.

Dr Nixon went through a routine which would produce hyperventilation and which did little or nothing to diagnose what was
wrong with Hughes. The idea was to make the patient think
about anger or other negative emotions. He told Hughes to get
'hugely angry, frustrated and trapped'. He did not ask to see
Hughes' medical records, nor was he an expert in the treatment
of AIDS. At the end of the consultation Nixon recommended
nothing more effective than valium and phenergen and two
weeks of sleep.

Nixon sued for libel. The trial was scheduled to last for five
weeks before Mr Justice Morland. Nixon's case was destroyed in
cross-examination by Desmond Browne QC. The plaintiff admitted that his articles in the *Journal of the Royal Society of
Medicine* were based on a number of other articles, some of
which he had neither written nor read. He was forced to admit
that he had 'no honest grounds' for his claims that a 'hypnotic
challenge' test for diagnosing hyperventilation was reliable.
Questioned about the results of a paper on his 'think test' – the

procedure he had used on the unfortunate Hughes – he admitted he had reached a false conclusion that it was more effective than the standard forced hyperventilation-provocation test. Pressed about the application of different percentage criteria to two groups of patients which produced results to back his claims, Nixon conceded that they appeared 'to be more than a honest slip of the pen'. When he was asked if there was any explanation other than scientific fraud, he replied 'Carelessness.'

On the sixth day of his evidence, 9 May 1997, in the fifth week of the trial, Nixon failed to turn up in court owing to 'ill health'. He was given until 14 May to decide whether to continue with the case. He chose not to do so, and the matter was then settled on humiliating terms. Nixon had to pay Channel 4's legal costs of £765,520, as well as his own, which were estimated to be of a comparable amount; he agreed not to sue if the programme was rebroadcast; he even had to write to two doctors who had drawn attention to his practices, and whose confidential notes had had to be produced at the trial, in order to show that Campbell had not breached any duty of confidentiality as a journalist, but had been compelled by the court to produce the notes. Nixon also agreed that all documents disclosed in the trial should be passed to the General Medical Council unless he voluntarily retired from practice in the meantime.

Occasionally the price of victory in a libel action is too great to make it worthwhile. In 1989 Professor Frederick Hartt, professor emeritus of history of art at the University of Virginia, was awarded £7,500 damages against the *Independent* for two articles written in December 1988 which suggested that he was dishonest or reckless in identifying a seven-inch figure as Michelangelo's model for his statue of David. Although Professor Hartt won the action, he was at a disadvantage in that the case had been heard by a judge alone. This meant that the judge, Mr Justice Morland, gave reasons for his conclusion. He held that the articles were indeed defamatory, as it had been suggested that there were reasonable grounds for suspecting that Hartt had been dishonest and reckless in the matter, and that he had not objectively assessed the evidence in his attribution or in a book he had written on the subject. Neither allegation, the judge ruled, was true or fair comment. However, he said he would have awarded Hartt substantial damages but for the fact that he had broken with the general custom and ethics of his profession by obtaining a financial interest – namely a 5 per cent cut from the French art dealer from the proceeds of the sale of the figure in addition to his $1,000 fee plus expenses – which depended on his attribution, and then concealing that interest. It was scant consolation to the professor that the damages exceeded the £5,000 paid into court by the *Independent* when the judge castigated him: 'He had in my judgement justifiably been exposed as a person who, despite his eminence as a Michelangelo scholar, has prostituted his genuinely held scholarly attribution of the statuette for a disreputable joint commercial venture.' This was indeed a case in which the cure seemed worse than the illness.

Others have come unstuck in libel actions by failing to win damages which exceed or even match the amount they have already paid into court. Not only does this leave the plaintiff substantially out of pocket, as he or she will have to pay all the legal costs incurred after the date of payment in, but the reports of the case will concentrate on the financial consequences – occasionally hinting that the plaintiff has been greedy – rather than on the vindication he or she has achieved. In March 1991 Charles Golding, a *Sunday Mirror* features editor, was left with a costs bill of £40,000 when he recovered £1,500 damages from *Private Eye* for the false suggestion that he had got his job from Eve Pollard, the editor, through favouritism, and that his appointment had been 'astonishing'. Pollard had given evidence on his behalf, stressing his suitable experience as a deputy features editor at TVam and his work at Channel 4 and as editor of the *Jewish Herald*, while *Private Eye* had claimed that the article did not allege favouritism or incompetence. As *Private Eye* had paid £5,000 into court, Golding was left to pay the bulk of the legal costs.

The same fate befell Dr Paul MacLoughlin, who successfully sued the *News of the World* in July 1991 for a 1988 story headlined 'FERGIE BABY DOCTOR IS DUPED BY FAKE CLINIC'. After a seven-day action in which he represented himself, he was awarded £50,000 damages for what he described as the 'monstrously scurrilous' allegations. However, as in the Roache case, detailed later in this chapter, the newspaper had, prior to the trial, paid into court precisely the sum that the jury awarded. MacLoughlin therefore had to bear the legal costs of the trial. He was more successful, however, when in May 1993 he was awarded £85,000 against a Dr Kells, who, he claimed, had denigrated him in a campaign of vindictive, anonymous letters sent to the media and potential financial backers over a period of ten years.

The risks involved in not paying a sum for damages into court when there is a likelihood of a modest sum being awarded were illustrated by a bitterly contested case between two warring Bedford neighbours, Alan Kingston and Raymond Ward, in July 1995. The law of libel is not well suited to the resolution of such disputes. After wearily hearing evidence of uprooted fences, the mysterious deaths of dogs, complaints about car parking, posters on lamp-posts, friendship with the chief constable and membership of the Freemasons, and having observed that the evidence was rather too improbable for a storyline in the TV soap *Neighbours*, Sir Michael Davies awarded Mr Ward £1,000. Mr Kingston, who had represented himself, was left with a bill of £20,000 as he had not thought to pay money into court to protect himself against the consequences of a modest award of damages.

Graham and Barbara Rush were awarded £4,750 against their neighbour Dagmar Coward for harsh words uttered during a boundary dispute, but before the verdict was secured in December 1998, the case had taken three trials and nine years and incurred £100,000 in costs. Coward also won £4,750 in a counterclaim for assault.

Some cases have happier endings. In a variant of the general rule in libel that at least the lawyers come out smiling, when the solicitor Anthony Julius needed to gather evidence for an action against an Israeli newspaper, he took his client's daughter, Dina Rabinovich, to Israel with him. Romance blossomed. The case was won, he billed his client for £40,000 and Ms Rabinovich got legal aid for her divorce.

## A Load of Bullish Advice

Libel is often defined as bringing a person into hatred, ridicule or contempt. In the case of allegations made in humorous or satirical publications or broadcasts, it is, on the whole, better for a victim to take the ridicule on the chin. The libel action Derek Jameson unwisely brought against the BBC in 1980, which arose out of a light-hearted skit on the radio programme *Week Ending*, exemplifies the perils of suing in respect of a satirical sketch. It also shows how a litigant can suffer when he is not brought in on discussions between his solicitor and his barrister. Jameson was editor of the *Daily Express* and became editor of the *Star* after sacking the previous incumbent, Peter Grimsditch, a Greek classical scholar and former deputy editor of *Reveille*. 'One of us had to go, and you can guess who that was,' Jameson joked on Radio Manchester.

This comment encouraged the *Week Ending* team to get stuck into their 'Man of the Week', Derek Jameson, 'to pay tribute to an editor who sees reality with half an eye, humour with half a wit and circulation figures with half an aspirin'. He was described as 'the archetypal East End boy made bad. Narrowly surviving a term of active service on the *Mirror*, he retired from newspaper work to become editor of the *Daily Express*. He arrived uncluttered with taste or talent and took to his new role like a duck to orange sauce.' His motto was said to be: 'All the nudes fit to print and the news fitted to print.' He had, taunted *Week Ending*, 'reduced the *Express* to the role of the thinking man's bin liner. But tonight we salute him for his promotion to the lofty obscurity of the *Star* – a man who still believes that erudite is a glue.' There was more in this vein, all of it clearly designed to caricature Jameson as a fool, a man ready to speak his mind, however small. He found being called an East End boy made bad particularly hurtful. He was proud of what he had achieved after his inauspicious beginnings as the illegitimate son of a poor laundry hand.

Lord Matthews, the chairman of Express Newspapers, advised Jameson to consult Peter Carter-Ruck, who, in response to a message from Jameson, telephoned him and advised him that the programme was highly defamatory and that he would recover damages. It was, in his opinion, a very serious libel. 'Don't worry,' Jameson was reassured by the solicitor, 'I know the BBC, they'll settle out of court.' Subsequent events showed this to be a miscalculation. As it turned out the BBC decided, as a matter of principle, to defend their right to broadcast satirical material. Jameson was to observe ruefully after the case that he should have taken the advice of his mum: find out who wrote it and go and punch him on the nose. The worst that could happen would be that you would be fined fifty quid.

Initially, Jameson was backed by Express Newspapers. However, in 1981 he himself experienced the notorious insecurity of the job of newspaper editor, and he found himself on his own financially. He then became editor of the *News of the World*, but by the time of the trial he was unemployed again. Four years were to pass before the case came to court, by which time the matter of his capabilities at Express Newspapers was a thing of the past and he was in no position to bear the risks involved in this uncertain litigation. He had in the interim discovered how expensive libel actions can be, how easy it is to rush into them and how costly it can be to get out. By 1982 his costs were £8,000, and by 1984 they had risen to £14,000. If he pulled out without securing a settlement, he might have to pay the BBC's costs as well. He was becoming increasingly nervous about the case, and wanted to settle for modest damages plus costs. Carter-Ruck was telling him that the BBC would settle, even on the steps of the court. 'Why,' Carter-Ruck pointed out, 'should you have to pay £5,000 to be insulted?' The lawyer explained that in negotiations he was hanging out for at least £1,000 in damages and a letter of apology. On 13 October 1983 Carter-Ruck had written to Jameson saying, 'I still take the view that if this action did go to trial, you could be awarded between £25,000 and £50,000 in damages. It is in my opinion a very serious libel.' With the mention of such figures, Jameson felt that he had a good case and that it would be satisfactorily settled.

The BBC would have been aware of the risks of litigation and of the element of irrecoverable legal costs involved in any action. Even if they won the case, the court would probably only allow them to recover 70 per cent of their legal costs from Jameson. As so often happens in such cases, the legal costs were becoming an impediment to the settlement of the action. With the uncertainty and expense of libel litigation, it is probable that the BBC would have been prepared to settle the case on reasonable terms.

The BBC's defence was that this was all light-hearted stuff and not defamatory, and that it was in any event fair comment on a matter of public interest. When the case began, in February 1984, it became clear that, with the assistance of the most formidable cross-examiner of the day, John Wilmers QC, the BBC proposed to run a defence that tabloid newspaper editors should not be too thin-skinned and that they should get as good as they gave – a tactic sometimes employed against erring editors on holiday with their bimbettes to gauge their equanimity when their own privacy is invaded. Over six days of costly and gruelling cross-examination, Jameson was reminded of the stories he had published and of his nickname in *Private Eye*, 'Sid Yobbo'. He was asked about a story published in February 1980 in the *Star* about Soraya Khashoggi and her relationship with Winston Churchill MP. 'The faster you go, the more I'll take off . . . in no time at all Winston was doing 100 mph.'

Jameson was also cross-examined at length about Joyce McKinney, who, in the 1970s, had jumped bail after being accused of kidnapping a Mormon missionary, Kirk Anderson, for sex. She had, it seemed, hit upon what she believed to be the Mormon missionary position, which involved chaining him to the bed. 'I loved Kirk so much I would have skied down Mount Everest in the nude with a carnation up my nose,' she was memorably reported as saying. Jameson was also accused by Wilmers of using sexual titillation by illustrating an article in the *Express* on Spain with a girl wearing a bikini. 'What should I have put there?' Jameson retorted. 'A picture of General Franco?'

The judge, Mr Justice Comyn, left it to the jury to decide whether the BBC had gone too far in poking fun at Jameson, or whether he was the last man who should be complaining about such jibes. It was, one would have thought, a fairly straightforward issue. However, the jury were left with five detailed questions to answer and four guidelines to consider. The fourth guideline was whether any of the imputations were (i) both factual and defamatory, or (ii) comment, but could not be made by an honest person on the facts, or (iii) comment which an honest person could make but which in this case involved malice on the part of the BBC. If the jury came up with the answer yes to any of the three options they would then be asked what damages they would award the plaintiff. Faced with this complexity, the jury, rather disconcertingly, returned after five hours' retirement to ask what imputation meant. After a further two hours they decided that the broadcast was defamatory, but was fair comment and broadcast without malice.

The BBC had paid £10 into court to ensure that they would recover their legal costs in the event of an award of nominal damages to Jameson. As we saw in Chapter 1, paying money into court normally means that the plaintiff will have to pay the legal costs of *both* sides after the date of payment into court if the damages he is awarded are no more than the amount paid in. The reasoning is that the plaintiff should have accepted the sum offered, plus his legal costs, up to that point. If he continues and does not recover a greater sum, he has to pay the legal costs incurred after that date.

The legal costs were therefore horrendous for Jameson. His final bill from Carter-Ruck was £41,342.50. It was little consolation to be told that he had been spared a further £20,000 as things had gone so badly. The BBC's costs were £33,500. Jameson did not have £75,000, but his financial bacon was saved by the BBC, which waived its claim to costs against him, and an appeal fund which raised £10,000.

With the benefit of hindsight, it is clear that the advice Jameson received was overoptimistic. As far as he was concerned, he had not been sufficiently advised of the risk-benefit ratio. He felt he should have been more clearly warned of the risk of losing the action and of the irrecoverable legal costs which could leave him out of pocket even if he won and the damages were modest, particularly as this was litigation he could ill afford.

Worse was to follow. After the case Jameson said in an interview with the *Guardian* that all his lawyers had been saying throughout what a good case he had. His barrister, David Eady QC, later to become a High Court judge, read this with considerable surprise. He was well aware of the risk that the BBC might not settle as Carter-Ruck had led Jameson to believe, and of the dangers of the case being lost if it were to be defended in the way it was. When the BBC paid £10 into court to ensure they would recover their legal costs in the event of an award of nominal damages to Jameson, Eady had given a written opinion, dated 20 September 1983, to Carter-Ruck in the expectation that it would, in accordance with normal practice, be passed on to Jameson: under the rules of the profession, barristers do not communicate directly with their clients but through their instructing solicitors. Eady pointed out that this was a 'high-risk piece of litigation. The payment into court needs to be taken seriously, not because £10 is a realistic figure for damages by way of compensation or vindication but because it presents one means of avoiding the considerable financial exposure now confronting Jameson.' He drew Carter-Ruck's attention to the danger of Jameson being more substantially out of pocket even after he won the case than he would be after accepting the £10 paid into court. 'If he should lose, the prospect is bleak indeed.' Eady noted that Carter-Ruck was best placed to point out the detailed financial implications, but that Jameson should be aware that he was in effect gambling with many thousands of pounds. If Jameson needed any more discouragement, Eady recommended that 'he has no more than an even chance of winning and even then the chances of his recovering a sufficient sum of damages to cover his irrecoverable legal costs are remote'. He felt that 'the BBC might well consider they have a better than even chance of winning the case. A jury might think the case represented a personal reaction to the attack and an oversensitive interpretation of its message – in other words it was really a satire on his brand of journalism and personal style rather than an attack on his intellectual capacity and technical competence.' A strikingly accurate forecast, as events were to show.

Concerned as a result of the publicity after the trial that his warning might not have been seen by Jameson, Eady wrote on 19 March 1984 to Carter-Ruck asking for an explanation as to what had happened to his opinion of 20 September 1983. On 2 April 1984, Carter-Ruck dispatched a somewhat delphic reply which stated that 'the client is fully aware of the situation of your advice, which he has seen'. Jameson, however, was adamant that he had not been shown Eady's advice by Carter-Ruck before the trial, although he does recollect Carter-Ruck telling him afterwards, 'Look here, Derek, you mustn't go around saying all your lawyers said you had a strong case. David Eady is most upset, he never thought so.' Jameson's recollection is that he did not realise how damning Eady's opinion had been until his new solicitor obtained a copy of his written opinion after the trial. There was no way, he maintained, he would have gone ahead if he had known about it.

Carter-Ruck's account of this state of affairs is to be found in his memoirs, *Reflections of a Libel Lawyer*. Although David Eady had advised that it was a high-risk case, he had, Carter-Ruck wrote, changed his mind when he had heard the broadcast and taken a more optimistic view. Jameson, however, evidently felt that it would have been surprising for a QC of Eady's skill and experience to have given such a forthright opinion on the case in the first place without a comprehensive grasp of the facts, particularly when it had by then been running for over two years.

His conduct after the action suggested his view had *not* departed significantly from his written advice of 20 September 1983.

When Jameson asked Carter-Ruck why he had not been shown the opinion, he received the extraordinary reply that he, Carter-Ruck, thought it would have been bad for his morale. In his memoirs Carter-Ruck made the point that he does not advise a client to take a libel action through to trial unless he considers the chances of success to be at least 85 per cent (the other 15 per cent is a contingency to take account of the unpredictability of the jury's verdict, the prejudice of the judge, a misdirection or a bad witness). Evidently Carter-Ruck, unlike Eady, was well wide of the mark on this occasion. In this case he claimed that Jameson was a bad witness – a matter on which others disagreed – and that the directions given to the jury were unduly complex.

Carter-Ruck did not sue Jameson for libel when Jameson criticised his handling of the case in his autobiography, *Touched by Angels*, or the journalist Adam Raphael, who attacked the lawyer's treatment of the Eady opinion in his book *My Learned Friends*. Carter-Ruck did, however, complain to Donald Trelford, Raphael's editor at the *Observer*, that Raphael was conducting 'a vendetta' against him in the paper.

Carter-Ruck had worked on the case with his legal executive and former secretary Mrs May Richards. In his memoirs he described her as meticulously careful, and her preparation of Jameson's case as exemplary. She was someone, he wrote glowingly, who would never let anything past unless it was perfect according to her standards. Mrs Richards, however, indicated to Jameson that she considered Carter-Ruck's handling of the case to be most unsatisfactory and that she was threatening to complain to the Law Society.

Carter-Ruck dispatched one of his senior partners to negotiate with the emotionally distraught Mrs Richards and, more importantly, to get her to withdraw any complaint to the Law Society. Carter-Ruck, a former council member of the Law Society, told them he had acted entirely as he considered was in the best interest of the client, and that he had substantially reduced his fees because of the outcome and the crisis faced by Jameson. He added that May Richards was suffering from a major nervous breakdown, as indeed was the case. Mrs Richards did not pursue her complaint and a cynical Derek Jameson was not altogether surprised.

Jameson did not himself take action against Carter-Ruck. The track record of those who have tried is not good, as is demonstrated by the next case we shall examine. More sensibly, he concentrated on establishing his career as a broadcaster at the BBC.

## Up Street Creek

Until some sanity was introduced into the level of damages awarded in the case of Elton John v. Mirror Group Newspapers in 1997 (see Chapter 15), libel damages were a complete lottery. This made it difficult to calculate the appropriate awards. It was the big ones that attracted the most publicity, and therefore remained uppermost in the public's mind: Jeffrey Archer, £500,000 in 1987; Koo Stark, a former girlfriend of Prince Andrew, £300,000, Lord Aldington (covered in Chapter 17), £1,500,000 and Elton John £1 million in 1988. Most cases, however, resulted in much more modest damages, and even many of the high awards were not enforced or were privately settled for lesser sums prior to appeal. A notable victim of the uncertainty of libel awards was Bill Roache, the actor who plays Ken Barlow in *Coronation Street*, who sued the *Sun* in 1990.

The origin of the libel was a piece written after a chance meeting at Euston Station between Roache and Ken Irwin, a showbusiness writer. The journalist's career had flourished since 1960, when, as the *Daily Mirror*'s Manchester TV critic, he had predicted that the new series *Coronation Street* would not last. Irwin's article was headlined 'BORING KEN WAS GIRL CRAZY STUD' and carried the strapline: 'Hated by the Cast: 30 Years of *Coronation Street* by the Man who Knew'. It was suggested that Roache was

known as BKB – Boring Ken Barlow – an nickname which Irwin
later admitted in court that he had made up. The report did not
simply claim that Roache was boring; it implied that he had
nearly been fired several times, and was regarded as a joke by the
producers and scriptwriters. He was said to be self-satisfied and
smug like Ken Barlow and hated by his colleagues. The passage
about his earlier love life was headed 'Cockroach'.

The drivel Irwin produced was based on the false assumption
that soap stars are like the characters they play. Hence Roache
was said to be at daggers drawn with Johnny Briggs, who played
his screen wife's lover, the smooth-talking entrepreneur Mike
Baldwin. It highlighted the endless fascination of the tabloids
with behind-the-scenes glances at soap stars, and their ability to
confuse the real and the fictional. At the trial one of the witnesses, Amanda Barrie, who plays Alma Sedgwick, the
café-owner, explained that her character had been having an
affair with Ken Barlow before ditching him for Mike Baldwin.
Incredibly, she had to make the point that it was Alma's love life,
not her own, and that in reality it had caused no bad blood
between the actors playing Baldwin and Barlow.

As Bill Roache had been with *Coronation Street* for over thirty
years, and indeed was the sole surviving member of the original
cast, this nonsense posed a serious threat to his livelihood. The
*Sun* had no real defence at trial, except that the whole thing had
got out of proportion and that it was a matter of fair comment
on a matter of public interest, namely the shortcomings of the
cast and characters of *Coronation Street*. Five members of the
cast gave evidence for Roache after he told the jury that he and
his wife had been to hell and back. He did not think it was right
that anyone should have to go through what he and his wife had
been through to justify their good name. Betty Driver, the bar-
maid Betty Turpin at the Rovers' Return, said that Roache was
the least boring person she had ever met in her life. He was a
lovely man, and she was the godmother of his son William.
William Waddington, who played old codger Percy Sugden, said
he had never heard the initials BKB. Johnny Briggs, Roache's

alleged rival, described him in glowing terms, adding, 'He is my golfing partner, and we are the best of friends, actually.' Amanda Barrie said it was quite wrong that Roache was hated by the cast. He was the last person anyone would hate.

The *Sun* was able to cross-examine Roache about the fact that he had in the past given interviews to Irwin about *Coronation Street* and co-operated with another journalist, Derek Shuff, for an article entitled 'SECRETS OF THE STREET'. It was suggested that he was being a little thin-skinned. The *Sun* also raised the issue that Roache had not sued in respect of the allegations about his private life and sexual exploits before his second marriage. This might well have backfired on the paper. It headlined one of its court reports 'STAR BILL TEARFUL AT SEX LIFE QUIZ', which may have influenced the jury's view of the paper's conduct. It certainly affected the judge's decision at the end of the case to award costs against the newspaper. The *Sun* had enthusiastically described Roache's youthful romances even though they had not been detailed in open court.

Anticipating that it would probably lose the case, on 13 September 1991, six weeks before the trial, the *Sun* paid £25,000 into court. Roache was advised by his solicitor, Peter Carter-Ruck, that the sum paid in was totally inadequate: had it been in the order of, say, £75,000 to £100,000, it would have been well within the risk area. Plaintiffs such as Roache need to realise that the cost of libel trials is so enormous that, to all except the extremely rich, it is an unwise and uneconomic gamble to go to trial to try to squeeze an extra £25,000 or so out of a defendant. The plaintiff also has the problem that even if he wins he is likely to recover only 70 per cent of his legal costs. So he has to bring into the financial calculation the 30 per cent of irrecoverable costs in deciding whether such a gamble is worthwhile.

Roache's final position was later the subject of some dispute between him and his solicitor. Although Roache was earning £160,000 a year, he had a £100,000 overdraft. Roache claimed that he had pointed out his financial limitations, which Carter-Ruck denied, and that Carter-Ruck had introduced him to Coutts

& Co., his bankers, to seek a loan. Furthermore, said Roache, his solicitor had personally offered to lend him £10,000, but had asked him not to tell anyone for fear people might think he was a big softy.

In any event, on 18 September Roache had a conference with his barristers, Charles Gray QC and Tom Shields, who said that they would be surprised if damages were less than £25,000. They were, however, a little more cautious, estimating that if the payment in was increased to £50,000, 'the risk would really begin'. Aware of some of the high awards recently made by libel juries, Roache believed he was likely to be awarded something in excess of £100,000. In 1989 Carmen Proetta, a witness to the SAS killings of three IRA suspects in Gibraltar, had received six-figure settlements from the *Sun* and *Mirror*, and Teresa Gorman MP and the Northampton doctor Malcolm Smith had earlier in 1991 each got £150,000 for a defamation published to only a handful of people. Counsel felt that although Roache might be awarded as much as a six-figure sum, this was very much at the top end of the scale and that the £75,000 to £100,000 bracket was more realistic. Negotiations took place, without success, to settle the case at an all-in figure of £200,000, which would include £60,000 legal costs.

On 7 October, the defendants increased their payment to £50,000. Those who knew the tough way in which News International, the *Sun*'s proprietor, conducted their litigation would have appreciated that this was their final word, as had been indicated to Carter-Ruck on 1 October. Carter-Ruck outlined to Roache the various alternatives open to him. His immediate reaction to the payment in was that Roache ought not to have to accept less than £100,000 by way of damages, but he made it clear that this would have to be the subject of very careful consideration and advice at a later stage. With the benefit of hindsight it was an unfortunate piece of advice, given that counsel had the previous month taken the view that upon payment in of £50,000 the serious risk would begin. Roache and his legal team hoped to recover more, but the stakes had been raised.

Unfortunately, the conference to review the case and the payment in did not take place until the afternoon of 24 October, with the trial due to start on the following Monday, 28 October. By that time Roache felt that the die was cast. He was told that the prospects of getting a higher award were 60–40. With those sort of odds he could ill afford to take the great financial risk of continuing the action. However, remarks he had made about being a gambler in golf and going for his shots seemed to have led the legal advisers to the view that he considered the gamble worth taking – which was, in fact, to be the analysis of Mr Justice Newman in the subsequent negligence action.

Indeed, Roache's instinct seems to have been to press for a higher award, but it was a high-risk strategy. Roache's subsequent complaint that the extent of the risk was not made sufficiently clear to him was unsuccessful. In retrospect he felt that what was to follow might have been avoided if this conference had taken place earlier and the precise financial consequences had been spelled out.

In any event, the case proceeded for five days in front of Mr Justice Waterhouse. Roache won, but the jury awarded him £50,000, precisely the sum already paid into court. The judge, who evidently had considerable sympathy for Roache, awarded him all his legal costs on the basis that part of his claim was for an injunction, that the newspaper had given no indication that it would not repeat these allegations, and that it had indeed published lurid details of the case during the trial.

But Roache's relief was short-lived. In November 1992, after examining all the correspondence relating to the negotiations between the parties, the Court of Appeal concluded that reason for the non-acceptance of the payment into court was not to obtain an injunction but in order to win a large amount of damages. Roache was therefore ordered to pay the newspaper's costs from the date of payment in. The consequences of this were appalling for Roache. He now faced a bill from News International of £61,007.69 for the newspaper's costs since the date of payment in, plus costs covering that period from his own solicitors of £55,000. Over £115,000 had been gambled with for the prospect of £25,000 to £50,000 damages over and above the £50,000 paid into court.

Roache felt very aggrieved at the advice he had received from his solicitors, and sued them for negligence. The happier moment at the beginning of the trial when Carter-Ruck had been photographed on the set of *Coronation Street* with members of the cast and crew now seemed a long way off. However, in July 1998, Mr Justice Newman, who heard the case in Manchester, concluded that his solicitors had not been negligent. He said that Roache had been very unlucky in the amount of damages he was awarded by the jury, but rejected Roache's claim that he had continued with the case because of negligent advice from Peter Carter-Ruck. He concluded that Roache had not been motivated by greed, but that his decision to reject the £50,000 paid into court had been dictated by hopes of being awarded a higher sum at a time when the level of awards was very unpredictable.

The loss of this case is said to have cost Roache a further £80,000 in legal bills. With some bitterness, Roache said that the judgement represented the continuation of a seven-year nightmare. To help pay his legal bills he devised a board game called Libel, the principal feature of which was the bank drafts used to pay lawyers. Ultimately, however, he had to declare himself bankrupt.

## The Costly Guest

The previous cases have outlined some of the traps which await the unwary plaintiff, and which could have been avoided with a little more thought. In some situations, though, problems arise which could not have been foreseen, as happened in the action brought by Mona Bauwens, which came to be dominated by extraneous considerations unrelated to the litigation – namely the political career and judgement of the Cabinet minister David Mellor. It also features another danger that may not have been bargained for: a deadlocked jury, which means that a further trial will be required if the case is to be resolved.

In the summer of 1990 David Mellor seemed to be riding high. He was chief secretary to the Treasury in the Thatcher government and, to all appearances, well house-trained. What could be more natural than that Mona Bauwens, the daughter of a leading Palestinian political figure, should include the Mellor family among her house party of twelve in the Marbella villa she had rented for a month for $20,000? The fact that the Mellors were to stay for a month, that Bauwens paid for the family's four air tickets and that Mellor had accepted similar hospitality over Christmas and the New Year from Sheikh Zayed in Abu Dhabi was to be ruthlessly exploited in the subsequent libel action.

Mona Bauwens, a film producer, had met David Mellor at a charity dinner for the Palestinian Medical Fund in 1986 and had become a family friend. She was married first to a Belgian property developer and subsequently to Mohammed Shourjabi, a banker. Her father, Jaweed Al Ghussein, was chairman of the Palestinian National Fund, an elected government body with thirty members. He was a moderate who advocated an Arab as opposed to a United Nations settlement of the Gulf crisis.

With infelicitous timing, Mellor managed to start his holiday with the daughter of the man described in the tabloid press as the 'top paymaster of the PLO' one day before Iraq invaded Kuwait. Iraq's aggression was supported by the Palestinians. Understandably, Mellor felt that there was little he personally could do to liberate the 4,000 British hostages in Kuwait and Iraq as he applied the Ambre Solaire in Marbella, and that he had obtained sufficient clearance for the trip. He was, however, a sitting duck for a press looking for politicians to blame. In September 1990 the *People* launched into Mellor with its report 'TOP TORY AND THE PLO PAYMASTER', supported by an editorial by the *People*'s proprietor, Robert Maxwell. Mellor had not endeared himself to the Jewish lobby when he had been filmed in 1988, as a Foreign Office minister on an official trip to Israel, berating an army officer in the Gaza Strip for his treatment of Palestinians.

Bauwens consulted her solicitors, Peter Carter-Ruck and

Partners, and issued a writ. She felt that the article branded her a social leper and outcast, not fit to be seen in decent company, and that it picked on her as an Arab woman. At the trial George Carman QC, with some force, made the point for the *People* that the article was designed to question David Mellor's political wisdom and judgement, and not to attack Bauwens. The report seemed more defamatory of her father than of her. Greater reflection might have focused Bauwens' mind on the fact that the *People*, for all its sales of 2.75 million and readership of 7 million, was not a major opinion-former and was probably read by few of Bauwens' friends and acquaintances.

Mrs Bauwens had successfully sued the *Observer* in respect of a piece in April 1989 which suggested that the BBC had rejected a film deal in which she was involved after fears of a link with the PLO. It was wrongly alleged that the PLO was the source of the finance and that she had tried to conceal this. The *Observer* paid damages into court which Mrs Bauwens accepted in April 1991.

This time, however, as often happens in libel actions, events took an unexpected turn. In July 1992, two months before the trial, Mellor, by then heritage secretary, had come under great pressure to resign from the government after his affair with a little-known actress, Antonia de Sancha, was reported in the tabloid press. His reputation had been undermined as he struggled to remain in the Cabinet. The amorous activities of the aptly named minister of fun – allegedly conducted in his replica Chelsea football strip – were retailed in the tabloid press and his telephone calls to Miss De Sancha were bugged. By the time the trial started in September, he had suffered a considerable loss of status. His evidence was not necessary for Bauwens' case and neither party called him as a witness. The *People* did subpoena him, but did not call him for fear of the damage his answers might do their case. Nevertheless, as the political pressure on Mellor mounted, the key issue in the trial increasingly became his wisdom in accepting Bauwens' hospitality rather than her links or otherwise with the PLO. Bauwens justifiably complained that she had not done anything wrong. She had been caught up in something that was bigger than her, and had been left to cope on her own.

The defence tactics were to concentrate on Mellor to seek to support what had been written and to establish that it was fair comment. As Carman put the matter, somewhat portentously, to the jury: 'When the clouds of war gather around the country and the nation takes the strain, you expect, do you not, unambiguous loyalty and conduct, and never ever for a minister to put himself in any association with a friend of the enemy?' He later observed, memorably, that 'Marbella has sand, sea and sunshine, and if a politician goes there and, in the honest view of some, behaves like an ostrich and puts his head in the sand, thereby exposing his thinking parts, it may be that a newspaper is entitled to say so.' It was felt by many that the revelation that Mellor had allowed Bauwens to pay for his family's air tickets sealed his fate as a Cabinet Minister.

The defence also tried to smear Bauwens by hinting, without ever directly suggesting it (as there was no basis for doing so), that there was an improper relationship between David Mellor and herself. Carman's tactics – 'behaving like a stand-up comic and music-hall act' – came under acrimonious attack from Bauwens' counsel, Richard Hartley QC. They were 'cruel, because at no time did he spare her feelings. No stick was too small to beat her with. It was cowardly, because he was prepared to wound but afraid to strike. Innuendos were left hanging in the air insinuating many things. Mr Carman is a past master of the wink-wink nudge-nudge, but he never puts a specific allegation. It's a classic smear tactic. She suffered a verbal mugging as the defendants decided to put the boot in and go for broke.' Carman's questions relating to Bauwens taking tea with Mellor and referring to private photographs which showed her sitting in a leotard on a rocking horse were 'pure, unadulterated prejudice'.

Bauwens' attempt to protect her reputation inexorably became side-tracked by prurient tabloid speculation as to the exact nature of her relationship with Mellor, notwithstanding the absence of any evidence of impropriety. *Today*'s headline was 'I HAD MELLOR FOR TEA' and the *Sun*'s, 'MR MELLOR'S MONA TEA-SER'. Carman's response to the judge, Mr Justice Drake, who wanted to know what was being suggested, was unconvincing. 'I did not suggest hanky panky or anything more dignified.' It led the judge to observe that he did not know if the press reports of the trial were supposed to be fair and accurate, but only one subject was addressed in them. Even the two visits of Mrs Mellor to court were criticised by the defence, who implied that they had been stage-managed for the press. Hartley was not having any of that. 'You may think that's a bit rich coming from Mr Carman. In the courtroom he has been the stage manager, producer and leading actor. If Mrs Mellor had not attended, George Carman would have drawn an inference from that as well. She was damned if she did and she was damned if she didn't.'

Bauwens can hardly have imagined that the case would become an opportunity to attack a discredited minister, or that unforeseeable events after she had issued her writ in September 1990 would come to dominate the case. She complained at the trial about the damaging press coverage, saying it had made her physically ill.

In summing up, Mr Justice Drake told the jury that they had to decide whether the fact that Mrs Bauwens was her Palestinian father's daughter justified the report and the public interest in Mr Mellor. The jury did not have to award football pools figures – 'Bear in mind they are wounded feelings. How long they will last is a matter for you. There may not be a permanent wound which will last for ever: perhaps more like a nasty bruise than a complete loss of a limb.' The judge perhaps felt that the case was something of a storm in one of Bauwens' elegant teacups.

After an eight-day trial, the jury were not able to agree on a verdict, being split 6–6. A retrial was ordered but never took place, and the action was settled on undisclosed terms in March 1993. Bauwens' costs were estimated at £250,000. The paper turned down the suggestion that the second trial should be by judge alone, evidently feeling that their chances were best served by floating their prejudicial allegations past another jury.

On 24 September 1992, two days after the trial ended, Mellor was compelled to resign from his post as heritage secretary – a job he had held for a mere 167 days. He had, as the *Sun* put it, gone 'from toe job to no job'.

As for Mrs Bauwens, the action not only left her poorer, it also focused disagreeable publicity on her life. In 1993 she attended a press conference in support of Clive Soley MP's Privacy Bill to provide an effective and speedy remedy for those wronged by the press. She complained that intrusive press coverage of her libel action against the *People* had turned her into a commodity and damaged her, her family and those who lived around her.

It seems that she decided to take action as she felt that it would establish her as a person to be reckoned with. That, unfortunately, is not a service which the law of libel often provides. Although it would have been difficult for Mrs Bauwens to have anticipated the course the case would take in court, her story is a salutary reminder that it is worth suing for libel only over things that really matter.

# 12

# SKELETONS IN THE CUPBOARD

### Should Sleeping Dogs Be Let Lie?

When a plaintiff is in the public eye, it is more likely that if his or her action is contested any hidden secrets will be brought into the light of day. The lessons of the Reynolds case (see Chapter 16) may prove to be a disincentive to such plaintiffs.

The libel action brought by the Conservative MP for Leicestershire North-West in 1994 against *The Sunday Times* was a classic example of needless self-destruction – particularly as David Ashby was a barrister himself. He should certainly have known better. Had he fully discussed with his solicitors, Peter Carter-Ruck and Partners, the skeletons that lurked in the Ashby family cupboard, it is difficult to imagine that he would have been advised to issue a writ. Deeper reflection might have brought it home to him that he was always going to have difficulty in persuading a jury that nothing untoward was happening when he shared a 4ft 8in bed with a man of thirty-two, especially when, as it was unkindly suggested at the trial, he was, at fifty-five, old enough to be his father. Add to that Ashby's distinctly bizarre domestic arrangements – an estranged Italian wife who, he claimed, not only described him in no uncertain terms as a 'poofter', but had also set about him when she found him with an elderly retired civil servant with whom she believed he might have been having a homosexual relationship, not to mention a visit to a gay pub – and it is clear that it was a very foolish case to bring.

Win or lose, the litigation was going to be very distressing, with Ashby's family divided into two camps and the MP himself having to relay intimate details of his sexual capabilities and proclivities. Moreover, the Cassandra factor would come into play: Ashby ran an unacceptably high risk of being disbelieved by the jury, even when he was telling the truth, simply because the facts were such that an innocent explanation was improbable. Experience might have told him that *The Sunday Times* was unlikely to back down in the face of his writ and would indeed take the case to court. And given the unpopularity of the John Major administration at the time, it was hardly the moment to be a Conservative MP appealing to a jury for damages with a somewhat ropey case.

The article which gave rise to the case was published by *The Sunday Times* in January 1994. It was based on an anonymous call from someone identifying himself only as 'Steve', who told them that Ashby had left his wife for another man. There had been, he added, a nasty incident at Ashby's London flat when Mrs Ashby had tried to persuade him to spend Christmas with her and their daughter. It was never established who exactly 'Steve' was, although suspicion was to fall on a relative of Ashby's – a suggestion that was firmly denied.

In the general atmosphere of sleaze and the Conservatives' 'Back to Basics' policy, the story proved irresistible to *The Sunday Times*. Unlike the tabloids, broadsheets do not publish stand-alone sexual tittle-tattle. When such a story arises they read an MP's electoral address and look for signs of hypocrisy which would justify such revelations before they publish them. In the 1992 General Election Ashby had laid emphasis on the importance of the family. He was married with a family, he had told the electorate, and therefore understood their needs. He was a man of integrity who believed in traditional moral values, discipline and effective law and order. So, in accusing Ashby of hypocrisy, the newspaper felt it had a valid point.

Towards the end of 1993, Ashby had left his wife after thirty turbulent years of marriage. To recover from an unhappy Christmas, and as an antidote to the Maastricht Treaty, he decided to go to France for a break, following the route taken by Henry V's army and visiting Agincourt and the battlefield of Crécy. Ashby's companion on the trip was Dr Ciaran Kilduff. They spent the first night in a twin-bedded room in the Hotel Bristol in Le Touquet. More problematic was their second night spent away, when they repaired to the Château Tilques Hotel in St Omer. Their room contained a double bed, apparently offered at a special rate. Ashby was never able to explain satisfactorily why he did not ask for another.

Ashby's London flat was above Kilduff's in Westleigh Avenue, Putney. Early on Friday 7 January a *Sunday Times* photographer parked his car outside the building and recorded Kilduff coming out of Ashby's flat and going into his own. When Ashby himself emerged, he held his briefcase up in front of his face.

On Sunday 9 January *The Sunday Times* ran an article about the break-up of Ashby's marriage. They then interviewed Mrs Ashby, who claimed that it had been caused by her husband's friendship with another man ('WIFE'S FURY OVER ERRANT MP'). On 16 January 1994, the newspaper published another piece headlined: 'ASHBY SHARES A DOUBLE BED ON GOA TRIP'. It was alleged that he had spent the night with an unnamed man at the Indian resort at the Silver Sands Hotel, described at the trial as a 'lovenest' where few questions were asked. In fact the MP had been alone in the hotel. The newspaper accepted that he had not holidayed in Goa with another man, but had been on his own. In April it apologised for its error. But it would not retract its allegation that Ashby was a homosexual.

Many people would feel that an allegation of homosexuality is not in itself defamatory, and in some cases it would not be. But in these circumstances, levelled at a family man and charging him with hypocrisy, there is little doubt that it was. Ashby felt confident that he would win his libel action after the paper admitted it had made a mistake with its Goa story. Unwisely, he took advantage of the burden of proof which rested on the newspaper to prove its case and chose to overlook the fact that he had indeed shared a queen-sized double bed with a man in an hotel – but in France, as *The Sunday Times* knew all too well.

As we have seen, the cases in which it is imperative for a plaintiff to bring a libel action are rare. It would have been unpleasant but not impossible for Ashby to have accepted *The Sunday Times*'s correction and apology for its error in suggesting that he had shared a bed with a male friend in Goa. There are two ground rules for plaintiffs in such circumstances. The first is to ask what the reaction of a newspaper to the issue of a writ is likely to be and what will be the consequences of that reaction for the plaintiff. The second is to ask the plaintiff to picture the journalist with a blank piece of paper and to ask him how it was that the journalist came to fill that piece of paper with the offending story. That should flush out any underlying element of truth in a story which may contain a number of errors.

As a barrister, Ashby should have been aware of the likelihood of what would emerge in such a high-profile action. Clearly he gambled on his wife not testifying against him. He wrote to her before the trial to discourage her from giving evidence for *The Sunday Times*. 'If I lose, then consider the situation. Personally, I will be destroyed as a member of Parliament and as a barrister. My total means of support will have been lost and my ability to support you in any way with it. It will have been you who have done it and you will be seen to have done it.' Ashby's forecast was not that wide of the mark.

At the trial Ashby sought to justify his sleeping arrangements in France by saying that it was something he had done on rugby trips in the past. Moreover, male MPs on occasion roomed together on foreign visits to save money. He even handed the trial judge, Mr Justice Morland, a note containing the name of an

MP with whom he had shared a room in the past. The MP's name was not disclosed, but the reason for this frugality was apparently the tight limits set on expenditure by the Commons fee office. Although Ashby admitted to financial problems, he said he could have afforded another room very easily, but he wouldn't have dreamed of wasting money in that way. The room had cost £44, but the two men had spent £50 on dinner. Ashby gave Kilduff cash to pay the bill. He later complained that the receipt had been stolen from his dustbin by the press.

He was asked by Richard Hartley QC why he had taken the terrible gamble of sharing a double bed with Dr Ciaran Kilduff. It was pointed out to him that the Château Tilques Hotel had had thirty-three vacant rooms that night, many of which were single or twin-bedded. Rather unconvincingly, Ashby said that to have done so would have been rude to Dr Kilduff. 'I didn't see any great thing about it. What was I supposed to do, say to Dr Kilduff, "I am not sleeping with you?" It didn't even enter my head. The fact was that we were not in the state of mind to think of traipsing back down to reception to say it wasn't good enough.' As it was, they had dinner together and played cards. Ashby went up to bed fifteen minutes before Kilduff and fell asleep.

Besides, 'I wasn't going to be dictated to by my wife. Frankly, I didn't see why she should dictate who I saw and how I lived after I left her. I was rather determined I should be able to lead my own life.' Nothing untoward had apparently happened as Ashby had worn a grotesque mask with a hosepipe attached to it – not as any form of sexual apparatus, but as a device to help him sleep – which was understandably said to have ruled out the possibility of any homosexual acts.

The hapless Ashby was then obliged to tell the jury that he could not have had a homosexual affair in any case as he was impotent. Even so, it was put to him by Hartley, 'Impotence doesn't prevent two men sharing a bed together and it wouldn't prevent the showing of affection.'

Ashby found himself exposed to close cross-examination

about his relationship with Kilduff. Although he already owned a house in West Hill, Putney – and another in Leicestershire – he had bought the Westleigh Avenue flat above Kilduff's – to get away from his wife, he explained. A video was produced which showed Ashby arriving outside Kilduff's flat on the August Bank Holiday of 1995 and leaving the following morning. Ashby strongly disputed the interpretation *The Sunday Times* sought to put on this. He explained that he had simply dropped off Kilduff after collecting him from the airport the night before and had gone round to Westleigh Avenue at around 6.30 the next morning for a potter round the garden before having a cup of coffee with Kilduff.

Kilduff's evidence confirmed that there had been no physical intimacy between the two men. He had suggested the French trip as a means of relieving Ashby's stress following the break-up of his marriage. In cross-examination, however, Richard Hartley QC was able to leave a few questions about his proclivities hanging in the air. 'I have many friends both male and female,' Kilduff said. When he was asked how intimate his relationships with women were, he replied: 'I don't presume to discuss my love life in public view.' Questioned about whether he had ever shared a room with a woman on holiday, he declared, 'That's not fair.' He hadn't considered it risky to share a double bed with Ashby in a French hotel; indeed, he had already successfully sued three tabloid newspapers for suggesting that he had behaved improperly with Ashby. Kilduff's solicitors had successfully brought his actions to conclusion before Ashby's was heard, the defendants having rapidly made offers to settle when an early trial date for the doctor's case was fixed. And whereas Ashby was to lose his action, all Kilduff's cases were settled out of court for a total of £22,000. Newspapers, it seemed, were not as interested in taking on a doctor as they were a Conservative MP.

Kilduff told the jury he had met Ashby in 1992. Evidently they hit if off, as one month later they flew to the USA together. 'You must have been amazed,' Hartley suggested. 'A person you met casually, you mention you are going to America and the next thing you know, he is booked on the same flight. You didn't think he was being a little forward? Brash?'

'You know what politicians are like! Some people might,' Kilduff answered, 'but as a doctor my business is to establish a rapport with people within a ten-minute conversation, so I tend to be quite open with people.'

There were further horrors for Ashby before he had finished giving his evidence. He described his 'distressful' marriage to a woman who called him a 'poofter'. 'I am bound to say,' Ashby related as he lapsed into barrister-speak, 'that for the last five or six years we fought every single day, at least once, maybe twice a day, and the fights were vicious.' He said that his wife, Silvana, had made false allegations that he beat her. When she returned to their home in Leicestershire and found him there with a retired civil servant – who, said Ashby, had recently had a stroke – plates and knives had, he claimed, started winging in his direction. She had broken his glasses, but it was she who called the police and he had waited in his car till they arrived. 'I would characterise myself as a victim of domestic violence,' said the former rugby player. He said he had never rugby-tackled her but had on a few occasions wrestled her to the ground. 'On one or two occasions I found it effective to get hold of her and bring her to the ground. She can't scratch, she can't kick, she can't grab my glasses or hair when she is on the ground. She is like a Jekyll and Hyde. If I am very upset she suddenly flips.' Ashby then broke down in tears, as he added 'and then she's wonderful.'

He said he had been attacked very frequently by Silvana but denied throwing a wet sponge at her when his mother-in-law was staying, or brandishing a carving knife at her, or threatening to kill her. Whatever the truth of the matter, this was a sorry picture of middle-aged, middle-class marital discord.

To add to his discomfiture, there was much disputed evidence during Ashby's five days in the witness box about his alleged homosexuality. He denied that in October 1993 he had confessed to his wife: 'I've got to tell you something. I've changed,' or that he had admitted to a brief homosexual encounter many years before adding that, although he had put it out of his mind for a very long time, he was no longer able to do so. He even suffered the indignity of having to call his doctor, Lewis Sevitt, whom he had consulted in May 1993 complaining of headaches and an inability to get an erection in the morning. Dr Sevitt's evidence scarcely helped Ashby. When he was asked by Hartley, 'If a person is having a mid-life crisis and is discovering he is more homosexual than heterosexual, that would lead to the symptoms you have been describing?' Dr Sevitt replied: 'That is a possibility'

Some support for Ashby's case came from his daughter, Alexandra, a stockbroker living in Milan. However, her evidence underlined the deep split in the Ashby family. She said her mother often accused Ashby of having homosexual affairs, citing among others a young researcher and a barrister friend. She had even herself been accused of lesbianism by her mother when, at the age of fifteen, she had got changed in a beach hut on holiday in Italy with a friend. The bitterness between Ashby and his sister, Lynne Granling, who was clearly sympathetic to the defence, was exploited by Hartley when he questioned Ashby. 'I am not prepared to take my sister's word on anything,' said the MP.

'What, not even her age?'

'That's the last thing.'

'When you refer to your beloved sister, you are, I presume, being sarcastic?'

'Very, I'm afraid.'

Worse was to come when Ashby's wife, Silvana, gave evidence for the defence. She was described with old-world courtesy by her husband as 'a vicious, sick woman, motivated by malice, who despises me'. She described how, when Ashby returned from America in September 1992, where he had she said, been visiting his homosexual brother Brian and his partner, he had declared he could stand things no longer. She denied that she had asked him if he was a poof like his brother. She did, however, admit to leaving very unpleasant messages on his answering machine when she was very upset and cross. She complained that she was treated like a maid, not like a wife. She claimed that when she had asked Ashby to spend more time at home, he had replied: 'No, I will buy you a dog instead.' When he had been elected to the House of Commons, she alleged he had said: 'Remember, Silvana, from now on for you I am dead. I don't exist for you any more. I will dedicate myself to my work. Don't count on me, I can have whatever I want now.'

Like most of the evidence, this was disputed. It would in any case have been a poor prediction. In Ashby's fourteen years in Parliament, he achieved little more than service on various Commons committees, such as those on the housing bills, where, to his credit, given the accusations of hypocrisy, he backed a move by Glenda Jackson MP for gay couples to be granted the same rights as heterosexuals to inherit the tenancy of partners' homes.

In an example of how even routine events can be used in libel cases to discredit someone, Ashby was asked about a three-day official trip to America, for which his expenses had been paid by the controversial lottery operator, Camelot. 'I always find these visits very informative but very hard work,' he told a visibly unimpressed jury.

Silvana gave graphic evidence of her suspicions of her husband's homosexual affairs. She claimed that Ashby had pointed a kitchen knife at her chest and threatened to kill her after she found him with a male friend she thought might have been a lover. They had thrown water at each other and she had venomously told him, 'My God, David, you make me sick. First of all you go for young boys, now you are going for old and crippled men.' When she had gone round to see Ashby at Kilduff's flat on Christmas Eve, there was more violence, she claimed. Ashby had grabbed her by the neck and Kilduff had called the police, telling them, 'We have an intruder in the flat. Can you send someone round?'

After this emotional testimony, the evidence of Andrew Pierce, a journalist with *The Times*, came as some welcome light relief,

although it was damaging to Ashby's denials about his prefer-
ences. Pierce claimed to have seen Ashby in the aptly named
Queen's Head pub in Tyron Street, Chelsea. He described this
establishment as 'one of London's oldest and best-known gay
pubs – men holding hands and the bar staff as camp as a row of
tents. Their voices gave the game away. They call each other
"dear" and "love". You would be under no illusion whatsoever.'
Ashby had apparently wandered in unsuspectingly for a drink.
'Whether it's a gay pub I don't know, but [the defence] solicitors
have shown me a homosexual guide to London,' he said. 'I didn't
know such things existed which show it's a homosexual pub, and
I think I must accept that.'

In final submission to the jury, Richard Hartley QC was dis-
missive of Ashby's explanation of the choice of a double-bedded
room. 'You are in the realm of people believing in Father
Christmas or that babies are delivered by storks.' Ashby's counsel, Geoffrey Shaw QC, called into question Silvana's motives,
referring to 'the green-eyed monster which doth mock the flesh
it feeds on'. In summing up, Mr Justice Morland pinpointed the
difficult decisions the jury had to reach. 'You have been wit-
nessing a family really exposing its misery to the full glare of
publicity. You've heard the details of verbal abuse and physical
abuse between husband and wife. Both claim to still love each
other very much, although they have given evidence on opposite
sides.'

After a retirement of five hours, the jury by a 10–2 majority
found in favour of *The Sunday Times*. This was one of the fairly
rare cases in which a paper discharges the burden of proving that
what it has written is true. The stakes had been very high. Ashby
was said to be facing legal costs of £500,000 for the four-week
trial. Had the jury accepted his case, he could have expected to
have recovered damages of between £50,000 and £120,000. Mr
Justice Morland had suggested to the jury that less than £50,000
would have been niggardly and more than £120,000
extravagant.

As it was, the case demonstrated how a determined newspaper

defendant can turn up devastating evidence. As voters are increasingly willing to accommodate their MPs' personal short-comings or sexual foibles, it is difficult to see why Ashby felt constrained to sue, particularly when he would have known what evidence existed for the newspaper to discover. If he had been gambling on his wife not testifying, and on the newspaper not uncovering the evidence on which it relied at the trial, it was a gamble which any prospective plaintiff would be mad to emulate.

The final chapter to the story was Ashby's ignominious deselection after the case. He dismissed his former constituents as 'a bunch of homophobics. They were behaving rather like Smithfield porters – or is that being unfair to Smithfield porters? – love the Queen Mum and bash the queers.' Before he departed Parliament, Ashby fired Silvana as his secretary. And the voters of Leicestershire North-West showed in 1997 that they had had enough of the Conservatives altogether.

## A Case Blown Out of All Proportion

One June evening in 1992 PC Terence Talbot approached a Range Rover parked in a layby on a slip road off the A1 near Borehamwood. PC Talbot's eye was caught by a woman with blonde hair who was lying with her head in her passenger's lap. Her head was moving up and down slightly and the passenger's eyes were closed. He was in no doubt that the woman's head was on the man's groin and that he had seen an erect penis. He immediately arrested the man for gross indecency.

The woman was Gillian Taylforth, better known as Kathy Beale, the café-owner in the BBC soap *EastEnders*. The man was her partner, Geoffrey Knights, the father of her child. The couple were well known for their stormy relationship. Knights was a self-made millionaire. He had made his money from office furniture and building businesses and had worked as property dealer and car salesman. He had convictions for burglary and criminal damage, and had received a prison sentence for assault after a fracas in a curry house. He had also been jailed for breaking a non-molestation order against Taylforth.

Knights and Taylforth had spent a well-lubricated day at Royal Ascot and as a result he had suffered an attack of pancreatitis. Taylforth had pulled into the layby and he had loosened his trousers to lessen the pain. Taylforth was simply leaning over to place her hand on his stomach to find where it hurt when PC Talbot had come and tapped on the car window, saying, 'I saw what you were doing. You were committing an act of gross indecency.' Taylforth indignantly replied, 'You've got to be joking – my boyfriend's ill.' Unfortunately the constable did not recognise a case of pancreatitis triggered by heavy drinking when he saw one.

After his arrest, Knights had done Taylforth's cause little good at the police station, either by threatening, 'Take your uniforms off and I will fucking fight you outside,' or by signing a caution admitting outraging public decency. That alone should have deterred the couple from bringing a libel action, whatever the truth of the matter.

As all too often happens with the famous, word of Knights' arrest leaked from the police to the press. Stuart Higgins from the *Sun* was soon on the phone. The upshot was 'TV KATHY'S SEX ROMP FURY'. Ostensibly reporting her outrage at Knights' arrest by the police, the story also suggested to its readers that Knights had been looking for some other kind of relief than that required for a pancreatic attack. An upset Taylforth rushed to her lawyers and a writ was issued against the *Sun*. The paper claimed their story was true; alternatively, if they had libelled Taylforth, it was all down to the Metropolitan Police, who had given them the information.

The facts were fiercely contested. Taylforth would not have dreamed of bringing the case unless she was convinced that PC Talbot was mistaken in what he believed he had seen. After all, people do not usually give blow jobs in broad daylight on the side of the A1, let alone to men with whom they have had a seven-year relationship and with whom they live but a short distance away. Taylforth would have been advised that as a well-known TV personality she stood to recover very substantial damages.

Yet bringing the action was a disastrous miscalculation, for it rested on the word of herself and Knights against that of the police. Moreover, Knights' behaviour at the scene and at the police station increased the probability that the police would be believed. The lurid subject matter of the case made it tempting for the paper to contest the case, particularly as it had manoeuvred itself into a position where it should win on one of two grounds: either against Taylforth because it *was* a blow job, or against the police because they had *said* it was a blow job, when in fact it was a nasty case of pancreatitis. And the trial would give the *Sun* a rich seam for copy to boot. A well-informed betting man would have given Taylforth odds of no more than 60–40 in her favour. Such odds did not make the cost or the publicity generated by the case worthwhile.

What happened in the layby dominated the trial. PC Talbot was adamant that when he had tapped on the window the gentleman had looked at him and the woman had resumed her position in the driver's seat. He saw, for a fleeting moment, that Knights was holding his erect penis with his right hand and trying to replace it in his trousers. Taylforth's counsel, Michael Beloff QC, suggested that the policeman had either made a complete mistake or had embroidered the incident. It was pointed out that his notes did not mention seeing Taylforth's head moving up and down. Talbot was unmovable. 'No, sir. I made no mistake. I recorded what I saw.'

With some force Beloff argued that any man who wants sex will open his trousers, but not every man who opens his trousers wants sex. The judge, Mr Justice Drake, asked PC Talbot: 'If you want to go somewhere quiet for a kiss and cuddle and a bit more besides, you could find somewhere better than a slip road?'

'Definitely, sir,' Talbot agreed.

Tests were conducted in the court car park to determine whether a blow job as described was physically possible. The results were inconclusive. 'YES, YOU CAN DO IT IN A RANGE ROVER' the *Sun* trumpeted – but not, apparently, if you were wearing a seatbelt. Taylforth disagreed: 'I would have had to have had a neck like a giraffe in the position I was in, or he would have had to have been really well endowed.' Clearly Taylforth was no giraffe, but there were limits to what the judge would allow to be demonstrated. The roles had in any event been played by averagely endowed *Sun* journalists.

Knights, giving evidence on Taylforth's behalf, explained that they had endured a nightmare and it had had a horrible degrading effect. On the matter of his conduct at the police station and his signing of the caution, Knights said he had been too ill and too drunk to know what he was signing, and had thought it was papers relating to the return of his belt and money, and a slap on the wrist for being abusive. He added that he had been half asleep. The police, on the other hand, claimed that Knights had been in full possession of his mental faculties. Professor Farndon, consultant surgeon at Bristol Royal Infirmary, testified that from Knights' description of his condition, which had caused five previous attacks, and his own professional experience, he would expect someone suffering such an attack to want to rest in bed and take pain-relieving drugs. But he did not think Knights was genuinely ill in any serious way.

Knights, for his part, entertained the jury with his reply to the question asking him to list his criminal convictions – 'What, all of them?'

In her evidence Taylforth angrily rejected the suggestion there had been any hanky panky. 'Geoff and I share a deep, mutual loving relationship and what we get up to in our relationship is entirely up to us. That is what we do behind closed doors. We are not exhibitionists and we respect one another and love one another. I have got a private life and I am entitled to have one.'

The odds had probably moved to 70–30 in her favour. The judge seemed sympathetic, and that counts for a lot in libel actions. Things, however, changed over the weekend, when something came to light which served as a reminder that high-profile libel actions can result in skeletons being dragged from cupboards. Two men had turned up at the offices of the *Sun*, clutching in their sweaty palms a thirty-five-minute video of the twentieth-anniversary lunch party of the Anna Scher Theatre School in Islington, at which Taylforth had been a student. Like everything in this case, it seemed, this was a record of a well-lubricated occasion. When one of the luvvies held up a sausage, Taylforth could be seen asking for a battery – it was, apparently, her vibrator joke. She was also shown putting a wine bottle between her legs and uttering the words – particularly unfortunate in the context of the case – 'Yeah, a lot of people say I give good head'.

Rather surprisingly, the *Sun*'s barrister, George Carman QC, on seeing the video, had telephoned his junior to ask what 'giving good head' meant. 'Fellatio, George,' his junior helpfully explained, with a barrister's fondness for Latin. 'Is that all?' exclaimed Carman. It was rather different in court. 'What does "good head" mean?' demanded Carman sternly of Taylforth.

'I suppose it means holding a man's penis and doing what I was supposed to be doing on the A1. I think they are words everyone uses in this day and age. "Giving good head" means giving a man a blow job.'

Suddenly, the judge seemed less sympathetic to the plaintiff. She was shown on the video appearing to unbutton her blouse and joking that she might be able to raise the £2.50 needed for a bottle of wine by selling her services. The court persona of George Carman swung into overdrive and affected suitable shock on behalf of the *Sun*. 'By anyone's standards, for a young woman in a public place in daylight to put a wine bottle near her vagina after placing it near her bottom and then simulating masturbation is pretty disgusting behaviour.'

'Had I been sober it would not have happened. It's not very nice, no. It was a private video, if someone had said it was for public use I would not have done it. I had known these friends since I was seventeen. I was very, very drunk. I think the party had been going on for about three hours.'

For good measure the video finished with a display of the men at the party making some politically incorrect comments about the women's behaviour. The video was of no evidential value for the *Sun*'s case, but distinctly prejudicial. In vain did Taylforth protest that the remark about £2.50 for her services was obviously a joke. Carman turned the knife. 'The whole impression of your evidence, the language you selected and the expression of outrage and disgust you have given the jury, I suggest all this has been a great show misleading the jury and the true Gillian Taylforth, when you are in drink, emerges in this video.' She was not, Carman suggested, 'the demure lady her counsel has painted to the jury. Miss Taylforth was behaving in a way [in which] one hopes the majority of young women in this country would never behave.' In other words, Taylforth had blown it. And so the jury decided, by a majority of 10–2.

Taylforth collapsed in court, hyperventilating, and needed medical treatment. Her sister launched into the Masonic judge, Mr Justice Drake, who had presided over the case, 'Which bloody lodge do you belong to?' He had on an earlier occasion made it clear that his freemasonry did not affect his work as a judge in any way: 'If I were trying somebody and they tried to signal to me or whatever, I would have to restrain myself from increasing the sentence.' Taylforth had to pay the legal costs not only of the *Sun* but also of the Metropolitan Police. With her own legal bills, these were estimated to amount to £500,000. Knights, who may by then have been feeling embarrassed about the whole débâcle, had sold his Ferrari Testarossa to finance the case, and that looked like being followed by his six-bedroomed house in Epping.

Knights gained one benefit from the case. He faced trial in September 1995 at Harrow Crown Court for wounding a Martin Davis with intent to do him grievous bodily harm. He was able to persuade a rather timid judge that the lurid pre-trial publicity – which included the *Sun*'s references to his violent past and previous convictions, and to treatment Gillian Taylforth had received, allegedly after being beaten up by him; plus a headline in the *Mirror* accusing, 'KNIGHTS BEAT ME TO A PULP', illustrated with a picture of him in handcuffs – made a fair trial impossible. Knights therefore walked free. Attempts to fine the newspapers for contempt of court failed, as it was felt that none of the publications created a greater risk of serious prejudice to the course of justice than already existed. In any event, juries are better at disregarding prejudicial material than Crown Court judges sometimes realise.

Taylforth did not have to sue. It was a needless gamble. Beloff had, very properly and with great prescience, warned her before the action about Carman's reputation for finding skeletons in cupboards. A libel action is an imperfect way of establishing the truth. If the hope was to recover enormous damages, it was a massive miscalculation. The ridicule which Taylforth suffered was exemplified by her selection as the subject of a *Sun* limerick competition. The newspaper helpfully pointed out, in case such a handy word should not occur to potential contestants, that an abbreviation for Gillian was Gilly.

## Boer Wars

Jani Allan, a thirty-eight-year-old UK-based columnist for *The Sunday Times of South Africa*, and a former teacher and part-time model, had done well out of suing the media. She had obtained £20,000 libel damages, plus her legal costs, from *Options* magazine and £15,000 from the *Evening Standard* for allegations that she had had an affair with Eugene Terre Blanche, the leader of the extreme right-wing Afrikaner Weerstandsbeweging (AWB) in South Africa. She also had writs outstanding against the *Daily Mail* and the *Daily Telegraph* over the same matter. So when, in 1991, Channel 4 broadcast a profile of Terre Blanche – *The Leader, His Driver and His Driver's Wife* – in which they repeated the allegations, she decided to sue them too. At the trial George Carman QC, for Channel 4, observed: 'If you win this and win the other two, libel is going to prove a very fruitful source of income for you.'

This was a case with a distinctly Afrikaner flavour, overshadowed by the unattractive but absent eighteen-stone figure of Terre Blanche. The jury was to hear allegations of cavorting in a Lancia sports car at the town of Krugersdorp, an escapade for which Terre Blanche had arrived in his 'very stupid little furry hat with ear flaps', and at which shots of whisky and peach schnapps were being dispensed; of an assignation at the Paardekraal Monument, an Afrikaner shrine (which, incidentally, Terre Blanche had been arrested for, but subsequently acquitted of, damaging). The jury was also to learn that the graffiti artists who scrawled on the walls of Johannesburg 'Jani Allan loves *boerewors*' were not referring only to the Afrikaner sausage which Allan and Terre Blanche used to eat together, but also to the word's secondary meaning as a slang word for the male sex organ.

Allan complained that the programme portrayed her as a woman of easy virtue. Channel 4 denied they had suggested an affair between Allan and Terre Blanche – something much rumoured in South Africa – but at the same time, in a strategy puzzling to the lay person, asserted that if the jury did think the programme suggested such an affair, it happened to be a fact.

The case had started promisingly enough, before Mr Justice Potts and a jury, in July 1992. Allan described how she led a celibate life and maintained that she had never been intimate with Terre Blanche, whom she described, with some justification, as 'repulsive' and as 'looking rather like a pig in a safari suit'. She was horrified, appalled and nauseated at the references in the programme to her having had an affair with him. Moreover, to substantiate this, she had had treatment for her lack of interest in sex. She called her psychologist, Dori-Anne Weil, who spoke of Allan's difficulties in forming meaningful long-term relationships with men.

In theory, suing for libel for an allegation of an affair should not present great difficulties for a plaintiff. Since the burden of proof is on the defendants, they are likely to face considerable difficulties if both the alleged participants deny any such relationship. Jani Allan's problem was that a number of her friends claimed to have witnessed the affair in intimate detail or to have discussed it with her. Terre Blanche was given to leaving messages on her answerphone, pleading with 'the loveliest girl with the most beautiful brain' to call him. He had also, Allan told the court, developed an obsession for ringing her in the middle of the night and turning up uninvited at her flat. On one occasion he had even bent the burglar bars on her window to get in. She herself was given to keeping an explicit diary which, unfortunately for her, fell into the hands of the defendants and completely destroyed her case.

Jani Allan's diary for 1984–5, recorded in a notebook, arrived dramatically in a parcel delivered to the court by a dispatch rider. It had been acquired in mysterious circumstances and the identity of the person who produced it was never revealed. This was yet another example of a plaintiff foolishly suing for libel when he or she was well aware of the existence of documents which, in the wrong hands, could blow the case apart. The diary covered a period predating her alleged affair with Terre Blanche by a few years. Providentially, it turned up shortly after her firm denial of any adultery.

But in the notebook were details of what appeared to be affairs with a married Italian pilot called Ricardo and an Italian gun-smuggler called Mauro. Entries included: 'On the way home he [Ricardo] cried. I stayed the night and it was heaven. We were stoned. We made love twice. It was freaky.' 'I remember us laughing about the freckles on our backs. I remember it hurting when he was in me. I remember the silk of his skin, and the way he kissed my ****.' 'Went to the flat, it was heaven.' Another entry described how Allan went to an hotel and made love to Ricardo.

She claimed the diary was fantasy and had been written when she was in a traumatic state and under psychiatric care. She had recorded her worst fears and her worst desires as a way of dealing with her sexual problems. She said it had absolutely, categorically not been written for public consumption and was deeply embarrassing. Carman, however, accused her of desperately inventing this story of a fantasy diary to protect herself against the consequence of perjury. Allan admitted to a degree of sexual foreplay with other men, but was adamant that she had never gone the whole way with Ricardo. The explanation for this in her diary – whether imagined or real – was that her gay clair-voyant had warned her to be careful not to get pregnant when Ricardo visited her. She admitted that she had been infatuated with Ricardo, and that she had a real letter from him containing the legally unhelpful observation: 'I love you for ever – you are the best thing in my life, all my love, your Ricardo.' Asked by Mr Justice Potts whether she had had an affair with Ricardo, she gave an unconvincing answer about not being sure if foreplay, fantasy and flirtation made it into an affair. 'I suppose you would call it an affair. There wasn't absolute sexual intercourse.' She was accused by Carman of being a liar and hypocrite. She remarked wryly to him: 'Whatever award is given for libel, being cross-examined by you would not make it enough.'

The picture Allan tried to paint of herself as a *hausfrau*, totally obedient to her husband, was further undermined when she was cross-examined about what she had written in her newspaper column about Terre Blanche. 'He speaks with a rich earth brown voice. Sometimes it has the loamy texture of a newly ploughed mealie field. I am impaled on the blue flame of his blowtorch eyes.' She was asked what she meant by this. 'His eyes bore into me much the way your eyes are boring into me,' she told Carman. This did not mean she found him attractive. Charles Moore, the editor of the *Daily Telegraph*, had referred to piercing blue eyes, but he was not accused of having a relationship with Terre Blanche, she added rather lamely.

Allan's case was further damaged by the evidence of Linda Shaw, her former flatmate. Shaw's falling out with and subse-quent testimony against Allan arose in an extraordinary way befitting this bizarre case. Allan had asked a recording producer, Andrew Broulidakis, so he claimed, to try to prove that Shaw had fabricated a story about Allan having group sex with a bunch of neo-Nazis. He invited Shaw to lunch and was, he said, assisted in his sleuthing inquiries by her announcement that she never trusted a man until she had had sex with him. Shaw described herself as having been struck through the heart when she discovered that the ensuing energetic sexual encounter was purely in the line of duty as far as Broulidakis was concerned. What was in his right-hand trouser pocket was not evidence of his being pleased to see her, but a tape-recorder which, or so he claimed, in the event failed to operate, during their lovemaking. Broulidakis had gained the impression that, much as Shaw felt it would be 'a scream to have that frigid bitch jailed for gang-banging Nazis', she would not be coming to London to give evidence.

Predictably, when Shaw learned what her lover had been up to and heard the sanctimonious claptrap with which he was attempting to justify what he had done, she needed no encouragement to fly to London to testify. Broulidakis piously asserted that he was a practising member of the Greek Orthodox Church, and that he had told a considerable number of lies to win her trust. His motive had been to find out the truth. For evil to triumph it is necessary only for good men to do nothing. He felt Allan was the victim of evil forces and the means justified the end. He was disparaged by George Carman QC as a downmarket Greek version of James Bond.

Shaw, meanwhile, told how she had known Allan since 1981 and how she and Allan had gone to an AWB rally at which Terre Blanche had been speaking. Allan had told her that she would not be happy to live under a black government in South Africa and had called black people 'kaffirs'. Shaw described the scene at Krugersdorp on Allan's birthday in September 1988, the occasion on which the six-foot Terre Blanche and Allan had clambered into the back of Allan's Lancia Spider sports car. They had drunk copious amounts of alcohol, enabling them to perform remarkable feats in the space available, which was little more than a luggage rack. They did not actually have sex, but they were 'doing a sexual number with a lot of fumbling, kissing and embracing'.

She described a distinctly unromantic approach made to her by Terre Blanche. At 3 o'clock one morning she had been woken in her bedroom by a large man in khaki undoing his shirt. When

Shaw inquired what he was doing, he claimed Jani Allan had told him that Linda liked sex very much, that she was a whore and that she would not mind if he came upstairs for sex. Before he could oblige, Shaw, unimpressed by this gambit, screamed, and he escaped. Later she heard loud music coming from Allan's room. Concerned that someone might be hurting her and playing the music to cover up her screams, she investigated. Finding the door locked, Shaw looked through the keyhole. She could see Allan's feet on the floor, which she recognised by her gnarled toe. Allan was on the floor with her knees apart and pointing upwards, and there was a large, white bottom moving up and down on her which seemed to be the right size and shape to be Terre Blanche. Shaw also spotted the toes of boots on either side of the couple, which she took to be those of his bodyguards. When she mentioned this to Allan the next day, Allan said, 'Sweetie, you had a nightmare.' Allan's counsel, Charles Gray QC, produced a section of door 1ft square and applied to the judge to see if Shaw really could have seen such goings-on. Disappointingly, Mr Justice Potts disallowed this piece of theatre.

Gossip about Jani Allan's relationship with Terre Blanche had, it was claimed, started when the police had stopped the two of them near the Paardekraal Monument. According to Shaw, the relationship had blossomed. Allan told her that he was 'a great lay but a little heavy'. Shaw claimed Allan had told her that she wanted to marry Terre Blanche. 'Jani Allan always regarded sex as a trump card which could be played at the last moment,' she said. Other witnesses supported Shaw's account of the alleged affair. Cornelius Kays Smit, formerly a bank manager, was chief secretary of the AWB and Terre Blanche's right-hand man. He testified that he had no doubt that Terre Blanche and Allan were having an affair. His suspicions had been aroused when he found Terre Blanche, dead drunk in Allan's flat, naked apart from a khaki jacket around his shoulders, a pair of green underpants with holes in them and a pair of khaki slacks belonging to Allan which he could get no higher than his knees. The lovers had, he said, met at his home, where they had danced, doing the twist, rock and roll and, on one occasion, as good right-wingers, the goose-step. On another night Allan had telephoned him at 3am to ask him to remove a snoring and drunken Terre Blanche from her flat. Smit, who had been in bed with his wife at the time – 'a rare species,' Carman was moved to observe – had gone to Allan's flat, covered Terre Blanche with a blanket and bundled him into his car.

Marlene Burger, news editor of *The Sunday Times of South Africa*, had seen Terre Blanche at Allan's flat on three occasions. Allan had been cooking him the notorious *boerewors* sausage and calling him '*ounooi*', an Afrikaans term of endearment. Burger had also seen her belabouring him with a riding crop after he reneged on his promise to leave his wife and marry her.

Against all this evidence, Terre Blanche sent a statement from his farm at Ventersdorp in the Transvaal. He wanted to respond to the despicable attack on his character by Kays Smit. He categorically refuted the scandalous allegations that he had ever had any kind of sexual relationship with Jani Allan, whom he described as the first English journalist to give him a fair hearing. He had never proposed marriage to Jani Allan, even in jest. He did not know of Ms Linda Shaw. 'Our enemies know no Christian morality,' he concluded. 'All these attempts to exaggerate the extent of my relationship with Jani Allan will ultimately be seen for what they are, a pack of lies.' And Allan's former husband, Gordon Pschaehat, testified on her behalf, confirming that their marriage had broken up because of her total obsession with her career and her complete lack of interest in sex. She had an inability to form relationships and she was not an extreme right-winger.

This evidence was, unsurprisingly, insufficient to rescue her case. The jury threw out her action, and her libel victories came to a dramatic end. She now faced a bill of costs of over £250,000.

It hardly needs to be said that this was a case she should never have brought. She had miscalculated the resolve of Channel 4 to uphold the integrity of its programme and to be prepared to spend the money necessary to gather evidence from South Africa which could be produced in England.

# 13

# BLINDFOLDED JUSTICE?

## Tales of Gloucester

On occasions the law of libel is used as an expensive blunt instrument by somewhat tacky individuals. It moves at a ponderous pace and shows an uncanny tendency to be imprecise at arriving at the truth. The case of Anthony Gilberthorpe, a Gloucester city and county councillor, highlighted the imperfections of the law. It was also unusual in that it is a rare example of an action in which one ends up feeling sorry for the tabloid newspapers involved.

In January 1987 the *Sun* published in its first edition a story entitled 'AIDS RIDDLE TORY GAVE MAGGIE A SMACKER', which was shortened in later editions to 'AIDS MAN KISSED MAGGIE'. The *Mirror* ran a rival piece, headlined 'AIDS SCARE TORY TO QUIT'. The reports centred on twenty-four-year-old Conservative councillor, Anthony Gilberthorpe, who had enthusiastically broken through a police cordon at the Conservative Party Conference to plant a kiss on the prime minister, Margaret Thatcher. They originated from a story put out by the Gloucester and County News Service that

Gilberthorpe was going to resign from Gloucester Council amid allegations that he was being treated for what the agency described as 'the sex plague AIDS'. It was also published in the local paper, the Gloucester *Citizen*. Gilberthorpe sued, alleging that the wording suggested that he had AIDS and that he had caught it as a result of promiscuous homosexual activity.

It was the background to the case, rather than the sorry details of Gilberthorpe's sexual proclivities, which illustrate the inefficiency of the law of libel at arriving at the truth. In 1986 the news agency's reporter, Mark Mitchell, had telephoned Gilberthorpe at the Cavendish Retirement Home in Stroud, which he then owned, asking him why he had been absent from a number of council meetings. Gilberthorpe blamed a blood disorder. On 15 January 1987, another conversation took place between Gilberthorpe and Mitchell. Mitchell claimed that Gilberthorpe had contacted his agency saying that he was planning to retire as a councillor, and that the *Sunday Express* was threatening to publish a piece about him receiving AIDS treatment in New York. The *Express* was also, according to Gilberthorpe, making noises about running a story on his financial relationship with Peter Haywood, a wheelchair-bound pensioner who had died at a nursing home the previous year. The man's family had begun a legal action for the repayment of £250,000.

On this, as on many matters concerning Gilberthorpe, the facts were in dispute. Gilberthorpe, it seemed, admitted having accepted gifts from the elderly bachelor of £18,755 and £25,000, but maintained he was under no obligation to repay them. The agency's version was that Gilberthorpe had volunteered this information to Mitchell, and that the otherwise libellous content of the subsequent articles had therefore been published with the leave and licence of Gilberthorpe. Mitchell recollected Gilberthorpe admitting that he had visited an AIDS clinic in New York, but ducking the question of whether or not he had AIDS himself.

Gilberthorpe, meanwhile, claimed that Mitchell had concocted the story. The reporter had contacted him and had raised all these suggestions about AIDS. There was no question, he said, of his having volunteered this information. Unhappily, in the light of subsequent events, Piers Merchant, the Conservative MP for whom Gilberthorpe had been a Commons researcher, was present in the room when the telephone call between Mitchell and Gilberthorpe took place. Merchant, a noted moral crusader for the protection of the unborn child, family life and similar causes, was able to confirm Gilberthorpe's version of the conversation.

Gilberthorpe had up to this point been eager to create publicity in the local press: his ambition was to succeed Conservative MP Sally Oppenheim when she retired. He would tell the media about his girlfriends 'MEET MY DALLAS GIRL', was one local headline, although there was some suspicion she may have been his 'beard'. A subsequent announcement of his engagement in *The Times* turned out to be a hoax, and it was reported that the lady in question was a figment of his imagination. When a door fell on Gilberthorpe at the Shire Hall in Gloucester, the incident had been given full coverage, as had an occasion when he had been hypnotised on stage and thereafter challenged to a boxing match by a fellow councillor.

Like many libel plaintiffs, Gilberthorpe realised that his best prospect of success was to bring the case on for trial as soon as possible. So in November 1987 he applied for an expedited hearing, as he wanted to stand in local elections in both 1988 and 1989. His action came on for trial in May 1988 and lasted eight days at a hearing before Mr Justice Jupp and a jury. Such was his confidence in his claim that when he was asked whether he was a homosexual, Gilberthorpe firmly replied, 'No, I am not.' It was an answer too far. The issue, as limited by the pleadings, was not whether or not he was gay – the newspapers had not sought to prove that such allegations were true – but rather whether or not he had volunteered the AIDS information to Mitchell, and had therefore consented to the publication of the stories about him. Here his bacon had been saved by his independent witness to the conversation, Piers Merchant MP.

As the case proceeded to its conclusion, it attracted some publicity locally. One Gloucestershire Conservative reported that he

had left the party after a homosexual approach from
Gilberthorpe. This evidence unfortunately emerged at too late a
stage in the trial for there to be any realistic prospect of it being
usable. The court will seldom allow a late amendment at the trial,
particularly if it raises a new line of defence. The basis of the rule
is that cases should proceed swiftly to trial and defendants
should be required to put forward their defence at an early stage.
Increasingly, substantive amendments tend to be allowed only if
a satisfactory explanation can be put forward as to the delay in
raising the defence, and if the court is satisfied that the plaintiff
has sufficient time to answer the defence that is now raised. The
rule laid down by Lord Justice Edmund Davies in Associated
Leisure v. Associated Newspapers (1972), that 'amendment ought
to be allowed if necessary to do justice between the parties so
long as any hardship can be compensated in money', is more and
more often being circumvented. While there is much to be said
for not allowing cases to be delayed or adding to the costs of the
trial with late amendments, there are cases in which it would
have been better if all the facts had been placed before the court
in the first place rather than being raised at a series of appeals at
a later date. This was such a case.

As it was, the jury was persuaded by the evidence of the independent witness, Piers Merchant, and Gilberthorpe was awarded
a total of £49,080: £28,750 libel damages against the *Sun*,
£10,580 against the *Mirror* and £9,750 against the Gloucester
*Citizen*. In a separate action against *Today* newspaper, he recovered a further £10,000 for the false allegation that he had AIDS.
*Today* had unsuccessfully attempted to amend its defence to
plead allegations of homosexuality.

The newspapers appealed. They claimed that Gilberthorpe had
lied when denying his homosexuality, and were able to produce
initially three and subsequently five young men who had not
given evidence at the trial, but who were now able to describe
sexual activity with or propositions from Gilberthorpe, usually at
his nursing home.

Some of the actual – or as Gilberthorpe claimed, fantasy

attempted buggery and fellatio had a distinctly Conservative context. One incident was said to have happened at a party to celebrate the Tory victory in the June 1987 General Election and to mourn Merchant's loss of his Newcastle seat. A man who claimed to have been bedded by Gilberthorpe said that the unappetising incident had ended with Gilberthorpe seeking reassurance that the man would continue to canvass for him. Another witness produced a diary of a homosexual affair with Gilberthorpe. Yet another claimed to have been buggered by him from New York to Windermere, and places in between, and to have been told by Gilberthorpe of his Stuarts, Brendans and Ians round the world. Even a reporter on the Gloucester *Citizen* claimed to have been propositioned by Gilberthorpe while investigating a story.

One of the witnesses, Duane Hoffman, had a record of nonpayment of hotel bills which had resulted initially in a fine from the Gloucester magistrates and latterly in a ten-week stay in Pentonville, followed by deportation to the United States. Gilberthorpe relied on the fact that Hoffman was a man of bad character and of a deceptive nature who was desperate for money. Hoffman may have got it right when he recollected Gilberthorpe confiding that the main thing in life was to get your name in the headlines. Significantly, in light of the events to follow, Hoffman spoke of secret taping taking place at the nursing home.

When the case came before the Court of Appeal in May 1989, the issue was whether the discovery of this new evidence required that, as a matter of justice, the verdict should be set aside. Under the principles of Ladd v. Marshall (1954), the test was whether the new evidence could have been obtained with reasonable diligence for the original trial; whether it would have had an important, even if not ultimately decisive, influence on the result of the case; and whether it was apparently credible, even though not necessarily incontrovertible.

The Court of Appeal accepted that there had been no lack of diligence regarding the obtaining of this evidence, which had effectively emerged in a usable form only after the conclusion of the trial. Although there were doubts about the credibility of Hoffman, the mere fact that he had a conviction for not paying his hotel bills did not, for the purposes of the appeal, discredit an apparently credible and detailed statement which suggested that Gilberthorpe had had many homosexual partners before Hoffman and that he had, in the words Hoffman remembered him using, pulled the wool over the eyes of the jury about his homosexuality. If the jury had heard this evidence, it might have disbelieved his account of the 'leave and licence' (that he had consented to the publication of the defamatory words) defence at the trial.

The Court of Appeal chose to adopt a statement made by Lord Atkin in Ras Behari v. King Emperor (1933) that finality is a good thing, but justice is better. After hearing much evidence seeking to discredit a number of the new witnesses, the court felt that the evidence of two of them was important as it tended to support the contention that Gilberthorpe was a homosexual at all material times, and had deliberately misled the court on this matter at the trial. Gilberthorpe's claim that these witnesses had a vendetta against him, and that one of them was wont to shout in Gloucester public houses, 'Quick, backs against the wall' when Gilberthorpe came in, failed to dissuade the Court of Appeal from sending the case for retrial.

Although the Court of Appeal is normally slow to deprive a litigant of a judgement in his favour on account of the discovery of new evidence, it will do so where the evidence raises such high doubts about the soundness of the verdict that it would be unjust to permit it to stand. The wretched Gilberthorpe, who must by now have been wondering why on earth he had felt it necessary to sue for libel in the first place, suffered the additional indignity of submitting to the court a report showing that the HIV test he had had proved negative, and the result of a physical examination which did not 'suggest over-indulgence in ano-receptive sexual intercourse'.

Little then happened for three and a half years. As the defendants were about to strike out the case for want of prosecution, Gilberthorpe produced an affidavit explaining that financial hardship had befallen him. He had sold his nineteen-roomed nursing home and both the proceeds of the sale and the libel damages he had received had gone in legal fees. He pointed to the unfairness of there being no legal aid to enable him to pursue the case. A number of the witnesses who had been under the impression that they had been propositioned by Gilberthorpe had by now recanted. Allegations about him making passes at a student party were, it seemed, a misunderstanding – he had apparently been flirting with men and women alike.

Hoffman now admitted that he had told lies, and claimed that he had been coerced by the defence into giving evidence. The newspapers, however, submitted evidence of Hoffman complaining to them that he had been offered £5,000 by Gilberthorpe to withdraw his evidence. This had earlier led them to write to Gilberthorpe's solicitors protesting that Hoffman was being harassed. To add to the general seediness, in 1991 Hoffman was reported not only to be dying of AIDS, but also to have sold false stories to an American supermarket tabloid about the sexual exploits of a royal prince in the New York hotel where he claimed to be in charge of VIP services. He had, however, sworn an affidavit in 1989, after the trial, confirming that his evidence had been true.

Gilberthorpe's case was at first struck out for want of prosecution by Mr Justice Drake. While the Court of Appeal was more sympathetic to his difficulties in progressing the case, he never did bring it back to court for retrial. In October 1997 he wrote a curious note to the *Mirror* stating, 'I acknowledge that since the beginning of 1997 I have recognised my choice to live as a gay man.' It looked as if his heart was no longer in the fight against allegations of homosexuality.

Even though Gilberthorpe's case ultimately proved unsuccessful, he had much for which to be grateful to Piers Merchant MP. Merchant had employed him as a researcher; he had given evidence which had convinced the jury of Gilberthorpe's account of the conversation with Mitchell. Furthermore, Merchant had also perhaps saved his life by summoning the emergency services when Gilberthorpe had telephoned him after taking an overdose and said, 'I am just calling to say goodbye, Piers.'

But whether Merchant was still willing to be a witness at any retrial was not clear. In any event, the two men fell out and there was some suggestion that that was the reason behind the breach. However, when, in March 1997, before the General Election, the *Sun* published details of an affair between forty-six-year-old Merchant and Anna Cox, seventeen, illustrated with pictures of them canoodling in a London park, Gilberthorpe made a surprising moral stand against the hitherto morally crusading MP. He took it upon himself to cast doubt on the teenager's claims to be a researcher for Merchant and friend of the family, and on the assertion of Cox and Merchant that they were jointly writing a book on tabloid intrusion. It was ridiculous, he said, to suggest that Anna – a former nightclub hostess and member of the Orpington Young Conservatives – was the MP's researcher: she could hardly spell. After himself looking into the matter, Gilberthorpe announced to a breathless world: 'Anna made it quite clear to me that, whatever Piers was saying, they had had a sexual affair. It was a shock to me. I had not questioned his honesty when the affair became public. Piers continued with his story that they were writing a book, but I knew they had resumed their affair.' He also informed the press that a trip to Merchant's Pimlico flat suggested that rather more than research was going on under the duvet. Despite the appearance in the media of stories which seemed to emanate from Anna Cox, one of which had Merchant tied to the bed with her stockings, the MP elected to mitigate the boredom of life in opposition by spending his sleeping hours away from the Tories' Blackpool Conference in Gilberthorpe's flat in York – accompanied by Anna Cox.

An inglorious political career was abruptly ended in October 1997 by a stab in the back. In circumstances which never became entirely clear, closed-circuit cameras installed to protect an antiques shop below Gilberthorpe's flat came to be focused instead on a duvet in one of the bedrooms. Not only did the camera capture some reassuringly heterosexual Tory activity,

but it recorded Merchant giving Cox a description of William
Hague's shortcomings – ranging from his ugliness to the view
that he was 'nineteen going on ninety' – which differed somewhat from the MP's Blackpool speech in praise of Hague's good
start as leader of the opposition. The film also featured a creditable impersonation by Merchant of Adolf Hitler.

To the *Mirror*'s astonishment, Gilberthorpe felt that this was
information he should – at a price (£25,000) – share with the
public, over sixteen lurid pages. Merchant's days as MP for
Beckenham, a seat he had won in May 1997 by a majority of
4,953 notwithstanding the *Sun* story, were over. He bowed out
complaining, 'Gilberthorpe was a man I thought was a close
friend who set us up. He is deceitful, and I can't believe we
trusted him as a friend.'

Gilberthorpe, meanwhile, fared little better, having stood down
in September 1991 during a local dispute from the position of
chairman of the Gloucester City Council Planning Sub-
Committee and as vice-chairman of the Leisure Services
Committee, and headed for the obscurity he richly deserved.

Ultimately the tabloid press had triumphed – albeit at a considerable financial cost which they would never recover. But
perhaps the press got its money's worth in the sense that the
case destroyed Gilberthorpe's reputation and, coincidentally, the
career, such as it was, of the Tory MP Piers Merchant. The case
seemed to be far removed from the business of protecting reputation. If Gilberthorpe had, as he ought to have, been required as
part of bringing a case in libel to spell out the particulars of
what was false in the articles and to verify his claim on affidavit, this futile and ruinous litigation would never have taken
place.

## A Strangely Uncomic Tale

Tom O'Connor, a highly successful and wealthy comedian and
TV personality, the star of *Name that Tune* and the *Tom
O'Connor Roadshow*, was a happily married Roman Catholic

with four children and known as 'Mr Clean'. On 12 October
1988, he relaxed with a stroll along Blackpool Pier, having finished his last show at the South Pier Theatre. Unfortunately, on
his arm was not his wife of twenty-five years' standing but a
teenage prostitute and drug-addict called Tracey Cummings. A
word of warning from a security guard gave him just enough
time to remove his arm from Tracey's before Nick Pritchard and
Boyd Milligan, respectively a journalist and a photographer
with the *News of the World*, introduced themselves, with the
inevitable consequences.

The words 'it's a fair cop, guv' appear to have been singularly
absent from O'Connor's vocabulary. Nor, it seems, did he have the
good sense to realise that the appetite of the British public for
tawdry tales of the sex life of a comedian who lives out of a suitcase is distinctly finite. Stories such as these are soon forgotten,
and the damage they cause to a career is not necessarily lasting:
indeed, many readers gain some reassurance from the fact that
well-loved entertainers have feet of clay. Yet after some equivo-
cation and a certain amount of poor advice, O'Connor opted to
tough it out with the tabloid press, gambling on them being unable
to prove their case. It was an unwise decision which not only
proved expensive, but also came close to landing him far deeper in
the mire than the original insubstantial tabloid reports had done.

O'Connor failed to realise that media resources to fight such
an action were greater than his. And at some stage he forgot that
libel is about the protection of reputation. It is self-defeating to
sully your reputation while trying to defend it, and O'Connor's
attempts to manipulate and muzzle the press served merely to
give a new lease of life to what would otherwise have been a
story with a limited shelf-life.

A hard-bitten *News of the World* journalist who had seen the
pair arm in arm was hardly likely to buy the 'Gladstone
defence' – that Tracey was a sad case whom O'Connor was trying
to help. O'Connor had, however, paid £1,000 to Peppers Massage
Parlour, whence Tracey hailed, apparently to save her from a
bleak future of prostitution and drug-addiction. A mixture of

evidence of his canoodling and admissions, coupled with an offer from O'Connor of £10,000 to the *News of the World* reporter to drop the story, all ensured that the incident received maximum coverage.

From 16 October to 27 November, the tale was repeatedly rehashed in the *Sun*, the *News of the World*, the *Sunday Mirror*, the *People* and the *Mirror*. No detail or feeling of O'Connor or his family was spared. 'Tom O'Connor in sex romps shock. Sauna girls tell of frolics with TV's Mr Clean. Tom had 4 girls but one was special. Kinky sex with 49-year-old former deputy head-master – she wore school uniform and he fed her wine gums' screamed the *Sunday Mirror*. The *People*'s headline was: 'I LOVE VICE GIRL, 18, SAYS TOM O'CONNOR. Tom O'Connor paid vice girls to spank his bottom.' The *Sunday Mirror* returned to the subject the following week with 'My spanking nights with Tom O'Connor', replete with details of girls in school uniforms punishing O'Connor for getting his sums wrong. The papers, it seemed, were determined to work him over: 'I SOLD MY WIFE TO TOM O'CONNOR – PIMP TELLS OF HOTEL SEX ORGY'. Slightly better from O'Connor's stand-point was 'SEX-SHAME TOM FACES THE FANS – COMIC JOKES ABOUT VICE GIRL STORIES'. Unfortunately, O'Connor later changed tack and stopped trying to laugh the whole thing off. Then the public were treated to: 'I JUST LOVE HIM SAYS MRS TOM O'CONNOR', and 'TOM'S GOOD BOOK – EVEN THE POPE GETS IN ON COMIC'S ACT', which was accompanied by a picture of O'Connor shaking the Pope's hand.

This orgy of prurient articles had been fuelled by some crass handling of the press. The story which was being fed to them was that Tracey Cummings was a whore on drugs, that O'Connor was getting her off drugs, and that his wife was a friend of hers (the 'Piers Merchant defence'). However, simultaneously Cummings was telling the *Sun* and the *News of the World* the true story. Demonstrating an almost unerring knack for doing the wrong thing, O'Connor's lieutenants approached the *People* with the offer of an O'Connor exclusive if they published an interview with Cummings. This resulted in Tracey Cummings, 'the teenage temptress', announcing on 20 November: 'I lied about sex with

Tom O'Connor. I am sorry if his life is ruined.' Phil Hall, the journalist who wrote the piece, doubted that it was true, but the view was taken that it was a good story anyhow. Exactly how the confession came to be made emerged during the preparation for the libel trial.

There was a limit to the number of tales that could be written about O'Connor, and tabloid interest in the comedian flagged at the end of November. Nevertheless writs were issued in February 1989 against Mirror Group Newspapers and no fewer than ten of its journalists, and News International. Evidently O'Connor was satisfied that Cummings would not now testify against him, and that the papers could not therefore justify their undoubtedly defamatory allegations. Revenge, he doubtless felt, was a dish best eaten cold.

The case duly came on for trial before Mr Justice Michael Davies in June 1990. He delayed proceedings after hearing that the director of public prosecutions had ordered Merseyside Police to investigate allegations of interference with witnesses.

What had emerged when Cummings agreed to give evidence for the defendants was that a number of sticks and carrots had been put her way to help her decide how she should testify. In November 1988 she had been offered (though was not paid) £25,000 through an intermediary to retract what she had earlier said to the papers. The upshot had been the Phil Hall article in the *People*, for which O'Connor had telephoned Hall and thanked him. The intermediary had then approached Cummings to get her to sign a statement denying she had any sexual relationship with O'Connor.

There followed a series of unpleasant threats to Cummings, and then offers of trips abroad to remove her from jurisdiction.

In December 1988 she was offered £10,000 or more by the intermediary to keep her mouth shut. Cummings was also asked to telephone the various newspaper defendants to indicate that she could be persuaded, for cash, to give evidence on their behalf. This was a crude gamble to try to discredit the defendants and undermine their prospects of defending the case. In May

1990 the defendants managed to serve a subpoena on Cummings. At that stage it was suggested to her by the intermediary that she should go abroad. Instead she took legal advice and decided to give a statement to the defendants.

When the matter came before Mr Justice Drake in December 1990, he allowed the defendants to amend their defence to include a plea that O'Connor had conspired with others to pervert the course of justice by seeking to persuade witnesses to give false evidence to the court, and had supplied the defendants with statements made by Cummings which he had known to give a false denial of any sexual relationship between her and himself. These allegations were vigorously refuted by O'Connor.

The case was relisted for trial on 14 January 1991. In the meantime the Merseyside Police decided to take no further action on the allegations of conspiracy to pervert the course of justice. Tracey Cummings and another witness were moved to a safe house in the south of England, where they lived in comfort under the protection of the Mirror Group. On the appointed day, O'Connor blanched as he arrived at court and realised that Cummings would be testifying against him. He immediately withdrew his action. He had to pay his own legal costs, and received no withdrawal or apology. He fared even worse against News International, to whose legal costs he had to contribute.

While it is undoubtedly difficult for defendants to get witnesses to court to testify, this case is yet another example of the folly of suing in the hope that the witnesses who could prove the defendants' case will dematerialise. Satisfactory as it was for the papers to win their cases, it was expensive for them to do so. Had O'Connor been required to verify on affidavit the truth of his claim to have been libelled, he surely would not have launched these proceedings.

When O'Connor published his memoirs, *Take a Funny Turn*, in 1994, he remembered his encounter with the Pope but seemed to have forgotten his brush with the libel law.

## Sailing Close to the Wind

Owen Oyston was a man who brought one libel action too many.
His belief that he had a grievance against a former and a serving
Conservative MP and minister, Lord Blaker, along with sports
minister Robert Atkins and a Lancashire businessman, William
Harrison, became almost all-consuming. His eagerness to pursue
a claim against the three men led to corners being cut and his
action being thrown out for serious procedural irregularities.
Given that he had sued three individuals, each with his own
separate legal teams incurring three lots of costs, and given that
the case went to the Court of Appeal, he is believed to have faced
a total bill of £400,000.

Oyston had made his money in the Oyston Estate Agency in
Lancashire, which he had sold at the top of the market to Royal
Insurance for £30 million in 1987. His company, Trans World
Communications, had acquired the rights to the Miss World competition. He had taken over the Piccadilly and Red Rose radio
stations in Manchester and Preston and had interests in cable television. Oyston had successfully sued *The Sunday Times* for
allegations made in September 1989 about share dealings at the
time of the Piccadilly Radio takeover, and for suggestions of an
improper business relationship with the Derbyshire County
Council pension fund. He complained that his name had been
severely damaged in the City. Newspaper reports suggested that
he had recovered damages of over £100,000. He also sued the
*Daily Telegraph* regarding an article published in July 1991 concerning the takeover of Piccadilly Radio.

Oyston then became owner and chairman of Blackpool
Football Club and planned to develop a £130 million astrodome
at the club. He installed himself in Claughton Hall near Preston,
surrounded by parkland grazed by his herd of bison. Life had
certainly moved on for the failed actor whose biggest role had
been a bit part in *Crown Court*. Unhappily, his next appearance
in the Crown Court was after his arrest in 1995 on four charges
of rape in the period April 1988 to December 1992, three of

indecent assault and one of procuring under-age women for sex. He was convicted of one of the charges of rape and sentenced to six years. Up till that point, however, he was a powerful man with a tendency to turn swiftly to his lawyers if material he disliked was published about him. Oyston continues to protest his innocence and the case has been referred to the Criminal Cases Review Commission. In August 1995 he recovered substantial damages for a reference to him made by a financial news service as a 'disgraced tycoon'.

Oyston's property interests and his plan to redevelop Preston Docks attracted criticism and controversy. Chief among his detractors was a single-minded crusader called Michael Murrin, a fish-and-chip shop proprietor and founder and chairman of the Preston and District Ratepayers' Association. Murrin succeeded in interesting a number of Oyston's opponents in supporting his investigations into the entrepreneur's activities. One of his habits was to tape-record conversations with Oyston's detractors, adopting a role as an *agent provocateur* as he outlined his extravagant allegations against Oyston and sought to implicate them in his schemes. In June 1988 Murrin produced a dossier entitled the 'Preston Dock Redevelopment Statement', which made very defamatory allegations about how Oyston had got to where he had in the planned development. Oyston indignantly denied any impropriety and immediately obtained an injunction against Murrin.

In the course of his proceedings against *The Sunday Times*, Oyston got to hear of the existence of Murrin's tapes. He subpoenaed them in January 1991 and eventually got hold of them on 23 September. The tapes related to the period April 1986 to July 1988. Oyston considered some of the recorded comments made about him by three of his opponents – Blaker, Atkins and Harrison – to be libellous. After his action against *The Sunday Times* was settled, he had forty hours of the tapes transcribed and made the tapes and transcripts available to *World in Action*, *Private Eye* and *Esquire*, who published his allegations of a conspiracy against him. His problem was that there was then a

three-year limitation period on bringing libel actions under
Section 4A of the Limitation Act of 1980. He had to rely on
Section 32A of the act, which allowed him, with the leave of the
court, an extension of one year to bring a libel action from the
earliest date he had first become aware of all the facts relevant to
the cause of action. That gave Oyston a year until 23 September
1992.

Oyston did not instruct his solicitors, Peter Carter-Ruck and
Partners, on the question of issuing proceedings until May 1992,
seven months after the receipt of the tapes and six months after
their transcription, although the firm had already been advising
him on other matters. Precisely why he did not bring his libel
action against his three *bêtes noires* sooner was never satisfactorily explained. The court seems to have suspected that he might
have held back until his opponents had been suitably worked
over in the press. In any event, in the meantime, he was trying
without success to interest his MP, Dame Elaine Kellet Bowman,
in their alleged nefarious activities. Had a writ been issued at the
outset, the likelihood is that he would have been unable to publicise his grievances with proceedings pending. It was a tactic
which backfired disastrously. In the Court of Appeal, Lord Justice
Henry was to observe that the essence of a genuine complaint in
libel is prompt action, particularly in those who need leave from
the court, because the cause of action is by definition (in a limitation case) a stale one.

For reasons that similarly never became clear, his solicitors
took three months to advise and a further month to appear before
the master, on 15 September 1992, to seek leave to bring the
action – a matter of eight days before the expiry of the year's
period of grace. And once again for reasons that were never properly explained, the action was launched amid such a miasma of
irregularities and non-disclosures of relevant material to the court
that it was struck out by Mr Justice Ognall in August 1993. His
decision was upheld by the Court of Appeal in November 1995.

Only rarely can the procedural conduct of a libel action have
been more ferociously criticised. The case had progressed no

further than the service of the statement of claim. Leave had to be obtained to issue the writ under the Limitation Act 1980. Instead of notice of this hearing being given to the defendants as required by the rules, Oyston, on legal advice, applied to the High Court master for leave, ex parte, that is to say privately, without giving the other side a chance to attend the hearing and to object. This was a serious irregularity and one which the Court of Appeal held prejudiced the defendants, as they were improperly prevented from seeking to defeat Oyston's claim at the earliest opportunity.

The hearing before the master was roundly condemned by the Court of Appeal. Oyston evidently felt aggrieved, for he consulted other solicitors after this legal débâcle, and in September 1997 they issued a writ on behalf of Oyston – whose address was now HM Prison, Wymott – against Peter Carter-Ruck and Partners, seeking reimbursement of the £261,101.81 plus interest he had had to pay Blaker, Harrison and Atkins in respect of their legal costs. He also claimed damages for the lost opportunity to sue the trio for defamation and malicious falsehood. The hearing before the master had lasted only ten or fifteen minutes. He was given the impression that the application for leave was a formality. There was, after all, a claim for slander spoken on 16 October 1990 in the writ. This would have indicated to the master that there was a claim which was *not*, as at September 1992, statute-barred by the three-year limitation period and that there was going to be a trial anyhow, whatever his decision on the limitation issue. That claim was dropped after the master gave leave and had apparently been included 'by mistake'. As it was the only instance in thirty-two allegations of libel and slander where the claim was *not* statute-barred, this was potentially an error of some significance. The evidence showed that Oyston had the relevant knowledge to bring any libel claim relating to the Preston Docks Statement by at latest June 1991. As over a year had by then elapsed since the acquisition of knowledge, leave would not have been given for that, had the master been told all the facts, so both Mr Justice Ognall and the Court of Appeal found.

Three claims for conspiracy, which had a six- as opposed to a three-year limitation period, and which likewise did not require leave, had been included. The conspiracy claims, the court held, were a transparent and specious attempt to circumvent the clear prohibition on running conspiracy in tandem with defamation proceedings, and were an abuse of process. The conspiracy to injure claim required proof of direct pecuniary loss, and there was none. Mr Justice Ognall was moved to observe that it was beyond doubt that Oyston's solicitors had 'sailed very close to the wind'. The solicitors' problems in the proceedings were self-inflicted. Nevertheless, Ognall used the same firm of solicitors himself a year later when he felt he had been libelled as a result of remarks made about him by the undercover police officer involved in the Rachel Nickell Wimbledon Common murder case, which were published in the *Daily Mail*. Ognall had been very critical of the officer's conduct and a draw – in terms of a contribution to his legal costs – seemed a fair outcome.

The finding by Mr Justice Ognall in Oyston, that the nature and extent of the concealment of the full facts amounted to a manipulation of the discretion of the master, was upheld by the Court of Appeal. The judge was, the Court of Appeal held, entitled to find that there was a breach of the requirement of full and frank disclosure and to view that as a serious and substantial irregularity seriously infecting the proceedings.

The master, the Court of Appeal ruled, would not have viewed the case as straightforward if he had known about the existence of a subpoena for Murrin to produce the tapes, and that the court's consent to the use of the subpoenaed tapes had not been obtained. If the tapes had been produced under the compulsion of the subpoena, the action would have been struck out as an abuse of process (Riddick v. Thames Board Mill, 1977). Whether Murrin had acted under the compulsion of the subpoena was contested on the affidavit evidence and could not be resolved without a full hearing. The court's complaint, however, was that the plaintiff had not disclosed the fact of the subpoena to the defendants, who had discovered it independently. Nor had the plaintiff disclosed a solicitor's letter, written to Murrin a week before he handed over the tapes, undertaking not to use them for any purpose other than Oyston's litigation against *The Sunday Times* or any other litigation that might arise to which the tape-recordings had relevance.

Murrin had also been sued, but in a separate writ, as the court commented, 'for good reason or bad, but probably not for no reason'. Indeed, Murrin's absence from the Blaker, Atkins and Harrison action was described by the court as *Hamlet* without the Prince, a flattering analogy for the Preston fish-and-chip shop owner. The existence of the subpoena would, the court felt, have been more likely to emerge if Murrin had been a party to the main action. It was nowhere satisfactorily explained why Murrin was sued separately, and it was another feature of the plaintiff's conduct which the court felt did not help his cause. There was no attempt to explain the delay in bringing the proceedings.

After the striking out of this claim by Mr Justice Ognall, but before the hearing in the Court of Appeal, Oyston once more sought to air his grievances in the press – on this occasion in the May 1995 issue of *Business Age*. So pleased was he with the piece that he had 4,800 copies handed out at his Blackpool Football Club, to the bemusement of the fans.

Despite this setback, and before his incarceration, Oyston showed no loss of appetite for libel litigation, although in fact he did not pursue that particular action against Murrin. However, the condemnation by the courts of the way in which he had sought to bring the action against Blaker, Atkins and Harrison did call into question the appropriateness of seeking to litigate matters of such antiquity.

# 14

# DAMAGES

The law of libel does provide remedies other than damages. As
detailed in Chapter 1, a statement, approved by a judge, can be
read in open court, exonerating the plaintiff and including an
apology from the defendant, or the plaintiff may obtain an
injunction preventing the publication or repetition of a libel.

Yet in spite of these provisions, the object of virtually all libel
actions is the recovery of damages coupled with the reimbursement of the legal costs which the plaintiff has incurred. Few
litigants are satisfied with a mere correction and apology.
Damages, they argue, are necessary to show that their reputation
has been vindicated. However, most plaintiffs are coy about the
amount they actually recover. Damages are often described as
'substantial' or 'appropriate', but seldom specified, and sometimes the figure is jacked up by the inclusion of the reimbursed
legal costs. While juries may award large sums based on sizeable
damages they have heard about, most libel claims are settled for
considerably more modest sums. Often these are smaller than the
plaintiff cares to admit.

The problem with awards of damages in libel cases is that libel is a very imprecise science with no arithmetical formula. There is not the degree of similarity between one libel and another as exists between different cases where people have suffered the same, specific personal injury, such as the loss of an eye. An award of libel damages has a number of objectives and depends on a variable set of factors. It is compensation for damage to reputation, vindication of a person's good name and a measure of the distress, hurt and humiliation which the defamatory publication has caused. It is looked at from the plaintiff's point of view: the tendency of defamatory words to damage reputation is assumed in the plaintiff's favour, and he does not have to prove actual damage. Not only are the facts significantly different in each case, but a court can take account of the way the action has been defended – whether, for example, there has been a defence of justification, the extent of the publication and the absence or otherwise of any apology. The conduct or state of mind of the defendant may aggravate the damages: are there circumstances, such as the way the defendant has handled the plaintiff's claim, which increase the injury to the plaintiff?

Plaintiffs are normally wise to settle their claims. Libel actions, as we have seen, are notoriously expensive to bring. The Court of Appeal has now placed limits on damages, capping them initially at £125,000 and latterly at £150,000, which has made the jackpots of recent years a thing of the past and reduced the odds in the gamble for a lucrative outcome. Without the prospect of enormous damages, the plaintiff has to consider not only the financial consequences if he or she loses the case and has to pay all the legal costs, but also the element of irrecoverable costs even if he wins. As he would normally recover only 70 per cent of his legal costs from the other side, and might have to go through the expensive and time-consuming procedure of having his costs claim assessed by a costs judge, the damages he may have been awarded in a court action lasting perhaps a week will be rapidly eroded. It is by no means unknown for a winning plaintiff to end up out of pocket, even after winning substantial damages, once he has kept his lawyers suitably provisioned.

Exceptionally, the plaintiff may recover exemplary or punitive damages if it can be proved that at the time of the publication the defendant knowingly or recklessly libelled the plaintiff and decided to publish the libel because the prospect of material advantage outweighed the prospect of material loss. There must be some evidence of such a cynical calculation other than simply that a defendant is in business to make a profit. This was established in 1970 against David Irving and Cassell, the publisher of his book *The Destruction of Convoy PQ17*. In that case a memorandum surfaced in which a member of Cassell's staff injudiciously calculated that a libel action would be good for sales. Likewise, recklessness was present in the *Mirror*'s decision to publish in 1992 their bulimia story about Elton John under a 'world exclusive' headline. It was less clear that it was present in 1979, when the *News of the World* printed as an exclusive, 'SIEGE MAN TELLS US WHY HE DID IT' – the allegations of the unbalanced David Brain against the members of Banbury CID detailed in Chapter 6. Unhappily for the officers concerned, the Court of Appeal set aside for a retrial the £25,000 exemplary damages each stood to collect.

At the opposite end of the scale are derisory or contemptuous damages. These were awarded to an Auschwitz doctor, Wladislaw Dering, who, astonishingly, sued Leon Uris, the author of *Exodus*, for a suggestion that he had carried out 17,000 experiments without anaesthetic. It was not the experiments themselves that were at issue – the number, it seemed, was considerably smaller. In 1964 Dering won a halfpenny after being identified as the anti-Semitic violator of human guinea pigs and the possessor of a tobacco pouch made from a tanned human scrotum. Lady Docker received the same sum in 1974 for a trivial complaint against the *Sunday Express* that the use of naughty words had got her evicted from a Jersey hotel. In the same year Colonel Elliot Brooks, a solicitor and one-time mayor of Kensington, also increased his bank balance by a halfpenny for his complaint about an article headed: 'EXPOSED' – THE TOP LAWYER WHO TRAPS GIRLS FOR SEX'. Unwisely, he had tried to interest a *Sunday People* journalist in a spot of spanking. For a solicitor who was a serial philanderer not above slipping girls a Mickey Finn, libel litigation was a distinct hazard. The press eagerly reported the case, especially when Brooks' counsel had to explain to a judicially curious Mr Justice Bristow what 'goosing' was. In recent times, derisory damages have been recovered in far less exotic or reprehensible circumstances by businessman Sir Rupert Mackeson against a firm of solicitors; by Dr Jagit Chohan, a Sikh historian, against Oxford University Press; by the former Taoiseach of Ireland Albert Reynolds, against *The Sunday Times*; by the chainstore Dixon's against Thames Television; by landlord Maurice Lubin against Harlech TV, and by Peter Oates, Broadmoor patient, against the *Mirror*.

Unless the case is one of particular complexity, involving the examination of considerable documentary evidence, or the parties have agreed to trial by judge alone, damages will be assessed by a jury. Under the Defamation Act 1996, more cases will be heard by judges alone, who will fix damages if they feel that the case is suitable for summary procedure or that there is no real defence, or if damages are to be assessed following an offer of amends by a defendant (see Chapter 21). A jury still receives precious little guidance as to the sum it should award; previously it was given virtually none. In Elton John v. Mirror Group Newspapers, Lord Bingham, in the Court of Appeal, likened the position of the jurors to that of sheep loosed on an unfenced common with no shepherd.

The problem was that no one was able to suggest suitable figures or even appropriate ranges for damages to the jury. Judges and advocates were not allowed to do so. Instead they bemused juries with references to, say, 'a substantial sum to vindicate a person's reputation', without suggesting what that sum might be, or with more familiar comparisons such as the price of a house, a holiday, a night out at Tramp nightclub, a clapped-out Volvo or a new Porsche. These formulations were always vague. The jury had to decide whether to award, for example, the value of a house (and no one told them which part of the country they should be thinking of) or of a car (again, without much guidance as to which model to go for). Judges sometimes added to the confusion by asking the jury to consider the purchasing power of their award or what income it might produce if invested at 10 per cent, but never suggesting the base figure.

Telly Savalas, the actor who played the eponymous cop in the TV series *Kojak*, was awarded £34,000 in 1976 for the not very serious allegation that his wild nightlife on location in Berlin caused him to forget his lines and keep his co-stars waiting. This sum was reduced prior to an appeal. The foreman of the jury wrote to *The Times* explaining the difficulties of jurors in such circumstances. He had entered the Royal Courts of Justice 'with not the remotest idea what compensation is paid for anything except perhaps a dented boot and wing; haloes are outside our normal terms of reference. Apparently that is why we were asked. If that is so, the court had the outcome it deserved from the appointed procedure.' Many juries might have been unable to improve on the method used to solve the problem in the case brought by Sir Oswald Mosley against the *Star* in 1934: each juror wrote down a figure, these were added together and divided by twelve and an award of £5,000 was arrived at.

As jurors tended to remember the big awards, and were likely to be unaware of any reductions to them on appeal or settlement, damages grew ever higher. Some of the large awards coincided with the launch of £1 million-prize bingo and other competitions by the tabloid newspapers, and were likened to such. The sums were inconsistent and considered by many to be disproportionate and unjust when compared to personal injury awards and compensation for criminal injuries. Yet until 1990 the courts did little to remedy matters and much to make things worse.

Although there were fluctuations, libel damages really reached a peak in the period from 1987 to 1989, in the sense of consistently high six-figure sums being awarded in cases falling some way short of the most serious. That period included Commander Martin Packard's £450,000 against the Greek-language newspaper *Eleftherotypia* – of which only forty copies were sold in

England – in June 1987. Very serious allegations had been unjustifiably made against him, but they related to events in Greece and, bearing in mind the minute circulation in the UK, these damages were wholly disproportionate. In July of the same year Jeffrey Archer was awarded his £500,000 against the *Star* for their speculations about his payment to a prostitute, and in November Lieutenant Narendra Sethia recovered £260,000 against the *Mail on Sunday* for a false allegation that he had stolen the log from the submarine HMS *Conqueror* after it sank the *General Belgrano* in the Falklands War.

In March 1988, Charles Freeman Group Ltd was awarded £300,000 against *Stationery Trade News*, a trade publication selling only 8,475 copies, for claims about counterfeit Basildon Bond paper. In terms of general public perception of libel awards, it mattered little that this case was in fact quietly settled for £17,500. In June the eleven Metropolitan Police officers met in Chapter 6 shared £160,000 for false allegations about their involvement in the beating-up of schoolboys. Again, it was the combined £160,000 sum which was reported rather than their individual cuts. In July Fox and Gibbons, a firm of London solicitors with a strong Arab clientele, netted after a two-day trial an award of £310,000 against an Arab magazine called *Sourakia* (worldwide circulation 1,000 copies) for allegations that it had helped to finance Zionist causes. In November Koo Stark recovered £300,000 from Mirror Group Newspapers for false claims that she was consorting with Prince Andrew after her marriage, and David and Carol Johnson were awarded £350,000 against Liverpool's Radio City for allegations of fraud in the way they ran their caravan holidays in France.

In April 1989 Kevin Maddocks won £150,000 against *Angler's Mail*, who wrongly accused him of cheating in a fishing competition, and that July father and son Tobias and their company, Tobias Cash 'n' Carry Ltd, shared £470,000 against the *Mail on Sunday* for allegations that they had repackaged and sold out-of-date food. In October 1989 Kit Miller, a former journalist, was awarded £165,000 against Mirror Group Newspapers for a series of articles falsely linking him with a slimming fraud. And in December Lord Aldington was awarded £1.5 million against Count Tolstoy.

The Aldington award marked the high-water mark of jury awards. It was the moment when the realisation dawned that libel jury awards had to be reined in and that guidance needed to be given on appropriate levels of damages. There were certainly high awards after 1989, among them the examples covered elsewhere in this book: Teresa Gorman v. Anthony Mudd (£150,000), Dr Malcolm Smith v. Dr Alanah Houston (£150,000), Esther Rantzen v. Mirror Group (£250,000) in 1991; Vladimir Telnikoff v. Vladimir Matusevitch (£240,000), Jason Donovan v. *The Face* (£200,000), Wafic Said v. Misbah Baki (£400,000), Rupert Allason (£200,000 on a settlement) in 1992; Elton John v. Mirror Group (£350,000) in 1993; Walker Wingsail (£1.485 million) in 1994; Souness v. Mirror Group (£750,000) in 1995; Percy v. Mirror Group (£625,000) in 1996, and Mr and Mrs Wilmot-Smith v. *Daily Telegraph* (£350,000) in 1997. However these were, for the most part, aberrations, and most of them were settled for, or reduced on appeal to, a much lesser sum (Gorman and Smith £50,000 each, Rantzen £110,000, Walker Wingsail £160,000, Percy £125,000 and the Wilmot-Smiths a figure believed to equate to £125,000 by virtue of cost orders not being enforced), or were simply not pursued.

The change came about in a number of ways. First was the greater perception that the size of libel awards was too large and too variable. Many of the larger ones were made against tabloid newspapers which the jury considered had behaved badly. While this did have some effect in curtailing the worst excesses of the popular press, it tended to set a yardstick for other cases in which the conduct of the defendant had not been nearly so bad, and produced some disproportionately high damages. Secondly, the Court of Appeal was given power under Section 8 of the Courts and Legal Services Act 1990 to substitute for a jury's award such sum as appears to the court to be proper. Previously the Court of Appeal could only intervene if the award was out of all proportion to the circumstances of the case or was divorced from reality. And if the court reached that conclusion, it had to order a retrial – something it was reluctant to do because of the expense involved – unless both parties to the appeal agreed that the court could substitute the figure it felt appropriate for damages. This was what happened in 1992 in the case of Gorman v. Mudd, in which the court made the point that the award of damages was something of a lottery if the judge could not give any meaningful direction on it.

The Court of Appeal's powers are much wider under the 1990 Act. Nonetheless, the jury still has to be allowed a considerable degree of flexibility to tailor the award to the injury done, as was recognised by the court in the case of Kiam v. *The Sunday Times* discussed later in this chapter. The court does not intervene simply because it would have arrived at a different figure: it asks whether a reasonable jury could have considered the award necessary to compensate the plaintiff and re-establish his or her reputation (Lord Justice Neill in Rantzen v. Mirror Group).

Thirdly, the Aldington case led to a challenge in the European Court of Human Rights to the system of jury awards in 1995. The European Court recognised that allowance had to be made for an open-ended variety of situations and that it was inherent in this area of the law that there could not be specific guidelines or legal rules for the assessment of damages in all cases. The European Court criticised the lack of judicial control over jury awards. It concluded that this was capable of infringing the freedom of speech provisions in Article 10 of the European Convention of Human Rights. The almost limitless discretion conferred on a jury failed to provide a satisfactory measurement for deciding what was necessary in a democratic society or justified by a pressing social need. The European Court was entitled, under the case of Lingens v. Austria in 1986, to determine whether the action taken by a national court was proportionate to the legitimate aim pursued. The £1.5 million award in the Aldington case was, it held, disproportionate to the protection of reputation.

The decision of the European Court led to a change of

approach by the Court of Appeal. In the Rantzen case in 1993, the Court of Appeal decided that specific guidance on the amount of damages should not be given to juries. They should not be referred to previous jury awards, nor should comparisons be made with personal injuries as happened in some jurisdictions such as Australia, with the aim of preventing disproportionately large libel damages, as has been the practice there since the case of Carson v. Fairfax & Sons Ltd in 1993. Instead the Court of Appeal would intervene where awards were excessive by any objective standard of reasonable compensation or proportionality. It was envisaged that as more cases went to the Court of Appeal, a body of case law would evolve which would enable judges to give some specific guidance to juries as to what the Court of Appeal had recommended. However, few cases have since gone to the Court of Appeal: if a jury awards an excessive amount, the parties normally agree a lower sum without going to appeal. It is extremely rare for damages to be increased on appeal (one of the few cases in which they were was the Tesco litigation covered in the Appendix).

After the European Court's decision in Aldington, the Court of Appeal in the Elton John case (see Chapter 15) reached a significantly different conclusion to that in Rantzen two years earlier. Personal injury cases *could* be referred to as yardsticks for damages. Juries could be told that damages for serious libels should be within the range of awards for serious personal injuries of £52,000 for loss of a limb to £125,000 for grave brain injuries (the personal injury awards the court had in mind were those for pain and suffering, not the special damages awarded for loss of wages and the expense of a new lifestyle which, in serious cases, could produce seven-figure sums). Advocates were now permitted to suggest a range of damages to juries.

Where the Court of Appeal has reviewed damages, the tendency has been to reduce them. In 1993 Dr Smith's £150,000 damages for slander – false allegations of sexual harassment and assorted groping of the defendant, Dr Alannah Houston, and female members of staff at his surgery – were reduced to

£50,000. This was said by Lord Justice Hirst to be at the very top
of the range for slander and only appropriate because of the very
grave and aggravating features of the case. Had the slander
remained within the confines of the waiting room, or had the
defendant promptly apologised, the sum would have been a very
small fraction of the original £150,000. Also in 1993, television
presenter Esther Rantzen's award of £250,000 against the Mirror
Group, for what she described as terrible, terrifying lies, was
reduced to £110,000. She had been attacked in vituperative terms
in a series of articles in the *People* suggesting that she had,
despite her role as founder of Childline, the helpline for abused
children, acted in a hypocritical and insincere manner by
allegedly protecting a man called Alex Standish, described as a
depraved religious studies master, so that she could secure his
assistance in exposing child abuse at Crookham Court School,
which resulted in the jailing of three teachers.

Rantzen's case was that she had done everything she could to
bring the attention of the authorities to Standish, and that she
believed the police were keeping a careful watch on him.
Childline had helped 190,000 children in fifteen years, and she
feared its activities could be imperilled by the articles. The *People*
claimed that Standish had composed twenty-one pages of 'sick-
ening pornography' about young boys and instructions on how
to deal with 'naughty lads'. The jury accepted Rantzen's case
and rejected the paper's after a mere ninety minutes' retirement.
The Court of Appeal recognised that the trial must have been a
terrible ordeal for her, but as she had suffered no financial loss or
social damage as a result of the case, and remained a distinguished and highly respected figure in the world of broadcasting,
it reduced her damages.

Standish, too, sued the *People*, claiming that his scribblings
were simply fantasies. Here the jury decided that he had indeed
been libelled but awarded him no damages, and he was left with
a £50,000 bill for legal costs after a two-week hearing.

In 1993 Elton John was awarded £350,000 damages, of which
£275,000 was exemplary, or punitive, damages, because the jury

felt that the newspaper which had libelled him, the *Mirror*, had behaved so badly over the affair (see Chapter 15). Moreover, the jury appears to have been persuaded that the whole story – which falsely alleged that John had been seen spitting out food at a party and interpreted this as evidence of an eating disorder – was an invention rather than a case of mistaken identity, as was claimed. In 1995 the Court of Appeal reduced the compensatory damages from £75,000 to £25,000, indicating that the libel, while not trivial, was not the most serious, either. Elton John was a man with an international reputation and he had struggled to overcome previous personal difficulties. Although the article was false, offensive and distressing, it did not attack his personal integrity or damage his reputation as an artist. However, the court did award £50,000 exemplary damages, as opposed to the jury's figure of £275,000, taking into account the recklessness of the *Mirror* with regard to whether or not the story was true and their apparent attempt to pressurise him not to sue.

In the previous year the Court of Appeal had upheld the £45,000 awarded to Victor Kiam against *The Sunday Times*. Kiam was an American entrepreneur best known in the UK for telling commercial television viewers that he liked Remington razors so much he had bought the company. Among his many other accomplishments was the launch of the Playtex Cross Your Heart bra and the purchase of the New England Patriots football team in the USA. Contrary to what the paper claimed, Kiam had not defaulted on a £13.5 million loan to buy his football team, nor had he filed for bankruptcy. The paper apologised within three weeks and offered to pay £10,000 damages, but the parties could not agree. It was ruled that the newspaper was not allowed to mention the figure of £10,000 to the jury as part of their argument that Kiam's demands were unreasonable. *The Sunday Times* was accused of using Kiam's name to give prominence to their article and of making no effort to check the accuracy of the story. They countered that they had apologised, and that the report had clearly done Kiam no harm in the years it had taken for the case to come to trial. The Court of Appeal upheld the award. It was not excessive, using the criteria of reasonableness and proportionality. The court agreed that it was hard to imagine a more damaging allegation against a successful entrepreneur than this grave and irresponsible assertion of insolvency.

This was a case which would be well suited to the offer of amends procedure under the Defamation Act 1996, where a judge can swiftly, and at less cost, determine the level of damages if the parties cannot agree. It is very likely that a judge at first instance, sitting without a jury, would have awarded a lower sum than £45,000. Moreover, in the wake of the Elton John case, a court might have allowed mention to be made of *The Sunday Times* offer of £10,000.

In 1997 the Court of Appeal reduced the £100,000 damages awarded to Barry Jones to £40,000. Additionally he recovered £15,000 for loss of wages – he had claimed £133,926. Jones, an interpreter and business consultant in Moscow, had been accused in two consecutive issues of the *Sunday Mirror* of assisting the KGB by organising sex sessions for jaded visiting businessmen. 'ORGIES TO ORDER IN KGB SEX TRAP', 'SEXPIONAGE' and 'BRITISH MR FIXIT SETS UP VICE GIRLS FOR OUR MEN IN MOSCOW', ran the headlines. These were very grave allegations which the paper failed to justify. Indeed, the judge was so unimpressed by the evidence relating to the KGB and the exposure of businessmen to blackmail that he had withdrawn these defences from the jury. The defendants did produce a tape on which Jones appeared to be arranging an assignation with a prostitute for the paper's undercover journalists ('Do you wanna bosh this brunette? I can fix it.'). Jones admitted to being a persistent womaniser and heavy drinker. He explained that he had been drunk and fantasising when the conversation had taken place.

In the Court of Appeal Lord Justice Hirst observed that, except possibly in the most exceptional case, it was difficult to imagine any defamation action where severe damage to reputation accompanied by maximum aggravation would be comparable to physical injuries such as quadriplegia, total blindness or deafness, for which the top limit for general damages was £130,000.

The court felt that there was no justification for an award twice the size of those of Kiam and Smith, and comparable to Rantzen's. Although the *Sunday Mirror*'s allegations and their robust defence of the action were aggravating features, damages were reduced by the fact that Jones' reputation had principally been harmed only by the very limited circulation of the newspaper in Moscow, and because the jury had not been greatly impressed by his large special damages claim or, perhaps, by some of his conduct.

The ceiling on damages and the more interventionist approach of the Court of Appeal has effectively put an end to windfall damages. As I have discussed, awards are likely to be further depressed when judges start awarding damages under the summary judgement and offer of amends procedures of the Defamation Act 1996.

Libel litigants who have experienced varying degrees of success.
*Clockwise from top*: Linford Christie, Gillian Taylforth, Elton John, Mohamed Fayed, Jeffrey Archer, Richard Branson.

Not a wire in sight: one impression of *Vanity Fair*'s Nicholas Coleridge and Harrods PR man Michael Cole discussing the litigation of Mohamed Fayed (*right*) in the steam room.

*Top left*: The comedian Tom O'Connor, whose case came to a sudden end.

*Top right*: Jonathan Aitken, whose libel action led to his stay at HMP Standford Hill.

*Right*: EastEnder Gillian Taylforth and her boyfriend Geoff Knights: did the policeman spot a little fellatio on the hard shoulder, or was it pancreatitis?

*Above left*: Judge 'Maximum Mike' Argyle, who libelled the 'very much less intelligent' Felix Dennis, later a millionaire publisher. *Above right*: The Oz defendants – Dennis (*left*), Richard Neville (*centre*) and Jim Anderson – pictured shortly before their conviction and (*below*) after their release on appeal, sporting prison haircuts.

Dave Morris and Helen Steel, the victors in the McDonald's case despite being ordered to pay £40,000 damages.

Mona Bauwens' libel action was torpedoed by her generosity to the Mellor family.

Derek Jameson lost his action after his solicitor kept him in the dark about his barrister's gloomy opinion of its prospects.

Jeffrey Archer, finally caught up by his past, faces a criminal investigation and the possibility of being required to reimburse the libel damages he recovered from the *Star*.

Imran Khan, accompanied by his wife, Jemima, arrives at the High Court, where he dispatched Ian Botham (*below left*) and Allan Lamb (*below right*) to the boundary.

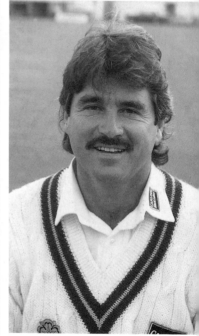

*Right*: Armand Hammer, oil
magnate and nonagenarian libel
forum-shopper.

*Below*: Robert Maxwell the ultimate
libel terrorist.

ANDRE BRUTMANN/REX FEATURES

David Ashby MP was unamused at his domestic arrangements being photographed by *The Sunday Times*.

*Coronation Street* star Bill Roache with the board game he invented after he was ruined by his legal action.

# 15

# MULTIPLE DAMAGES

There is no limit to the number of times a plaintiff can sue for republication of a libel. As if to prove the adage that mud sticks, sometimes a false allegation which has already been the subject of a court case lodges in the minds of writers, reporters or commentators to re-emerge years later as fact. So it is vital for news organisations to keep a record of libel verdicts and apologies in an appropriate databank to reduce the risk of repetition of libels.

It passed into legend that a British police officer in Palestine by the name of Morton had been responsible for shooting Abraham Stern, head of the Stern gang, in cold blood. W. H. Allen was the first publisher to pay Morton damages when the allegation was made in 1951 in the book *The Revolt* by Menachem Begin, then best known as the leader of the Irgun gang, but later prime minister of Israel. In 1972 Morton collected £4,000 from Secker and Warburg when the story resurfaced in *The Terrorists* by Roland Gautier. And in 1978 Weidenfeld and Nicolson had to pay him damages for repeating the libel in Michael Bar Zohar's *Ben Gurion*.

The importance of keeping records is illustrated by the number of cases where a libel is repeated by the same organisation. In April 1988 property developer Harry Hyams received his fourth apology and set of damages from the BBC, which had again repeated the canard that he was deliberately keeping empty a development at Centrepoint in heart of London. And in the same year the BBC was also apologising and paying damages to George Ward, managing director of Grunwick Processing Laboratories – in this instance for the third time – for unwarranted accusations of providing appalling pay and conditions.

In 1975 Princess Elizabeth of Toro was the victim of scurrilous allegations of misbehaviour in a lavatory at Orly Airport in Paris, which led *Private Eye* to invent the euphemism 'Ugandan discussions'. The mendacious allegations rested on the notoriously unreliable say-so of the despot President Idi Amin of Uganda. Princess Elizabeth brought six libel actions in the UK, against the *Daily Express*, the *Daily Mail*, the *Mirror*, the *Sunday Telegraph*, the *Sun* and the German magazine *Der Spiegel*, all publications which should have known better. She recovered £50,000 plus 23,000 Deutschmarks, and undisclosed damages in France and Italy.

On occasions it is difficult to escape the conclusion that a plaintiff is repeatedly hoovering up tax-free damages. The record for the number of libel actions still seems to be held by Dr John Bodkin Adams, renowned for easing the passing of wealthy widows in Eastbourne after suitable adjustments had been made to their wills. He sued thirteen newspapers after he had been acquitted of the murder of a former patient, Mrs Morrell. Taking advantage of the lack of restrictions on pre-trial publicity which existed in the late 1950s, the press had a field day. The *Daily Mail*'s story was unambiguous: 'YARD PROBES MASS POISONING. Twenty-five Deaths in the Great Mystery of Eastbourne – Enquiry into 400 Wills – Rich Women Believed to Have Been the Victims'. In 1961 the newspapers collectively paid Adams £50,000 damages. He periodically sued other papers who repeated the accusation in the belief that he was no longer alive. In fact he did not die until 1983, leaving £402,970 in his will, largely the product of his successful libel actions – and bequests made to him in the wills of an astonishing 132 of his patients.

Multiple libel claims nowadays are often the product of sloppy, ill-researched attacks by tabloids on well-known personalities they believe are unlikely to sue. On occasions the libels are simply a rehash of stories already demonstrated to be libellous.

The most scandalous example was the attack launched by the *Sun* on the pop star Elton John in 1987. It appeared to have no more substance than editor Kelvin Mackenzie's dislike of homosexuals, whom he dismissed as 'poofters' and 'bum bandits'. Elton John had been open about his sexuality; indeed, in an interview in *Rolling Stone* he had been quoted as saying, 'There's nothing wrong with going to bed with someone of your own sex.' Based on the very dubious and venal evidence of a rent boy, the *Sun*, from February to September 1987, published increasingly malicious stories about Elton John, ignoring written advice from its own lawyer not to publish. It started with 'ELTON IN VICE BOYS SCANDAL'. The piece was written in sanctimonious terms, in which the rent boy confided hypocritically to the *Sun*: 'I am ashamed of what I did. I am speaking out to show how widespread this sort of thing is and to warn other gullible kids to steer clear of people like this.' The *Sun* did not find space to mention that they had paid him £2,000 plus a weekly retainer of £250 for the ensuing months during which he was to dish the dirt on John.

A writ was immediately issued by the star's solicitors, Frere Cholmeley. This served only to spur on the paper to print further libels. 'THE STORY THEY ARE ALL SUING OVER – ELTON'S KINKY KINKS AND DRUG CAPERS'. By the time the campaign had ended, John had issued no fewer than seventeen writs. Among the garbage being printed was 'ELTON'S PORN PHOTO SHAME', which reproduced, in coyly cropped form, Polaroid pictures of Elton with a consenting male, which the paper mistakenly thought would force him to drop his action. Again there was no space to tell readers that it had paid £10,000 for the photographs. Other lurid stories, such as 'STAR'S LUST FOR BONDAGE' and 'YOU'RE A LIAR, ELTON', unleashed more writs and reinforced John's determination to take the paper to the cleaners.

The *Sun*'s owner, Rupert Murdoch, was sufficiently concerned at these outpourings to call his editor. 'Kelvin, are you all right on this Elton John business?' he inquired.

'Yes, boss,' Mackenzie reassured him.

But behind the scenes the *Sun* was becoming increasingly nervous. A fraudster with a quashed conviction for attempted murder was the rather unpromising choice to rake up more dirt which could be substantiated. The deal was that he collected £1,750 for each affidavit he obtained from a rent boy, who himself got a cut of £500. As the stories became more specific, Elton John was able to establish that he had been in the United States when he was alleged to have been trawling London gay clubs. There were signs of increasing jitters at the *Sun* when it failed to run its trailed story 'Tomorrow: Elton's Pink Tutu Party'. Worse was to follow. After their last attack on Elton John, 'MYSTERY OF ELTON'S SILENT DOG', a fictitious account of 'Elton's vicious Rottweiler silenced by a horrific operation' – appeared on 28 September, their great rival, the *Mirror*, gleefully published the *Sun*'s original rent boy's retraction: 'It's a pack of lies. I made it all up. I only did it for the money and the *Sun* was easy to con. I have never met Elton John.'

The dog story, as inaccurate as the others – Elton John's dog was not even a Rottweiler but an Alsatian, and it still packed a good howl – was a grave tactical error. It enabled John to bring this writ on for trial first, so that he could sue without any risk of his sexuality being picked over in court. The *Sun*, noting the £500,000 recently awarded by a jury to Jeffrey Archer against the *Star*, realised that the time had come to capitulate. Mackenzie admitted: 'We were totally duped. Elton John was a big error.'

On 12 December 1988, a statement in open court was read in which the *Sun* apologised unreservedly and agreed to pay £1 million damages to Elton John. The paper's headline that morning was 'SORRY ELTON'. 'We are delighted that the *Sun* and Elton have become friends again and are sorry we were lied to by a teenager living in the world of fantasy.' Sir Michael Davies, the judge hearing the statement, expressed his disapproval and distaste that the settlement had been reported before it was finalised, referring sarcastically to the mutual admiration society of the *Sun* and Elton John.

That, one would have thought, would have been the end of tabloid libels against this particular victim. However, the *Mirror* had failed to learn the *Sun*'s lesson. In December 1992 it published a bizarre story, trumpeted as a world exclusive: 'ELTON'S DIET OF DEATH. SECRET OF ELTON'S SPITTING IMAGE'. John was described as having been seen to spit seafood canapés into his napkin at a Hollywood party. Porky pies might have been more appropriate. John's complaint was that it was outrageous that a recovered bulimic who had also fought against various other addictions and been a member of Alcoholics, Narcotics and Overeaters Anonymous, and who had latterly been giving encouragement to other sufferers, should be accused of being a sham. It was perhaps not the most earth-shattering of libels, but the jury took exception to the newspaper's conduct in the matter and their attempt to defend the case – particularly when it was established that Elton had been at his home in Atlanta and not at the party in question at all.

Furthermore, unfortunately – and expensively – for the *Mirror*, they had been warned in a carefully documented telephone conversation with Elton's solicitor that, from the sound of things, it was most unlikely that their story was true and that they should not publish. They afterwards offered to apologise and make a donation to a charity on the star's behalf, but their sincerity was called into question when they wrote to him intimating that he was fortunate not to have been prosecuted for drug abuse. The jury clearly felt that the whole story was a fabrication and perceived this letter as an attempt to frighten off the star.

Mr Justice Drake advised jurors to keep a sense of proportion in any damages they awarded and to resist the temptation to add a nought or two to the figure. The jury nevertheless willingly adopted George Carman QC's suggestion that they should award

a sum which would wipe the smile off the faces of the board of
Mirror Group Newspapers. After a retirement of five hours and
on a majority of 10–2 they awarded an unhumorous £75,000 for
the libel, plus £275,000 punitive damages for the way the paper
had behaved. Elton announced that the damages would go to an
AIDS charity. 'I would have accepted an apology much earlier in
the case if they had said that their story was fictional. I am
pleased about the punishment part of it because I think it will
make newspapers think twice before doing such things,' he
added. As we have seen, the Court of Appeal reduced the damages to a total of £75,000.

It is, however, principally against women that the tabloid
press has unleashed a mass of libels. For some reason, the press
seems to have been unable to write about Prince Andrew's
former girlfriend Koo Stark in anything other than defamatory
terms. The tabloids seem to have imagined that people like Stark
who had previously been awarded very large libel damages could
somehow be exposed if they kept on digging. Yet some elemen-
tary research might have persuaded journalists that what they
were reporting was probably untrue and that she would not be
slow to protect her reputation. Precisely why the tabloids felt it
necessary to attack Stark in the first place was unclear. She was
a talented photographer and the soul of discretion, and seemed a
distinct improvement on the woman Prince Andrew did eventually choose to marry. The tabloid press were, it seems,
overexcited by a lurid movie in which Stark had appeared in her
youth.

For two successive weekends in December 1985 the *People*
accused Stark of having deceived her husband, Tim Jeffries, by
continuing secretly to date Prince Andrew. In fact she had met
the Prince only once since her marriage, and then in the company of her husband. 'I was horrified and shocked,' she said. 'I
did not know why they wanted to manufacture a story about me
which was so cruel.' The newspaper's attack was particularly
unpleasant given that her marriage had failed. The *People* took it
upon itself to publish pernicious rubbish about her continuing

love for the Prince being the reason for the break-up. She had, they claimed, improbably, needed an exorcism ceremony to rid her of her love for Andrew. In court in November 1988 the paper did not claim that their reportage was true. Rather lamely they argued that Stark was being oversensitive and that she had misinterpreted the meaning of the articles.

The judge suggested that the jury should assume the stories in the *People* were a tissue of lies. Stark's counsel, Desmond Browne, intimated that damages should be right at the top of the scale. It took the jury only a hundred minutes to award her £300,000. As part of the final settlement of the case it was agreed that the *People* would not pursue its appeal against the award.

The *Sun* likewise had to pay substantial damages to Koo Stark for publishing the same story; the *News of the World* had to pay her damages for both libel and breach of copyright for misuse of some photographs she had taken for a calendar, which it contrived to use to libel her. The newspaper had seemingly mistaken a mouse tattooed on one of the models for a cat, and had concocted the peculiar headline: 'VEILED DIG AT HER OLD DATE ANDREW?' This was its second run-in with Koo Stark: in March 1986 she had been awarded damages against the paper in respect of a purported interview following the break-up of her marriage. This was in fact a rehash of a conversation she had had seven years previously.

The *Mirror*, part of the same group as the *People*, forked out substantial damages, also in November 1988, and had to apologise for the story it had published in December 1986, headlined 'KOO SPARKED JOAN'S DIVORCE'. This had falsely alleged that Stark had been frolicking with Joan Collins' husband on a Mediterranean holiday. Again, no attempt was made to justify the piece, but no apology was offered. The incident had simply never taken place.

In 1986 Stark had recovered damages from *Penthouse*, for what it had claimed was an interview about her love life, and from the *Observer*, for suggestions that she had exploited for her personal advantage her relationship with Prince Andrew. In March 1988 the *Star* had to pay her libel damages for allegations that she had made bitter remarks about Prince Andrew and Sarah Ferguson. And the press had still not finished with her: in February 1990 she received substantial damages for a suggestion in Nigel Dempster's diary in the *Daily Mail* that she had unjustifiably reneged on a divorce agreement. All told, Koo Stark was awarded £150,000 in eight libel actions, in addition to the £300,000 from the *People*. At last the message had got home to the tabloid press that she could not be libelled with impunity.

Another victim of such coverage was Carmen Proetta. She is estimated to have recovered £350,000 libel damages plus costs in libel actions against five British newspapers. Proetta was an interpreter for a Spanish law firm who appeared in the Thames TV documentary *Death on the Rock*, which dealt with the shooting of three suspected IRA terrorists, Mairead Farrell, Sean Savage and Dan McCann, in Gibraltar on 6 March 1988. She described how she had seen two of them raise their hands in surrender before they were shot by the SAS. Whether or not her account of events was correct, she had voluntarily given a statement to the police, and it represented her honest recollection. But the English media were convinced she was making it up and that there was no misconduct of which she was not guilty. They effectively declared open season on Carmen Proetta.

Proetta believed that she was the victim of a smear campaign. *The Sunday Times*, the *Mirror*, the *Sun*, *Express* and *Mail* accused her of a wide range of misdeeds, the common thread being that she had fabricated her account. The tabloids in particular vied with each other to blacken her name. The *Mirror*, in two articles published in April and September 1988, accused her for good measure of knowingly associating with wanted Britons, involvement in vice and drugs, misleading the inquest and assaulting a photographer. The *Sun* jumped on this bandwagon, labelling her the 'Tart of Gibraltar' in two pieces they ran, in April and May 1988. They subsequently publicly withdrew their unfounded statements and apologised to Proetta for the distress and embarrassment generated by their allegations, which they acknowledged should have never been made. Although Proetta ended up with substantial damages, she commented with some feeling: 'No amount of money could compensate for the suffering this has caused. Not so much for me, but for my three children and my mother. I feel very happy my name has been cleared and the truth has prevailed. I have prayed very hard for this day.'

Her hope that this put an end to the matter was premature. Channel 4's *Hard News*, which broadcast a sympathetic account of the way Proetta had been treated, was obliged to pay substantial libel damages to Nigel Bowden, a freelance journalist working for *The Sunday Times*, for suggestions that he had taken part in a deliberate smear campaign against her, and to Alastair Brett, the *Sunday Times*' lawyer, for criticisms of the paper's defence of Proetta's libel action. *The Sunday Times* continued to publish articles accusing Proetta of criminal conduct. Neither *The Sunday Times* nor its sister paper, the *News of the World* – which in 1992 alleged that she had tried to sell passports to one of its reporters – was sued, but she did produce an affidavit from a Spanish inspector showing that she had kept the police informed of the newspaper group's campaign. The next chapter in the saga is the hearing of her action in Ireland against Andrew Neil, the former editor of *The Sunday Times*, for remarks he made about her on the Gay Byrne show. Court appearances seem to have taken over her life.

In very different circumstances, Sara Keays, the mother of a child by Conservative Cabinet minister Cecil Parkinson, received a similar working over from the English press. Her relationship with Parkinson had broken up amid bitter recriminations, and it seemed that certain sections of the media were incapable of addressing the matter without libelling her.

In 1988 the *Daily Express* had to apologise and pay damages for an article entitled 'Bittersweet Revenge' which falsely suggested that Keays had arranged for the press to be present when her disabled daughter left hospital after an operation. The same year Peter Jenkins and his publishers also had to apologise, for references to her in his book *Mrs Thatcher's Revolution*. In 1990

substantial libel damages were forthcoming from the
Conservative peer Lord Tebbit for an unfounded allegation in his
autobiography, *Upwardly Mobile*, that she had broken an undertaking not to comment on her relationship with Parkinson. In
1991 Keays began further libel proceedings, against the bookseller Waterstone's, for continuing to sell Tebbit's book in its
legally objectionable form. And in February 1992 she was
awarded £105,000 damages against *New Woman* for suggesting
that, in writing her own book, *A Question of Judgement*, she had
behaved like a kiss-and-tell bimbo, producing a lurid account
calculated to make money and cause Parkinson maximum
embarrassment. The editor of *New Woman*, Frankie McGowan,
indignantly asserted that she 'would not do that to another
woman'. However, as the offending article had been headlined
'LAUGHING ALL THE WAY TO THE BONK', it was not surprising the jury
thought otherwise. Their award comfortably exceeded the
£50,000 paid into court, and Keays was estimated to have recovered £100,000 damages from her other libel actions.

Keays explained that she had written her book to set the
record straight, particularly as Parkinson's friends had set about
denigrating her in the media. She wanted to correct newspaper
stories that her relationship with Parkinson had been a mere
dalliance. If she had simply wanted to make money, she said, she
could have accepted an offer of £250,000 from the *News of the
World* for her story. In fact she made no more than £50,000
from the book and its serialisation, which ran in the *Mirror* at the
time of the Conservative Party Conference in 1985. She had conducted negotiations herself with Robert Maxwell. Her memorable
conversation with the old villain was taped for posterity: 'Trust
me if you will. You know my record speaks for itself. Can I say
to you that you are talking to Robert Maxwell? I am not Rupert
Murdoch. I am not a hired hand. You are as safe as you would be
in the Bank of England. If there's anybody more powerful than I,
then you must go and find them. What else can I do other than
tell you that my record speaks for itself, and that nobody on
earth or in heaven or hell will prevent me from publishing your

book?' Clearly Keays made quite an impression on Maxwell, who can be heard to declare: 'You're quite a tough lady, well done.'

In July 1992 she also recovered substantial damages from the Birmingham *Sunday Mercury* for false suggestions that she had wrecked Cecil Parkinson's career in revenge for a breach of promise of marriage.

The same kind of resolve eventually stopped the press from recycling libels of the socialite Lady Colin Campbell, author of *Diana in Private – The Princess No One Knows, Lady Colin Campbell's Guide to Being a Modern Lady* and an autobiography, *A Life Worth Living.* Lady Colin's upbringing in Jamaica had been a little unusual. As she recounted, fused labia and a deformed clitoris had led to her being mistakenly registered and brought up as a boy – a rare but not unknown occurrence. An operation in New York and an amendment to her Jamaican birth certificate had put matters right. The operation was not a sex change, but the correction of a wrongly assigned gender; an all-important alteration was made to George Ziadie's name, and Georgia went on to marry Lord Colin Campbell. The marriage unfortunately ended in an acrimonious divorce, and stories about her past were fed to the press. In 1976 the *People*, the London *Evening News* and the *Daily Express* agreed not to repeat libels about her marriage to Lord Colin Campbell and her private life.

Publication of her book *Diana in Private* in 1992 brought Lady Colin back into the spotlight and prompted other journalists to regurgitate these libels. In 1995 she received an apology and damages from Mirror Group Newspapers for falsely describing her as a Jamaican transsexual, with an undertaking not to repeat the libel. She received what she called 'a massive sum' from Associated Newspapers for untrue suggestions in three articles by Peter McKay and Nigel Dempster in the *Evening Standard* and *Daily Mail* respectively that she had been born a man and had had a sex change operation, and that Lord Colin Campbell had found out only after their marriage that she had been born a boy. This was in breach of an undertaking given by the newspapers' parent company in 1989 that it would not repeat any such allegations. The newspapers apologised and accepted that the reports were not only untrue but most hurtful. By dint of years of litigation, Lady Colin Campbell had established the truth and put an end to the prurient misinformation about her gender.

A less meritorious plaintiff who repeatedly sued the press was Sonia Sutcliffe, the wife of the 'Yorkshire Ripper' who was jailed in 1981 for multiple murder. In 1990 she was calculated to be receiving £50,000 a year tax-free in respect of her libel and copyright claims. Her libel awards included £5,000 from the *Bradford Telegraph and Argus* in June 1983; £25,000 from the *Yorkshire Post* in November 1988, plus another £7,500 in May 1989; £100,000 and £60,000 from *Private Eye* in October 1989; £35,000 from the *Star* in November and December 1989; £75,000 from the *Express* in December 1989 and £26,500 from News Group in September 1990. Most notoriously, in May 1989 she had been awarded £600,000 against *Private Eye*, which resulted in their 'Ripperballs' and 'Bananaballs' appeals for funds. The *Eye* had alleged that Mrs Sutcliffe had negotiated a £250,000 deal with the *Daily Mail* to sell through an intermediary, Barbara Jones of the *Mail on Sunday*, the story of her life with her husband. The Court of Appeal held that the award was unreasonable and excessive, and it was reduced by agreement to £60,000. Even so the sum compared favourably with the compensation paid to Sutcliffe's surviving victims – an average of £7,000. The court would not, however, allow *Private Eye* to produce freshly discovered evidence said to show that Sutcliffe had received £25,000 as a 'loan' from the *Mail on Sunday* reporter, which was in fact a disguised payment for the story. Sutcliffe had also received £100,000 in respect of two subsequent libel actions for false suggestions that she had defrauded the Social Security authorities. Proceedings had been unsuccessfully taken by the attorney-general against *Private Eye* for contempt of court in respect of the DHSS articles.

After appeals Sutcliffe had won £334,00 in damages, yet she

lost virtually all the fruits of her litigation when, in December 1990, she lost a fifteen-day libel action against the *News of the World*, having declined to accept a payment into court of £50,000. Their story, headlined 'SONIA LOVES A RIPPER DOUBLE', claimed she had had a passionate affair with one George Papoutsis, who was said to be the spitting image of her husband. It was highly defamatory, intimating that she had deceived Papoutsis by not telling him who her husband was. He was quoted as saying, 'I felt sick. I have been kissing and caressing the wife of a monster.' She was also accused of leaving him to pay two hotel bills. Sutcliffe denied the affair, which was alleged to have taken place during a trip to Greece in May 1988. However, the *News of the World*, using the same tactics employed by the *Sun* in the Taylforth case, joined Barbara Jones, the source for the report, as a third party to the proceedings on the basis that if Sutcliffe won the case they should be able to recover the damages and costs from her.

The *News of the World* had paid Rex Features £25,000 for the story, for which Rex said they had paid £23,500 to Barbara Jones. She in turn claimed that she had paid Mr Papoutsis £10,000 for his account of his fling with Sonia Sutcliffe. Ms Jones also produced receipts for £15,000 and £10,000, which she asserted represented payment for Mrs Sutcliffe's co-operation in a book she had planned to write.

George Carman QC accused Sutcliffe of having committed perjury in her 1989 libel action against *Private Eye* when she said that an agreement for the loan she needed to save her family house was not recorded in writing but only by word of mouth, and that the £25,000 was a loan from a personal friend. The jury evidently believed Barbara Jones, and Sutcliffe was left having to pay several hundreds of thousands of pounds in legal costs.

Sutcliffe remained undeterred by this setback. In July 1997 she recovered damages estimated to be between £10,000 and £20,000 for false allegations in a book about her libel cases and her dealings with her husband. It was her ninth libel action.

## The Trials and Tribulations of Rupert Allason

Anyone planning to write about Rupert Allason, Conservative
MP for Torbay from 1987 to 1997 and author, under the name
Nigel West, of a number of books on security and intelligence,
would do well to remember that he has brought eighteen libel
actions and has defended another six. Experienced in the ways of
the laws of libel he may be, but even he has encountered some
setbacks in these less plaintiff-friendly times.

Allason's early books explored the operations of MI5 and MI6
in unprecedented detail. Almost invariably they attracted a
number of legal complaints, which formed the basis of Allason's
libel training. His book *MI5 British Security Service Operations
1909–45*, published in 1981, produced a complaint from Eric
Glass, a theatrical agent who had come to the UK from Austria in
1936 and whose identity had, unknown to him, been used in
1942 by MI5 to provide funds for the double agent Wolf
Schmidt, operating under the code name 'Tate'. MI5 needed to get
money to Tate using a New York bank account without arousing
the suspicions of the Germans, and decided that Glass's name
would provide the cover they required. Lord Goodman threatened
to obtain an injunction on behalf of Glass, but after much huff-
ing and puffing the claim disappeared.

Allason's history of MI6, *The Friends: Britain's Post-War
Secret Intelligence*, published in 1988, attracted a writ from
Greville Wynne, who had worked for MI6 and had been impris-
oned as a spy by the Russians. In his book Allason questioned
the veracity of Wynne's account, given in his autobiography, *The
Man from Odessa*, of the important role he had played in the
defection of a Soviet military intelligence major, Sergei Kuznov.
It suffered, according to Allason, from the slight difficulty that
no such person existed. Moreover, Wynne's claim to have
accompanied Oleg Penkovsky, who spied for the West, to the
White House was, Allason pointed out, a fantasy. Neither did
Allason's depiction of Wynne's alcoholism and 'post-usefulness
syndrome', implying that he was on the scrapheap, endear him to

the former MI6 man. Such allegations are difficult to prove, at the best of times, but particularly when they require evidence from the shadowy figures of the intelligence world. Allason's publishers were advised to settle and paid Wynne £80,000. Allason's barrister informed him that damages could be in the region of £100,000 to £150,000. A jury might well, he said, feel sorry for Wynne, who had not only served his country in MI6 and suffered at the hands of the Soviets, but also now had cancer of the throat.

But Allason refused to apologise to Wynne. He subpoenaed Wynne's wife, a photograph of whose black eye had earlier bedecked the *Daily Express*. He collected evidence of Wynne's drunken activities in Majorca, which included being arrested for throwing beer crates off a balcony, and obtained an affidavit from a former director of the CIA, who swore that Wynne's account of the trip to the White House was false. The intelligence community was appalled: such cases did not go to court. Although Allason received two public-interest immunity certificates preventing the court from hearing certain parts of the defence evidence on grounds of national security, his tactics produced the desired result: Wynne dropped his action the weekend before it was due to be heard. Thus was Allason's appetite for do-it-yourself litigation whetted.

In October 1991, Allason and George Galloway, Labour MP for Glasgow Hillhead, tabled an early day motion in the House of Commons calling for an inquiry into the arms-dealing activities of Robert Maxwell and his role in the betrayal of Mordecai Vanunu, an Israeli nuclear technician, as described in Seymour Hersh's book *The Samson Option*. Maxwell and his newspaper, the *Mirror*, went on the attack, headlining their allegations 'DIS-HONOURABLE MEN AND DIRTY TRICKS'. Allason and Galloway counterclaimed when Maxwell was cavalier enough to sue them. Allason scoured the country to uncover the questionable evidence used by the *Mirror* to ridicule Vanunu's claims about an Israeli nuclear plant at Dimona (they had even suggested that it might be an egg-packaging factory). Allason also got wind of the

*Mirror*'s internal investigation into the activities of its foreign editor, Nicholas Davies, who had featured in Hersh's book. One Saturday a Porsche turned up at 7am at the country home of the executive who had investigated Davies. It was Allason the process-server with a subpoena demanding production of the Davies report. That Sunday evening Arthur Davidson QC, the *Mirror*'s in-house lawyer, was on the telephone to Allason wanting to settle the case.

Allason recovered £200,000 damages, a record for a counterclaimant acting in person, plus £30,000 costs for his favourite lawyer – himself.

Galloway also recovered very substantial damages and costs reported to be £150,000. The Labour MP has himself been a frequent visitor to the libel courts. In June 1991 he had been awarded undisclosed damages against the *Today* newspaper for an allegation that he had neglected his duties to pursue his own pleasures. In November 1994 he successfully sued the *Sunday Telegraph* for their story 'SOMETHING COOKING IN THE HOUSE'. The paper had confused him with another MP who had become disorderly after attending what was described as a 'whisky bash'. In 1996 he recovered damages first from the *Evening Standard*, for allegations it published about his financial affairs which it subsequently acknowledged were above suspicion, and then from the Arabic paper *Al Hayat*, which repeated the *Standard*'s story. And in June 1999 he was awarded a further £20,000 after another Arab newspaper, *Al Ahram*, for allegations that he was a prominent supporter of terrorism in Parliament. A similarly bizarre charge which linked him with British intelligence was also levelled at the Liberal peer Lord Avebury, who recovered £35,000 damages.

The Maxwell case spawned further battles for Allason. Nicholas Davies' own book, *The Unknown Maxwell*, was successfully sued for its suggestion that Allason had made reckless and unfounded allegations in the House of Commons and had sheltered behind parliamentary privilege to protect himself from litigation. In fact Allason had no fear of litigation and was happy

to recount his allegations. More damages were paid. And impu-
tations in *Maxwell's Fall*, by former *Mirror* editor Roy
Greenslade, concerning the manner in which Allason and
Galloway had raised the arms-dealing allegations in the House of
Commons, and their motives for doing so, resulted in yet another
payment of damages,

After the *Mirror* had settled the Maxwell libel action in
November 1992, staff at the newspaper contrived to prompt
friendly members of Parliament to table a motion asking Allason
to hand over the libel damages he had been awarded to
Maxwell's deprived pensioners. The *Mirror* reported this as 'a
challenge by fifty MPs last night to demonstrate his concern for
Maxwell pensioners by giving them his £250,000 [sic] libel damages'. The story was also passed to the *Western Morning News*
where it could be read locally by Allason's constituents. In fact
only seven MPs had signed the motion, and it was *Mirror* journalists who had drafted it. The *Mirror* had published the story
before the motion had appeared on the Commons order paper.
Allason sued MGN and Alastair Campbell, then the *Mirror*'s
political editor, for malicious falsehood, claiming that as a consequence of this he had lost a publishing agreement with Holmes
Protection Inc. in New York worth £75,000.

Much of the evidence at the trial centred on whether Alastair
Campbell, by that stage Tony Blair's chief press secretary, had
been involved in drafting the motion. Allason had had a spirited
correspondence with Campbell, being moved to write on one
occasion, 'I console myself with the knowledge that the proprietor for whom you lied probably stole your pension.' George
Galloway MP gave evidence for Allason, telling the court he
had seen Campbell urging an MP to sign the motion. In a testimony which did little to advance his political prospects,
Galloway said he took 'a special interest in the perambulations of
Mr Campbell, because I have regarded him for years as the hired
character assassin for Robert Maxwell'. Now that Campbell held
an important position as chief press secretary to the leader of the
opposition, 'I have to keep these comments to myself', but before

he left the subject he added: 'My feelings are the same: that a man who could serve with such gusto the greatest thief of the twentieth century in this country is the kind of person to be kept a wary eye on.'

The judge, Sir Maurice Drake, while describing Galloway as 'an impressive witness', concluded that there was no evidence of malicious involvement by Campbell or the other *Mirror* journalist accused, Andy McSmith, but that MGN had published a false and malicious article. However, the behaviour of the *Mirror*'s deputy political editor David Bradshaw was criticised, and the judge said he did not find Campbell by any means a wholly satisfactory or convincing witness, although he did accept his evidence. Allason's claim failed because he had not been able to prove that he had lost the book contract as a result of the *Mirror*'s report.

The *Mirror* took their revenge by mounting surveillance on Allason and then publishing a grossly intrusive story: 'TORY MP CHEATS ON HIS WIFE WITH A BLONDE VIOLINIST'.

Undaunted, Allason appealed successfully, and the case was reheard in July 1998 before Mr Justice Popplewell. He ruled that the *Mirror*'s behaviour entitled Allason to rescind the earlier settlement agreement and had been calculated to cause financial damage to the MP. However, he too found Allason's claim about the book contract unpersuasive. He awarded him nominal damages of £1,050 and 75 per cent of his legal costs, figures he based on the £100 (with increases to allow for inflation) recovered by the impresario Claude Fielding thirty years earlier for malicious falsehood when the musical *Charlie Girl* was described as a 'disastrous flop' (which in fact caused no damage). The judge observed that it was no part of his function to express a view about current standards in public life, noting that both Campbell and Bradshaw (as a member of the strategic development unit) had ended up at 10 Downing Street. The *Mirror* then appealed and eventually the case was settled on confidential terms.

In his earlier dispute with the *Mirror* and its journalists, Allason had written to Joe Haines, Maxwell's biographer and leader-writer for the paper, demanding an apology. The answer he received was short and to the point.

> Dear Mr Allason,
>
> I regard you with the utmost contempt. Rather than apologise to you for your wickedness, I'll see you in hell first.

By 1995 Haines had moved his pithy talents to *Today*. There he accused Allason of behaving in a dishonourable and cowardly manner. Commenting on a ban preventing Allason from naming, in a House of Commons motion, past and present MPs who were alleged to have been KGB agents, Haines referred back to the Maxwell saga of October 1991. Allason sued. Haines obtained a stay of the proceedings under Article 9 of the Bill of Rights, 1689, under which courts were not empowered to question proceedings in Parliament. However, help was at hand for Allason in Section 13 of the Defamation Act 1996, which allows an MP to waive his or her privilege under the Bill of Rights to bring libel proceedings. The case continues.

In 1990 Allason sued John Pilger for allegations in his book *Distant Voices* that Allason had worked for MI5, manufactured stories at their request and had blackened the name of Farzad Bazoft, the journalist executed by the Iraqis in 1990. Allason subsequently received £25,000 damages.

In October of that year Allason sued a reviewer who attacked his book *Wartime Secrets – The Story of SOE, Britain's Wartime Sabotage Organisation* in *Contemporary Review*: 'appallingly researched, one error on every page . . . his approach to the subject matter is offensive and negative. Did he write the book as a friend or foe?' The reviewer could not establish fair comment for her review, as she had attributed to Allason passages which were in fact quotations from other people. Allason again recovered damages.

The following year it was the turn of the *Guardian*, which published an article entitled 'The Guts of a Louse, Which is

Altogether a Higher Form of Life'. This was a quote which had
already been the subject of litigation and an undertaking not to
repeat it. The story recycled the 1991 *Mirror* allegations. And in
1994 Allason sued the *Independent* for a diary piece wrongly
claiming that he had made overtures to the Liberal Democrats'
chief whip, Archie Kirkwood, about joining the party after his
Conservative whip was suspended as a result of his refusal to
support the Maastricht Treaty Bill. It was also falsely suggested
that Allason had accused the autoeroticist MP Stephen Milligan
of compromising national security. The *Independent* apologised
in a statement in open court and had to find more damages.

It was not only the print media which fell foul of Allason. In
1995 Westcountry TV had to apologise to him for repeating allegations made by the Torbay Liberal Democrats that he had been
reported to the director of public prosecutions for possible breach
of the electoral laws. The libel arose out of the thorny issue of the
recording of votes in old people's homes in Torbay, which formed
a significant part of the electorate in this highly marginal seat (so
marginal, in fact, that Allason was to lose it in 1997 by just
twelve votes). His opponents sought to make political capital out
of his jocular remarks: 'They all vote Conservative, and, more
importantly, vote Conservative whether they know it or not.'

Allason's crusade through the libel courts suffered a setback in
December 1996, when he sued the BBC over a book published as
a spin-off to the satirical quiz show *Have I Got News for You*. It
featured a photograph of him with the caption: 'The maverick
Tory MP when he is writing spy novels is called Nigel West and
when he is fighting against his own government is called something unprintable. Indeed, given Mr Allason's fondness for
pursuing libel actions, there are excellent legal reasons for not
referring to him as a conniving little shit.' Allason had in fact
appeared on the show, and the first sentence of the caption had
been used by quizmaster Angus Deayton to introduce him. The
BBC's lawyers had struck out the second from the script. The BBC
paid £50 into court and resisted Allason's complaint that this was
'a vicious libel and a revolting slur'.

The case came on in January 1998, not an ideal time to be a Conservative MP – and indeed, Allason no longer was, his Torbay constituency having demonstrated just how marginal it was, old people's homes notwithstanding. The jury concurred with Charles Gray QC's argument that MPs must accept public criticism, whether it is made in the columns of *The Times* or on satirical television programmes. The jury probably felt that the offending words were mere abuse which did not carry any actual defamatory meaning. Thus Allason notched up his first libel loss.

Allason also featured in the background of, though was not himself made a party to, one of the strangest libel actions of recent times. This was brought by Anthony Cavendish, a former MI6 officer, against the publishers of Allason's *Faber Book of Espionage*. The offending words were a reference to the officer as 'the Swiss who changed his name to Anthony Cavendish'. The complaint was not about the change of name, but the suggestion that he was Swiss. It was pursued with characteristic vigour by Peter Carter-Ruck, the third solicitor selected by Mr Cavendish, and was all the more curious given the evident affection in which the British-born Cavendish held Switzerland. He had, as he had described in his memoirs, *Inside Intelligence*, been taken to Switzerland by his mother after the death of his father. By the age of fourteen he spoke Swiss German fluently and passed for a Swiss among foreigners.

Allason's book was published in hardback in 1993 and in paperback in 1994. The hardback had jocularly referred to Cavendish as 'the Bulgarian'. He was, of course, nothing of the kind. Letters about this inaccuracy had been exchanged but no legal action taken. Indeed, Allason and Cavendish remained friends, lunching together and occasionally indulging in 'Bulgarian' jokes, and Allason had even been invited to contribute the foreword to the paperback edition of *Inside Intelligence*, due to be published in 1997. There he wrote of a remarkable book by a man of independent mind and means with a backbone of steel. It was odd that Cavendish continued this amicable relationship even after he had discovered that Allason had 'libelled' him.

Cavendish's complaint was that people who knew him and had read his book would wrongly believe that in claiming to be British he was concealing his true or original Swiss nationality. It was a tenuous interpretation, and it was most unlikely that any reader of the two books over the ten-year period in question would even retain the salient facts in order to draw such an alarming conclusion about Anthony Cavendish, who had, in the meantime, enjoyed a distinguished career as a British subject, not only in the service of the crown but also in business.

Before the application to strike out his claim for defamation and malicious falsehood, Cavendish decided to discontinue his action and to pay Allason's publisher's legal costs. The whole exercise is said to have cost him £35,000, a sum he could ill afford and which would undoubtably have been better spent on something other than this peculiar piece of litigation. Indeed, he later filed for bankruptcy.

Meanwhile, Peter Carter-Ruck himself fell out with his partners at the firm which bore his name – the third time he had been embroiled in a major partnership dispute. Undaunted, at the age of eighty-six he joined another law firm, and went into competition with his colleagues who, gallingly, continued to practise under the name Peter Carter-Ruck & Partners. In the process he became England's oldest practising solicitor.

# 16

# ALBERT REYNOLDS:
## A Libel Too Far

The Reynolds case is far more important than a simple example of the shortcomings of the English legal system. As we have seen, in 1993 in Derbyshire County Council v. Times Newspapers Ltd, *The Sunday Times* secured a ruling that a county council could not sue for libel for injury to its governing reputation. However, it was still open to politicians to exercise an unfettered right to sue newspapers, and the chilling effect of the threat of libel actions from politicians still pervaded the press.

The case brought by Albert Reynolds, the former Taoiseach (prime minister) of Ireland produced a judgement by the lord chief justice, Lord Bingham, which significantly changed the balance in favour of freedom of speech and will make the bringing of libel actions by politicians more perilous. Bizarrely, Reynolds effectively lost on the facts of the case but should have won, while the press, who should have won on the legal issues, in fact lost – but such are the idiosyncrasies of the law of libel.

Reynolds had taken exception to a *Sunday Times* report, 'Goodbye Gombeen Man. Why a Fib Too Far Proved Fatal for

Ireland's Peacemaker and Mr Fixit', which appeared in November
1994. The front-page piece pulled no punches.

> In another age Albert Reynolds could have been the classic
> *gombeen* man of Irish law – the real fixer with a finger in
> every pie. His slow fall last week, his fingernails scratching
> down the potential cliff-face, has been welcomed with a
> whoop of delight by many Irish people who want to see
> their country dragged out of the past. The full story of this
> eclipse, however, has sullied Ireland's reputation, damaged
> its Church, destroyed its peacemaking and provided its
> unionist neighbours with a fistful of new reasons to avoid
> the contamination by the South.

At any rate, that is what you would have read in England,
Scotland or Wales about the sequence of peculiarly Irish events
of the week of 11 November 1994 which resulted in the resignation of Reynolds and Harry Whelehan, the former Irish
attorney-general and briefly president of the High Court, and in
the break-up of the coalition between Fianna Fail and the
Labour Party which had been in power since February 1992.
The government had disintegrated over the issue of the extradition of Father Brendan Smyth to Northern Ireland to face
charges of sexual abuse over a twenty-four year period from
1964 to 1988. In October 1994 it had been revealed in the Irish
press that the attorney-general, Harry Whelehan, had taken a
leisurely seven months to ponder the extradition issue.
Whelehan claimed that the delay was due to the extremely
complex legal situation. This contention was somewhat undermined by the existence of an earlier case of extradition to
England of another sexually erring former cleric, John Duggan.
The general atmosphere of economy with the truth was compounded by Reynolds' wish to appoint Whelehan to the second
most senior position in the Irish judiciary in the face of the
protests of the Tanaiste (deputy prime minister), Dick Spring,
leader of the Labour Party, and by Reynolds' apparent failure to

disclose the fact that Whelehan was likely to have to resign after a few days in office.

As the issues were to emerge in Reynolds' libel action against *The Sunday Times*, the questions were as follows. Had he misled the Irish Parliament, the Dail, on Tuesday 15 November 1994, by suppressing vital information about the extradition issue which might have cast doubt on Whelehan's explanations? Had he deliberately and dishonestly misled his coalition Cabinet colleagues, especially Dick Spring, by withholding information from Monday 14 to Wednesday 16 November? And had he lied to them as to when the vital information about the Duggan case had first come into his possession?

Reynolds had learned of the Duggan case on Monday 14 November and had appreciated that it might be relevant to the Smyth situation. He had accordingly requested the new attorney-general, Eoghan Fitzsimons, to investigate and report back. He had unsuccessfully asked Whelehan to defer being sworn in as president of the High Court until the matter had been clarified. Reynolds said, however, that it was only when he received Fitzsimons' written advice, after the debate in the Dail, that he realised the true significance of the Duggan case.

With its references to the Taoiseach, Tanaiste, *offig an ard-aighne* (office of the attorney-general) and the *gombeen* man (a usurer or extortionate middleman or speculator who had profited from corn prices during the Irish potato famine), this case might have been thought to be one for the plaintiff-friendly Irish courts. *The Sunday Times* had, however, anticipated that particular obstacle. In recent years while minister of finance and minister for industry and commerce, Reynolds had netted £140,000 in libel damages in out-of-court settlements in Ireland. He had collected £60,000 on the steps of the court from *The Sunday Times*, a total of £50,000 from *The Irish Times* for two libel claims, £10,000 from the provocatively named *Guinness Book of Political Blunders* (over its chapter 'The Last Gombeen Man', itself a bad omen for *The Sunday Times*) and £20,000 from Radio Tara, based in County Meath. Such were his successes that wits had named the house he bought in Dublin 'Litigation Lodge'. *The Sunday Times* calculated, correctly, that the fact that Reynolds was by then prime minister would not prevent him from suing. While mainland readers were informed by Alan Ruddock, the paper's Irish editor, that Reynolds' fall was due to his 'fibs', Irish readers were told by Irish journalist Vincent Browne, in a markedly less defamatory piece called 'House of Cards', that it had been caused by confusion, error and shambles. At the trial, John Witherow, editor of *The Sunday Times*, unconvincingly claimed that the Ruddock article was inappropriate for their Irish readership because of their greater background knowledge.

In any event, the Ruddock article was read by Reynolds' daughter in Scotland. After the Dail Select Committee into the Whelehan appointment had reported in March 1995 with its full account of what Reynolds did or did not know at the time, Reynolds issued a writ for libel in England. The case lasted twenty-four costly days in October and November 1996 before Mr Justice French. Unhappily, he was not up to the rigours of a five-week trial. He was recovering from a recent triple heart bypass operation and was to take early retirement, albeit at the youthful age – for a judge – of seventy-one, in April 1997 on the grounds of ill health.

*The Sunday Times*' defences were justification – that what they had written was true – and qualified privilege – that the paper was covering events in the Irish Dail, and that they had a duty to report the political upheavals in a government which was helping to broker a settlement of the conflict in Northern Ireland.

The central issue was whether or not Reynolds had acted dishonestly. He had, it seemed, handled the affair in an inept and insensitive manner, and the English jury was unimpressed by his conduct. If the jury found in favour of Reynolds, his counsel, Lord Williams of Mostyn QC, argued, damages should be in the range of an 'absolute base minimum' of £45,000 up to £125,000 for this 'shoddy and shabby journalism'. For *The Sunday Times*, James Price QC suggested that if the paper lost, damages should be no more than £3,000 – about the sum Reynolds would have received if he had been mugged and had his jaw broken.

As it was, the jury, after three days' deliberation in which they sought guidance as to the distinction between a lie and a fib, concluded by a majority of 10–1 (having lost one of their number through illness) that the article was *not* true in substance and that Reynolds had *not* been dishonest, but that neither Ruddock nor Witherow had been malicious: the paper had correctly reported the reasons for Dick Spring's withdrawal from the coalition government. They therefore disconcertingly announced that they had awarded zero costs. It was explained that they meant pounds zero, pence zero. To reflect their finding on the issue of truth, the judge increased this to one penny. Reynolds had been vindicated by being acquitted of dishonesty and the article had been found to be defamatory. He was, however, saddled with paying all his own costs, plus the costs of the newspaper at trial. It was calculated that he faced legal costs of £800,000.

How had this bizarre result come about? It was almost entirely due to a wholly inept summing-up by Mr Justice French. Lord Justice Hirst has defined the job of a judge, in a nutshell, as making sure the jury sees the wood for the trees, and marking the right trees. In summing up, the judge's role is, so far as he or she can, to ensure that the jury understand and apply the law relevant to their decision, identifying the facts not in dispute and summarising significant factual issues and the admissible evidence relevant to each issue. Mr Justice French took over two days to sum up the case, filling 170 pages of transcript with a further sixty pages of legal applications, often to correct errors he had made. As Lord Bingham pointed out in the Court of Appeal, the events of that week of November 1994 had been fast-moving and called for a clear chronology from the judge.

On any view the judge had failed miserably. He had started by marking the wrong trees. Reynolds complained that the summing-up was unbalanced and grossly unfair. This was put more politely in the appeal, where it was described as 'confusing and unstructured'. Mr Justice French had just read out the evidence, giving no summary, and the jury had been left to make sense of large tracts of undigested material. The judge had not fairly reflected Albert Reynolds' evidence, and on one passage he unwittingly misrepresented it, the Court of Appeal observed.

Reluctantly, in view of the expense involved, the Court of Appeal had to set aside the verdict and order a retrial. In England there is no provision for compensating the parties for wasted costs as a result of judicial shortcomings as there is under the New South Wales Suitors Fund Act 1951, for example: the legal costs of the first trial are added to the pot at stake in the second.

The important question which arose in the Reynolds case was whether the media could establish a defence of qualified privilege on the basis that they had a duty to promote an ample flow of information to the public and the vigorous discussion of matters of public interest among those who had a corresponding interest in receiving it. The events surrounding the fall of the Irish government during the search for peace in Northern Ireland was clearly of great public interest. If such a defence could be established, the plaintiff would not succeed even if the defendants could not prove the truth of what they had written, unless he could establish malice on the part of the defendants.

The starting point was that certain communications should be protected in the general interests of society. People should, for example, be able to give references about former employees without the risk of being sued for libel, unless they act maliciously, as discussed in Chapter 1. The courts have developed the concept that there must be a legal, moral or social duty to make the communication and a corresponding interest in the person receiving it (Pulman v. Hill & Co., 1891). This could protect a newspaper which published in good faith inaccurate and defamatory information about, say, suspected contaminated food or a terrorist alert. The old legal cases establish that communications may be protected for the common convenience and welfare of society, if fairly warranted by any reasonable occasion or exigency (Stuart v. Bell, 1891). Qualified privilege can arise in a wide range of cases, ranging from reports made by credit agencies, through replies to a public attack, to fair and accurate reports of the findings of disciplinary bodies where there is a public interest in their decisions.

The question here was how far this could be extended to the reporting of political controversies if the facts published turned out to be incorrect. The competing legal argument had been set out by Chief Justice Cockburn in Campbell v. Spottiswood, 1863: 'The public have an equal interest in the maintenance of the public character of public men; public affairs could not be conducted by men of honour with a view to the welfare of the country if we were to sanction attacks upon them, destructive of their honour and character, and made without foundation.' The same idea was put in more twentieth-century terms in 1958 by Mr Justice Diplock in Silkin v. Beaverbrook: 'Every man, whether he is in public life or not, is entitled not to have lies told about him . . . A newspaper reporter or a newspaper editor has exactly the same rights, neither more nor less, than any other citizen and the test is no different whether that comment appears in a Sunday newspaper with an enormous circulation, or in a letter from a private person to a friend, or is said to an acquaintance in a train or a public house.'

Early attempts to tilt the balance in favour of free speech enjoyed only brief success. When Bessie Braddock MP sued her Conservative opponent for libel in his election address, the Court of Appeal in 1948 considered it 'scarcely open to doubt that statements contained in the election address of one candidate concerning the opposing candidate, provided they are relevant to the matters which the electors will have to consider in deciding which way to cast their votes, are entitled to the protection of qualified privilege' (Braddock v. Bevins). This was promptly overruled by Section 10 of the 1952 Defamation Act. In 1960, *The Times* published a report of the murder trial in Switzerland of Donald Hume, who had earlier served a term of imprisonment for dumping the dismembered corpse of Stanley Setty over the Essex marshes from a plane. The paper established a defence of qualified privilege against Hume's former wife, who sued them for reporting Hume's false claim at the trial that he was not the father of one of their children. The subject matter of the trial was closely connected with the administration of justice in England and was of legitimate interest to the English newspaper readership (Webb v. Times Publishing Co. Ltd).

Unfortunately, the courts showed little enthusiasm for extending the defence of qualified privilege into areas where there was a legitimate public interest. In 1982 the Court of Appeal had to consider the question in relation to a newspaper which had published reports of the proceedings of the Public Accounts Committee of the House of Commons concerning grants payable under a Department of Energy Committee. This report – 'Incompetence at Ministry Cost £52 Million' – damaged the reputation of the plaintiff. Faced with the choice between the ability to publish fearlessly what is necessary for the protection of the public and the need to protect the individual from falsehoods, the court chose to protect the individual (Blackshaw v. Lord) and the award of £45,000 to the plaintiff was upheld. The court recoiled from 'a startling licence to defame and on a grand scale'.

In the Reynolds case, the Court of Appeal was invited by Lord Lester of Herne Hill QC to look afresh at the issue in the light of Article 10 of the European Convention of Human Rights and the preliminary decisions in the cases brought by David Lange, the former prime minister of New Zealand, whose performance in office had been attacked in virulent terms. The preliminary points, which related to whether there could be a qualified privilege defence on matters of political discussion, are still to be resolved in New Zealand, where they went from the New Zealand Court of Appeal to the British Privy Council. In Australia, in a process notable for the employment it provided for no fewer than twenty-seven barristers, the High Court of Australia held that there could be a defence of qualified privilege where the material published related to government or political matters and the publication of the material was reasonable in the circumstances. Two earlier decisions, Theophanous v. The Herald and Weekly Times Limited and Stephens v. Western Australia Newspapers Limited in 1994, had reached similar conclusions by a different path on the basis that the Australian Constitution contained an implied principle of freedom of communication on political issues. Both were MPs, but they were suing on essentially political matters; in one instance allegations of bias against Greek immigrants, and in the other of participating in a junket of mammoth proportions.

The Lange cases themselves remain to be tried in both Australia and New Zealand. The unfortunate Mr Lange, who has had to endure such humiliations as a cartoon showing him in a hospital bed while assembled doctors comment that his is the worst case of false-memory syndrome they have ever come across, has nevertheless had to put his complaint before a jury, and in a context in which it is extremely difficult for politicians to recover damages.

In the Reynolds case, the Court of Appeal did not wish to adopt the American public figure defence in Sullivan v. *New York Times*, which requires any plaintiff who is a public figure to prove that the defendant either knew that what was published was false or was reckless as to the issue of truth or falsity. Indeed, it had been consistently rejected by English judges when raised by newspapers in relation to MPs, foreign politicians and police officers. The appeal court agreed with the 1975 Faulks and the 1991 Neill Committees, which concluded that the 1964 Sullivan rule would destroy the proper balance between protection of reputation and freedom of speech, and would mean that newspapers could publish more or less what they liked. This, it was felt, would create injustice, and it would be contrary to common law to effectively divide citizens into separate classes when it came to deciding what could be published about them. The court saw the Sullivan decision as a product of the First Amendment of the US Constitution.

The Court of Appeal deliberating on Reynolds preferred to adopt the approach of the European Court of Human Rights in 1986 in Lingens v. Austria, arising out of an earlier case in which the Austrian chancellor brought a private prosecution for criminal defamation against the publishers of a magazine which accused him of protecting former members of the Nazi SS for political reasons. In order to safeguard the reputation of individuals, the press must not be allowed to overstep the bounds, but it is nevertheless incumbent upon it to impart information and ideas on political issues of public interest. Moreover, not only does the press have a responsibility to disseminate such information and ideas, but the public has a right to receive them.

The Court of Appeal came close to following the decision of the Australian High Court in Lange, which upheld the interest of every member of the Australian community in disseminating and receiving information, opinions and arguments concerning government and political matters which affected the people. The publisher had, however, to prove the reasonableness of his conduct and to be able to show that he believed what he had published was true, that he had taken proper steps to verify it, and that he had given the plaintiff an opportunity to comment.

In a ringing endorsement of freedom of speech, the Court of Appeal noted that the land of Milton, Paine and Mill should recognise the ample flow of information to the public and vigorous public discussion of matters of public interest as a modern democratic imperative. The media will therefore be able to raise a defence of qualified privilege if they can establish that a report was part of their duty to inform the public and engage in public discussion of matters of public interest and that the public had a corresponding interest in receiving the information. Additionally, there is a circumstantial test which is effectively a requirement of reasonable conduct: what were the nature, status and source of the material and the circumstances of publication? A distinction may have to be drawn between, for example, publishing the contents of an official press release from a public company chairman and material from a hand-out produced by a politically motivated opponent of the plaintiff. Likewise, it will be relevant to see what steps have been taken to check the facts and to seek the comments of the plaintiff.

*The Sunday Times* had won an important point of principle. However, like Reynolds, they found themselves losing a point they appeared to have won. On the facts, the Court of Appeal concluded that *The Sunday Times* had *not* acted reasonably: they had relied on an unidentified political source; they had not reported Reynolds' justification of his conduct in the Dail; they had not come off the fence as to whether Reynolds was a victim of circumstance (their Irish version) or a devious liar (their English version); nor had they put the allegations in the article of Reynolds for comment.

The decision was upheld by the House of Lords on somewhat different grounds on 28 October 1999. They recognised the Court of Appeal's ruling, in the words of Lord Hope, as forward-looking and imaginative. What they disagreed with was over its creation of the circumstantial test as a third limb of the qualified privilege test. In the view of the Lords, there were only two requirements, namely a duty to communicate information and a corresponding interest in receiving it. In practice, however, the factors deemed relevant to circumstantial test would still be important in deciding whether the duty and interest situation gave rise to qualified privilege. The court would look at the seriousness of the allegation, the extent to which the subject matter was of public concern and the source of the information, considering such factors as whether the informant had direct knowledge of the facts, some axe to grind or was being paid for the story; the steps taken to verify the information; the status of the information (whether, for example, it was already the subject of an investigation); the urgency of the matter, bearing in mind that news is often a perishable commodity; whether comment was sought from the defendant, a factor not in itself conclusive; whether the article contained the gist of the plaintiff's side of the story; the tone of the article – was it simply raising questions, or was it making statements of fact? – and all the circumstances of the publication, including its timing.

The House of Lords rejected the idea of privilege deriving simply from the fact that information was political in nature.

They were not prepared to leave the ultimate decision on this to the editor: his or her decision would be reviewed by the courts taking into account all the relevant factors. They felt that it was appropriate to balance the corresponding right of reputation. If there was no additional safeguard for reputation, a newspaper anxious to be first with a scoop would in practice be free to publish serious, defamatory misstatements of fact on the slenderest of bases. They also had in mind the difficulty of establishing malice, which could effectively deprive plaintiffs of a remedy if the threshold of qualified privilege was set too high. There is no procedure in the UK, as there is in the United States, which allows for a pre-trial enquiry into the sources of a story and the editorial decision-making which would produce evidence of malice if it existed.

What was striking about the House of Lords decision was their ringing endorsement of freedom of expression, which, as Lord Nicholls noted, would be a hollow concept without freedom of expression for the media. In this regard it should be kept in mind that one of the contemporary functions of the media is investigative journalism. In general, a newspaper's unwillingness to disclose the identity of its sources should not weigh against it. Further, it should always be remembered that journalists act without the benefit of clarifying hindsight. The press discharges vital functions as a bloodhound as well as a watchdog. Courts, the Lords felt, should not be in a hurry to conclude that publication was not in the public interest and that the public therefore had no right to know – especially when the information in question was in the nature of political discussion – and any lingering doubts should be resolved in favour of publication. Lord Steyn referred to the new landscape mapped out by the Human Rights Act 1998, incorporating Article 10 of the European Convention of Human Rights, and the decisions of the European Court on the convention. Exceptions to freedom of speech have to be justified as being necessary in a democracy, and the exception must be underpinned by a pressing social need.

Two of the law lords would have allowed *The Sunday Times* to argue its defence of qualified privilege, bearing in mind what was in effect a change in the law during the course of the case. The rest upheld the Court of Appeal's ruling that, on the facts, the defence of qualified privilege was not justified. A retrial on the other issues was due to take place, but in September 2000 the case was settled on undisclosed terms bearing all the hallmarks of a draw: *The Sunday Times* accepted Reynolds' assurance that he had not lied, while he accepted that the newspaper had not acted maliciously.

The first application of the Reynolds decision came in an action brought, rather surprisingly, by one of Libyan leader Colonel Gaddaffi's sons, Saif Al Islam, against two reports published in the *Sunday Telegraph* in November and December 1995. The appeal, which was heard in October 1998, related simply to the question of how the defence could be formulated. The facts underlying Gaddaffi's complaint remain to be determined. The first article linked the young Gaddaffi, an architectural graduate of Al Fateh University in Tripoli, with a plan to flood Iran with fake currency, which was said to make the Great Train Robbery look like a teddy bear's picnic. The second was a complaint by the author of the first piece, Con Coughlin, that an invitation to fly out to Tripoli to discuss his article might lead to his being strung up from the nearest Libyan lamp-post. The pieces were highly defamatory; the court, however, recognised people's interest in receiving information on matters of public interest to the community and the need for an ample flow of information and vigorous discussion of such matters. The question was whether the *Sunday Telegraph* could meet the circumstantial test by simply asserting that their sources were unidentified security officials. The case was interesting for the details given of the care with which the article had been put together. However, no clue was given as to the identity of the informants – in reality members of MI6 – or how they had come by their information. Eventually, the *Sunday Telegraph* admitted that its sources were within a Western government security agency and made it clear that they had not been paid for their information. The court accepted that this was capable of being sufficient compliance with the circumstantial test – a welcome outcome for newspapers who had feared that such a plea of qualified privilege would be of little practical value if they had to disclose their sources, and a robust application of the principles laid down in the Reynolds case.

As Lord Nicholls had predicted, the ruling in Reynolds had the advantage of elasticity but the disadvantage of unpredictability and uncertainty. Two of the cases heard to date, GKR Karate (UK) Limited v. Yorkshire Post Newspapers Limited and Al Fagih v. HH Saudi Research and Marketing, could very easily have been decided differently, and indeed it has since been argued that both verdicts were wrong.

In the first of these cases, a free newspaper, the *Leeds Weekly News*, set about a local karate club: 'Give 'em the chop – doorstep salesman flogged dodgy karate lessons'. There was no evidence of illegal conduct by GKR Karate, nor had they attracted the attention of the local trading standards officer. Mr Justice Popplewell, however, felt it was important that the warning to the community was published as a matter of some urgency. He accepted that the paper had based its article on what the journalist who had conducted most of the inquiries on the telephone had honestly believed was reliable evidence. She had contacted karate's governing body, but there had been significant shortcomings in her attempts to take up the complaints with the claimants – she had attempted to ring them only once – or to canvas the matter with the trading standards officer.

There were also criticisms of the accuracy of some of the quotes in the article. The judge ruled that the story was covered by qualified privilege even though it had the potential to be very damaging to the claimants and the newspaper might have considered conducting a more thoroughgoing investigation before printing it. As the judge's ruling, upheld by the Court of Appeal, was that the issue of the application of qualified privilege, together with any evidence of malice, should be heard before the evidence of justification, the trial was concluded in three days as opposed to the four to six weeks predicted.

In Al Fagih, however, Mrs Justice Smith ruled that an article about a dissident group of which the claimant was a former member, although evidently a matter of great public interest in the Arab community, was not covered by qualified privilege because the journalist in question had failed to take sufficient steps to verify the information.

In James Gilbert Limited v. MGN, the first case in which the summary procedure available under Section 8 of the 1996 Defamation Act was used, Mr Justice Eady held that the defence of qualified privilege had no reasonable prospect of success. He ordered summary trial of the case and MGN agreed to settle for £10,000 damages. A series of articles in the *Mirror* had claimed that James Gilbert Limited, a rugby ball manufacturer, had subcontracted work to an Indian company that employed child labour and had broken an earlier promise to send representatives to India to investigate the allegation. In fact an investigation had been launched and an inquiry team had been dispatched. The judge considered that the paper's attempts to verify their information had been wholly inadequate, particularly since channels of communication had already been set up between the parties. No reasonable opportunity for comment had been afforded to the claimants, and in his view there was no urgency that justified publishing the story before it had been checked.

Nevertheless, with the Reynolds ruling has come a greater willingness on the part of the courts to uphold claims for privilege. In Regan v. Taylor, Simon Regan's attempt to sue an opposing solicitor for remarks he had made to the media about a libel case (see Chapter 18) failed because the court ruled that the comments were covered by qualified privilege. In November 2000, in Turkington v. Times Newspapers Limited, the House of Lords decided that a press conference could be a public meeting for the purpose of qualified privilege. Lord Bingham observed that press freedom was of cardinal importance, and that the restriction of that freedom had to be proportionate and no more than was necessary to promote the legitimate aim of the restriction. A modern, developed society required free, active, professional and inquiring media if the majority were to participate in public life.

In this case five partners in a Belfast law firm lost the £145,000 damages they had been awarded by a Northern Irish jury as a result of the reporting of criticisms of the defence team at a meeting on the Free Clegg Campaign. Lee Clegg was a paratrooper then in jail for shooting a civilian. The decision took the lustre off the £600,000 damages the claimants had previously received in other actions. The case was remitted to the Irish High Court for the accuracy of the newspaper report to be verified.

In Taylor v. the Serious Fraud Office, it was held that absolute privilege extended to statements made to the police to assist them with their inquiries and with criminal investigations, and to the passing of statements between investigators in the course of their work. In June 2000, in Mahon and Kent v. Rhan and Bodner, the Court of Appeal ruled that it also attached to communication between the Securities Association and its informants in connection with its investigations and regulatory hearings concerning the activities of financial organisations.

So the Reynolds case will make it very difficult for politicians and those in public life to bring libel actions where there is a legitimate public interest in the discussion of that particular topic, and where the media can show that they have acted reasonably. No longer can the politician rely on the fact that a media defendant would have to prove that what has been said is true. Now there will be a defence for the media even if the material published turns out to be untrue, provided that it was of legitimate public interest and responsibly researched.

# 17

# A PYRRHIC VICTORY IN SOUTHERN AUSTRIA

Lord Aldington's case against Nigel Watts and Count Tolstoy resulted in the largest-ever award of libel damages by a jury. Goaded into suing by shameful allegations that he was a war criminal, Aldington found himself, as one of the senior British officers who had been involved in the repatriation of Cossacks and Yugoslavs, enmeshed in an action whose defendants were supported by the Forced Repatriation Defence Fund. Although the jury vindicated his reputation and decisively rejected the accusations against him, evidently accepting that he had done no more than obey the orders of Field-Marshal Alexander and General Robertson in giving effect to the Yalta Agreement and to 'clear the decks' for operational reasons, the law of libel proved incapable of providing Aldington with an effective remedy.

At the end of the Second World War in May 1945, Toby Low was, at thirty-one, the second-youngest brigadier in the British army and had been awarded the DSO for gallantry in Greece. He was brigadier general staff attached to Lt-Gen. Charles Keightley, commander of the British 5th Corps, in charge of Carinthia in southern Austria, the largest area then unoccupied by Allied troops. The Russians had overshot the agreed demarcation line in Austria by 100 miles; they had already passed Vienna and were showing signs of taking over the whole of Austria. Tito of Yugoslavia was eyeing up Carinthia, as well as the Italian province of Venezia Giulia, which he claimed as Greater Yugoslavia. The strength of the 8th Army, of which the 5th Corps constituted three divisions, was only 25,000, yet hundreds of thousands of Germans and their Cossack and Yugoslavian allies were surrendering to them.

At the Yalta Conference in 1945 it had been agreed that all Soviet citizens liberated or captured by forces under Allied command were to be handed over to the Soviet authorities. The foreign secretary, Anthony Eden, had warned against succumbing to sentimentality which might anger Stalin and provoke Tito: there were real anxieties about the security of the British soldiers still in Soviet zones who were due to be handed over to the British under the Yalta Agreement. But were the 45,000 Cossacks under 5th Corps control Soviet citizens, and were they, and the 25,000 Yugoslavs who had surrendered, to be handed over? It was decided that they were. The consequence was a series of massacres at the pit of Kocevje, in the tank traps at Teharje and in the slave-labour camps of Siberia.

By 1987 Toby Low, a Conservative MP from 1945 to 1962 and a former deputy chairman of the Conservative Party, had been ennobled as Baron Aldington. He had been chairman of the insurance company Sun Alliance from 1971 to 1985 and warden of Winchester College from 1979 to 1987. Now, over forty years after the war, he found himself, to his horror, accused of being a major war criminal. The allegations appeared in a pamphlet which had been sent out to MPs, peers and members of the royal family, ranging from Prince Charles to Princess Michael of Kent; to his neighbours in Kent and to staff and the parents of pupils at Winchester College. Despite the scurrilous tone of the pamphlet, the confrontational behaviour of its authors left Aldington with little choice but to sue.

Unfortunately, the strategy of those authors had been to

provoke him to do just that. The upshot was a forty-one-day libel case and ensuing litigation lasting eight years and involving fifteen applications to court after the trial. He was awarded £1.5 million libel damages, but ten years later he had recovered only £10,000 from one of the defendants and incurred legal fees of nearly £1 million. In 1992 he observed: 'If you had told me in 1989 that this thing would still be dragging on I would not have believed you.' In fact it had many more unproductive but costly years to run. Aldington's reputation had been vindicated, but at the price of a continuing nightmare for a man in his late seventies.

In a sense the winner had lost and the loser remained unbowed. The man who was responsible for the publication of the pamphlet, Count Nikolai Tolstoy-Miloslavsky, had paid for nothing. He had, it is true, been adjudged bankrupt, with debts of £2,029,999, but sympathisers had set up a trust fund for him in his wife's name and he continued to live in the seventeenth-century farmhouse in Oxfordshire jointly owned with his wife, Georgina. Tolstoy had reduced the net value of his share by taking out a loan against it. His children completed their private education, at Eton and Downe House respectively, and went on to university. Tolstoy nonetheless complained to the European Court of Human Rights about a libel law which permitted an award of £1.5 million damages. The European judges agreed that this violated his right to freedom of speech under Article 10 of the European Convention and awarded him £70,000 costs and 40,000 Swiss francs against the British Government in June 1995.

None of this money found its way to Aldington. The European Court upheld his entitlement to an injunction against Tolstoy preventing him from repeating his allegations, and to an order requiring Tolstoy to lodge £124,000 security for costs before he could appeal the jury's verdict. Regrettably, perhaps, the European Court did not rule on the issue of the exorbitant libel costs which so often deprive a litigant of his rights.

The pamphlet, of which 10,000 copies had been printed, was

entitled 'War Crimes and the Warden of Winchester College'. It accused Aldington of having on his hands the blood of 70,000 innocent Cossack and Yugoslav men, women and children who had been handed over to Stalin and Tito in May 1945. His activities, it claimed, merited comparison with those of the worst of the Nazi butchers, which, it correctly pointed out, was as blatant a charge as could be conceived of. It was further suggested that he knew that his actions were disapproved of and unauthorised by higher command. It was a disgraceful libel. Aldington's case, which the jury accepted, was that he had acted throughout on orders – which he was satisfied in any event were lawful – his superiors received from the 8th Army and that he had kept his superiors informed of his actions.

Although Tolstoy had not acted alone, he was the moving spirit behind the pamphlet. A descendant of the great Russian novelist, he had progressed from right-wing politics through schoolmastering to becoming an historian, and had written extensively on the subject of the repatriation of the Cossacks and Yugoslavs. *Victims of Yalta* (1978) described how Cossacks and their families had been forced into trains at bayonet point by British troops. 'The Klagenfurt Conspiracy', an article written for *Encounter* magazine in 1979, revealed the fate of 20,000 anti-communist Yugoslavs who had been handed over to Tito and executed, and *The Minister and the Massacres* (1986) accused Harold Macmillan, political adviser for the Mediterranean area, of responsibility for these massacres.

In April 1985 an advertisement had caught Tolstoy's eye. 'Brigadier Toby Low 5 Corps 1945 Klagenfurt 12 May–3 June,' it read. 'Repatriation non-Soviet Cossacks. Researcher urgently requires information.' It had been placed by a Nigel Watts, a man of many occupations – property developer, piano-restorer, antique-dealer and accomplished pheasant-poacher – and soon to become a litigant. His brother-in-law, Christopher Bowden, had died after a fall, allegedly while drunk in his bath. Bowden's life had been insured with Sun Alliance, the company of which Lord Aldington was chairman, but they refused to pay out on the policy because Bowden had not disclosed on his renewal form that he was having treatment for alcoholism. Watts claimed that Bowden had been sober but had been suffering from a condition called Wilson's disease, the symptoms of which resemble those of alcoholism. The extreme measures to which Watts had then resorted – which included telephoning Aldington at home twenty-eight times over one weekend in March 1984 – undermined his credibility in the subsequent litigation. Tolstoy had responded to Watts' advertisement and as a result of this contact had come to rewrite Watts' draft of the offending pamphlet. Initially, Aldington had not even been aware of Tolstoy's involvement. It was not until the peer sued Watts that Tolstoy asked for his own name to be added to the writ and his role came to light.

Formidable problems beset the British forces in Carinthia in May 1945. It had to be decided whether the Nedics, the Slovene militia, Chetniks, White Guards, Russkii Korpus, Domobranci, Ustache, Serbian Volunteer Corps, Georgians, Azerbaijanis and others who had fought in German uniforms had to be handed over to the Titoists or the Soviets. Nigel Nicolson, then a captain in the Grenadier Guards, had divided them into 'Yugs', who were 'our' Yugoslavs, and 'Tits', the partisan Titoists and enemies of the Yugs. A request by General Keightley on 10 May for permission to use force against Titoist partisans infiltrating Carinthia if they disobeyed orders from British commanders had been refused by Field-Marshal Alexander.

Under the working definition of a Soviet citizen – any person who came from a place within the boundaries of the Soviet Union as constituted before the outbreak of war – most members of the 15th Cossack Cavalry Corps which had fought as a regular unit of the German army under General Helmulth von Pannwitz were *not* Soviet citizens. It was decided nevertheless to hand them back to the Soviets, and Von Pannwitz and other White Russian generals were hanged in Moscow in January 1947. No real attempt was made to distinguish Soviet from non-Soviet citizens.

On 14 May General Robertson, Alexander's chief officer, issued an order that all surrendered Yugoslav personnel of established Yugoslav nationality who had been serving in German forces should be disarmed and handed over to local Yugoslav forces. On 17 May the future Lord Aldington signed what came to be castigated over forty years later as the 'deception order', but which was to him simply a matter of military good sense. 'All Yugoslav nationals at present in the Corps area will be handed over to Tito forces as soon as possible. These forces will be disarmed immediately and will not be told of their destination.' The upshot of Aldington's order was that the Yugoslavs being loaded on to trains which took them to Yugoslavia – and in many cases to summary execution – were told they were bound for Italy.

Nigel Nicolson wrote in his daily situation report: 'The Croats have been given no warning of their fate and are being allowed to believe that their destination is not Yugoslavia but Italy until the actual moment of handover. The whole business is most unsavoury and British troops have the utmost distaste in carrying out their orders.' He was reprimanded for this frankness and was made to record the next day: 'The Croats were kindly and efficiently handled [by the Titoists] and provided with light refreshment before continuing their journey into Yugoslavia. A representative of Tito had told them that only the criminals among them would be punished and the remainder would be sent to work on farms. We have every reason to believe this policy, which accords with the previous practice of Tito's men, will be faithfully carried out.' Nicolson felt this was one of the most disgraceful operations British troops had ever been ordered to undertake. Colonel Robin Rose Price, commander of the 3rd Welsh Guards, viewed the 'deception order' as an order of the most sinister duplicity. Anthony Crosland, captain of the intelligence staff of the 6th Armoured Division and later Labour foreign secretary, described the repatriations as 'the most nauseating and cold-blooded act of war I had ever taken part in'.

Within hours of the so-called 'deception order' on 17 May, Field-Marshal Alexander had issued the 'Distone order': all Chetniks and dissident Yugoslavs were to be evacuated to the British concentration area in Distone (District 1), behind the lines in Italy. Alexander was concerned that returning them to their country of origin immediately 'might be fatal to their health'. There were similar anxieties about the Cossacks. Prime Minister Winston Churchill wrote to General Ismay on 20 May seeking a report on the 45,000 Cossacks, how they had come to be in their present plight, whether they had fought against Britain and reviewing the possibility of moving them into the SHAEF 12th Army Group for their safety. Alexander then appealed to General Eisenhower of the US army to take the 45,000 Cossacks into the SHAEF area.

Under the Yalta Agreement it had been intended only to return Soviet citizens. The Foreign Office had sent a telegram to Harold Macmillan on 19 February 1945 defining Yalta as meaning that 'all persons who are Soviet citizens under British law must be repatriated but any person who is not (repeat not) a Soviet citizen under British law must not (repeat not) be sent back to the Soviet Union'. On 21 May Aldington issued a definition order to clarify who was to be treated as a Soviet national. Any individual, even if of Russian blood, was not to be treated as a Soviet national if, prior to joining the Russian forces, he had not been in the USSR since 1930. Residence as well as place of birth could be considered. Individual cases would not be considered unless particularly pressed, and in all cases of doubt the individual would be treated as a Soviet national. Many officers, including General Krasnov, chose not to claim exemption and remained with their troops.

When the libel case came up for trial forty-four years later, in October 1989, the fact that Lord Aldington had been required to take part in a very inglorious episode in the aftermath of war was not in question. However, in attempting to justify what they had written in their pamphlet, the defendants, Nikolai Tolstoy and Nigel Watts, wanted to widen the case into an examination of

whether or not a war crime had been committed. Their counsel
had advised that their case was strong on paper; it would be
stronger still if they were able to place before the jury a significant number of witnesses to and victims of British actions in
southern Austria in May and June 1945. Yet even one of their
own witnesses, Nigel Nicolson, felt they had been intemperate in
their allegations. Had he been asked the question – probably
inadmissible, as it was the very issue the jury had to decide – he
would have said that what had happened was a war crime, but
that Aldington himself was no war criminal.

The plaintiff, on the other hand, was equally determined that
the case should be confined to the pamphlet's intemperate language. So, for that matter, was the judge. Mr Justice Michael
Davies said at the opening of the trial, 'This is a trial for an
action for libel, and not an historical commission or some sort of
inquisitorial process. This is not an inquiry into what happened
in May 1945 to the Yugoslavs or the Cossacks.'

The defence were outmanoeuvred by the admission for the
purpose of the trial that Cossacks and various Yugoslav groups
*had* been grossly ill-treated, as Tolstoy alleged. This allowed the
focus to be placed on the issue of whether or not Aldington bore
any responsibility for these atrocities.

Although attempts were made to clothe what had been essentially a political decision in the aftermath of Yalta with legality,
the reality of the situation was well expressed by Aldington,
who made the point that the British forces were not best pleased
with people who had joined the Germans and thereby prolonged
their country's agony. 'One had to harden one's heart. We had
been fighting against the Germans for six years, and we weren't
awfully sorry for people who had been fighting for the Germans.'
However, he hoped this had not influenced his attitude to the
extent that he did not mind what happened to them. He remained
'a human being, a good Christian'.

The case concerned, Aldington's counsel, Charles Gray QC
suggested, 'a vile attack on Aldington's honour and integrity'. As
Aldington put it: 'I thought it was monstrous that my family

should have to carry the stigma of having at their head a war criminal worse than the Nazi butchers.'

The defence asserted that in the two days preceding Aldington's 'deception order', 15 and 16 May 1945, there had already been massacres of Croats by partisans. Certainly there were mass killings of the surrendered troops at the end of the month, but Aldington firmly denied any knowledge of any such atrocities before the handover. As for the question of the Yugoslavs being told they were being sent to Italy, the attempts of the defence to suggest that this was a breach of Articles 20 and 26 of the Geneva Convention – which required that prisoners of war should, when being transferred, be told in a language they understood of their new destination – were rejected by the judge. Aldington's case was that he had not ordered lies to be told, simply that the truth be withheld – an early and dramatic example of economy with the truth.

Defence claims that Aldington's 'deception order', in requiring 'all Yugoslavs in the Corps area' to be returned to Tito, went further than General Robertson's edict, which specified 'surrendered Yugoslav personnel of established Yugoslav nationality', were denied by Aldington, who pointed out that Robertson's order referred to forces being disarmed.

Aldington was asked by Tolstoy's counsel, Richard Rampton QC, about Field-Marshal Alexander's Distone order and his comment that the repatriation of both Yugoslavs and Cossacks was likely to be 'fatal to their health'. 'That meant death, did it not?' suggested Rampton. Aldington disagreed. It meant no more than that some might be tried and executed. 'It was not for us,' he argued, 'to overrule the orders of the army commander and the theatre supreme commander.' The Distone order was in any case never intended to apply to 5th Corps, was never received by it, and he had not seen it at the time. It applied, he asserted, only to Chetniks infiltrating the area occupied by British troops around the River Isonzo in Italy. Judging by the size of the award, the jury accepted his evidence.

Aldington produced a distinguished collection of witnesses,

who some felt were treated in a more sympathetic manner than
the defence witnesses. They explained the undoubted appalling
difficulties that faced the British forces in May 1945 and their
ignorance of the massacres. Tito and Stalin were then allies, and,
they said, there had been no reason not to accept their assurances about the fate of the surrendered troops. Tito had on 13
May ordered that the most energetic measures were to be taken
to prevent the killing of prisoners of war and those arrested. It
was an order soon to be altered. In marked contrast to the
defence witnesses, Brigadier Tryon-Wilson was able to describe
how he won the DSO during the battle of Cassino; General Sir
James Wilson recounted how, as a young company commander,
he had had to clear Titoist partisans out of Klagenfurt Town
Hall, and had spent time looking for a suitable site for a cricket
pitch. Aldington's actions were also supported by two special
operations executive officers, Sir Charles Villiers and Robert
Lockhart. One of Charles Gray QC's successful tactics was to
commit Tolstoy to calling these witnesses either war criminals or
liars, or both, when they claimed not to know about the massacres. This, evidently, was not how the jury viewed them.

Moreover, much of Tolstoy's criticism of Aldington was based
on his having remained in Austria until 25 or 26 May 1945, and
having issued every order and arranged every detail of what the
author described as 'the lying and brutality which resulted in the
massacres'. His case was undermined by evidence emerging at the
trial from the son of Brigadier de Fonblanque, who had found his
father's journal showing that Aldington had left the country on
21 May.

It was further damaged, and to a greater extent, by Tolstoy's
involvement with Watts. When Tolstoy came to give evidence he
was reminded of what he had rashly written to his co-defendant.
'I wish you luck in your struggle with this evil man. Had he been
born a German he would have been strung up years ago' –
strange words for an historian. 'Please do not alert [Aldington]
about my contact with you. He has at least agreed to see me and
I think you will be astonished (I am) at the evidence which

proves Lord Aldington acted as Macmillan's hatchet man in sending 75,000 men, women and children to their deaths, and I want his guard to be lowered . . . I have caught him out in lie after lie.'

In cross-examination Tolstoy was cast as an extremist. He claimed that Aldington should have protested against his orders and tried to have them changed. He said that as his investigations had progressed, he had formed the view that Aldington had disobeyed his orders from General Alexander. He attacked Aldington for never having expressed any contrition, repentance or regret about the massacres. He agreed that he had made the most terrible charge that could be made against a public man. 'Yes, because I think it is probably the worst thing I can think of that has happened in recent British history.' He was accused of making a 180-degree swing in his interpretation at the trial of the Robertson order of 14 May from what he had written in *The Minister and the Massacres*. One of the main weaknesses of his case was that he was unable to offer any explanation as to why Aldington should have taken it upon himself to disobey his orders. He also experienced some difficulty in suggesting what Aldington's motives might have been for becoming involved in a war crime. Lamely, he said that Aldington was an inhumane officer who did not question an inhumane order.

The defence called twenty-eight witnesses, of whom twenty-three were foreigners. The judge was determined to rule out any emotional testimony. They were allowed only to say that they had been badly treated in Yugoslavia and that they had escaped, without going into traumatic detail. 'This trial may be looked upon by witnesses as an opportunity to get off their chests something they have had on their chests for forty-five years, but unfortunately this is not a place where we provide a soapbox. Please keep your witnesses under control,' he ordered Rampton, thereby holing the defence strategy below the waterline. The plaintiff's witnesses, on the other hand, were allowed to give the background evidence. One defence witness, Zoe Polanska-Palmer, a Cossack, complained after the trial, 'I was so mad I wanted to throw my knickers at the judge'. Another, Joro Miletic, a Slav, said, 'We were wogs, just like blacks, foreigners, jetsam; second-class people who never had an empire.' As they could at most prove only that a war crime had been committed, but not that Aldington had committed it, the judge gave them short shrift. The British witnesses fared little better. Philip Brutton, who had been a junior officer in the Welsh Guards, was able to say that he had found the extradition of the Chetniks and Croats nauseating. Nigel Nicolson spoke of the betrayal of trust involved in sending the men, women and children back to their enemies. One French-speaking Serb had asked him: 'Is it true that we are going back to Italy?' Nicolson replied, 'I am going to turn my back on you for thirty seconds, and if, when I turn back, you are still there, you are going to Italy.' When he turned back, he said, he was not there.

Watts' involvement in the trial was wholly in character. On day 13 he sacked his counsel with £23,400 fees on the clock, relying thereafter on *The Layman's Guide to the Law*. He was warned by the judge that it was a very ill-advised move to run a case of this complexity as a litigant in person. Judges prefer trials to stick to the rules of evidence and procedure. In any event Watts made little impact on the case. His apology to Lady Aldington for the distress caused by his constant telephone calls to her home cut little ice. 'You've heard what Mr Watts says, Lady Aldington,' the judge said.

'That's right,' she replied frostily.

All went reasonably well, however, until the judge started to comment on Watts' letter to Lord Aldington of 14 March 1985. 'On 14 March I had not met Count Tolstoy,' Watts exploded. 'It is an absolute disgrace, and everybody in this court thinks so.' Mr Justice Michael Davies had earlier warned he would not please all the parties, and so it proved. 'Keep your justice – you are a disgrace to the legal profession,' Watts shouted at the judge as he left court. The judge suggested that Watts' walk-out should not influence the jury in any way, and that Watts' letters to Sun Alliance bordered on blackmail.

Giving evidence in such a bitterly contested case was a terrible ordeal for Lord Aldington. He was constantly accused by Rampton of lying. Periodically he flared up. 'I know you think I am a liar, but I tell you I am not, and I find it very hard to keep an equable temper with a man who behaves to me in court in this way when I have stated these things to him on oath.' The judge, who made little secret of his sympathy for Lord Aldington, said, with some justification, 'I am not here to protect Lord Aldington. He is a man of seventy-five and to impose unnecessary strain by repeating the same question over and over again at hourly intervals is not really the proper way to do it.'

Aldington was cross-examined for thirty hours and emerged relatively unscathed, leaving it to his witnesses and the judge to put a seal on his victory, assisted by the poor impression made on the jury by Tolstoy and Watts. The jury no doubt took account of the way the case had been conducted against Aldington in their award of damages. Lady Aldington spoke of the strain of the trial in upper-crust terms. 'We had tears three nights, I think, and two when we didn't, but I think that's his safety valve. I mean, I was brought up rather differently. I was brought up not to boo, but I think his family have Celtic blood.'

Mr Justice Michael Davies' summing-up was favourable to Aldington. He suggested that the jury might accept that the plaintiff had not seen the 'fatal-to-health' order signed by Field-Marshal Alexander, and that they might think that his definition order was an honest, conscientious and successful attempt to apply the Yalta Treaty. The defence did not fare so well. Captain Nicolson, the judge intimated, with no evident qualification from his war experience, was, they might think, rather a wet. He was not for a moment suggesting they should think so, but was he rather too oversensitive for a soldier? As for Tolstoy: 'Well, members of the jury, I put a question to you, and I am not suggesting an answer. Is that the letter [the 'evil man' letter] of a balanced historian, or is it the letter of a fanatic? He is a self-styled historian in the sense that he calls himself an historian; there is no sneer about that. Whether he is an impartial, balanced, unbiased historian is entirely a matter for you to decide. Again, you have to consider, did he become obsessed?' It was a summing-up which itself sounded less balanced than it appears on the page.

Charles Gray QC put it to the jurors that the only way to nail these lies was to award a sum of sufficient size by way of damages to demonstrate to the world at large that they had carefully considered and utterly rejected the charges against Lord Aldington. The judge tried to get the jury to exercise moderation if they awarded damages. Although it was obviously a very serious libel indeed – in effect the plaintiff had been defamed as a party to mass murder – one cannot deal in Mickey Mouse money, just reeling off noughts because they sound good, he explained. You have got to consider money in real terms. He offered the familiar unsatisfactory formula of the day: work out how much a house is worth, and what a sum would realise if invested at 10 per cent, and consider whether that seems rather a lot of money for the wrong done. With some foresight he observed: 'You are not doing the plaintiff any favours if you give a figure which is grossly too much, because it leads to appeal and further litigation.'

The jury awarded their £1.5 million: three times the previous highest jury award. Perhaps it was not that surprising when one considers that two years earlier Jeffrey Archer had recovered £500,000 for not sleeping with a prostitute to whom he had paid £2,000. Nevertheless it was a staggering figure, and Aldington tried in vain to compromise on £300,000 damages. The size of the award was attacked in the press as a mockery of British justice and served only to deflect attention from Aldington's exoneration.

There followed years of further litigation, which got Aldington no nearer his money. Watts bombarded the directors of Sun Alliance with false assertions that Aldington had committed perjury, and that he was guilty as the pamphlet claimed. In February 1991 he was found by Mr Justice Macpherson to be in contempt of the injunction imposed on him not to repeat the libellous allegations. It was unfortunate for Aldington that the judge did not at that point impose a custodial sentence on Watts. This did not happen until he came up before Mr Justice Morland after the publication of his second, unambiguously titled, pamphlet *War Criminal in the House of Lords*. Masochistically, Watts had commented in this effort about a corrupt judiciary. He must have realised that things were going badly when the judge asked what the maximum sentence was. On being told it was two years, he gave him eighteen months. Watts' letter of apology was felt not to be genuine or sincere, but the Court of Appeal reduced his sentence to nine months anyway. His next appeal persuaded Mr Justice Latham that he had purged his contempt, so he was out of prison after three months. The judge mournfully observed that the court could control Watts' actions but not his thoughts.

After he was made bankrupt, Watts had rather smartly got his mother to produce £10,000, which was accepted in full and final settlement by the Aldington side with an agreement not to oppose Watts' application for his release from his bankruptcy order. For a time it looked as if Aldington's advisers might have been outmanoeuvred legally, as it was asserted that this release settled the entire claim, including Tolstoy's liability. Some very arcane arguments were heard by Mr Justice Morritt and the Court of Appeal on the matter before the court held that it did not, and that it was a release subject to the implied term that Lord Aldington's rights against Count Tolstoy would be reserved.

But Watts continued to raise his complaints at the AGMs of Sun Alliance. In September 1995 he was removed in handcuffs by the City of London Police, but was not charged. As a result he recovered £5,090 damages against the police for false imprisonment. His triumph, however, was short-lived: the Court of Appeal set the judgement aside.

Things were not going much better with Tolstoy. Aldington began an action against him to discover the identity of the person financing his litigation. This proved a costly failure. Aldington was quoted in 1992 as saying: 'I wasn't a rich man when I started.

I haven't had to sell my home yet, and I hope I won't have to. I ask myself whether it is worth the expense and the time.' In fact the wolf was being kept from the door by the Earl of Portsmouth, who had contributed £500,000 to Tolstoy's funds, almost matching the £530,000 loan which Sun Alliance had written off to help Aldington meet his legal costs. Portsmouth also backed the publication of a book by Ian Mitchell, *The Cost of Reputation*, which argued that vital files had been withheld from Tolstoy by the Ministry of Defence and the Foreign Office. These painted a fuller picture of the sequence of orders. Douglas Hurd, then foreign secretary, investigated the matter of the missing files, which had subsequently resurfaced in a Foreign Office cupboard, and concluded that it was a cock-up rather than a conspiracy. For his part Aldington disputed the significance and extent of any documents the defence might not have sent. It is doubtful in any event that the files could have done any more than incline the jury to a more sensible award of damages.

In February 1994 Tolstoy's new lawyers – the previous firm had left the case after being paid £619,248, rather more than their original estimate of £225,000 – commenced proceedings claiming the libel verdict had been obtained by fraud. This received short shrift from Mr Justice Collins and the Court of Appeal, who were distinctly unimpressed by the saga of the missing government files. A new QC imported from the criminal bar because he was thought to know about fraud received a judicial roasting from the judge, who evidently thought Tolstoy's had gone on long enough. The court ordered that Tolstoy's solicitors had acted unreasonably and should pay 60 per cent of the legal costs. Thus, although the lawyers acted without a fee, they ended up having to find £60,000. Richard Rampton QC, who had advocated this line of attack, but who had departed to do battle on behalf of McDonald's burgers, did not himself suffer any costs penalty. The proceedings were simply struck out as a collateral attack* on the judgement of a court of competent

*A legally impermissible way of circumventing an earlier court decision.

jurisdiction and, most unusually, an order was made for the transcripts of the case to be destroyed.

Tolstoy's attempt to appeal against the main judgement failed as he had been ordered to lodge £124,090 security for costs, plus £33,000 for the costs of the application. This had involved Aldington in an expensive six-day hearing in the Court of Appeal. Lord Justice Russell paid tribute to the trial judge's summing-up. 'Count Tolstoy has singularly failed to persuade me that it was in any way biased, prejudiced or unfair. There is not in my judgement the remotest chance of a Court of Appeal interfering with the jury's findings.'

Attempts to seize Tolstoy's assets did not prove worth the effort. He, however, then obtained his July 1995 ruling from the European Court of Human Rights that the amount of damages was wholly disproportionate and violated his right to freedom of speech. Reviewing the Rantzen case of 1994, the court concluded that the scope of judicial control at an English libel trial did not offer adequate and effective safeguards against a disproportionately large award. The result was the English court did produce guidelines for damages in Elton John v. MGN to prevent such high damages.

In June 1989 Aldington had, by agreement, been paid £30,000 damages by Century Hutchinson for libels in Tolstoy's *The Minister and the Massacres*, and the book had been withdrawn. It was scant consolation. When the BBC regurgitated the same allegations in their programme *A British Betrayal*, Aldington issued a writ before the end of the limitation period. Understandably, however, he did not have the stomach to pursue his claim once he had failed to persuade the BBC not to broadcast the film.

The libel law had let down the parties, and the end result had little to do with justice. In some respects Tolstoy had been portrayed as the victim, but this was scarcely accurate – not even in the eyes of some of his supporters. Nigel Nicolson wrote to him in February 1991:

You persist in pursuing your case through the European Court and the British courts, putting yourself under great strain and incurring further expense and writing newsletters that are so slanted in your favour, so filled with venom against your opponent, so abusive of the English legal system that even those who support you must question whether your obsession with the case has not rendered you crazy. You have won the moral victory. Now you are in danger of throwing away that advantage by overstating your case.

Lord Aldington died in December 2000 without recovering any damages or costs from Tolstoy. Although Tolstoy had inherited £1.5 million from his stepfather, Patrick O'Brian, that March, he had no intention of paying his debt to Aldington. He had by then been discharged from bankruptcy, so he argued that money acquired afterwards did not come into account. In interviews he gave while Aldington was dying of cancer, he cheerfully acknowledged that Aldington would not get a bean. However, he did have to pay £57,000 in respect of a costs order made against him for his failed action over his unproved allegation of perjury against Aldington.

The Earl of Portsmouth, one of Tolstoy's benefactors, had, in an altruistic search for the truth behind the crime some felt had been committed in the repatriation of the Cossacks, initially put up £367,000 for Tolstoy's defence, plus a further sum for the appeal, and had contributed to his daughter's school fees. When he heard of Tolstoy's windfall, he expressed the hope that Tolstoy might repay the school fees. The Earl felt he would like to use the money to assist others – he had also been one of the backers of Neil Hamilton's libel action against Mohamed Fayed. The extent to which Tolstoy is willing to reimburse his supporters remains unclear.

Tolstoy continued to attack Aldington as a deeply embittered and vindictive man. When Aldington died, Nigel Nicolson observed: 'The most of which I would accuse Aldington is negligence and indifference. I hope Nikolai Tolstoy will act generously now that Aldington is dead, admit that he overstated his charges against him and that the jury's verdict was not unfair.'

In a curious footnote to this saga, Watts, by that stage an experienced litigant, managed to recover libel damages himself in 1992, when his photograph was mistakenly used to illustrate a diary item in *The Sunday Times* which falsely accused another Nigel Watts of having won the Betty Trask literary award with his book *The Life Game* by dint of plagiarising Ann Henning's autobiographical novel *To Hell or to Connaught*. In fact both Wattses sued *The Sunday Times*, as neither of them had plagiarised Henning's book. Watts the author had never even heard of it. The apology to 'War Crime' Watts published in the newspaper featured a phrase inserted at the insistence of his solicitors which was subsequently interpreted as a repetition of the libel of Watts the author, who promptly sued *The Sunday Times* again. *The Sunday Times* was unable to recover the second lot of damages it had to pay Watts the author from 'War Crime' Watts or his solicitors, as they had qualified privilege while acting in protection of their legitimate interests.

The abiding impression of the Aldington case is how the complexities of the law of libel failed to provide proper justice for the parties. The case cried out for a more streamlined procedure to resolve it and for a more generally acceptable level of damages. As it was, the case is likely to be remembered for the disproportionately large award of damages and the legal manoeuvring which deprived Lord Aldington of the fruits of his victory in court.

# 18

# POLITICIANS

As a group, politicians have been the most persistent libel litigants. This is, in a sense, inevitable, given the great exposure of politicians to coverage in the press. Attempts to import from America into English law a variant of the public figure defence in the 1964 Sullivan v. *New York Times* case, which would more easily enable discussion of public affairs without the risk of libel suits, met initially with strong judicial resistance. The Reynolds case has introduced a defence of qualified privilege and will afford the press the opportunity of defending cases on the grounds of public interest, even if some of the facts may be wrong or unprovable. The days when an error in the 'Crossbencher' column in the *Sunday Express* recarpeted an MP's home may be drawing to a close.

A few cases brought by politicians have become notorious for the lies told by the plaintiffs. The case of Jonathan Aitken in Chapter 4 is not the first. Richard Crossman admitted that the £2,500 apiece recovered, with Lord Goodman's help, in 1957 by three leading Labour figures of the day, Aneurin Bevan, Morgan Phillips and himself, was ill gotten. Damages were awarded after the three men brought a libel action against the *Spectator*, which had alleged that they were drunk during a party conference. A few weeks after the trial, Crossman revealed to the magazine's assistant editor, Brian Inglis, that Phillips had indeed been drunk, and that Bevan had been drinking heavily. In 1962 he told Iain Adamson, the biographer of their counsel, Gilbert Beyfus QC, that Bevan and Phillips had been drunk and had therefore committed perjury at the trial. Crossman claimed that he himself had been sober.

He cannot, however, have failed to notice that he and his colleagues were obtaining money by false pretences. In 1972 Crossman's account of the incident, retailed at a *Private Eye* lunch, led Auberon Waugh to write subsequently of all three having been 'pissed as newts'. In his diaries Crossman wrote of Phillips sweating with panic in the witness box as he'd been dead drunk for most of the conference. He claimed that Bevan had told him: 'I've been libelled too often. I can get them on this' – not such a wise assumption nowadays.

The case was an appalling example of how nerve and standing in society normally secure a verdict for a plaintiff who is confident that a defendant cannot discharge the burden of proving his or her allegations to be true. Moreover, these plaintiffs had the luxury of support from a socialist property millionaire who encouraged them not to accept the £525 paid into court by the *Spectator*. The *Spectator* concluded, probably correctly at the time, that a jury would not prefer the word of an Italian barman and a journalist to that of three privy councillors.

Seven years later, Lord Boothby trousered £40,000 of the *Sunday Mirror*'s money for their story 'Peer and a Gangster: Yard Inquiry', which suggested that a homosexual relationship existed between a peer said to be a household name and a leading London gangster responsible for West End protection rackets. It was reported that the pair went to parties together in Mayfair. The peer was helpfully named by the German magazine *Stern* as Lord Boothby, and the gangster was Ronnie Kray.

Boothby claimed in a letter to *The Times* that he was not a homosexual, that Kray was merely an acquaintance and brazenly denounced the allegations as a 'tissue of atrocious lies'. A suitcase of letters and photographs prudently kept by Kray subsequently proved otherwise. Despite the flamboyance with which Boothby conducted his friendship with Kray – they had socialised at the House of Lords and at White's – there were pressures to avoid another sex scandal, which could also have implicated the homosexual Labour MP Tom Driberg, before the 1964 election and Lord Goodman swiftly and skilfully obtained what was a huge award for the time. Even Kray was graced with an apology in the *Sunday Mirror*.

Goodman's biographer, Brian Brivati, is convinced his subject knew that his clients were lying. Whatever the truth, the case established Goodman's unmatched reputation for dissuading newspapers from printing defamatory articles about his clients.

Suing for libel is not the preserve of any one political party, nor of Westminster itself. David Bookbinder, Labour leader of Derbyshire County Council, issued many libel writs during his term of office. He enjoyed some success: his own claim against *The Sunday Times* in relation to its article on the investment policies of the council pension fund brought him substantial damages. However, the action of the council itself, which was brought at the same time, resulted in the establishment of the principle that a county council cannot sue for libel for damage to its governing reputation – plus a very substantial legal costs bill for the ratepayers of Derbyshire.

As well as *The Sunday Times*, Bookbinder has sued Norman Tebbit, the *Derby Trader* and its editor, Tony Mather, and Tory councillor Walter Marshall. Three of the *Derby Trader* writs Bookbinder had issued in 1989 were eventually struck out for want of prosecution. He said he could not afford to fight the cases. He had to pay costs estimated at £126,000 and faced having to sell his house. He lost his case against Philip Oppenheim, his opponent in the Amber Valley constituency in the 1987 election. Bookbinder claimed he personally had been libelled by a pamphlet issued by Oppenheim, which reproduced newspaper headlines such as 'BOOKIE'S BARMY BOOKLIST' and 'COUNCIL'S BOOKLIST FOR KIDS SLAMMED' in its criticisms of recommended school reading lists on subjects such as homosexuality, lesbianism and nuclear war. Bookbinder complained that the pamphlet alleged that he personally selected school books, was mad to do so, was encouraging homosexuality among children and was a member of the 'loony left'. Oppenheim's defence was not that he suggested that Bookbinder was any of these things; rather that the pamphlet did not allege them. Mr Justice Drake agreed in a ruling given in 1994 that the pamphlet was not capable of bearing any such meaning. In 1996, nearly ten years after the election in question, Bookbinder dropped his appeal against the decision. He was due to pay Oppenheim's costs of £80,000 as well as his own, but the parties reached a compromise.

Bookbinder was no more successful with his action against Norman Tebbit for comments the Conservative minister had made in the 1986 West Derbyshire by-election. At a speech at Matlock Bath, Tebbit had mocked the Derbyshire County Council policy of overprinting envelopes with the declaration that it was a nuclear-free zone. 'I hope he has told the Russians of Derbyshire's nuclear-free policy. If not, it is arguable he has lost £50,000 on this damn fool idea on school notepaper.' Tebbit wondered out loud whether Soviet generals targeting their SS20 missiles would refrain from aiming at the Rolls–Royce factory in Derby because it was in a nuclear-free zone. Bookbinder claimed that the cost of overprinting was minimal. There was some dispute as to what it actually had cost. Very unusually, and unwisely, Bookbinder did not go into the witness box, prompting more references to Hamlet without the Prince and allegations by George Carman QC that he lacked the strength of character, integrity, decency and courtesy to face the music – comments which were characterised by Bookbinder's counsel, Alan Newman QC, as the equivalent of a verbal napalm attack. The defence case was that this was an exercise of free speech and part of the cut and thrust of politics. The jury agreed, taking only ninety-five minutes to throw out the case after a five-day hearing. Bookbinder was left with a legal bill of over £100,000.

The case was memorable for its explanation of how Tebbit – who had, during his political career, been described as both a Chingford skinhead and a semi-house-trained polecat – had come to be known as Dracula. He had been spotted by Labour minister Denis Healey with a dark blue raincoat thrown round his shoulders. Healey had dropped to his knees and made the sign of the cross, scrabbling for some garlic to save himself.

Tebbit himself recovered £14,000 damages and £16,000 costs from the *Guardian* in 1988 when the paper falsely claimed he had once said that 'nobody with a conscience votes Conservative', which he had not.

The Derbyshire County Council case was followed in the action brought by Sir James Goldsmith and the Referendum Party against the *Daily Express* and one of its journalists prior to the 1997 general election. The paper had alleged that its under-cover reporter had been offered £6.50 an hour to canvass, something prohibited under the Representation of the People Act 1983. The party claimed this was wholly false and part of a dirty-tricks campaign. It would have been a regrettable extension of the law of libel if a political party, as opposed to its officials, could have sued for libel. Fortunately, Mr Justice Buckley threw out the Referendum Party's action. He held that the policy under-lying the decision in the Derbyshire County Council case should be extended to political parties. While he observed that prevent-ing defamation actions being brought was a power which should be exercised with caution, the public interest in freedom of speech was, in the circumstances of the case, sufficiently strong and should not be fettered. Individual candidates could sue when they were identified in material published about the party, but now, under the ruling in the Reynolds case, they would be likely to face a defence of qualified privilege. Slowly the law seems to have got back to where it was thought to be in the Bessie Braddock case (see Chapter 16).

The bringing of libel actions by politicians has become more risky, particularly if their party is unpopular at the time. This in part explained the loss in January 1995 by a majority of 10–2 of the action brought by Paul Judge, director-general of the Conservative Party, against the *Guardian* after a seven-day trial.

On 5 September 1993 the paper had published a front-page story headlined 'TORIES FACE COURT OVER NADIR CASH. CENTRAL OFFICE TRICKS OBSTRUCTING INQUIRY'. It accused the party of being guilty of obstruction in failing to respond speedily to the inquiries of the accountants Robson Rhodes into the donation made to party funds by the fugitive financier Asil Nadir. Judge was named four times in the article. Neil Cooper, a partner at Robson Rhodes and one of the trustees in the bankruptcy of Nadir, gave evidence that he had been driven to scribble the note 'Typical delaying tactics' on his file after Judge wrote to him saying he had to postpone a full response pending legal advice. Cooper felt that Central Office was trying to hinder inquiries by the trustees in order to obstruct investigations into Nadir's donation. He had felt compelled to give the Tories a final opportunity to provide information voluntarily before issuing a summons to force Judge to answer the necessary questions in the High Court. His solicitor had been reduced to delivering letters by hand to Judge at Central Office in Smith Square, saying, 'We hope this does not get lost between the front office and your desk.' The first request for information was made on 16 June 1993 and it was not concluded until 21 October 1993. At the trial Charles Gray QC, for the *Guardian*, was highly critical of the fact that it took eighteen weeks to hand over relatively limited information.

Judge said he had co-operated with the trustees and that at no time had he been aware of the threat of court action. He had written promising further investigations if Cooper had information that Nadir or his nominees had paid more than the £440,000 the party had already declared (there had been speculation in the press that Nadir might have given as much as £1.7 million).

Judge, a millionaire businessman, volubly asserted that he was 'amazed, stupefied, worried and concerned' by the allegations, which had caused him 'considerable distress, anxiety and embarrassment'. He alleged that the *Guardian* was motivated by

anti-Conservative scandalmongering, pointing to the fact that
the paper had had to apologise and pay 'hefty' damages for an
allegation that the Conservative Party had received a £7 million
donation from Prince Bandar Bin Sultan before the 1992
election. He complained that the article had been published without any opportunity being extended to him to comment on it.

The *Guardian* claimed that they were writing about a matter
of considerable public interest – the acceptance of funding from
dubious sources – and that what they had written was true and
a matter of fair comment. After four hours' deliberation, the jury
agreed. Judge was left facing costs of £300,000. The perils of
suing on what was essentially a political story – albeit with a
hostile slant – were evident.

A politician is, like any other citizen, entitled to protect himself against false allegations concerning his private life. It was on
that basis that, in January 1993, John Major, then prime minister, sued the *New Statesman*. Their article was undoubtedly
defamatory. Although it had been published in a political magazine and its subject was a political figure, it had no political
content or significance. It simply regurgitated ill-informed
rumour over three pages of gossip and nudge-nudge, wink-wink
innuendo. Had the purpose of the piece been to inform readers
that such rumours were doing the rounds, something which
might have been of legitimate public interest, that information
could, in suitably discreet terms, have been communicated in one
or two well-chosen sentences. Instead the *New Statesman*
decided to repeat them in breathless detail. Other journalists
were well aware of these false rumours but had understandably
decided not to repeat them.

The front cover of the *New Statesman* was undoubtedly
defamatory. It bore an unambiguous montage picture depicting
the prime minister enjoying a candlelit dinner with his caterer.
The story was headlined: 'THE CURIOUS CASE OF JOHN MAJOR'S "MIS-
TRESS" – It is the Story that Dare Not Speak its Name. Steve Platt
and Nyta Mann investigate'. Both the feature and the front cover,
where the picture was captioned with the headline, undoubtedly

left readers with the impression that there was some substance and fire to go with the smoke. In truth the rumours were a pack of lies and in the ensuing litigation the *New Statesman* did not suggest otherwise. Platt seemed to have assumed the role of Quintus Slide of the People's Banner, 'the surest guardian of the people's liberty', who libelled the prime minister in Trollope's *The Prime Minister.*

Underlying the libel was an attempt to commemorate the *New Statesman*'s eightieth anniversary issue: they wanted a good story to liven up the party. The magazine had been redesigned and 2,000 extra copies had been printed for the launch at the House of Commons. The print run was swiftly increased by 5,000 when the tale hit the headlines of the mainstream press – prompting some gems from the headline-writers, such as 'WRIT HITS THE FAN' (the *Sun*) and 'I DIDN'T GOOSE THE COOK' (the *Daily Record*).

Foolishly, the magazine seems to have thought it could get away with it by putting inverted commas round the word 'mistress'. The printers and distributors, who were also sued, in the light of the *New Statesman*'s financially parlous state, were advised by their counsel that the article was indeed libellous. They swiftly settled the claims against them, having formed the view that the defamatory front cover would deprive them of a defence of innocent dissemination which might have been available if the libel had been buried in the text of a reputable magazine.

After the distributors and printers had settled, the *New Statesman* paid £1,001 into court. The payment into court was therefore in effect £27,501, as £26,500 had already been forked out by the printers and distributors. Underlying this procedure is the legal notion that the plaintiff is suing for one libel and that the various parties responsible for it are contributing to a single pot of damages. Had the case proceeded, the prime minister would have had to have been awarded damages of over £27,501 to have recovered all his legal costs against the *New Statesman*. Had he fought the case and been awarded only, say, £20,000 against the *New Statesman* he would not have recovered more than the sum paid into court and would have had to pay the *New Statesman*'s as well as his own legal costs after the date of payment. In that case he would have ended up substantially out of pocket. Although he would most likely have been awarded more than £27,501, there was a strong probability that the *New Statesman* would have gone to the wall if it had fought and lost a contested libel action. Substantial damages plus costs *were* paid and recovered, although certain sections of the press misunderstood the effect of payment in by the *New Statesman*: the magazine was acknowledging its liability to pay £27,501 in damages, not £1,001.

Although the media no doubt relished the prospect of a contested libel action, it would have made no sense financially, or indeed in terms of the use of the prime minister's time, to have continued the action to seek to recover more than the £27,501 already tendered.

Having taken action against the *New Statesman*, it was not possible for the prime minister to ignore the libels emanating from *Scallywag*, which seemed to pride itself on the publication of defamatory material while its lack of assets deterred potential litigants. Instead, plaintiffs sued its printers, distributors and retailers. In this case, after taking legal advice, the printers and distributors paid substantial damages to the prime minister and proceedings against the magazine itself were settled. The settlement included an undertaking by the magazine not to repeat the allegations.

Finally, in 1994, Julian Lewis, who was later to become a Conservative MP, used his skills in strategic studies to put *Scallywag* out of business. He was understandably aggrieved by its wholly false accusations – that he was preparing a dossier on the (non-existent) homosexual activities of Tony Blair, then leader of the Labour opposition, and that he was himself a secret homosexual, transvestite and frequenter of male dens of iniquity who used women from escort agencies to accompany him to political events – but *Scallywag*'s editor, Simon Regan, who was living on income support and disability benefit, made it clear that neither he nor the magazine was worth suing.

However, when Lewis denied these allegations, *Scallywag* added insult to injury by accusing him of lying, leaving him with the problem of how to nail these demonstrably false claims to protect his prospects of remaining a parliamentary candidate. Either he had to tolerate them, running the risk of a whispering campaign, or he had to sue for libel without piling up huge costs that would be irrecoverable from an assetless libeller.

Lewis decided to sue the printer, six distributors and two retailers and in the end he recovered £39,500 damages plus a much larger sum in costs. The printer and distributors could have been in little doubt as to the libellous content of *Scallywag*. Lewis supplied details of the magazine's distributors and printers to former police superintendent Gordon Anglesea who, as we saw in Chapter 6, had also been libelled by *Scallywag*, and he too sued. Lewis was in turn sued by Scallywag Ltd for malicious falsehood, but after he defended the action as a litigant in person without incurring costs that claim was not pursued. Shortly afterwards the assetless company was struck off the register of companies.

There was a time when a plaintiff might have brought an action for criminal libel against an impecunious publisher of such libels, but the High Court nowadays is unlikely to give the necessary leave for such a prosecution. Unable to bring a worthwhile action for libel against the magazine's editor, Lewis resorted to the arcane provisions of Section 106 of the Representation of the People Act 1983. He obtained taped evidence of Regan, who had set up his own website, making false statements on the Internet about his character and conduct and got Regan to admit at a public meeting that his aim was to reduce Lewis's votes at the election. The unsuspecting editor was trapped by a recording of his admission. After a four-day trial, he was fined £250 with £50 costs for a breach of this obscure electoral law.

Lewis was also able to successfully sue Regan's Internet

provider, Demon Internet Services Ltd, who paid him libel damages and closed the website. The obtaining of damages from an Internet service provider was very rare; the criminal prosecution of a person for something he had published on the Internet unprecedented. The prosecution was only possible because the libel had been published during an election campaign. However, Regan's conviction was overturned by Southwark Crown Court on the grounds that Lewis had been merely the prospective as opposed to the adopted parliamentary candidate at the time the allegations were posted on the Internet. Information broadcast on the Internet remains very difficult to suppress, and indeed the offending website later reappeared via a Dutch service-provider. But increasingly, in cases where the primary libeller is insufficiently solvent to make suing him or her worthwhile, determined plaintiffs like Lewis will have to look to the secondary libellers – that is to say, distributors, printers and Internet providers – to vindicate their reputation, provided that they are on notice of the likelihood of defamatory material in publication complained of.

Regan, meanwhile, unsuccessfully sued a solicitor, Barton Taylor, who was held by the Court of Appeal to be covered by qualified privilege in respect of remarks he had made in response to press inquiries concerning litigation he was conducting on behalf of his clients. Taylor had forthrightly observed that Regan was a suitable candidate for a case of criminal libel. When Regan died, his obituary in *The Times*, published in August 2000, included the comment: 'He never quite knew where to stop or grasped where sensation ended and fantasy began.'

John Major is not the only prime minister to have sued for libel. In 1967 Labour premier Harold Wilson sued the pop group The Move over a postcard depicting him in nude caricature which had been produced to promote their highly successful record *Flowers in the Rain*. The court ruled that royalties on sales of the record should be paid into a charitable trust set up to distribute funds to good causes. As the royalties totalled £200,000 over the next thirty years, it turned out to be a huge libel award. Attempts by members of the group to get the settlement set aside on the grounds that they had, in law, been infants at the time (that is, under twenty-one), came to nothing. Wilson was represented by Quintin Hogg QC, who, appropriately, prepared his notes for the case in classical Greek. In the same year, Wilson also recovered damages from the *International Herald Tribune* for comments about his relationship with his personal assistant, Lady Falkender.

And in 1964, just before he became prime minister, Wilson was himself sued after accusing Herbert Hill, the chairman of Hardy Spicer Ltd, of fomenting a strike for improper political motive. He had to apologise to Hill and pay his legal costs.

Paddy Ashdown was also involved in a libel suit when leader of the Liberal Democrats. He recovered substantial damages against the *Western Daily Press* in a case which was settled within twenty-four hours after allegations were made about him and an unnamed woman. The case produced a forthright apology: 'We apologise unreservedly . . . and accept the allegations are completely untrue. If people tend to think there is no smoke without fire, we are happy to accept that this is the exception.'

There have been cases where politicians have brought libel actions which fall somewhere between their public and their private lives. Teresa Gorman, MP for Billericay, sued local accountant Anthony Mudd, the chairman of the Billericay Conservative Businessmen's Association, for a mock press release, ostensibly issued on behalf of Gorman and attributing to her a number of unflattering and highly personal remarks on such matters as hormone implants. It had been sent in May 1988 to ninety-one prominent figures in the local Conservative community.

Mudd offered US tourists an £1,800-a-week package holiday based at his seventeenth-century electronically gated moated mansion, Stockwell Hall, near Billericay. It was unashamedly first-generation money, Dralon sofas and Jeffrey Archer novels (Mudd had a taste for personalised number plates: MUD 2 on the Rolls and MUD 317 on the Range Rover). His dispute with

Gorman arose over her refusal to follow the practice of her predecessor, Harvey Proctor (who had resigned the seat after
admitting indecency with teenage boys), of hosting dinners for
the American visitors at the House of Commons. At the libel trial
Proctor denied that a brochure which advertised House of
Commons dinners to the tourists constituted any breach of parliamentary rules. The scheme had been approved in draft by Sir
Charles Irvine, chairman of the Commons Catering Committee.

Gorman complained that the pamphlet depicted her as vain,
deceitful and unconcerned with the wellbeing of the local
Conservative Party, and claimed the newsletter was unpleasant,
spiteful and motivated by malice. She explained that she got no
pleasure out of the litigation. It was not a satisfactory way for
members of the Conservative Party to carry on. Dining at the
Commons was a strictly controlled privilege. To do it on a regular basis four times a year as if you were popping into a local
café seemed almost an abuse of privilege. Mudd's association,
she said, was a private club and its usefulness to the
Conservative Association was limited. She would have been content if he had apologised, but her offer to settle the case for an
apology and costs without damages had been rejected. Mudd
had treated this gesture not as an olive branch, but as a case of
Gorman having, as he put it, 'got herself on a hook and wrig-
gling to try to get off it'. She branded Mudd a chauvinist and a
bully. The press release had made her blood run cold. She knew
it was not a tease or a joke, but a serious attempt to undermine
her position and reputation; indeed, there had already been an
attempt to deselect her.

The case was bitterly contested and the rancour in the end
rebounded on Mudd. He sought to attack Gorman in court for
having sent personal details to the Conservative Selection
Committee for Billericay showing her date of birth as 1941 when
1931 was rather nearer the mark. The defence thought they were
on to a winner when they caught Gorman out on this untruth,
but the nine women on the jury evidently sympathised with her
reason: that it was extremely difficult for women of over fifty to

be taken seriously in life. Women are considered to be over the hill at an age when men are thought to be in their prime, she explained.

Mudd's attempts to justify his thoroughly unpleasant pamphlet by accusing Gorman of conducting a personal vendetta against him served only to escalate the damage. She kept saying dreadful things about him, he complained. This attitude undermined Mudd's best point – that it would be a sad day when one could not write about one's MP in the time-honoured form of a lampoon. Gorman's claim was, his counsel, David Eady QC, claimed, an almighty cheek for an MP who had on any view behaved quite appallingly to Mr Mudd, and who valued her own robust freedom of speech as much as anyone. When Eady described the case as a clash between strong, overripe personalities reminiscent of the studies in provincial life immortalised by the 'Mapp and Lucia' novels of E.F. Benson, his allusion seemed to go over the heads of the jury. It brought to mind the Irish judge asking Sergeant Sullivan at the turn of the century, 'Surely your client has heard of the maxim *Volenti non fit iniuria*?'

'My Lord, in Tipperary they talk of little else.'

In any event, the jury apparently did not care for Mr Mudd. They awarded a staggering £150,000 for the ninety-one pamphlets. On appeal the damages were reduced to £50,000, but the costs were estimated to be £200,000, and by the time the case had gone to the Court of Appeal it proved an unprofitable and costly business for all concerned. As Gorman later observed: 'You don't come into a case like this for fun. You do it because you think there is a principle at stake, and that's why I did it.'

Michael Meacher, the Labour MP for Oldham West, subsequently shadow spokesman on employment and later minister for the environment, was notably less successful when he felt he had been libelled by Alan Watkins' column in the *Observer* of 25 November 1984. In a mocking piece, Meacher was accused of playing down his middle-class origins and of hounding the chairman of the Islington Health Authority, Eric Moonman, out of the Labour Party by sending out questionnaires asking chairmen to report their members' political views. Watkins poked fun at Meacher's claims to be the son of a farmworker and adopted the words of Dr Johnson to suggest that the choice between Meacher and Moonman was a choice between a louse and a flea. The words carried an offensive but somewhat meaningless ring. Watkins' point, which appeared to be misunderstood by Meacher's counsel at the trial, was that, as with Johnson's contemporaries, the writer and louse Samuel Derrick, and the poet, occasional resident of a lunatic asylum and flea Christopher Smart, there was no real difference between the two.

The case revolved round the first issue, which came to be characterised as 'prolier than thou'. It was extraordinary that Meacher thought this matter sufficiently offensive to merit action. He had been mocked a year previously in very similar terms by Peter Hillmore in the *Observer*'s 'Pendennis' column but had not sued. On that occasion Hillmore had commented that it was a nonsense to say that Meacher's father was a farmworker: he had trained as an accountant and gone on to work on his brother's farm, which was not quite the same thing.

It should have proved possible to negotiate a settlement of the case without recourse to proceedings. It appears that Meacher became involved perhaps without realising what he was letting himself in for. It was fully two months before his solicitors complained about the piece – and ironically at a time when Meacher was himself trying to get an article published in the *Observer*. A correction was published on 24 February 1985, but it was in shorter form than appeared to have been agreed. The *Observer* recorded that they were satisfied that Meacher had never claimed to be the son of an agricultural labourer. They offered to pay his legal costs, but in April Meacher's solicitors requested £1,500 damages and a full apology. In October this had decreased to £1,000. By 1986, Meacher would have been prepared to settle for no more than £500. Nevertheless he had been advised that he had a 75 per cent chance of success if the case went to court, and that the jury might award him £50,000. Unfortunately, the *Observer* was receiving rather similar but more accurate advice.

Their case got stronger as Meacher's got weaker. In fact, with the exception of a brief interlude when a clergyman, Canon Wilkinson, gave evidence of the deprivations of the Meacher family, it was pretty obvious to people in court that Meacher would lose.

In an unhappy chapter of accidents which reflected little credit on the legal profession, it seems that communications between solicitors broke down and neither party fully realised the terms on which the other would settle. Had they done so it is most unlikely that the case would have gone to trial. At the beginning of 1986, the *Observer* paid £225 into court – a sum not very far from the figure at which Meacher was willing to settle. Unfortunately, it seems that the payment in was not communicated to Meacher. The first he heard of it was just before the jury returned its verdict, when, of course, it was too late. So he lost the chance of accepting the money and having most of his costs paid. Meacher said he would have accepted the money paid into court rather than take the matter to a full trial, and in 1990 he sued his solicitors, Seifert Sedley Williams, for negligence. Those proceedings were later settled to Meacher's satisfaction. The firm collapsed in 1991 with debts said to total £1 million.

The case which had taken three and a half years to lumber into court lasted for no fewer than fourteen days in June 1988, as opposed to the estimated five to eight days. In four days of gruelling cross-examination, Meacher said that his social origins would not have made any difference to the Labour Party anyway. Horny hands were not, it seems, then essential in the Labour Party.

At the trial the *actualité* about Meacher's background emerged both in cross-examination and in yet another legal mishap, this time one which forced him to disclose the contents of his witness statement. He was from a third generation of tenant farmers and his mother had inherited the then very sizeable sum of £40,000 from his father in 1969. His family had connections with brewery ownership in Hertfordshire and in his childhood they had had a maid in the family house. Young Meacher had, like his father, gone to Berkhamsted Public School. The Meachers played bridge and owned a Ford Prefect in the 1950s, pleasures then confined to the middle classes. But his family had had to take in lodgers, who had had the use of the bathroom while the Meachers made do with the outside lavatory and a bath in the kitchen.

Meacher denied he had ever claimed that his father was a farm labourer. He admitted that he had acquiesced in that description, but it was his practice to qualify this with a potted family history – something which must have won him many new friends. His father had gone to London to train as an accountant, but a few months later, after suffering a nervous breakdown, he had returned to work on the family farm, where he remained for twenty-five years. Meacher himself had gone to Berkhamsted only because he won a state scholarship. His priv-ileged education was crowned by a first-class degree at Oxford, and made him determined to help those less fortunate, he explained.

The case, involving Meacher as it did in an agonising trawl through his social origins which left him looking somewhat sanctimonious, was a particularly fruitless exercise – particu-larly as by that stage all he wanted was for the litigation to end, and to get married. As it turned out, he married before the end of the trial and part of his honeymoon was spent in the law courts.

His prospects of success in the case seem to have been fatally undermined when, during cross-examination, his barrister unwisely asked whether he had told his solicitors about his mother's explanation that he would not have been sent to public school if he had not won a scholarship. The purpose of the ques-tion was the ostensibly reasonable one of disproving the suggestion made by the *Observer*'s counsel, Richard Hartley QC, that Meacher had made up the story in the witness box. Meacher was doing no more than truthfully answering the question posed by his barrister. In those days, witness statements were not exchanged, as is now the practice. That meant the jury would be unlikely to know whether a witness had given a different version of the facts to his solicitors in his witness statement. Statements therefore tended to contain material which a party might not wish the other side to see, but which was useful for his barrister to know.

This question enabled the *Observer*'s barrister to apply to have Meacher's witness statement produced to the jury. The judge, Mr Justice Hazan, ruled that the jury were entitled to examine his entire witness statement. Out of Meacher's statement popped the Ford Prefect, the brewery, the bridge and the £40,000 legacy. And unhappily for him it showed that he *had* described his father as a farmworker. He claimed the sentence had been taken out of context. Whatever the case, it gave a rather different impression from the much fuller explanation he had given in evidence. Furthermore, two journalists called by the *Observer*, Robert Taylor and John Knight, did not recollect the qualifications Meacher said applied to his description of himself.

The introduction of his witness statement therefore reinforced the feeling that the MP had been equivocal about his social origins, and that he had no business to be suing the *Observer* over this relatively unimportant matter. The jury was evidently inclined to the view that politicians have to be prepared to take the rough and tumble of political life.

As for the questionnaire sent out to the health authority chairmen, Kenneth Clarke, who had been minister of health at the time, gave evidence for the *Observer* that this was 'a shabby episode'. Meacher said he had circulated it because he feared that the Tories were trying to impose political composition on the health authorities.

In civil cases juries tend to pay rather more heed to the judge than in criminal cases. Meacher was therefore not assisted by Mr Justice Hazan's comment that, although Watkins had laid about Meacher with considerable vigour, 'you should keep out of the kitchen if you cannot stand the heat'. Sending out the questionnaire was, the judge felt, decidedly un-English. After a retirement of ninety minutes, the jury threw out Meacher's case, leaving him with a bill of £50,000 for his own legal costs. He also had to

pay the *Observer* £80,000 towards their costs of £130,000. It was
a notable victory for the press: the last libel action won by a
newspaper had been forty cases before, when the *Daily Mail* had
defeated the religious cult the Moonies in 1981. As for Michael
Meacher, neither his experience in the libel courts nor his ownership of a cottage in rural Ampney Crucis and a string of other
properties deterred him from pontificating eleven years later on
the morality of possessing a second home.

It is certainly possible for politicians to sue successfully for
libel in respect of articles which attack their political integrity
and principles. In December 1995 Peter Bottomley, then
Conservative MP for Eltham and a leading member of the all-
party New Dialogue movement seeking peace in Ireland, was
awarded £40,000 against the *Sunday Express* for a story headed:
'TOP TORY SHARES PLATFORM WITH IRA MOUTHPIECE – THE FINAL BETRAYAL'. This
attacked him for sharing a platform with Martin McGuinness of
Sinn Fein in a debate on the ending of violence in Northern
Ireland and accused him of fraternising with the IRA. The meeting had been organised by the Irish Peace Initiative and Clive
Soley MP was also on the platform. In truth Bottomley was, as a
former Northern Ireland minister, engaged in the thankless task
of speaking for and writing about the need for peace and a further inquiry into the events of Bloody Sunday, a principled stand
which was justified by subsequent events: an inquiry was set up
and McGuinness became a minister in the power-sharing administration. Nevertheless, Bottomley's efforts had earned him a
place on two IRA death lists. He complained that the article
depicted him as having acted in treacherously disloyal and disreputable manner and as having dishonourably abused his
position as a former minister.

The case revealed some fairly unattractive journalistic practice – the headline had been written before Bottomley had been
interviewed, and the interview itself, which was never used, had
been conducted by a reporter with a hidden tape-recorder. There
was more than a suspicion that this 'exclusive' was being used
simply as a peg on which to hang a story about the failure of the

House of Lords to release a British soldier, Private Lee Clegg, from his conviction for murdering a Belfast teenager. Whatever the intention, this important front-page denunciation was shifted in later editions to page two when former showjumper Harvey Smith's horsebox was involved in a fatal road accident. It was an action that could have been avoided in the first place through more balanced reporting, or at least before it reached court – Bottomley's attempts to resolve the situation at the outset with the editor were rebuffed. Instead it will have cost the newspaper well over £250,000

In 1989 Bottomley had already successfully sued the *Mail on Sunday*, reputedly recovering £100,000 damages, and the *Daily Express* and *News of the World* (£25,000 each) for allegations connected with his support of a social worker in his constituency accused of misbehaviour in a children's home. The £40,000 award was one of the first made under the guidelines laid down in the Elton John case.

In July 1995 Michael Foot MP received an unreserved apology and substantial damages said to be in the region of £30,000 from *The Sunday Times*, with a further £35,000 from the *News of the World*, a sum reputed to reflect the paper's genuine regret, for an article headlined 'KGB: MICHAEL FOOT WAS OUR AGENT', which described how Soviet intelligence services had targeted Labour leaders and trades union officials in the 1960s and had hoped to use Foot as an unwitting agent of influence. What the paper was seeking to do was simply to report what the KGB asserted. It unequivocally accepted that there was no truth in the serious allegation that Foot might have propagated Soviet views in the left-wing newspaper *Tribune* and betrayed the democratic principles he had always upheld. Foot was said to be known as Agent Boot. Ironically, the Heath government's expulsion of 105 Soviet intelligence personnel was known as Operation Foot – presumably because some wit in British intelligence services noted they were being given the boot. On this occasion, though, the boot was on another Foot.

The article illustrated the danger in repeating such allegations

in a way which might lead readers to conclude that there is
some substance to a story.

Newspapers have frequently run into libel difficulties when
they have tried to criticise a particular group under some catchy
headlines. The prospect of Conservative MPs being bankrupted
by losses at the insurance underwriters Lloyd's, being required to
resign their seats and thus reducing the government majority to
vanishing point proved irresistible to various papers, and as a
result a number of hard-up MPs recovered damages to help them
meet their Lloyd's commitments. When the *Standard* published
an article in January 1992 about the 'Dozy Dozen' whose departure from the Palace of Westminster might not significantly
deprive or denude it, it was not surprising that they received a
number of writs. The paper found itself apologising to and withdrawing suggestions that certain MPs, including two
Conservative, David Atkinson and Sir Fergus Montgomery, and
one Labour member, Robert Parry, were inactive or ineffectual or
did not merit re-election. The report, it acknowledged, did not
reflect the contributions each made to Parliament and their constituents and, in the case of Mr Parry and Mr Atkinson, to the
Council of Europe. The MPs were paid libel damages to mark the
falsity of the allegations against them.

The *Daily Express* had to pay libel damages to three
Conservative MPs, John Townend, Iain Duncan Smith and
Bernard Jenkin, when it published an attack on a number of Tory
MPs who, it felt, were undermining John Major's attempts to
implement the Maastricht Treaty. This was, unfortunately, a case
of a story failing to match the headlines, which were borrowed
from Hollywood: 'TWELVE ANGRY MEN OUT TO GET MAJOR', and 'DIRTY DOZEN
TRYING TO UNDERMINE THE PM'.

The Conservative Party itself suffered the same problem in
February 1993, after its chairman had named twenty-seven
Labour MPs as being associated with or supporters of Militant
Tendency. Bob Wareing MP, who had never been a member of
Militant Tendency and had denounced them as Stalinists, recov-
ered substantial damages. The fact that others named as members

of the group did not take action did not mean that the allegations against them were true: as we have seen, there are many good reasons for not suing, not least a lack of funds.

Libel actions do pose a threat to politicians who make attacks on individuals, even if they are on political topics. In 1994 John Patten, then education secretary, had to pay damages said to be in the region of £30,000 for describing the chief education officer of Birmingham, Professor Tim Brighouse, as 'a madman let loose, frightening the children'. Brighouse received an apology and generously used the money to fund equal opportunities projects. In 1995 Michael Heseltine, the deputy prime minister, had to pay £40,000 damages plus £15,000 costs to Martyn Gregory, who had produced a programme on Channel 4 exposing the secret British trade in torture equipment – a very rare libel victory for the citizen against the government. Heseltine had signed letters to MPs and their constituents accusing Gregory of scaremongering and of producing a contrived programme by fabricating his story. Gregory had even been threatened with prosecution and interviewed under caution by MoD police for possession of the very electric batons and shock shields which he had ordered from an English company to show that the trade in such instruments did indeed exist.


## The Perception of Sleaze

Neil Hamilton MP was a great letter-writer. As a supporter of businessman Mohamed Fayed, with whose dealings we are already familiar from earlier chapters, his enthusiasm had shown few bounds. When Fayed was being subjected to the DTI inquiry which was to find that he and his brother had produced evidence under solemn affirmation, including written memoranda, birth certificates and documents, which they knew to be false, and that they had repeatedly lied about their family background, their early business life and their wealth, Hamilton was writing to Mohamed Fayed in very different terms. 'Everyone knows the Al Fayeds to be among the world's most significant businessmen. I have no doubt that were it not for the paranoid and personal vendetta pursued against you by Tiny Rowland, you would not now be enduring the indignity of this inquiry.'

When, at the beginning of October 1993, Hamilton discovered that the *Guardian* was making inquiries into a six-day stay he had had at the Ritz in Paris as a guest of Fayed in September 1987, for which his bill, if rendered, would have amounted to £3,604, he wrote a spirited warning letter to the paper. He told them he had stopped at the Ritz en route to a motoring holiday in Alsace, and that he had come to know Fayed – 'a convivial person whom I liked' – reasonably well. Fayed, Hamilton wrote, had pressed him and his wife to spend some time driving round Paris, to go and see the Villa Windsor (which Fayed now owned) and to stay in his private rooms at the Ritz. More to the point, Hamilton reminded the paper that litigation was both time-consuming and expensive for all parties. He had, he pointed out, fought a libel action against *Panorama* some years earlier, which had cost the BBC a total of £500,000. If the newspaper were to print any of the untrue claims or insinuations which it seemed to be planning to publish, he would have no hesitation in pursuing the legal route again; indeed, it might become more necessary now, because of his ministerial position. Just in case the *Guardian* should miss the point, Hamilton copied in Peter Carter-Ruck and Partners.

The previous action Hamilton mentioned was the £20,000 damages plus costs that he and his fellow Tory MP Gerald Howarth had each recovered in October 1986 for their depiction in the *Panorama* programme 'Maggie's Militant Tendency'. The BBC had falsely linked the two MPs with an extreme right-wing organisation, said to hold anti-Semitic and racist views, which had allegedly infiltrated the Conservative Party. Hamilton had disproved claims that he had done the goose-step outside a Berlin hotel and given the Nazi salute at the Reichstag. He had, however, mimicked Adolf Hitler quite passably in the witness box. It was his fellow delegates who had performed the goose-step, and then only in imitation of the East German border guards. The BBC's case collapsed after three days, when their governors and board of management ordered the case to be settled. On that occasion, Hamilton had had a safety net in that the Goldsmith Foundation had met his legal costs. With the *Guardian*, however, he would be on his own financially.

Hamilton's letter seemed to work, as the article published in the *Guardian* of 5 October 1993 focused instead on the lobbyist Ian Greer, referring only in passing to Hamilton having 'stayed at a European hotel' at the expense of 'a leading British company'. However, the paper was in fact biding its time until its source, Mohamed Fayed, was prepared to emerge from under his stone.

The *Guardian* got what it wanted within a year, when Hamilton's relationship with Fayed foundered. The seeds of Hamilton's difficulties with Fayed seem to have been sown by his failure to reply when the businessman wrote to congratulate him on his appointment in April 1992 as minister for corporate affairs at the DTI. In his letter Fayed also drew attention to his own case against the DTI in the European Court of Human Rights. On advice Hamilton did not reply, and thereby joined the ranks of those Fayed perceived as 'shitting on me from a great height'.

Fayed now began to speak out about the nature of his relationship with Hamilton. He claimed that he had been advised by Ian Greer, whom he retained as a public relations consultant, that he needed to hire an MP in the same way as you hire a London taxi. He cast his bread on the waters by contributing sums of between £500 to £5,000 to the election funds of twenty-one MPs, but his strategy depended on the handful of MPs who he hoped would become his consultants. Hamilton had been recommended by Greer as a supportive MP. Hamilton and Greer had a business relationship spawned by an attempt to protect the somewhat politically incorrect business interests of US Tobacco Inc. against proposals in 1986 to ban the sale of a chewing tobacco called Skoal Bandits through the Protection of Children (Tobacco) Bill. Hamilton knew US Tobacco, having assisted them in a controversial libel action they were bringing against BBC's consumer programme *That's Life*. Ian Greer Associates had earned £120,000 in fees from this, and Hamilton had received a cut by way of his introductory commission of £6,000.

Hamilton sympathised with Fayed who, he felt, was the victim of an unjustified campaign by Tiny Rowland over his purchase of Harrods. Fayed's claims about his background had, Hamilton believed at the time, been verified by leading city institutions. Hamilton's toadying to Fayed started before he received any benefits from him. In February 1986 the Labour MP Clare Short had tabled an early-day motion condemning Harrods' treatment of its staff. By contrast, on 10 March 1986 Hamilton applauded the agreement Harrods had reached with its staff and congratu-lated the government on its decision to allow the purchase of Harrods by AIT (Al Fayed Investment Trust) (UK) plc, which he saw as especially pleasing in view of the enormous investment being made by the owners. Time was to show that Short was nearer the mark than Hamilton.

Exactly what Hamilton received from Fayed was a matter of bitter controversy. Hamilton has always denied receiving any cash at all from Fayed, let alone in the 'brown envelopes' which were to become notorious. The hotel room at the Ritz was recorded for internal accounting purposes as having cost 14,760 francs (£1,483.46), and the extras for which Hamilton had signed were claimed by Fayed to amount to a self-indulgent 21,104.45 francs (£2,121.05). Hamilton, a tax barrister by training, liked benefits in kind: he had also spent, courtesy of Fayed, a few days in a holiday cottage at Balnagown Castle in 1989 and a few days in an apartment in Paris in 1990, and had received two Harrods hampers, each worth £185. As part of his commission from Greer he had accepted air fares to New Orleans, a selection of wrought-iron garden furniture from Peter Jones costing £959.95 and some Cornish watercolours valued at £700. In addition Fayed claimed to have given Hamilton thousands of pounds in cash and Harrods vouchers between 1987 and 1989, which Hamilton strongly denied. Another Conservative MP, Tim Smith, who rep-resented Beaconsfield, admitted that he had received between

£18,000 and £25,000 in cash from Fayed – a surprisingly imprecise figure for an accountant, and more, in fact, than Fayed said
he had given him.

Hamilton proved assiduous in Fayed's cause. He asked costly
parliamentary questions of a distinctly parochial and partisan
nature, such as whether Dr Ashraf Marwan, an enemy of Fayed
and a close friend of Colonel Gaddaffi of Libya, was an accred-
ited diplomat representing the Arab Republic of Egypt – a matter
which a telephone call to the Egyptian Embassy might have
resolved. On another occasion he asked the secretary of state for
defence what representations he had received on the effect of the
attempts of Lonrho, Tiny Rowland's company, to frustrate British
arms sales to Kenya. 'None,' a junior minister replied tersely,
perhaps wondering of what benefit this information might be to
taxpayers. Hamilton had also tabled early day motions deploring
the barrage of libellous and vicious propaganda emanating from
Tiny Rowland and urging the completion of the inquiry into the
House of Fraser by the DTI (July 1988), and noting with concern
(May 1989) the close links between Lonrho and Dr Ashraf
Marwan, and asking for an immediate investigation into Lonrho.
The latter EDM was sent in draft by Greer to Fayed before it was
tabled. Hamilton had also been a member of a delegation to the
DTI.

Precisely how much value Fayed derived from Hamilton's parliamentary work is open to question. The success of lobbying,
like that of advertising, is difficult to quantify. Hamilton, the MP
for Tatton, was at the time progressing through the ranks of the
Conservative Party, becoming a party whip in 1990 and a junior
minister in 1992. For the record, Hamilton's support for Fayed –
he was to make the point that this began well before his trip to
the Ritz – took the following form between 1985 and 1989 (the
total numbers of particular activities are given, with the numbers
of these which took place after he stayed at the Ritz in brackets):
12 (8) written questions, 3 (0) meetings with Fayed relating to
parliamentary matters, 3 (2) early day motions tabled, 3 (3) early
day motions signed, 2 (0) parliamentary delegations, 7 (7) letters

to ministers, 3 (2) meetings with other MPs to discuss Fayed's
business, 1 (1) oral parliamentary question. Whatever the efficacy
of these interventions, they would, coupled with favourable articles in the press, have been of at least some assistance.

It was after the rejection of Fayed's appeal by the European
Court of Human Rights that he prevailed upon Brian Hitchin,
editor of the *Sunday Express*, to approach John Major to report
that he would blow the gaff on Hamilton and others unless the
DTI report in which he was criticised was withdrawn or revised.
The prime minister, contacted on 29 September 1994, made it
abundantly clear that he would not be dictated to in this manner.
Hitchin's newspaper, meanwhile, continued to champion Fayed's
cause. 'Fayed is more British than most of the people you and I
will ever meet,' purred Hitchin. 'Unlike the riff-raff upon whom
we bestow British passports willy-nilly, Mr Fayed pays his way.
So let's cut out the envy and malice and give Mohamed Fayed
the thing he would treasure most: British citizenship. He has
earned it several times over.'

On 20 October 1994 the *Guardian* published an article headlined 'TORY MPS WERE PAID TO PLANT QUESTIONS SAYS HARRODS CHIEF', in
which Hamilton was named. It alleged that Hamilton and Tim
Smith had been paid in cash, at a rate of £2,000 for each of
seventeen parliamentary questions, from Ian Greer Associates'
monthly retainer. Greer and Hamilton immediately sued. They
were no doubt encouraged by the fact that, relying as it was on
Fayed's word alone, the *Guardian* would be unable to prove that
this had happened. Indeed, by the time of the trial, Fayed's
account of how Hamilton had been paid had changed three
times.

His second version was that the money to pày Smith and
Hamilton had come from two cheques given by Fayed to Greer in
May 1987, topped up by a cheque to Ian Greer Associates of
£13,333 plus VAT in February 1990. Hamilton was able to show
that the 1987 payments were for other MPs' election funds and
the £13,333 for additional work Greer had had to undertake
when the DTI report was published.

The third scenario was that Fayed had paid Hamilton directly in face-to-face meetings between the two men alone, to the tune of £20,000 in cash and £8,000 in Harrods vouchers, on eight separate occasions between June 1987 and July 1989. Hamilton had visited him at Harrods or at 60 Park Lane. Touchingly, Fayed said he felt it would have been impolite to have allowed Hamilton to leave empty-handed, so he invariably gave him cash. That account was undermined when Hamilton was able to produce a witness, Timothy O'Sullivan, who asserted that he had been present at the meeting of 20 February 1989 and had not seen Fayed giving the MP £1,000 in vouchers as Fayed had claimed. Finally, three Fayed employees appeared and said they had prepared and handed over the cash to Hamilton.

As happened in the Aitken case, the *Guardian*'s relationship with Fayed became surprisingly close in their common pursuit of their quarry. The editor, Peter Preston, met Fayed on seven occasions in 1993 and 1994. Two drafts of the proposed article were sent to Fayed for his approval – a luxury not afforded to many. As it was, Fayed's famous allegation about brown envelopes did not surface in the *Guardian* article of 20 October, first seeing the light of day on 5 December.

Hamilton no doubt believed that the *Guardian* had a very real problem with Fayed's credibility and that Fayed ultimately would not be willing to testify. Not only had he been condemned as a serial liar by the DTI inspectors, but he had made a number of extravagant claims of corruption against MPs – ironically, while doing his best to corrupt them – including the allegation that a £1 million bribe had been paid by Rowland to the DTI secretary of state at the time, Michael Howard, to order a DTI inquiry into the House of Fraser takeover – an allegation which was disbelieved by Sir Gordon Downey, the parliamentary standards commissioner. Fayed also spoke of a £500,000 bribe to a Conservative MP, whom he never named.

Hamilton probably had no choice but to sue for libel if he wished to preserve his political career. When Tim Smith was questioned about the *Guardian* allegations by the Cabinet secretary, Sir Robin Butler, he immediately confessed. He resigned on 20 October 1994 as a Northern Ireland minister and later as candidate for Beaconsfield for the next general election. Hamilton, with unfaltering confidence in his innocence, was determined to tough it out. He vehemently denied to Butler Fayed's allegations, and specifically that he had received cash from the Egyptian. Hamilton was also asked by his boss, president of the Board of Trade Michael Heseltine, the crucial question of whether or not he had had any financial relationship with Ian Greer Associates. Hamilton asserted he had not. He later claimed he had misunderstood the question, but it was straightforward enough and his answer unqualified. In reality Hamilton had received an unregistered £10,000 commission for introducing United States Tobacco and the National Nuclear Corporation to IGA. When the *Guardian* obtained evidence before the trial of Hamilton's exchange with Heseltine, they became convinced that he would lose the action. Even so, there were to be bizarre recriminations between Greer and Hamilton as to the discovery of whose untruths proved most fatal to their litigation.

Toughing it out did little good for Hamilton politically. After unwisely comparing his litigation to prime minister John Major's case against the *New Statesman* and *Scallywag*, Hamilton was unceremoniously dumped as a minister, as he was in 1997 by the voters of Tatton, who were persuaded by the anti-corruption candidate, Martin Bell of the BBC, to convert Hamilton's majority of 15,680 into a defeat by 11,077 votes.

Hamilton's case against the *Guardian* had always involved a very real risk. Early in 1995 he escaped severe censure by the Parliamentary Committee on Members' Interests. Although boycotted by Labour MPs, the committee held that it had been imprudent of Hamilton not to check whether he should declare his visit to the Ritz. It rejected Hamilton's argument that staying in the hotel at Fayed's invitation was, in the circumstances, no different in principle from staying in a sumptuous private residence. And the fact that Tim Smith had admitted receiving thousands of pounds in cash made it that much more likely that Fayed's account would be believed.

Indeed, this was very much the approach taken by Sir Gordon Downey when his report was published in July 1997. He concluded that there was 'a general obligation on members to the effect, if in doubt, register. Mr Hamilton seems to have adopted the opposite principle, and if in doubt, he gave himself the benefit of it. He fell well below the standards of conduct expected of an MP.' Sir Gordon found that a number of relevant statements by Neil Hamilton were 'in varying degrees untruthful'.

Hamilton also failed to latch on to the anti-Tory and anti-sleaze *zeitgeist*. He seems to have realised this problem, but too late. 'He accepted that he should have applied a more objective test and gave too little weight to the growing climate of suspicion, however unjustified, about MPs' interests,' wrote Sir Gordon. He now saw that 'regrettably, it is not so much the reality but the perception by suspicious third parties that matters about registration of interests'. The benefits in kind which Hamilton admitted receiving were sufficiently large and his documented services for Fayed of such a sycophantic nature that no one was going to be particularly sympathetic to his complaint.

Having taken the unwise decision to sue, Hamilton's fortunes went steadily downhill. In the belief that there was no conflict between their respective denials of Fayed's allegations about his cash payments, in the interests of economy Hamilton and Greer used the same barristers and solicitors. This understandable decision had disastrous consequences, particularly for Hamilton, when the flaws in the plaintiffs' stories were uncovered. It also had the unfortunate consequence, as events turned out, that both cases were ordered to be heard together. The decision by Mr Justice May in July 1995 that he should, in the light of the provision in Article 9 of the Bill of Rights 1689 prohibiting the courts from questioning parliamentary proceedings, stay Hamilton's proceedings, did not alert Hamilton to the omens. It was a section designed to protect the parliamentary privileges of MPs long before anyone thought of MPs suing for libel in respect of the performance of their parliamentary duties. The judge was persuaded by the *Guardian*'s lawyers that the whole basis of their defence of justification could not, by virtue of Article 9, be fairly put to the jury. The court would not be able to decide whether or not particular actions in Parliament by Hamilton had been influenced by any payment of money by Fayed. Hamilton's reaction was to lobby for the inclusion of Section 13 in the Defamation Act 1996, which enabled an MP to waive his privilege under the Bill of Rights 1689. The act came into force on 29 September 1996 and Hamilton's action was reinstated for trial at the beginning of that October.

Hamilton and Greer's lawyers were still advising them that their prospects of success were 'very good', as high as 90 per cent. Greer's company had made a claim for special damages of £10 million based on the business lost as a result of the *Guardian* piece. Hopes that a potential liability of this size would encourage the newspaper to settle proved illusory – even when it was suggested that Greer might see his way to settling at a modest £2.5 million.

Beneath the surface, however, Greer and Hamilton's cases were at the last moment being destroyed by the process of discovery of documents. There turned up in Greer's case on Thursday 26 September, days before the trial began the following Tuesday, the revelation that his records showed he had misled the House of Commons Select Committee in 1990. He had made six commission payments to Sir Michael Grylls MP, rather than the three he had disclosed. At this point Greer was advised by his counsel, Richard Ferguson QC (who had replaced Lord Williams of Mostyn QC, who was not available for the rescheduled trial date in October 1996), that his prospects of success had now declined to 'almost nil'.

The bad news was broken to the feuding plaintiffs at a conference with the barristers, Richard Ferguson QC and Victoria Sharp, and Peter Carter-Ruck and Partners who, as the day started, were acting for both men. Ferguson told Greer: 'Your entire credibility has gone. We are not going to put you in the witness box because you will be torn to shreds.' A shaken Greer later asked Sharp: 'You are making a very serious statement. What are our chances of success?' Sharp replied, 'Zero, but possibly 5 to 10 per cent.' Neil Hamilton and his wife, Christine, expressed their fury to Greer at his betrayal of their joint case by his failure to disclose this information. 'I did not realise there were skeletons in your cupboard,' Hamilton complained bitterly. It became apparent from these recriminations that an irreconcilable conflict of interest had arisen.

Lunchtime brought a yet more melancholy development – this time the uncovering of Hamilton's untruthfulness to Michael Heseltine. The Cabinet secretary's note of Hamilton's conversation with the president of the Board of Trade on 21 October 1994 had been disclosed to the *Guardian*. This stated starkly that Mr Hamilton had given Heseltine an absolute assurance that he had no financial relationship with Mr Greer and that the president had accepted this. Hamilton realised that this damaging document would put him in a dubious light before the jury. Now Hamilton's rancour towards Greer was reciprocated. The revelation of what Hamilton had said to Heseltine was, according to Greer, 'the killer blow for the trial. We could not proceed. I was horrified to think that Neil had not told me about this during two years of preparation. It would have been devastating if this had come to light during the libel trial.'

It was now necessary for each plaintiff to be found alternative, separate representation. At 3.45 that afternoon Hamilton was delivered by Andrew Stephenson of Peter Carter-Ruck and Partners to his new solicitor, Rupert Grey of Crockers. After effecting introductions, Stephenson left. Hamilton was informed that Crockers would require at least £100,000 on account to prepare for trial. Hamilton had already paid Carter-Ruck £100,000 and owed them another £100,000. He would have difficulty meeting the existing bill, let alone a third one. Clearly the case would, unless settled, have to be adjourned to enable his new lawyers to assimilate the papers. A similar melancholy procession led Ian Greer to the office of Mark Stephens at Stephens Innocent.

There was even more bad news to come later that evening. Geoffrey Robertson QC, for the *Guardian*, had taken note of some handwritten telephone messages from 1987 and 1989 written down for Mohamed Fayed by his secretaries. Fayed's Washington lawyer, Douglas Marvin, had arrived on the scene and was deputed to take statements from Fayed's secretaries which might cast some light on the cash payments allegedly made to Hamilton and Greer. This last-minute inquiry was to prove surprisingly fruitful, despite the fact that the accounts were somewhat at variance with some of Fayed's earlier versions. Iris Bond, his secretary since 1979, remembered Fayed stuffing £2,500 into envelopes. Philip Bromfield, a security guard on his staff for fourteen years, recalled Hamilton coming to collect envelopes from 60 Park Lane and Alison Bosek, thirteen years Fayed's PA but by this time a trainee solicitor with Allen and Overy, recollected putting several thousand pounds into brown envelopes on two or three occasions and Hamilton's plaintive telephone calls about money. Hamilton strenuously disputed this new evidence, and it was not then tested in court, but Sir Gordon Downey found these witnesses reliable and honest. They were later to give evidence in Hamilton's libel case against Fayed.

It was unfortunate that the assembled legal talent had not followed this paper trail earlier. By this stage Hamilton and Greer's cases were in such disarray that they did not get to read these three new witness statements until after the weekend. They had been sent late on the Friday evening to Peter Carter-Ruck and Partners in the belief that they were still representing both parties. Professional bodies had been consulted to determine who could properly act for whom. Peter Carter-Ruck now came back on to the scene to mediate on behalf of Greer and Hamilton with the *Guardian*'s lawyers. A stream of offers were made on behalf of the plaintiffs to settle. The *Guardian* was interested in settling so that it could publish the story without having to remain silent until the adjourned trial concluded – which would in all probability not be until after the 1997 election.

Unrealistically, Hamilton and Greer's solicitors initially wanted their legal costs paid and a statement read in open court withdrawing the main allegations against their clients, in return for which they would drop their claim for punitive damages. The *Guardian* sought £30,000 towards their costs – the amount of Geoffrey Robertson's brief fee. Ultimately, they accepted £15,000, but with no confidentiality agreement.

The result was complete humiliation for Greer, and particularly for Hamilton. The next day's *Guardian* was headlined 'A LIAR AND A CHEAT'. It was illustrated with a four-column picture of Hamilton. The strapline read: 'Disgraced Former Minister and Lobbyist Abandoned £10 Million Case at Last Minute'. For good measure the editorial trumpeted: 'A Pattern of Corruption and Deceit'. In vain did Hamilton protest that he had settled because he did not have enough money to pay for his new lawyers.

The *Guardian* had always been confident of their case against Hamilton, as there was more material on which to cross-examine him, and because he was a Conservative MP at a time of unprecedented unpopularity for the party.

Greer's companies, Ian Greer Associates Ltd, IGA (Europe) Ltd and IGA International Ltd, went into liquidation. Greer wrote a book about the *Guardian* case called *One Man's World – The Untold Story of the Cash for Questions Affair*. His feelings about Hamilton were evident from the way in which he described Hamilton's entreaties to him, in his capacity as an adviser to British Airways, for upgrades on flight tickets. Greer also wrote to the Tatton Conservative Association accusing Hamilton of a lack of candour about the case when he was reselected as a candidate for the 1997 election.

Hamilton found himself without a job and with a new role as a figure of fun, appearing on quiz shows such as the BBC's *Have I Got News for You*. He was, however, determined to clear his name. Following Channel 4's *Dispatches* programme 'A Question of Sleaze', broadcast on 16 January 1997, he issued a writ for libel against Mohamed Fayed. Here, he felt, was his opportunity to establish his innocence of the charges made against him by the Harrods boss, even though Fayed's credibility was already tarnished.

Hamilton's friends, spearheaded by Lord Harris of High Cross, raised £450,000 to fund the litigation. Fayed was unsuccessful in his attempts to persuade Mr Justice Popplewell that this libel action was a collateral attack on a parliamentary proceeding, namely the findings by Sir Gordon Downey.

Although in 1997 Downey had concluded that the evidence that Hamilton had received cash payments from Fayed in return for lobbying services was compelling, a committee on standards and privileges felt they had no mechanism for reaching a judgement which added to or subtracted from the commissioner's findings. In March 1999 Lord Woolf, the master of the rolls, ruled in the Court of Appeal that a libel action based on events outside the Houses of Parliament should be allowed to proceed. Such a trial would not be an attack on the parliamentary process so as to offend against the provisions of Article 9 of the Bill of Rights. Mr Justice Popplewell had felt that the findings of the MPs were delphic in the extreme. The Court of Appeal, which had no doubt that the admission of Tim Smith proved nothing whatsoever against Hamilton, appeared to accept that the law courts were better placed to determine the issue of whether or not Hamilton had been paid cash by Fayed, and indeed Hamilton viewed his libel action as the only route to clear his name of the allegations. The Court of Appeal awarded Hamilton £208,000 in legal costs following the fear expressed by his counsel, Desmond Browne QC, of a pre-trial 'war of attrition'. The House of Lords upheld the Court of Appeal's decision.

Fayed's attempts to defeat Hamilton on a technical knockout in the appeal courts prompted his adversary to ring in, calling himself simply Neil of Shropshire, when Fayed appeared on a talk radio phone-in in May 1999. Once Hamilton was unmasked, the benign shopkeeper set the tone of the ensuing conversation by greeting the former minister with the words : 'You liar, crook and bastard!'

Before the trial Hamilton was able to have a cartoon of

himself removed from Peter Brookes's second book, *Nature Notes*, a collection of caricatures, first published in *The Times*, that depicted politicians as members of the animal kingdom. He apparently didn't care for his representation as a lying toad, *Hamiltonus Corruptus*, which sported a spotted bow tie and was shown resting on a brown envelope containing £50 notes. He was even less impressed by the description of the mythical beast in the caption: 'A species once protected by the authorities, this clammy creature crawls out from under stones to seek exposure. The female is dominant.'

If Hamilton had hoped that Fayed would duck the confrontation in court when his case began in November 1999, he was to be disappointed. Not surprisingly, the five-week trial contained moments of pure farce and attracted much media coverage. The evidence given by Fayed, described by Desmond Browne, QC for Hamilton, as the Ali Baba of deceit, became increasingly erratic. Of Hamilton he said: 'He took maybe £30,000 in cash. He is a prostitute, a homosexual.' On another occasion he declared: 'Let MI5 and MI6 sue me. Let Prince Philip sue me. Then I will go through everything. They killed my son.'

Like all actions with a political flavour featuring bitterly contested evidence, it was a high-risk strategy for Hamilton; it was also likely to be expensive, as Fayed was cocooned by no fewer than eleven lawyers. And so it proved. In December the jury rejected Hamilton's action, leaving him with a £2.5 million bill for costs and facing ruin.

What did for Hamilton was the evidence of Lionel Blumenthal, tax adviser to the Mobil oil company, coupled with Hamilton's undisputed displays of greed and the fact that his fellow MP, Tim Smith, had confessed to taking cash from Fayed. Blumenthal had been so flabbergasted by Hamilton's request for a fee of £10,000 for tabling an amendment to a Finance Act proposal of concern to the oil industry, so outraged by his posturing as a man of honour in the wake of the *Guardian*'s cash-for-questions articles, that he had made it clear he would write to the prime minister if Hamilton did not resign. Fayed's legal team got wind of this letter and obtained Mobil's papers on the Friday night before the Monday the trial was due to start.

Initially Hamilton decided against appealing. However, the discovery that his barristers' dustbins had been raided by the notorious rubbish thief Benjy 'the Binman' Pell, and that the contents had been passed through intermediaries to Fayed for £10,000, changed his mind. But the master of the rolls, Lord Phillips, ruled that although Fayed had acted discreditably and must have known about the origins of the stolen documents, it would probably have made no difference if the jury had been aware of the way they had been obtained. Some indication of Lord Phillips' views could be inferred from his opening explanation that the appeal was 'about a load of rubbish'. The Court of Appeal concluded that the Mobil evidence had clearly carried considerable weight with the jury, as had the evidence of three Harrods' employees as to the handing over of cash to Hamilton. Hamilton's ruin was complete. The fact that he was not ordered to pay Fayed's costs for the appeal, a mark of the court's disapproval of Fayed's conduct, was scant consolation.

Hamilton was left facing bankruptcy proceedings and the sale of his house in Nether Alderley in Cheshire. Those who had subscribed £5,000 or more to his appeal for legal funds found themselves dealing with an application to make them pay such part of the costs as Hamilton was unable to discharge. He was declared bankrupt in May 2001.

As for Fayed, interestingly, his bad reputation actually helped him: in the court's view, the fact that he was prepared to pay for stolen garbage did little damage to his case, which was, after all, based on the proposition that he had bribed a politician to behave corruptly.

In the *Guardian* case, Hamilton had failed to appreciate the shortcomings of his admitted behaviour. In his libel action against Fayed, his problem was that it was all too easy for the jurors to conclude that Fayed was the sort of person who would bribe an MP, and that Hamilton was the sort of MP to accept a bribe.

# 19

# THE SERIOUS GAME
# OF LIBEL

### Sporting Libels

Sport has given rise to a large number of libel actions over the last decade. Some of these cases have related to the private lives of sports personalities and have resulted in significant libel awards, notably for Graeme Souness and Tessa Sanderson. Others have been brought to rescue a sports star's good name in the face of allegations which have threatened his or her career, like the case won by jockey Kieren Fallon. A number of sportsmen have, however, been unsuccessful in the law courts, including Terry Venables, Ian Botham, Allan Lamb and Sarfraz Nawaz, who would have been wiser to steer clear of litigation. On other occasions, defences of qualified privilege have been successfully raised in sporting controversies with the result that the plaintiff has lost even though he has established that what was said was incorrect.

On the face of it an interview with the Pakistan cricketer Imran Khan by Shekhar Gupta, editor of *India Today*, in June 1994, was defamatory of his English counterparts. It suggested

that a certain section of England players – notably those who
had not had an Oxbridge education or a privileged upbringing,
such as Allan Lamb and Ian Botham – were racist in their criticism of the Pakistan team, whom they had accused of tampering
with the ball to achieve reverse swing. The *India Today* article
further alleged that Botham had cheated in Test matches against
India in 1982, on one occasion using his thumbnail to pick the
seam of the ball, and on another throwing the ball to wicketkeeper Bob Taylor to remove the lacquer from it.

Botham was England's most successful Test all-rounder, with
5,200 runs and 383 wickets as opposed to Imran's 3,807 and 362,
and had almost single-handedly won the Ashes for England in
1981. 'I have never lifted a seam, not even in the nets. I have
never, so far as I am aware, broken the rules against tampering.
I have never felt it necessary,' he said. Lamb, a batsman who had
left South Africa to play for England, was likewise incensed by
the allegation of racism. Botham and Lamb decided to sue. Both
players had already enjoyed some success in the libel courts.
Botham had won substantial damages in 1989 against the *Star*
for a suggestion that he had been involved in a pub brawl; Lamb
had seen off the Pakistan fast bowler Sarfraz Nawaz, at one time
a playing colleague of his at Northamptonshire, in 1993. After
four days in the High Court Sarfraz had dropped his libel action
against Lamb, who had accused him in a piece in the *Mirror* of
illegal gouging of the ball during the 1992 Test series against
Pakistan in order to make the ball swing late and unexpectedly.
Lamb had acknowledged that Sarfraz played within the laws of
cricket and did not cheat, but Sarfraz had nonetheless been
ordered to pay Lamb's legal costs. These totalled £75,000.

The England players were confident of victory. Apart from
anything else, Botham bit his fingernails, which would consequently have been of little use in interfering with the ball. And
he had enlisted Bob Taylor, a veteran of fifty-seven Test matches,
as a witness – along with his gloves, which the wicketkeeper had
retrieved from the museum at Lord's as proof that no trickery had
taken place. The case came on for trial in July 1996 before Mr

Justice French. The general view that Botham and Lamb could not lose was reinforced when Imran Khan accepted Botham's assertion that he had never tampered with a cricket ball. Imran was adamant that he had not called Botham a cheat, and that his words had been taken out of context by *India Today*. He said in slightly incredulous terms, after listening to the evidence of Ian Botham and former England captain David Gower, 'I respect them both. And if they say they were squeezing the ball, fine, they were squeezing the ball.' He also conceded that the reason why Botham had thrown the ball hard to Taylor was to dry the sweat from – it had been kept in plastic – rather than to scuff it. 'I don't know why he didn't use his trousers, but I accept it,' he added, somewhat acidly.

All that Imran seemed to have going for him was that he was the son-in-law of one of the most determined libel litigants of all time, Sir James Goldsmith. It was a factor not to be underestimated: Imran was able to manoeuvre the case away from the unwinnable issue of whether Botham and Lamb were cheats to the safer ground of whether *India Today* had misreported him. The gentlemanly way in which he accepted Botham's explanation and apologised for doubting his actions stood him in good stead and enabled his counsel, George Carman QC, to undermine Botham's credibility and motives in bringing the action.

Evidently the jury felt that this was a case which need never have been brought. The libel court was no place for Test players, or for the emotions of the cricket pitch. Two years previously Imran had been prepared to write a letter to *The Times* clearing the name of both men. He would not, however, apologise for calling them racist, because he was adamant that he had not done so. He knew how friendly Botham was with the West Indian cricketers Viv Richards and Joel Garner, and he had himself spent time with Lamb in Pakistan. 'You know a racist. I know they are not racist, so I wouldn't make a statement like that. If they were, I would say so.' Botham had dismissed this statement as a smokescreen not made in good faith and said it was not the apology he had asked for.

Imran's case went well and he presented it with dignity; Botham's had its problems. He was accused by Carman of having an obsessive attitude towards the Pakistan team. His famous description of Pakistan as a place to which you'd like to send your mother-in-law may have been made in jest, but he did give the impression that he harboured ill feeling against the Pakistan cricketers. After England's defeat by Pakistan in the World Cup final of 1992 he had smashed his bat, gone on a drinking spree and declared that he would never play against them again. He had said he wanted revenge, but claimed in court that that was only in a cricketing sense. He evidently did not care for Imran's review of his autobiography, *Don't Tell Kath*, in which the Pakistani had wished Kathy Botham all the luck for the remainder of her marriage. 'I thought it was an extremely arrogant remark and I would inform Imran that my wife and I have a very successful marriage, thank you.'

Carman relished burrowing into Botham's earlier libel actions. 'Are you a truthful man?' he asked.

'I think so, so often as you can be. We are not all saints. I might have broken a window at school or something,' Botham replied guardedly. He had earlier sued the *Mail on Sunday* for allegations that he had smoked marijuana with two girls and offered to have sex with them during the England tour of New Zealand in 1984. Botham had indignantly denied these charges at a press conference, saying that he had never smoked marijuana. 'That was a lie, wasn't it?' Carman probed. 'No, as I had to take legal advice. I was confronted by journalists and when you do that you tend to freeze – it was a natural reaction.'

'It was a lie, wasn't it?'

'Yes, sir.'

There was not much else Botham could say, because he had settled that libel action by writing an article headlined: 'BOTHAM: I DID SMOKE POT'. His legal costs had been paid by the newspaper in return for this piece, but he had been suspended from professional cricket for two months. His next tour, to the West Indies, had produced a crop of wickets and one more libel writ, this time against the *News of the World* over allegations that he had enjoyed sex and cocaine with Miss Barbados. His counsel, Charles Gray QC, complained that this was all muck-raking, but it was damaging muck nonetheless.

The jury might have found Lamb's evidence more compelling. It was, however, suggested to him that he had a grievance against Pakistan as a result of having been fined £6,000 by the Test and County Cricket Board (reduced on appeal to £2,500) and £650 by his county for a *Mirror* article in 1992 exposing what he considered to be an official cover-up of ball-tampering by the Pakistan team. This controversy had hastened the end of his test career. Lamb said he had been upset at the time, 'but all that's blown over, and it doesn't bother me now'.

A large number of distinguished cricketers were called to give evidence on the practice of picking the seam of the cricket ball, and whether a breach of law 42 of the rules of cricket constituted cheating. On balance, it was an argument that Imran won. Atherton, then the England captain and himself the subject of some controversy in 1994, when he had been shown on television using dirt in his trouser pocket to dry the ball, testified that raising the seam was against the laws of the game, but he was pretty relaxed about it and players tacitly accepted it. In a book he had written in 1995, he had said that cricketers had always tried to alter the condition of the ball during matches in order to change its flight through the air or its bounce. Geoffrey Boycott's evidence also helped Imran. The former England opening batsman did not regard ball-tampering as a hanging matter. It was like speeding on a motorway, not like bashing old ladies on the head – an analogy he later repeated, before his own conviction in a French court of beating up his girlfriend. 'It's definitely technically a breach of the rules, but cheating – no, it's too emotive a word.' Boycott agreed with Imran and Atherton that the laws on ball-tampering should be reviewed, but told the court that the International Cricket Conference took a long time to do anything. 'It's slower than a tortoise.' However, his evidence degenerated when he was asked about the claim of his former

Yorkshire colleague Brian Close that ball-tampering was not common and he launched into a diatribe against Close. 'I said Yorkshire would be no good until he left the club. He left last year and they are now doing well.' He was shut up by Mr Justice French, and sent off to commentate on the Test match.

David Lloyd, a former England batsman and later the England coach, described the controversy as a mountain being made of a molehill. 'We have all been there and done it and ticked it off.' He did not agree with ball-tampering, and did not accept that it was rife. Derek Pringle, a former England bowler, testified that picking at the ball with a fingernail was fair play, although the use of bottle tops was beyond the pale. This was a reference to Imran's admission in 1994 that he had himself done just that in 1981. Imran's stated aim had been to bring the issue of ball-tampering out into the open. His argument was that it was not illegal, but that the action he took with the bottle top definitely was. He had, he said, never called anyone a cheat other than himself on that occasion in 1981. Pringle added to the confusion by describing a variant of ball-tampering, the application of lip salve to the ball. This was a clear breach of the laws, but an acceptable breach. Boycott, puzzlingly, claimed that Pringle had got away with ball-tampering because 'he's white, he's Essex and he's not that good'.

The bemused jury heard more evidence from Don Oslear, an umpire, that ball-tampering was not an accepted practice. He said that he carried a set of circular metal hoops to measure the shape of the ball. David Gower asserted that he had never seen Botham tamper with the ball. He explained that in a video recording in which Botham appeared to be picking at the seam in the 1982 Pakistan series he was in fact repairing the ball. Gower had seen ball-tampering on a few occasions, but it was not habitual. Bob Taylor denied that there had been any attempt to get the lacquer off the ball during the Test match against India in 1982. John Emburey, the England bowler who had played alongside Botham, said he would have noticed if the seam had been lifted, and that pushing a misshapen ball back into its original form, as Botham was doing in the video clip, was not against the laws.

But in the end all this heavyweight cricketing evidence did not count for much. The jury seems to have accepted that Imran had been misquoted by *India Today*. He had neither accused Lamb or Botham of racism or cheating nor cast aspersions on their class or upbringing, he asserted.

I have never at any stage in my life believed in the class system. I don't look at people and decide what class they belong to. I believe in an egalitarian society. We are Pathans, a tribal group, we have always been egalitarian. I have never called any cricketer a cheat simply because the law is very straightforward. The umpire is the sole author- ity to decide what is fair and unfair play. Raising the seam is against law 42.5, but as a cricketer, and knowing that it has gone on over the years, I wouldn't regard it as cheating.

He had nothing to apologise for; he had written what Carman described as perfectly decent, kind letters to Botham and Lamb to which they had not bothered to reply. In his closing address to the jury, the QC made the point that the actions were ill consid- ered, ill founded and based on the false proposition that every contravention of the laws of cricket constituted cheating. There was, he argued, overwhelming evidence that technical breaches of the rules were part and parcel of the game. The lifting of the seam had gone on since time immemorial.

Given the choice between Botham and Lamb's contentions – that this had been an offensive personal attack supported by plain old-fashioned smears, and that they had never been offered a proper public apology – and Imran's argument – that his words had been taken out of context, that he had been responding to nasty tabloid attacks and that the knives had been out for him despite his attempts to resolve the case at an early stage – the jury preferred the case made by Imran Khan. After a thirteen-day hearing and a retirement of five hours they found in his favour,

and Botham and Lamb were left facing legal costs of £400,000.
It was the 1981 Headingley Test in reverse.

Botham and Lamb appealed against the verdict, but in May
1999 decided to discontinue the litigation.

The case was followed by a number of arguments about the
legal costs. Although Allan Lamb resolved his differences with
his solicitors, Ian Botham was invloved in a dispute over the
amount of those costs and the issue of whether he or his promotional company was liable to pay them. Imran Khan, too, was
reported to be in dispute with his solicitors about his legal costs.

Later in 1996, the former England captain Mike Gatting
received damages for false suggestions in Ivo Tennant's biography of Imran Khan, published by Gollancz, that he was an
uneducated Englishman, racially prejudiced and had unjustifiably accused the Pakistani umpire Shakhoor Rana of cheating.
Imran was not involved in the action, and wrote to Gatting to
make it clear that he held him 'in respect as a sportsman'.

Very much more successful were the cricketing libel actions
brought by Phillip DeFreitas and Devon Malcolm. Astonishingly,
not to say offensively, under the heading 'IS IT IN THE BLOOD?',
*Wisden Cricket Monthly* had published an article which suggested
that Asian or black players brought up in England could never
play for their country with the same pride as white English players. Some people thought this was simply a reflection of the
'Norman Tebbit' test: whether immigrants to the UK supported the
English national side or the teams of their country of origin. But
Lord Tebbit hastened to condemn the article, and in October 1995
DeFreitas recovered substantial damages, believed to be in excess
of £50,000, a large part of which he planned to donate to the
burns unit of Birmingham Hospital, where his daughter had been
treated. Devon Malcolm appears to have recovered £25,000, and
used some of the money to set up the Devon Malcolm Cricket
Centre for Young People in Sheffield. The magazine accepted that
it had been guilty of misjudgement. It is noticeable that cricket is
a game better understood by Her Majesty's judges than other
sports, and on this occasion Malcolm was congratulated by Mr

Justice Morland on his heroic bowling feats against the South Africans (9 for 57) as he left the court.

Football libels have tended to be a little murkier. In 1982 Billy Bremner, formerly of Leeds and Scotland, was awarded the then enormous sum of £100,000 against the *People* for allegations that he had offered bribes to other footballers to fix the results of matches – an accusation now widely believed to have been true. Bremner was reputed to have said to the former Wolves player Danny Hegan, 'Give us a penalty and I'll give you a grand.' Bremner was certainly an abrasive character and had an appalling disciplinary record. He had once shouted at an opponent with an unfortunately pock-marked complexion, 'Go and get your face filled in with Polyfilla.'

Terry Venables, the former England coach and Tottenham Hotspur manager, has spent much of his off-field time in the law courts. His book *Venables: The Autobiography* resulted in payments of £100,000 libel damages to Tony Berry, the vice-chairman of Tottenham, in October 1995 for false allegations about stolen documents. Venables had to pay costs estimated at £350,000. He found himself out of pocket to the tune of another £100,001 in damages in October 1996 to Alan Sugar, the Tottenham chairman, who complained of fifteen libels in the book, which was then pulped. Sugar was himself served with a libel writ from Venables' lawyers as he left the court, this time concerning comments he had made in a Channel 4 *Dispatches* programme nearly three years previously. He was held liable to pay the costs incurred by Venables since the £100,001 had been paid into court in March 1996. A number of Venables' actions await hearing, including one against the *Mirror*, two against the BBC for *Panorama* programmes about the £1 million he raised to buy shares in Tottenham and another against a Radio 1 disc jockey, Simon Mayo, for witty but unflattering suggestions for a design for Venables sportswear, coupled with a comparison, again unflattering, of Venables' footballing and accounting skills. Additionally Venables had an order made against him in 1998 at the instance of the DTI which banned him from acting as a director of a company for seven years under the Company Directors Disqualification Act 1986.

The football manager Graeme Souness was awarded £750,000 in July 1995 for false allegations in the *People* that he had behaved like a rat in his treatment of his first wife, Danielle, and had failed to make proper provision for her after their divorce. The jury disregarded Mr Justice Morland's warning that the damages should be fair and reasonable, and could range from the value of a family saloon to a Rolls–Royce or, if appropriate, a house. They opted for a luxury house, but by agreement the damages were reduced to a Rolls–Royce – £100,000. As £250,000 of the damages had by that stage already been paid out to Souness, he had to write out a cheque for £150,000. During the trial George Carman QC sought unsuccessfully to bring in claims of 'bungs' allegedly paid to Souness while he was at Liverpool and Glasgow Rangers. Mr Justice Morland ruled out the evidence as being prejudicial and not relevant to the issue of how Souness treated his wife. Danielle did her own cause little good by selling her story to the *People* for £20,000. She claimed that she had told Souness about this and that he had replied: 'I hope you do it, because I'll sue them and make even more money.' She had not actually used the words 'dirty rat', but admitted that they reflected her views of her ex-husband at the time.

The evidence ranged over the sorry story of the Souness marriage. Graeme was criticised for the way he sought to exercise control over his family and for trying to evict Danielle from his £1 million Surrey farmhouse. He retorted that 'a Bengal tiger' couldn't control his former wife. She, meanwhile, was accused of spiriting £533,693 out of their joint bank account in Majorca. But clearly the jurors' hearts failed to bleed as they heard how Danielle had had to sell her jewellery to make ends meet – despite, it was claimed, having received a cash sum of £560,000 plus land valued at £500,000 in Majorca – and how Graeme had tried to prevent her from living with anyone else in the family home through the terms of her tenancy agreement. Graeme's counsel, Lord Williams of Mostyn QC, memorably attacked the

*People* for having shown 'all the courage of a dead chicken and less decency than an elderly skunk' in failing to check the story with the plaintiff, and in not giving evidence about its story. Newspapers who do not call any journalist as a witness tend to fare badly, and this case proved no exception.

The paper would have done no better even if it had been permitted to question Souness about 'bungs': the *Mail on Sunday* which had accused him in 1994 of profiting by £130,000 in this way while at Rangers and Liverpool had to pay him £100,000 libel damages in 1996.

Another soccer case was one brought by Bruce Grobbelaar, the Liverpool goalkeeper, who netted £85,000 after a thirteen-day trial costing £800,000 after the *Sun* accused him of taking bribes to let in goals. He was subsequently acquitted of criminal conspiracy, and although he succesfully sued the newspaper for libel, he experienced some uncomfortable moments during the trial. The jury was shown a secretly filmed video, on which he could be seen discussing money and sex. Grobbelaar's explanation was that he had simply been stringing along the man who was offering him money. The jury evidently accepted this, and registered their dislike of tabloid tactics and the failure of the *Sun* to call their informant, Grobbelaar's former partner, as a witness.

But Grobbelaar's triumph turned out to be short-lived. In January 2001, in an unprecedented decision, the Court of Appeal overturned the criminal conspiracy verdict. Analysing what they praised as a lengthy and penetrating cross-examination by George Carman QC, who had died shortly before the result of the appeal was announced, the court concluded that the jury had been skilfully deflected from the path of logic. Grobbelaar's explanations for such questions as his acceptance of a £40,000 payment in relation to Liverpool's 3–0 defeat by Newcastle, the film of him taking £2,000 from an *agent provocateur* and his taped account of how he lost £125,000 by inadvertently diving the wrong way and saving a goal he was being paid to let in were described by Lord Justice Simon Brown as 'beggaring belief at every turn'. Too many improbabilities were piled one upon another to begin to be credible. Although the Court of Appeal would 'inevitably be reluctant to find the jury's verdict perverse, and would be anxious not to usurp their functions', Grobbelaar's story was 'incredible, and an affront to justice'. Lord Justice Thorpe considered that Grobbelaar's words on tape 'proved corruption to the hilt'.

Grobbelaar was left with a legal bill estimated at £1.2 million. The *Sun*, meanwhile, recovered only half its legal costs in the Court of Appeal because it had tried to establish a Reynolds-type defence of qualified privilege. Its conduct was savaged in unequivocal terms by the judges, but the newspaper was beyond caring. Although it devoted fifteen pages of triumphalism to the outcome of the case, nowhere did it find space to cover the court's condemnation of its emotive language; the lamentable involvement of Grobbelaar's family; the prejudgement of guilt to its uttermost limits; investigative work described by the court as amateurish, to say the least; its failure to verify the allegations of match-fixing against recordings of the matches in question or the ambush of Grobbelaar at Gatwick Airport. Indeed, the case gives a good guide as to the circumstances in which the defence of qualified privilege as laid down in the Reynolds case is likely to fail, not to mention as to how the press should *not* behave if it seeks to establish such a defence. Factors which counted against the *Sun* were the parading of allegations as fact, its mocking and abusive tone, its carelessness with the truth, the promotion of self-interest, and its failure to seek proper comment from Grobbelaar on the allegations against him.

As the Souness case shows, attacking the private lives of sports personalities can be a costly exercise for the tabloid press. Tessa Sanderson, the former Olympic javelin champion, recovered £30,000 from the *Sunday Mirror* and the *People* in March 1991, a sum which comfortably exceeded the £20,000 they had paid into court. They had alleged that Sanderson had enticed Derrick Evans, TV's 'Mr Motivator', away from his nine-year marriage to his wife Jewel. The judge, Mr Justice Michael Davies, told the jury this was not a football pools case. They had to decide whether they should award Ms Sanderson nominal damages for a Chinese meal or enough to pay for a holiday in Jamaica. As they chose to give her £30,000, the jurors obviously did not find the direction particularly helpful.

In May 1995 Channel 4 and the *New Statesman* had to pay Chris Brasher and John Disley, the organisers of the London Marathon, and the London Marathon Company, a sports equipment firm, £380,000 damages for allegations of fraud and dishonesty made in the programme *Keep on Running*. The case ran for four years and it is believed that the costs ran to £720,000. It ended with an apology broadcast on Channel 4 which exonerated Brasher and Disley of any suggestion that they had used the marathon to enrich themselves. Brasher said that the allegations had been so outrageously untrue and hurtful that they had no choice but to seek retribution through the courts. Duncan Campbell, who had presented the programme and had himself run in the event three times, ungraciously commented that the insurers had dictated the settlement. Wisely, however, he did not again claim that the allegations were true.

Racing has produced its share of libels, particularly when jockeys and trainers have been accused of trying too hard to win or of not trying to win at all. In 1955 Lester Piggott recovered £250 from the *Mirror* for allegations that he had used unsporting tactics to win the Edward VII Stakes at Ascot. As he was, despite this distinctly adult behaviour, treated in law as an infant because he was not yet twenty-one, a judge had to approve the award of damages. In 1963 champion jockey Scobie Breasley was awarded £250 damages after the *Sunday People* claimed that he had not been trying in the Byfleet Stakes. He argued that it was simply a case of being beaten on an odds-on favourite. He proved not to be a good gambler, however, as he had turned down a settlement offer of £500. By the early 1980s when the same allegation was made against Michael Dickinson, then a jockey, the going rate for such libels had increased to £7,500.

More recently, in 1998 the jockey Kieren Fallon was awarded £70,000 after an eighteen-day case for the suggestion that he had

held back the favourite, Top Cees, in the Swaffham Handicap at
Newmarket in April 1995. Top Cees had gone on to win the
Chester Cup at 8–1 three weeks later, beating two of the horses
who had finished in front of it at Newmarket. The horse's trainers, Lynda Ramsden and her husband Jack, were awarded
£75,000 and £50,000 respectively, she unanimously and he by a
majority of 10–2. Channel 4 commentators, including the tipster
John McCririck, had expressed outrage at the result of the
Swaffham Handicap. The cause had been enthusiastically taken
up by the *Sporting Life* in its editorial 'Contempt for the Punter',
which fulminated about 'a seedy and deeply unpopular victory
with the damning patter of perhaps three sets of hands clap-
ping – all hands presumably attached to relations by blood or
marriage to Jack and Lynda Ramsden'. This accompanied a front-
page report headed: 'PUNTERS FUME OVER FALLON'. The Ramsdens were
accused of putting two fingers up at the Jockey Club and exploiting a system that rolled over and let them tickle its tummy like
some soppy puppy.

The Ramsdens had in their time attracted some controversy.
When finishing third at Edinburgh, Top Cees had been the subject of a stewards' inquiry, which had concluded that there was
no suggestion that the horse had not been ridden to achieve the
best placing. There had been some suspicion about the Swaffham
Handicap in the form of a local stewards' inquiry and a Jockey
Club probe. A dope test had proved negative. The jockey's explanation, that he simply could not find a way through and that he
had not held the horse back, had been accepted by the Jockey
Club disciplinary committee. A letter from Nigel McFarlane, the
secretary, told Fallon that they had reviewed the running of the
race but had decided not to instruct the committee to hold an
inquiry. There was nevertheless a mild rap on the knuckles:
'However, you should not assume from this decision that the
stewards were satisfied with your riding.' Fallon later commented: 'I wasn't satisfied with my riding, either. I went for the
wrong gap. The Jockey Club have every right to say that.'

Once the jockey had been acquitted of the serious offence of

holding back the horse, it was rash of the *Sporting Life* to level
the grave charge of cheating and manipulating the odds against
Fallon and the Ramsdens. Fallon had been the Ramsdens'
retained rider until he was engaged by Henry Cecil in 1997, and
had been champion jockey, riding 196 winners and taking two
classics. It is true that he did not have the best of disciplinary
records. However, his brushes with the racing authorities arose
not from holding back, but out of an overenthusiastic use of the
whip – a common habit with other libel litigants in rather less
sporting circumstances.

The Ramsdens and Fallon had had little choice but to sue:
their comfortable livelihoods were at stake. Mrs Ramsden had
held a training licence since 1987. In 1995 she had trained fifty-
six winners and in 1997 the Ramsdens' horses had earned prize
money totalling £440,998. Jack Ramsden admitted having made
£100,000 in his best year from gambling: their swimming pool
was known as the Arbory Street pool in honour of Ramsden's
£2,000 bet at 14–1 on the horse of that name. However, he had
not bet on Top Cees in the Chester Cup, choosing instead to
place his money on the second-placed horse. The alleged motive
for his conduct was thus fatally undermined.

The *Sporting Life*'s case seemed to rest on the evidence of
Derek Thompson, a racing presenter with Channel 4 who also ran
a telephone tips line. He claimed that a few hours after the
Swaffham Handicap Fallon had admitted to him, in a two-
minute conversation in the Old Plough near Newmarket, that he
had been told by Jack Ramsden to stop the horse. But Thompson
was a reluctant witness whom the *Sporting Life* had to subpoena. Under the rules, the newspaper had to serve a notice
giving the gist of what they believed he was going to say. As he
had not co-operated with the *Sporting Life*, this entailed a degree
of guesswork. When Thompson's evidence differed from what
was in the gist notice, the judge, Mr Justice Morland, warned the
jury to treat it with caution. Thompson's claim was indignantly
denied by the Ramsdens and Fallon. He said he had mentioned
the conversation in what he described as a 'corner-of-the-mouth

confession' at a Channel 4 production meeting. Thompson had interviewed Fallon the next day, but had not asked him about the race. Fallon said with some force that he would not have discussed his racing arrangements in this casual way with a man he knew only as a TV presenter. Thompson was committed to revealing his conversation with Fallon but he did so with no enthusiasm. And the jury was not going to find the very serious allegations proved on the say-so of a man who was alleged not only to have invited *Hello!* magazine to his wedding but to have charged his guests for their drinks at the reception as well.

Once the judge had, not unexpectedly, ruled that the *Sporting Life* could not establish that its report was covered by qualified privilege on the basis that the paper had a duty to publish criticism because of public concern about the alleged activities of the Ramsdens and Fallon and the pusillanimity of the Jockey Club, the only defence could be that the article was true. This defence might have had a better prospect of success if the case had been heard after rather than before the Court of Appeal ruling on the Reynolds case. However, it would probably have failed anyway, as the paper would not have been able to establish that it had dealt with the allegations reasonably. Alastair Down, the associate editor of the *Sporting Life*, said that he was fully aware of the gravity of the accusations the paper was making. But he felt that the racing public had had their noses rubbed in it and that it was the *Sporting Life*'s job to look after the interests of punters. The horse was not 'off' (not trying to win). He did, however, agree he had been wrong to say that the Chester Racecourse switchboard had been jammed with calls complaining about the result of the Chester Cup. He had been writing for effect, and was prone to a vivid turn of phrase (he had once written about a horse running in the Cesarewitch 'with all the success of a veal butcher at a vegan food festival').

Faced with the vigorous denials of the Ramsdens and Fallon's evidence that there had been no gaps for his horse to take to get to the front in the Swaffham Handicap, and that when eventually they had appeared the horse would not quicken, the *Sporting Life* was bound to lose. As for Top Cees, the horse went on to win the Cesarewitch in 1999.

Not all sporting libels involve such high-profile names. In April 1994 John Buckingham, an amateur golfer, lost the action he brought against two players, Graham Rusk and Reginald Dove, who reported him for allegedly moving a ball with his foot and putting a lost ball back by dropping it down his trouser leg at successive holes during a tournament at the Sherwood Forest Gold Club in 1990. The allegations were, not surprisingly, indignantly disputed by Buckingham, who said he had found the ball quite close to his golf trolley. The jury forewoman made it clear that the jury did not believe that Buckingham had cheated. But his accusers had not acted maliciously, and their complaint to the committee was covered by the defence of qualified privilege.

There was a similar outcome to a four-day libel case heard in Hull County Court in August 1995, when Bruce Hibbard, a retired IBM executive, complained that there had been a campaign to oust him from the Driffield Bowls Club. A letter had been sent to the league chairman by the club secretary and eight committee members accusing him of bias in his role as league secretary and of harassing an elderly lady member by using the word 'bloody' when she breached match etiquette by taking drinks on to the green during a game. Hibbard told the jury, 'Once one plays bowls, one is hooked,' but serious as these matters undoubtedly were, they did not merit a libel action and the jury decided that the letter was covered by qualified privilege.

In July 1998 the sprinter Linford Christie OBE recovered £40,000 from the printers and distributors of *Spiked* magazine for a piece written by retired armed robber John McVicar entitled 'How did Linford Christie get so good?', which suggested that the athlete was a cheat who used performance-enhancing drugs. The article was highly defamatory and found to be untrue. *Spiked*, which belonged to the *Scallywag* school of journalism, had by then gone out of business, and Christie found himself involved in a fourteen-day trial conducted by McVicar in person.

Although Christie was exonerated, he had to bear a significant portion of the £150,000 costs, having turned down an offer of £2,500 from one of the distributors, Johnsons News Ltd of Bath, who, unlike their co-defendants, refused to increase their settlement terms. Christie was a wealthy man and needed to clear his name, but the case underlined the financial perils of proceeding against impecunious defendants. McVicar proposes to ask the European Court of Human Rights to condemn the unavailability of legal aid to defendants in libel actions and the burden of proof placed upon them.

The case is perhaps best remembered for Mr Justice Popplewell's question: 'What is Linford Christie's lunchbox?'

'They are making a reference to my genitalia, your honour.'

Outside the courtroom, Christie was less successful in defending his stance against drugs: in August 2000, the International Amateur Athletics Federation upheld a two-year ban on him following a positive test for Nandrolone at an indoor athletics meeting in Dortmund in February 1999.

In October 1998 Penny Little of the League Against Cruel Sports was awarded £1,500 damages against Janet George, a press officer for the British Field Sports Society, for allegations made on a live phone-in about her behaviour at a Vale of Aylesbury hunt. The BBC successfully raised a defence of innocent dissemination under Section 1, of the Defamation Act 1996. Fox-hunters have in recent times had mixed results in their libel actions. In December 1994 Howard Jones, the master of the Tredegar Farmers Hunt, sued one of his former huntsmen, Clifford Pellow, who claimed at a House of Commons press conference organised by the League against Cruel Sports that foxes were being put in bags before being released to the hounds. Jones lost the action at Cardiff Crown Court.

## Libel in the World of Make Believe

Fiction, as a product of imagination, the creation of something not real, ought not to give rise to libel. However, since the case of Hulton v. Jones in 1910, it has been clearly established that an action for libel can be brought if reasonable people might conclude that defamatory words refer to a real-life plaintiff. Such actions tend to have a touch of the absurd about them – does anyone actually think the worse of a friend or acquaintance as a result of what they read about a character with similarities to their friend? There was a time in the 1970s and 1980s when it was difficult to read a novel set in London's Holland Park which did not feature a character bearing a striking resemblance to Lady Antonia Fraser, but, being a writer herself, she never bothered to sue.

Such cases can be costly and are difficult to defend once it is established that the words in question are defamatory, and once witnesses have been produced to say that they understood them to refer to the plaintiff. It is hard to rebut such evidence, and the defendant cannot, because the reference is fictitious, claim that what has been written is true or fair comment without laying him- or herself open to the charge that the words were indeed aimed at the plaintiff. Under English law, the plaintiff has to prove only that a reasonable reader has understood a passage to refer to him or her. He does not have to produce witnesses who believed that the defamatory references were in fact true of him. Actions for libel based on fiction therefore proceed on a somewhat artificial basis.

The absurdities of such litigation were illustrated by the facts of the test case, Hulton v. Jones, an action brought by a Welsh barrister called Artemus Jones, who evidently suffered no damage as a result of the libel since he later became a County Court judge and was knighted. Jones complained about a satirical sketch in the *Sunday Chronicle* in which a fictional Peckham churchwarden called Artemus Jones was attending Dieppe Motor Week.

'Whist! There is Artemus Jones with a woman who is not his wife, who must be, you know – the other thing!', whispers a fair neighbour of mine excitedly into her bosom friend's ear.

'Really, is it not surprising how certain of our fellow

countrymen behave when they come abroad? Who would suppose, by his goings on, that he was churchwarden at Peckham?'

Although neither a churchwarden nor a resident of Peckham, the Welsh barrister sued for this humorous Edwardian sketch of infidelity. After the case had gone to the House of Lords, his verdict of £1,750 libel damages was upheld. There was a faint suspicion that the use of his unusual name was not entirely coincidental. Jones had been a sub-editor on the *Sunday Chronicle* seven years earlier, and there was something rather pointed about the apology published in the newspaper: 'It seems hardly necessary for us to state that the imaginary Mr Artemus Jones referred to was not Mr Thomas Artemus Jones, barrister, but, as he has complained to us, we gladly publish this paragraph in order to remove any possible misunderstanding and to satisfy Mr Thomas Artemus Jones that we had no intention whatsoever of referring to him.' It was a notice that his counsel was to describe as 'a mere sarcastic postscript to the original libel.'

It is easier to sympathise with a plaintiff where there is a suspicion that a work of fiction may have been deliberately used as a means of denigrating him or her. There was a suggestion of that with Artemus Jones; more recently, such allegations surfaced in a claim brought by the investigative journalist Duncan Campbell who in 1990 recovered libel damages of £50,000 plus £50,000 costs and a broadcast apology for a drama shown by the BBC called *Here is the News*. This featured a journalist called David Dunhill who, like Campbell, worked on newspaper and television stories about secret government defence plans. Like Campbell, Dunhill had had a television programme banned and his office and home raided by the Special Branch. The character even appeared to frequent the same two north London supermarkets where Campbell did his shopping. It seemed that the BBC were well aware of the libel risk the drama posed, and knew where it was sailing close to the wind. For example, the sex of the fictional prime minister – who knew that explosives had been planted on unarmed terrorists to provide an excuse for them to be shot outside Chelsea Barracks, an incident featuring some purported parallels with the real-life shooting in Gibraltar of three suspected IRA terrorists – had been changed from female to male to avoid incurring the wrath of Mrs Thatcher. On the other hand, they were able safely to recast Sir Maurice Oldfield, security co-ordinator in Northern Ireland, as Sir Michael Newfield, and to give their character AIDS and a predilection for buggering boys at King's House Hostel – a thinly disguised fictionalisation of the Kincora Home, which had been the focus of child abuse allegations. Since Sir Maurice Oldfield was dead, he could be libelled with impunity.

Having established similarities between Dunhill and Campbell, the film depicted its character in a way which was highly defamatory. He was shown not only as a journalist who let down his sources, but as a compulsive shoplifter, transvestite fetishist and repressed homosexual whose only company was a cat and a domineering mother, and who was given to wearing black silk underwear. Understandably, Campbell made the point that some, though of course not all, of the similarities to himself were more than coincidence, and that viewers would not know where the fiction ended and fact began. The result was one of the highest awards ever for a claim in respect of fiction.

This was not, however, a modern phenomenon. In 1934 Princess Irena Alexandrovna Youssoupoff recovered what was the enormous sum in those days of £25,000 against MGM for their film *Rasputin the Mad Monk*, which depicted a Princess Natasha Chegodieff being seduced by Rasputin. From the context of the film it was evident that Princess Natasha's husband, the character Prince Paul, was intended to represent Princess Irena's husband, Prince Felix Youssoupoff, the man who killed Rasputin in December 1916. It was a situation in which the factual background had been embroidered with fictional detail, and one in which a filmgoer acquainted with the well-known manner of Rasputin's death would readily make the association between Youssoupoff and Chegodieff, and might well conclude that the seduction of Chegodieff's wife was a true story.

Sometimes it is difficult to escape the conclusion that a plaintiff sees in an unwise choice of name for a fictional character the opportunity to benefit from something of a windfall. This was certainly the case when a Princess Chegodieff, observing the good fortune of Princess Youssoupoff, decided to sue MGM herself, even though it was clear that Princess Natasha Chegodieff was a fictional character. Fact and fiction have become increasingly blurred with the growth of 'faction' and 'docudrama' films, and as fictitious characters meet real people and participate in actual events. In extreme cases, such as Youssoupoff, the plaintiff will argue with some force that the work of fiction is little different from a libellous mis-statement of the facts. In others, it might not be quite so easy to decide where fact ends and fiction begins.

Libel in fiction can arise in a number of different ways. Some novels are thinly veiled autobiography, making identification a relatively simple matter for those acquainted with the author's life. In *Cider with Rosie*, Laurie Lee drew heavily on the events of his childhood and described how he and his friends would climb a hill to look down on a factory. 'There was a fire at the piano works almost every year. It seemed like a way of balancing the books. When we got to the fire, we found it a particularly good one.' In fact the local piano factory had suffered only one fire, fifteen years previously, and understandably its proprietors felt compelled to take action to establish their innocence of any such behaviour. They recovered £5,000 in damages and Lee's factory rapidly became a boilerworks.

The permutations are considerable. Characters may be identifiable even in purely invented scenes when an author draws on people known to him or incidents in his life. A *roman à clef* may invite the reader to draw conclusions as to the identities of the characters, and books like *Primary Colors* can therefore give rise to considerable libel worries when published in the UK. In July 1999, Pan accordingly decided not to publish a novel featuring a character who was the wife of a Labour prime minister described as 'a young chap with a phoney smile'. Here fact and fiction were so inextricably linked that readers might have inferred that the steamy sexual infidelities in the plot related to an identifiable person. The book therefore could not have been defended in the event of a libel claim.

A novel which appeared in slightly different form on either side of the Atlantic was Nora Ephron's *Heartburn*, a scarcely concealed portrait of real-life dalliance between the author's husband, the celebrated investigative journalist Carl Bernstein, and Margaret Jay, wife of Peter Jay, the former British ambassador in Washington. The book did not give rise to a libel action, but nonetheless it did prompt a complaint, with the Jays taking the unusual step, for a husband and wife, of retaining his-and-hers libel lawyers.

A key part of the improbable plot has the Peter Jay-based character's feet sticking out of a rhododendron bush, where the narrator trips over them. In the original version of the text – as published for American readers – the wronged husband, described in the book as the American under-secretary of state for Middle Eastern affairs, is ostensibly gardening in the depths of a flowerbed but in fact listening out for any extramarital noises in the house by means of a specially adapted Walkman. After much expensive legal advice, this was changed to involve the character in clipping the rhododendrons so that English readers encountered the more seemly scenario of the narrator tripping over the flex of the electric trimmer as opposed to the protruding legs of the politician. Unpleasant as this all was, and overlaid as it may have been with personal acrimony, it was difficult to imagine that any reader of the book could possibly have believed that the Jays might have behaved in this fashion. Nevertheless, Jay did persuade one publisher not to go ahead with the book, somewhat unconvincingly citing possible upset to his children as the reason for his complaint – notwithstanding his own dalliance with their nanny. Jay was to do rather more damage to his reputation on his own account by hitching his star to the Robert Maxwell wagon. Margaret Jay, meanwhile, survived this unpleasantness and became a government minister in the House of Lords.

Husband-and-wife libels are, not surprisingly, very rare. There was one in 1935, although here each spouse was libelled separately. The Duchess of Marlborough recovered damages for a horticultural libel which had her in bed with the Rev. F. Page Roberts (like the Duchess, a variety of rose bush). Unfortunately, the article mistakenly referred to the Rev. H. Robertson Page, who was not a rose bush, and consequently added to the general confusion and *double entendre* of the article. A few years later the Duchess's husband, the Duke of Marlborough, sued the communist paper the *Daily Worker* for allegations about his wartime efforts to have poachers sent to prison to protect his pheasants. At a time when the English should all have been pulling together, this was seen as particularly defamatory, and he too was awarded damages.

Husbands and wives can in theory sue each other for libel, but are on the whole well advised not to do so (see the 1994 case of Wraith v. Wraith in the Appendix).

American law has a remedy for the intentional infliction of emotional distress, which seems an admirable way of dealing with any settling of scores in the guise of fiction. In 1988, when *Hustler* magazine published a spoof liquor advertisement depicting Jerry Falwell, the leader of the moral majority, drinking and engaging in sexual practices, he recovered $200,000 for infliction of emotional distress, a satisfactory award, if somewhat less than the $45 million he had claimed for libel.

Libel in fiction may be the product of pure accident rather than the result of the author drawing, either consciously or subconsciously, on episodes and people from his or her earlier life. The classic example of such an accident arose in 1988 in relation to a character in Jilly Cooper's book *Rivals*. Her larger-than-life TV tycoon, who was described in the complaint as 'an impossibly corrupt television magnate', had originally been called Lord Daglingworth, after a nearby village. But this non-existent title seemed a bit of a mouthful, and Cooper's publishers suggested changing it. A name was substituted which had been used without problem for a character in one of John Mortimer's books.

Unhappily, it was the name of a local government dignitary who by an unfortunate coincidence was a director of a non-operational cable television company which itself had a similar name to the fictitious franchise terrestrial television company in the book. In bringing a claim for libel, a number of other less striking similarities between the character and the plaintiff were prayed in aid, such as a love of gardening and ownership of a BMW. Less convincing was the claim that the complainant's wife, like the character's, also had a Rottweiler. This betrayed a lack of a grasp of the intricacies of Jilly Cooper's plot: in her book the tycoon had a mistress who behaved like a Rottweiler. The offending name was changed by three letters in the paperback edition, although no damages were paid.

Tom Sharpe experienced a very similar problem with *Porterhouse Blue* in 1974. In satirising high-profile television presenters, he selected a name for his character which he felt, wrongly as it turned out, was outlandish. Lo and behold, from a far-flung corner of the BBC empire, someone of that unusual name emerged. The relevant research, which Sharpe had believed unnecessary for a work of fiction, could have revealed the existence of the namesake on the corporation's payroll. Sharpe was advised that he had no defence to the claim as he could not produce any notes as proof that he had scoured the appropriate directories to check there was no one of this name at the BBC. Damages of £250 were paid to the plaintiff, and his lawyers received twice that sum for grappling with the plot of *Porterhouse Blue.* The situation may well have been distressing and annoying to the complainant, but the book was unquestionably a work of fiction and use of his name a pure coincidence. That being the case, it is difficult to see what this litigation had to do with the protection of reputation.

The potentially serious consequences of accidental libel were illustrated by the case brought in 1994 by Old Etonian Alex Wilbraham against the Anglo-American author Paul Watkins, who described his experiences at Eton in the early 1980s in his book *Stand Up Before Your God: Growing Up to be a Writer.*

Watkins was a serious novelist who had twice been nominated for the Booker Prize. There was no question here of settling scores, and the complainant accepted that the libel was inadvertent. But it was very near the knuckle and one can see why Wilbraham was upset.

The two men had overlapped at Eton, but, being two academic years apart, had not known each other. Unhappily, the author had chosen Wilbraham, not the most common of names, for a drug-taking homosexual – a character who couldn't have been more different from the blameless and clean-living Alex Wilbraham. He recovered damages reputed to be in the order of £15,000 and the name was changed to something less Etonian. Here was a case where one can see that reputation could be damaged as the distinction between fact and fiction might be blurred. In fact, adopting a method used by Sir Compton Mackenzie, Watkins had selected the name from a 1940 New Jersey telephone directory. He explained that he had changed the physical traits of his characters to prevent identification of the real people who had inspired them. There was, however, a school list of names which the author should have checked to avoid just such a mishap. As in the situation in which Tom Sharpe found himself, there is unlikely to be a defence to a claim where there is a failure to consult a directory which would readily establish whether it is safe to use a particular name in a work of fiction.

A similar problem befell Piers Paul Read in 1976. He had created an unsavoury character for his novel *Polonaise*, calling him Lord Derwent in the belief, it seems, that peers are not named after stretches of water. Again, a check would have established the existence of a real and unreproachable Lord Derwent. The book had to be pulped and the name changed when it transpired that there were some parallels between the two – although not, of course, any traits in the real Lord Derwent relating to the misdeeds of his fictional namesake.

Paul Erdman experienced similar difficulties with his book *The Last Days of America*, published in 1981, which dealt with events taking place from 1985 to 1987. He drew on his time as a banker in Basel to construct a stream of unattractive characters, including a lawyer who, under some provocation, had drawn his Walther PPK on the principal character before his legal brain came terminally into contact with the door of his office safe. Unhappily, the author had chosen the distinctive name of a respected lawyer who was still very much alive. There was nothing to indicate that this was anything other than accidental, although, yet again, more rigorous checks would have informed the author of the lawyer's existence. Despite the self-evidently fictitious events, the living lawyer's continuing good health and an author's disclaimer note, the plaintiff was still able to establish a claim for libel. Under existing libel law, it was not too difficult to spell out the potentially damaging effects of such references on a discreet Swiss lawyer. They would certainly be annoying, but would they actually be damaging, and could they have affected his reputation?

The mixing of fact and fiction inevitably has its perils. In Simon Raven's part-fiction, part-memoir *Is There Anybody There Said the Traveller*, the thinly disguised names of the characters resulted in 1990 in the payment of damages and costs totalling £17,000. The book was withdrawn after various complaints, including one about a humorous suggestion that a character who could have been readily identified had added a personal ingredient – his own seed – to a stew. In reality his culinary expertise had not, it seems, progressed beyond tossing the salad.

Ill-chosen fictionalised pseudonyms can lead to problems in straightforward non-fiction, too. Derek Jameson explained in the preface to his autobiography, *Touched by Angels*, that some names had been changed to avoid pain and embarrassment. One of them was that of a small, skinny, Scottish staff sergeant who had been convicted of treason and sentenced to seven years. Unhappily, Jameson inadvertently borrowed the name of a *Daily Mail* journalist of the highest integrity, who was also Scottish and of similar physical appearance to the staff sergeant. Jameson even used a variant of the Christian name – Harry rather than Henry – but this is, of course, a common diminutive; moreover, it turned out that the real Henry Longmuir was the only man to have been christened in this name in Great Britain during the relevant period.

Longmuir specialised in crime stories, and was the man who had tracked down the fugitive Labour minister John Stonehouse, subsequently jailed for fraud in the 1970s. The traitor had been a staff sergeant who had manned a petrol pump outside Villach in southern Austria and married a girl from Czechoslovakia. Longmuir had never been in the army and had no connections with Austria. The idea that a crime reporter working around Scotland Yard had, in a misspent youth, served seven years for treason seemed ludicrous. Nevertheless Longmuir's son had been asked at his golf club whether Jameson's Harry Longmuir was his father. Longmuir sued and recovered £3,000. While one may feel the greatest sympathy for the annoyance and distress caused to Mr Longmuir after a distinguished career in journalism, it is difficult to see what an author wishing to change a name in this particular situation could have done to avoid such a coincidence. There may be directories of bishops, lawyers and schools, but they do not exist for most occupations – and Jameson was writing about a soldier, not a journalist.

This case showed how names can be dredged up from the depths of a writer's subconscious memory – as a newspaper editor, Jameson is likely to have heard Longmuir's name at some stage of his life and then to have forgotten it, to all intents and purposes. Such situations can be real headaches for authors. One solution would have been to have specified in the preface exactly which names had been changed, or to have included a footnote in the text stating that Longmuir was not the traitor's real name. But this is easy to suggest with the benefit of hindsight. At the time, Jameson evidently believed that he had covered the risk in his generalised preface.

In cases where there is no evidence that a name has deliberately been chosen to cause distress, there is much to be said for setting a higher threshold for the recovering of libel damages. No one knowing Henry Longmuir could have believed he could have been guilty of such conduct. It is therefore artificial to proceed on the basis that he was being accused of such behaviour just as if this were a false statement written about his career, and there were potentially some unidentifiable people who might actually have thought the worse of him after reading the book.

There is much to be learned from the much stricter approach of the US courts to libels in fiction. In Bindrim v. Mitchell, the author of the novel *Touching* had recreated and embroidered, under the auspices of a fictitious doctor, Simon Herford, a peculiarly American nude group-therapy session he had attended with the real-life psychologist Dr Paul Bindrim. Although Bindrim's 1979 case did succeed, the jury was directed to decide whether the literary incidents were understood by readers as strictly fictional or to be based on facts – a higher threshold test than that employed in England. Where the events described were evident fantasy, a plaintiff would not succeed. In the case of Pring v. Penthouse International Ltd in 1982, a verdict for a modest $26.5 million in favour of a baton-twirling beauty queen – portrayed in *Miss Wyoming Saves the World* as the giver of blow jobs of such near-presidential excellence that the recipients levitated – was set aside, since the passage was pure fantasy.

In Springer v. Viking Press in 1983, Lisa Springer, the former girlfriend of Robert Tine, author of *State of Grace*, alleged that after the break-up of their relationship he had gratuitously added to his plot a totally immoral character, Lisa Black, based on herself. There were indeed a number of striking similarities – her first name, where she lived and her studies as a psychology student – which had been adversely commented upon by the writer Nadine Gordimer when she was sent a copy of the book. Nevertheless, the New York Court of Appeals ruled that in such a case it must be established that a reasonable reader would not only conclude that the fictitious character was an actual portrayal of the plaintiff, but also attribute to the plaintiff the defamatory aspects of that character. Springer's claim failed, as she had a different lifestyle and could not show that the defamatory references could be attributed to her. With such a test, many of the successful English cases would likewise have been lost.

Some of the older cases involving fiction failed because the courts took the robust view that reasonable people could not have concluded that the offending passages referred to the plaintiff. In the 1930s two humourless stockbrokers, William Lewis Rowland Paul Sebastian Blennerhassett and Captain John Canning, both lost their actions for this reason. Blennerhassett had taken exception to an advertisement in the London *Standard*:

BEWARE OF THE YO-YO. IT STARTS AS A HOBBY AND ENDS AS A HABIT

Take warning of the fate of Mr Blennerhassett. As worthy a citizen as any that ever ate lobster at Pimm's or holed a putt at Walton Health. 'Sound man, Blennerhassett,' they said on Throgmorton Street.

Canning had objected to parts of a book entitled *People in Cages*, which was set in London Zoo and depicted a Captain John Canning, a City financier wanted by the police, running panic-stricken from cage to cage. His case had not really survived the question: 'Captain Canning in the book was making over to the doctor's wife and kissing her parlourmaid when he came to call at the doctor's house. No one would think that was you?'

'No one who knew me,' replied the Hove stockbroker ponderously, 'but I am continuously making new acquaintances, and it might be by some people with whom I might seek to do business.'

Unfortunately, given that there is nearly always something which, with the benefit of hindsight, an author might have done to avoid publishing a libel, not to mention the mounting cost of contesting libel actions, most such claims now have to be settled. In one of the few libel-in-fiction cases tried in recent times, Longmore v. BBC in 1981, the plaintiff recovered £8,000 damages. The BBC broadcast two plays about a disreputable fictitious firm of solicitors, Longmore, Page and Longmore, based in Birmingham. The first was heard by a lady doing her ironing, who thought it must be a portrayal of the very reputable solicitors Longmores, who practised in Hertfordshire. The BBC persisted in its second broadcast notwithstanding a complaint. The judge concluded that reasonable people might think this was a reference to the real Longmores, and reiterated the point made by Mr Justice Ormerod in the case of Ross v. Hopkinson in 1956. 'If anyone wished to libel a person in a book, they would not do it by faithfully representing details of that person's life and age.' As anyone making this association might conclude, unjustly, that Longmores was not the kind of company to which they would wish to entrust their business – and as he was unimpressed by the BBC's handling of their reasonable complaint after the first broadcast – the judge found in the solicitors' favour.

In support of the actions of such plaintiffs it must be said that the boundaries between fact and fiction have become more and more indistinct – and not only as a consequence of the advent of 'faction' and 'docudrama'. Numerous pages of tabloid newspapers are devoted to the antics of soap-opera stars, and it is often unclear whether these relate to the actors themselves or their soap personas. Indeed, it was such coverage that prompted the case brought by Bill Roache of *Coronation Street*, discussed in Chapter 11. The blurring of reality and fantasy was further illustrated by litigation which in 1991 resulted in the award of £5,000 damages plus costs of about £20,000 to the member of Parliament Edwina Currie. Her complaint centred on a preview in the *Observer* of the film *Paris by Night*. Here Clara Paige, a particularly unattractive character – even for a thrusting, ambitious Euro MP – whose behaviour apparently extended to bumping off, blackmail and appalling behaviour towards her family was described by the actress Charlotte Rampling as 'an Edwina Currie, if we must'. It was scarcely a flattering reference, but on the other hand the activities of Clara Paige were so outlandish that it is doubtful that this unpleasant comparison could actually have impacted on the faultless reputation of the respected MP and former health minister. No one, of course, suggested that there were any resemblances to her own character; indeed, the defence argument was just the opposite: that nobody would attribute Paige's traits to Currie. Currie explained that it was not her intention to take the newspaper to the cleaners; the preview cast a slur on her capabilities as a wife and mother, and she considered it important to redress that. 'I was really upset about it, and still am. I couldn't just let it lie.' The jury decided in her favour, after a retirement of only forty-five minutes, perhaps as much because of the very aggressive way in which George Carman QC cross-examined her in pursuit of his contention that this was a trivial case – he grilled her about her good-natured participation in a *Punch* quiz headed 'Are You a Good Flirt?' and her fondness for Janet Reger underwear – as for any real belief that this was a damaging reflection on her reputation. Her counsel, Richard Hartley QC, complained in terms reminiscent of the Mona Bauwens (see Chapter 11) case of 'the most eloquent character assassination' he had ever heard.

Clearly it is a dangerous practice to compare living people with unattractive characters in fiction. *The Sunday Times* had to pay libel damages to a man of letters unfortunately equated with one of John Mortimer's less attractive Chiantishire characters in its review of *Summer's Lease*. Once meaning and reference are established, there is not likely to be a defence unless it can be proved that what has been written is true and, almost by definition, that is impossible.

As things stand, authors of fiction need to go through a checklist to lessen the risk of a claim by a plaintiff of whom they have never heard. They should consult any listings which may exist relating to the particular profession or group about which they are writing. Unusual names should be checked against telephone directories. Authors should be asked by their advisers on whom their characters are based, whether any of the surrounding events actually happened and to what extent they are autobiographical. Do they know anyone of the same name, or might they ever have had any dealings with someone of that name? A carefully worded disclaimer of reference to living individuals is advisable.

In cases of accidental non-negligent libel, it was in the past possible to make an offer of amends under Section 4 of the Defamation Act 1952. As demonstrated by the case of Ross v. Hopkinson, which arose out of Antonia White's book *The Sugar House*, this defence was, however, extremely difficult to use, involving as it did the admission of liability and an offer of compensation to be made more swiftly than lawyers were in the habit of moving. A young actress, June Sylvaine, sued in respect of the almost contemptuous depiction of a young actress with an identical name in *The Sugar House*. The character, described as being decidedly fat, was cast as the comic elderly cook and referred to as 'that bloody bitch Sylvaine'. The defence under Section 4 of the Defamation Act 1952 required an offer of amends to be made as soon as practicable: a delay of over six weeks was not soon enough.

A more practical and effective version of the defence has now been substituted in Section 2 of the 1996 Defamation Act. This enables a defendant who has made a mistake – provided that he or she did not know it referred to and was false and defamatory of the plaintiff – to offer a correction and apology and to pay appropriate compensation and costs. If the plaintiff does not accept the offer, a judge will fix the compensation. The substantive law is not altered, but errors can be put right quickly and at less expense, and it is now unlikely that a plaintiff will be able to extract large damages from a defendant.

# 20

# SHOPPING AND SUING

London has become known to many foreign 'forum-shoppers' as a Town named Sue – a place where you can launder your reputation on the basis of a few sales in the UK of some overseas publication. This is a trick that did not escape Robert Maxwell, who sued the *New Republic* in the UK, where it had 135 subscribers, rather than in the USA, where its circulation was 98,000.

As publication has grown more global, English courts are in danger of growing more insular. Plaintiffs take advantage of the libel laws of the country, under which the burden of proof is on the defendants and there is no necessity to prove actual damage. It may also be difficult and expensive – indeed, completely uneconomic – to persuade overseas-based witnesses to come to England to substantiate the defence.

A defendant cannot subpoena witnesses and documents from abroad except by the elaborate letters rogatory system, whereby an official request has to be sent via a foreign court. The forum-shopper may therefore obtain a verdict in his favour to which his reputation in his own country would not entitle him. Forum-shoppers take two principal forms: American plaintiffs who benefit from the absence of a Sullivan (public figure) defence, or other foreign nationals who calculate that, given the difficulties of proof combined with a minute circulation of a libel in the UK, it will simply not be worthwhile for a defendant to try to fight the claim, whatever the truth of the matter. Under Sullivan, a US plaintiff who is a public figure will not succeed unless he or she can establish by clear and convincing evidence that the defendant published the libel with knowledge of its falsity, or with reckless disregard as to its truth or falsity. Even a private figure is required to prove fault on the part of a media defendant.

Libel is different from other civil wrongs, which will normally involve only one act of negligence or one breach of contract. If there is a dispute as to where the case should be heard, the court will have to decide which of the contending countries is the most appropriate. In libel, however, an actionable wrong is committed in every jurisdiction in which the offending words are published. The issue in forum-shopping cases, therefore, is to persuade the English court that even though a wrong has technically been committed within its jurisdiction, the case should be heard in the country with which the publication has its most natural affinity, rather than in England. As information becomes increasingly transnational and widely available in cyberspace, it is usually possible to find a handful of copies of most leading foreign publications in the UK, if only for the purpose of being circulated among the overseas businesses based there or among foreign nationals in England. This has been accentuated by the Internet, where downloading a foreign publication in England is itself an act of publication within the jurisdiction of the English courts. Indeed, foreign publications are likely to be downloaded as a matter of routine during due diligence research in commercial transactions.

The difficulty of confining libels to one jurisdiction is illustrated by the litigation brought by the reclusive brothers David and Frederick Barclay who, despite being the owners of the *Scotsman* and the *European*, sued BBC Radio Guernsey and its contributor, the journalist John Sweeney, over false allegations about their involvement in the troubles of the Crown Agents. They sued not only in the English courts – recovering £15,000, which they donated to charity – but also in Brittany, where the programme could have been picked up. The appeal court in Rennes awarded them 20,000 francs (£2,200), with the requirement that the defendants advertised the judgement at the cost of a further 5,000 francs in a St Malo paper.

In choosing between conflicting jurisdictions, the English court will look for the forum with the most real and substantial connections with the action. The determining factors include convenience, expense, the availability and compellability of witnesses and documents, and the places where the parties reside or carry out their business. A distinction is drawn between cases where the plaintiff is entitled to sue *as of right*, that is to say where he or she can directly issue a writ against a defendant resident in the UK, or a company which has a place of business under Section 691 of the Companies Act 1985, and those where the plaintiff must seek leave to serve the writ abroad.

When the plaintiff can sue as of right, the burden is on the defendant to show that England is not the natural or appropriate forum for trial and that there is another forum available which is clearly more appropriate than England where substantial justice can be done. Once he has done so, the burden shifts to the plaintiff to show why the case should not be heard in that country.

If the defendant resides abroad or does not have a place of business in England, leave to serve the writ out of the jurisdiction is required under Order 11 of the civil procedure rules. The plaintiff has to establish that the damage results from a wrongful act within the jurisdiction of the English court and that there is a serious issue to be tried. The burden is on the plaintiff as opposed to the defendant to show that England is *clearly* the most appropriate forum for the trial of the action. The principles for resolving such conflicts of jurisdiction were set out by Lord Goff in Spiliada v. Cansulex in 1987. Defendants in such cases are well advised not to accept the jurisdiction of the English courts.

A prime example of the potential injustice of forum-shopping is the case of Armand Hammer, head of Occidental Petroleum of Los Angeles, a man who was obsessed with massaging his reputation. In his last years he devoted large sums to trying to secure a libel verdict in England in the vain hope of establishing a lasting monument to his good name. Like Robert Maxwell, Hammer tried to control what was written about him.

There was considerable interest in the man who turned Occidental Petroleum into the USA's sixteenth-largest industrial corporation before his death. He had contrived to maintain good relations with both Israel and Colonel Gaddaffi and acquired an honorary knighthood in Britain as well as twenty-five honorary degrees worldwide. His early business career had ranged from receiving manufacturing concessions from the Soviet government to the production of tincture of ginger, which was said to make a passable highball during prohibition. His family life was no less exotic. His father had been sent to Sing Sing for manslaughter after being convicted of performing an illegal abortion; his son had been charged with, but acquitted of, murder. Hammer himself had been convicted of, and subsequently pardoned for, making a secret $54,000 donation to Richard Nixon's 1972 presidential campaign. He received a very lenient sentence of one year's probation and a fine of $3,000, possibly because of his frail appearance: he had been pushed into the Los Angeles court in a wheelchair. Afterwards he made a remarkable and speedy recovery. He wrote in one of his autobiographies of his blissful marriage with his wife, Frances, but in reality relations were very strained between them at the time of her death in controversial circumstances. Hammer refused to allow a post-mortem, and her estate thereafter engaged in four years of unsuccessful litigation against him.

In 1975 Hammer commissioned Bob Considine to write *The Remarkable Life of Dr Armand Hammer*, which was distributed by Occidental's PR department to any journalists researching articles about him. He also wrote several autobiographies, including *The Quest of the Romanoff Treasure* in 1932 and *Armand Hammer*, in conjunction with Neil Lyndon, in 1987. Armand

Hammer Productions released films and books about Hammer's global activities. Nearly $100 million of Occidental's funds went into the Armand Hammer Museum of Art and Cultural Center, whose entrance boasted a seven-foot-high portrait of its bene-factor. When he bought, with Occidental's money, Leonardo da Vinci's *Codex Leicester* it was renamed *Codex Hammer*.

The case the old rogue brought in 1988 was a cynical attempt to exploit the English laws of libel for his own benefit. When a biography of him – *Armand Hammer: The Untold Story* by Steve Weinberg – was published in the UK by Ebury Press, Hammer sued. A mere 3,000 copies had been published, of which only 2,000 had been sold, compared with a very much larger print run in the USA. Yet Hammer did not sue Little, Brown, the American publisher, in the country where his reputation had been forged. Ebury Press was at that time part of a small to medium-sized publishing group. Unfortunately for Hammer, before the case came to court it was taken over by the publishing giant Random House, which was not prepared to be bullied.

Hammer took advantage of the facts that his good reputation would be assumed in his favour, that he would not have to prove specific damage and that the book had been written to conform with American rather than English libel laws. Weinberg, the author, was chief executive director of Investigative Reporters and Editors and associate professor at the University of Missouri School of Journalism. His book was the product of five years' work and 700 interviews – none of which was with Hammer, who had refused to talk to him. Jokes about using a nut to crack a hammer were misplaced. The book examined allegations made against Hammer during the course of his life: that he was a KGB paymaster and money-launderer; that he had in the 1960s bribed the Libyan government to obtain oil-drilling con-cessions and that he had been involved in the murder by poisoning of a former business associate. In many instances Weinberg found the charges to be unsubstantiated. However, the way they had been repeated in the book left it open for claims to be made under English law that Hammer was either being said to be guilty, or could reasonably be suspected of being guilty, of them.

Actions for libel cannot, as we have seen, be continued on behalf of a plaintiff after his death. It is therefore unusual for people beyond the age of eighty to bring such cases. Hammer was ninety when he sued in 1988 and died at the age of ninety-two in December 1990.

Hammer's solicitors, Peter Carter-Ruck and Partners, argued that he was a very old man and much offended that towards the end of his life he should be attacked in this way. As he was suffering from chronic anaemia, bronchitis, prostate enlargement, kidney ailments, irregular heartbeat and advanced bone-marrow cancer, he must have appreciated when he commenced the litigation that the end was near. This dictated the means by which he tried to browbeat the defendants. He asked for a staggering £3 million damages. His lawyers went into overdrive, producing a massive statement of claim which ran to 118 pages, encompassing the whole of the twentieth century and complaining of passages on 155 of the book's 426 pages. Even the number of accidents and alleged unsanitary conditions in the pencil factory that he ran in Russia in the 1920s were among the myriad issues. The defence solicitors, Crockers, scoured the United States for evidence. Everywhere they found witnesses who had been persuaded by Hammer not to speak to them, even though they had been willing to talk to Steve Weinberg. By the time of Hammer's death the legal costs were said to exceed £1.5 million. It was predicted that the trial would take over three months, and Hammer would be likely to be in the witness box for six weeks. Final costs were forecast at something of the order of £5 million and the number of documents to amount to about 40,000.

In spite of his murky past, it seemed that the English libel law was almost tailor-made for Armand Hammer. As a precaution the defendants had paid £2,000 into court. As Hammer's health deteriorated his lawyers indicated that he might be prepared to settle in the region of £25,000 to £50,000. Sensing that the case did not have much longer to run, the defendants stood firm. When

Hammer died, Peter Carter-Ruck was reported as saying that he would have expected damages upwards of £500,000. 'He was a very good client who was unjustly treated in the book. I don't deny that this was a very remunerative case for the lawyers involved.' The underlying unfairness of English libel law was borne out by the fact that Random House, whose principled stand had been vindicated by what emerged about Hammer, were left to pay their own heavy legal costs.

There are, however, a number of compelling arguments which can be raised in favour of the foreign defendant. Mr Justice Pearson, on Société Générale de Paris v. Dreyfuss Brothers in 1885, pointed out: 'It becomes a very serious question . . . whether this court ought to put a foreigner who has no allegiance here to the inconvenience and annoyance of being brought to contest his rights in this country, and I, for one, say, most distinctly, that I think this court ought to be exceedingly careful before it allows a writ to be served out of the jurisdiction.' Furthermore, it was stated in 1995 in the case of Trade Indemnity plc that an unwilling foreign defendant should not be forced into an English court by the beguiling superiority of English law or judicial expertise.

Equally, an English court is unlikely to be sympathetic to any argument by a plaintiff that the courts of his own country would perpetrate injustice. In Jeyaretnam v. Mahmood, a libel writ issued in England by a citizen of Singapore, who had lived and worked there nearly all his life, against a Singaporean newspaper which distributed no more than twelve copies in England, was set aside. His complaint that as he was an opponent of the government of Singapore he would not get a fair hearing there fell on deaf ears.

If proceedings are already taking place in the foreign country, a plaintiff is unlikely to be able to persuade an English court to allow him to bring them in England as well. In the same year as the Singaporean case, 1992, in Oraro v. *Observer*, a libel claim brought by a senior lawyer over a report implicating him in the alleged murder in 1990 of Robert Ouko, foreign minister of Kenya, was rejected and sent for trial in Kenya by Mr Justice

Drake. Notwithstanding the fact that the *Observer* then had a circulation of 500,000 in the UK and sold only a handful of copies in Kenya, the court, in a robust decision, took the view that the action had virtually no connection with England, that the damage to the plaintiff's reputation would have taken place in Kenya, and that the plaintiff had already brought other libel proceedings in respect of these allegations in Kenya.

The action brought in 1992 by Captain Tojo Tsikata, the former head of the Ghanaian security service, against the *Independent* was, however, permitted to proceed by Mr Justice Newman. The case clearly belonged to Ghana, just as Oraro had to Kenya, but the judge felt that the *Independent* could scarcely complain about being sued in this country since they had chosen to publish a report about the public inquiry into the murder of three Ghanaian High Court judges in 1982. Tsikata complained that the *Independent* had failed to mention, in reporting an official recommendation to prosecute him, that the attorney-general of Ghana had subsequently concluded that there was insufficient evidence to proceed against Tsikata and that one of the conspirators had, before facing a firing squad, admitted making false allegations against him.

The case established that qualified privilege could attach to the official Ghanaian report. Tsikata had therefore to prove malice, and in September 1998 he gave up the unequal struggle. The *Independent* published a correction making it clear that they had never intended to suggest Tsikata was guilty of any crime, and that they regretted it if this had been inferred by anyone. Tsikata v. the *Independent* was notable for the unusual way in which Tsikata chose to pay his legal bills: by funnelling £327,000 from miscellaneous Libyan sources into the Abbey National account of Victoria Brittain, the unobservant deputy foreign editor of the *Guardian*. Brittain seems not to have noticed what was going on, but MI5 was sufficiently disturbed that it made money-laundering inquiries before the truth was established. Brittain was blameless, but had, in the view of the paper's ombudsman, made a 'silly mistake' and exercised 'poor judgement'.

Tsikata was more successful in the courts in April 1997, when he recovered substantial damages from *New African* for false allegations about involvement in the drugs trade.

Justice would appear to dictate that a plaintiff should, in the normal course of events, be required to sue in the country where he has established his reputation or where the events took place. These basic rules should not be varied in favour of the rich and powerful, who are precisely the people who are able to indulge in forum-shopping. Through their international activities they can establish some connections with England in pursuit of a jurisdiction in which they believe they can secure a favourable verdict. Courts ought to be cautious about paying too much heed to such persons producing hotel bills and business cronies as evidence of spurious links with England. They ought also to look at where the events occurred, where the relevant documents and witnesses are likely to come from, what language the latter speak and where the bulk of the publication took place. They should consider why the plaintiff is not suing in the country where he acquired his reputation. There is a very strong argument for requiring a plaintiff to sue for a libel in one country rather than allowing him to fire off writs around the world in order to bring home to the defendant the exorbitant cost of defending the case worldwide.

It is sometimes said that there is a justification for bringing an action in more than one jurisdiction in order to obtain an injunction against the defamatory publication, since a court in one country cannot ban publication in another. However, this is likely to be of practical significance only in the rarest cases. Normally a court can assume jurisdiction over an author or publishing company based within its jurisdiction and can prohibit the further publication worldwide by the author or publisher of the defamatory words. Moreover, a foreign company may be taking a considerable risk in publishing a work that has been proved to be defamatory elsewhere. A plaintiff suing in England can include in his claim relief for a libel committed in a foreign country, provided he can show that it would be actionable under English law and under the law of the foreign country. He is

entitled to assume that foreign law is the same as English law in
the absence of evidence to the contrary.

Three recent decisions – by Mr Justice Popplewell in
Berezovsky and Glouchkov v *Forbes*, by Mr Justice Morland in
Wyatt v. *Forbes* and by Mr Justice Popplewell in Parvinder
Chadha v. Dow Jones – indicated a growing reluctance among
judges to allow forum-shopping. All of these plaintiffs failed at
first instance, but unfortunately, in a retrograde step, the Court of
Appeal overturned the decision of Mr Justice Popplewell in the
Berezovsky and Glouchkov case. Wyatt did not appeal. The issues
in the cases remain to be tried, and the applications proceeded on
the basis that the allegations were defamatory. The sole question
was whether, in cases concerning US-based publications with a
limited circulation in England, the plaintiffs should be permitted
to sue in the English courts.

Berezovsky, a Russian tycoon, had visited England on thirty-
one occasions in the three and a half years leading up to the
case; he had business activities in the country and maintained a
flat in London through an offshore company. His estranged wife
and children lived in London and his daughters had been to
Cambridge University. Glouchkov, a deputy manager of the
Russian national airline, Aeroflot, a company with which
Berezovsky had close links, travelled to London to negotiate
their insurance contract. He also was said to keep a London flat,
although it was not clear whether it was simply a company flat.
Mr Justice Popplewell found that these connections were, in the
circumstances, tenuous. Here were Russians suing an American
publication with a circulation in the United States and Canada of
over 785,000 compared with under 2,000 copies in the UK, and
these predominantly serving the expatriate American community. The events described in the article had nothing whatsoever
to do with England: they involved a series of detailed allegations
about Berezovsky's extraordinary rise to power and wealth and
his business methods in Russia.

The Court of Appeal acknowledged that these were matters
within the scope of the judge's discretion and that it should

interfere only if the judge had erred in principle, had seriously misapprehended relevant issues or had taken into account irrelevant ones. Having said which, it proceeded to interfere. The decision was of enormous significance as, in an era of global communications, most important publications will find their way into England by subscription or on the Internet since people in England need to know what American business executives are reading. The Court of Appeal may not have appreciated the practical implications of their ruling in dismissing such criticisms as 'jejune'. Essentially, American publications like *Forbes* have to choose between not publishing in England because of its oppressive libel laws and gambling on whether someone like Berezovsky or Wyatt will decide to try to secure himself a libel verdict in England in relation to stories which have nothing whatsoever to do with the country. Foreign-based publications may wish to take advice on English libel law when they are writing about English people or events, but they are placed in an impossible position if articles which are perfectly permissible in their American market, and which have nothing to do with England, can nevertheless be the subject of an action in England. The enormous expense and difficulties associated with conducting such litigation will mean that either information is not made available in England, or publishers will have to factor in the cost of libel actions when publishing in the UK.

There are very real practical problems in dealing with what is essentially Russian litigation in England, where a majority of the witnesses are likely to be Russian-speaking and the documents will require translation from Russian. The fact that witnesses in Russia cannot easily be subpoenaed, either to testify or to produce documents, underlines the need for the greatest caution in litigating these matters in the UK. The appropriate forum to understand and rule upon the present turbulent conditions in Russia is the Russian courts.

The impracticality of requiring an English jury to make sense of shifting Russian sands was underlined by the events that took place before any trial of the libel action. Berezovsky had found himself embroiled in the allegations in connection with his handling of the Aeroflot finances. First he was threatened with arrest in Russia. After that threat was lifted, he claimed that elements in the security services were planning to kill him. He left Russia amid renewed risk of arrest. By February 2001 Glouchkov had been arrested by the Russians investigating allegations of money-laundering and Berezovsky had declined to return to Russia to assist those authorities with their inquiries.

Hitherto the track record of newly rich Russians suing American publications in the UK has not been particularly successful, but the claims are very costly to dispute. In October 2000 Mr Justice Gray upheld the right of another Russian businessman, Grigori Loutchansky, to bring an action against Times Newspapers even though he had, on the application of the British Home Office, been barred from entering the UK on the basis that his presence in the country was not conducive to the public good. So, subject to providing security for costs, Loutchansky was permitted to sue *The Times* – which is of course a British publication, not a foreign one – in Britain. Arguments that Loutchansky's connections with the UK were tenuous and that the probable cost of the action would be disproportionate to the damages he would be likely to recover did not persuade the judge, and Loutchansky, who was suing on allegations of links with international crime, was given a restricted visa enabling him to come to the country to conduct his case. Similar issues arose in a libel action brought by an Uzbekistani businessman, Gafur Rakhimov, who sought to vindicate his reputation in England. He had been barred from entering Australia for the 2000 Olympic Games in Sydney, even though he was a senior national Olympic representative.

As a justification of the ability of the English courts to grapple with complex foreign cases, the Court of Appeal in Berezovsky and Glouchkov v. *Forbes* referred to the case of the Auschwitz doctor mentioned in Chapter 14. It was an odd one to choose. By the time Dr Dering sued the English publishers of Leon Uris' novel *Exodus*, in the 1960s, he was a doctor practising in north London, so no issue of jurisdiction arose. He had performed surgical experiments on the inmates of Auschwitz, although only hundreds of them rather than, as the book suggested, thousands – figures which emerged from the carefully tabulated records in Dr Dering's hand. Two of his colleagues, Dr Rohde and Dr Entress, had been hanged – and rightly so; Dr Dering had, however, gone on to receive an OBE for his work in the colonial medical service in Somaliland, something his libel counsel, Colin Duncan QC, with a greater sense of irony than he perhaps intended, called 'a somewhat strange decoration for a war criminal'. As a mark of their disgust, the jury awarded contemptuous damages of one halfpenny, as we have seen. Dr Dering, seeing the opportunities afforded to libel plaintiffs by English libel law, had asked for £7,000 damages, and at the time of his death some years later he had failed to pay £17,000 of the legal costs which had been awarded against him. He had, however, managed to lift £500 from the book's printers, who had considered it prudent to settle.

The approach of the Court of Appeal in the Berezovsky and Glouchkov case seems to have been influenced by a distaste for the American style of the offending article, which was quoted at length in the court's judgement, and which was hotly disputed by Berezovsky and Glouchkov. It was headlined: 'IS HE THE GODFATHER OF THE KREMLIN? POWER, POLITICS, MURDER. BORIS BEREZOVSKY COULD TEACH THE GUYS IN SICILY A THING OR TWO'. Another passage read: 'These guys are criminals on an outrageous scale. It's as if Lucky Luciano were chairman of the board of Chrysler.' The court observed that the article throughout abounded with allegations against Mr Berezovsky of complicity in corruption and fraud on a massive scale, and drew attention to two photograph captions, 'Was Berezovsky behind the killing?' (of a TV producer, Vladislav Listiev), and, with a picture of Mr Berezovsky, 'A buccaneering capitalist, he seems to have learned some of his tactics from the old KGB.' This was certainly not the usual language of magazines in England, and in the view of the court it was highly defamatory.

Wherever the case was heard, there would be a heavy burden upon the defence in view of the nature of the allegations made. The Court of Appeal was prepared to accept that a plaintiff could tailor his case by confining himself to the tiny proportion of copies published in England. The fact that Berezovsky had not sued in either the country where he had established his reputation, Russia, or where nearly 99 per cent of the publication of the alleged libel occurred, the USA and Canada, was of no real consequence. The approach of the court was to follow the words of Lord Pearson in 1971 in Distillers v. Thompson: 'It is manifestly just and reasonable that a defendant should have to answer for his wrongdoing in a country where he did the wrong.' Lord Justice Ackner had said the same thing in the Albuforth case of 1984. 'The jurisdiction in which the tort has been committed is prima facie the natural forum for the determination of the dispute.' The Court of Appeal did not draw a distinction between cases where there is effectively one act of civil wrongdoing, namely negligence or the breaking of a contract, and libel, where a minute fraction of the entire publication can be artificially selected.

The court pointed out that each publication is a separate act of wrongdoing. Certainly, under the Brussels Convention, which applies predominantly to countries within the European Union, a plaintiff can choose under Article 5 (3) to sue the publisher either in the court of the state in which the publisher is established for *all* the harm caused by the libel, or in the courts of any contracting state in which the publication took place, in which instance the court may award damages only for the harm caused *in that state*. No doubt what was envisaged was that a plaintiff would use these provisions to sue in the state in which he or she lived, and that within Brussels Convention countries it should therefore be easier to marshal the evidence required to defend the claim. A plaintiff who sued successively in different countries for the harm done in those countries might run foul of the provisions in Article 21, preventing a multiplicity of actions. However, the Brussels Convention did mean that a plaintiff was able to sue

*France Soir* for the 230 copies which circulated in England and Wales – of which five were sold in Yorkshire, where the plaintiff lived – as opposed to the 237,000 published in France, in respect of defamatory allegations about money-laundering in Shevill v. Presse Alliance in 1992.

In May 2000, the House of Lords upheld the Court of Appeal ruling on Berezovsky and Glouchkov v. *Forbes* by a majority of 3–2. The issue turned on a nineteen-word judgement by Lord Hobhouse. Lord Steyn rejected the defence argument that in multi-jurisdictional libel claims there should be one cause of action and that it was artificial for the plaintiffs to confine their claim to the number of copies sold in a particular jurisdiction. He felt that the Russians did have reputations in the UK to protect, and that it was not unfair for a foreign publisher to be sued there. The judgements of the two dissenting judges, Lord Hoffmann and Lord Hope, however, are likely to be viewed as the more intellectually compelling and will probably herald a curbing of forum-shopping.

Lord Hoffmann had little doubt that Berezovsky and Glouchkov were forum-shoppers in the most literal sense. He and Lord Hope were convinced that Mr Justice Popplewell had reached the correct decision when he held that the Russians' links with the UK were 'tenuous'. It mattered not that Berezovsky had a truly international reputation, that he had lectured at Princeton, dined with George Soros and attended Rupert Murdoch's wedding in the United States: his reputation in England was an inseparable segment of his reputation worldwide. Lord Hoffman observed that the English courts should decline the role of international policeman and should not be an international libel tribunal for disputes between foreigners who had no connection with the UK.

Lord Hope felt it would be a matter of regret if orders for service on publishers out of the jurisdiction were to be regarded as available on demand to those who had established international reputations by what they had said or done elsewhere and who themselves had no longstanding or durable links with England.

There is bound to be a considerable difficulty in fairly assessing damages in cases in which the plaintiff has not sued in respect of the bulk of an offending publication elsewhere, or in a country or countries with which he has the closest connection.

Plaintiffs who actually live in England are likely to be allowed to sue foreign publications in the country. In Schapira v. Ahronson (1987), the plaintiff, who had lived in England for fourteen years and had been a UK citizen for ten and whose wife was English by birth and whose children went to English schools, was able to sue an Israeli Hebrew newspaper in respect of events in Israel notwithstanding the fact that only 121 copies out of 58,900 were sold in the UK. The principle laid down by Lord Justice Peter Gibson was that 'an English resident is entitled to bring proceedings here against those foreigners and to limit his claims to publication in England, even though the circulation of the article alleged to be defamatory was extremely limited in England and there was much larger publication elsewhere.' It was felt to be unjust to compel an English citizen in those circumstances to have to litigate abroad.

Oscar Wyatt, the founder and co-chairman of the US-based energy company Coastal Corporation, failed in his attempt to sue *Forbes* magazine in England for reports about 'Saddam's Pal Oscar' and the alleged destruction by arson of documents required by a US federal inquiry. The story had originally been published in the *Houston Chronicle*, which was already the subject of separate proceedings brought by Coastal Corporation. As one would expect of an international businessman, Wyatt was able to point to his business, family and social connections with England, which included the close friendship of his stepson with the Duchess of York, an unusual toehold for jurisdiction. However, the focus of the dispute was Coastal's headquarters in Houston, which had mysteriously combusted in the early hours when, unhappily, its sprinklers were out of commission. The surviving documents, witnesses and parties were all based in the United States. Mr Justice Morland noted that while there were some juridical advantages to Wyatt in having the case heard in

England, it could more suitably, for the interests of all the parties and the ends of justice, be heard in Texas.

A similar conclusion was reached in the Chadha case. The plaintiff was a United States citizen living and working in California who sued in respect of an article in *Barons* magazine, of which 283,520 copies were sold in the United States and only 1,257 in the UK. Chadha was accused of fraud and of laundering money through the Channel Islands and the British Virgin Islands. He sought to confine himself to events which could in some way be connected to England. He had no family or real social connections with the country, just some friends and business contacts and a small office in Windsor with three employees. The judge viewed with some scepticism the plaintiff's claim that the business in the UK was a key strategic link to the UK and European market. The fact that some of the money from an alleged fraud had ended up in a London bank account was purely incidental to the main thrust of the *Barons* article, which focused on Chadha, his company, Osicom Technologies Inc., and their alleged fraudulent business activities in the United States.

In May 1999 the Court of Appeal upheld the judge's ruling, remaining unconvinced that the plaintiff had a reputation which required vindication in England, as opposed to the United States, or that such reputation as he did have in England was likely to be harmed by the UK publication.

The complexities of this area of law have recently been underlined by the decision of Mr Justice Drake in Cumming v. *Scottish Daily Record*. The question was whether a plaintiff could choose to sue a Scottish newspaper for libel in England as opposed to Scotland for its not inconsiderable circulation in the former. Although the UK is a party to the Brussels Convention, which gives the plaintiff the option of choosing the country where the harmful event has occurred and of suing in respect of only that damage, the convention does not differentiate between England and Scotland. The test is therefore which is the most convenient forum for the case to be heard, which is what Mr Justice Drake decided after the point was fully argued in the Cumming case in

1995. He opted for Scotland. The previous year, in Foxen v. Scotsman Publications Ltd, he had reached the opposite conclusion in refusing to stay proceedings brought in England by a plaintiff domiciled in Scotland regarding an article published in *Scotland on Sunday*. With a wry elegance, the judge observed as he granted leave to appeal: 'It will be an odd situation in which, whatever the Court of Appeal decides, I shall be held wrong, although it is some consolation that I shall also be held right.' There was in fact no appeal, and academic opinion was that the decision in Cumming was correct.

A libel verdict which a plaintiff may obtain in England may prove to be of little value if it has to be enforced in the United States. The battle of the two Vladimirs, which extended over nine years, was a salutary warning lesson in the way that some libel actions benefit only the lawyers involved. Both Vladimirs were Russian-Jewish émigrés who knew each other; both had suffered persecution before coming to England. Vladimir Matusevitch had been born in New York to Belorussian parents who had, astonishingly, taken him to the Soviet Union as a child in 1940. His father was falsely accused by the Soviet regime of being an American spy and spent fifteen years in the gulag. Matusevitch defected in 1968 while in Norway, and in 1969 he began working as a journalist for Radio Free Europe and Radio Liberty. Vladimir Telnikoff was imprisoned twice during the Khrushchev regime for agitating against the state. He was able to emigrate to Israel in 1971, and later became an Israeli citizen.

In February 1984, Telnikoff wrote an article in the *Daily Telegraph*, 'Selecting the Right Wavelength to Tune into Russia', which stressed the importance of distinguishing between Russia and communism. He voiced the opinion that the Russian service of the BBC recruited too many employees from the ethnic minorities of the Soviet Union and not enough from among those people who associated themselves ethnically, spiritually or religiously with the Russian people. He criticised the confusion he believed existed at the BBC which, for many, made Russians synonymous with communists. It was not perhaps the most

sensible course of action for someone who was then a proba-
tioner at the BBC, and indeed his employment with the
corporation lasted only three years, after which he did not renew
his contract. Nevertheless it seemed a legitimate topic for discussion, even if only of real interest to a limited readership.

Matusevitch, however, was incensed. He wrote to the
*Telegraph* claiming that Telnikoff was demanding, in the interests
of more effective broadcasting, that the management of the
BBC's Russian services should switch from professional testing to
blood-testing as part of its recruitment policies. Telnikoff, he
said, was trying to rid the BBC of ethnically alien people. His
complaints were so outlandish that it might have been
considered self-evident that they were not allegations of fact
but the expression of strongly held opinions. Telnikoff, though,
took the view that Matusevitch was accusing him of being a
racist, an anti-Semite and a proponent of doctrines of racial
superiority. He replied to Matusevich's outpourings through the
*Telegraph*'s letters page, demanding an apology. When he failed
to receive one, he sued, and what had seemed simply a spat
between fellow émigrés became a full-blown libel action.

The case came on for trial before Mr Justice Michael Davies in
October 1988. Matusevitch did not turn up, and the jury awarded
Telnikoff £65,000. But victory was never going to be that simple,
and the judgement was set aside in April 1989 after Matusevitch
persuaded the judge that he had not been aware of the hearing
date.

The matter then came before Mr Justice Drake in May 1989.
He had little doubt that Matusevitch had an unassailable defence
of fair comment. As there was no evidence of express malice on
the part of the defendant, he dismissed Telnikoff's action. The
judge held that Matusevitch was doing no more than commenting on the employment policies of the BBC's Russian service. He
ruled that a fair-minded person might honestly hold these views;
it mattered not that many might disagree with them, or even that
they may have been of a bigoted or extreme nature.

Telnikoff took the matter to the Court of Appeal, to no avail.

The question was whether the jury should consider the letter by itself – in which case it might appear that Matusevitch was making allegations of fact – or in conjunction with the article which had prompted Matusevitch's letter – in which case it would become more apparent that Matusevitch was not making allegations of fact so much as commenting on what Telnikoff had written. The Court of Appeal felt that it was always permissible, and indeed essential, for the court to have regard to the context of the libel.

But the defence of fair comment raised points of sufficient complexity to take the matter to the House of Lords, who, after three days of debate, seemingly financed by the Goldsmith Foundation, accepted by a majority of 4–1 the argument against Matusevitch: that a number of people reading the letter would probably not have read the original article. They held that the letter therefore had to be considered on its own. This analysis does seem to have failed to take proper account of exactly what Matusevitch's letter was. Considerations of freedom of speech appeared to have been swamped by an intellectual study of the defence of fair comment.

The House of Lords did, however, define fair comment in a manner which would assist in establishing the defence. A defendant merely has to show that the facts upon which his or her comments were based are true, and that the comment was objectively fair in the sense that any individual, however prejudiced and obstinate, could honestly hold the views expressed. There is no obligation on the defendant to substantiate or in any way to justify his comment or to explain why he holds his opinion. The Court of Appeal had noted that some might think it odd to refer to the protection of what might be prejudiced, wrong-headed and grossly exaggerated opinion as fair comment. The court thought another possible formulation might be to call the defence honest comment, but that had the disadvantage that it might bring into play questions about the defendant's state of mind which are not relevant unless and until the plaintiff seeks to defeat the defence of fair comment by alleging malice on the part of the defendant.

Armed with the House of Lords ruling, a retrial took place, and in March 1992 – a mere eight years after the offending article was published – Telnikoff was awarded the staggering sum of £240,000. By this time Matusevitch had moved to the Washington office of Radio Free Europe. Telnikoff therefore had to try to enforce his judgement through the American courts. It was perhaps something of an omen that the dollar equivalent of his award, which had originally been $416,000, had shrunk to $370,800 by the time he tried to register the judgement. Worse was to follow. Telnikoff then had to go through the discovery and interrogatories procedure of US law, which established that there was no evidence that it was actually being suggested that he wanted to introduce blood-testing, or that he had made any statements inciting racial hatred. By this stage, the American media had interested themselves in the case. Amicus briefs* were filed by the *New York Times*, the Hearst Corporation and fourteen other organisations.

In January 1995 District Court Judge Urbina gave summary judgement precluding the enforcement of an English judgement. In so doing he was following the decision in Bachchan v. India Abroad Publications Inc. that the enforcement of a claim for libel under the English law of defamation would, in these circumstances, be antithetical to the First Amendment to the US Constitution, which protects freedom of speech. In the United States the plaintiff has to prove that the statements were false, and the court would look at the defendant's state of mind and intention. The constitutional right to free speech prevented this type of hyperbole from being actionable, and required proof of actual malice in relation to statements about public figures. Foreign judgements need not be recognised if the cause of action on which the judgement is based is repugnant to the public policy of the United States. The presumption under English law that defamatory words are false, and the fact that a defendant in

---

*A procedure enabling interested parties who are not parties to the case to make representations to the court.

an English court could be held liable for a statement which proved to be false but which he or she honestly believed to be true, and had published without any negligence, are alien to US law. This decision was upheld in the most forthright terms by the Maryland State Appeals Court, which considered that the published comments were rhetorical hyperbole and part of a vigorous public debate.

The case thus proved to be disastrous for Telnikoff. He faced a liability for costs of £150,000. He said that his life had been devastated by allegations of racism and that other human-rights campaigners had shunned him.

The case on which the US decision was based itself featured many of the problems that arise in litigation which has no real connection with England. The action was brought by an Indian businessman, Ajitabh Bachchan, against a Swedish newspaper, *Dagens Nyjeter*. In 1990 the paper reported that Bachchan had a Swiss bank account into which commissions from the Swedish company Bofors had allegedly been paid as a kick-back for a large arms contract with the Indian government. At no stage in the subsequent proceedings was it suggested that the report was true, and Bachchan vehemently denied any wrongdoing. It seemed that he was the innocent victim of an alleged political scandal involving former prime minister Rajiv Gandhi.

The question was not whether he had been libelled, but whether he should be allowed to sue in England. *Dagens Nyjeter*, being a Swedish-language paper, had a circulation of 400,000 in Sweden and sold at most 200 copies in England, presumably to assorted Swedes. But Bachchan, having lived in England for two years, was able to sue there. He won damages and an apology in *Dagens Nyjeter* stating that the paper had been misled by the Indian authorities. This exoneration was not, it seems, enough for Bachchan. He also sued a New York news agency, India Abroad Publications Inc., whose reporter in London had wired it to two Indian newspapers, a few copies of which were sold in England – as was *India Abroad*, the company's New York newspaper. Bachchan secured a judgement for £40,000 in 1991 against India

Abroad Publications Inc. and the reporter, Rahul Bedi. He endeavoured to enforce the judgement in New York, but Judge Shirley Fingerhood struck out the claim on the basis that the restrictive principles of English libel law made the enforcement of such a judgement repugnant to public policy and contrary to the freedoms protected by the First Amendment of the Constitution. The upshot of this decision is that, unless American defendants have assets in the UK, it is not worth suing them.

# 21

# LIBEL IN THE NEW MILLENNIUM

We have examined all the angles of the law of libel as it has been applied in the past, but what direction will it take as we enter the new millennium? The most significant influence on future libel cases will be the effects of the Defamation Act 1996, parts of which have been touched on throughout this book.

The first attempt to reform the Defamation Act of 1952 came in the 1975 report of the committee chaired by Mr Justice Faulks, which was left to collect dust. More effective was a bill prepared by Mr Justice Hoffman in 1989, although not enacted, which proposed the introduction of a swift procedure for small libel claims. Underlying Hoffman's approach was the theory that inflexible insistence on perfect justice could mean that for many people there would be no justice at all. Hoffman's proposals were rejected in 1991 by Lord Justice Neill's committee, which reviewed the law of libel. However, the bill was to form the basis of the changes introduced by the Defamation Act 1996.

The new Defamation Act had the laudable aims of updating and simplifying the law of libel and making litigation less costly. Unhappily, however, it was the legislative equivalent of the

Friday-afternoon car off the assembly line. It was largely procedural and did not address fundamental issues such as the need to
establish damage to reputation. It was hastened into force in
September 1996 to alter the rules governing parliamentary privilege, thus enabling, as we have seen, Neil Hamilton to bring his
ill-starred libel action. Its crucial provisions relating to summary
procedure and the defences of offer of amends and privilege did
not come into operation until 28 February 2000 and were consequently overtaken by the proposals made by the master of the
rolls, Lord Woolf, for the reform of civil procedure in other cases.

The latter, enshrined in the Civil Procedure Act of 1997, came
into effect in April 1999. The new rules provide for active case-
management by the court – potentially good news for defendants
in that plaintiffs who issue gagging writs will be compelled to
bring them to court. However, the balance of the new Woolf
changes is firmly in favour of the claimant (as the plaintiff has
come to be known under the Woolf regime). Their aim is to make
justice more accessible, fair and efficient. Courts are commanded
to give effect to the overriding objective that the parties should
be on as equal a footing as possible, that expense is where possible saved and that cases are dealt with in a way that is
proportionate to the amount of money involved, the importance
of the case, the complexity of the issues and the financial position of each party. Less advantageous to a defendant is the fact
that whereas the claimant is required to prepare his or her case
more fully before issuing proceedings, and to explore alternative
means of resolving the matter, the defendant will find him or
herself under pressure from the court and from the plaintiff to
respond swiftly to the claim, and may well thus be deprived of
the time necessary to prepare a proper defence.

A plaintiff will also be able to urge a defendant to settle by
making a formal offer stating a sum for which he or she would
settle their claim even before proceedings are issued. Suppose the
claimant says he would be prepared to settle for £15,000, the
defendant declines the offer and a court decides upon £20,000
damages. The claimant can be awarded interest at a punitive rate

of 10 per cent over base rate on both the damages and the costs (assessed on the higher indemnity scale) as from the end of the twenty-one-day period which runs from the making of such a settlement offer. In as uncertain and as plaintiff-friendly an area of litigation as libel, it is going to be a brave defendant who risks taking his case to court.

The provisions in the Defamation Act relating to privilege came into force on 1 April 1999, with the remainder taking effect on 28 February 2000. The excuse for the delay was the time it has taken successive governments to implement the changes in the court rules necessary to accommodate the new, but not startlingly radical, procedures introduced by the act.

In line with the simplification of civil procedure under the rules laid down by Lord Woolf, judges will increasingly take control of libel actions to ensure that they are swiftly and less expensively brought to court, or are settled or otherwise disposed of at an early stage. The use of juries is restricted under the Defamation Act, as a judge alone will deal with the summary procedure and offer-of-amends cases described in this chapter. If damages are limited to £10,000, a cheap, fast-track claims procedure can be used. High court judges who were specialist libel practitioners have been appointed to deal with such cases. However, defendants are quite likely to find that they incur substantial costs in defending claims of up to £10,000 under a regime which will require their defence to be ready within a couple of weeks rather than months, if they are to prevent summary judgement being ordered. Moreover, courts face a growth in the number of small claims and defendants will need to devise effective strategies to deal with fast-moving claims of up to £10,000 without spending too much money in the process. For plaintiffs, the act introduces a number of significant benefits. Under Sections 8 to 10, a claimant will be able to obtain summary judgement thereby avoiding the costs and delay of a full trial, just as has been possible in ordinary money claims, if he can establish that the defence has no realistic prospect of success and there is no other reason why the case should be tried.

In a case which had originally been decided before the summary procedure under Section 8 had come into force, Safeway Stores plc v. Albert Tate, the Court of Appeal held that the right to trial by jury, and in particular to have the jury determine the question of libel or no libel, was not a matter of procedure but an important substantive legal right which could be changed only by statute and not by the procedural alterations to the court rules. This may lead to a reluctance on the part of the courts to deprive a litigant of his right to trial by jury, although the Court of Appeal did observe that if the matter had come on for trial on or after 28 February 2000, it would have been within the judge's power to determine that the words in question were defamatory of the complainant, to give summary judgement for Safeway, to award damages of up to £10,000 and to issue an injunction.

Given the expense of libel litigation, and the fact that legal aid is not available in libel cases, this is a significant improvement for a plaintiff. A fanciful hope of success or an unrealistic arguable defence will not be enough for a defendant to defeat a claim for summary judgement. Reasons justifying a full trial in spite of a somewhat ropey defence could include the seriousness of the accusation, the need to resolve conflicts of evidence or the existence of similar claims against other persons.

Even if there is an arguable defence, the judge may nevertheless use the fast-track procedure to enable him to decide the case without a jury, provided the plaintiff limits his damages to £10,000. The court is given a new power, following the model of Section 4 New Zealand Libel Act 1992, to declare that a statement is false and defamatory. This is potentially alarming for defendants, as a finding could be made under pressure from a Maxwell-type litigant to dispose economically of a claim without any real consideration by the court of the facts, and as a means of circumventing any public interest or qualified-privilege defence. Thereafter the media would republish such statements very much at their peril. The court can order that the defendant publish a suitable correction and apology. If the parties cannot agree the terms of the apology, the court will not dictate how and where it is to be published but can direct that a summary of its judgement be published. It can also make an order preventing any further publication of the libellous statement.

There are benefits for defendants as well. If they can persuade the judge that the plaintiff has no realistic prospect of winning and that there is no other reason why the case should be heard, it will be struck out without a full trial. Furthermore, the limitation period for bringing libel claims has, under Section 5, been reduced from three years to one (except, curiously, in Scotland, where they seem to need longer to ponder such matters). There is, however, a greater discretion to extend the limitation period. The court can look at the length of and reason for any delay in bringing proceedings, and at matters such as when the plaintiff learned of the libel, how promptly he or she then acted and whether the evidence still exists to enable a fair trial to take place.

In January 2000, Mr Justice Gray refused to permit Grigori Loutchansky, the Russian businessman he had allowed to sue *The Times* in the UK (see Chapter 20), to amend his claim to seek a declaration of falsity, which the claimant doubtless felt provided a better remedy in his situation than a claim for damages. In Hinks v. Channel 4, in which the claimant's solicitor had used an out-of-date textbook showing the old three-year limitation period as opposed to the new one of a year, the claimant was debarred from pursuing his claim, though in all probability the court took into account the fact that he should have a claim in negligence against his lawyer.

With publications such as books, each sale will, unfortunately, still constitute a new act of publication for the purpose of calculating the limitation period. It will therefore continue to be possible to follow the example of the Duke of Brunswick and send one's manservant to a bookshop (although the twenty-first-century equivalent is likely to be an order through the Internet) to buy a copy of an offending work years after its publication. In the United States there is a more sensible system of measuring the limitation period from the date of first publication.

There are provisions under the civil procedure rules for summary judgements which will apply to defamation cases, but these have been in the nature of a stopgap to allow the Defamation Act 1996 to be fully implemented. It is unfortunate that, after Parliament laid down a special 'summary disposal' procedure under Section 9 of the act, the courts were unable to devise the relevant procedural rules to give effect to the changes in the law. Instead summary disposal became entangled with Lord Woolf's somewhat different summary judgement procedure. Libel law, with its freedom of speech implications and human rights aspect, does need to be dealt with separately in court procedure and as a specialist jurisdiction.

Defendants now have to say why they deny the claimant's allegations, and to set out any different version of the facts upon which they seek to rely. Both sides have to sign statements of truth in any pleading or witness statement. This still falls some way short of requiring a plaintiff to verify on oath which of the facts in the disputed article are false – something which would deter the institution of mendacious proceedings. The likelihood is that statements of case by the claimant will continue to be sparse, short on particulars and on occasion distinctly economical with the truth. The burden of great specificity is still likely to fall on defendants as opposed to claimants.

Under the Woolf proposals, litigation is intended to be a last resort and the parties are meant to go through various stages designed to explore the possibility of settlement. These are known as pre-action protocols. They lay down the specific matters that should be set out in correspondence between the parties within a timetabled framework so that each side is able to form a realistic assessment of the case against them and may thereby avoid having to go on to court. So, rather than firing off a libel writ as a reflex action, a claimant will normally have to show that he or she has set out the claim in detail and taken appropriate steps to try to resolve the dispute before issuing proceedings.

Costs must be kept proportionate to the nature and gravity of the case and to the stage that the complaint has reached. In

Times Newspapers Limited v. Singh and Choudry, in which the claimants had accepted an offer of £12,000 damages, the legal costs of £1.05 million they were optimistically hoping to recover from the newspaper were described by the court as 'astonishingly disproportionate' and were disallowed virtually in their entirety.

In May 1999, Lord Woolf did preside over an appeal, in his capacity as master of the rolls, in the case of McPhilemy v. Times Newspapers Limited, which concerned an alleged conspiracy to murder Republicans in Northern Ireland. McPhilemy had produced a television programme on the subject called *The Committee*, and an accompanying book has subsequently been published in the US. The court, asked to rule on the complexities of the pleadings in the case, made it clear that it wished to discourage contests over pleadings (or statements of case, as they are now known) and generally to make them less technical. Its purpose would henceforward be simply to mark out the parameters of the case whose particulars would be apparent from the witness statements, and it expected to see proper case-management to ensure that libel actions were kept within manageable and economic bounds to minimise the burden on parties of slender means.

*The Committee* spawned a considerable amount of litigation. Although, owing to its content, it was not sold in the UK, David Trimble, Northern Ireland's first minister, is suing the Internet retailer Amazon UK for fulfilling an order for the book – a case likely to set the rules for libel in the field of e-commerce.

The defence of innocent dissemination has also been amended by the Defamation Act. This is designed to protect those not primarily responsible for a libel but who are deemed in law nevertheless to have published it – defendants such as printers, distributors, booksellers, the presenters of live broadcasts and talk-in shows and Internet service-providers. The praiseworthy aim here is to bring the law up to date, since modern technology has effectively deprived a printer, for example, of the opportunity he had in the days of hot metal to study what he was printing. For the same reason the act restricts the liability of a person who merely provides an Internet bulletin board for what is actually posted on it without his or her knowledge. A ruling in June 1999 by Mr Justice Gray indicates that the courts will view such a defence in terms of upholding freedom of expression. This case, brought by the opinion-poll researchers MORI against the BBC, concerned a live pre-election broadcast containing characteristically forthright comments by the Eurosceptic Sir James Goldsmith. It showed that a broadcaster is likely to have a defence if it can prove that it had no effective control over a person making a contentious statement. The fact that there was a seven-second profanity delay did not stop this broadcast being deemed 'live'. The case ended rather dramatically in July when, after a two-week trial, MORI accepted a walkaway settlement just as the jury was about to return its verdict, having deliberated over it for five hours.

Unfortunately, however, some of these good intentions have been lost in some ineptly drafted legislation. To avail himself of the new-style defence of innocent dissemination, the defendant needs to establish that he was not the author, editor or primary publisher of the statement complained of, that he took reasonable care in relation to its publication and that he did not know, or have reasonable cause to believe, that his involvement caused or contributed to the publication of the defamatory statements. In assessing what constitutes reasonable care, one would look at the circumstances of the publication and the extent of the defendant's responsibility for it, together with the past history and track record of the primary publisher. Is it, for example, a magazine which regularly libels people? Thus publications in the *Scallywag* mould will continue to have problems.

It seems that the new defence is aimed at amending the common law of libel rather than supplementing it. The unfortunate consequence is that instead of liberalising the law, the act has blunderingly restricted it. The problem lies in the use of the words 'defamatory statements'. Here the drafters of the legislation seem to have overlooked the fundamental difference between the terms 'defamatory' (the mere tendency to damage reputation) and 'libellous' (the publication of a legally indefensible statement damaging a person's reputation). For example, if someone is accused of dishonesty, the allegation remains defamatory whether or not it is true, and whether or not it is in the public interest to publish it. If the accusation can be proved to be true, there is a defence in libel, but while it may not therefore be libellous it is still defamatory. A secondary publisher would therefore know – or would learn when his attention was drawn to the matter – that he was contributing to the publication of a defamatory statement, even if he believed it to be true or defensible under the law of libel.

Under the old common law, a printer or bookseller could rely on the defence of innocent dissemination if he took reasonable care to ensure that he was not publishing something libellous. Lord Denning spelled out this defence in dealing with Sir James Goldsmith's actions against *Private Eye* in Goldsmith v. Sperrings in 1977: 'Common sense and fairness require that no subordinate distributor should be held liable for a libel contained in the newspaper or periodical unless he knew or ought to have known that it contained a libel on the plaintiff himself, that is to say that it contained a libel that could not be justified or excused.' Under the new law such justification or excuse will not be sufficient, as the words will still be defamatory, even if the distributor has obtained legal advice that there is a good defence to the claim.

Since this part of the Defamation Act came into force in September 1996, there have been successful attempts to stop the publication of defamatory material. Neil Hamilton persuaded booksellers not to stock David Leigh's *Sleaze: The Corruption of Parliament*, and controversial historian David Irving even sued branch managers of Waterstone's who were selling *Denying the Holocaust: The Growing Assault on Truth and Memory*. It is unlikely that this legislative change would survive a concerted challenge under Article 10 of the European Convention of Human Rights, which is dealt with later in this chapter.

It is already far too easy for a litigant using the Maxwell style to complain about booksellers continuing to sell an allegedly

defamatory book. A plaintiff does not have to give any undertaking as to the damage he may cause to an author's sales or a
shop's profits when he demands that a book be withdrawn from
sale, even if his claim subsequently proves spurious. With the
cost of obtaining specialist legal advice, many booksellers feel
they have no alternative but to remove the offending material
from their shelves, no matter how villainous the complainant. It
is a pity that a suggestion by the Faulks Committee that such an
undertaking should be given if a plaintiff wants to claim additional damages for the failure to withdraw a book fell on deaf
legislative ears. Likewise the responsible Internet service-provider
who polices his website runs the risk, through the exercise of
some editorial control, of being held to be an editor of the website, or of having contributed to the publication of defamatory
statements, and as a result of falling foul of the new defence
under Section 1.

More promising for defendants is the new defence of offer of
amends, which replaces the needlessly technical and useless
defence of accidental defamation under Section 4 of the 1952
act, which was rarely called upon. The new defence provides a
defendant with the means of resolving a case where a mistake
has been made. It prevents the gold-digging tactics of certain
plaintiffs, assisted by their solicitors, who run up legal bills with
abandon in the knowledge that they will ultimately win their
case, and who may try to insist that the not-so-small matter of
their costs is attended to before the claim can be settled.

The offer of amends must be made in writing. It must be
plainly expressed that it is such an offer and made clear whether
it relates to every alleged libel, or whether it is qualified in some
way. The offer has to be tendered before a defence is submitted.
The defendant who makes an offer of amends in relation to a
particular libel has in effect to admit liability. He cannot at the
same time put in a defence that what he said was nevertheless
true or fair comment. The defendant proposes a suitable correction and apology and payment of such compensation (if any),
and of any agreed or determined costs. Any dispute about

damages is heard by a judge alone, sitting without a jury. He will not be restricted to £10,000, as with summary procedure, but the court will take account of any apology which has been published. The awards judges make in such cases will set a useful yardstick for the resolution of libel claims in future and are likely to result in a lower and more consistent system of libel damages.

If an offer of amends is accepted, the action is brought to an end. If it is not, the defendant has a defence to the claim, unless the claimant can prove that he or she published it knowing, or having reason to believe, that it was false and defamatory. No oversight of the sort mentioned in relation to the innocent dissemination defence was made here: the plaintiff has to prove not only that the defendant knew that the reference was defamatory but also that it was false. If the claimant is playing hardball, the defendant can apply to a judge to fix fair terms of resolution, including damages and a statement in open court.

The Defamation Act 1996 also widens and clarifies the law of privilege. As we have seen, Section 13 already permits MPs to waive parliamentary privilege in order to bring libel actions. Now publishing fair and accurate contemporaneous reports of court proceedings, including those of European and certain international courts, will attract absolute privilege. It matters not that what has been said in court may have been a malicious lie – and it may well extend to reporting an outburst from the public gallery. Reports of public proceedings or extracts from certain official documents will attract qualified privilege, but sometimes with an obligation to publish a reasonable statement in explanation or contradiction – a form of statutory right of reply. This privilege now extends to all publications, including books, magazines and television programmes. Previously it was confined to newspapers (although for this purpose any publication published at least every thirty-six days qualified as a newspaper). This change makes it easier for the media to report public information without having to be sure that the truth of the material could be proved in court. A notable extension covers documents circulated to members of a UK public company, hitherto a fruitful source of work for libel lawyers.

One of the justifiable complaints against the law of libel is that it is a rich man's sport. Those advising tabloid newspapers on libel risks factor in the virtual financial impossibility of an erring vicar and/or bimbette suing a powerful news group. Even though the court is now required to take account of the relative strengths and weaknesses of each side's position in formulating the appropriate procedure, a claimant's lack of funds will inevitably remain a consideration when a media organisation is deciding whether or not to run a contentious story. Legal aid is still not available in libel actions, either to plaintiffs or to defendants, and hitherto all complaints about the unfairness this occasions to the weaker party, particularly when this is the defendant, have failed to impress the European Commission of Human Rights.

A system of contingency fees, whereby a lawyer needs to win to get paid, taking his fee as a percentage cut of any damages, has never been allowed in the UK for fear of an upsurge in the number of ambulance-chasing lawyers and to prevent the worst excesses of US plaintiff attorneys taking root here. This anxiety has perhaps been misplaced, as civil actions other than defamation and false imprisonment are tried without juries (defamation cases in any event tend to be handled by specialist lawyers and heard by specialist judges), and the judges presiding alone should be able to sniff out an over-rehearsed case. Furthermore, with damages being fixed by judges, the tendency of American juries to award millions of dollars will not spread across the Atlantic. One of the main arguments against contingency fees in the UK is that they provide no protection for the successful defendant who would normally be reimbursed his legal costs. So if an impecunious claimant legally represented on a no-win, no-fee basis were to lose an action, the defendant would not be able to recover those costs. Additionally there has been no political appetite for extending legal aid to defamation when government policy has been to cut back on such expenditure rather than to increase it.

Conditional fees, a variation of contingency fees, are, however, permitted in the UK. With this system, the lawyer still needs to win to get paid, but his fee is linked to the legal costs rather than to damages (subject to the capping rule discussed below). Conditional fee agreements were first allowed by Section 58 of the Courts and Legal Services Act 1990. Initially they were applied mainly to personal injury cases but the Conditional Fees Agreement Order of 1998 has now extended them to almost all types of litigation, including libel actions. Given the fact that in libel cases legal costs are often greater than the damages – the reverse of the situation with personal injury cases – the British lawyer, unlike his or her American counterpart, would probably get a better deal under conditional fee agreements than from a contingency fee. In essence, the plaintiff will not have to pay his lawyer's charges if he loses. If he wins, his lawyer can recover his legal costs from the losing defendant, although he may claw back out of the claimant's damages certain costs which prove to be irrecoverable from the defendant. If the plaintiff loses the case, he pays the defendant's costs either from his own pocket or out of the insurance he has taken out as part of the arrangement. The claimant's lawyer, however, is entitled to increase his basic fee by up to 100 per cent, in theory to cover his losses in those cases where a claimant's case fails. So theoretically he can hike up his basic £250 an hour to £500.

It is not, however, all good news for lawyers. The Law Society has given some indication that the increase on basic charges should not exceed 50 per cent, and that indeed this may become the maximum. So rates of £500 an hour are likely to be challenged not only by the defendant, if he is having to pay the costs, but also by the claimant, if his lawyer is trying to claw back his fee out of the damages. The fee can be assessed by the courts, which will take into account whether it is proportionate to the sums involved and to the importance of the case. And in a climate in which attempts are being made to reduce legal fees, the courts may well not allow a fee if a lawyer has tried to double the rate of £250 an hour. This is likely to make lawyers even more wary about the cases they take up on behalf of claimants on conditional fee agreements.

It remains to be seen how the courts will assess legal costs that include a success fee, but they will have to be proportionate to the sum recovered. As claimants' solicitors may want to settle at a lower figure to ensure that the case is indeed won, the level of fees may not prove to be a bonanza for lawyers.

The Law Society has recommended that a cap is placed on the success fee a claimant's lawyer can charge for both barrister and solicitor, namely that it shall not exceed 25 per cent of the damages awarded. This, too, may become mandatory. So if the damages awarded amounted to were £20,000, the success fee would be capped at £5,000. That may not present a great problem in personal injury claims, where the inherent risks are fewer and the costs lower, but in libel the lawyers would be bearing potentially high costs: £50,000 for a five-day trial would not be unusual. The problem for libel lawyers acting under conditional fee arrangements is that since the ruling in the Elton John case, libel damages have fallen. Today virtually the maximum awarded in libel damages would be in the region of £150,000. So conditional fees will be fine for libel lawyers as long as they keep winning, but one loss will more than wipe out their profits. As libel litigation is notoriously unpredictable, and as a number of firms who operate conditional-fee agreements are undercapitalised, there may be casualties.

The concept of a success fee is by no means unknown in commercial transactions, where a larger fee is likely to be payable if a particular deal comes to fruition, but are conditional fees a valid means of addressing the balance in favour of libel plaintiffs with limited resources? Plaintiffs may well be encouraged that a lawyer is prepared to bear most of the financial risk of litigation, which certainly sounds more attractive than finding out at a late stage, having paid large fees, that your legal representative always thought your case was weak. However, in practice, I suspect that conditional fees will not in the immediate future have a significant impact on this area of law. If, as may happen, they become widely used elsewhere, there may be pressure to adapt libel to follow suit, but if so, the ratio of legal costs to damages will have to be brought into line with the position in other fields, or a different success fee made allowable for more complex litigation. In the meantime, such arrangements may prove to be little more than a marketing gimmick by lawyers who have already been willing to take on speculative cases and will continue to do so.

A prudent lawyer will usually take on only cases with a very good chance of success. We have seen that the increase in a lawyer's normal fees to reflect the risk inherent in conditional fees is likely to become effectively capped at 25 per cent of the damages. The Law Society has calculated percentage increases that would be required to allow for the uncertainties of litigation and the inevitable lost cases. Thus a careful plaintiff's lawyer who is 80 per cent confident of his case would statistically require an uplift of 25 per cent to cover the 20 per cent area of risk and the probability that other cases will be lost with no fees being paid to him. If one then brings into the equation an often-quoted statistic – that even in the strongest libel claim there may be a 15 per cent chance of failure owing to the unpredictability of jury verdicts, the prejudice of the judge or bad witnesses – it soon becomes apparent that realistically, only the safest cases will be undertaken on contingency fee agreements. If the sure-fire libel winner can only engender 85 per cent confidence, that 15 per cent area of uncertainty will require an increase on the fee of 18 per cent. In personal injury litigation, on the other hand, it is much easier to envisage where there really is a 100 per cent prospect of winning.

In libel litigation, the claimant's lawyer also has to factor in potential difficulties of enforcing the judgement. When conditional fees funded a case against the tobacco company Gallaher which collapsed, the plaintiff's solicitors agreed not to act for a number of years in any such litigation. There appears to have been some fear that liability could have attached to the solicitors themselves for the legal costs, even though in principle a solicitor acting on a conditional fee basis should be in the same position as a solicitor acting for a legally aided client. So at present there do seem to be some risks for solicitors who undertake these arrangements. However, they may find their smarter clients will insist on conditional fee arrangements rather than paying as the fees are incurred.

The real comfort – in theory, at least – is to the plaintiff, who will be able to call on his insurers if he loses rather than face bankruptcy. It is uncertain whether many insurance companies will continue to be prepared to underwrite such cases, at any rate until conditional fees have become widespread and there is an acceptable level of business over which to spread the risk. Insuring a libel action is very different from underwriting the costs of a personal injury claim, where the insurer is well placed to assess the risk and the costs are fairly consistent. If, for example, a motorcyclist wishes to sue for a road accident in which he broke his leg, the insurance company will have police, medical and other expert reports. There is also likely to be a sufficient volume of such claims to calculate with reasonable accuracy the likely outcome. Moreover, damages for that type of injury will fall within a clearly defined bracket. Insurers may require their own lawyers to evaluate the chances of success, which will in itself add to the cost of the insurance and hence the litigation.

Libel claims, by contrast, are individual in nature. Each case is quite different and the level of damages will depend on the impression formed by the jury, having taken into account the behaviour and reputation of the parties concerned. Legal costs also vary enormously. And all these factors will probably not be known until late on in the litigation process. So how does the cautious underwriter provide for the unmasking of a former Cabinet minister's perjury after the expenditure of some £2 million of legal costs, or for a ruling by the Court of Appeal, as in the Reynolds case, which significantly alters the interpretation of the qualified privilege defence?

It is, then, an odd business for insurers to be involved in.

Whereas, for example, if you insure your house against fire, the insurer hopes there will be no claim at all, here there will already have been an adverse event, namely the institution of libel proceedings in the first place. The insurer will have to hope that the claimant's lawyer has called it right. And even then, sometimes the most promising cases can be lost, and occasionally the most experienced lawyers lend their support to distinctly unpromising cases. Not only do insurers have to set against those uncertainties the enormous legal costs they may have to pay if the case fails, but they may also wonder whether they should be in the business of generating libel litigation, because that is what they will in effect be doing – particularly when, as a specialist insurer, they may be asked to cover a claimant while they are already insuring the defendant against libel risks.

Insurance companies are likely to find that there is not the turnover, in comparison with personal injury claims, to justify moving into this high-risk and very unpredictable area of the law. Premiums may amount to between 10 and 35 per cent of the ascertainable defence costs. Under Section 29 of the Access to Justice Act 1999, premiums for conditional fee arrangements can be recovered from the unsuccessful defendant. If this was to extend to libel litigation, it could swell the costs considerably, since defendants would run the risk of having to pay the enhanced fees of the plaintiffs as well as the high premiums. Insurance companies are now suspicious that they will only be asked to insure very risky cases, and this fear will inevitably be reflected in the premiums they charge. In practice, it is likely that they will refuse to insure many actions. The stiff premiums will make claimants think twice about buying insurance when they are confident of winning, and they may even be dubious about it where there is a high probability that the litigation will be settled.

In other types of libel insurance, a substantial five- or six-figure excess before the insurance cuts in is increasingly being stipulated – and even then the insurer may require the insured to pay a percentage of the remainder of the claim. If this course is followed, conditional fee insurance will have little attraction for the middle- or low-income plaintiff, unless the solicitor is prepared to underwrite that part of the risk. The probability is that a media group will successfully fight a case against a conditional-fee plaintiff, leaving his insurers with a legal bill which will send shockwaves through the industry.

A litigant may also experience difficulties with his or her solicitor. The plaintiff may want no more than an apology, whereas the lawyer might seek damages in order to establish that the case has been won – and that the necessary condition for collecting his or her enhanced fees under the conditional agreement has been triggered. If there are no damages, there is no fund from which the lawyer can recoup the increased costs. Alternatively, the claimant may wish to pursue high libel damages to restore his reputation, whereas the lawyer may be keen to settle for a lower figure to ensure that he gets paid. And as we have seen, the tendency towards lower damages is likely to be accentuated by the Defamation Act 1996.

The uncertainty of libel litigation and the risk of operating conditional fee agreements was illustrated by a case brought by a barrister, Luisa Morelli, and her businessman friend Vincent Coyle, which, it was revealed in December 1998, had been the subject of a conditional fee agreement. The claimants recovered £30,000 and £15,000 respectively from *The Sunday Times*, which had suggested that their County Court action against the airline Unijet, for what had been described as the flight from hell, had been a try-on. Yet although the action ended in victory, it was by no means all plain sailing for the plaintiffs' solicitors. What had appeared to them to be an open-and-shut case seemed much less so when, after the proceedings had been underway for some time, they discovered that Coyle had earlier served a jail sentence for an unrelated fraud. Another high-profile case was that of Labour MP Helen Brinton, who was reported in December 1998 to have successfully sued on a conditional-fee basis and received substantial damages after she was wrongfully featured in an article in the *Sun* headed 'WHY CAN'T THE LABOUR PARTY KEEP ITS KIT ON?'

The paper had rashly misinterpreted the noise coming from an innocent dinner party.

Another development which will have an impact on libel in the new millennium is the explosive growth over the last five years of one particular medium for disseminating information worldwide, namely, of course, the Internet. In the final two years of the twentieth century this vast expansion encompassed a huge increase in the use of the Internet for business as well as for purely information-gathering purposes, and the 1999 Computer Industry Almanac estimated that there were then 259 million Internet users worldwide.

The 'information superhighway' is likely to produce very real problems in the fields of jurisdiction and enforcement.

There is no significant difference between a libel on a printed page and one which can be electronically accessed on a computer screen. The jurisdictional problems, however, can be complex. 'Publication' takes place where the information is downloaded, but the material may originally have been posted elsewhere. However, it may be argued that where information has been put on a website in a foreign jurisdiction, say the United States, and some activity on the part of an Internet-user is required to download it, there is no more an act of publication in the user's jurisdiction than there would be if that person had flown to the United States and purchased a book that was not otherwise available in his or her own country.

But the fact remains that what might have been free of libel risks in the United States – the biggest source of information on the Internet – might be found to be libellous when downloaded in England (which is if nothing else a strong argument for greater harmonisation of the libel laws in different jurisdictions). There are potentially a number of people who can be held to account for libel on the Internet, including the provider of the service, the content or the access as well as the website host. So the person who put the information on the net may be held responsible for a libel in some foreign country with hostile libel laws even though he has no control over where it is published.

At an equal disadvantage are claimants, who may find it almost impossible to prevent further publication of a libel on the Internet in another country. They may also be unable to discover who placed the libel on the net. English courts are likely to follow their American counterparts in compelling Internet service-providers to reveal the identity of such offenders, but this is not always known to them. Even if the perpetrator of the libel is rooted out, the claimant may find that taking proceedings in a foreign jurisdiction, where the prospects of successfully enforcing the judgement are doubtful, is going to be prohibitively expensive. The majority of Internet service-providers are based in the USA, and as we have seen, courts there will not enforce UK libel judgements. In any event, the determined Internet libeller will simply engage in jurisdiction-hopping ending up in a country where his defamatory message is litigation-proof. This was what appears to have happened in Julian Lewis's litigation against *Scallywag* magazine in Chapter 18.

If the publisher of a libel on the Internet is a man of straw or someone adept at evading liability a claimant may feel that the only worthwhile course of action is to sue the service-provider. Under English common law, the basis of liability for Internet service-providers is that a person who allows a defamatory message to remain on a noticeboard over which he has control after receiving a complaint is guilty of libel. This principle was established in 1936 in Byrne v. Dean, a case in which a man successfully sued his golf club for allowing a defamatory notice (it suggested that he had caddishly called in the police to remove a gambling machine at the club) to remain on display.

One school of thought is that libel on the Internet does not matter; that the very idea of defamation is anathema to the freedom of the medium. That may well be true of discussion groups, and of the vast quantity of scarcely digested information to be found in cyberspace. There are, however, databanks offering information which, if libellous, would do serious harm and would, for example, show up on any due-diligence research in a major company deal. Indeed, this was one of the factors which enabled Berezovsky to establish jurisdiction in the UK in his action against *Forbes* magazine, recounted in Chapter 20.

Litigation over defamation on the Internet seems to have begun in Western Australia, where an anthropologist recovered Aus$40,000 for allegations posted on a bulletin board about the shortcomings of his research into aboriginal culture and, of rather less academic interest, his own sexual proclivities. Cases have been brought in England for libels on the Internet. Dr Laurence Godfrey, an English nuclear physicist, has issued writs against Demon Internet Limited, Cornell University, New Zealand TeleCom, the online *Toronto Star*, the University of Minnesota, Minneapolis StarNet, two individuals (researcher Michael Dolenga and student Kratchel Quanchairut) and the Melbourne PC Users Group for imputations against his professional competence, in the process earning himself in some quarters the soubriquet 'the Don Quixote of cyberspace'. In April 1995 Godfrey accepted 'significant' damages for remarks made on a Usenet newsgroup by researcher Dr Philip Hallam-Baker of the European Swiss Nuclear Physics Laboratory. He has also obtained a default judgement for £15,000 against Michael Dolenga, who now lives in Canada. Whether, in the light of a comment Dolenga is reported to have made – 'I am not recognising the British Court's jurisdiction, and to hell with it,' Godfrey will harvest the fruits of his litigation remains to be seen. Some of the defendants have settled, including the Melbourne PC users, who agreed to pay him Aus$6,190, but for the most part the cases have been disputed and the Internet defence under Section 1 of the Defamation Act 1996 has been raised.

However, liability for libel could become very wide-ranging. Website-owners could be held responsible not only for the contents of their own sites but also for material accessible via a hyperlink. Judges may be tempted to follow the example of Judge Jean-Jacques Gomez who ordered Yahoo! to remove an advertisement for Nazi paraphernalia in France in January 2001. It had been thought that the Internet precluded such an order but, having appointed an independent expert and having reached

the conclusion that there was a good prospect of an order proving reasonably effective, the judge banned Yahoo! from
displaying the advertisements in France on pain of a penalty of
100,000 francs (£9,200) per day.

Mr Justice Morland held that Demon was not protected by the
innocent dissemination defence in relation to one claim by
Laurence Godfrey. This concerned a message to a newsgroup
which appeared to originate from Dr Godfrey but turned out to
be a forgery. The judge described the message, posted in the
United States on 13 January 1997, as 'squalid, obscene and
defamatory'. Godfrey had complained to Demon on 17 January,
asking for its removal, a request which appears to have been
ignored. Whatever the case, the libellous message remained on
the Internet until 27 January, at which point it was automatically
erased.

The English court, relying on the Byrne v. Dean golf noticeboard case, held that Demon's failure to remove the message
after Godfrey's complaint demonstrated a lack of the necessary
knowledge and exercise of reasonable care required of a service-
provider under Section 1. The judge did, however, indicate that
the level of damages was likely to be very small. Yet in March
2000, two claims arising out of Demon's failure to remove libels
about Godfrey, relating to the January 1997 complaint and a further one in July 1998, resulted in agreed damages of £5,000 and
£15,000 respectively for Godfrey, in addition to the payment of
his legal costs, which were said to total £230,000.

As a result, service-providers are now more likely to remove
material they have displayed on the Internet on receiving a libel
complaint, as happened when it was claimed that the Outcast
website had published, and threatened to continue publishing,
defamatory statements about the *Pink Paper*. Net Benefit, the ISP
host for Outcast, closed down the website. A challenge is being
made under Article 10, asserting that Outcast's freedom of speech
has been infringed.

Another case was successfully brought by a computer-games
designer, David Brabin, against Ian Bell in December 1995. This

concerned allegations made on the Worldwide Web casting doubt on Brabin's claim to copyright in the Elite game. The matter was settled on amicable terms involving the retraction of the statement and an apology.

In the United States, meanwhile, a New York District court in the case of Cubby Inc. v. Compuserve in 1991 held that Compuserve was not liable for highly defamatory allegations about the creators of a computer database called Scuttlebutt, which was designed to publish news and gossip about the television, news and radio industries by an outfit called Rumorville. The very name would probably be enough to disqualify Compuserve from an innocent dissemination defence under Section 1 of the British Defamation Act, but the evidence showed that the service-provider had had no opportunity to review the material, which was provided by a subcontractor with whom it had no direct contractual relationship. More alarming, however, for the computer industry was another New York decision, in 1995: Stratton Oakmont Inc. v. Prodigy Services. In this case the plaintiffs were very seriously libelled in a newsgroup called Money Talk, which accused them of fraud. However, the question at issue here was not whether the allegation was true, but whether Prodigy was liable. The court held that they were, as they had advertised the fact that theirs was an online service and a family-orientated computer network which exercised editorial control with a board leader and an automated software-screening service. Prodigy subsequently apologised to the plaintiffs.

After these uncertain beginnings in the United States courts, legislation was enacted to protect the computer industry in general and service-providers in particular. Section 230 of the Communications Decency Act 1995 states that no provider or user of an interactive computer service shall be treated as the publisher of any information provided by another publisher. Section 509 of the Telecommunications Act reinforces this, while Section 509 (c) 2 enacted what is known as the 'good Samaritan defence', which should have been a model for this country's Defamation Act 1996: 'An interactive computer service-provider shall not be liable for taking good-faith steps to restrict access to or availability of material which may be obscene, lewd or violent.'

This legislation dramatically changed the law in a country given to publishing extraordinary libels on the Internet, and it is likely that pressure will be brought for the same standards to be set in the UK and elsewhere in Europe to reflect the transnational nature of such publications.

This should happen when Articles 12 to 15 of the European e-commerce directive are implemented, which is due to take place by 17 January 2002. These will require member states to provide greater protection for intermediary service-providers who merely 'host' or 'cache' (temporarily store) information. However, Internet service-providers will have to expeditiously remove or bar access to problematical material. To that extent their obligations may be even stricter in Europe than they are in the USA.

The European Union's desire to harmonise all matters relating to e-commerce has its dangers in terms of the preservation of free speech and the discouragement of forum-shopping. The Rome II green paper, published in March 2001, seeks to regulate disputes involving a citizen of one country and a company marketing goods or services from another. In this instance, Europe seems to favour the consumer as far as the choice of jurisdiction is concerned. This could have implications for libel, in that a newspaper published online could be exposed to claims in the country where the person alleging the libel lives. So an English online newspaper that might have assumed that its libel risks were confined to England could in fact find itself being sued under the significantly different libel laws that appertain in the fifteen countries of the European Union.

The US legislation, meanwhile, was not good news for plaintiffs like the unfortunate Kenneth Zeran, who, as a result, was unable to recover damages against America Online for malicious hoax messages suggesting that he was selling T-shirts glorifying the Oklahoma city bombers and, for good measure, providing his telephone number. Poor Mr Zeran, who received a number of death threats, was not even a subscriber to AOL. On the facts he should have been compensated, but the American courts were adamant that the poster of the message rather than the service-provider should be held responsible. As that person's identity was unknown, Zeran was left without a remedy. Sidney Blumenthal, a senior adviser to President Clinton, was another casualty in 1998. He sued for wholly false allegations of spouse abuse made by one Matt Drudge, whom Judge Friedmann described not as a reporter, journalist or newsgatherer, but as Drudge himself admitted, simply a purveyor of gossip. Drudge had retracted the allegations within two days of Blumenthal's complaint and accepted them to be without foundation, but the Federal District Court in Washington decided that the service-provider, AOL, was not liable under the terms of the Communications Decency Act, even though they had been paying Drudge a $36,000 retainer. And in December of that year Alexander Lunney's claim against Prodigy Services was rejected by way of summary judgement by the New York Appeal Division. Lunney, not himself a subscriber to Prodigy, was a highly respectable prospective Eagle Scout who found to his horror that as a cruel practical joke someone had posted on a bulletin board vile and obscene messages, including threats to sodomise the scout leader's sons. Again, there was no question the allegations were false: Lunney's problem was that Prodigy had been unaware of the content of the message until it was brought to their attention, at which point it had immediately been withdrawn. Their position was likened to that in earlier cases of telegraph and telephone companies who simply provided the equipment by which libellous messages were communicated. There was no obligation on Prodigy to police their service to prevent such outrageous libels being published.

As well as the information posted on websites, electronic messages, now used by many people as an alternative method of communication to the memo or telephone, can of course give rise to libel litigation. In terms of libel, e-mails are no different from the written page, but the ease with which they can be sent often encourages a dangerous spontaneity. The consequences can be exacerbated by the capacity of the technology to copy information to a large circulation list – not to mention the ability of any of the recipients to forward a message elsewhere – at the click of a mouse. It therefore seems likely that e-mails will provide much work for hungry libel lawyers in the new millennium.

Insurers Norwich Union had to pay £450,000 in damages and costs to Western Provident, a healthcare company, in July 1997 for completely false allegations circulated internally by e-mail that it was insolvent, being investigated by the DTI and unwilling to accept more policies. Norwich Union also apologised and acknowledged these charges to be completely untrue. The damaging nature of such accusations is obvious, but the appreciation of the consequences in what appears to be a transient and all-too-easy-to-use medium operating within the office may not have been. Western Provident was able to obtain an order at an early stage in the proceedings to preserve copies of the offending e-mails, which would in any event have been retrievable from Norwich Union's database.

In April 1995 an Asda customer recovered substantial damages from the supermarket chain for e-mails posted to their Derbyshire branches headed: 'Refund fraud – urgent, urgent, urgent'. The messages falsely accused him of making a fraudulent claim for a refund of the cost of a joint of meat. Needless to say, Asda had not been aware that the customer they were maligning was a police officer. Ironically, it was only because the plaintiff, PC Eggleton, was giving Asda crime-prevention advice at one of their stores that he found out about the e-mails at all.

In July 1999, Exoteric Gas Solutions accepted £101,000 in damages and £125,000 costs for a libellous e-mail distributed by BG, a gas company, to the employees of one of its subsidiaries, Transco, warning them not to have any dealings with EGS and falsely accusing the company of misusing information confidential to Transco.

And in October 2000 libellous e-mails were sent to a company by an ex-employee using a false name. The messages made a number of allegations about the firm and in particular about the private life of the defendant's former boss. The case was notable for the wide-ranging orders for disclosure against the service-providers that enabled the claimants to trace the messages to the defendant's laptop in Turkey. Mr Justice Alliott did not accept the defendant's claim that someone else, using software called Back Orifice, must have gained access to his computer to send the e-mails. He awarded £1,000 damages to the company and £25,000 to the defendant's former boss.

The incorporation of the European Convention of Human Rights into English law via the Human Rights Act 1998, which came into force in October 2000, is also likely to have a very significant impact on the law of libel and to go some way to redressing the balance in favour of defendants in the future. English courts are now required under Section 2 to apply the convention and to take it into account in making its decisions. Article 10 of the convention, which has become the cornerstone of the protection of freedom of speech, was in large measure intended to safeguard the individual's rights against the state rather than to be an adjunct to the libel law. This states that everyone has the right of freedom of expression, which shall include the freedom to hold opinions and to receive and impart information and ideas without interference by public authority, and regardless of frontiers. The exercise of these freedoms may be subject to such restrictions as are prescribed by law and as are necessary in a democratic society. Article 8 incorporates a right of privacy, under which everyone is entitled to respect for his or her private and family life, home and correspondence. Again, there should be no interference by a public authority in this except in such circumstances as may be necessary in a democratic society.

The creation of the convention was a reaction to the excesses of the Second World War. For almost thirty years after it was ratified by the United Kingdom in 1951, the convention had little impact. The decision of the European Court of Human Rights condemning English restrictions on reporting the Thalidomide drug disaster in the 1970s led to the enactment in the UK of the

Contempt of Court Act 1981. In the Tolstoy case, the European Court deplored the lack of judicial control over awards of libel damages and this led to guidelines being laid down by the Court of Appeal in the Elton John case. In the Goodwin case, a fine imposed on a journalist who refused to reveal his source was held to be a violation of his rights of freedom of expression. Prior to the incorporation of the European Convention of Human Rights into United Kingdom law, the attitude of English judges to its effect on English law has been somewhat equivocal. In the Spycatcher litigation the master of the rolls, Sir John Donaldson, expressed the view that the substantive right of freedom of expression contained in Article 10 is subsumed in our domestic law. In Derbyshire County Council v. Times Newspapers Limited, the House of Lords reached its decision without seeing any need to rely on the European Convention, whereas the Court of Appeal had taken the opposite view, justifying its decision by reference to the convention. Increasingly, the English courts have endeavoured to find a solution which accords with Article 10.

Both the right to privacy and the right to freedom of speech have over the years been developed far beyond the original declarations of protection against the excesses of the state. They now provide protection both against and for the activities of the media. The incorporation of the European Convention will expand the freedom of the press to discuss matters of public interest without fear of libel writs, and it will enable the English courts to apply the principles laid down by the European Court of Human Rights to challenge long-established restrictive rules in English libel law. The incorporation of Article 8 is likely to lead to the development by English judges of a law of privacy, which may restrict the publication of what can at present be printed by tabloid newspapers with impunity.

This process was begun by the decision of the Court of Appeal in December 2000 in the case of Douglas v. *Hello!*, which was essentially a dispute as to whether *OK!* magazine could enforce the exclusive rights it had bought to the photographs of the wedding of film stars Michael Douglas and Catherine Zeta Jones.

The leading judgement was that of Lord Justice Sedley, who felt there was a powerfully arguable case to advance at trial (this being a preliminary hearing for an injunction) that Douglas and Zeta Jones had a right to privacy that English law will today acknowledge and, where appropriate, protect. The judge observed that we have reached a point at which it can be said with confidence that the law recognises that it has to protect not only those people whose trust has been abused but also those who simply find themselves subjected to an unwarranted intrusion into their personal life.

The dispute remained to be tried and the level of damages, if awarded, to be fixed. Whatever the outcome, the case is likely to open the floodgates to further claims, extending beyond outright intrusion to interference with the rights of individuals to regulate their privacy, even when they are prepared to allow chosen photographers take pictures for a particular publication.

The procedure for taking a case to the European Court of Human Rights has been elaborate and protracted. The claim had to be brought after all national remedies had been exhausted. It had to be approved as suitable by the European Commission of Human Rights, which weeded out unsuitable cases. There was on average a five-year delay between lodging a petition with the commission and the delivery of a judgement. Some improvement was achieved by cutting out the commission's role, but the procedure is still slow and expensive.

The impact of the adoption of Article 10 is likely to be considerable. The European Court pays greater heed than English law, which set its face against the American public-figure defence, to American decisions, even though there is still no Sullivan-type defence (under which a public figure can only sue if he can prove the defendant published with knowledge of falsity). Restrictions on freedom of speech have to be justified as being necessary in a democratic society, and the court must be satisfied that the restrictions are proportionate to the requirements of competing rights, such as the prevention of crime or the protection of information obtained in confidence. In Lingens v.

Austria (1986) the European Court underlined the importance of the freedom of the press. It 'affords the public one of the best means of discovering and forming an opinion of the ideas and attitudes of political leaders. More generally, freedom of political debate is at the very core of a democratic society which prevails through the convention. The limits of acceptable criticism are accordingly wider as regards a politician as such and as regards a private individual'. While the media should not overstep the bounds set for the protection of reputation, their task is nevertheless to impart information and ideas on political issues and on other matters of general interest (Oberschlick v. Austria, 1995).

The likelihood is that the principles laid down in the Reynolds case will be greatly expanded by the English courts by reference to European decisions. It will become increasingly difficult for politicians to sue for libel in respect of their public lives. Many of the European judgements arose out of the consideration of libel actions brought under criminal legislation, where one would expect the European Court to be quick to protect those who express unwelcome opinions, such as condemning an Austrian chancellor for his too-cosy links with a former SS man. The principles established will, however, be of general application and will affect civil libel cases brought in England.

Public officials will also find it harder to bring libel actions. Thorgeirson v. Iceland was a 1992 case involving accusations of police brutality in terms which would scarcely have commended themselves to the British Police Federation – 'Beasts in uniform . . . allowing brutes and sadists to act out their perversions'. The upshot was a prosecution backed by the Reykjavik Police Association. The resultant conviction was, however, felt by the European Court to be in breach of Article 10 since the offending piece had not identified particular police officers and had been aimed at achieving reforms in the police service in general. The court held that 'there is no warrant in case law for distinguishing between political discussion and discussion of other matters of public concern'. Application of the decisions of the European

Court in England will make the bringing of police actions that much more perilous, and any case involving coverage of political figures in the context of public issues of general importance is likely to involve a greater reliance on defences crafted from those decisions.

Recent judgements by the European Court go even further than the Reynolds decision in protecting newspapers against libel claims when they are acting in the public interest and in good faith. In Bladet Tromso v. Norway, a newspaper was able to rely on the contents of an official report alleging violations of seal-hunting regulations even though the Ministry of Fisheries had decided not to publish it. The paper had printed, in sensational fashion, allegations that seal pups had been kicked and skinned alive, which were subsequently found to be unsubstantiated. Bearing in mind the vital public interest in ensuring informed, open debate of an issue of local, national and international interest, the court concluded that there was no reasonable relationship of proportionality between the restrictions placed by the initial judgement in favour of the seal-hunters and the newspaper's right to freedom of expression and the legitimate aim pursued.

To similar effect was another judgement against the state of Norway, in May 2000, in favour of Bergens Tinende. Here a newspaper had reported allegations made against a cosmetic surgeon by dissatisfied patients that clearly raised questions as to the surgeon's professional competence. Although the patients' accounts of the effects of their treatment were expressed in strong and graphic terms, they were held to be correct and matters of public interest. The decision indicated a greater willingness to find that the reporting of allegations is essentially a matter of opinion rather than a claim to fact – journalists must act 'in good faith to provide accurate and reliable information in accordance with the ethics of journalism'.

The court ruled that the surgeon should not have recovered damages against the newspaper. Had a similar case been brought in the UK, one would have expected the surgeon to have won it.

These two cases suggest that the boundaries set out in the Reynolds decision may be extended in favour of the media.

The other practical effect of the European Convention will be the opportunity it provides to ask the court to override some of the more restrictive rules of English libel law on the basis that they were decided before the incorporation of the convention. For example, the Blackshaw case in Chapter 16, in which a public-interest defence was disallowed, might have been decided differently under the new system. Increasingly, there may be challenges in Europe to the basic tenets of English libel law, such as the assumption of good reputation and of that reputation being damaged by the defamatory words. Furthermore, litigants will be able to request that British courts directly apply European law to avoid the lengthy process of having to take the case to Strasbourg.

The Human Rights Act also empowers a court to declare under Section 4 that a piece of legislation is incompatible with the European Convention. Freedom of expression is specifically protected under Section 12 of the act, which will make pre-publication injunctions more difficult to obtain. A court must not now grant such injunctions in the absence of the defendant unless it is satisfied that all practicable steps were taken to notify him or her, unless there are compelling reasons why he or she should not have been notified. It is required to have particular regard to the right to freedom of expression, to the extent to which the material in question is already or is about to enter the public domain and to whether its publication is in the public interest.

A court has also to consider whether a journalist has compiled with any relevant code of conduct relating to privacy. It will be interesting to see whether judges take the opportunity to restrict the granting of injunctions and whether they adopt Lord Hoffman's words in the Central Television case referred to in Chapter 1: A freedom [of expression] which is restricted to what judges think to be responsible in the public interest is no freedom. Freedom means the right to publish things which governments and judges, however well-motivated, think should not be published.' The court has to be satisfied that the person seeking the injunction is likely to establish at trial that publication should not be allowed. This restriction of prior restraint, which brings together a number of common-law principles, is a notable endorsement for freedom of speech in the new millennium.

My final reflection on libel on an era of global publishing moving towards uniformity in such matters as copyright and trademarks concerns the need for Europe as a whole to decide how it will balance the protection of reputation with rights of freedom of speech and privacy. A brief look at the position in France, the Netherlands and Germany shows just how far away we are from harmonisation.

French law is the most restrictive of freedom of speech. The sanctity in which the private lives of public figures is held prevented the publication of details of President Mitterrand's distinctly extended family, which would have been considered a matter of public interest elsewhere. There does, however, seem to be a deep-rooted dislike in France of the publication of details of such private matters. Defamation is predominantly a criminal matter involving an allegation of a specific and precise fact attacking the personal honour or reputation of the complainant and published in bad faith. An action must be started within three months of the libel, and legal aid is available.

The law of the freedom of the press was passed in 1881 to protect free speech and to cut the death toll resulting from the resolution of disputes by duelling. It has proved rather more successful in solving the latter problem than the former. Financial penalties in both civil and criminal cases tend to be low, measured in the hundreds or low thousands of pounds, although criminal penalties of up to FF80,000 (£8,000) and/or six months' or more imprisonment (normally suspended) can be imposed if a libel relates to the courts, the armed forces, civil service or has some racial or religious element. In assessing good faith, the court would look at why the material was published, the terms in which it was written and the quality of the research – a test which gives the courts a degree of control over what appears in the press.

Only rarely would a fine exceed FF100,000 (£10,000). One of the higher penalties of recent times was imposed in 1997 on the publishers of a book which suggested that two former government ministers, Francois Leotard and Jean-Claude Gaudin, had been involved in the murder of a *depute* (MP) called Yann Piat. They were ordered by the Tribunal Correctional to pay a fine of FF100,000 and FF1,000,000 (£100,000) in damages. There is a summary procedure which enables a judge to stop the distribution of defamatory material and to order its seizure and destruction, though this would be implemented only when a financial penalty alone is deemed insufficient. Truth is a defence, but this is offset by the requirement that full particulars of the defence, including copies of the documents relied on and details of the intended witnesses, have to be given within ten days. A plea of truth cannot include matters protected by the law of privacy, nor material that is more than ten years old. Actions can be brought in respect of an attack on the dead if it reflects on the reputation of the deceased's family.

Foreign publications which are unobjectionable elsewhere in Europe are liable to both civil and criminal action once they are sold in France. Surprisingly, though, Robert Maxwell's attempts to prosecute Bower's biography of him in France ultimately failed. The old rogue singled out Bower's reference to the fact that he had a damaged lung as an unwarranted invasion of his privacy. Although he succeeded at the first hurdle, after the French appeal court heard the penchant of his newspapers for printing pictures of Prince William peeing in a park, and of an unclad Princess Stephanie of Monaco by a swimming pool, he was sent packing with a swingeing order for costs against him. In practice claims like this are very difficult to defend in the light of the importance attached to *la vie privée*.

The approach to libel is more pragmatic in both Germany and Holland, whose systems are likely to form the backbone of any future Euro-libel law. In Holland freedom of speech is guaranteed by Article 7 and article 94, which incorporates Article 10 of the European Convention of Human Rights, of the Constitution. Libel can be a criminal matter, ranging from simple insult to slander (meaning a deliberate libel known to be untrue). The most serious offences carry a maximum penalty of two years in jail and fine of Dfl25,000 (£8,000) with, curiously, a potential increment of one third on the jail sentence if the person libelled is a civil servant or a member of a foreign government. However, criminal law requires the consent of the public prosecutor, who decides whether or not it is in the public interest to prosecute – is it, for example, a libel of a minority group which needs protection – and in practice it is rarely used. Generally penalties range from Dfl100 to 5,000 (£30 to £1,500), with the occasional suspended prison sentence of up to six months. Libels with an anti-semitic or neo-nazi flavour, though, may attract an immediate jail sentence.

The possible use of criminal law, the fact that a plaintiff can sue even if what has been published is true, provided that there was some evidence of an improper motive in publishing it, the facility for bringing claims on behalf of the dead and a five-year limitation period are restrictive features of the Dutch laws. However, the approach to civil claims for defamation is essentially pragmatic. Freedom of speech is weighed against the right of privacy, and libel involves an infringement of honour and reputation. There is an acceptance that the lives of public figures command greater scrutiny. A Dutch court looks at the effect of the libel on the private life of the complainant, the thoroughness of the investigation of the underlying facts, the words used and the underlying intention of the publication in question. It may be possible to obtain an interim injunction at an early stage and a rectification and submission of the offending materials. The aim is to produce practical remedies, for example, a declaration that the claimant has been wronged, rather than large compensation. Damages tend to be lower than in England. Emotional damages – based on the seriousness of the allegations, the publicity given to them and the intrusion into private life – usually fall into the Dfl1,000 to 20,000 (£300 to £6,000) bracket, but have been as high as Dfl125,000 (£35,000). Economic damage may also be ordered, but these are normally low (Dfl100 to 5,000/£30 to 1,500) in the absence of a clearly established financial loss.

Free speech is likewise enshrined in Article 5 of the German Constitution, while Articles 1 and 2 protect the right of personality and private life. Accordingly, although truth and public interest are defences to libel claims, they are subject to the right of privacy. Certain areas of private life, such as sexual matters and personal beliefs, are absolutely protected; others are weighed against any public interest in their being revealed. The courts can grant an injunction or order the publication of a statement contradicting the facts complained of, and offending material can be seized and destroyed. There is also a statutory right of reply available to those aggrieved by what is published about them in the media. Legal Aid is available, provided a judge is satisfied that the case has a reasonable prospect of success, and actions can also be brought on behalf of or by relatives of the deceased.

As in other mainland European countries, libel encompasses insult, slander and malicious defamation, and carries a penalty of a maximum of five years' imprisonment. A prosecution requires the consent of the public prosecutor and must be brought within three months. There are provisions under criminal law for the seizure and destruction of offending material. Fines tend to be modest, related to the defendant's means, and might represent up to twenty days' earnings. As in the Netherlands, neo-nazi or anti-semitic statements, such as denying the Holocaust, might result in a prison sentence. Civil cases have not attracted the large awards seen in England, though compensation can be ordered for specific financial loss as a result of a libel. In 1964, for example, Princess Soraya of Iran recovered DM15,000 (£6,000) when a false interview was published, and in 1969 Josef Strauss, a former defence minister, received only DM25,000 (£10,000) for allegations that he had received a briefcase full of cash from an arms-dealer. In 1994, however, the German

Supreme Court ruled that an award of DM30,000 (£12,000) for a fictitious interview with Princess Caroline of Monaco was insufficient, and that there should be a punitive element to the damages in addition to the compensation given for pain and suffering. Accordingly, later that year Steffi Graf received DM60,000 (£24,000) for false allegations of incest in a pop song, 'I Wanna Make Love to Steffi Graf', still a considerably lower sum than she would have got in England.

Attitudes in mainland Europe still seem to be influenced by the legacy of the Second World War. While freedom of speech is enshrined in a country's Constitution, there remains a regrettable willingness to resort to the criminal law. Libel is a matter that belongs in the civil courts. Some of the Woolf and Defamation Act changes may go some way to encouraging British courts to adopt the more pragmatic approach of continental Europe, for example, inexpensive, practical remedies such as an early publication of an apology rather than large damages later in the day. But the twenty-first century must usher in a greater degree of agreement in Europe as to the boundaries between freedom of speech and private reputation, and those between public interest and private life.

# Appendix 1

# DAMAGES

The vast majority of libel actions are settled. Damages are not normally disclosed, but the description 'substantial' is a form of legal shorthand for £10,000 or over. It is difficult to obtain accurate statistics: more often than not, both parties have some interest in leaving the world at large guessing about the amount actually paid. Sometimes claimants inflate the figure by lumping together the damages and costs, and sometimes there is an element of wishful thinking involved. Readers are invited to send in any details of libel awards they may have – and which they are not precluded from disclosing – to me at 1 Gresham Street, London EC2V 7BU or by fax to 020 7731 8462, or to SooperHooper@dial.pipex.com.

In the following breakdown of cases, no further comment will be made on those which have already featured in the main text of the book, and of the remainder, accounts are necessarily brief and may not do full justice to the unpleasantness of the libel. It is important to bear in mind that the plaintiffs receiving damages were exonerated of the charges brought against them. People remember the high awards, but these summaries show serious libels are often settled for sensibly modest sums.

# 1988

1988 was one of the last years of consistently high awards.

| | | |
|---|---|---|
| 1. | Adam Raphael v. Stewart Steven | £25,000 |
| 2. | Charles Freeman Ltd v. *Stationery Trade News* | £300,000 |
| | *Stationers falsely accused in* Stationery Trade News *(circulation 8,745) of dealing in counterfeit Basildon Bond paper. To save a retrial on damages, a figure of £17,500 was substituted by agreement.* | |
| 3. | Anthony Gilberthorpe v. *Today* | £10,000 |
| 4. | Anthony Gilberthorpe v. *Sun* | £28,750 |
| 5. | Anthony Gilberthorpe v. *Mirror* | £10,580 |
| 6. | Anthony Gilberthorpe v. *Gloucester Citizen* | £9,500 |
| 7. | Inspector James McNally (and 10 others) v. *Evening Standard* | £160,000 |
| 8. | Michael Murphy v. *Sunday Telegraph* | £10,000 |
| | *Michael Murphy, a union official suffering from motor-neurone disease, won the surprising low figure of £10,000 for allegations in the* Sunday Telegraph *that he had been drunk during pay negotiations. The slurring of his speech was attributable to his medical condition.* | |
| 9. | Norman Tebbit v. *Guardian* | £14,000 |
| 10. | Fox and Gibbons v. *Sourakia* | £310,000 |
| | *A London firm of solicitors with many Arab clients who were falsely accused in an Arab magazine (worldwide circulation 1,000) of supporting Zionism. They were awarded £310,000 after a two-day trial.* | |
| 11. | Neil Hamilton MP v. BBC | £20,000 |
| 12. | Gerald Howarth MP v. BBC | £20,000 |
| 13. | Robert Blair v. BBC Radio Humberside | |
| | *The chairman of Grimsby Area Health Authority recovered damages from Radio Humberside for derogatory comments about his work on a radio phone-in.* | £5,000 |
| 14. | Koo Stark v. *People* | £300,000 |
| 15. | Sethia v. *Hindustani Times* | £40,000 |
| 16. | Vladimir Telnikoff v. Vladimir Matsusevich | £65,000 |

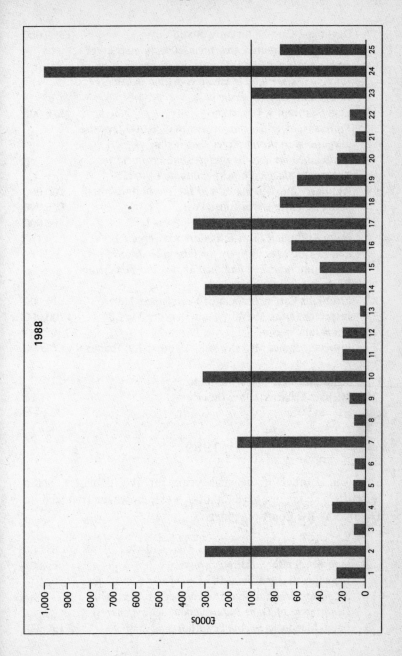

17.  David and Carol Johnson v. Radio City                £350,000
     *The Johnsons represented themselves in a six-week*
     *action against Radio City, who had accused them of*
     *running a disreputable business selling worthless*
     *caravan holidays in France.*
18.  Roger Scruton v. *Observer*                           £75,000
     *Professor Roger Scruton recovered £75,000 for false*
     *allegations in the* Observer *that he had given a*
     *National Front activist preferential treatment in*
     *securing a place on a post-graduate course.*
19.  P.C. Barry Bawden v. *News of the World* (inc. costs)  £60,000
20.  Sonia Sutcliffe v. *Yorkshire Post*          .         £25,000
21.  Dolly Kiffin v. Associated Newspapers Ltd.             £9,000
     *Dolly Kiffin and Errol Ellis Carr recovered £9,000*
     *and £14,000 respectively for false allegations*
     *suggesting that they had mishandled the Broadwater*
     *Farm Association's funds.*
22.  Errol Ellis Carr v. Associated Newspapers Ltd.        £14,000
23.  Inspector James McNally (and 15 others) v. BBC       £100,000
24.  Elton John v. *Sun*                                  £1 million
25.  Inspector James McNally (and 15 others) v. Thames TV £75,000

**Lost or abandoned cases/mishaps**
26.  Michael Meacher MP v. *Observer*                          Lost

# 1989

This was another of the peak years for libel damages. Sonia
Sutcliffe's damages of £600,000 were, however, reduced to
£60,000 by the Court of Appeal.

1.  Gross v. Goodman                                        £3,000
2.  Maureen Smith v. *Daily Express*                        £5,000
    *A public-relations consultant recovered £5,000 for*
    *the false allegation that she had been subject to a*
    *Department of Trade inquiry about selling shares.*
3.  Kevin Maddocks v. *Angler's Mail*                     £150,250

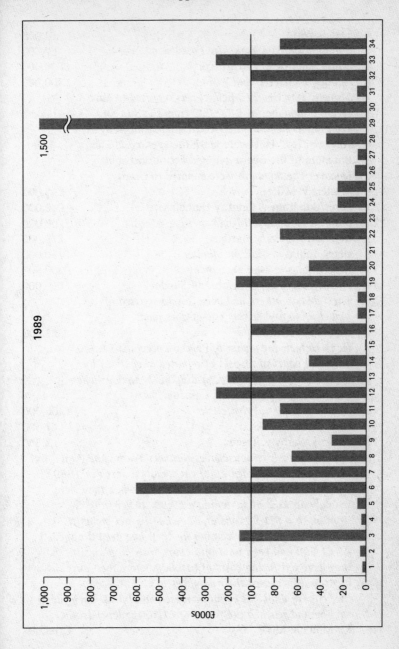

| | | |
|---|---|---|
| 4. | Trevor Ward | £4,000 |
| 5. | Sonia Sutcliffe v. *Yorkshire Post* | £7,500 |
| 6. | Sonia Sutcliffe v. *Private Eye* | £600,000 |
| 7. | George Michael v. *Sun* | £100,000 |

*The pop star George Michael was reported to have received damages of £100,000 from the* Sun *for suggestions he had gatecrashed a party given by Andrew Lloyd Webber to mark the opening of* The Phantom of the Opera *and had been drunk and abusive. The damages were donated to charity.*

| | | |
|---|---|---|
| 8. | Masters v. MGN | £65,000 |
| 9. | Lord Aldington v. Century Hutchinson | £30,000 |
| 10. | Smith & Holland v. MGN | £90,000 |
| 11. | Ken Bates v. Harry Harris | £75,000 |
| 12. | Derek Tobias v. *Mail on Sunday* | £250,000 |
| 13. | Nigel Tobias v. *Mail on Sunday* | £200,000 |
| 14. | Tobias Cash'n'Carry v. *Mail on Sunday* | £50,000 |

*The Tobias brothers had been falsely accused of repackaging and selling out-of-date food.*

| | | |
|---|---|---|
| 15. | Hugh Hefner v. *People* | £1,000 |

*Hugh Hefner, the owner of* Playboy *accepted £1,000 paid into court in respect of reported allegations by the model Fiona Wright regarding his behaviour when she visited his Californian mansion.*

| | | |
|---|---|---|
| 16. | Sonia Sutcliffe v. *Private Eye* | £100,000 |
| 17. | Ann Chastell v. Tesco | £7,500 |
| 18. | Frances Warby v. Tesco | £7,500 |

*Two Hertfordshire housewives, Frances Warby and Ann Chastell, were awarded £800 each against Tesco in 1989 for libel, slander and false imprisonment when they were wrongly accused of switching a £9.99 sticker from an iron on to a £11.99 toaster. They had in fact bought £70 worth of goods. A prosecution for theft had been dropped. As £1,500 had been paid into court for each plaintiff, they were left facing costs of £10,000 before the Court of Appeal increased their damages to £7,500 each – a very rare case of damages being increased on appeal. Each judge said he had reached the figure of £7,500 independently.*

| | | |
|---|---|---|
| 19. | Kit Miller v. MGN | £165,000 |

*A former journalist recovered £100,000 from the*
Mirror *for five articles and £65,000 from the* People
*for falsely suggesting that he was behind a slimming-*
*pill fraud.*

20. McCarthy and Stone v. Channel 4                     £50,000
    *McCarthy and Stone accepted £50,000 paid into*
    *court by Channel 4 for allegations about the quality*
    *of service and conduct of their employees at two of*
    *their sheltered-accommodation developments. They*
    *did not do so well in 1993.*

21. Sir Rupert Mackeson v. Willis                          1p
    *Sir Rupert Mackeson was awarded 1p for the contents*
    *of a solicitors' letter sent to his business address and*
    *read by members of his staff.*

22. Mardas v. *Mirror*                                   £75,000
23. Peter Bottomley MP v. *Mail on Sunday*              £100,000
24. Peter Bottomley MP v. *Daily Express*                £25,000
25. Peter Bottomley MP v. *News of the World*            £25,000
26. Andrew Wadsworth v. Matthew Freud                    £10,000
27. Professor Frederick Hartt v. *Independent*            £7,500
28. Sonia Sutcliffe v. *Star*                            £35,000
29. Lord Aldington v. Tolstoy                         £1,500,000
30. Trebith v. Sunday Sport                              £60,000
31  Trevor Clay v. MGN
    *The former general secretary of the Royal College of*
    *Nursing recovered £8,000 against the* Mirror *for*
    *suggestions linking him with a government job while*
    *he negotiated nurses' pay. He was said to be facing a*
    *bill for £25,000 costs after rejecting £10,000 paid*
    *into court.*                                         £8,000
32. Sonia Sutcliffe v. *Private Eye*                    £100,000

33.  Frederick Wright v. BBC                          £250,000
     *The owner of Barry Island resort accepted £250,000*
     *damages plus the same in costs against the BBC's*
     *That's Life which had wrongly given the impression*
     *that the resort was so squalid and dangerous that no*
     *sensible person would spend their time there. 10,000*
     *people had cancelled their holidays after the programme,*
     *which was based on the opinions of an unrepresentative*
     *handful of holidaymakers.*
34.  Sonia Sutcliffe v. *Express*                     £75,000

## Lost or abandoned cases/mishaps
35.  Brian Sedgmore MP v. Robert Kilroy-Silk      Abandoned
     *Kilroy-Silk had criticised Sedgmore's motives in wanting to*
     *extend the law of blasphemy to Muslims. The jury failed to*
     *agree and the case was subsequently settled.*

# 1990

The most bizarre case of 1990 was that brought by Andrew Neil,
editor of *The Sunday Times*, against Peregrine Worsthorne, editor
of the *Sunday Telegraph*, described by the judge as two great
steam locomotives crashing head on. Times Newspapers Limited
also sued and recovered 60p (the cost of a copy of *The Sunday
Times*). The judge had suggested that the jury might think of
awarding Neil enough for a good night out at Tramp nightclub
(where his pursuit of Pamela Bordes, by day a House of
Commons researcher, had taken place). Neil complained that two
articles and a cartoon charting his relationship with Bordes libel-
lously suggested that he was unfit to edit his paper. He was
awarded £1,000 damages.

1.  *Sunday Times* v. Peregrine Worsthorne              60p
2.  Andrew Neil v. Peregrine Worsthorne              £1,000

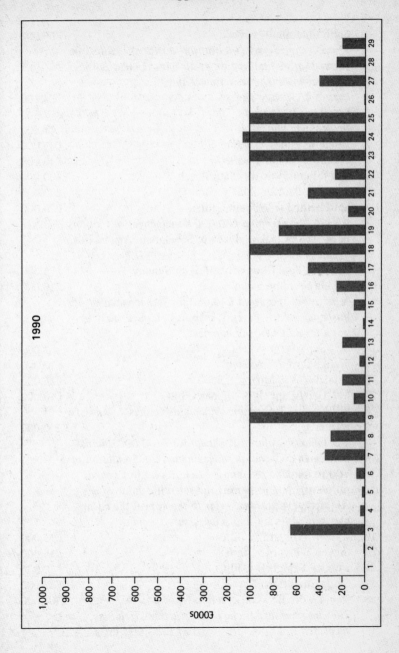

3.  Carlo Colombotti v. *Today*                   £65,000
*A banker recovered £65,000 for untrue allegations in*
Today *that he had had an affair with Pamela Bordes*
*when he knew she was a prostitute.*

4.  Carroll v. *Sunday Times*                     £4,000
5.  Ken Bates v. *Mirror*                        £2,500
6.  Noah v. Shuba                           £7,500
7.  Viscount Linley v. *Today*                  £35,000
8.  Tessa Sanderson v. MGN                £30,000
9.  San Klibansky v. *Ha Olam Hazeh*        £100,000
10.  Sergeant Paul Douglas v. *Sun*           £10,000
11.  Lord Bethell v. William Collins          £20,000
*A Euro MP accepted £20,000 damages for allegations*
*in the book* Cloak and Gown: Scholars in American's
Secret War.

12.  Sergeant Paul Douglas v. *Mail on Sunday*    £5,000
13.  Zahida Seemi v. Sadiq                 £20,000
*Miss Seemi recovered £20,000 for slander against her*
*husband and his parents, who had claimed she was*
*not a virgin when she married.*

14.  Det. Supt. Peter Whent v. *Today*         £2,000
15.  Frank Warren v. *Mirror*              £10,000
16.  Grudzinkas v. *Mirror*                £25,000
17.  Det. Chief Supt. Jack Slipper v. BBC     £50,000
18.  Sir Ranulph Twistleton-Wykeham-Fiennes v. Maclean
Hunter                           £100,000
*The famous explorer was awarded £100,000 against*
Maclean's *a Canadian magazine with a circulation of*
*400 in England as opposed to 600,000 in Canada,*
*for an article questioning the scientific value of his*
*Antarctic expeditions. Prior to the appeal the case*
*was settled for an undisclosed sum.*

19.  Gaynor Winyard v. *Tatler*              £75,000
20.  Steven Winyard v. *Tatler*              £15,000
21.  Duncan Campbell v. BBC             £50,000
22.  Sonia Sutcliffe v. News Group        £26,500
23.  David Morrell v. *Construction News*     £101,000
*The chairman of Mitchell Constructions Holdings*
*recovered £101,000 plus costs of £222,000 for a*

*review of his book chronicling the collapse of the*
*company which falsely suggested that he might have*
*concealed the true state of Mitchell's profitability in*
*the wake of difficulties with a hydroelectric contract in*
*Zambia.*

| | | |
|---|---|---|
| 24. | James Rowland Jones v. Andrew Greystoke | £130,000 |
| 25. | David Prendergast v. NUM | £100,000 |

*The leader of the Union of Democratic Mineworkers*
*was awarded £100,000 against the NUM and their*
*Nottinghamshire area secretary over a forged letter*
*which suggested he had betrayed union members.*

| | | |
|---|---|---|
| 26. | Warwick Seymour-Hamilton v. *Orpington Times* | £1,000 |

*An Orpington vet recovered £1,000 when he was*
*wrongly accused in his local paper of negligently*
*causing the death of a ten-year-old girl's dog. £5,000*
*had been paid into court, so he was left with legal*
*costs of £10,000.*

| | | |
|---|---|---|
| 27. | Earl of Stradbroke v. Gilbey | £40,000 |

*The Earl of Stradbroke was awarded £40,000 for*
*accusations made against him by his son-in-law in a*
*letter to the* Daily Telegraph *about the running of his*
*estate.*

| | | |
|---|---|---|
| 28. | Shiner v. BBC | £25,000 |
| 29. | PC Nurthen v. MGN | £20,000 |

*A police constable recovered damages for unfounded*
*criticisms of his arrest of a man who made chocolate*
*penises.*

## Lost or abandoned cases/mishaps

| | | |
|---|---|---|
| 30. | Sonia Sutcliffe v. News Group Newspapers Ltd. | Lost |

# 1991

This year contained a number of high awards, notably those to Rantzen, Gorman and Smith, but these were substantially reduced on appeal to £110,000, £50,000 and £50,000 respectively. The trend towards lower awards can be detected in the £50,000 awarded to Bill Roache.

1. Oliver Reed v. *Sun*     £50,000
   *Oliver Reed was awarded £50,000 for a front-page article headed 'OLIVER REED BEATS HIS WIFE'.*
2. Charles Golding v. *Private Eye*     £1,500
3. Tessa Sanderson v. *Mirror*     £30,000
4. PC Michael Seaston v. Spery     £10,000
   *A Derbyshire police constable recovered £10,000 from a motorist who falsely accused him of offering to accept a bribe to ignore a speeding offence – a salutary warning to pub jokers who believe they can resort to this defence when all else fails.*
5. Wyckham Laboratories v. Central TV     £40,000
6. David Walker v. Central TV     £40,000
   *David Walker, a vet and director of Wyckham Research Laboratory, which undertook research for the pharmaceutical industry, recovered £40,000 against Central TV for false accusations that their animal experiments were cruel and unnecessary. The company was awarded £5,000.*
7. Gavin Campbell v. *Today*     £15,000
   *The* That's Life *presenter received £15,000 from* Today *when they settled this bizarre libel action after five days in court. In what was described as spiteful character assassination, Campbell was falsely accused of ruining a Wembley couple's underwater wedding off Key Largo in Florida by being sick over the head of the Rev. Amy Slater, who was officiating in her flippers. The unfortunate presenter had been seasick, but had coped discreetly with this difficulty over the side of the boat and well away from the padre.*

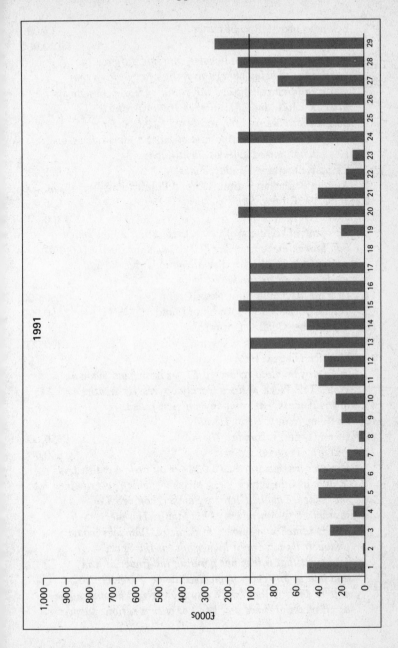

1991

8.  Edwina Currie MP v. *Observer*                                    £5,000
9.  Ray Honeyford v. CRE                                             £20,000
    *A former Bradford headmaster who had suffered the*
    *misfortune of being obliged to retire after writing that*
    *white children constituted the ethnic minority in many*
    *urban schools, and of a number of unwarranted*
    *political attacks on him, recovered £20,000 for a*
    *pamphlet falsely accusing him of having racist views.*
    *He was not named but was identifiable.*
10. Carman Proetta v. *Sunday Times*                                £25,000
11. Ajitabh Bachchan v. India Abroad Publications Inc.             £40,000
12. Jonathan Hunt v. *Sun*                                          £35,000
13. James Welsh v. TGWU                                            £100,000
    *The general secretary of Cabin Crew 89, a union which*
    *had broken away from the TGWU, was awarded £100,000*
    *against the TGWU for false allegations that he had*
    *made off with its funds.*
14. Dr Paul MacLoughlin v. News Group                              £50,000
15. Teresa Gorman MP v. Anthony Mudd                             £150,000
16. Christopher Geidt v. Central TV                               £100,000
17. Anthony de Norman v. Central TV                              £100,000
18. Maurice Lubin v. HTV                                               £1
    *A Cardiff landlord recovered £1 for criticisms made on*
    Wales This Week *of his allegedly oppressive treatment*
    *of his tenants. His company's action failed.*
19. Paul Leighton v. *Derby Herald*                                £20,000
20. Owen Oyston v. *Sunday Times*                                 £150,000
21. Anthony Pargeter v. *Sport*                                    £40,000
    *Pargeter was awarded £40,000 for an article entitled*
    'Riddle of Gun Which Went Missing', *which re-examined*
    *the evidence against Jeremy Bamber, convicted of*
    *murdering five members of his family. The piece*
    *falsely attached suspicion to Pargeter. Damages would*
    *undoubtedly have been higher but for the* Sport's
    *argument that it was not pointing the finger at him*
    *and had in any event apologised twice. Pargeter was*
    *able to show without difficulty that he had been at home*
    *at all material times and had not been a serious suspect.*

| 22. | Jennifer Noble v. Steel | £15,750 |
| 23. | Robert Noble v. Steel | £9,975 |

*Dr Jennifer Noble, a senior lecturer, and her husband Robert were awarded £15,750 and £9,975 for libel and slander against their former neighbours for false allegations to the police and press.*

| 24. | Dr Malcolm Smith v. Dr Alanah Houston | £150,000 |
| 25. | Bill Roache v. *Sun* | £50,000 |
| 26. | George Nye v. Channel 4 | £50,000 |

*A farmer recovered damages believed to total £50,000 for false suggestions in Channel 4's Disciple of Chaos that he had allowed the National Front to carry out military exercises on his land. Channel 4 acknowledged there was no truth whatsoever in the allegations.*

| 27. | Dusty Springfield v. TVS | £75,000 |

*The singer was awarded £75,000 for a sketch by comedian Bobby Davro in which she was portrayed as performing while drunk.*

| 28. | Gunasekera v. Samco Agencies | £150,000 |
| 29. | Esther Rantzen v. MGN | £250,000 |

## Lost or abandoned cases/mishaps

| 30. | PC Brian Williams and PC Antony Baker v. *People* | Lost |
| 31. | Cordelia Lim v. Lawless | |

*Cordelia Lim lost a twenty-nine-day action against the News of the World after they had accused her of incompetent use of laser surgery.* Lost

| 32. | Alex Standish v. *People* | Won, but no damages or costs |
| 33. | Tom O'Connor v. *People* and *News of the World* | Abandoned |
| 34. | David Bookbinder v. Tebbit | Lost |

# 1992

The trend of libel damages was again downwards in 1992. The largest successful awards were the £230,000 and £150,000 (inclusive of legal costs) recovered by the MPs Rupert Allason and George Galloway. However, there was a 'Maxwell factor' in that the MGN management were particularly anxious to get out of these cases, which carried unwelcome reminders of craven subservience to their former boss which a jury might have punished in any damages award. The £240,000 awarded to Telnikoff against Matusevich would not have survived an appeal. Telnikoff's attempt to enforce the judgement in the USA ended in disaster.

1. Jason Connery v. *Sun*      £35,000
   *The actor was awarded £35,000 after a five-day*
   *hearing after a jury retirement of only forty-five*
   *minutes for an article written at the time of the Gulf*
   *War headlined 'I COULDN'T FIGHT IN GULF, SAYS 007'S SON'.*
2. Spittle v. Hughes      £20,000
3. PC Robert Taylor v. Chapman      £2,500
   *A police officer recovered £2,500 for false allegations*
   *of corruption broadcast by a scrap-metal merchant on*
   *his sandwich board.*
4. Sarah Keays v. *New Woman*      £105,000
5. Vladimir Telnikoff v. Vladimir Matusevich      £240,000
6. Terry Dicks MP v. John McDonnell      £15,000
   *The MP received £15,000 damages from his Labour*
   *opponent John McDonnell for false allegations in an*
   *election leaflet linking him with the Iraqis at the time*
   *of the Gulf War.*
7. Rex Makin v. Merseyside Police      £750
8. Jason Donovan v. *Face*      £200,000
   *The actor and pop star did not seek to enforce all of*
   *his £200,000 award against the* Face. *Otherwise it*
   *might have been reduced on appeal. The magazine*
   *claimed this was simply an article about 'outing' gays.*
   *'If there was any ambiguity, I can only apologise', the*

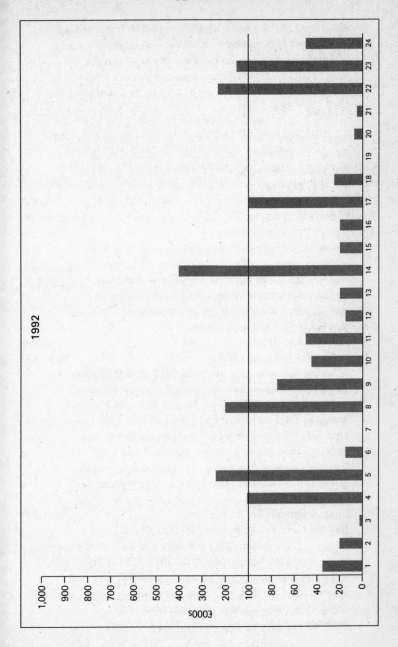

1992

*editor said. As the piece was illustrated by a mocked-up
photograph of Donovan in a T-shirt emblazoned* 'Queer
as Fuck' *and he was described as* 'the boy with the
bleached hair whose life has been subject to constant
speculation', *the room for ambiguity seemed limited.
Mr Justice Drake urged the jury to exercise moderation
in their award. What would a miner with damaged
lungs think of a huge libel award in such circumstances?
But as often happens with a well-known television
and stage personality, the jury chose to ignore these
words of caution.*

| | | |
|---|---|---|
| 9. | Faragi v. al Hayat | £75,000 |
| 10. | Webster v. al Hayat | £45,000 |
| 11. | Weiner Hotels v. al Hayat | £50,000 |

*The managing directors and an executive of a hotel
company were awarded £75,000 and £45,000 and the
company £50,000 for false allegations in a Saudi
newspaper (circulation less than 2,000 in the UK)
that they had avoided Egyptian exchange control.*

| | | |
|---|---|---|
| 12. | Jani Allan v. *Evening Standard* | £15,000 |
| 13. | Jani Allan v. *Options* | £20,000 |
| 14. | Wafic Said v. Misbah Baki | £400,000 |

*A Syrian financier was awarded £400,000 following
an eight-day action against Misbah Baki over letters
written to Prince Khalid bin Sultan. Said had lent
money to Baki and there had been previous litigation.
Said indicated that he would not enforce the award.
Baki defended himself, noting that Said had used
fourteen lawyers. In view of the restricted publication
of the libel, this would have been greatly reduced on
appeal.*

| | | |
|---|---|---|
| 15. | Duncan Campbell v. *Pink Paper* | £20,000 |

*Duncan Campbell recovered £20,000 after he was
falsely accused of pursuing a vendetta in his articles
in the* New Statesman *against an alternative AIDS
treatment organisation in an article captions* 'The Sick
Statesman'. *This was held to be damaging to
Campbell's standing as a researcher into AIDS
treatment and in the gay community. Libel was*

*admitted and the trial related only to the amount of
damages.*

16. Peter Clarke v. *Independent* £20,000
   *A former Conservative candidate was awarded
   £20,000 for the recycling of false rumours circulated
   by his enemies and previously published in* East
   Lothian News, *including the accusation that he
   advocated the reduction of the school-leaving age to
   twelve.*

17. Irving Scholar v. *Daily Mail* £100,000
   *Irving Scholar, chairman of Tottenham Hotspur, was
   awarded £100,000, but this was by agreement
   reduced prior to the appeal. He was falsely accused
   of misconduct over the transfer of Paul Gascoigne to
   Lazio.*

18. John Cleese v. *Sun* £25,000
   *John Cleese recovered £25,000 for false allegations
   that he had been haunted by lifelong fears about sex
   in their article: 'I WAS 24 BEFORE I FINALLY LOST MY VIRGINITY',
   which purported to be a review of an unauthorised
   biography. The damages were donated to the Fulbright
   Foundation for British screenwriters to study in the
   USA.*

19. Dixons v. Thames TV £1
   *The store pocketed a mere £1 against Thames TV over
   allegations that misleading statements had been made
   about a camera. £5,000 had been paid into court.*

20. Sir Oliver Popplewell v. *Today* £7,500
21. Sean Hannan v. Thames TV £5,000
   *A plumber received £5,000 for suggestions on Thames
   Television that he was a cowboy.*

22. Rupert Allason MP v. MGN (inc. costs) £230,000
23. George Galloway MP v. MGN (inc. costs) £150,000
24. Peter Martyn v. BR £50,000
   *The former head of a company which made railway
   track maintenance equipment received £50,000 from
   the British Railways Board for false allegations of
   corruption.*

## Lost or abandoned cases/mishaps

25. Jani Allan v. Channel 4                                                Lost
26. Laura Watson v. Argles and Court
    *Watson lost her slander action when it was ruled that
    the act of dismissing and escorting her from the solicitors
    where she worked was an occasion of qualified privilege.*   Lost
27. James Hewitt v. *Sun*                                          Abandoned
28. Frank Warren v. Terry Marsh                                          Lost
29. Mona Bauwens v. *People*              Jury failed to agree, settled.
30. Mitch Mitchell v. Book Sales Ltd.
    *The jury decided that a biography of Jimi Hendrix did
    not suggest that his drummer was a racist.*                    Lost.

# 1993

The awards in 1993 appear to suggest a higher trend of damages
than was in fact the case.

1. Richard Branson v. BA                                          £500,000
2. Bill Morris v. Lady Seear                                       £10,000
   *Lady Seear paid the general secretary of the TGWU
   £10,000 in costs and damages for allegations
   concerning his voting intentions in the 1992 election.*
3. Virgin v. BA                                                   £110,000
4. Corporal Brian Cooper v. Central                               £105,000
   *A corporal in the Black Watch recovered damages in
   the region of £105,000 when his claim against the
   Cook Report on Central Television for a piece of film
   captioned 'Bullied to Death' was settled after eight
   days. It was alleged that one of the witnesses had a
   conviction for wasting police time. Central TV
   apologised to Cooper and accepted that their accusations
   were completely untrue and without foundation.*
5. Dr Paul MacLoughlin v. Dr Gordon Kells                          £85,000
6. Steve Turnbull v. *Shooting News*                                £2,000
7. Julia Charlton v. Streetlife                                    £75,000
8. Joe Lee v. *Mail on Sunday*                                     £14,000

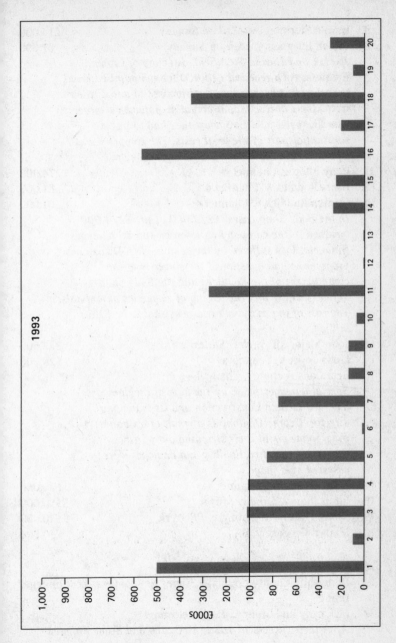

9.  Harold Sternfield v. *Mail on Sunday*          £14,000
10. Crown Eyeglass v. *Mail on Sunday*          £7,000
    *Joe Lee and Harold Sternfield, directors of Crown*
    *Eyeglass, each received £14,000 following false claims*
    *that they had broken into the premises of one of their*
    *franchisees during a contractual dispute. As a larger*
    *sum had been paid into court they had to pay a*
    *substantial part of the legal costs. The company was*
    *awarded £7,000.*
11. Body Shop v. Channel 4          £274,000
12. Anita Roddick v. Channel 4          £1,000
13. Gordon Roddick v. Channel 4          £1,000
    *In the Body Shop cases, £273,000 of the £274,000*
    *awarded to the company represented special damages*
    *(financial loss suffered by the company). A* Dispatches
    *programme had questioned the sincerity of the*
    *commitment of the Roddicks and the Body Shop to*
    *animal welfare and the testing of cosmetics on animals.*
    *The cost of the five-week trial was said to be £1.5*
    *million.*
14. John Major MP v. *New Statesman*          £27,500
15. Linda Joyce v. Sengupta          £25,000
16. Beta Construction v. Channel 4          £566,000
    *Special damages made up the bulk of the damages*
    *awarded to Beta Construction and its managing*
    *director, George Denton, as a result of a Channel 4*
    *programme about their stripping out of asbestos.*
    *Channel 4 admitted liability and damages were*
    *assessed by a judge.*
17. Nigel Bowden v. Channel 4          £20,050
18. Elton John v. *Sunday Mirror*          £350,000
19. James Fraser-Armstrong v. *PR Week*          £10,000
20. Martyn Gregory v. BA          £30,000

## Lost or abandoned cases/mishaps

21. Derbyshire County Council v. Times Newspapers   Lost on legal
    ruling
22. McCarthy and Stone v. *Daily Telegraph*
    *After their success in 1989, McCarthy and Stone dropped*

*their action over an article concerning their allegedly
confusing service charges. The paper denied that the
article reflected badly on the integrity of the company.
The case was settled with each side bearing its own
costs following an application by George Carman QC
to admit evidence relating to a £3,500 fine on a
subsidiary company for an advertisement suggesting
that prices for their accommodation started at £55,950
when the lowest was in fact £69,950. The paper
accepted that the company never intended to deceive
purchasers.*                                    Abandoned

23. Alex Standish v. *People*          Won, but no damages or costs
24. Sarfraz Nawaz v. Allan Lamb                    Abandoned.


# 1994

| | | |
|---|---|---|
| 1. | Professor Ian Oswald v. Upjohn | £50,000 |
| 2. | Andrew Halpin v. Oxford Brookes University | £60,000 |
| 3. | Upjohn v. BBC | £60,000 |
| 4. | Upjohn v. Professor Ian Oswald | £25,000 |
| 5. | Dr Royston Drucker v. Professor Ian Oswald | £75,000 |
| 6. | David Wraith v. Shirley Wraith | £69 |

*Wraith sued his former wife Shirley for slander for
falsely suggesting that he had caught VD from a tart
he had picked up on a business trip to Holland. £69
seemed a particularly appropriate award to the jury.
The polite explanation was that it represented the
cost of a bottle of champagne in a clipjoint. Mr
Justice Drake felt that the case, which lasted ten
days, should never have been brought and refused to
order costs against Mrs Wraith. Wraith admitted
visiting sleazy nightclubs, but only to play roulette.
The jury did not find proved claims that his former
wife had slandered him in their disputes over the
proceeds of their Majorcan home and Porsche. In
retrospect Wraith agreed that he should not have
brought the action and acknowledged that it ended up
doing immense damage to his reputation. His*

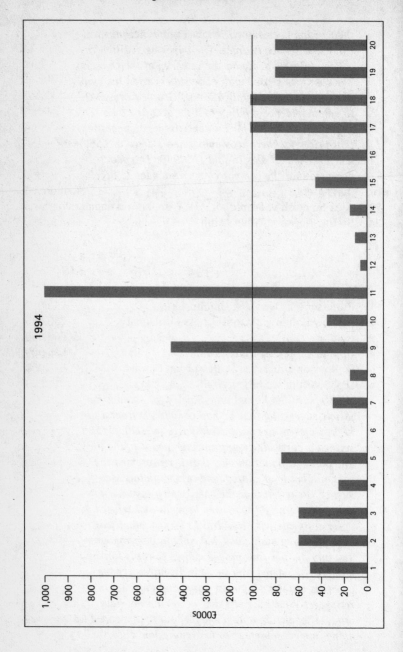

*jaundiced view of the legal system can be gauged
from the title of the book he is writing:* Trust Me –
I'm a Lawyer.

| | | |
|---|---|---|
| 7. | Professor Tim Brighouse v. John Patten MP | £30,000 |
| 8. | Alex Wilbraham v. Paul Watkins | £15,000 |
| 9. | John Walker v. *Yachting World* | £450,000 |
| 10. | Jean Walker v. *Yachting World* | £35,000 |
| 11. | Walker Wingsail v. *Yachting World* | £1,000,000 |

*Damages in the Walker Wingsail case distorted the
overall downward trend. The award of £1 million to
the company reflected the jury's distaste for the
attack on the manufacturers of the revolutionary
Wingsail design by* Yachting World. *As the company
could not prove actual loss as a result of the
offending article, the award for the company should
have been a low five-figure sum. The case
highlighted the need for juries to be given directions
as to the appropriate level of damages. The case was
settled for £160,000 damages plus payment in full of
all legal costs which, with the element of
irrecoverable costs inherent in litigation on that
scale, was the equivalent of damages of £250,000.*

| | | |
|---|---|---|
| 12. | Law for All v. *Coventry Evening Telegraph* | £6,000 |
| 13. | Ken Bates v. *Sunday Mirror* | £10,500 |

*The chairman of Chelsea FC recovered damages of
£10,500 for false suggestions that he had interfered
in matters which were the team manager's
responsibility.*

| | | |
|---|---|---|
| 14. | Richard Adams v. Associated Newspapers Ltd | £15,000 |
| 15. | Victor Kiam v. *Sunday Times* | £45,000 |
| 16. | Jim Rowland Jones v. Andrew Greystoke | £80,000 |

*Greystoke was ordered to pay Rowland-Jones £45,000
damages plus £35,000 exemplary damages over
accusations in a takeover circular regarding the sale
of 600,000 shares. Greystoke had been trying to
acquire the Bremner property company through City
and Westminster Financial. The case spanned seven
years. The original award of £130,000 had been set
aside as excessive by the Court of Appeal.*

| | | |
|---|---|---|
| 17. | Gordon Anglesea v. HTV | £107,500 |
| 18. | Gordon Anglesea v. *Independent on Sunday* | £107,500 |

| 19. | Gordon Anglesea v. *Private Eye* | £80,000 |
| 20. | Gordon Anglesea v. *Observer* | £80,000 |

## Lost or abandoned cases/mishaps

| 21. | Gillian Taylforth v. *Sun* | Lost |
| 22. | John Buckingham v. Graham Rusk and Reginald Dove | Lost |
| 23. | Ann Charleston and Ian Smith v. *News of the World* | Lost on legal ruling |
| 24. | Howard Jones v. Clifford Pellow | Lost |
| 25. | David Bookbinder v. Phillip Oppenheim MP | Lost on legal ruling |
| 26. | Dr Frank Skuse v. Granada Television | Abandoned |

# 1995

The lower trend of libel damages was again obscured by one freak result, the Graham Souness case against the *People*. Damages were by consent reduced to £100,000. There were also, however, very high damages – £380,000 – shared between Chris Brasher and John Disley and their company against Channel 4. This was out of line with the trend, but reflected the massive scale of that litigation.

| 1. | Natasha Erokhina v. MGN | £60,000 |
| 2. | Barry Jones v. Eve Pollard | £115,000 |

*Barry Jones' £115,000 damages included £15,000 special damages. General damages were reduced from £100,000 to £40,000 by the Court of Appeal.*

| 3. | Prince Bin Sultan Bandar v. *Guardian* | £10,000 |
| 4. | Chris Brasher & John Disley v. Channel 4 | £380,000 |
| 5. | Dr Mudiame Giwa-Osagie v. Smithson | £5,000 |
| 6. | Dr Mudiame Giwa-Osagie v. Hall | £40,000 |

*Dr Giwa-Osagie was a gynaecologist falsely accused of sexually harassing two midwives at the Doncaster Royal Infirmary. He recovered £40,000 against one and £5,000 against the other. His innocent acts had been misunderstood. His career had suffered but his claim for £1 million loss of earnings failed.*

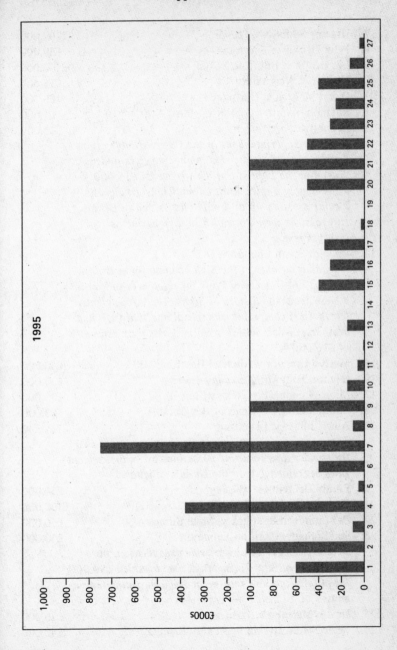

1995

| | | |
|---|---|---|
| 7. | Graeme Souness v *People* | £750,000 |
| 8. | Felix Dennis v. *Spectator* | £10,000 |
| 9. | Bio Health v. BBC (inc. costs) | £100,000 |
| 10. | Newton v. New World | £15,000 |
| 11. | David Morgan v. Haringey | £6,000 |
| 12. | Raymond Ward v. Alan Kingston | £1,000 |
| 13. | Bennett v. *For Women* | £15,000 |

13. *A former superintendent in the Obscene Publications Squad, by then a solicitors' managing clerk and deacon in the Baptist Church, recovered £15,000 for a thoroughly unpleasant and malicious article. His jocular dressing-up at family parties and in Benny Hill routines were portrayed in a magazine as transvestism.*

| | | |
|---|---|---|
| 14. | Dr Jagit Singh Chohan v. OUP | 1p |

14. *A leading member of the Sikh community in Britain sued Oxford University Press for references to him in a book about the history of Sikhs. The jury evidently felt that his complaint was trivial and that OUP had dealt responsibly with his claim. Costs were estimated at £50,000.*

| | | |
|---|---|---|
| 15. | Martyn Gregory v. Michael Heseltine MP | £40,000 |
| 16. | Michael Foot MP v. *Sunday Times* | £30,000 |
| 17. | Michael Foot MP v. *News of the World* | £35,000 |
| 18. | Philip McHugh v. *News of the World* | £3,000 |
| 19. | Albert Miller v. Osbourne | £40 |

19. *The secretary of the Showman's Guild recovered £40 for slander as a result of allegations by an amusement-rides operator made to the Guild's solicitor.*

| | | |
|---|---|---|
| 20. | Phillip DeFreitas v. *Wisden* | £50,000 |
| 21. | Tony Berry v. Terry Venables | £100,000 |
| 22. | Baron Steven Bentinck v. Nigel Dempster | £50,000 |
| 23. | Joe Homan v. *Mail on Sunday* | £30,000 |

23. *The former head of a charitable organisation, the International Boys Town Trust, was awarded £30,000 for false allegations that he had abused young Indian boys.*

| | | |
|---|---|---|
| 24. | Devon Malcolm v. *Wisden* | £25,000 |
| 25. | Peter Bottomley MP v. *Sunday Express* | £40,000 |

| 26. | PC Christopher Wright v. BBC | £12,500 |
| 27. | PC Peter Callaghan v. BBC | £4,000 |

## Lost or abandoned cases/mishaps

| 28 | David Ashby MP v. Times Newspapers Ltd | Lost |
| 29. | Bruce Hibbard v. Driffield Bowls Club | Lost |
| 30. | Paul Judge v. *Guardian* | Lost |
| 31. | Matthews and Mattex v. Hill and Bristol Uniforms | Abandoned |

# 1996

The damages awarded during the year were once again distorted by a freak result, this time in the case brought by Dr Anthony Percy against the *Mirror* over three articles. He was labelled 'Dr Doolittle' and accused of declining to attend a patient with serious head injuries at Queen Mary's Hospital, Sidcup. The patient was flown to Leeds, where he died. Dr Percy said that if he had been asked to go in to Queen Mary's, he would have done so like a shot. A follow-up article headlined: '*I DID IGNORE CRISIS CALL*' suggested that he had gone back to sleep, and a third falsely reported that he was responsible for the decision to send home another patient, who also later died. Mr Justice French did not give the recommended direction to the jury following the Elton John case, which would have indicated to them that damages for serious libels should be in the bracket of £50,000 to £125,000 in each case. The total sum awarded should have borne a proper relationship to the nature of the allegation, even given that there were three very serious libels. Instead the jury awarded £250,000, £200,000 and £175,000 for the three articles. The case was subsequently settled for £150,000, nearer the figure the trial judge should have recommended. Legal costs were estimated at £500,000. The jury evidently accepted Dr Percy's contention that he had been used as a sacrificial lamb to cover up the unpopular Conservative government's failure to provide enough neurosurgical beds.

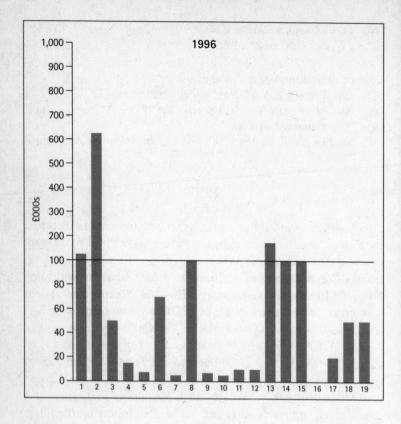

1. Christopher Bettermann v. Mohamed Fayed     £125,000
2. Dr Anthony Percy v. MGN     £625,000
3. Earl Spencer v. *Express*     £50,000
   *Earl Spencer recovered £50,000 damages for a wholly*
   *false suggestion that he had played some part in*
   *laundering the proceeds of his friend Darius Guppy's*
   *fraudulent gems insurance claim.*
4. George Howarth MP v. *Guardian*     £15,000
5. Sam Lucas v. Building (inc. costs)     £7,500
6. Stefanie Powers v. *Sun*     £70,000
   *The actress was awarded £70,000 over wholly untrue*
   *allegations that she was an alcoholic who had sexually*

*harassed and assaulted a male assistant. She donated*
*her settlement to the William Holden Wildlife*
*Foundation and Conservation Trust.*

7.   Dolores O'Riordan v. *Sport*             £5,000
*The lead singer of the Irish pop group The Cranberries*
*agreed to forward to charity £5,000 damages from*
*the* Sport *for false suggestions that she cavorted on*
*stage in Hamburg with no knickers in a story*
*headlined 'DOLORES DRAWERS A CROWD'. The same charity*
*benefited to the tune of £10,000 when the* Star
*repeated the allegation (no. 11).*

8.   Graeme Souness v. *Mail on Sunday*     £100,000
9.   Thoday v. *Evening Standard*           £7,000
10.  Allen-Turner v. *Evening Standard*      £5,000
11.  Dolores O'Riordan v. *Daily Star*       £10,000
12.  Albert Reynolds v. Guinness Publishing   £10,000
13.  Dusko Doder v. *Time*             £175,000
*The former Moscow correspondent of the* Washington
Post *received agreed damages of £175,000 from* Time
*magazine for false allegations accusing him of*
*accepting money from the KGB.*

14.  Anthony Steen MP v. Morris        £100,000
*The MP accepted £100,000 for false allegations*
*about missing charity money. These were recognised*
*to be utterly untrue, mistaken and without foundation.*

15.  Alan Sugar v. Terry Venables       £100,000
16.  Albert Reynolds v. *Times*              1p
17.  Brian Basham v. Martyn Gregory      £20,000
18.  Professor David Reeves v. *Spectator*   £50,000
*The professor accepted damages reported to amount*
*to £50,000 for completely untrue allegations that he*
*had given false expert evidence in court.*

19.  Martha Pope v. *Mail on Sunday*      £50,000
*Pope, a deputy to Senator George Mitchell, the*
*peacebroker in Northern Ireland, accepted agreed*
*damages of £50,000 for false accusations of trysts*
*with a member of Sinn Fein.*

## Lost or abandoned cases/mishaps

20. Ian Botham and Allan Lamb v. Imran Khan       Lost
21. British Coal v. National Union of Miners
    *Mr Justice French ruled following the Derbyshire County
    Council case that as a public body (as opposed to a
    private trading corporation), British Coal could not
    bring a libel claim for allegations about the
    way it ran its pension fund.*     Lost on legal ruling.
22. Neil Hamilton MP and Ian Greer v. *Guardian*    Abandoned
23. Dr James Sharp v. BBC
    *Dr Sharp abandoned his claim for malicious falsehood
    regarding comments made by Duncan Campbell on
    the BBC's* Watchdog *programme relating to an AIDS
    clinic he was running.*     Abandoned.

# 1997

The lower trend for damages continued in 1997.

1. Reynold Bennett (and 7 others) v. *Time Out*    £120,000
2. Melanie Spires v. Carlton TV    £10,000
   *Spires accepted £10,000 damages for allegations
   made about her when she was wrongly identified in
   a film about the Church of Scientology.*
3. Princess Diana v. *Sunday Express*    £75,000
4. Martin Clunes v. *Express*    £1,000
   *The star of* Men Behaving Badly *accepted £1,000
   paid into court following an ill-mannered attack on
   the programme by Sir Bernard Ingham. Sir Bernard
   seems to have confused the actor with his television
   persona as he pontificated about a 'stupid, nasty,
   foulmouthed, posturing juvenile with limited
   command of the language'.*
5. Richard Wilmot-Smith QC v. *Daily Telegraph*    £250,000
6. Jenny Wilmot-Smith v. *Daily Telegraph*    £100,000
7. Stephen Kirby v. *Daily Telegraph*    £80,000
   *Richard Wilmot-Smith and his wife Jenny were*

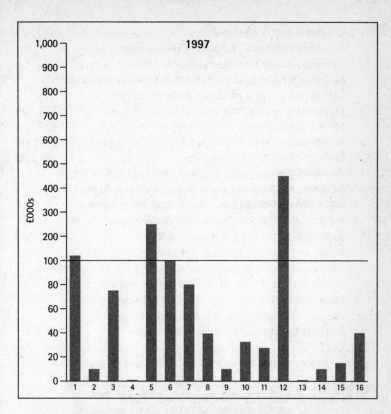

1997

awarded £250,000 and £100,000 against the Daily
Telegraph *for false allegations that they had
brainwashed a solicitor, Stephen Kirby, into leaving
his wife. Kirby was awarded £80,000. In view of an
appeal against the size of the award, the judge only
allowed £100,000 and £25,000 to be paid to the
Wilmot-Smiths prior to their appeal. It was initially
reported that they settled the appeal on payment of
the £125,000, but it seems they received all the
damages awarded but forwent their legal costs, which
may have amounted to the same thing.*

8.  Lewis v. RJB Magazines and 8 others                £39,500

9.    Katalin Blanc v. *Observer*                          £10,000
       *The psychotherapist ex-wife of the renowned chef*
       *Raymond Blanc recovered damages believed to exceed*
       *£10,000 for the false allegation that she was in some*
       *way to blame for a stroke he suffered in 1991.*

10.   McDonalds v. Dave Morris                     £32,500
11.   McDonalds v. Steel                              £27,500
12.   Western Provident v. Norwich Union (incl. costs)    £450,00
13.   Michael Winner v. Kensington                   £1,000
       *The film director and food writer donated the £1,000*
       *he recovered from the Royal Borough of Kensington*
       *and Chelsea for an unjustified notice about unpaid*
       *rates to the Diana Princess of Wales Memorial Fund.*

14.   Judith Ward v. Paragon Book Services          £10,000
       *Ward, freed on appeal from her conviction for the*
       *M62 coach bombing when, as we have seen, the*
       *evidence of Dr Frank Skuse was called into question,*
       *recovered £10,000 in respect of a book which failed*
       *to state that her conviction had been overturned.*

15.   David & Frederick Barclay v. BBC            £15,000
16.   Robin Katz v. Virgin Radio                    £40,100
       *A music journalist accepted £40,100 paid into court*
       *for comments about her on Virgin Radio by a disc*
       *jockey Nick Abbott. She was attacked in the most*
       *personal, unpleasant and offensive terms and falsely*
       *depicted as a pathetic and laughable figure following*
       *comments she had made in the* Independent *and on*
       *Radio 4 about Virgin Radio.*

## Lost or abandoned cases/mishaps

17.   Dr Peter Nixon v. Channel 4                     Lost
18.   Kirk Brandon v. George O'Dowd (Boy George)     Lost
19.   PC Reynold Bennett and others v. *Guardian*       Lost
20.   Jonathan Aitken v. *Guardian*             Abandoned

# 1998

| | | |
|---|---|---|
| 1. | Richard Branson v. Snowden | £100,000 |
| 2. | Luisa Morelli v. *Sunday Times* | £30,000 |
| 3. | Vincent Coyle v. *Sunday Times* | £15,000 |
| 4. | Lynda Ramsden v. *Sporting Life* | £75,000 |
| 5. | Jack Ramsden v. *Sporting Life* | £50,000 |
| 6. | Kieren Fallon v. *Sporting Life* | £70,000 |
| 7. | Marks and Spencer v. Granada | £50,000 |
| 8. | Christopher Bodker v. Associated Newspapers | £30,000 |
| 9. | David Colver v. Associated Newspapers | £10,000 |
| 10. | Alan Eisner v. Associated Newspapers | £10,000 |
| 11. | Margaret Mortlock v. George Mason | £7,500 |

11. *A councillor received £7,500 in respect of a draft press release sent out in error which falsely suggested that she was a hypocrite and guilty of back-door politics.*

12. Brooke Shields v. *Mail on Sunday*          £100,000
*The actress recovered £100,000 plus a front-page apology, continued on page 3, and a personal apology from* Mail on Sunday *editor Jonathan Holbrow accepting that a grave error had been made. The paper had published a false story, splashed as an exclusive on the front page, claiming that Shields had been questioned by police after leaving the Cannes International Film Festival. Her flight was said to have been delayed for two hours while she was searched. She had not even been stopped and was for good measure a committed campaigner against drugs.*

| | | |
|---|---|---|
| 13. | Linford Christie v. John McVicar | £40,000 |
| 14. | Rupert Allason v. *Mirror* | £1,050 |
| 15. | Gillian Stanton v. *Mirror* | £5,000 |

15. *A barrister's wife accepted £5,000 damages for false allegations that she had dressed in a sexually provocative manner. The* Mirror *accepted that she had not, but argued that their article did not make that claim. There was a suggestion that the matter had arisen after her husband described a witness in a criminal trial as a 'Pamela Anderson look-alike'.*

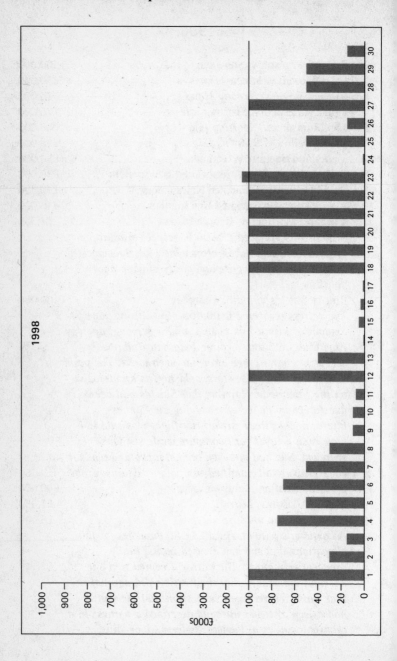

1998

£000s

| | | |
|---|---|---:|
| 16. | Graham Rush v. Dagmar Coward | £3,500 |
| 17. | Barbara Rush v. Dagmar Coward | £1,500 |
| 18. | Sergeant Peter Bleakley v. Channel 4 | £100,000 |
| 19. | PC Emlyn Welsh v. Channel 4 | £100,000 |
| 20. | Paul Giles v. Channel 4 | £100,000 |
| 21. | Tom Cruise v. Express Newspapers | £100,000 |
| 22. | Nicole Kidman v. Express Newspapers | £100,000 |

*The actor Tom Cruise and his wife, actress Nicole Kidman, were believed to have each received £100,000 damages for what was described as a recycling of wholly unfounded rumours of a highly offensive nature in an* Express on Sunday *magazine feature entitled: 'Cruising for a bruising . . . What's the Inside Story on Hollywood's Golden Couple?' Some extremely unpleasant allegations were made about their marriage, their links with the Church of Scientology and their sexuality. An abject apology was obtained for the allegations, which were accepted to be wholly false. The damages were to be distributed to charities.*

23. Liam Neeson and Natasha Richardson v. *Daily Telegraph*                    £130,000

*The actor Liam Neeson and his wife, actress Natasha Richardson, recovered damages reputedly totalling £130,000 for false allegations that their marriage was breaking up. £50,000 was recovered in a separate action against the* Mirror. *The couple were reported to be giving the money to the victims of the Omagh bombing.*

24. Penny Little v. Janet George                    £1,500

*Little, an anti-blood sports campaigner, was awarded £1,500 when she was falsely accused of appalling swearing in a live radio interview by the British Field Sports Society press officer.*

25. Liam Neeson and Natasha Richardson v. MGN                    £50,000
26. Brenda Solomons v. *Daily Telegraph*                    £15,000

*Solomons was awarded £15,000 for a false suggestion that she had persuaded her son to sue her estranged husband in a bid to recover money given to him on his bar mitzvah. The* Telegraph *apologised, making it clear that she had no involvement whatsoever in the decision to take action.*

| | | |
|---|---|---:|
| 27. | Peter Brooke-Smith v. Anglo Georgian | £100,000 |
| 28. | Vyacheslav Kolodyazhniy v. Anglo Georgian | £50,000 |

*Brooke-Smith and Kolodyazhniy recovered £100,000 and £50,000 respectively for false suggestions that they had unlawfully diverted payments belonging to a shipping company to the Cayman Islands.*

| | | |
|---|---|---:|
| 29. | Dr Barry Robson v. Drs Andrew Llewelyn, Lindsay, Slater and Forbes Watson | £50,000 |

*A doctor received £50,000 for false allegations of misconduct in his practice in a press release.*

| | | |
|---|---|---:|
| 30. | Graham Baldwin v. *Guardian* | *£15,000* |

*A director of a charity counselling cult victims was falsely accused of being self-promoting, self-aggrandising and obsessive and of using false religious credentials. He was awarded £15,000. Comments in an article by the* Guardian's *editor about the outcome of this case have spawned another writ.*

## Lost or abandoned cases/mishaps

| | | |
|---|---|---:|
| 31. | Jessye Norman v. Classic CD | Lost on legal ruling |
| 32. | Dept. Insp. Trevor Gladding v. Channel 4 | Lost |

## 1999

| | | |
|---|---|---:|
| 1. | Irving Scholar v. *People* | £7,501 |

*Scholar, a director of Nottingham Forest FC, accepted £7,501 libel damages when he was falsely accused of undermining the authority of the manager.*

| | | |
|---|---|---:|
| 2. | Julian O'Neill v. *Guardian* | £7,500 |

*A Rugby League player recovered £7,500 when he was mistaken for another sportsman said to have urinated under a blackjack table and damaged a motel room.*

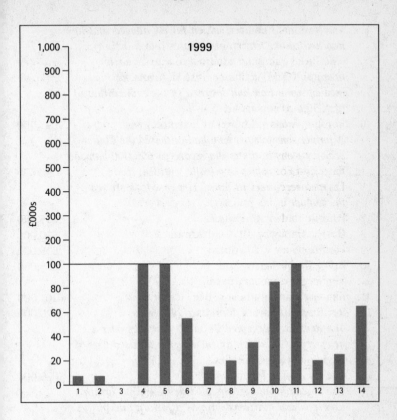

3.  Peter Oates v. *Sunday Mirror*                              1p.
    *A Broadmoor patient was falsely accused of*
    *possessing hard-core pornographic videos. The fact*
    *that he was serving a sentence for having kidnapped*
    *a teenager whom he had tied up and whose genitals*
    *he had threatened to shoot off seems however to have*
    *counted against him. He recovered 1p from the*
    Sunday Mirror *and lost his action against the* Mirror
    *(no. 18) altogether.*

4.  Paul McKenna v. *Star*                              £100,000
5.  Paul McKenna v. *National Enquirer*                £100,000
    *The TV hypnotist accepted undisclosed libel damages,*
    *said in both cases to be six-figure sums, from the* Star

*and* National Enquirer, *which falsely alleged that he
had turned one Christopher Gates into a 'helpless
child' who had to be admitted to a psychiatric
hospital. Gates' action against McKenna for his
medical condition had resulted in the exoneration of
McKenna of any blame.*

6.  Bonnie Woods v. Church of Scientology £55,000
    *A former scientologist who had criticised the Church
    of Scientology in the media recovered £55,000 damages
    for forty-eight copies of a leaflet entitled; 'Hate
    Campaigner Comes to Town'. Her case took six years
    to conclude.*

7.  Patti Boulaye v. *Guardian* £15,000
8.  George Galloway MP v. Al Ahram £20,000
9.  Lord Avebury v. Al Ahram £35,000
10. Bruce Grobbelaar v. *Sun* £85,000
    *Verdict set aside on appeal.*
11. Exoteric Gas Solutions v. BG £101,000
12. Rev Royston Such v. Meridian TV £20,000
    *The Rev. Such accepted £20,000 damages over a
    news report in which an interviewer accused him of
    having destroyed families.*
13. Mickey Duff v. *Mirror* £25,000
    *The boxing promoter was awarded £25,000 for an
    article which portrayed him as a forlorn and pitiful
    figure.*
14. Clive Everton v. WPSBA (inc. costs) £65,000
    *The snooker commentator and editor of* Snooker Scene
    *accepted agreed damages and costs against the World
    Professional Billiards and Snooker Association and
    two of its officials for comments in their in-house
    magazine* In the Frame *which led to his temporarily
    being banned from WPSBA venues except for the BBC
    commentary box.*

## Lost or abandoned cases/mishaps
15. Bill Cash MP v. *Sunday Mirror*
    *The jury could not agree over the allegation that Cash
    was a gutless turncoat who had ditched the miners in*

*their hour of need when thirty-one mines were being*
*closed. A retrial was ordered.*                Jury failed to agree

16.  Keith Schellenberg v. *Guardian* and *Sunday Times*
*The former Laird of Eigg dropped his action after five*
*weeks, paying £300,000 of the* Guardian's *and the*
Sunday Times' *costs. His own were estimated at*
*£750,000. He was accused of being an appalling*
*landlord and a playboy. Schellenberg also abandoned*
*his case against BBC Radio's* Breakaway *programme,*
*which was said to have involved a further £50,000*
*costs. In addition he failed to prevent Channel 4*
*profiling him in their* Filthy Rich *series.*          Abandoned

17.  Glyn Kirpalani v. Miss B.
*An immigration officer faced a retrial when he sued his*
*former girlfriend for allegations of rape.*     Jury failed to agree

18.  John Hickey v. BBC
*A holistic doctor who had been struck off by the GMC*
*in 1990 lost his libel action against the BBC in*
*respect of their programme* Doctors in the Dock,
*which accused him of irresponsibility in prescribing*
*drugs to one of his patients, who had subsequently*
*died. The judge accepted that Hickey had a sincere*
*belief in the benefits of holistic treatment and was*
*acting in good faith, but said that the prescription*
*of Diconal for the patient was medically indefensible*
*and dangerous.*                                        Lost

19.  Keith Schellenberg v. BBC                       Abandoned
20.  Neil Hamilton v. Mohamed Fayed                       Lost
21.  Taylor v. Serious Fraud Office                       Lost

# 2000

1. Martin Garfoot v. Lynn Walker                                    £400,000
   *A pharmacist at Boots in North Shields was falsely
   accused of raping a colleague in the store's staff
   room. The judge suggested that damages should be in
   the £50,000 to £100,000 bracket; costs totalled
   £150,000. The defendant was declared bankrupt. The
   judge also lifted the anonymity that would normally
   attach to an alleged rape victim.*

2. DNV Petroleum Services v. CBC Marine
   Publications                                                      £45,000
   *The award was made by a judge hearing the case
   without a jury to a shipping fuel-bunkering service
   accused of dishonest practices and publishing
   misleading information. CBC did not appear at the
   trial.*

3. Betty Boothroyd v. Express Newspapers and the
   *Spectator*                                                       £10,000
   *The speaker of the House of Commons received
   £5,000 from each publication, which she donated to
   charity, in respect of false suggestions that she had
   been the mistress of a Labour peer.*

4. Stephen Scott v. Orion Publishers             £59,000 (inclusive
                                                    of £50,000 costs)
   *A television producer was accused in a book of
   having driven a paedophile to suicide as a result of a
   documentary he had made. In fact the man was alive
   and living in Kent.*

5. Keith Burstein v. Times Newspapers                                £8,000
   *Burstein was falsely accused of organising hecklers
   at a concert of modern atonal music. On appeal the
   award was upheld, but the judge was considered to
   have been wrong to refuse to allow evidence that the
   claimant had co-founded a group of campaigners
   against such music, particularly* Gwain *by Sir
   Harrison Birtwistle, although he was not guilty of
   any such conduct on this occasion.*

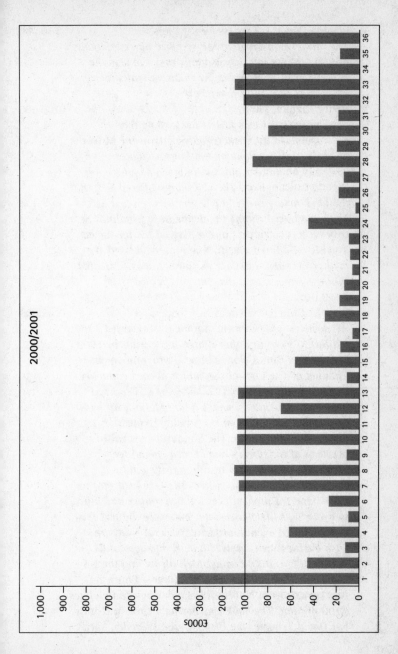

2000/2001

6.  Edwina Currie v. Express Newspapers                 £30,000
    *The former Conservative MP received agreed damages*
    *of £30,000 for false accusations that she was the*
    *vilest lady in Britain and for rumours that she*
    *planned to join the Labour Party.*

7.  Victor Kiam v. MGN                                   £105,000
    *The industrialist was falsely accused by the*
    *controversial City Slickers journalists in the* Mirror
    *of having lost millions on the Ronson lighter*
    *company he had bought and of being about to pull*
    *the plug on the firm. The newspaper offered £50,000*
    *the week before the trial but this was rejected as too*
    *little, too late. Echoing the defamatory headline, 'MY*
    *COMPANY HAS BOUGHT IT', and a play on his renowned*
    *Remington advertisement, Kiam joked: 'I liked the*
    *verdict so much, I bought the jury.' It was estimated*
    *that the paper would also have to pay costs of*
    *£250,000.*

8.  Sean McPhilemy v. Times Newspapers                   £145,000
    *A television producer and author was awarded*
    *£145,000 by a jury after a nine-week trial. In 1993*
    The Sunday Times *claimed that a programme on*
    *Channel 4,* The Committee, *which alleged collusion*
    *in the murder of Roman Catholics of RUC-backed*
    *loyalist death squads, was a hoax. McPhilemy had*
    *recovered £50,000 from the* Sunday Express *in 1996*
    *for similar allegations. The Sunday Times called*
    *nineteen of the twenty-one alleged committee*
    *members at the trial to testify that they did not*
    *belong to any such committee. The jury held that on*
    *the balance of probabilities the newspaper had failed*
    *to prove that the clandestine committee did not exist.*
    *Costs totalled £1 million. Later, several Northern*
    *Irish businessmen received agreed damages of $1*
    *million (£630,000) against McPhilemy and the US*
    *publishers of his book* The Committee – Political
    Assassinations in Northern Ireland. *They had claimed*
    *$100 million. The book was not published in Britain*
    *but David Trimble, the Ulster Unionist leader, sued*

     *Amazon Books for copies they had supplied to the*
     *UK.*

9.  Dr Lawrence Godfrey v. Demon             £15,000

10.  Peter Gadsby v. Stuart Webb          £150,000
     *After four days of a libel action the vice-chairman of*
     *Derby County FC received agreed damages of*
     *£150,000 and £200,000 costs in a settlement from a*
     *former board member following a poison-pen letter*
     *sent to eleven prominent Derbyshire people*
     *containing allegations of fraud, corruption and*
     *arson. Webb had made it clear he dissociated himself*
     *from the letter.*

11.  Marco Pierre White v. *New York Times*     £15,000
     *A review of White's career as a chef and restaurateur*
     *falsely referred to a well-publicised bout with drugs*
     *and alcohol.* The New York Times *sold only 140*
     *copies in England. White had never been a drug-*
     *taker or alcoholic. The newspaper's tactics of hiring*
     *private investigators to dig up dirt to try to justify*
     *some of the allegations in the article and claiming*
     *that White was greedy for a large award of damages*
     *backfired. This line of defence was withdrawn a*
     *couple of weeks before the trial. Mr Justice Morland*
     *awarded indemnity costs believed to total £480,000*
     *to mark his disapproval of the way the defendants*
     *had conducted the case.*

12.  Marco Pierre White v. *International Herald Tribune*  £60,000
     *For the same allegations.*

13.  Penny Marshall v. *Living Marxism*       £150,000

14.  Ian Williams v. *Living Marxism*        £150,000

15.  ITN Limited v. *Living Marxism*         £75,000
     *An article entitled 'The Picture that Fooled the*
     *World' falsely suggested that pictures of emaciated*
     *Bosnian Muslims behind barbed wire at the Serb-run*
     *Trnopolje prison camp were the product of selective*
     *filming. The magazine was given every opportunity*
     *to retract. There was no attempt to check the facts*
     *with ITN and the report was puffed by a press*
     *release. The magazine went into liquidation.*

16. Chris Mile v. Neil Turner MP                                     £20,000
*An environmental activist was awarded £20,000
libel damages against the MP for Wigan over letters
sent to the Green Party and the local press attacking
his integrity.*

17. Peter Cunningham v. Essex County Council, Patricia
Elliot and Peter Ayre                                                £9,500
*False allegations of theft against a teacher were
republished by the Assistant Education Officer.*

18. Caroline Coon v. Jonathon Green                                  £40,000
*The co-founder of the drugs-related charity Release
was falsely accused in Green's book* All Dressed Up:
The Sixties and the Counterculture *of offering George
Harrison oral sex in return for a £1,000 donation to
Release. Earlier Harrison had himself recovered
substantial damages for the same allegation. It had
also been falsely claimed that Mick Jagger had been
made the same offer but had refused to pay. Coon's
damages were donated to Warwick University to
establish a Release archive. She was also awarded
£33,000 costs.*

19. John Steven v. West Country TV                                   £25,000
*A property developer accepted £25,000 paid into
court for a very critical account of his business
methods.*

20. Mike Hollingsworth v. Associated Newspapers                      £20,000
*The showbusiness agent received £20,000 for
suggestions in the* Mail on Sunday *that personal
problems following his separation from the television
presenter Anne Diamond were affecting his
professional abilities.*

21. Jane Proctor v. Associated Newspapers                            £5,000
*The former editor of the* Tatler *received agreed
damages of £5,000 plus costs for false allegations
that she had behaved unsympathetically to an
employee whose mother had been diagnosed with
cancer.*

22. Kelly Antonucci v. *What's On TV*                                £7,500
*A wife was falsely accused of spending her husband's*

*£2.8 million lottery win on herself and friends,*
*reducing him to homelessness and insolvency.*

23. Brendan Ingle v. BBC                              £13,000
*The trainer of the boxer Prince Naseem received*
*£13,000 agreed damages for suggestions made by*
*Naseem on the* Parkinson *programme that Ingle had*
*manipulated and exploited him. Frank Warren, the*
*boxing promoter, was awarded substantial damages*
*for similar allegations made against him in the same*
*programme.*

24. Tim Blackstone v. Mirror Group Newspapers        £50,000
*Blackstone, a PR consultant, brother of a government*
*minister and one-time porn star, was awarded*
*£50,000 for an 'horrendously inaccurate' account of*
*a dispute with his estranged wife.*

25. Takenaka (UK) Limited v. Frankle                   £1,000
26. Brian Corfe v. David Frankle                      £25,000
27. Marc Tufano v. MGN                                £20,000
*An actor and screenwriter sued for allegations in the*
People *concerning the actor Danny de Vito and*
*himself. He conducted the case in person and the*
*award included the costs he had incurred.*

28. Lynn Walker v. *Newcastle Chronicle and Journal*  £100,000
*Walker received damages of £100,000 for the false*
*allegation that she had tried to murder the wife of*
*her alleged lover, a former Scotland football captain.*

29. Shan Hunt v. *Bedfordshire on Sunday*              £19,950
*The leader of the Labour Group on Bedford Borough*
*Council accepted £19,950 damages and a front-page*
*apology over a claim that she proposed to squander*
*£1 million of public money in a bid to gag the press*
*by fitting new doors to social housing with*
*letterboxes too small to take newspapers.*

30. Sir Alan Sugar v. News Group                      £80,000
*On the day before the libel action was to begin, the*
News of the World *paid the Tottenham Hotspur*
*chairman £80,000 for allegations about his*
*treatment of the player Gary Mabbutt and his own*
*failure to buy top players.*

31.   Dr Ruth Dudley Edwards v. Tim Pat Coogan and
      Random House                                          £25,000
      *An Irish historian and political commentator was
      falsely accused of hypocritically ingratiating herself
      with the English establishment to further her writing
      career and of having been responsible for the collapse
      of the British Association of Irish Studies.*

## 2001

32.   Marco Pierre White v. Tony Allan                      £100,000
      *The restaurateur recovered what was publicly
      described as a very substantial sum of damages and
      all his legal costs from Tony Allan, the owner of the
      Fish! restaurant chain, for false suggestions in a
      newspaper interview that White had substituted real
      ink for squid ink in a dish of braised cutlets. The
      case, which was surprisingly scheduled to last three
      weeks, was settled at the court door. Amid
      allegations that reports of £100,000 damages had
      breached the confidentiality terms of the settlement,
      an order was obtained from Mrs Justice Hallett
      binding the parties to preserve them. White had
      shown himself to be amenable to reasonable
      settlements in February 2001, when he accepted a
      more modest £1, plus his legal costs, for a claim
      against Declan Molloy. Misplaced remarks in
      Flooring magazine had wrongly suggested that he
      had taken a damaged oak floor from his Mirabelle
      restaurant and relaid it in his country home.*

33.   Kevin Keegan v. News Group                            £150,000
      *The former England coach received damages of
      £150,000 plus £30,000 costs for false allegations
      that he was the ringleader of a betting school among
      the England squad during the European
      Championships and acted as bookmaker for gambling
      nights at the team hotel.*

34. Sir Alan Sugar v. Associated Group Newspapers          £100,000
*Another libel action by the chairman of Tottenham Hotspur. This time he sued over an article in the football pages of the* Daily Mail *which accused him of general miserliness and in particular of an unwillingness to provide the manager, George Graham, with money to buy players. Sugar complained that the newspaper took the mickey out of people just to increase its circulation. The* Mail *turned down his offer to settle for £20,000, claiming the article was fair comment. In fact £100 million had been spent during Sugar's ten years at the club. Damages were to be donated to Great Ormond Street Hospital. Costs totalled £400,000. An appeal was settled by adjusting the damages to £60,000.*

35. Terry Marsh v. News Group                              £30,000
*The boxer Terry Marsh, whose earlier libel success is described in Chapter 1, received damages of £30,000 for a completely false allegation that he had been one of the 'thuggish sidekicks' who had intimidated witnesses during the trial of* London's Burning *star John Alford. Alford had been convicted of supplying drugs to a newspaper reporter posing as an Arab prince. The defendants did not try to justify their claim and had tried to negotiate a settlement, but Marsh, who represented himself, had rejected this as too little, too late.*

36. Dr Rahamin v. Channel 4 and ITN
*A consultant accused of being unqualified and incompetent recovered £175,000 agreed damages for references to him in a news broadcast and archive footage. Costs were said to total £1 million, including a claimed £250,000 success fee as the case had been taken on a conditional-fee basis.*

## Lost or abandoned cases/mishaps

37.   Victoria Gillick v. Brook Advisory Centre                    Lost on
                                                                                        legal ruling

*The campaigner against the provision of*
*contraceptives to girls under sixteen without parental*
*consent lost her case alleging libel in a factsheet*
*distributed by Brook Street Advisory Centre which*
*she claimed implied that she was responsible for the*
*rise in teenage pregnancies. Mr Justice Eady ruled*
*that the pamphlet did not have this meaning.*

38.   David Irving v. Professor Deborah Lipstadt and
        Penguin Books                                                            Lost

*Irving sued Lipstadt for allegations in her book*
Denying the Holocaust: The Growing Assault on
Truth and Memory *that he was a rabid anti-Semite*
*and one of the most dangerous spokespersons for*
*Holocaust denial. After a thirty-two day trial Mr*
*Justice Gray, whom Irving once inadvertently called*
*Mein Führer, rejected his claim, ruling that Irving*
*had persistently and deliberately misrepresented and*
*manipulated historical evidence and was an active*
*Holocaust denier. The judge also found that he was*
*anti-Semitic and racist and that he associated with*
*right-wing extremists who promoted neo-Nazism.*
*The judge reached this conclusion after hearing the*
*ditty Irving recited to his daughter – 'I am a baby*
*Aryan/I have no plans to marry an ape or*
*Rastafarian' – and a repulsive joke he had cracked*
*to an audience in Canada about forming the*
*Association of Auschwitz Survivors of the*
*Holocaust and Other Liars, or ASSHOLS. The judge*
*acknowledged that Irving was beyond question able*
*and intelligent, that he had remarkable mastery of*
*the detail of historical documents and that his*
*knowledge of the Second World War was*
*unparalleled. This was, however, a crazy action for*
*Irving to bring and the destruction of his reputation*
*as an historian was completed by the fact that the*
*judge gave a reasoned judgement for his findings*

*against Irving. He was left with a bill estimated at
£2.5 million.*

39. Jupiter v. Johnson Fry      Lost
40. Geoff Foulds v. Mirror Group Newspapers      Lost
*The former chairman of the World Professional
Billiards and Snooker Association lost his case for
libel against the* Mirror *by a majority after a two-
week trial. He alleged that the newspaper had
suggested that he had defrauded the association by
making false expense claims. He was said to be
facing a bill for costs of £350,000.*
41. Police Constable Robert Bridle v. Mirror Group
Newspapers      Abandoned
*Following rulings by the judge, Bridle dropped his
case, which arose out of complaints about a
newspaper article after he was cleared of indecently
assaulting two female colleagues. Each side bore
their own costs.*
42. Simon Regan v. Barton Taylor      Lost on legal ruling
43. Patrick Mahon and Andrew Kent v. Rhan
and Bodmer      Lost on legal ruling

# Appendix 2

# CASE SOURCES

| | |
|---|---|
| Adams v. Associated Newspapers | (1999) EMLR 26 |
| Al Faghi v. HH Saudi Research and Marketing | (unreported) 28 July 2000 |
| Al Fayed v. Observer Ltd | *The Times* 14 July 1986 |
| Albuforth The | (1984) 2 Lloyds List 91 |
| Allason v. Haines | *The Times*, 25 July 1995 |
| Aspro Travel v. Owners Abroad Group | (1996) 1 WLR 132 |
| Associated Leisure v. Associated Newspapers | (1970) 2 QB 450 |
| Attorney General v. Guardian Newspapers Ltd | (1999) EMLR 904 |
| Attorney General v. MGN Limited | (1997) 1All ER 456 |
| Bachchan v. India Abroad Publications Inc. | 585 NYS 2d 561 (1992) |
| Bennett v. News Group Newspapers Ltd | Court of Appeal, (unreported) 8 July 1998 |
| Bergens Tinende v. Norway | (2000) 29 EHRR 125 |
| Berkoff v. Burchill | (1996) 4 All ER 1008 |
| Bestobell Paints Ltd v. Bigg | (1975) FSR 421 |

| | |
|---|---|
| Bindrim v. Mitchell | (1979) 155 CAL.RPTR.29 |
| Blackshaw v. Lord | (1984) QB 1 |
| Bladet Tromso v. Norway | 2 May 2000 |
| Blumenthal v. Drudge | (1998) 992 F.Supp 44 |
| Bognor Regis Urban District Council v. Dutton | (1972) 2 QB 169 |
| Bonnard v. Perryman | (1891) 2 CH 269 |
| Bookbinder v. Tebbit | (1989) 1All ER 1169 |
| Braddock v. Bevins | (1948) 1 KB 580 |
| Brunswick Duke of v. Harmer | (1849) 14 QB 185 |
| Byrne v. Deane | (1936) 1QB 818 |
| Campbell v. Spottiswood | (1863) 3 B+S 769 |
| Carson v. John Fairfax and Sons Ltd | (1993) 178 CLR 44 |
| Chadha v. Dow Jones | (1999) EMLR 724 |
| Charleston v. News Group Newspapers Ltd | (1995) 2WLR 450 |
| Cornwell v. Myskow | (1987) 1WLR 630 |
| Crest Homes Ltd v. Ascott | (1980) FSR 396 |
| Cruise v. Express Newspapers | (1992) EMLR 780 |
| Cubby Inc. v. Compuserve Inc. | (1991) 776 F Supp 135 |
| Cumming v. Scottish Daily Record | 1995 EMLR 538 |
| Daniels v. Griffiths | (1998) EMLR 489 |
| Derbyshire County Council v. Times Newspapers Ltd | (1993) AC 534 |
| Distillers v. Thompson | (1971) AC 458 |
| Douglas v. Hello! Ltd | Court of Appeal, 18 January 2001 |
| Fayed v. Al Tajir | (1988) 1 QB 712 |
| Fayed v. United Kingdom | (1986) 18 EHRR 393 |
| Fielding v. Variety | (1967) 2QB 841 |
| Forbes v. Berezovsky | (1999) EMLR 278 |
| Forbes v. Berezovsky | (2000) 1 WLR 1004 |
| Foxen v. Scotsman Publications Ltd | *The Times*, 15 February 1994 |
| Gaddaffi v. Telegraph Group Ltd | Court of Appeal, 28 October 1998 |
| Gay News Ltd and Lemon v. UK | (1983) 4 EHRR 123 |
| Geenty v. Channel 4 | (1998) EMLR 524 |
| Gilberthorpe v. Hawkins | Court of Appeal, *The Times,* |

| | |
|---|---|
| Loutchansky v. Times Newspapers Ltd | 24 October 2000 |
| Lucas-Box v. News Group Newspapers Ltd | (1986) 1WLR 147 |
| Lunney v. Prodigy Services Co. | 28 December 1998, Second Appellate Division, New York |
| Mahon v. Rhan | (2000) 2 All ER 1 |
| Mapp v. News Group Newspapers Ltd | (1997) EMLR 397; (1998) 2 WLR 260 |
| Marks and Spencer v. Granada | 3 March 1998, Mr Justice Popplewell (unreported) |
| McDonald Corporation v. Steel | (1995) 3 All ER 615 |
| McPhilemy v. Times Newspapers Ltd | (1999) EMLR 751 |
| Mori v. BBC | Mr Justice Gray, *The Times*, 6 July 1999 |
| New York Times v. Sullivan | (1964) 376 US 254 |
| Norman v. Future Publishing | (1999) EMLR 325 |
| Oberschlick v. Austria | (1995) 19 EHRR 386 |
| Oraro v. Observer | 10 April 1992 |
| Pamplin v. Express Newspapers Ltd | (1988) 1 WLR 116 |
| Parmiter v. Coupland | (1840) 6 M and W 105 |
| Plato Films Limited v. Speidel | (1961) AC 1090 |
| Pring v. Penthouse International | (1982) 695 F.2d 438 |
| Pulman v. Hill | (1891) 1 QB 524 |
| R v. Bromell ex parte Coventry Evening Newspapers Ltd | *The Times*, 24 July 1992 |
| R v. Central Independent Television plc | (1994) Fam192 |
| Ras Behari v. King Emperor | (1933) 50 TLR 1 |
| Regan v. Taylor | (2000) EMLR 549 |
| Reynolds v. Times Newspapers Ltd | (1999) 3 WLR 1010 |
| Riddick v. Thames Board Mill | (1977) QB 881 |
| Rindos v. Hardwick | Sup. Ct Western Australian, 31 March 1994 |
| Roache v. News Group Newspapers Limited | (1998) EMLR 161 |
| Ross v. Hopkinson | *The Times*, 16 October 1956 |
| Safeway Stores plc v. Tate | Court of Appeal, 18 December 2000 |
| Schapira v. Ahronson | (1999) EMLR 735 |

Wallersteiner v. Moir                    (1974) 1WLR 991
Webb v. Times Publishing Co.             (1960) 2QB 535
Winyard v. Tatler Publishing Co. Ltd     Court of Appeal,
                                         *Independent,* 16 August
                                         1991
Wyatt v. Forbes                          2 December 1997, Mr
                                         Justice Morland
                                         (unreported)
Yousoupoff v. MGM Pictures Ltd           (1934) 50 TLR 581
Zeran v. Diamond Broadcasting Inc.       (1997) 129 F.3d 327

# BIBLIOGRAPHY

Adamson, Ian, *A Man of Quality*, Frederick Muller, 1964.

Aitken, Jonathan, *Pride and Perjury*, HarperCollins, 2000.

Alletzhauser, Albert J., *The House of Nomura — The Rise to Supremacy of the World's Most Powerful Company*, Bloomsbury, 1990.

Barendt, Professor Eric, *Libel and the Media: The Chilling Effect*, Clarendon Press, 1997.

Barendt, Professor Eric, *Defamation and Fiction, Law and Literature*, Oxford University Press, 1999.

Barendt, Professor Eric, *Yearbook of Copyright and Media Law: 1999*, Oxford University Press, 1999.

Booker, Christopher, *A Looking Glass Tragedy*, Duckworth, 1997.

Bower, Tom, *Maxwell: The Outsider*, Aurum Press, 1988.

Bower, Tom, *Maxwell: The Final Verdict*, HarperCollins, 1995.

Bower, Tom, *Fayed: The Unauthorised Biography*, Macmillan, 1998.

Branson, Richard, *Losing my Virginity*, Virgin, 1998.

Braithwaite, Nick, *The International Libel Handbook*, Butterwirth Heinemann, 1995.

Bresler, Fenton, *Lord Goddard*, Harrap, 1977.

Brivati, Brian, *Lord Goodman*, Richard Cohen Books, 1999.

Campbell, Lady Colin, *A Life Worth Living*, Little, Brown, 1997.

Carter-Ruck, Peter, *Reflections of a Libel Lawyer*, Weidenfeld & Nicolson, 1990.

Carter-Ruck, Peter and Starte, Harvey, *Carter-Ruck on Libel and Slander* (5th ed.), Butterworth, 1997.

Cavendish, Anthony, *Inside Intelligence*, Palü Publishing Ltd. 1997.

Chippindale, Peter and Horrie, Chris, *Stick it up your Punter*, Heinemann, 1990.

Connor, Robert, *Cassandra*, Cassell, 1969.

Considine, Bob, *The Remarkable Life of Dr Armand Hammer*, Harper & Rowe, 1975.

Crick, Michael, *Jeffrey Archer – Stranger than Fiction*, Penguin 1996.

Cudlipp, Hugh, *Publish and be Damned*, Arthur Barker, 1953.

Davies, Nicholas, *The Unknown Maxwell*, Sidgwick & Jackson, 1992.

Dean, Joseph, *Hatred, Ridicule and Contempt*, Constable, 1953.

Neill, Sir Brian and Rampton, Richard, *Duncan and Neill on Defamation*, Butterworth, 1983.

Ephron, Nora, *Heartburn*, Heinemann, 1983.

Epstein, Jay, 'The Last days of Armand Hammer' *New Yorker*, 23 September 1996.

Erdman, Paul, *The Last Days of America*, Secker & Warburg, 1981.

Faulks, Neville, *No Mitigating Circumstances*, William Kimber, 1977.

Faulks, Neville, *Law Unto Myself*, William Kimber, 1978.

*Gatley on Libel and Slander* (9th ed.) Sweet & Maxwell, 1998.

Garbus, Martin, and Kurnit, Richard, 'Libel Claims Based in Fiction', 51, Brooklyn Law Review 401.

Greenslade, Roy, *Maxwell's Fall*, Simon & Schuster, 1992.

Greer, Ian, *One Man's World – The Untold Story of the Cash for Questions Affair*, André Deutsch, 1997.

Gregory, Martyn, *Dirty Tricks*, Warner Books, 1996.

Grove, Valerie, *Laurie Lee: The Well-Loved Stranger*, Viking, 1999.

Haines, Joe and Donnelly, Peter, *Malice in Wonderland*, Macdonald & Co., 1986.

Haines, Joe, *Maxwell*, Macdonald & Co., 1988.

Hamlyn, Michael, 'How the Dering Dossier Was Built Up', *The Sunday Times*, 10 May 1964.

Hammer, Armand, and Lyndon, Neil, *Armand Hammer*, Perigee Books, 1988.

Harding, Luke, Leigh, David and Pallister, David, *The Liar – The Fall of Jonathan Aitken*, Penguin, 1977.

Hersh, Seymour, *The Samson Option*, Faber & Faber, 1991.

Hill, Mavis and Williams, Norman, *Auschwitz in England*, McGibbon & Kee, 1965.

Hodgson, Godfrey, *Lloyd's of London: A Reputation at Risk*, Allen Lane, 1984.

Hooper, David, 'Forum Shopping in Libel Actions', *The Yearbook of Copyright and Media Law*, Oxford University Press, 1999.

Hooper, David, *Public Scandal, Odium and Contempt*, Secker & Warburg, 1984.

Hoskins, Peter, *Two Men were Acquitted*, Secker & Warburg, 1984.

Hunt, Jonathan, *Trial by Conspiracy*, GreenZone, 1998.

Irving, David, *The Destruction of Convoy PQ17*, Popular Library (New York) 1968.

Jameson, Derek, *Touched by Angels*, Ebury Press, 1988.

Keays, Sarah, *A Question of Judgment*, Quintessential Press, 1986.

Leigh, David and Vulliamy, Ed, *Sleaze: The Corruption of Parliament*, Fourth Estate, 1997.

Marnham, Patrick, *The Private Eye Story*, André Deutsch, 1982.

Michie, David, *The Invisible Persuaders*, Bantam Press, 1998.

Mitchell, Ian, *The Cost of a Reputation*, Topical Books, 1997.

Montgomery, Hyde, *Patrick Hastings: His Life and Cases*, Heinemann, 1960.

Montgomery, Hyde, *Their Good Names*, Hamish Hamilton, 1970.

Morgan, Janet (ed.), *Back Bench Diaries of Richard Crossman*, Hamish Hamilton/Jonathan Cape, 1981.

Napier, Michael, and Bawden, Fiona, *Conditional Fees – a Survival Guide*, The Law Society, 1997.

Neville, Richard, *Hippy Hippy Shake*, Bloomsbury, 1995.

Nicolson, Nigel, *Long Life*, Weidenfeld & Nicholson, 1997.

O'Connor, Tom, *Take a Funny Turn*, Robson Books, 1994.

Palmer, Tony, *The Trials of Oz*, Blond and Briggs, 1971.

Pasternak, Anna, *Princess in Love*, Bloomsbury, 1994.

Pearson, John, *The Profession of Violence: The Rise and Fall of the Kray Twins* 1972.

Price, David, *Defamation Law, Procedure & Practice* (2nd ed.), Sweet & Maxwell, 2001.

Raphael, Adam, *The Ultimate Risk*, Bantam Press, 1994.

Raphael, Adam, *My Learned Friends*, W H Allen, 1989.

Raphael, Adam, *Grotesque Libels*, Corgi, 1993.

Rhodes James, Robert, *Bob Boothby*, Hodder & Stoughton, 1991.

Roache, William, *Ken and Me*, Simon & Schuster, 1993.

Robertson, Geoffrey, *The Justice Game*, Chatto and Windus, 1998.

Robertson, Geoffrey and Andrew, Nicol, *Media Law* (3rd ed.), Penguin, 1992.

Rubinstein, Michael, *Wicked, Wicked Libels*, Routledge & Keegan Paul, 1972.

Scott-Bayfield, Julie, *Defamation Law and Practice*, FT Law and Tax, 1996.

Scott-Bayfield, Julie, 'Damages – The Beginning of the End', *the Yearbook of Copyright Media Law*, Oxford University Press, 1999.

Sykes, Christopher, *Evelyn Waugh*, Collins, 1975.

Taylforth, Gillian, *Kathy and Me*, Bloomsbury, 1995.

Thompson, Peter and Delano, Anthony, *Maxwell: A Portrait of Power*, Transworld, 1988.

Tolstoy, Nikolai, *Victims of Yalta*, Hodder & Stoughton, 1978.

Tolstoy, Nikolai, *The Klagenfurt Conspiracy*, Encounter, 1983.

Tolstoy, Nikolai, *The Minister and the Massacres*, Century Hutchinson, 1986.

Toro, Elizabeth, *African Princess*, Hamish Hamilton, 1983.

Venables, Terry, *The Autobiography*, Michael Joseph, 1994.

Vidal, John, *McLibel – Burger Culture on Trial*, Pan, 1997.

Watkins, Alan, *A Slight Case of Libel*, Duckworth, 1990.

Weinberg, Steve, *Armand Hammer: The Untold Story*, Ebury Press, 1989.

West, Nigel, *British Security Service Operations 1909–45*, Bodley Head, 1981.

West, Nigel, *The Friends: Britain's Post War Secret Intelligence*, Weidenfeld & Nicholson, 1988.

West, Nigel, *Secret War – The Story of SOE*, Hodder & Stoughton, 1992.

West, Nigel, *Faber Book of Espionage*, 1994.

## Libel Awards

I acknowledge with thanks the comprehensive material in the *Media Lawyer* and the assistance of its editor, Tom Welsh, together with the schedules found in the books of Julie Scott-Bayfield, David Price and Peter Carter-Ruck. I likewise acknowledge the annual surveys which are produced by Richard Shillito in the *Law Society Gazette* and the reports of libel actions in the local and national press, including reports in the *UK Press Gazette*.

# INDEX

Douglas, Kirk, 488–9
Dove, Anne, 59
Dove, Reginald, 421
Down, Alastair, 420
Downey, Sir Gordon, 92, 395, 397, 400, 402
Drake, Mr Justice, 148, 254, 268, 271, 285, 291, 315, 328, 371, 454, 456
Driberg, Tom, 370
Driver, Betty, 246
Drucker, Royston, 197, 199–200, 201
Drudge, Matt, 485
Duff, Mickey, 538
Duggan, John, 334, 335
Dukes, Graham, 204
Duncan, Colin, 450
Dunhill, David, 424

e-mails *see* Internet
Eady, David, 153, 242–4, 381
Eaton, Patricia, 229, 232–3
Ebury Press, 442
*Economist*, 133
Eden, Anthony, 350
Edinburgh, Duke of: and McDonald's, 171
Edward VII, King, 28
Edwards, Dr Ruth Dudley, 546
Eggert, Gerhardt, 79
Eggleton, PC, 486
*Eleftherotypia* (newspaper), 302–3
Elizabeth of Toro, Princess, 312
Elliot, Patricia, 544
Elmi, Gillian, 75–6
Elwyn-Jones, Lord, 51, 53
Embury, John, 410–11
Ephron, Norma, 427
Erdman, Paul, 430–1
Essex County Council, 544
European Commission of Human Rights, 164, 472, 489
European Convention of Human Rights, 4, 154, 305, 340, 344, 469, 487–92
European Court of Human Rights, 71, 305, 341–2, 344, 487–8, 489–92
European e-commerce directive, 484
Evans, Derrick, 416
Evans, Harold, 45, 46–7
*Evening Standard:* and Alec Cairncross, 20; 'Dozy Dozen' story,

388; and Fayed case, 83; and George Galloway, 326; sued by Metropolitan Police officers, 144–5
Everton, Clive, 538
*Exodus* (Uris), 300, 449
exoneration statement, 15–16, 298
Exoteric Gas Solutions, 486
*Express see Daily Express*; *Sunday Express*
Express Newspapers, 540, 542

*Faber Book of Espionage*, 331
Faber and Faber: and Maxwell, 38, 43, 63–4
*Face, The*: and Donovan, 304, 514, 516
Fahd, King, 115
Fahd, Prince Mohammed Bin, 99, 102, 105, 109, 112, 113, 115–16, 119
Fairfax & Sons Ltd, 306
Falkender, Lady, 379
Fallon, Kieren, 405, 417–21
Falwell, Jerry, 428
Fane, Lady Camilla (later Hipwood), 28–9
*Far Eastern Economic Review*, 71
Faulks Committee, 461, 470
Fayed, Dodi, 82, 86–7, 93
Fayed, Mohamed, 66–87; and Aitken case, 99, 102–3, 104–5; and Bandar Bin Sultan's libel action against the *Guardian*, 101–2; and Bettermann case, 87–93; death of son, 82–3, 93; hostility towards by media after *Vanity Fair* case, 82, 83; and industrial tribunals, 75–6; involvement in Harrod's safety deposit box break-in, 83–5, 93; libel action against Mahdi Al Tajir, 67–8; libel actions taken, 67–8; payment of cash to Hamilton allegation, 392–4, 394–5, 396, 397, 400, 402; purchase of House of Fraser, 66, 70, 72, 392; refusal by British government to grant citizenship, 72–3, 93, 394; relationship with Hamilton, 101, 389–90, 391, 392, 393; and Rowland, 66–7, 70, 72, 392, 393, 395; sued by Hamilton, 86, 401–4; sues the *Observer*, 17, 68–9, 70–1; and Swami Tapes, 72; *Vanity Fair* profile and subsequent libel case, 73–82, 83, 86

Gowrie, Lord, 11, 15
Graf, Steffi, 497
Graham, George, 547
Granada Television: and Aitken case, 95, 96, 97–8, 111, 112–13, 118–19; and Docherty, 119; and Marks & Spencer, 7, 8; suing of by police officers, 139; and *World in Action* programme *see World in Action*
Granling, Lynne, 263
Gravett, Paul, 159
Gray, Charles, 114, 248, 331, 356, 362, 373, 449, 465, 468, 548
*Great Paper Chase, The*, 24
*Greatest Treason, The* (Deacon), 16
Green, David, 170–1
Green, Jonathon, 544
Greenslade, Roy, 327
Greer, Ian, 391, 392, 394, 396, 397, 398–401
Gregory, Dr Neville, 174
Gregory, Martyn, 217, 389
Grey, Rupert, 399
Greystoke, Andrew, 523
Griffiths, Judge, 29
Griffiths, Lynne, 22
Griffiths, Mark, 84
Grimsditch, Peter, 238
Grobbelaar, Bruce, 415–16
Grott, Richard, 104
Grundberg, Ilo, 190–1, 192, 194, 205
Grylls, Sir Michael, 398
Gtech: Branson's libel action against, 219–28
*Guardian:* and Aitken case, 95, 96–7, 98, 99–100, 104–5, 106, 108, 109–10, 111, 113, 115, 116–17, 118; and Fayed, 100–1; and George Howarth, 20; and Graham Baldwin, 536; and Hamilton case, 394–404; and Julian O'Neill, 536; and Keith Schellenberg, 536; and McDonald's, 163; and Norman Tebbit, 372; and Patti Boulaye, 21; and Paul Judge, 373–4; and Prince Bandar, 101–2; Rupert Allason, 329–30; and Stoke Newington Police Station case, 139, 146–7, 148
Guardian Assurance, 22–3
*Guinness Book of Political Blunders*, 335

Guppy, Darius, 30

Haines, Joe, 52–3, 54, 58, 328–9
Halcion, 167, 190–209; banning of, 209; decline in sales, 194; FDA investigation and report, 191, 193–4, 198, 200, 201–3, 207–8; and Grundberg case, 190–1, 192, 194, 205; history of development, 191–2; Jackson Prison study, 192–3, 193–4, 199, 201; and *Panorama* programme, 194, 195, 196, 197, 199, 206; popularity of, 191; side effects, 191, 192, 193, 198, 202; suing of Oswald by Upjohn, 195–6, 197–8, 200–6, 209; suspension of licence in Britain, 194
Hall, Phil, 290
Hallam-Baker, Dr Philip, 481
Hamilton, Neil, 67, 84, 86, 389–404, 469; controversy over money received from Fayed, 392–4, 394–5, 396, 397, 400, 402; facing bankruptcy, 404; loses seat, 396; and *Panorama*, 390–1; relationship with Fayed, 101, 389–90, 391, 392; stay at the Ritz, 390, 392, 396; sues Fayed, 86, 401–4; sues *Guardian* for cash for questions story, 394–401, 403; and US Tobacco, 391–2, 396
Hamilton, Roy, 84
Hammer, Armand, 441–4
Hammer, Frances, 441
Hammond, Jonathan, 55
Handley-Greaves, Paul, 79–81, 84
Hannan, Sean, 517
*Hard News*, 319
Haringey Council, 21
Harkess, Judge James, 30
Harlech TV *see* HTV
Harris, Harry, 61–2
Harris, Lawrence, 91
Harris, Leopold, 39
Harris, Lord, 402
Harris, Wendy, 114
Harrison, George, 544
Harrison, William, 292, 293, 295, 297
Harrods *see* Fayed, Mohamed
Hartley, Richard, 50–1, 52, 253, 254, 260, 261–2, 265, 436
Hartt, Professor Frederick, 229, 235–6

Unijet, 478
United Nations Association, 122, 123
United States, 3, 30; approach to libels in fiction, 433; discovery procedure, 5; Internet litigation, 483–4; and limitation period, 465; non-enforcement of UK libel judgements, 454–5, 479
United States Tobacco International, 25–6, 391–2, 396
*Unknown Maxwell, The* (Davies), 326
Upjohn: and Halcion *see* Halcion; merger with Pharmacia, 207–8
Uris, Leon, 300, 449

Van der Kroef, Dr C., 191, 193, 201, 204
*Vanity Fair*: profile of Fayed and subsequent libel case, 73–82, 83, 86
Vanunu, Mordecai, 63, 325
Venables, Terry, 405, 413–14
Vidal, John, 161
Vidal, Manon, 105–6, 115
Viking Press, 433
Virgin *see* Branson, Richard
Virgin Radio, 532

Wacaser, Nila, 194
Waddington, William, 246
Wales, Princess *see* Diana, Princess
Walker, David, 510
Walker, Denzil, 32
Walker, Judge Richard, 24
Walker, Lynn, 540, 545
Walker, Peter, 62
Walker Wingsail, 304, 523
Wallersteiner, Kurt, 43, 69–70
Walton, Robert, 147
Warbey, Adrian, 57
Warby, Frances, 504
Ward, George, 312
Ward, Judith, 230, 532
Ward, Raymond, 237
Wareing, Bob, 388
Warren, Frank, 27, 545
*Wartime Secrets* (West), 329
*Watchdog*, 530
Watkins, Alan, 381–2, 385
Watkins, Paul, 429–30
Watson, Laura, 518

Watts, Nigel, 349, 352–3, 355–6, 358, 360, 361, 362–3, 367
Waugh, Auberon, 369
Waugh, Eveleyn, 15
Webb, Frederick, 39
Webb, Stuart, 543
Webb v. Times Publishing Co.Ltd, 340
*Week Ending*, 238
Weinberg, Steve, 442–3
Weiner hotels, 516
Welsh, Emlyn, 149–50
Welsh, James, 512
West, Nigel *see* Allason, Rupert
Westcountry TV, 330, 544
Western Australia Newspapers Limited, 341
*Western Daily Press*, 379
Western Provident, 486
What's On TV, 544–5
Wheelock, Professor Verner, 172
Whelehan, Harry, 334–5
Whitaker, David, 55
White, Antonia, 437
White, Marco Pierre, 543, 546
*White Christmas* (tv programme), 76
Whitehorn, Will, 214
Wickman, Peter, 69, 71
Widgery, Lord, 32
*Wigan Observer*, 19
Wigan Rugby League Football Club, 19
Wilbraham, Alex, 429–30
Williams, Ian, 543
Williams of Mostyn, Lord, 26, 140, 336, 414–15
Wilmers, John, 46, 58, 120, 240, 241
Wilmot-Smith, Richard and Jenny, 304, 530–1
Wilson, Harold, 378–9
Wiltshire, Hensley, 151, 152, 154
Winner, Michael, 532
Winyard, Gaynor, 11–12
*Wisden Cricket Monthly*, 412–13
Witherow, John, 336, 337
Woods, Bonnie, 538
Woolf, Lord, 5, 41, 177, 402, 462, 463, 466–7
*World in Action*, 142–3; 'A Time to Kill' programme, 150; and Aitken, 96, 111; and Birmingham Six programme, 230